Street by Street

SOUTH HAMPSHIRE
PLUS BOURNEMOUTH, CHRISTCHURCH, FERNDOWN, POOLE, SOUTHBOURNE, VERWOOD, WIMBORNE MINSTER
Enlarged Areas Fareham, Gosport, Havant, Portsmouth, Southampton, Winchester

C000243016

Ist edition May 2001

© Automobile Association Developments Limited 2001

This product includes map data licensed from Ordnance Survey® with the permission of the Controller of Her Majesty's Stationery Office. © Crown copyright 2000. All rights reserved. Licence No: 399221.

Published by AA Publishing (a trading name of Automobile Association Developments Limited, whose registered office is Norfolk House, Priestley Road, Basingstoke, Hampshire, RG24 9NY.
Registered number 1878835).

Mapping produced by the Cartographic Department of The Automobile Association.

ISBN 0 7495 2360 3

A CIP Catalogue record for this book is available from the British Library.

Printed by G. Canale & C. S.P.A., Torino, Italy

Ref: MX007

Key to map pages	ii-iii
Key to map symbols	iv-1
Enlarged scale pages	2-15
Street by Street	16-245
Index – towns & villages	246-247
Index – streets	247-278
Index – featured places	278-282

ii

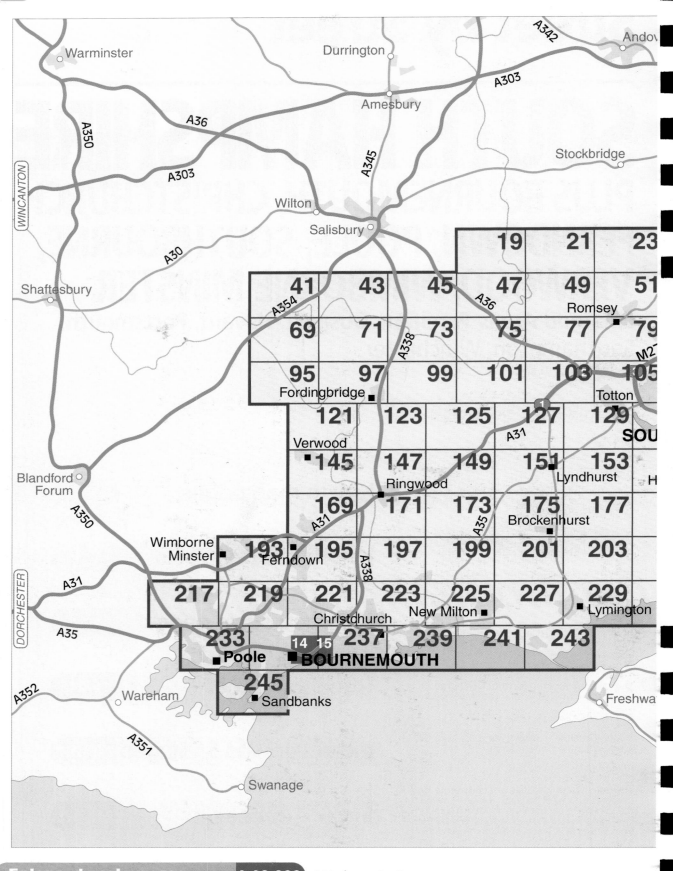

Warminster

Durrington

Amesbury

Stockbridge

A342

Andov

A303

A345

A36

A303

A350

Wilton

Salisbury

WINCANTON

A30

Shaftesbury

A354

Romsey

19	21	23
41	43	45	47	49	51
69	71	73	75	77	79
95	97	99	101	103	105

A36

A338

M2

Fordingbridge

Totton

| 121 | 123 | 125 | 127 | 129 |

Verwood

A31

SOU

Blandford Forum

A350

| 145 | 147 | 149 | 151 | 153 |

Ringwood

Lyndhurst

H

| 169 | 171 | 173 | 175 | 177 |

A31

A35

Brockenhurst

Wimborne Minster

| 193 | 195 | 197 | 199 | 201 | 203 |

DORCHESTER

A31

Ferndown

A338

New Milton

Lymington

| 217 | 219 | 221 | 223 | 225 | 227 | 229 |

A35

Christchurch

| 233 | 14 15 | 237 | 239 | 241 | 243 |

Poole

BOURNEMOUTH

A352

245

Wareham

Sandbanks

Freshwa

A351

Swanage

0   1/4   miles   1/2   3/4

0   1/4   1/2   kilometres   3/4   1   1 1/4

NEWBURY

BASINGSTOKE

Farnham

A303

A339

7

8

A31

A30

A34

M3

A31

Alton

A3

New
Alresford

A32

Haslemere

Liphook

17

Winchester 27

2 3

9

10

29

31

33

35

37

Liss

39

25

11

A272

53

55

57

59

61

63

39 *(67)*

67

Petersfield

12

81

83

85

A32

87

89

91

93

Midhurst

Eastleigh

Southampton

14

Bishop's Waltham

A3

107

109

111

113

115

117

119

HORSHAM

7

4

Hedge End

A286

8

133

135

137

139

1

141

143

4

5

THAMPTON

M27

Waterlooville

A3(M)

A285

155

157

159

161

3

163

167

WORTHING

6 7 11

Fareham

Portchester

Havant

8 9

ythe

179

181

183

185

187

4

189

191

Chichester

Fawley

5

Southbourne

205

207

Gosport

PORTSMOUTH

213

215

Bognor Regis

209

10 11 12 13

211

Southsea

South Hayling

231

Cowes

Selsey

Ryde

A3054

Newport

Bembridge

A3055

Isle of Wight

Shanklin

ter

Ventnor

3.6 inches to 1 mile

Scale of main map pages 1:17,500

| 0 | | 1/2 | miles | 1 |
| 0 | 1/2 | 1 | kilometres | 1 1/2 | 2 |

iv

Junction 9	Motorway & junction
Services	Motorway service area
	Primary road single/dual carriageway
Services	Primary road service area
	A road single/dual carriageway
	B road single/dual carriageway
	Other road single/dual carriageway
	Restricted road
	Private road
←	One way street
	Pedestrian street
	Track/ footpath
	Road under construction
	Road tunnel
P	Parking

P+	Park & Ride
	Bus/coach station
	Railway & main railway station
	Railway & minor railway station
	Underground station
	Light railway & station
	Preserved private railway
LC	Level crossing
	Tramway
	Ferry route
	Airport runway
	Boundaries- borough/ district
	Mounds
93	Page continuation 1:17,500
7	Page continuation to enlarged scale 1:10,000

River/canal
lake, pier

Toilet with
disabled facilities

Aqueduct
lock, weir

Petrol station

465
▲
Winter Hill
Peak (with height in metres)

Public house

Beach

Post Office

Coniferous woodland

Public library

Broadleaved woodland

Tourist Information Centre

Mixed woodland

Castle

Park

Historic house/ building

Cemetery

Wakehurst
Place NT
National Trust property

Built-up area

Museum/ art gallery

Featured building

Church/chapel

City wall

Country park

A&E
Accident & Emergency hospital

Theatre/ performing arts

Toilet

Cinema

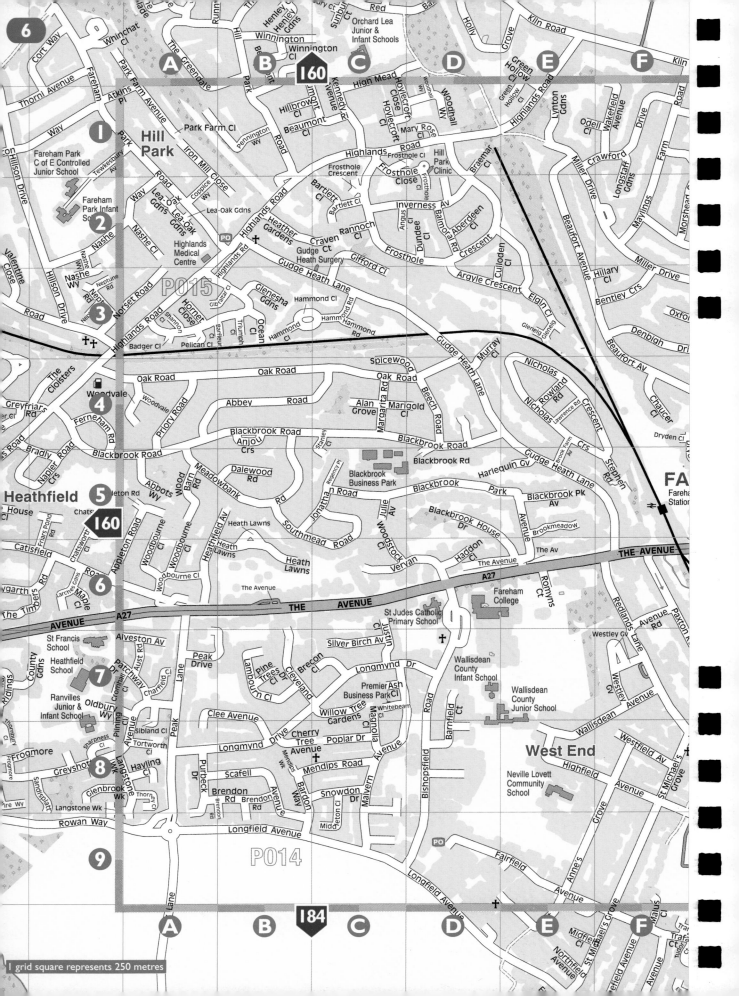

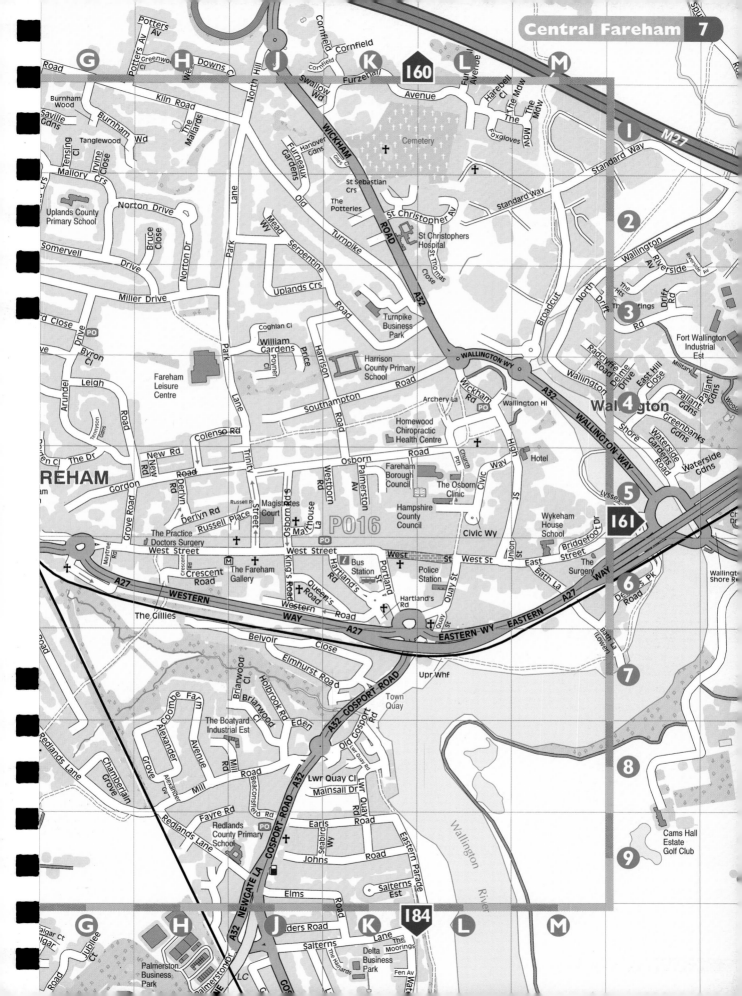

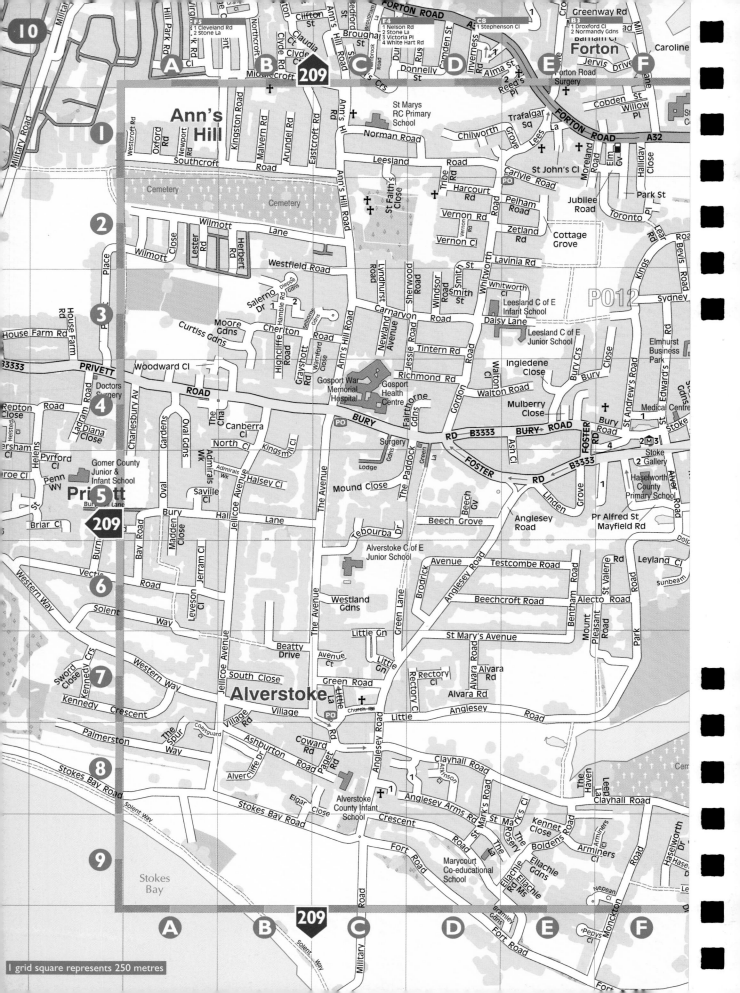

Forton

Ann's Hill

Priestt

Alverstoke

Stokes Bay

209

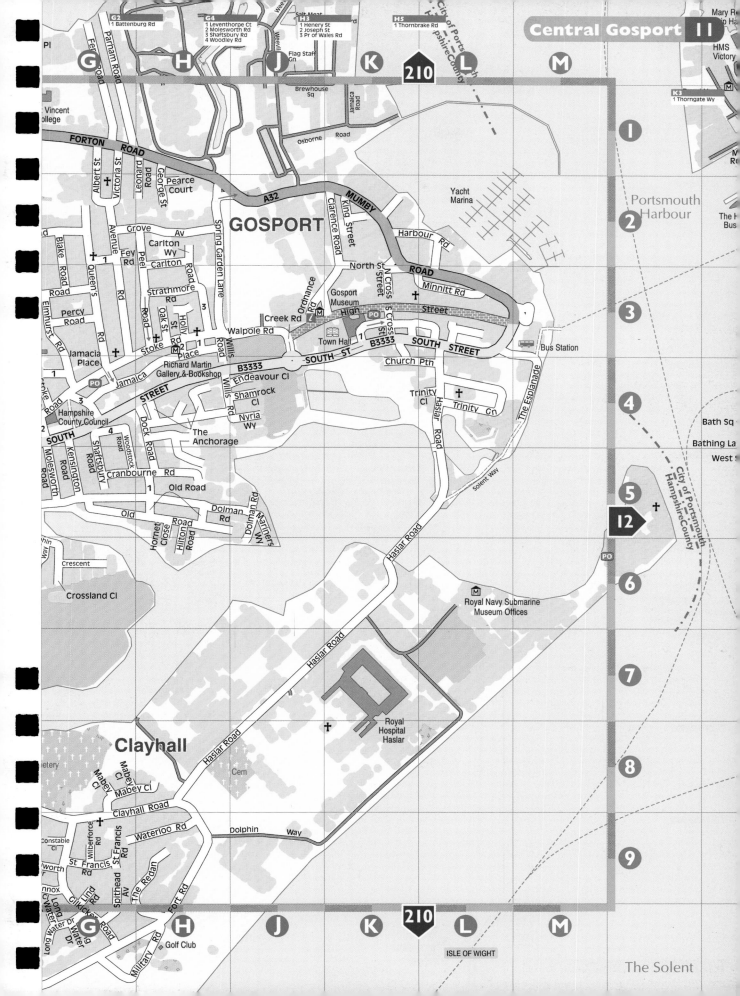

G2
1 Battenburg Rd

G4
1 Leventhorpe Ct
2 Molesworth Rd
3 Shaftsbury Rd
4 Woodley Rd

H3
1 Henery St
2 Joseph St
3 Pr of Wales Rd

H5
1 Thornbrake Rd

K3
1 Thorngate Wy

G **H** **J** **K** **210** **L** **M**

Mary R
ip Rd

HMS
Victory

M
Ro

1

Portsmouth
Harbour

The H
Bus

2

City of Ports
th
pshire Coun

Flag Staff
Gn

Salt Meat

Wee

Wevill

Brewhouse
Sq

Jamaica
Road

Osborne Road

Yacht
Marina

FORTON ROAD

A32

St Vincent
College

Albert St

Victoria St

Leonard Road

George St

Pearce Court

MUMBY

King Street

Clarence Road

Harbour Rd

GOSPORT

Grove

Av

Carlton Wy

Carlton

Spring Garden Lane

North St

N Cross Street

ROAD

Minnitt Rd

Street

Bath Sq

3

Bathing La

West

Fey Rd

Peel

Strathmore Rd

Oak St

Holly St

Ordnance Rd

Gosport Museum

High

S Cross St

M

PO

Blake Road

Queen's Avenue

Road

1

Creek Rd

Walpole Rd

Willis Road

Town Hall

B3333

SOUTH STREET

Bus Station

Percy Road

Elmhurst Rd

3

Stoke

M 2

1

Richard Martin
Gallery & Bookshop

Willis Rd

SOUTH ST

Church Pth

Haslar Road

Trinity Cl

Trinity Gn

The Esplanade

4

Jamacia Place

PO

1

Jamaica

STREET

B3333

Endeavour Cl

Shamrock Cl

3

Dock Road

Nyria Wy

Hampshire
County Council

2

SOUTH

4

Woodstock Road

The Anchorage

Solent Way

City of Portsmouth
HampshireCounty

5

12

Molesworth Road

Kensington Road

Shaftsbury Road

Cranbourne Rd

Old Road

1

PO

6

Crossland Cl

Crescent

Dolman Rd

Old Road

Hornet Close

Hilton Road

Mariners Wy

Dolman Rd

Royal Navy Submarine
Museum Offices

M

Haslar Road

7

Clayhall

Haslar Road

Cem

Cemetery

Mabey Cl

Mabey Cl

Mabey Cl

Royal Hospital Haslar

8

Clayhall Road

Wilberforce Rd

Waterloo Rd

Dolphin Way

9

Constable Cl

St Francis Rd

St Francis Rd

Spithead Av

The Redan

Fort Rd

Lind Rd

Gilkicker Road

Lennox

Long Water Dr

g Water Dr

Military Rd

Golf Club

ISLE OF WIGHT

The Solent

G **H** **J** **K** **210** **L** **M**

Pl

Fer
Road

Parham Road

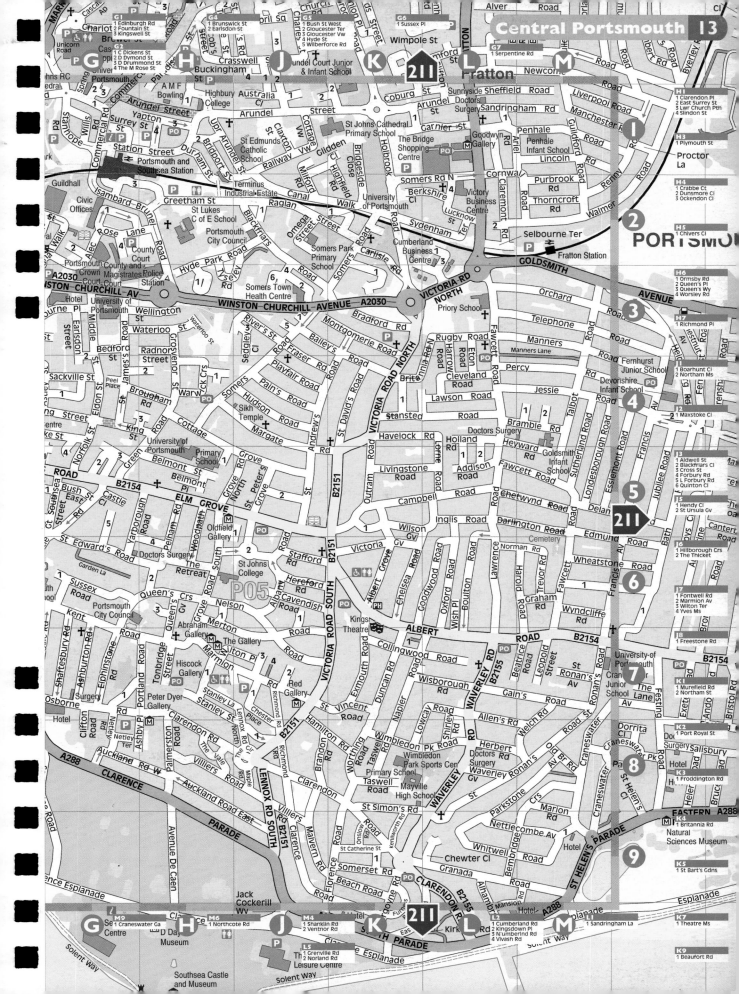

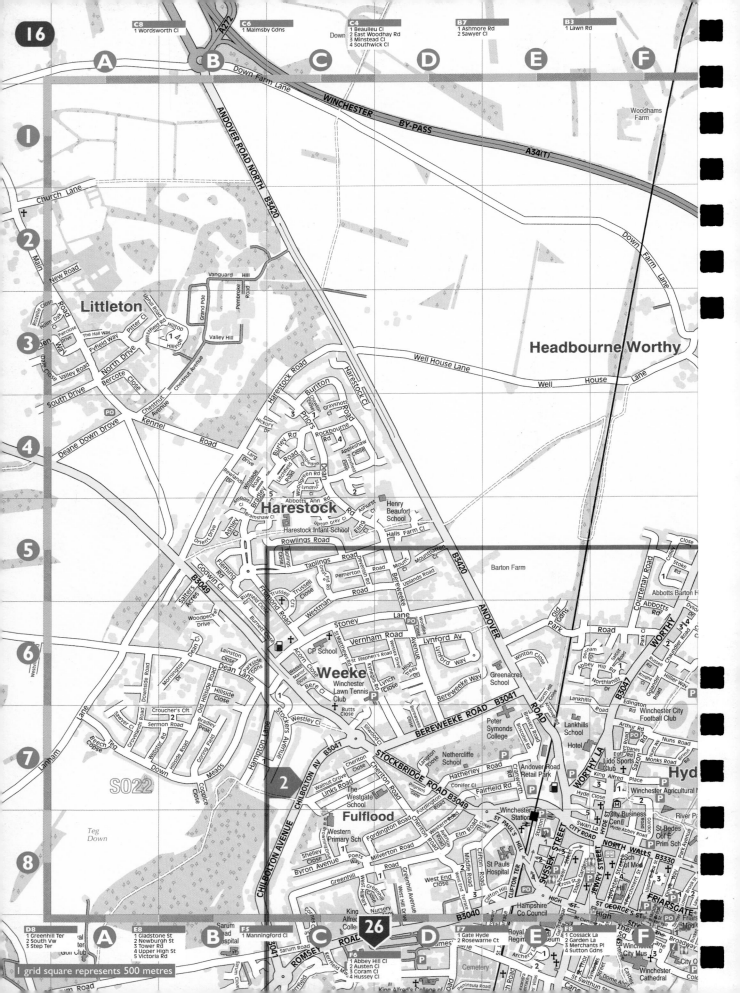

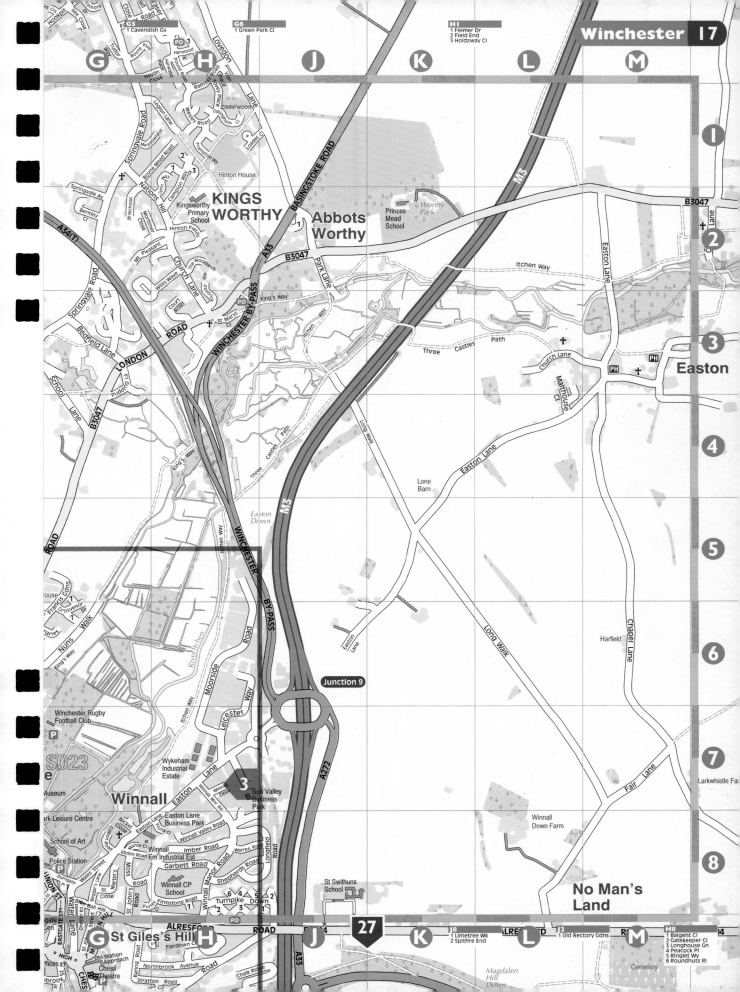

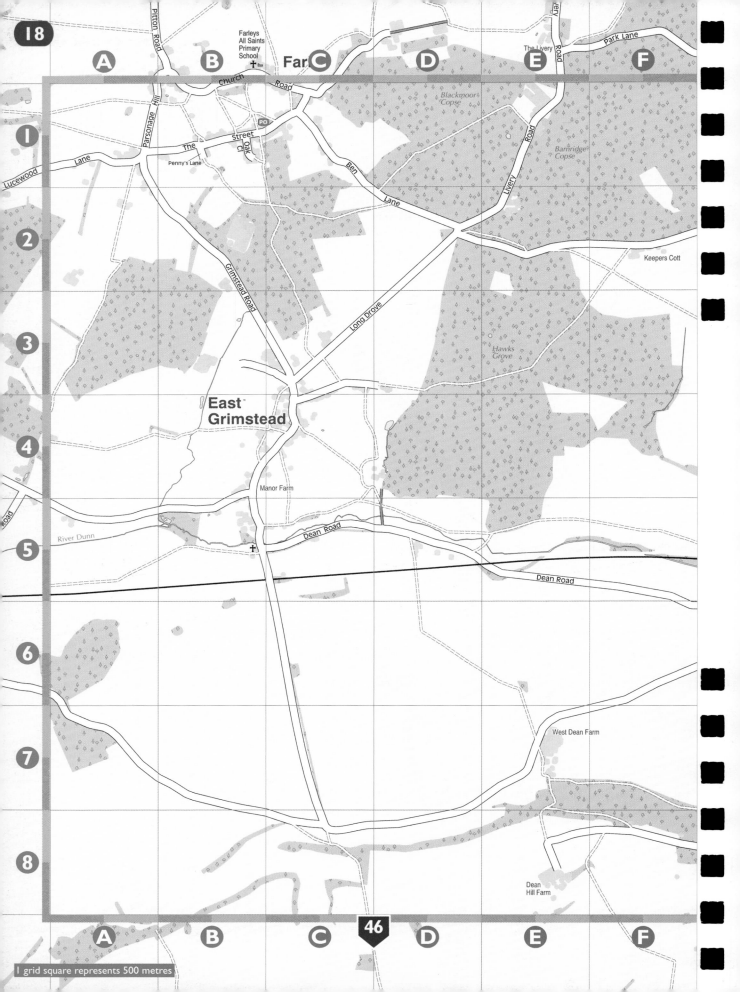

G H J K L M

I

2

3

4

20

5

6

7

8

Standing Hill

Home Farm

Dean Lane

The Gre

Pug's Hole

The L

Ty

Copse

Park

Howe Copse East

Wiltshire County
Hampshire County

Red Lane

Bulls Drove

Dean Road

Tytherley Common

Frenchmoor

Dean Copse

Dean Road

Drove Farm Ho

Frenchmoor Lane

Pilgrims Croft

PO

†

River Dunn

†

Rectory Hill

West Dean

Frenchmoor La

Park Farm

Dean Road

Moody's Hill

Dean Station

Ashmore Lane

Hillside Close

East Dean

†

Glebe Mdw

Deanhill Barn

Gatmore Copse

Hampshire County
shire County

Mean Wood

Ashmore Lane

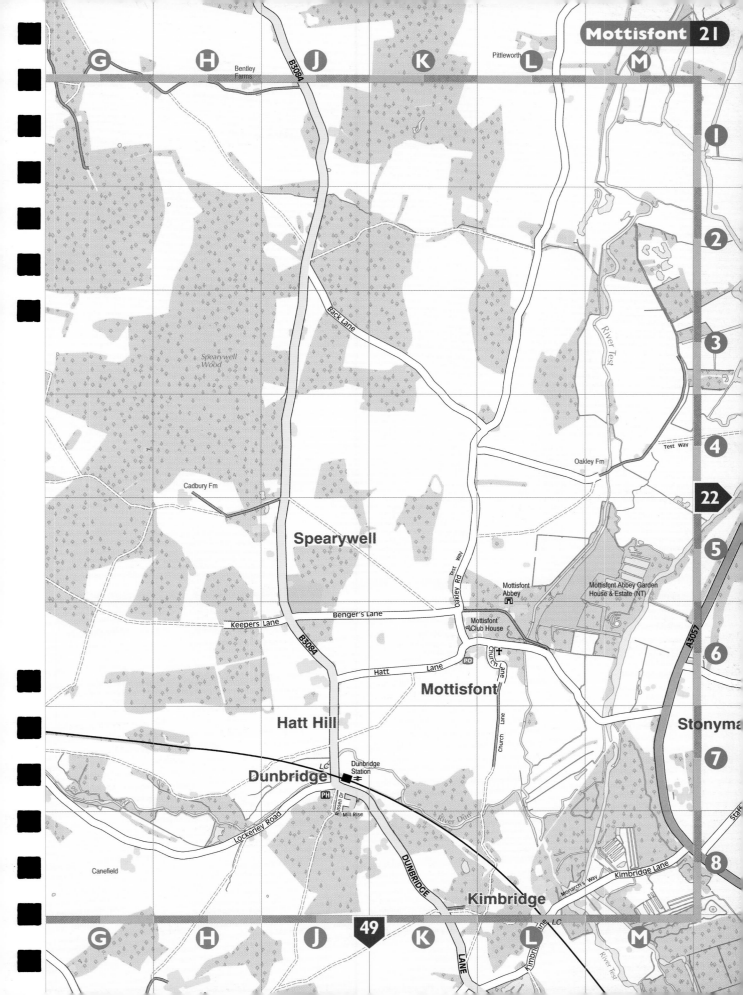

G H Bentley Farms B3084 J K Pittleworth L M

I
2
3
Test Way 4
22
5
A3057 6
7
8

River Test

Spearywell Wood

Back Lane

Cadbury Fm

Spearywell

Oakley Fm

Oakley Rd Test Way

Mottisfont Abbey

Mottisfont Abbey Garden House & Estate (NT)

Benger's Lane

Keepers Lane

Mottisfont Club House

B3084

Hatt Lane PO Church Lane

Mottisfont

Church Lane

Hatt Hill

Stonyma

LC Dunbridge Station

Dunbridge

PH Russell Dr Mill Rise

River Dun

Lockerley Road

DUNBRIDGE

Canefield

Kimbridge Lane

Monarch's Way

Kimbridge

River Test

LANE Kimbr Line LC

Staf

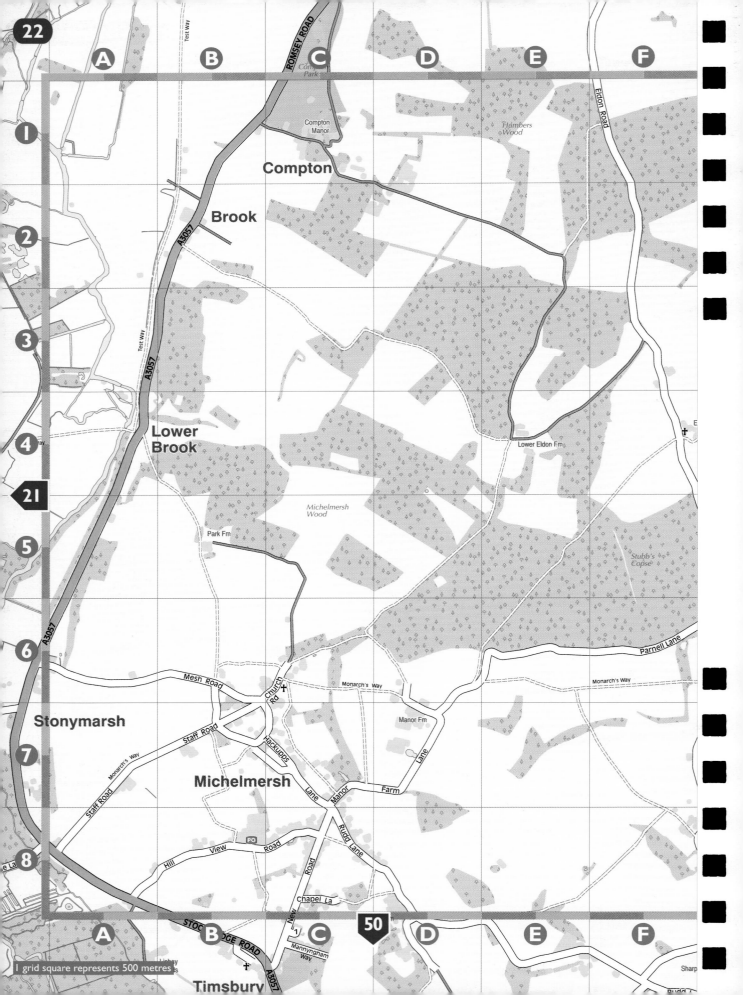

A B C D E F

1

Compton Park

Compton Manor

Humbers Wood

2

Brook

Compton

ROMSEY ROAD

A3057

Test Way

Eldon Road

3

4

Lower Brook

Lower Eldon Fm

21

Michelmersh Wood

5

Park Fm

Stubb's Copse

6

A3057

Parnell Lane

Mesh Road

Church Rd

Monarch's Way

Monarch's Way

Stonymarsh

Staff Road

Hackugps Lane

Manor Fm

7

Monarch's Way

Michelmersh

Manor

Farm

Lane

Staff Road

Lane

PO

8

Hill View Road

New Road

Rudd Lane

Chapel La

e La

STOCKBRIDGE ROAD

A3057

Mannyngham Way

50

Sharp

Timsbury

1 grid square represents 500 metres

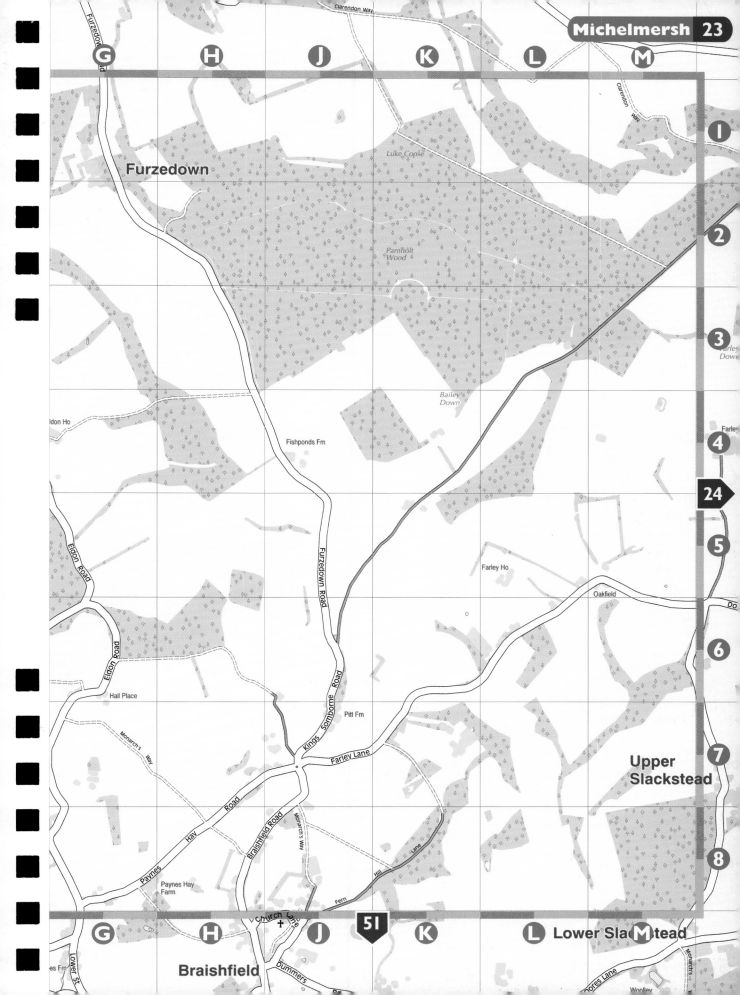

G H J K L M

I
2
3
4
24
5
6
7
8

Clarendon Way

Furzedown

Luke Copse

Parnholt
Wood

Bailey's
Down

Farle
Dow

Farle

Eldon Ho

Fishponds Fm

Eldon Road

Farley Ho

Oakfield

Do

Furzedown Road

Somborne Road

Hall Place

Kings

Pitt Fm

Farley Lane

Upper
Slackstead

Monarch's Way

Braishfield Road

Monarch's Way

Paynes

Hay

Road

Hill

Lane

Fern

Paynes Hay
Farm

Church Lane

G H J 51 K L Lower Sla M tead

Braishfield

Dummers

Monarch's

Woolley

Lower St

es Fm

24

A　B　C　D　E　F

Farley
Mount

Wood　Farley Mount
Country Park

Clarendon Way

I

Clarendon Way

*Pitt
Down*

*Mount
Down*

Farley Mount Road

2

3

*Farley
Down*

South
Lynch

4

Farley Fm

Berrydown Farm

23

†

*Southlynch
Plantn*

5

Dores Lane

Farley

Dores　Lane

6

*Gudge
Copse*

Merdon Manor Farm

7

ckstead

Dores　Lane

8

A　B　**52**　C　D　Home Farm　E　F

Claypl

Mon

1 grid square represents 500 metres

Hursley Park

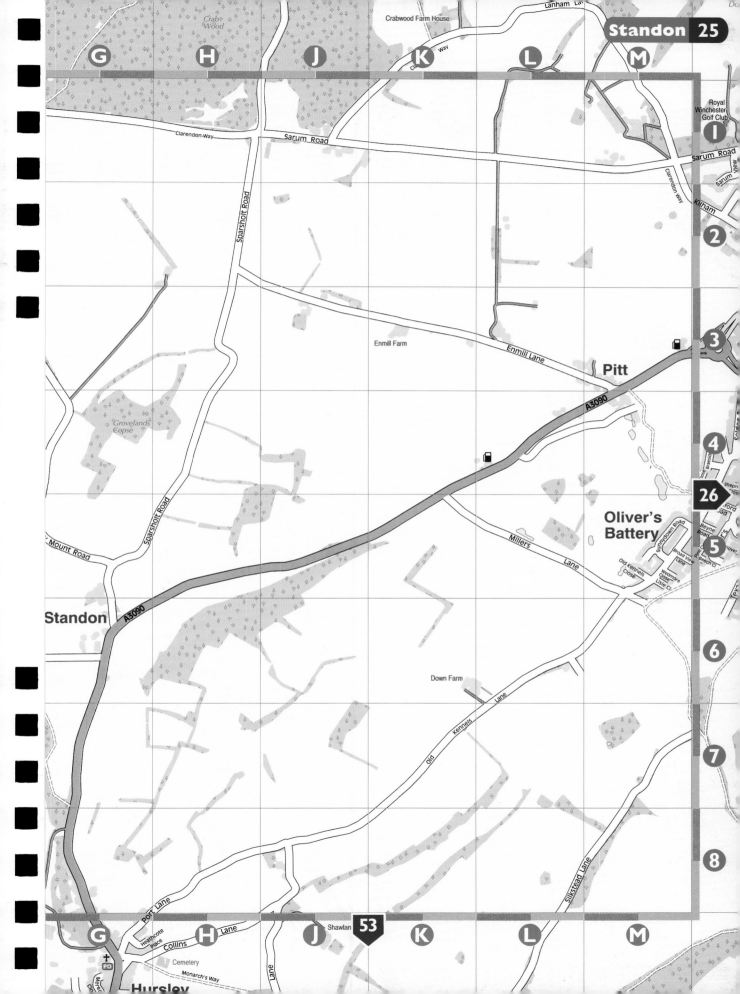

Crab Wood

Crabwood Farm House

Lanham La

Royal Winchester Golf Club

I

Clarendon-Way

Sarum Road

Sarum Road

Clarendon Way

Killham

Sarum

2

Sparsholt Road

Enmill Farm

Enmill Lane

Pitt

3

A3090

4

Grovelands Copse

Sparsholt Road

Oliver's Battery

Sunnydown Road

Beyne Road

Broad View

26

5

Mount Road

Millers

Lane

Old Kennels Close

Wedmore Close

Isle Cl.

Beech Cl.

Standon

A3090

6

Down Farm

Old Kennels Lane

7

Silkstead Lane

8

Port Lane

Heathcote Place

Collins   Lane

Shawlan

Lane

Cemetery

† PO

Monarch's Way

Hursley

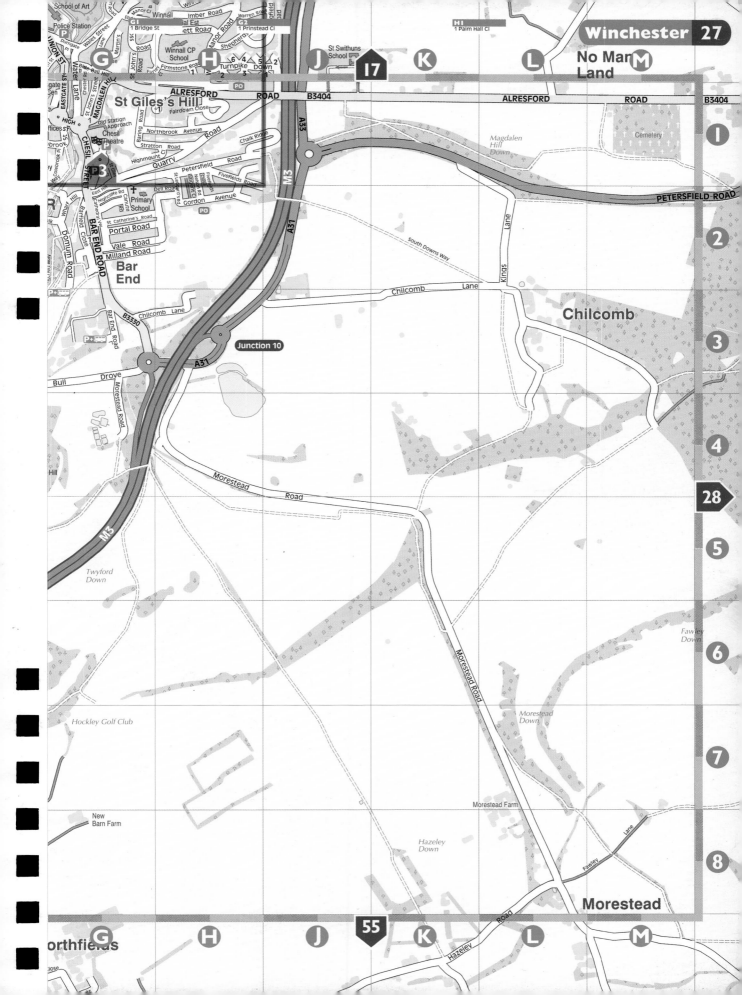

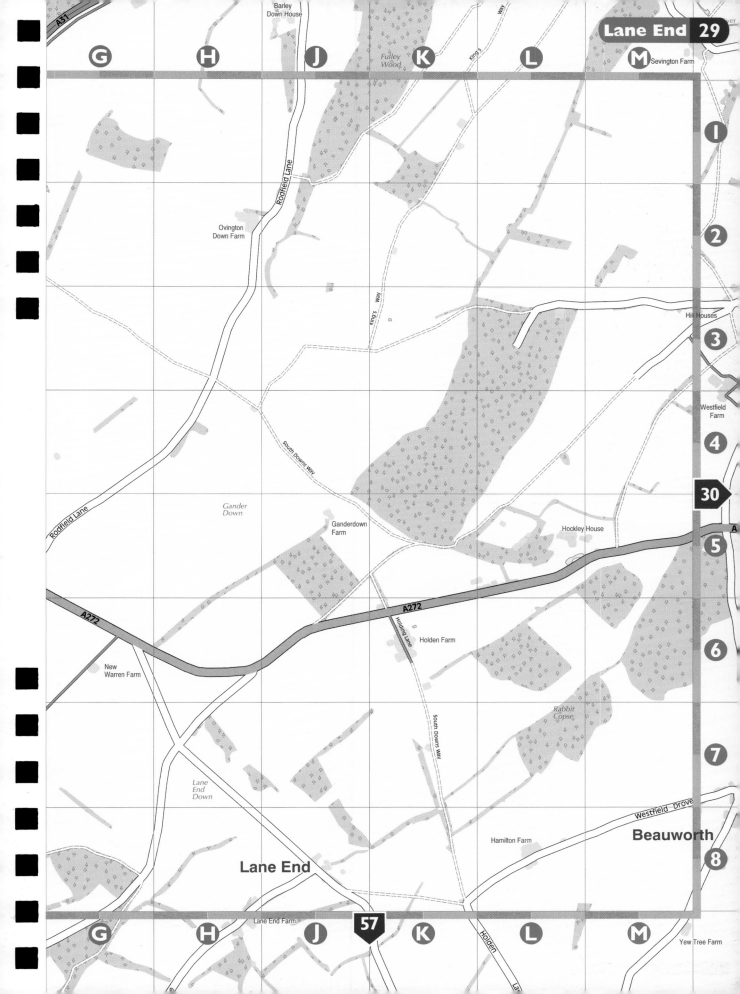

G · H · J · K · L · M

I
2
3
4
30
5
6
7
8

Sevington Farm
Barley Down House
Fulley Wood
Hill Houses
Westfield Farm
Ovington Down Farm
Rodfield Lane
King's Way
South Downs Way
Gander Down
Ganderdown Farm
Hockley House
Rodfield Lane
A272
A31
New Warren Farm
Holden Lane
Holden Farm
Rabbit Copse
South Downs Way
Lane End Down
Westfield Drove
Beauworth
Hamilton Farm
Lane End
Lane End Farm
57
Holden La
Yew Tree Farm

G H J K L M

Old Park Wood

Bramdean Common

1

Cheriton Wood

Wood Lane

Park Road

Marriners Farm

Wood Farm

2

3

Slys Farm

Bramdean

The spinney

Wood Lane

Woodlane Close

Woodcote Manor House

Tithelands Lane

Church Lane

A272

PH

4

32

Hint Woo

5

The Dean

A272

6

Joan's Acre

Brockwood Bottom

Joan's Acre Wood

Brockwood Park

7

Brockwood Bottom

8

Black House Farm

Bere Farm

Maldell Farm

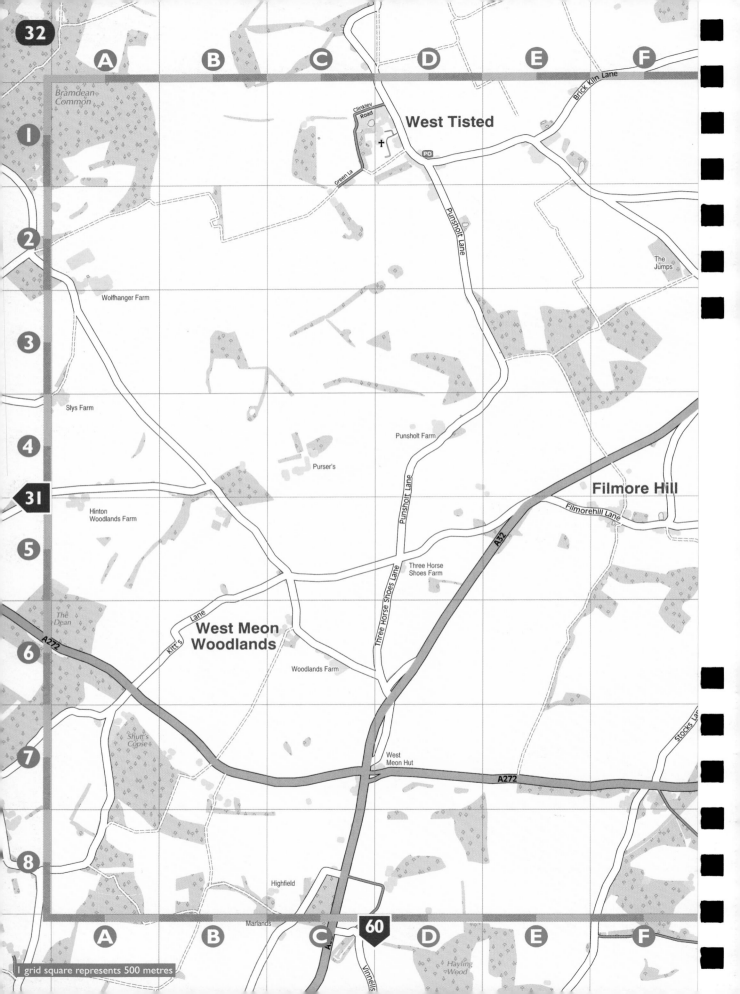

A B C D E F

I

Bramdean
Common

2

Wolfhanger Farm

3

Slys Farm

4

Hinton
Woodlands Farm

5

The
Dean

6

A272

Shutt's
Copse

7

8

A B C D E F

West Tisted

Clinkley
Road

Green La

PO

Punsholt Lane

Brick Kiln Lane

The
Jumps

Punsholt Farm

Punsholt Lane

Filmore Hill

Filmorehill Lane

A32

Three Horse
Shoes Farm

Purser's

Three Horse Shoes Lane

Kitt's
Lane

West Meon
Woodlands

Woodlands Farm

West
Meon Hut

A272

Stocks Lane

Highfield

Marlands

Vinnells

Hayling
Wood

1 grid square represents 500 metres

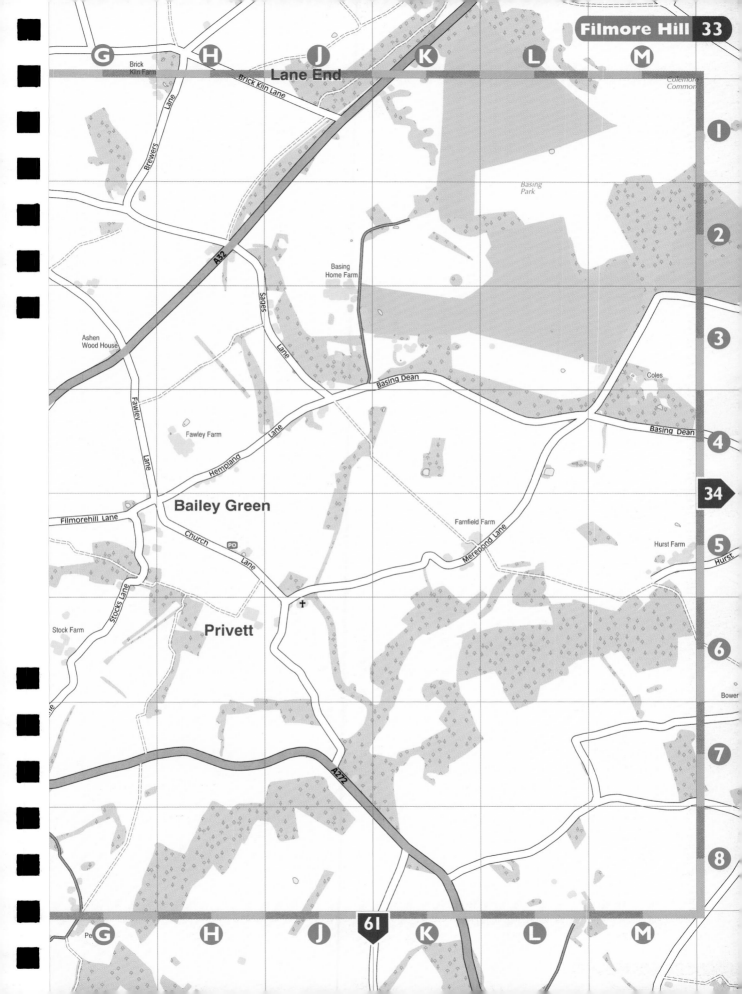

G   H   J   K   L   M

Brick
Kiln Farm

Lane End

Brick Kiln Lane

Colemore
Common

Brewers Lane

I

Basing
Park

A32

2

Sages Lane

Basing
Home Farm

3

Ashen
Wood House

Basing Dean

Coles

Basing Dean

Fawley Lane

Fawley Farm

Hempland Lane

4

34

Bailey Green

Farnfield Farm

Filmorehill Lane

Church Lane

PO

Merepond Lane

Hurst Farm

Hurst

5

Stocks Lane

Stock Farm

Privett

†

6

Bower

7

A272

8

Pe

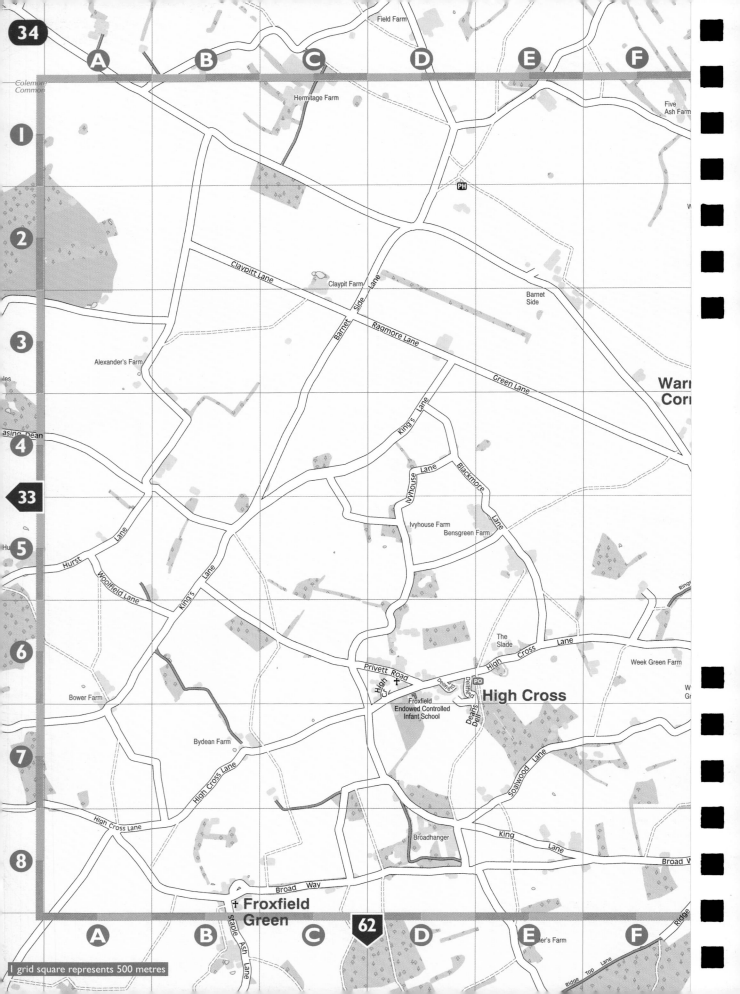

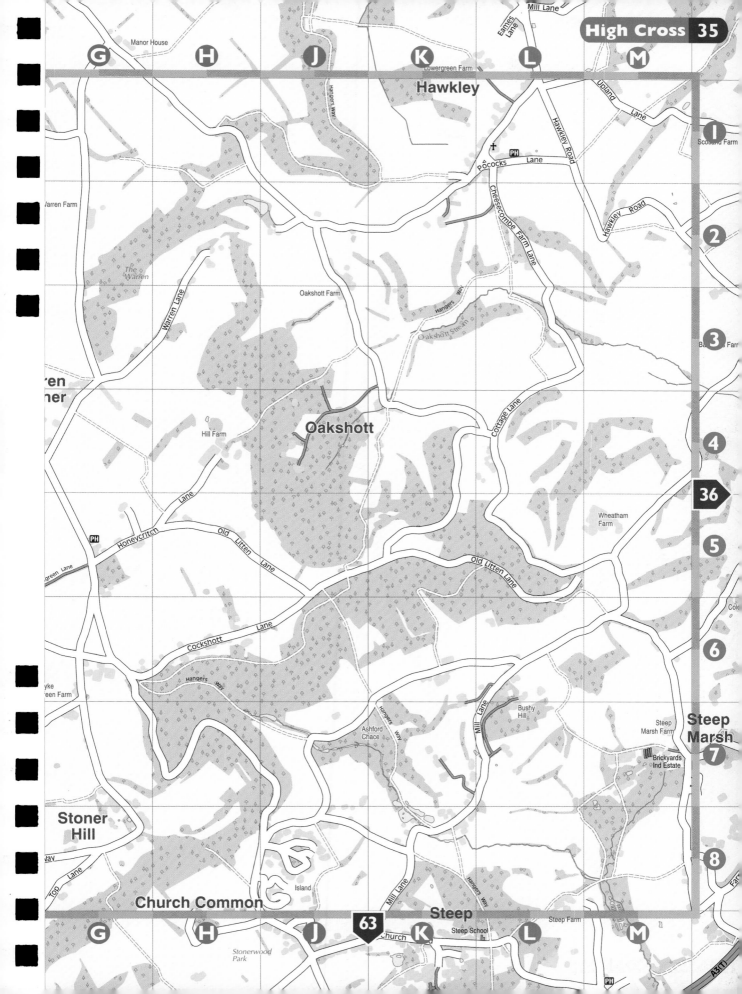

G H J K L M

Manor House

Mill Lane

Eames Lane

Hawkley

Lowergreen Farm

Upland Lane

Scotland Farm

1

Hangers Way

Warren Farm

Hawkley Road

2

Pococks Lane

PH

The Warren

Cheesecombe Farm Lane

Hawkley Road

Ba Farr

3

Warren Lane

Oakshott Farm

Hangers Way

Oakshott Stream

arren ner

Oakshott

Cottage Lane

4

Hill Farm

Lane

Wheatham Farm

36

Honeycritch

Old Litten Lane

PH

5

reen Lane

Old Litten Lane

Col

Cockshott Lane

6

yke een Farm

Hangers Way

Bushy Hill

Mill Lane

Steep Marsh Farm

Steep Marsh

Ashford Chace

Hangers Way

Brickyards Ind Estate

7

Stoner Hill

Way

op Lane

Island

Mill Lane

Hangers Way

8

Church Common

63

Steep

Steep Farm

Church

Steep School

PH

G H J K L M

Stonerwood Park

A3(T)

Far

PH

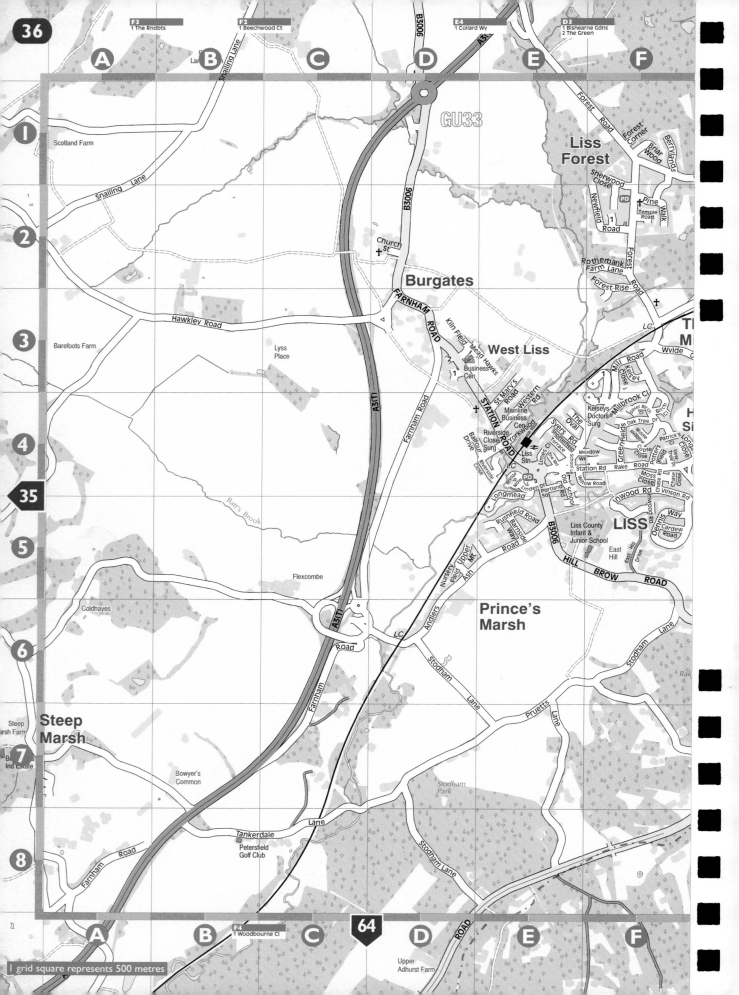

GU33

A B C D E F

1

Scotland Farm

Snailing Lane

2

Church St

Burgates

3

Barefoots Farm

Hawkley Road

Lyss Place

FARNHAM ROAD

Kiln Field
Mead Hawks

West Liss

Liss Business Cen

St. Mary's Road

Western Rd

Mainline Business Cen

4

A3(T)

Farnham Road

Balfour Drive

Riverside Close Surg

STATION ROAD
Norkwood

Riverside Close

Sydr's Rd
Shottermill Terrace

The Oval

Liss Stn

Kelseys Doctors Surg

Millbrook Cl

Greenfield

Oak Tree Dr

Patrick's
Yew Tree Pl

Mill Road

Kelsey Close

Wylde

LC

35

Batt's Brook

5

Flexcombe

PO
Bridge Mdw

Linden Dr
Umes Cl
The Mt

Old School
Portland Sq

Longmead

Rushfield Road

Barnside Way

B3006

Liss County Infant & Junior School

Meadow Wk

Station Rd

Willow Road

Rake Road

Moss Close

Vinson Rd

LISS

Inwood Rd

Dennis Way

Cardew Road

East Hill

East Hill Drive

HILL BROW ROAD

Coldhayes

6

A3(T)
Road

LC

Nursery Field
Upper Ash

Andlers

Prince's Marsh

Stodham Lane

Pruetts Lane

Stodham Lane

Stodham Park

Steep Marsh

Farnham Road

Steep Marsh Farm

Ind Estate

7

Bowyer's Common

Lane

Tankerdale

Petersfield Golf Club

8

Farnham Road

A B C D E F

ROAD

Upper Adhurst Farm

F4
1 Woodbourne Cl

Forest Road
Forest Corner
Briar Wood
Berrylands

Liss Forest

Sherwood Close
Newfield Road
Pine Walk
Temple Road
PO

Rotherbank Farm Lane
Forest Rise
Forest Road

LC

TH
M

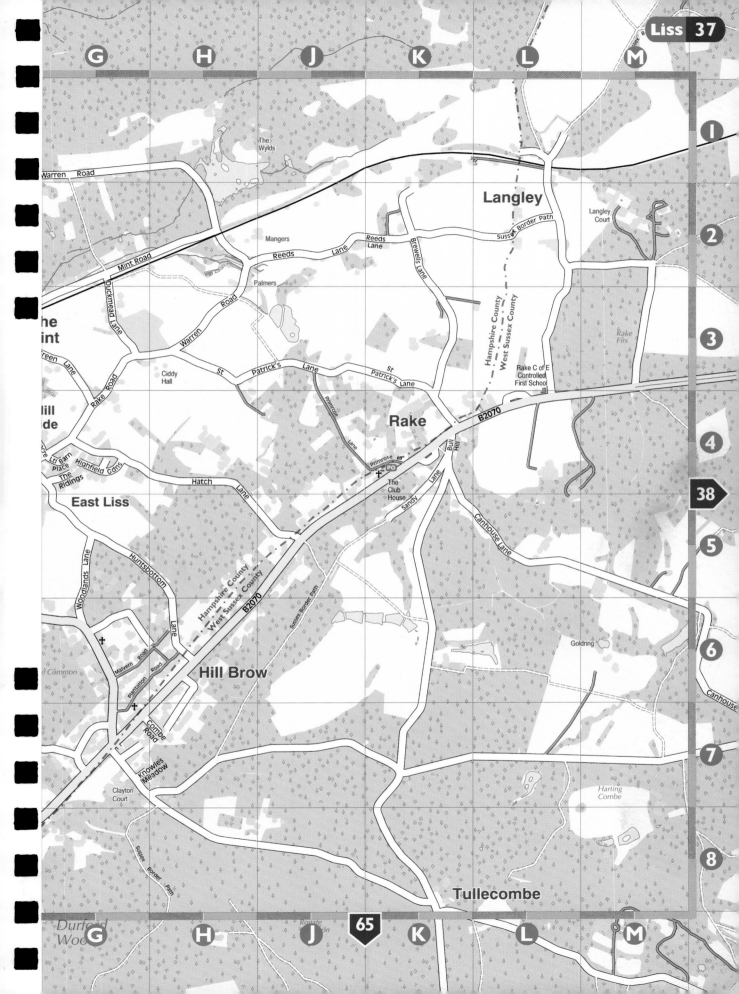

A   B   C   D   E   F

1

Home
Park

Border Path

Sussex

B2070

Liphook
Golf
Club

PORTSMOUTH

Hatch Farm

Ripsley House

2

Chapel
Common

Milland
Lane

Milland House

Upper
Wardley

3

Maysleith

Milland Lane

Wa

4

Maysleith
Wood

Hollycomb
School

37

Mill Farm

5

Mill Vale
Meadows

Fernhurst Road

6

Canhouse Lane

Great
Trippetts Farm

Chorley
Common

Rake Road

Stretcons
Copse

Milland
Rd

Greenland
Drawsey
Pennels
C
Rd
Meade
bahn

Ibing Road

Milland

Rake   Road

Lyford Farm

Waldergrove Farm ✝

7

New
Barn Farm

8

Cook's Pond Road

Bobbolds
Farm

Kingsham
Wood

A   B   66   D   E   F

Trotten Marsh

Borden
Wood

Rol

Rondle

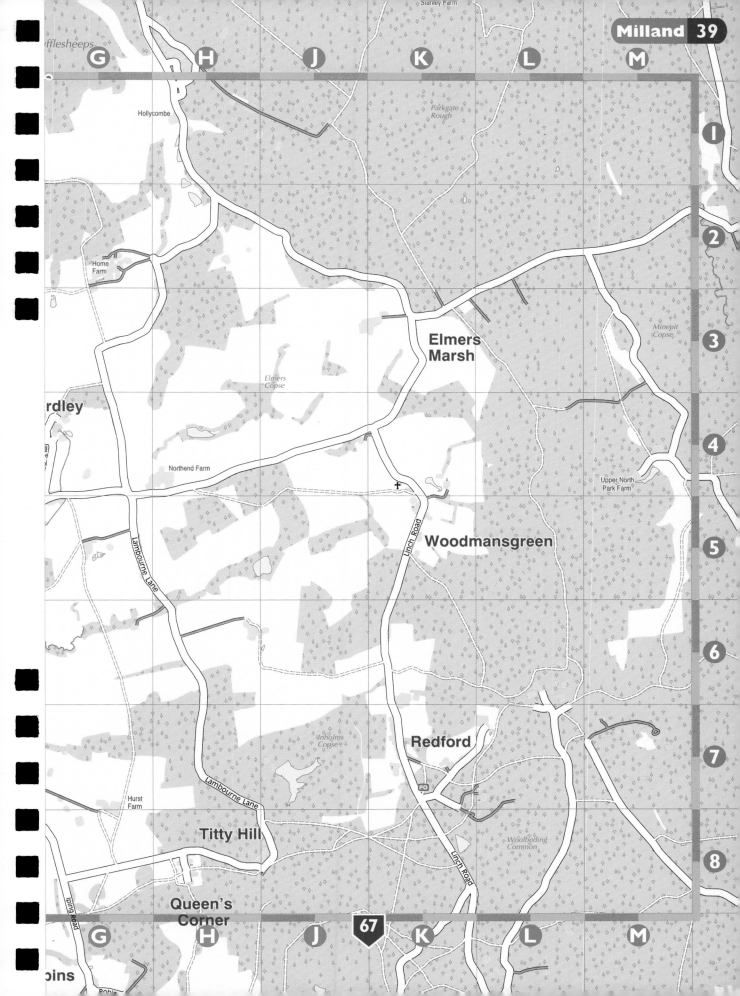

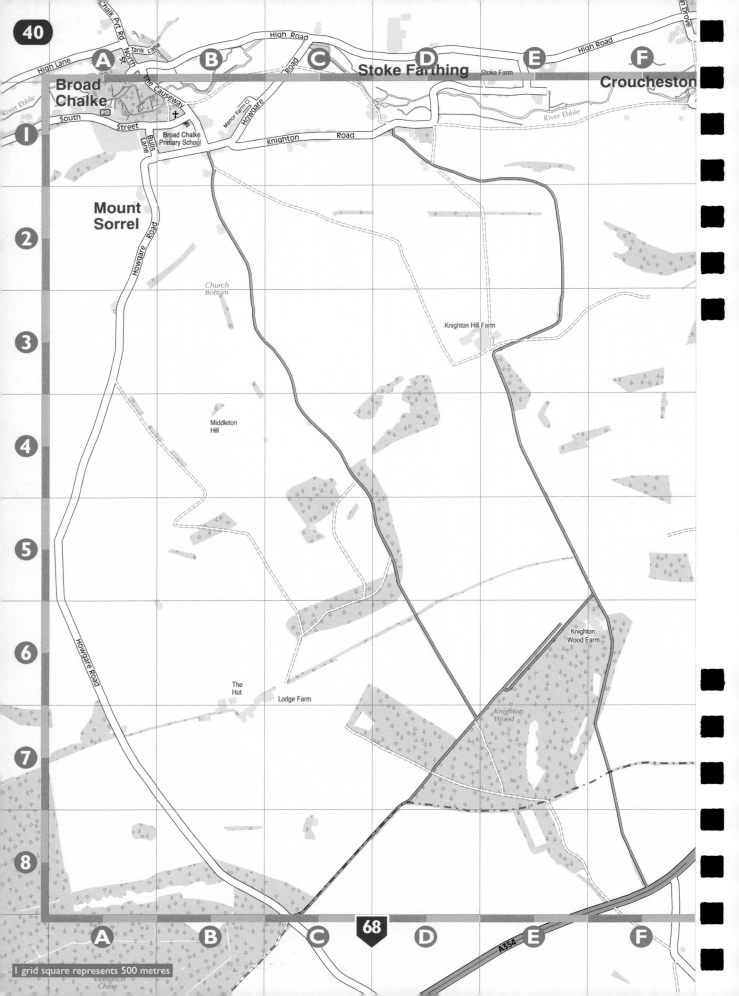

Chalk Pvt Rd

High Lane

Tank Lane

North St

High Road

A

B

Road

C

D

Stoke Farthing

Stoke Farm

E

High Road

F

River Ebble

Broad Chalke

The Causeway

PO

South Street

Bulls Lane

Manor Farm cl

Howgare

Broad Chalke Primary School

Knighton   Road

Crtoucheston

River Ebble

1

Mount Sorrel

Howgare Road

2

Church Bottom

Knighton Hill Farm

3

Middleton Hill

4

5

6

Howgare Road

Knighton Wood Farm

The Hut

Lodge Farm

Knighton Wood

7

8

A

B

C

68

D

A354

E

F

Verditch Chase

1 grid square represents 500 metres

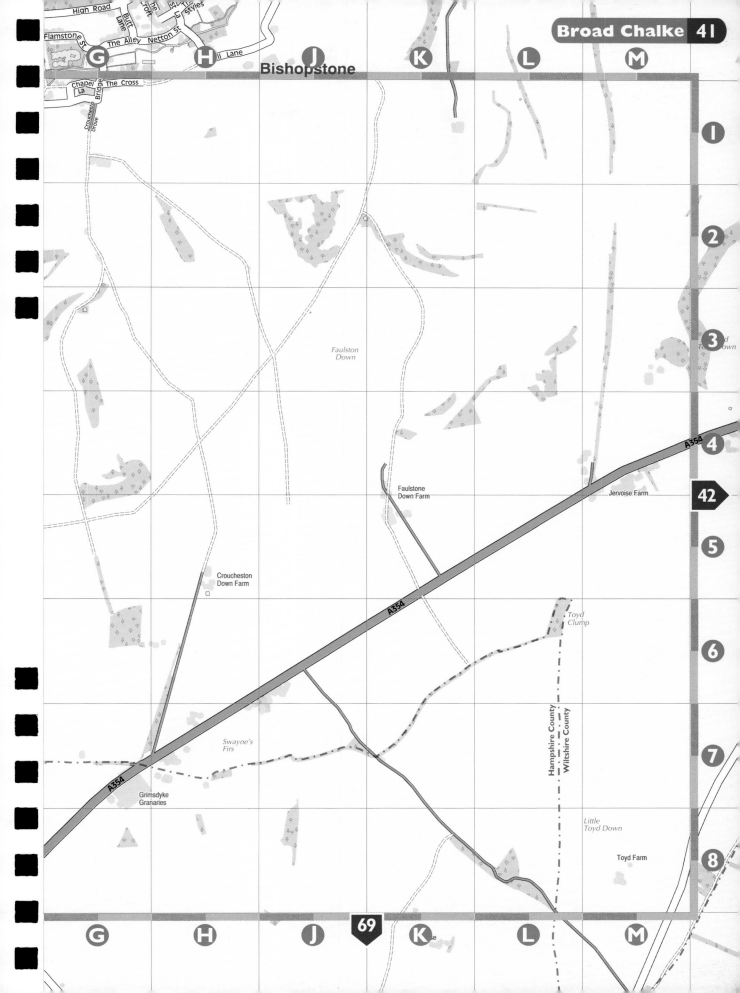

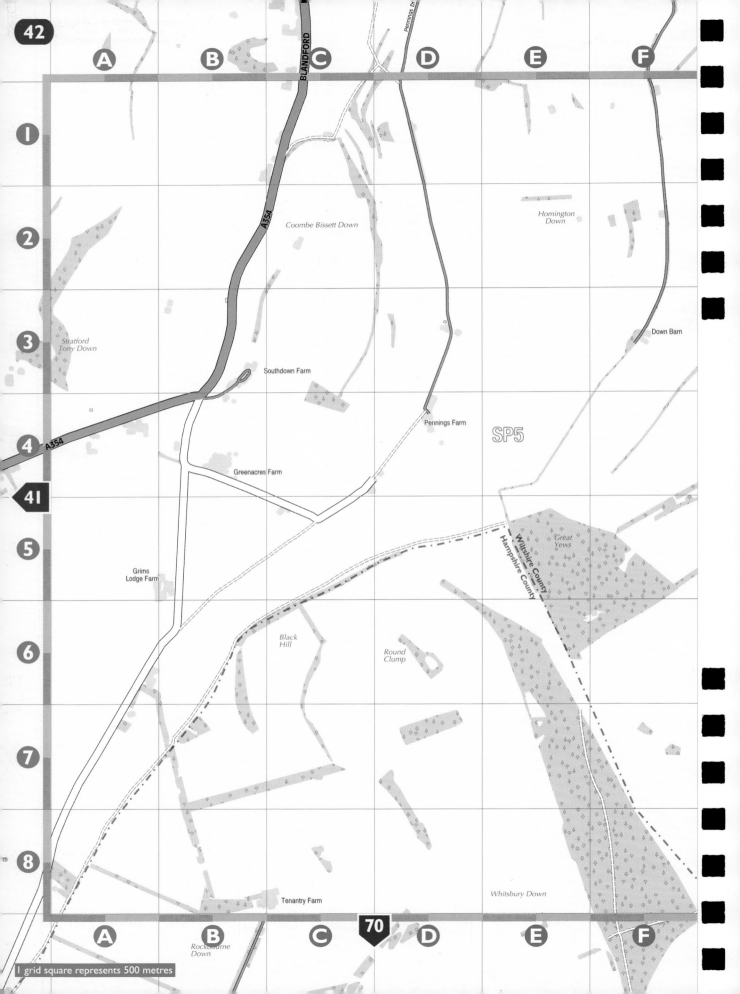

42

A   B   BLANDFORD C   D   E   F

1

A354

2   Coombe Bissett Down   Homington Down

3   Stratford Tony Down   Down Barn

Southdown Farm

Pennings Farm

4   A354   SP5

Greenacres Farm

41

Great Yews

5   Wiltshire County
Hampshire County

Grims Lodge Farm

6   Black Hill   Round Clump

7

8   Whitsbury Down

A   B   70 C   D   E   F
Rockbourne Down
Tenantry Farm

1 grid square represents 500 metres

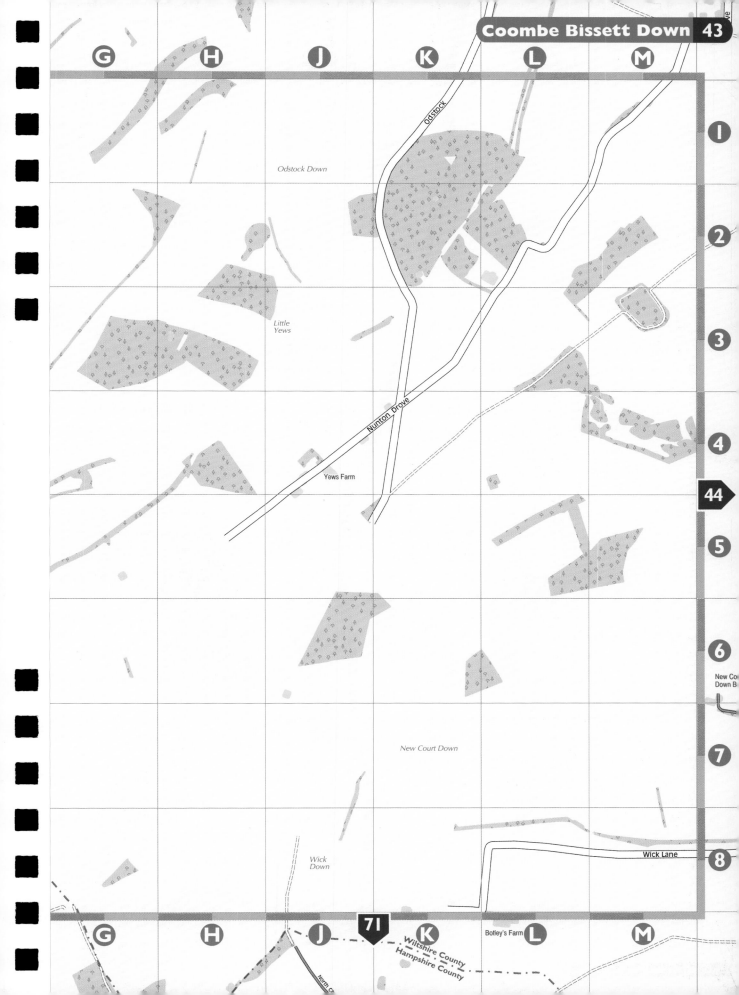

G   H   J   K   L   M

I

2

3

Odstock

Odstock Down

Little
Yews

Nunton Drove

4

44

5

Yews Farm

6

New Co
Down B

New Court Down

7

Wick Lane

8

Wick
Down

G   H   J   K   L   M

Wiltshire County
Hampshire County

Botley's Farm

North Ch

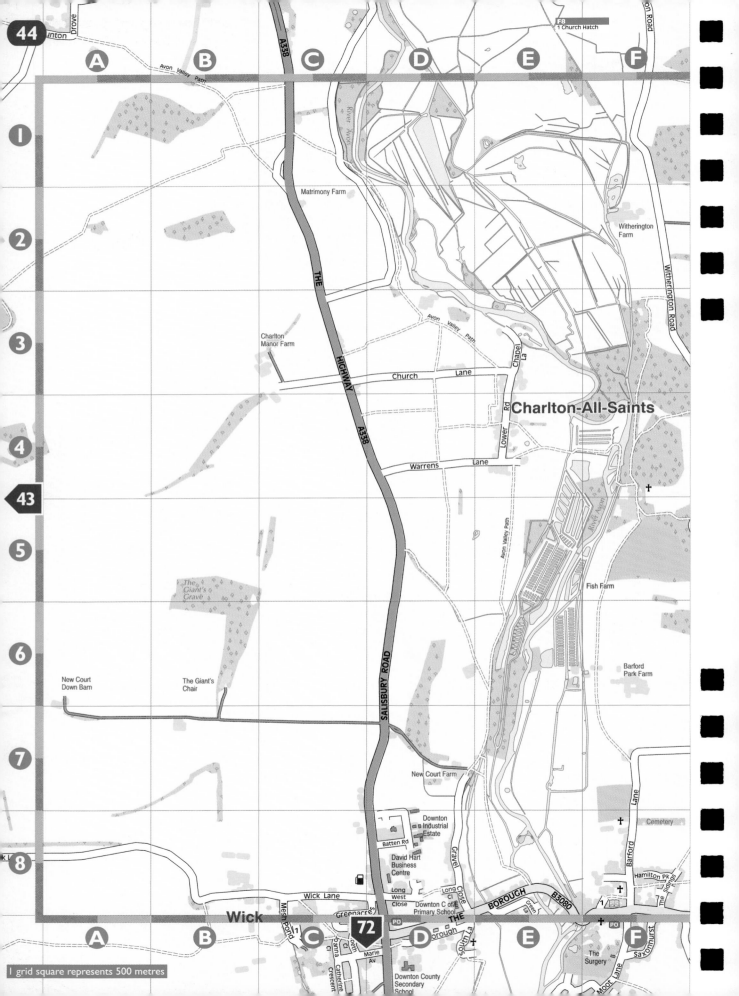

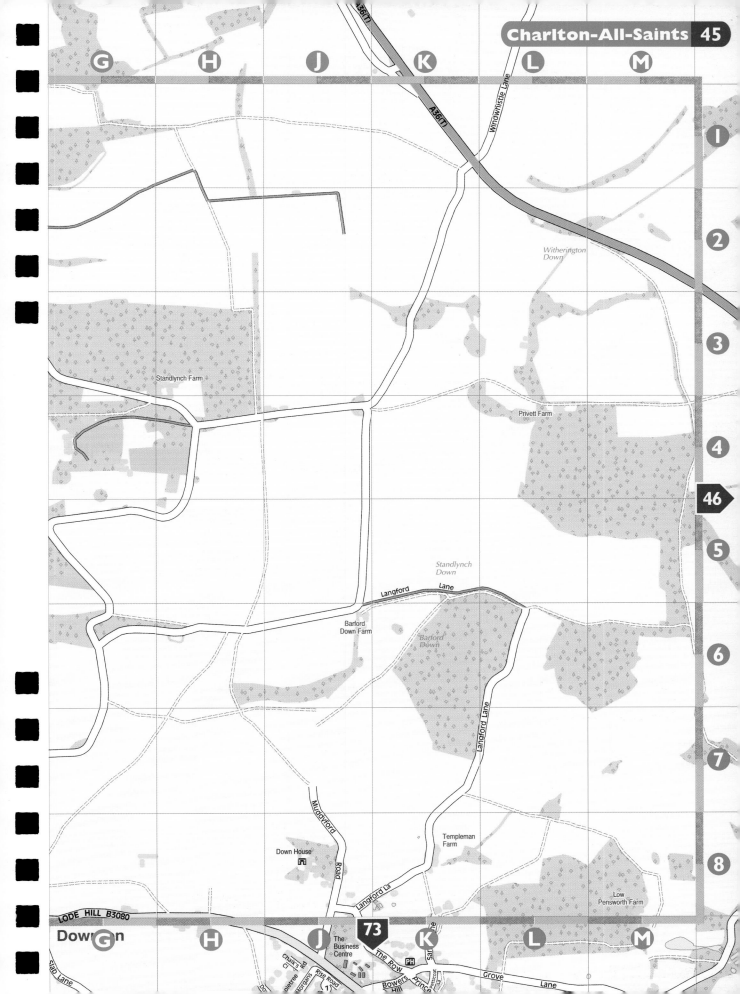

G H J K L M

I
2
3
4
46
5
6
7
8

Witherington Down

Standlynch Farm

Privett Farm

Standlynch Down

Langford Lane

Barford Down Farm

Barford Down

Langford Lane

Muddyford Road

Down House

Templeman Farm

Langford La

Low Pensworth Farm

LODE HILL B3080

Dow**G**n

73

The Business Centre

PH

The Row

Chalk's Rd

Morgans

Rise Road

Bowers Hill

Prince

Grove Lane

G H J K L M

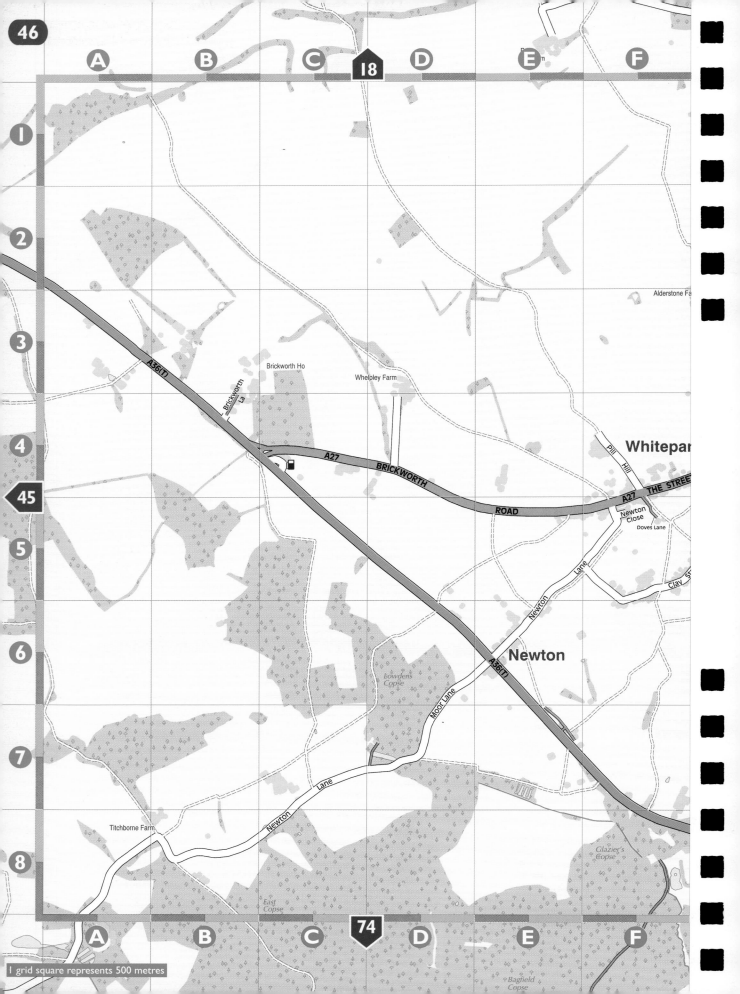

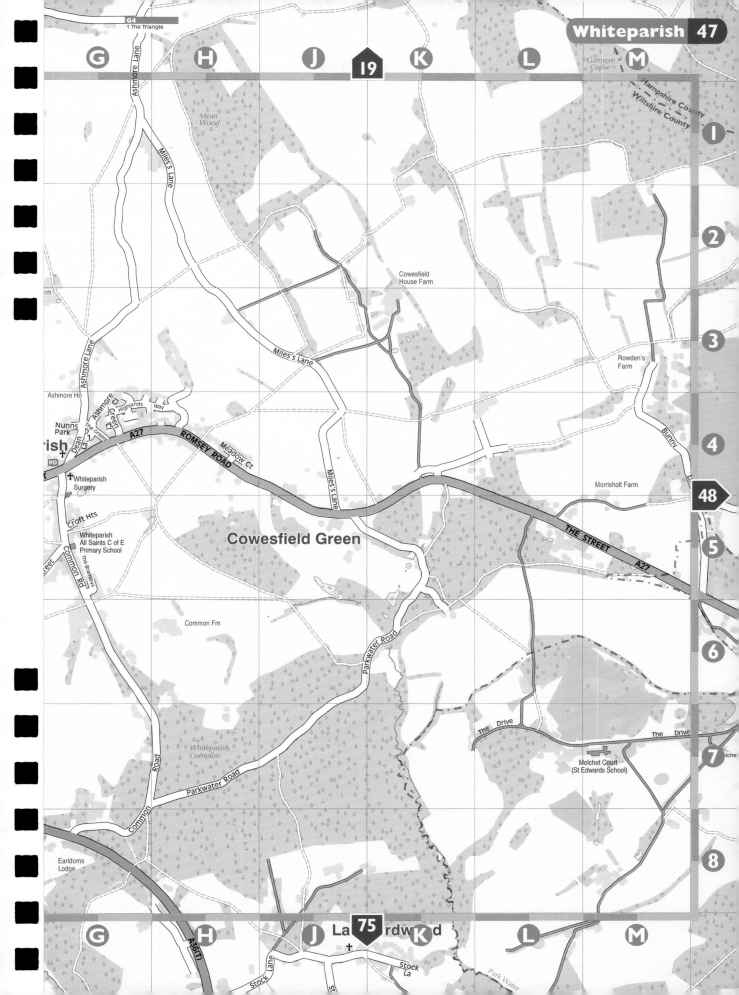

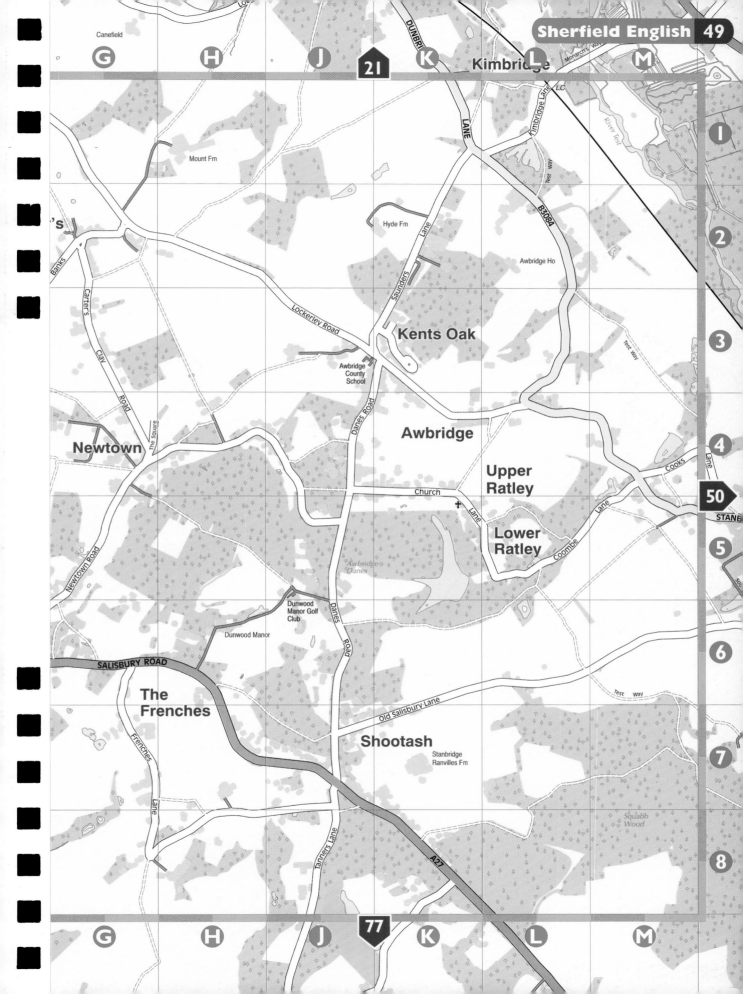

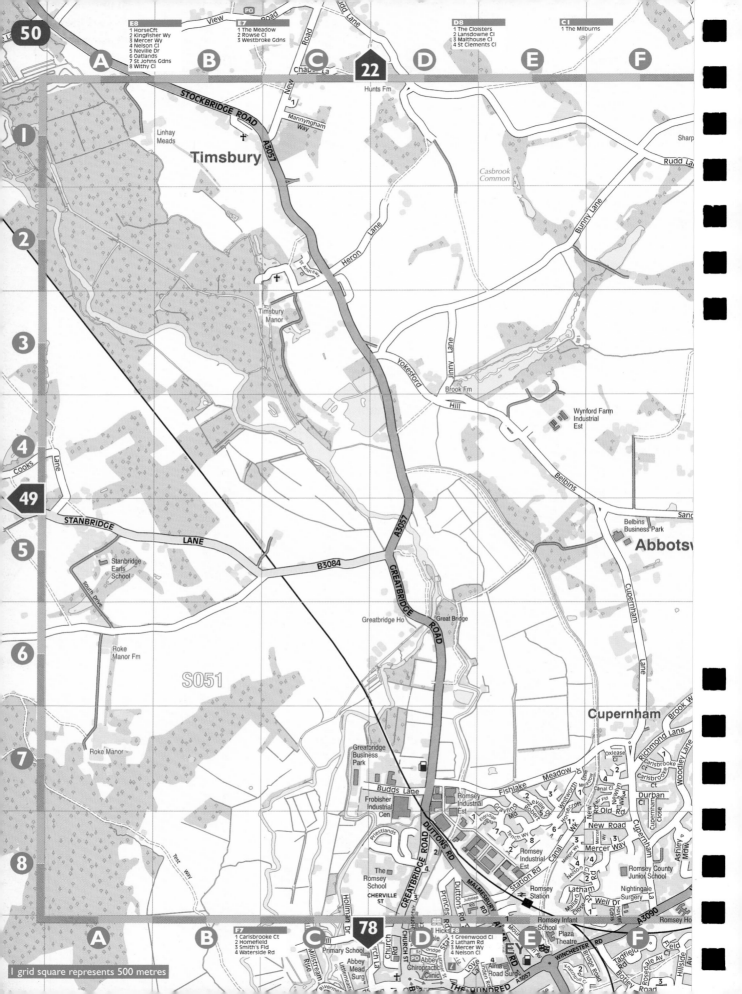

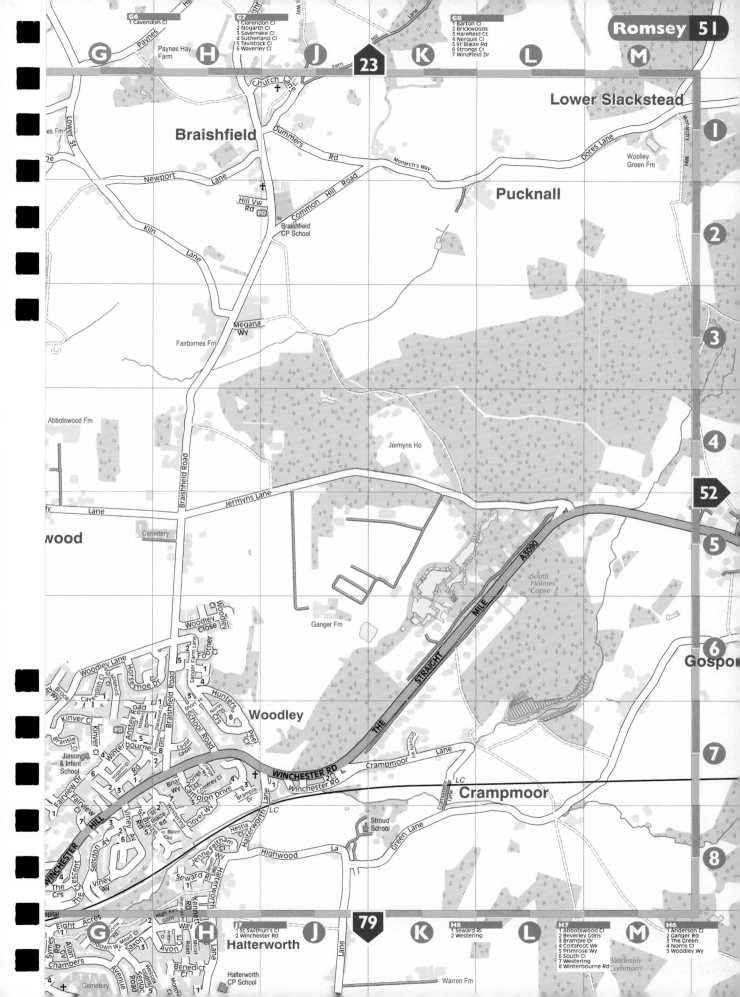

G6
1 Cavendish Cl

G7
1 Clarendon Cl
2 Nogarth Cl
3 Savernake Cl
4 Sutherland Cl
5 Tavistock Cl
6 Waverley Cl

G8
1 Barton Cl
2 Brickwoods
3 Harefield Ct
4 Nerquis Cl
5 St Blaize Rd
6 Strongs Cl
7 Windfield Dr

G H J K L M

23 52

Lower Slackstead

Braishfield

Pucknall

Paynes Hay Farm

Newport Lane

Hill Vw Rd PO

Braishfield CP School

Kiln Lane

Common Hill Road

Dummers Rd

Monarch's Way

Dores Lane

Woolley Green Fm

Monarch's Way

I

2

3

Megana Wy

Fairbornes Fm

Abbotswood Fm

Jermyns Ho

South Holmes Copse

4

52

5

wood

Braishfield Road

Jermyns Lane

Lane

Cemetery

Ganger Fm

A3090

THE STRAIGHT MILE

6

Gospor

Woodley Cl

Woodley Close

Fortner Cl

Ganger Farm Lane

Woodley Lane

Horseshoe Dr

Hunters

Cl

Woodley

Groom Wy

Lane

7

Kinver Cl

Anstey Road

Braishfield Road

School Road

Peel Ct

Winchester Rd

Crampmoor

Lane

LC

Crampmoor

Junior & Infant School

Winterbourne

Campion Drive

Winchester Rd

Stroud School

Green Lane

Highwood

La

Warren Fm

Halterworth CP School

Halterworth

Cemetery

G H J 79 K L M

J7
1 St Swithun's Cl
2 Winchester Rd

H8
1 Seward Ri
2 Westering

H7
1 Abbotswood Cl
2 Beverley Gdns
3 Bramble Dr
4 Coltsfoot Wk
5 Primrose Wy
6 South Cl
7 Westering
8 Winterbourne Rd

H6
1 Anderson Cl
2 Ganger Rd
3 The Green
4 Norris Cl
5 Woodley Wy

8

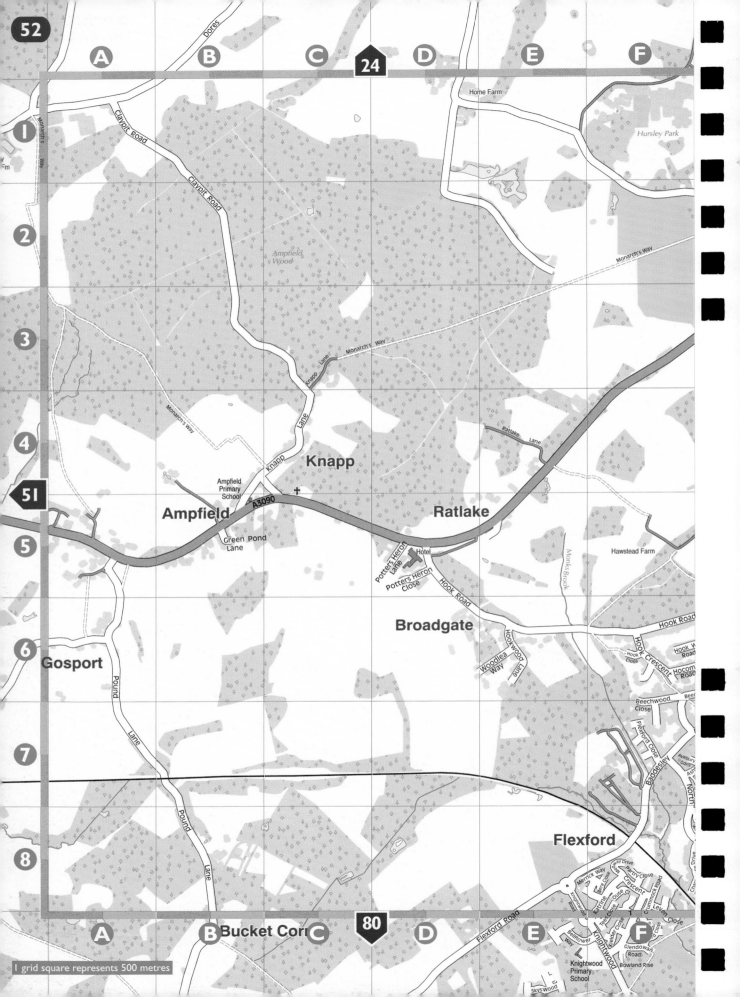

A B C 24 D E F

I
2
3
4
51
5
6
7
8

A B Bucket Corr C 80 D E F

Claypit Road
Claypit Road

Monarch's Way
Monarch's Way

Home Farm

Hursley Park

Ampfield Wood

Monarch's Way

Knapp Lane
Knapp Lane

Monarch's Way

Ratlake Lane

Knapp

Ampfield Primary School

Ampfield

A3090

Green Pond Lane

Ratlake

Potters Heron Lane
Potters Heron Close
Hotel

Hook Road

Monks Brook

Hawstead Farm

Broadgate

Hookwood Lane
Woodlea Way

Hook Road

Hook Crescent
Hook Close
Hook W Road
Hocomb Road

Beechwood Close
Beech

Gosport

Pound Lane

Pound Lane

Flexford Close
Baddesley

Avebury Gdns
Ash

North

Flexford

Flexford Road

Knightwood

Merrick Way
Oakley Drive
Pantry Close

Knightwood Road
Katrine
Bere Close
Ouse Cl
Crummock Road
Leven Close

Bellflower Way
Kielder Close
Glendowan Road
Bowland Rise

Knightwood Primary School

Skys Wood

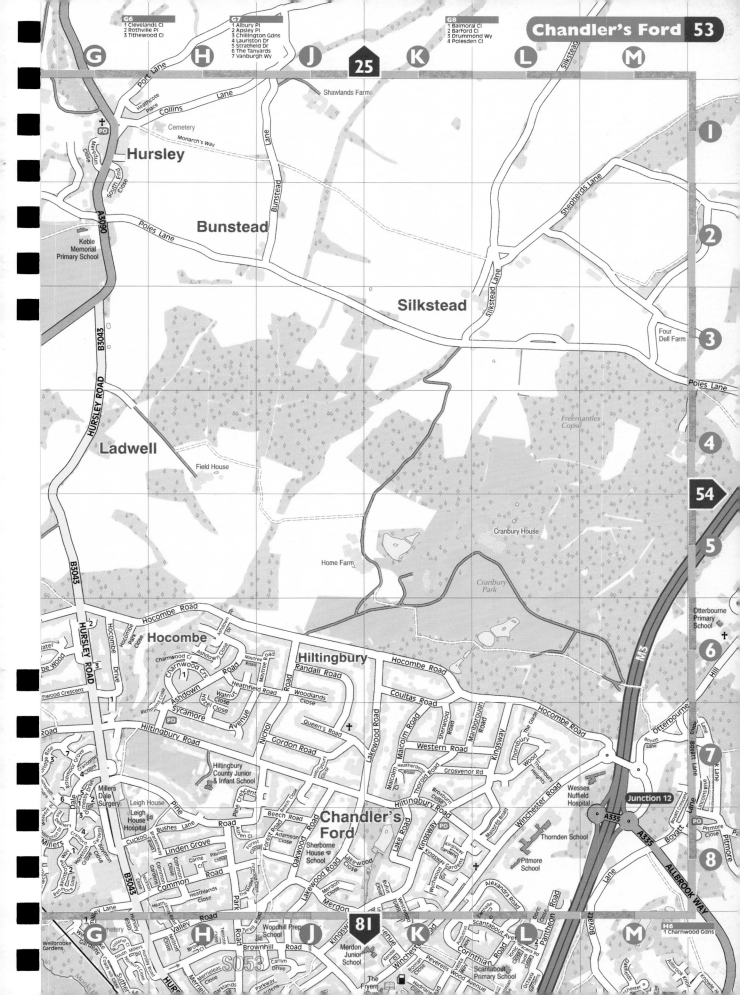

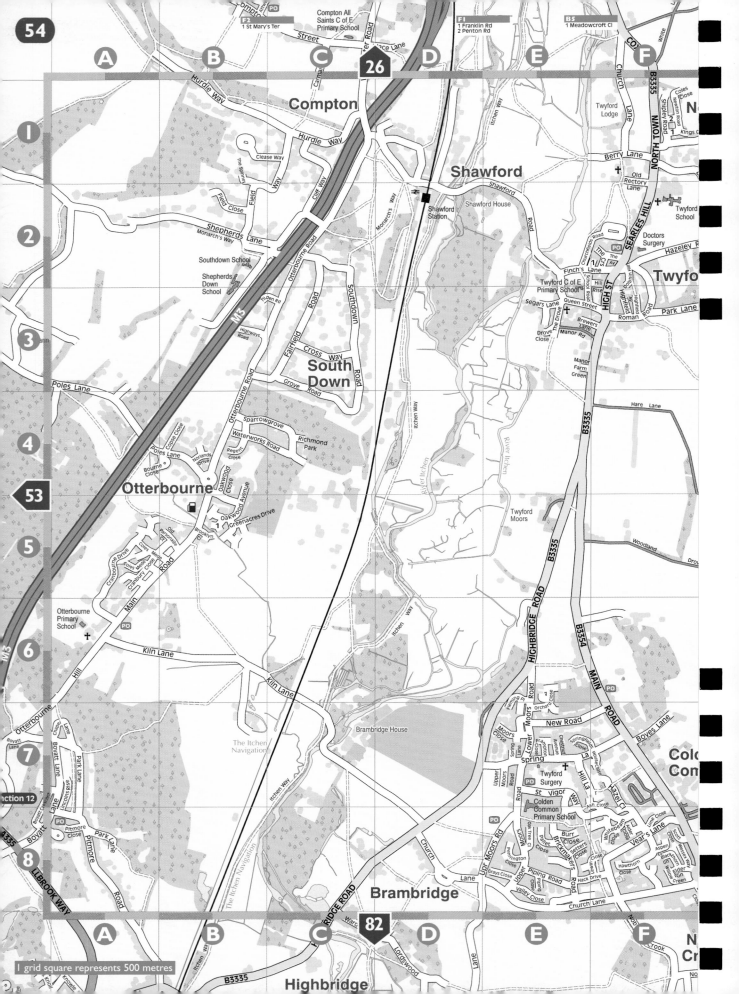

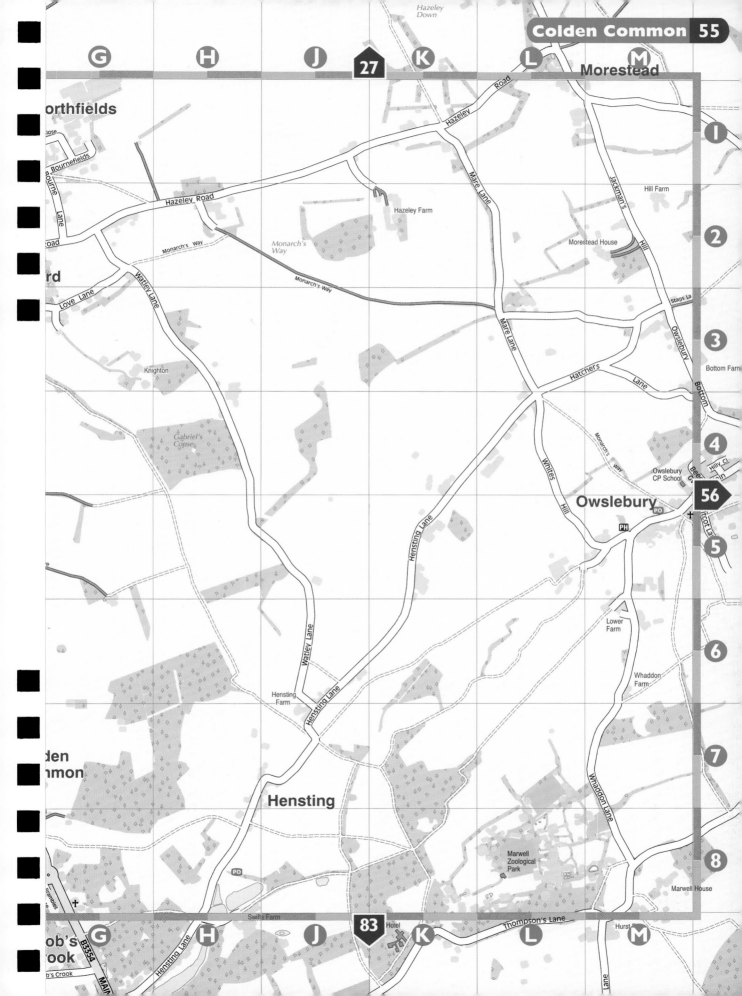

Baybridge

I grid square represents 500 metres

Lane End

G   H   J   29   K   L   M

Lane End Farm

Yew Tree Farm

I

Longwood Dean Lane

Lancen Cotts

Greendowns

PH

2

South Downs Wy

3

Salt Lane

Longwood Dean Farm

Dur Wood

4

58

Preshaw Hous

†

5

The Holt

Salt Lane

ore Lane

High Wood

Valley Walk

Stony Hard Farm

6

Monarch's Way

Preshaw

7

Belmore House

Lower Preshaw Lane

Ower Farm

Stephen's Castle Down

8

G   H   J   85   K   L   M

Monarch's Way

Stake's Lane

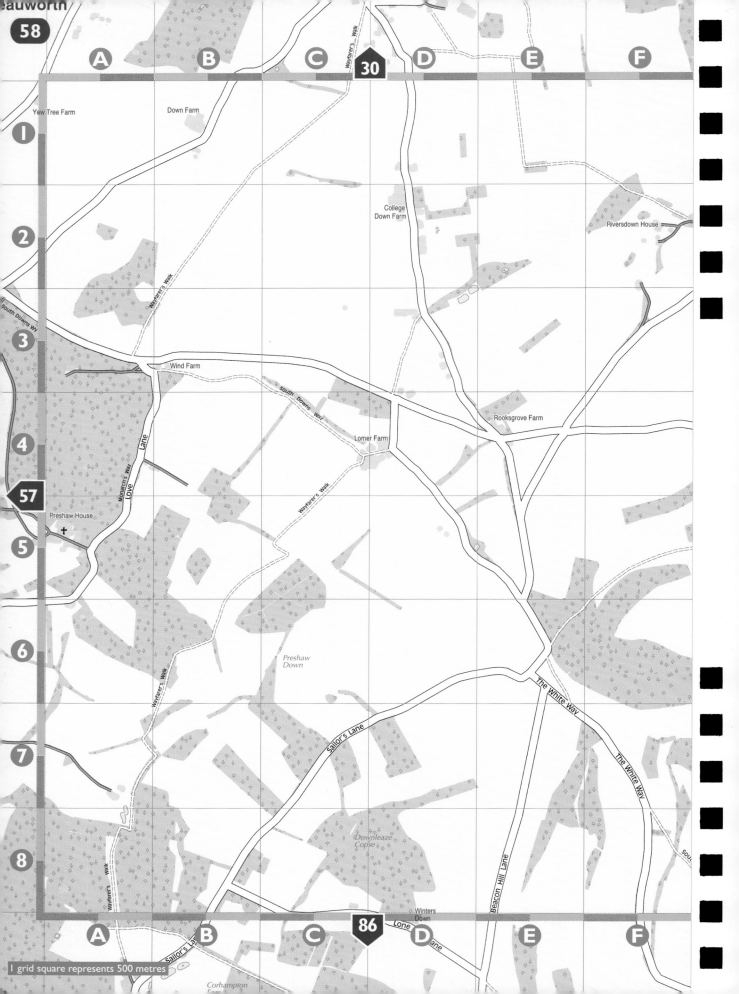

G   H   J   **31**   K   L   M

1

2

3

4

A32

60

5

6

7

8

Black House Farm

Bere Farm

Marldell Farm

Lippen Cotts

Wheely Farm

Lippen Lane

Warnford

We

Wheely Down

Monarch's Way

Old Winchester Hill Lane

Monarch's Way

Warnford Park

Old Wi

Monarch's Way

Peake New Road

Peake Farm

Monarch's

G   H   J   **87**   K   L   M

Exton

The White Way

South Downs Way

h Downs Way

A32

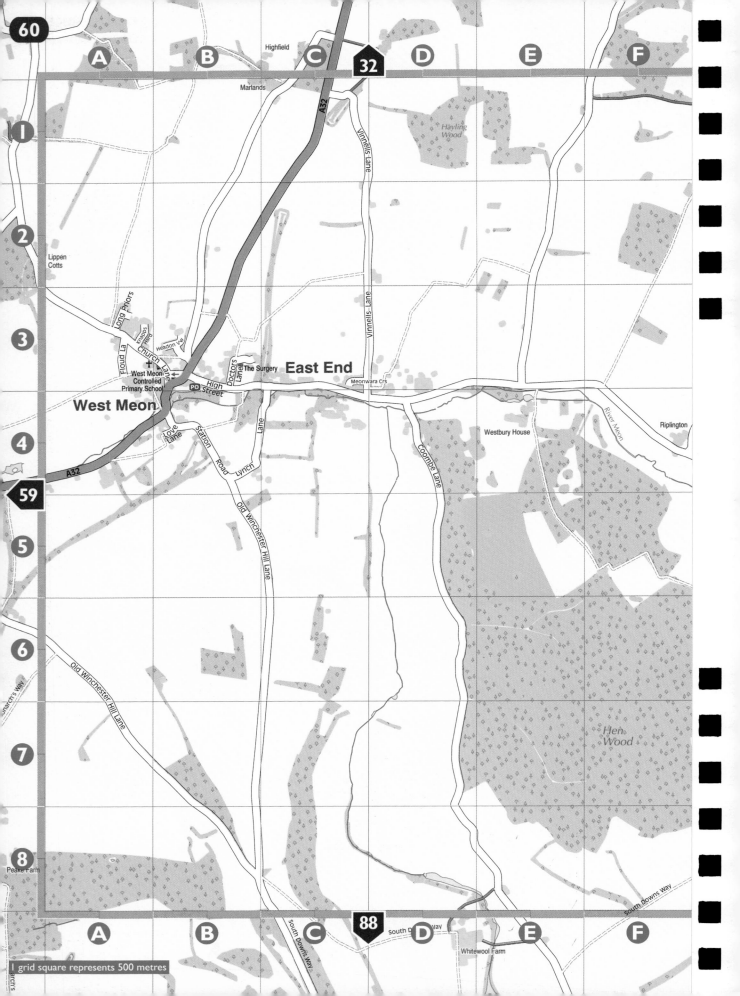

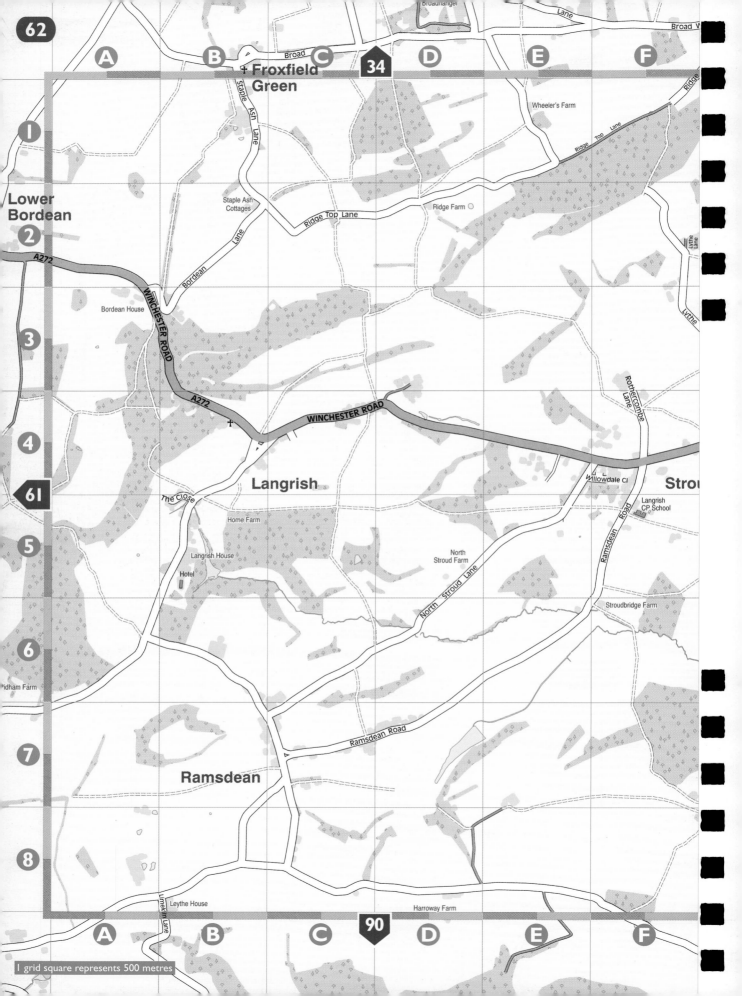

62

A   B   Broad   C   34   D   E   F

✝ Froxfield
Green

Wheeler's Farm

1

Ridge Top Lane

Lower
Bordean

Staple Ash
Cottages

Ridge Farm ○

2

A272

Bordean Lane

Bordean House

WINCHESTER ROAD

3

A272

Rothercombe Lane

WINCHESTER ROAD

✝

4

Langrish

Willowdale Cl

Strou

61

The Close

Langrish
CP. School

Home Farm

5

Langrish House

North
Stroud Farm

Ramsdean Road

Hotel

idham Farm

North Stroud Lane

Stroudbridge Farm

6

Ramsdean Road

7

Ramsdean

Limekiln Lane

Leythe House

8

Harroway Farm

A   B   C   90   D   E   F

I grid square represents 500 metres

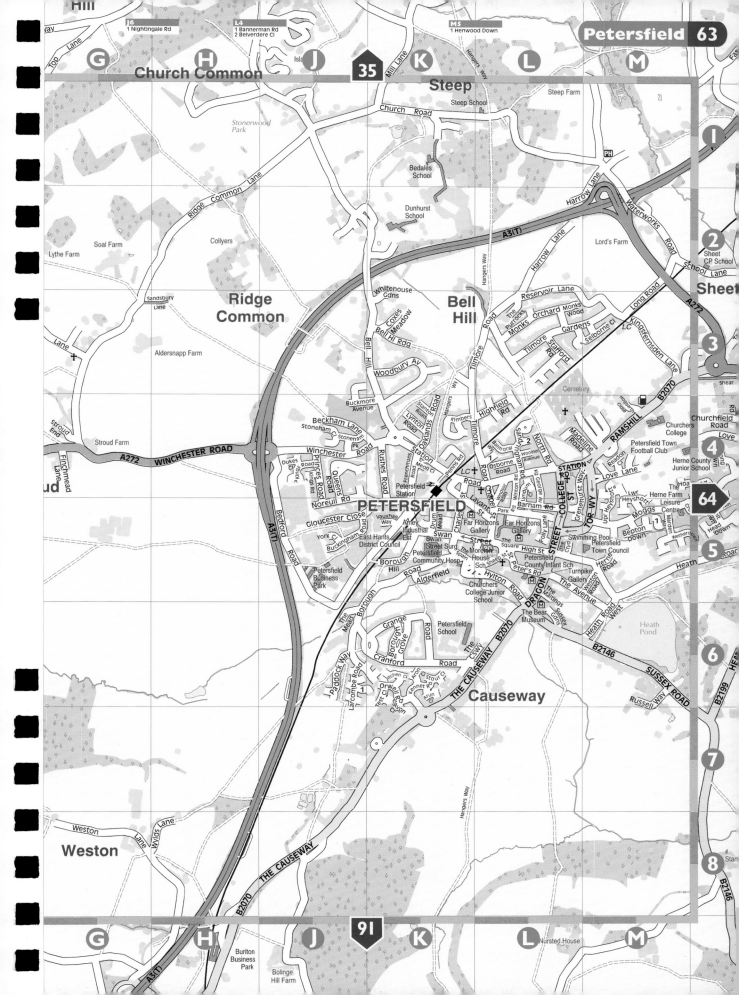

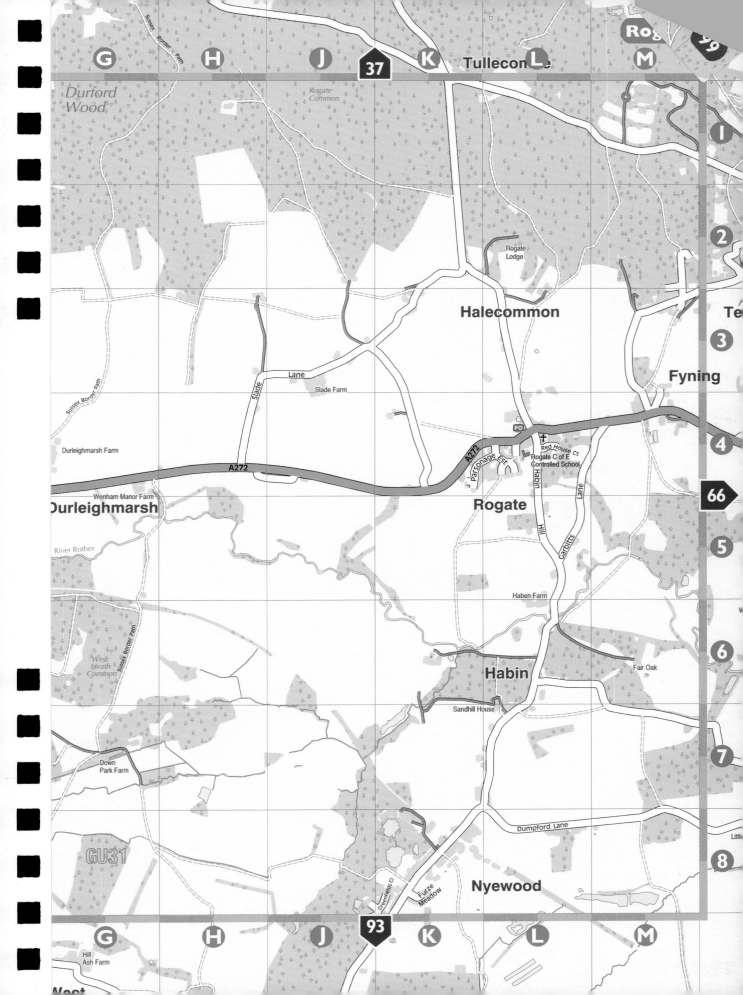

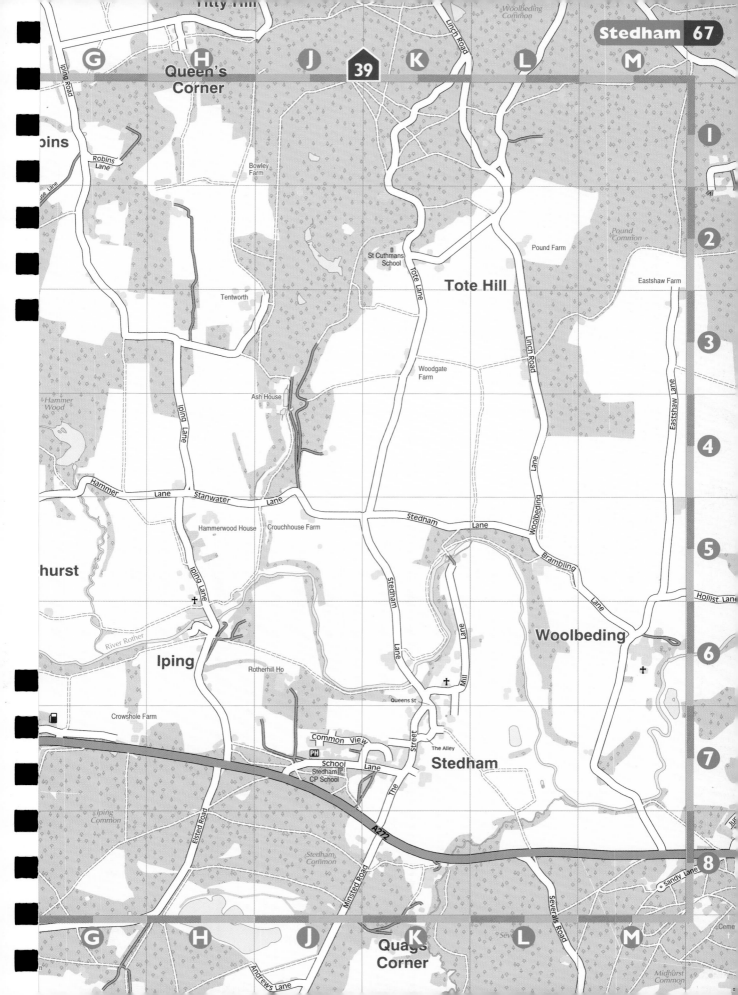

Titty Hill

Woolbeding Common

G H J **39** K L M

Queen's Corner

bins

Robins Lane

Bowley Farm

Lunch Road

I

Pound Common

2

St Cuthmans School

Tote Lane

Tote Hill

Pound Farm

Eastshaw Farm

Tentworth

3

Woodgate Farm

Linch Road

Eastshaw Lane

Iping Lane

Ash House

4

Hammer Wood

Hammer Lane Stanwater Lane

Stedham Lane

Woolbeding Lane

5

hurst

Hammerwood House Crouchhouse Farm

Iping Lane

Stedham Lane

Brambling Lane

Hollist Lane

River Rother

Woolbeding

6

Iping

Rotherhill Ho

Mill Lane

Crowshole Farm

Queens St

7

Common View

PH

School Lane

The Alley

Stedham

The Street

Stedham CP School

Iping Common

Elsted Road

A272

Minsted Road

Stedham Common

Severals Road

Sandy Lane

8

G H J K L M

Quags Corner

Andrews Lane

Midhurst Common

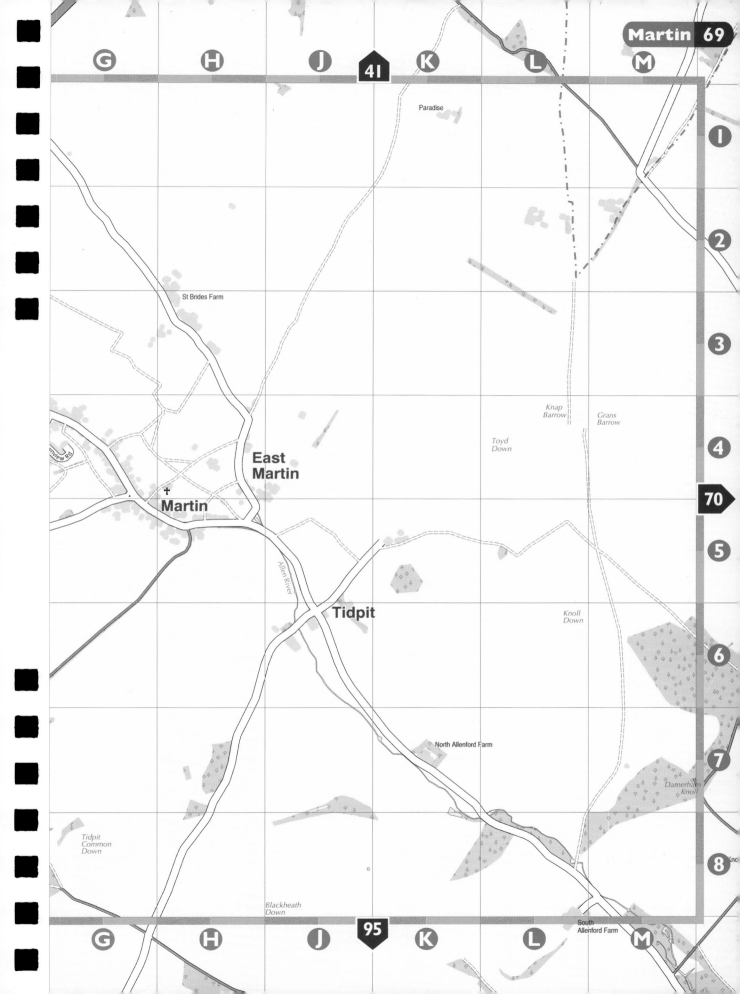

G H J 41 K L M

1
2
3
4
70
5
6
7
8

Paradise

St Brides Farm

Knap Barrow

Grans Barrow

Toyd Down

East Martin

Martin

Allen River

Tidpit

Knoll Down

North Allenford Farm

Damerham Knoll

Tidpit Common Down

Blackheath Down

South Allenford Farm

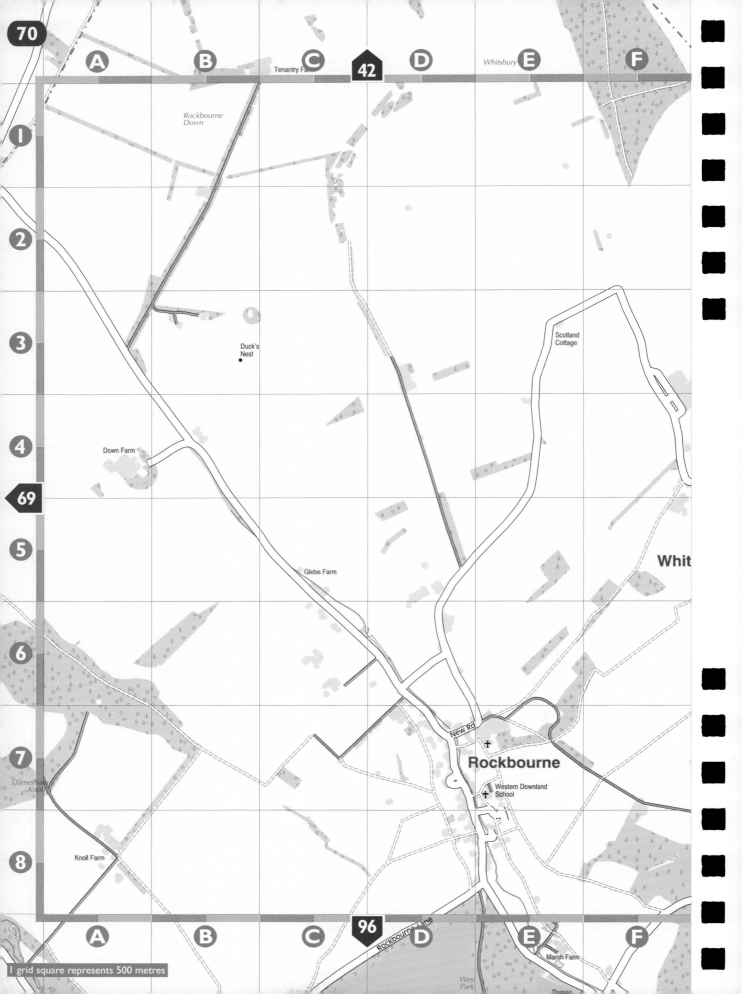

A   B   C   42   D   Whitsbury E   F

Tenantry Fa

I

Rockbourne
Down

2

3   Duck's
Nest

Scotland
Cottage

4   Down Farm

69

5   Glebe Farm   Whit

6

New Rd

7   Rockbourne

Damerham
Knoll   Western Downland
School

8   Knoll Farm

A   B   96   D   Rockbourne Lane   E   F

Marsh Farm

West
Park

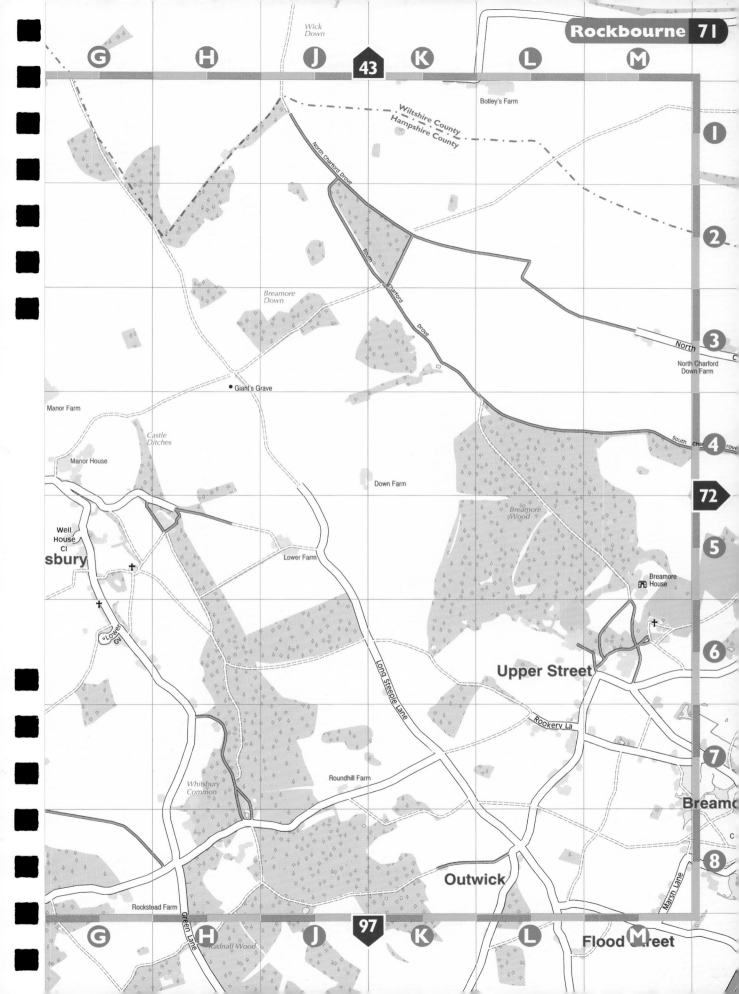

G H J 43 K L M

1
2
North 3
North Charford
Down Farm
South Cha rove 4
72
5
6
7
Breamo
8

Wick
Down

Botley's Farm

Wiltshire County
Hampshire County

North Charford Drove

South Charford Drove

Breamore
Down

Giant's Grave

Manor Farm

Castle
Ditches

Manor House

Well
House
Cl

sbury

Lower
Gv

Down Farm

Breamore
Wood

Breamore
House

Lower Farm

Upper Street

Rookery La

Long Steeple Lane

Whitsbury
Common

Roundhill Farm

Outwick

Marsh Lane

Rockstead Farm

Green Lane

Radnall Wood

G H 97 J K L M

Flood Street

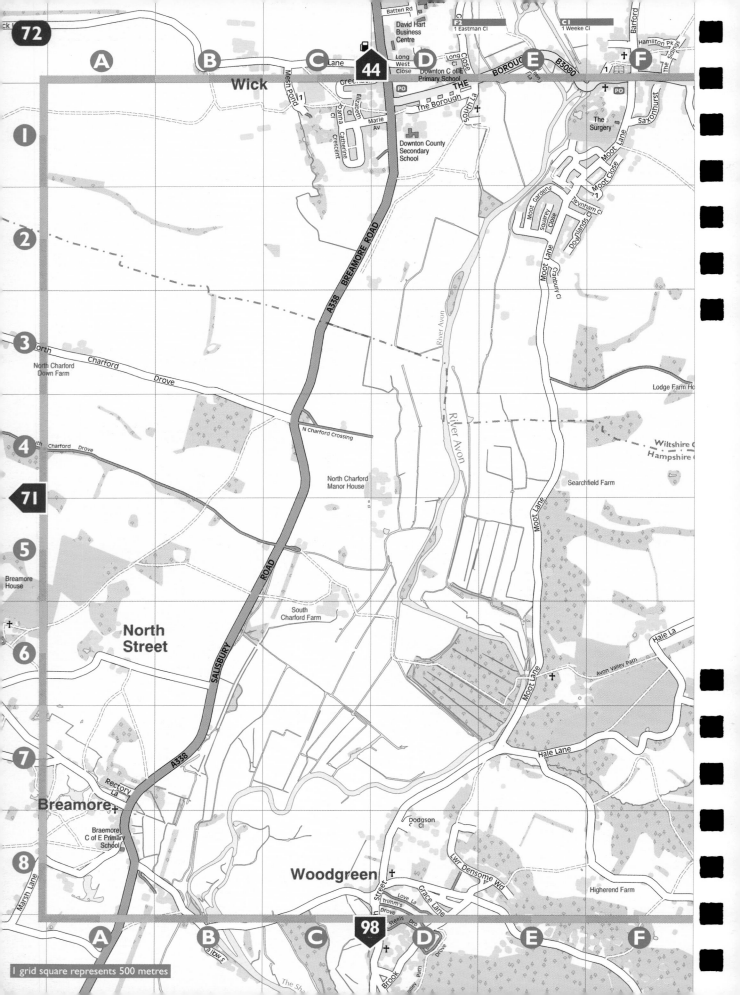

A B C 44 D E B3080 F

Wick

1

2

71

3

4

5

6

7

8

A B 98 C D E F

Batten Rd
David Hart
Business
Centre
F2 1 Eastman Cl C1 1 Weeke Cl Barford
Hamilton Pk
Long
West
Close Long
Close
Downton C of E
Primary School THE BOROUGH
The Borough PO
Downton County
Secondary
School
The
Surgery
Saxonhurst
PO
Moot Lane
Moot Close
Moot Garden
Squarey Close
Wynham Cl
Dowlands Cl
Moot Lane
Cranbury Cl
Lodge Farm Ho
River Avon
River Avon
Wiltshire C
Hampshire C
Searchfield Farm
Moot Lane
Hale La
North Charford
Down Farm North Charford Drove
Drove
N Charford Crossing
North Charford
Manor House
Breamore
House
North
Street
South
Charford Farm
Avon Valley Path
Hale Lane
Moot Lane
A338 BREAMORE ROAD
SALISBURY ROAD
A338
Rectory La
Breamore
Braemore
C of E Primary
School
Marsh Lane
Dodgson
Cl
Lwr Densome Wd
Higherend Farm
Woodgreen
Street
Trimm's
Drove
Love La
Circle Lane
Steels Dro
Brook
The Sha
Valley Path

Greenclose
Lane
Mesh Pond
Joanna Cl
Elizabeth
Marie
Av
Catherine
Crescent
South La

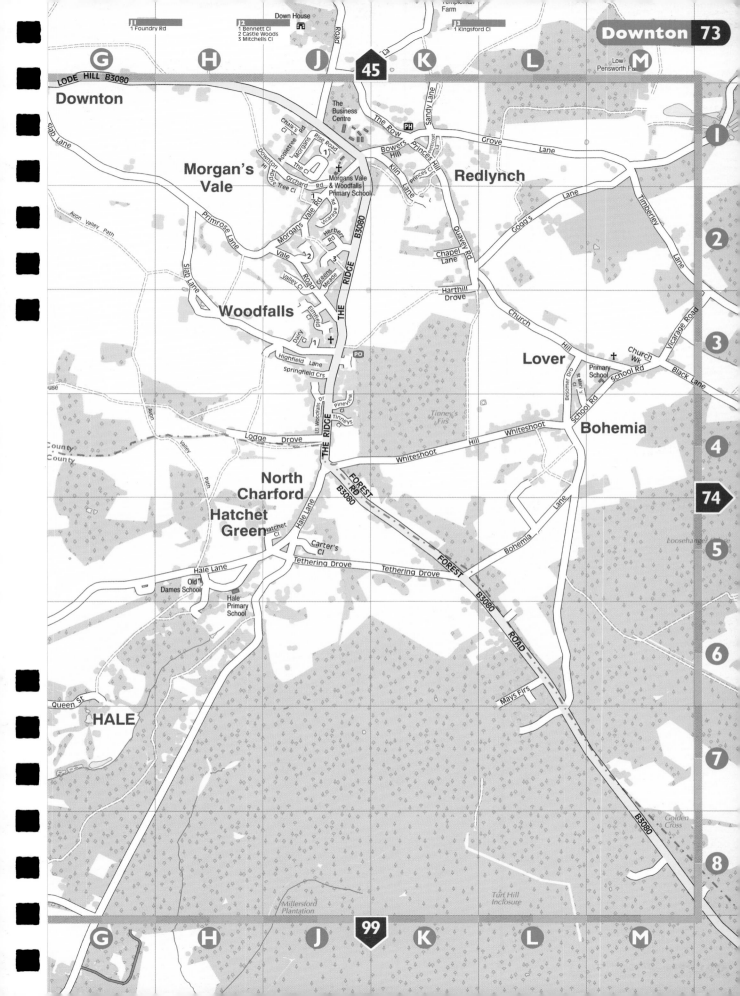

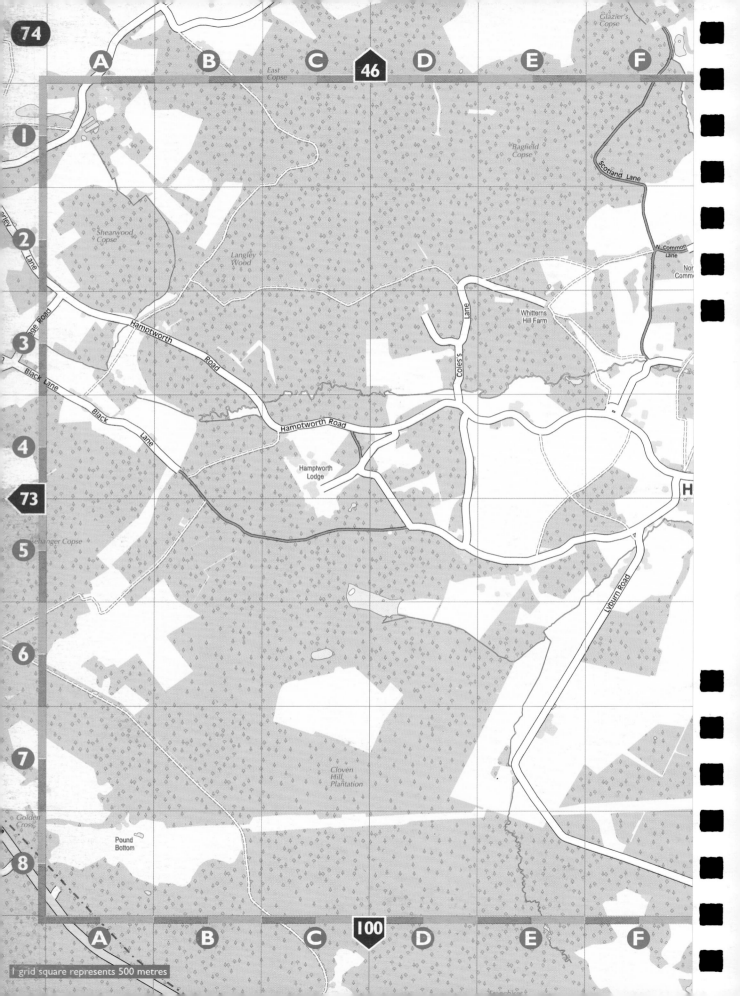

A B C 46 D E F

1

2

3

4

73

5

6

7

8

A B C 100 D E F

East Copse

Glazier's Copse

Bagfield Copse

Scotland Lane

W. Common Lane

Nor Common

Shearwood Copse

Langley Wood

Hamptworth Road

Black Lane

Black Lane

Coles's Lane

Whitterns Hill Farm

Hamptworth Road

Hamptworth Lodge

H

Lyburn Road

ehanger Copse

Cloven Hill Plantation

Golden Cross

Pound Bottom

1 grid square represents 500 metres

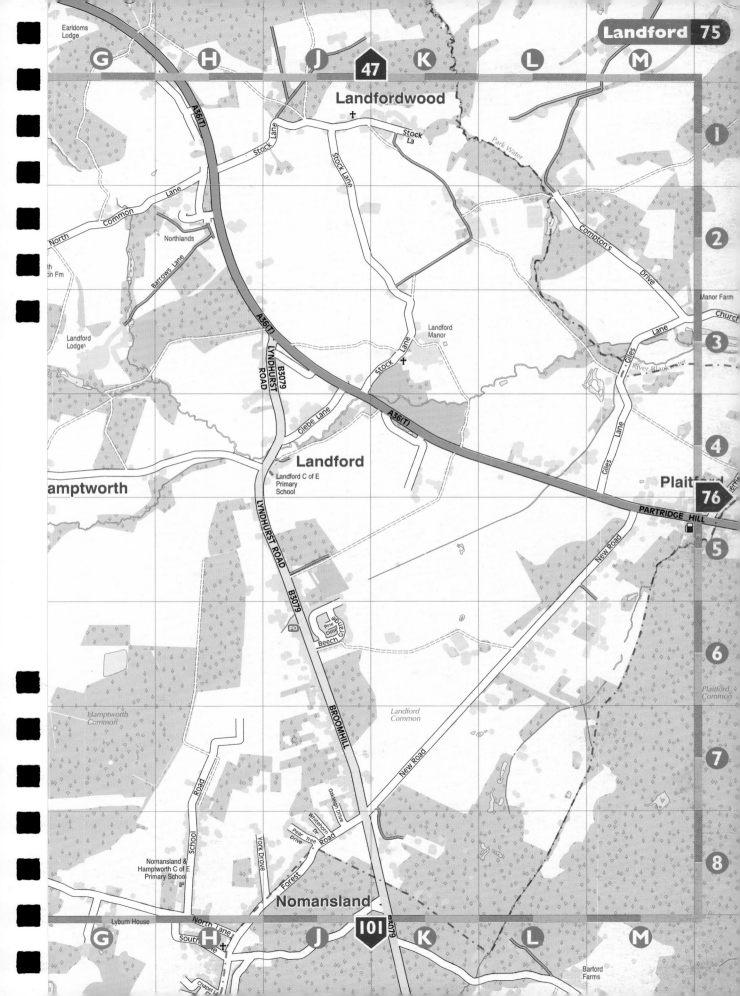

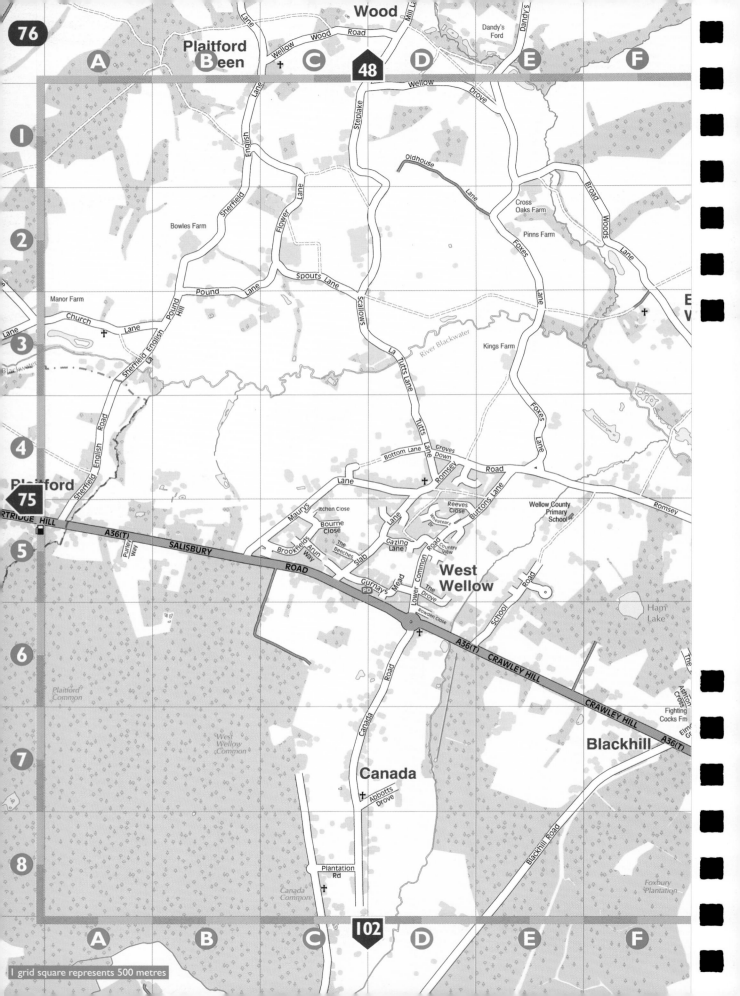

Wood

Plaitford Been

A   B   C   48   D   E   F

I

2

3

4

Plaitford

75

5

6

7

8

A   B   C   102   D   E   F

Wood Road

Wellow

Wellow Drove

Dandy's Ford

Dandy's Ford

Steplake

Oldhouse Lane

Cross Oaks Farm

Broad Woods Lane

Bowles Farm

Sherfield English Lane

Flower Lane

Pinns Farm

Foxes Lane

Spouts Lane

Pound Lane

Scallows

E V

Manor Farm

Church Lane

Pound Hill

Sherfield English La

Sherfield English Road

River Blackwater

Kings Farm

Blackwater

Tufts Lane

Foxes Lane

Bottom Lane

Groves Down

Tufts Lane

Romsey Road

Wellow County Primary School

Romsey

Maurys

Itchen Close

Lane

Reeves Close

Buttons Lane

Bourne Close

Wheatears

Country View

PARTRIDGE HILL

A36(T)

SALISBURY ROAD

Purley Way

Brookfields

Arun Way

The Beeches Slab

Gazing Lane

Mead

Lower Common Road

The Drove

West Wellow

School Road

Hap Lake

Gurnays

PO

Rowden Close

A36(T) CRAWLEY HILL

CRAWLEY HILL A36(T)

Blackhill

Ashton Cross

Fighting Cocks Fm

Elmo Gr

The

Plaitford Common

West Wellow Common

Canada Road

Canada

Abbotts Drove

Blackhill Road

Plantation Rd

Canada Common

Foxbury Plantation

I grid square represents 500 metres

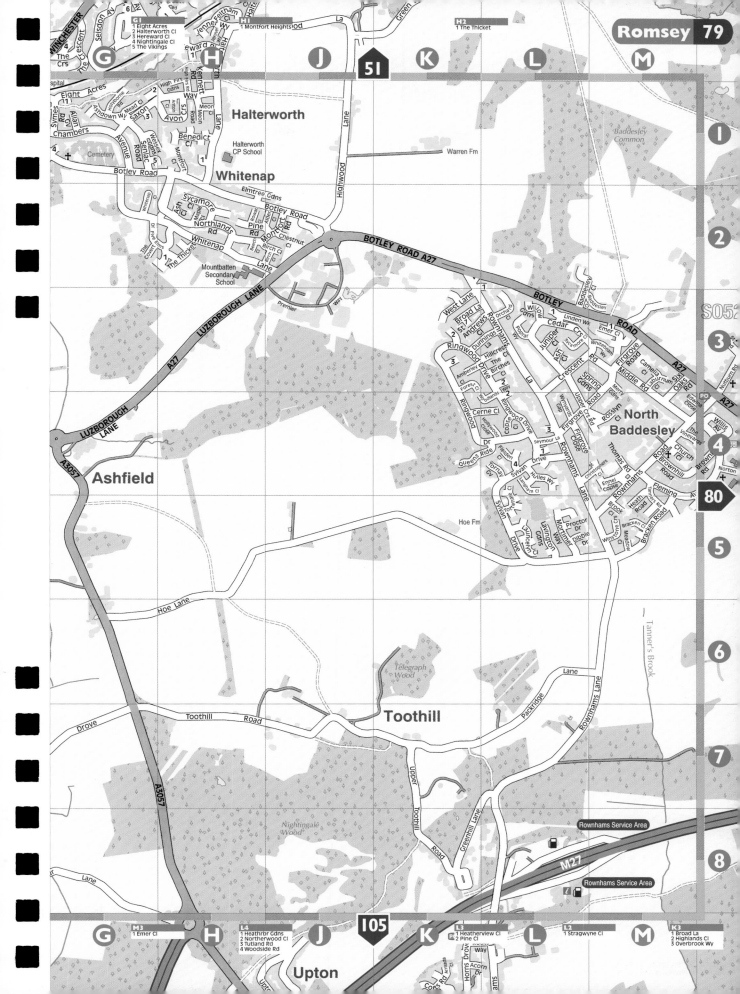

G | H | J | 51 | K | L | M

G1
1 Eight Acres
2 Halterworth Cl
3 Hereward Cl
4 Nightingale Cl
5 The Vikings

H1
1 Montfort Heights

H2
1 The Thicket

I
2
S052
3
4
80
5
6
7
8

Halterworth

Whitenap

Halterworth CP School

Cemetery

Botley Road

Mountbatten Secondary School

LUZBOROUGH LANE

A27

Ashfield

A3057

Botley Road A27

West Lane

North Baddesley

BOTLEY ROAD

Baddesley Common

Warren Fm

Hoe Lane

Hoe Fm

Telegraph Wood

Toothill Road

Toothill

Tanner's Brook

Lane

Packridge

Rownhams Lane

Rownhams Service Area

Nightingale Wood

Upper Toothill Road

Greenhill Lane

M27

Rownhams Service Area

Drove

M3
1 Emer Cl

L4
1 Heathrbr Gdns
2 Northerwood Cl
3 Tutland Rd
4 Woodside Rd

L3
1 Heatherview Cl
2 Pine Cl

L2
1 Stragwyne Cl

K3
1 Broad La
2 Highlands Cl
3 Overbrook Wy

Upton

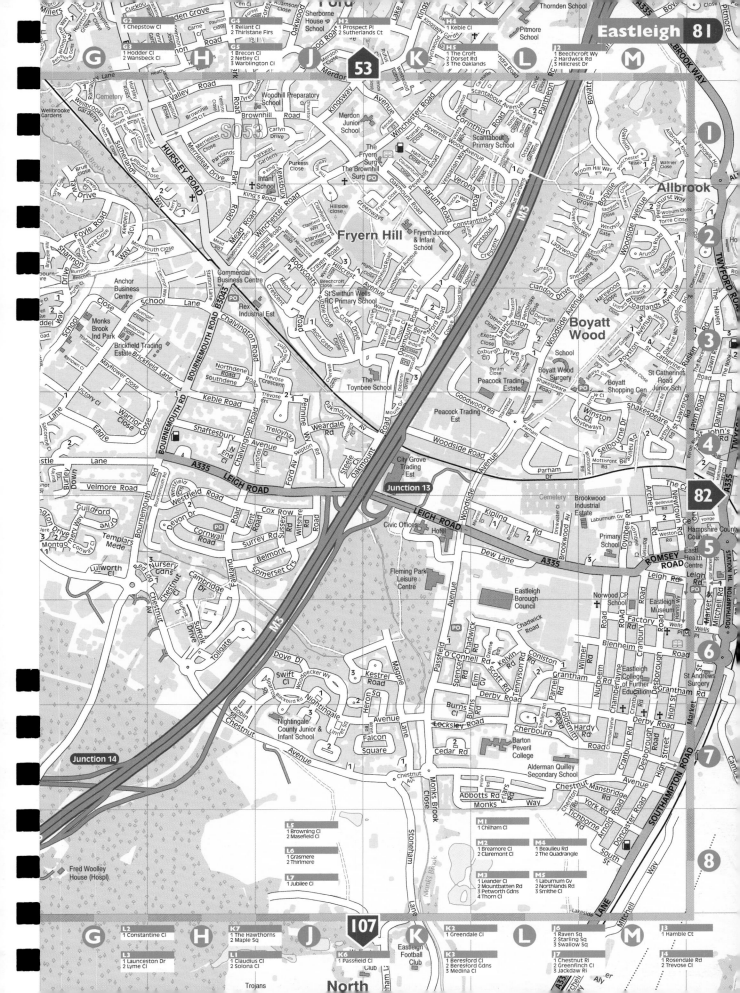

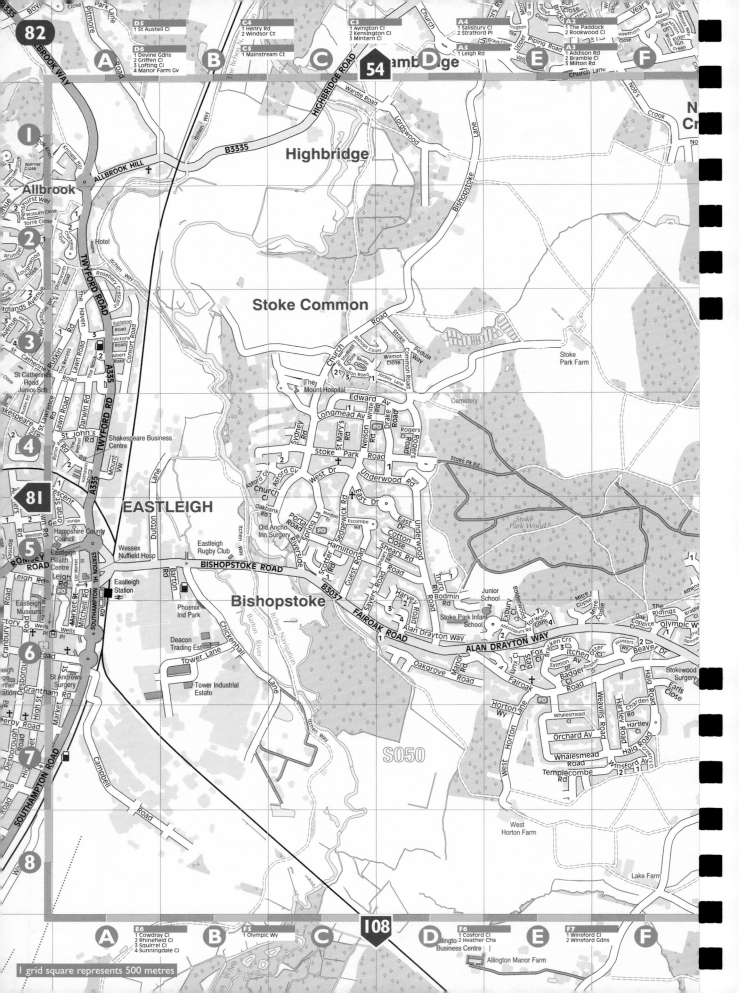

A B C D E F

D5
1 St Austell Cl

D6
1 Devine Gdns
2 Griffen Cl
3 Lofting Cl
4 Manor Farm Gv

C4
1 Henry Rd
2 Windsor Ct

C5
1 Mainstream Ct

C3
1 Avington Cl
2 Kensington Cl
3 Mintern Cl

A4
1 Salisbury Cl
2 Stratford Pl

A5
1 Leigh Rd

A7
1 The Paddock
2 Rookwood Cl

A3
1 Addison Rd
2 Bramble Cl
3 Milton Rd

Highbridge

Stoke Common

Allbrook

EASTLEIGH

Bishopstoke

S050

81

A B C D E F
1
2
3
4
5
6
7
8

Stoke Park Farm

Stoke Park Wood

West Horton Farm

Lake Farm

A B C D E F

E6
1 Cowdray Cl
2 Rhinefield Cl
3 Squirrel Cl
4 Sunningdale Cl

F5
1 Olympic Wy

F6
1 Cosford Cl
2 Heather Cha

F7
1 Winsford Cl
2 Winsford Gdns

1 grid square represents 500 metres

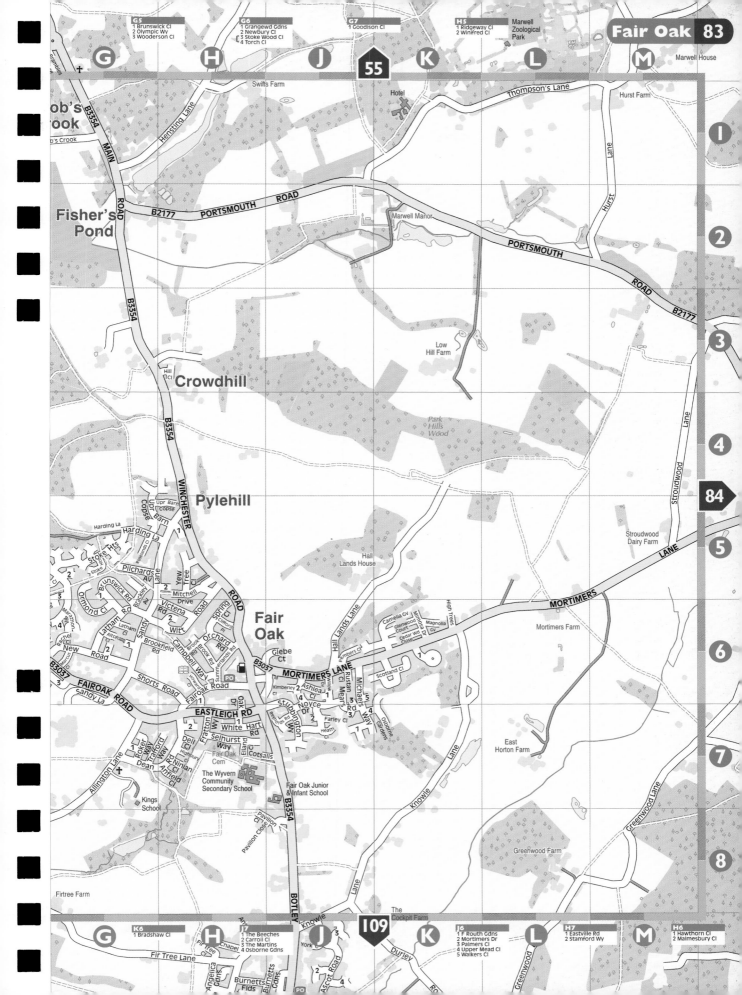

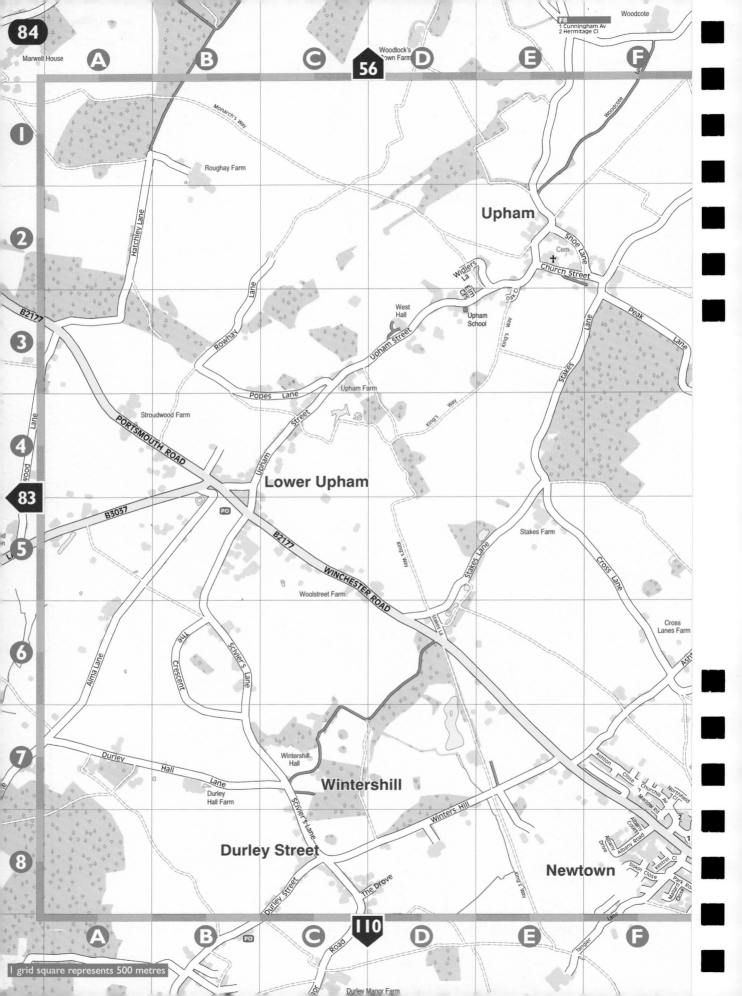

Marwell House

A   B   C   D   E   F

Woodcote

F8
1 Cunningham Av
2 Hermitage Cl

56

Woodlock's Down Farm

I

Monarch's Way

Roughay Farm

Upham

Hatchley Lane

shoe Lane

2

Cem

Church Street

Widlers La

West Hall

Upham Street

Upham School

Oak Cl

Peak Lane

Lane

B2177

Rownhay Lane

3

Popes   Lane

Upham Farm

King's Way

Stakes

Stroudwood Farm

Upham   Street

King's   Way

4

PORTSMOUTH ROAD

Wood Lane

83

B3037

PO

Lower Upham

B2177

Stakes Farm

Cross Lane

Cross Lanes Farm

5

WINCHESTER ROAD

King's Way

Stakes Lane

Woolstreet Farm

Ash

6

The Crescent

Sciviers Lane

Alma Lane

Stakes La

7

Durley   Hall   Lane

Wintershill Hall

Wintershill

Winters Hill

Ashton Close

Churchill Av

Northfield

Marlow Rd

Durley Hall Farm

Sciviers Lane

Albany Court

Albany Road

2

8

Durley Street

Durley Street

The Drove

King's Way

Newtown

Albany Drive

Kestrel Cl

Siskin Close

Park Rd

Mallard Close

1

A   B   C   D   E   F

PO

110

Road

Tangier Lane

Durley Manor Farm

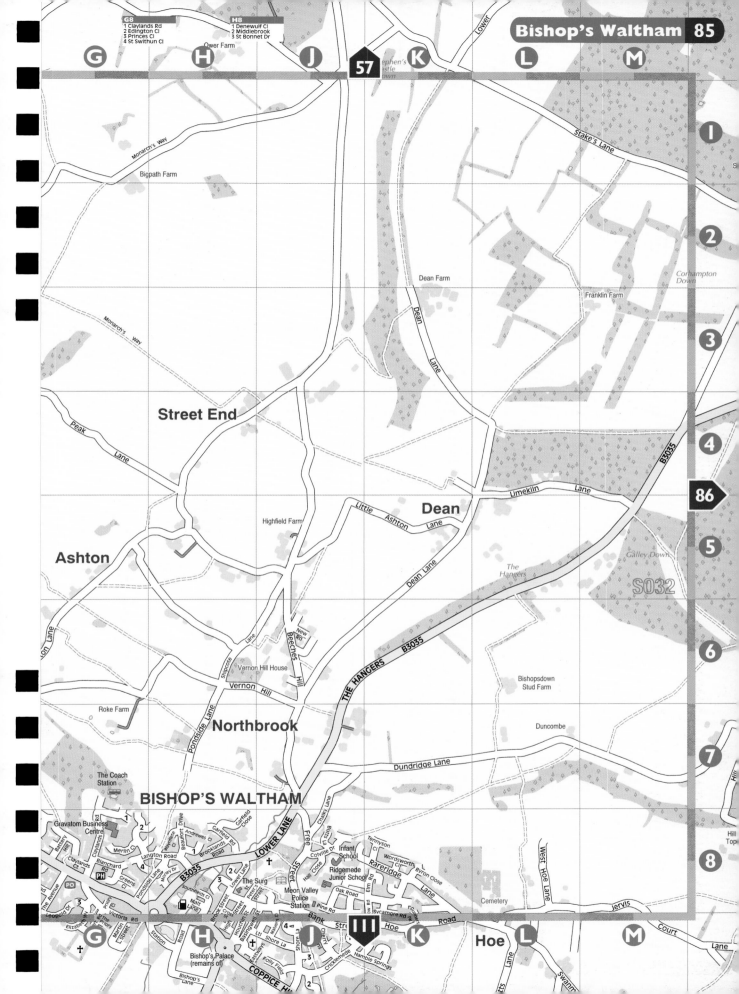

G8
1 Claylands Rd
2 Edington Cl
3 Princes Cl
4 St Swithun Cl

H8
1 Denewulf Cl
2 Middlebrook
3 St Bonnet Dr

G H Ower Farm J 57 K L M

Stephen's Castle Down

1

Stake's Lane

Bigpath Farm

Monarch's Way

2

Corhampton Down

Dean Farm

Franklin Farm

3

Monarch's Way

Dean Lane

Street End

4

Peak Lane

B3035

Limekiln Lane

Little Ashton Lane

Dean

86

Highfield Farm

5

Galley Down

The Hangers

SO32

Ashton

Dean Lane

New Rd

6

Snipcote Lane

Beeches Hill

Vernon Hill House

THE HANGERS B3035

Bishopsdown Stud Farm

Vernon Hill

Roke Farm

Pondside Lane

Northbrook

Duncombe

Dundridge Lane

7

The Coach Station

BISHOP'S WALTHAM

Garfield Close

Chalky Lane

Infant School

Tennyson Cl

Wordsworth Cl

8

Gravatom Business Centre

Bentley Hill

Claylands Rd

Merlin Cl

Wallace Cl

Beaufort Drive

Andrewes Cl

Garfield Rd

Brooklands Road

LOWER LANE

Free Street

Colville Dr

Hall Close

Ridgemede Junior School

Byron Close

Rareridge Lane

West Hoe Lane

Hill Top

Langton Road

Morley Dr

Lower Lane

St Peter's Street

Oak Road

Elm Rd

Blanchard Rd

Greens Cl

The Surg

Southfields Cl

Meon Valley Police Station

Pine Rd

Sycamore Rd

PH

PO

The Avenue

Leopold Dr

Elizabeth Av

Priory

Victoria Rd

Malt Lane

Brook Street

High Street

Houchin St

Basingwell St

St Stevens

Shore La

Bank Street

Hoe Road

Cemetery

Jervis

Court Lane

G Merlin Street Station Road H Bishop's Palace (remains of) Folly Field Shore Rd Cherry Drive J Cricklemede Hamble Springs K **Hoe** L Swanm M

Bishop's Lane

COPPICE HILL

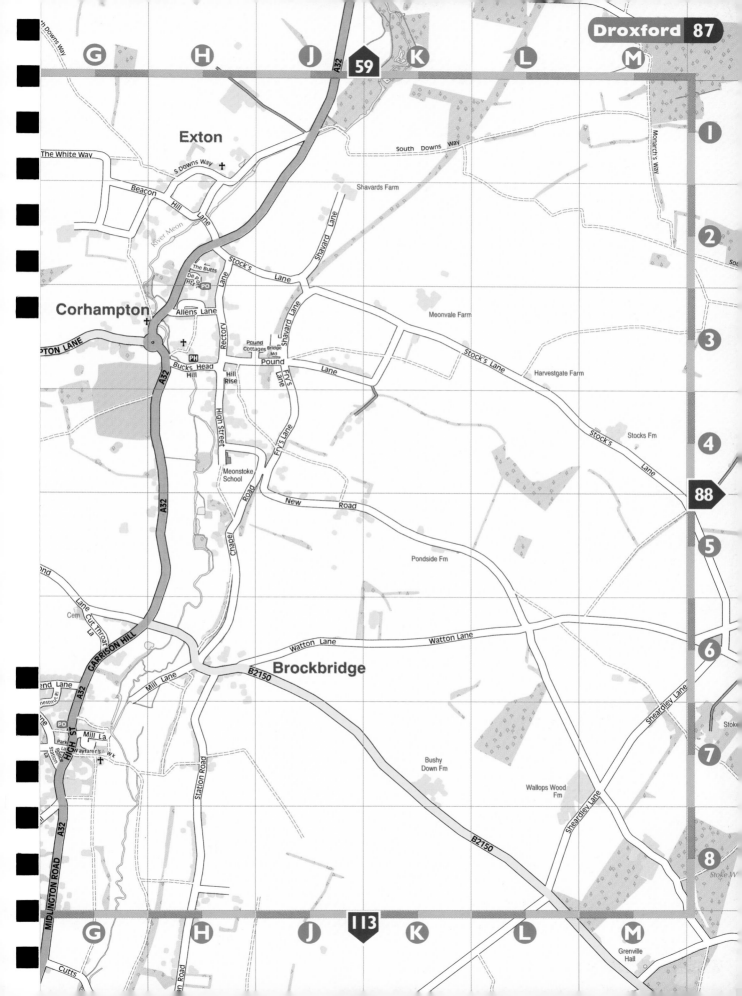

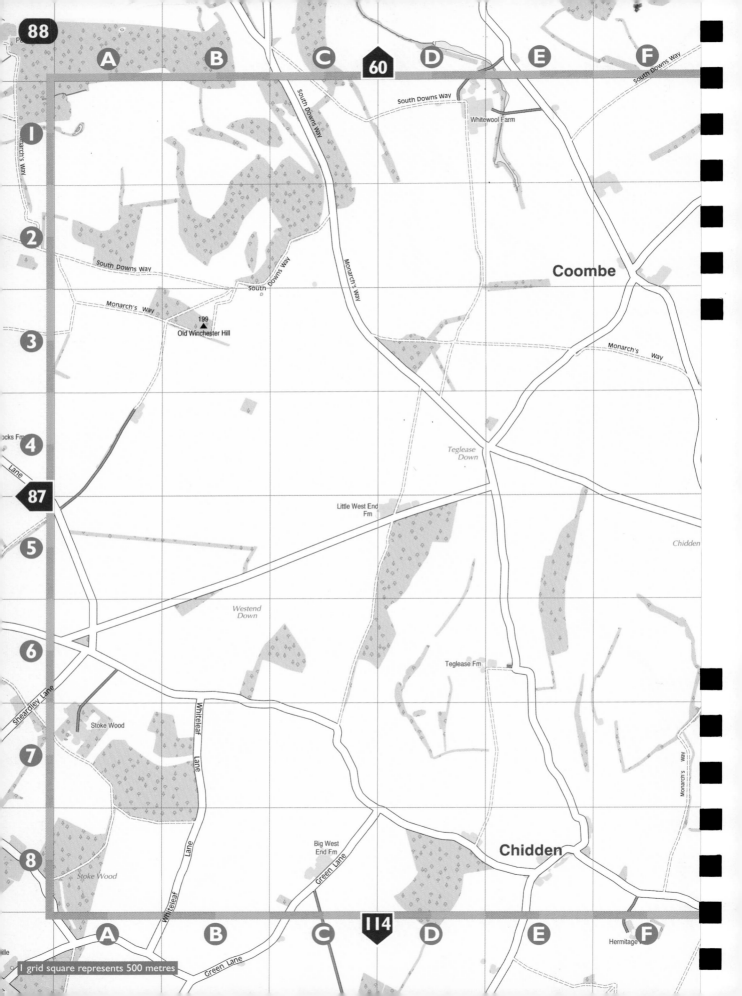

A B C 60 D E F

I

2

3

87

4

5

6

7

8

A B C 114 D E F

South Downs Way

South Downs Way

Whitewool Farm

Coombe

Monarch's Way

South Downs Way

South Downs Way

South

Monarch's Way

199
Old Winchester Hill

Monarch's Way

Monarch's Way

Teglease
Down

Chidden

Little West End
Fm

ocks Fm

Lane

Westend
Down

Teglease Fm

Sheardley Lane

Stoke Wood

Whiteleaf
Lane

Chidden

Whiteleaf
Lane

Stoke Wood

Big West
End Fm

Green Lane

Hermitage

ille

Green Lane

1 grid square represents 500 metres

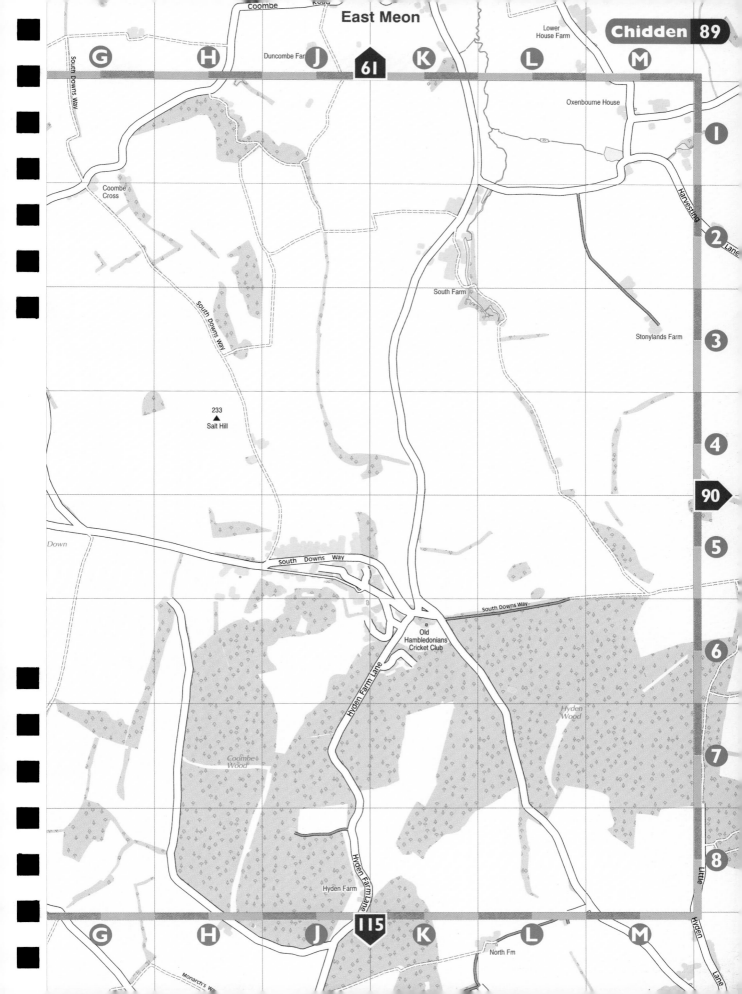

East Meon

Coombe Road

G   H   J   61   K   L   M

Duncombe Farm

Lower House Farm

Oxenbourne House

I

South Downs Way

Coombe Cross

Harvesting Lane

2

South Farm

Stonylands Farm

3

233
▲
Salt Hill

4

90

Down

5

South Downs Way

South Downs Way

Old Hambledonians Cricket Club

6

Hyden Farm Lane

Hyden Wood

Coombe Wood

7

8

Little Hyden Lane

Hyden Farm

G   H   J   115   K   L   M

North Fm

Monarch's Way

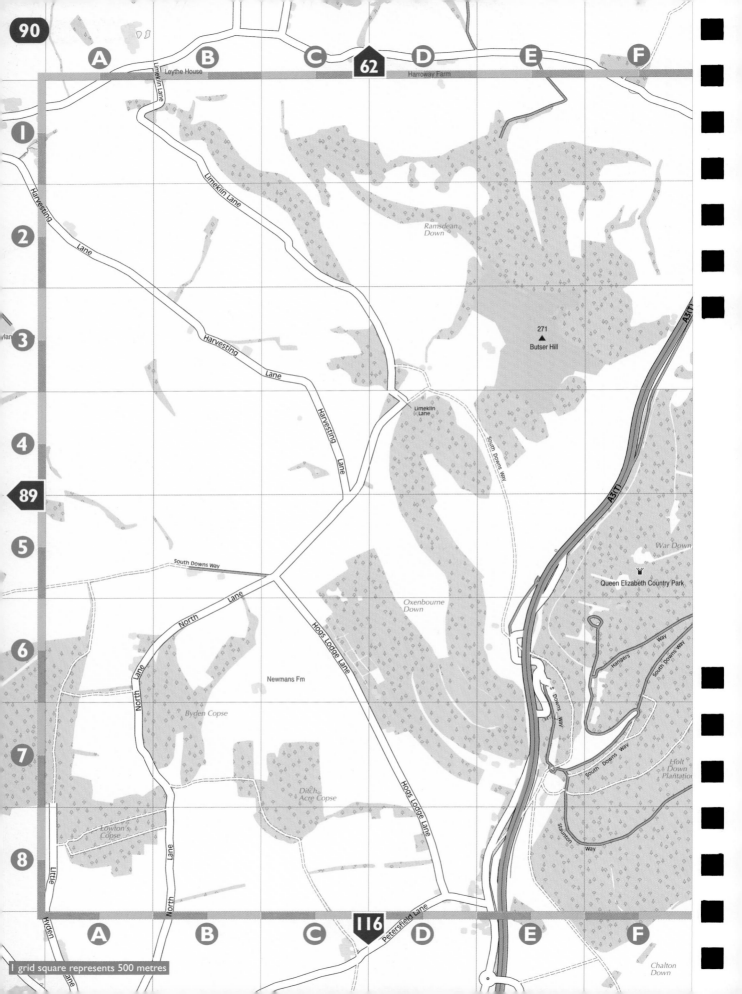

A   B   C   62   D   E   F

Leythe House   Harroway Farm

Limekiln Lane

1

Harvesting

Limekiln Lane

Lane

2

Ramsdean
Down

Harvesting   Lane

3

271
▲
Butser Hill

Limekiln
Lane

Harvesting Lane

4

South Downs Way

89

A3(T)

5

South Downs Way

War Down

North   Lane

Queen Elizabeth Country Park

Oxenbourne
Down

6

Hogs Lodge Lane

Newmans Fm

Hangers   Way

South Downs Way

North   Lane

Byden Copse

S' Downs Way

7

Ditch
Acre Copse

Hogs Lodge Lane

South Downs Way

Holt
Down
Plantation

Lowton's
Copse

Staunton

8

Way

A   B   116   C   D   Petersfield Lane   E   F

Little

Hyden   Chalton
Down

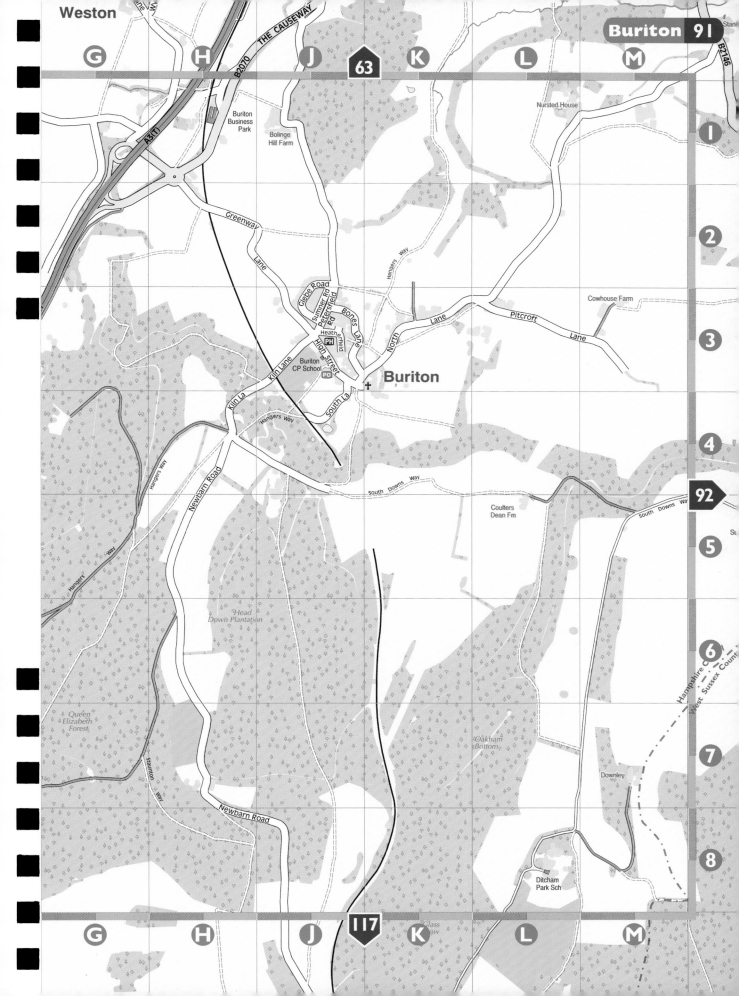

Weston

G H J 63 K L M

1

2

3

4

92

5

6

7

8

Nursted House

Buriton Business Park

Bolinge Hill Farm

Cowhouse Farm

Greenway

Lane

Hangers Way

Glebe Road

Sumner Rd

Petersfield Rd

Bones Lane

North Lane

Pitcroft Lane

Heathfield

PH

High Street

Kiln Lane

Buriton CP School

PO

Buriton

Kiln La

South La

Hangers Way

Newbarn Road

Hangers Way

South Downs Way

Coulters Dean Fm

South Downs Way

Hampshire co

West Sussex Count

Head Down Plantation

Queen Elizabeth Forest

Staunton Way

Newbarn Road

Oakham Bottom

Downley

Ditcham Park Sch

G H J 117 K L M

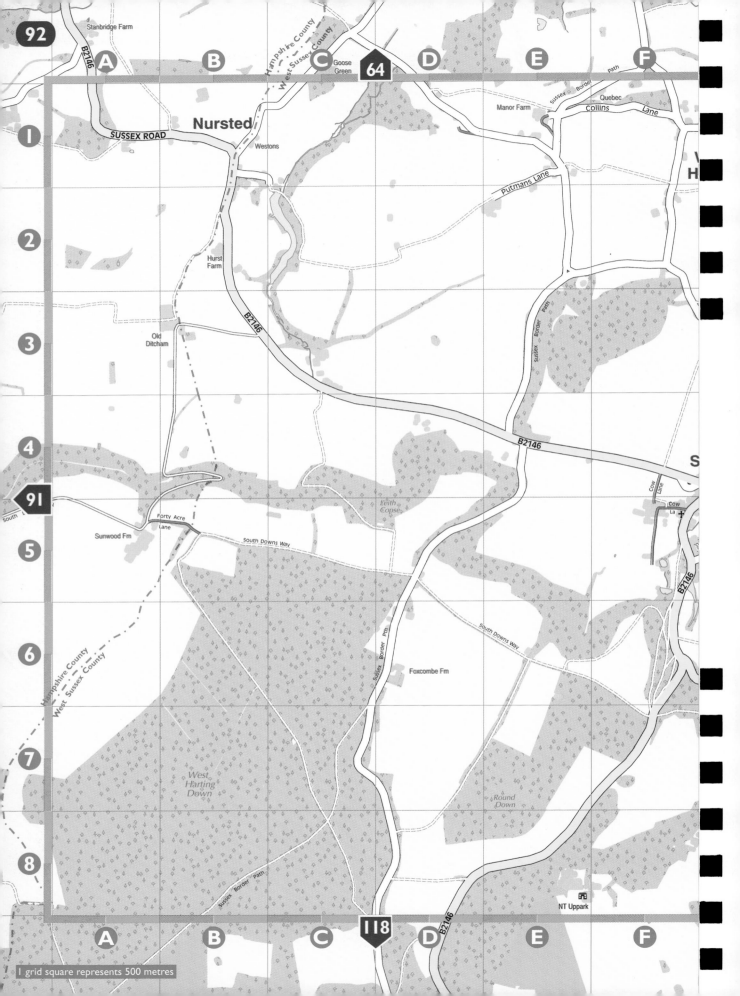

A   B   C   D   E   F

64

Stanbridge Farm

B2146

Hampshire County

West Sussex County

Goose
Green

Manor Farm

Collins

Quebec

Lane

Sussex Border Path

V
H

1   SUSSEX ROAD   Nursted

Westons

Putmans Lane

2   Hurst
Farm

3   Old
Ditcham

B2146

Sussex Border Path

4   B2146   S

91   Feith
Copse

Cow Lane

Cow
La

South

Forty Acre
Lane

5   Sunwood Fm   South Downs Way

B2146

6   Hampshire County
West Sussex County

Sussex Border Pth

South Downs Way

Foxcombe Fm

7   West
Harting
Down

Round
Down

8   NT Uppark

B2146

A   B   C   D   E   F

118

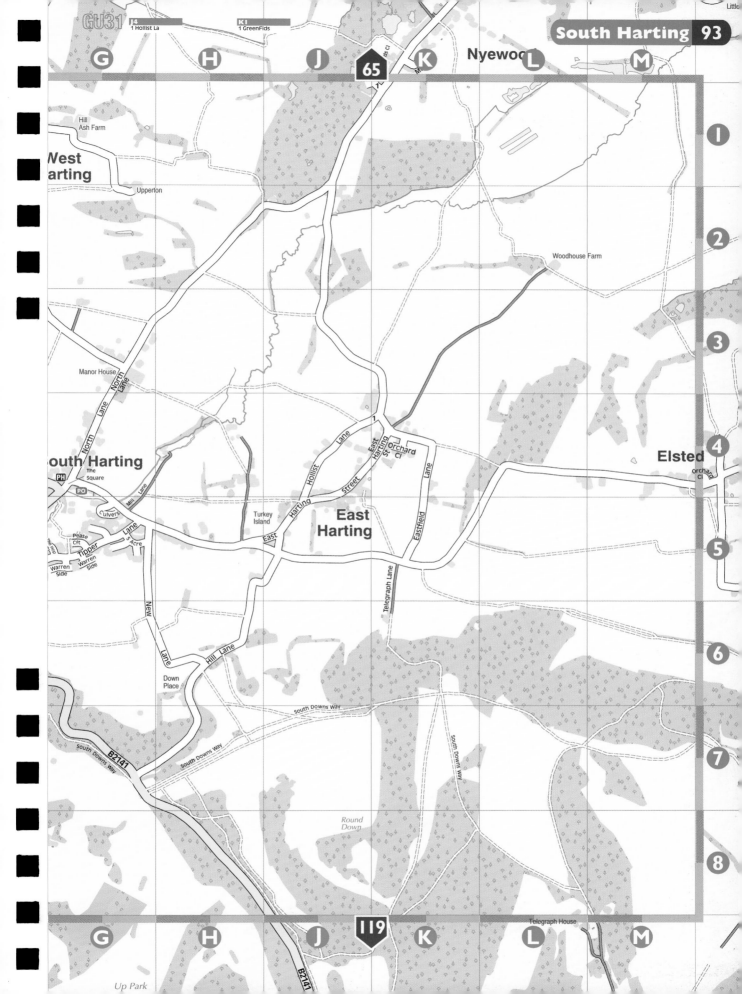

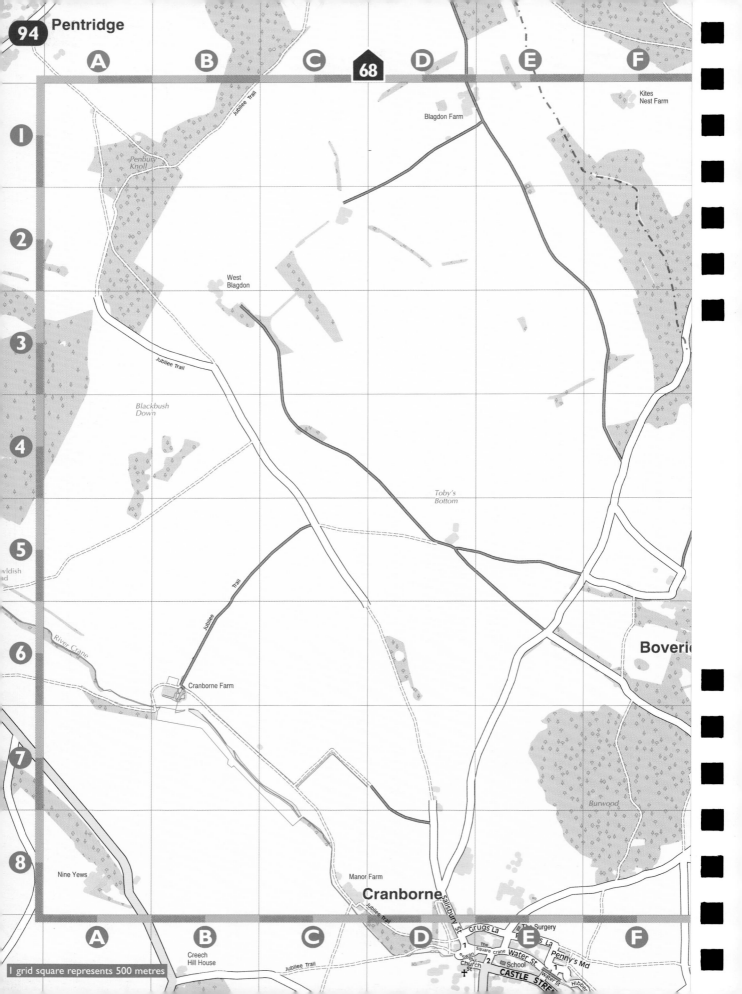

68

A B C D E F

1

Penbury
Knoll

Kites
Nest Farm

Blagdon Farm

2

West
Blagdon

3

Jubilee Trail

Blackbush
Down

4

Toby's
Bottom

5

wldish
ad

Jubilee Trail

River Crane

6

Cranborne Farm

Boveri

7

Burwood

8

Nine Yews

Manor Farm

Cranborne

A B C D E F

Creech
Hill House

Jubilee Trail

Salisbury St

Grugs La

The Surgery

The
Swan

Square

Crane

Penny's Md

Water St

Church
St

School

Water St

Hibber

CASTLE STRE

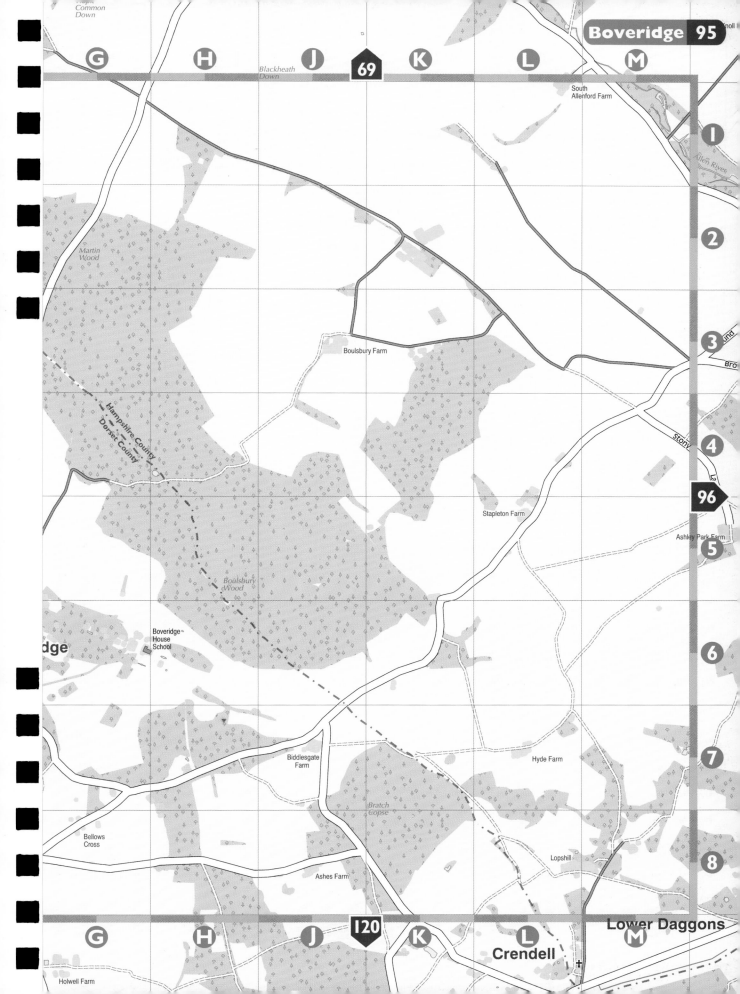

G H J **69** K L M

Jolpes Common Down

Blackheath Down

South Allenford Farm

I

Allen River

Martin Wood

Boulsbury Farm

Hampshire County
Dorset County

Stapleton Farm

96

Ashley Park Farm

5

Boulsbury Wood

Boveridge House School

6

Biddlesgate Farm

Hyde Farm

7

Bratch Copse

Bellows Cross

Lopshill

8

Ashes Farm

Crendell

Holwell Farm

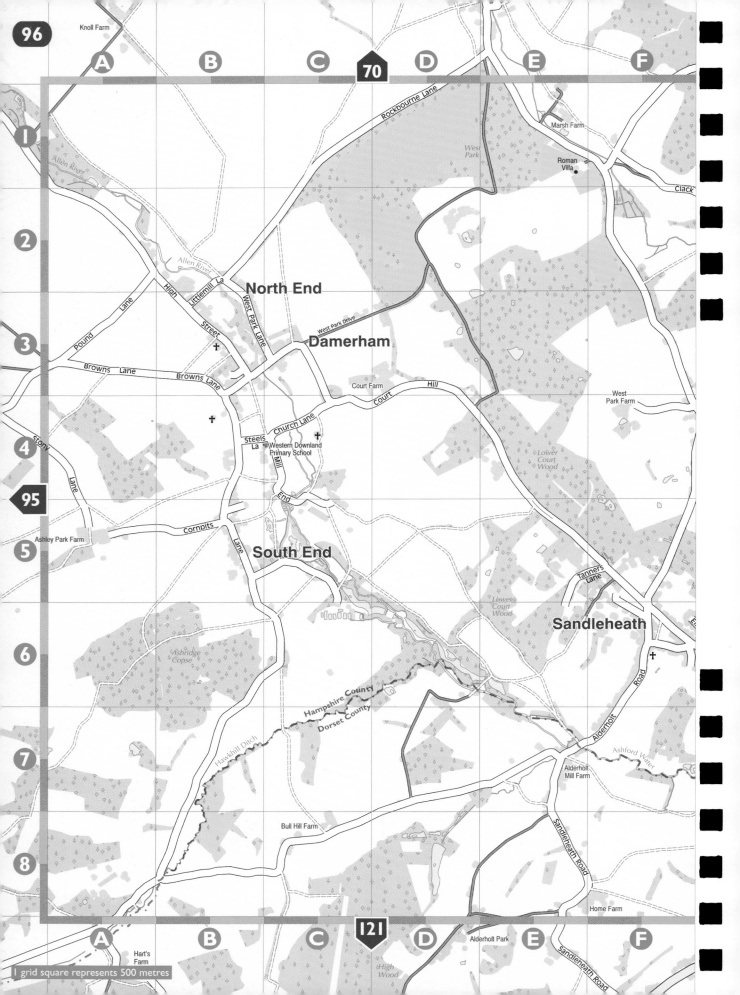

96

A   B   C   70   D   E   F

1

Knoll Farm

Allen River

West
Park

Marsh Farm

Roman
Villa

Clack

2

Allen River

North End

High Littlemill La West Park Lane Street Lane

West Park Drive

Rockbourne Lane

3

Damerham

Pound Lane

Browns Lane

Browns Lane

Court Farm

Court   Hill

West
Park Farm

4

Stony

Steels
La

Church Lane

Western Downland
Primary School

Lower
Court
Wood

95

5

Ashley Park Farm

Cornpits

Mill End

South End

Lane

Tanners
Lane

Lower
Court
Wood

Sandleheath

6

Ashridge
Copse

Hampshire County

Dorset County

Alderholt Road

7

Hawkhill Ditch

Ashford Water

Alderholt
Mill Farm

8

Bull Hill Farm

Sandleheath Road

121

A   B   C   D   Alderholt Park E   F

Hart's
Farm

High
Wood

Home Farm

Sandleheath Road

I grid square represents 500 metres

H6
1 Marbrean Cl

J7
1 The Old Vineries
2 The Pantiles

K6
1 Allen Water Dr
2 Avon Meade
3 Cottage Ms
4 Garendon Ct
5 Meadow Cl
6 Oaklands Cl
7 Pealsham Gdns
8 S Martin Gdns

K7
1 Mill Ct
2 Vimoutiers Ct
3 WestGv

Flood Street

I
2
SP6
3
Upper Burgate
Fryern Court Road
4
98
Lower Burgate
Avon Valley Path
5
6
FORDINGBRI
7
B3078
8

Rockstead Farm
Radnall Wood
Green Lane
Brookheath
Lane
Green La
Peasash Farm
Fryern Court Road
Fryern Court
Fryern Court Road
Allen's Farm
Wilkins's Coomb
Lane
Sweatsfords Water
Sandle Dairy Farm
Arch Farm Industrial Est
Fordingbridge Junior & Infant School
The Burgate School
Hertford Cl
Dudley Av
Penny's Crescent
Burgate Flds
Sandleheath Industrial Est
Marl Lane
Sharpley
Beacon
Whitsbury
Penys La
Waverley
Waverley Road
Langley Gdn
Player Ct
Pennington Gdn
Old Orchard Rd
ms Cl
Sandle Manor School
Marl Lane
Charnwood Cl
Willow Av
Riverdale
St Georges Rd
Orchard Cl
Albion Road
Vyster Rd
Salisbury Road
Bruyn Rd
Station Road
Sandle Manor
Elmwood Av
Downwood Cl
Ashford Close
Parsonade Park Dr
Normandy Way
Queens Gdns
Alexandra Rd
Park Rd
Sandle Copse
Mayfield Rd
Brympton Cl
Station Road
Jubilee Rd
Ashford
Green La
Lwr Bartons
Manor Ct
Manor Farm Road
Manor Farm Rd
Victoria Rd
Station Road
Victoria Gdns
Beechwood
Hotel
Bartons Rd
Fordingbridge Hospital
Salisbury Road
A338
BRIDGE ST
Ashford Road
West St
Shaftesbury St
Council Office
High St
PROVOST ST
CHURCH ST
Town Hall
RINGWOOD ROAD
Stuckton Road
Cemetery
BOWERWOOD ROAD
Padstow Pl
Mulberry Gdns
Church Farm
Lane
Frog
Ditchend Brook

L8
1 Brook Ter

L7
1 The Bartons
2 Highbank Gdns
3 Moxhams
4 Orchard Gdns
5 Round Hl

L6
1 Mayfly Cl
2 St Georges Crs

L5
1 Bedford Cl
2 Burnham Rd
3 Merton Cl

K8
1 Bushells Farm
2 Diamond Cl

Dorset County Coun
Hampshire Coun

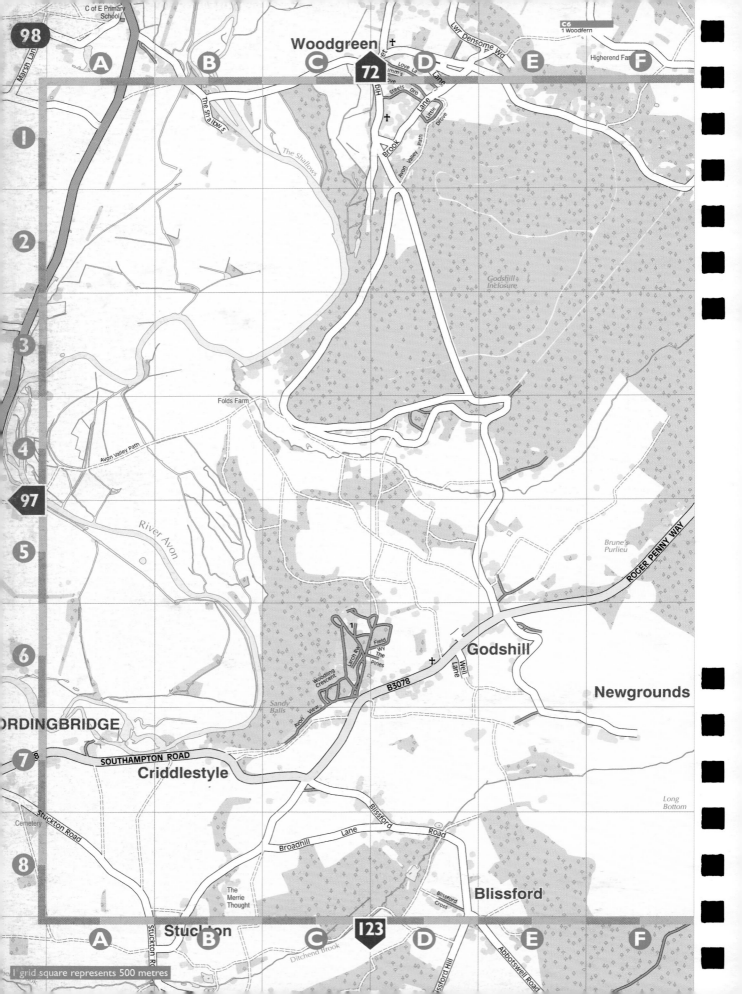

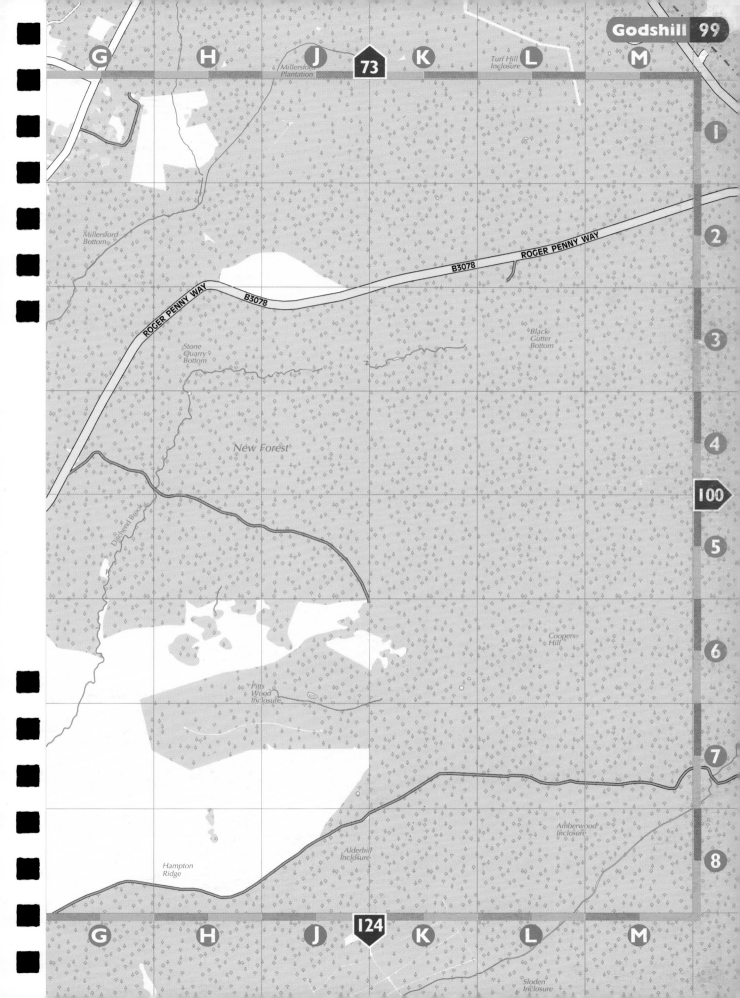

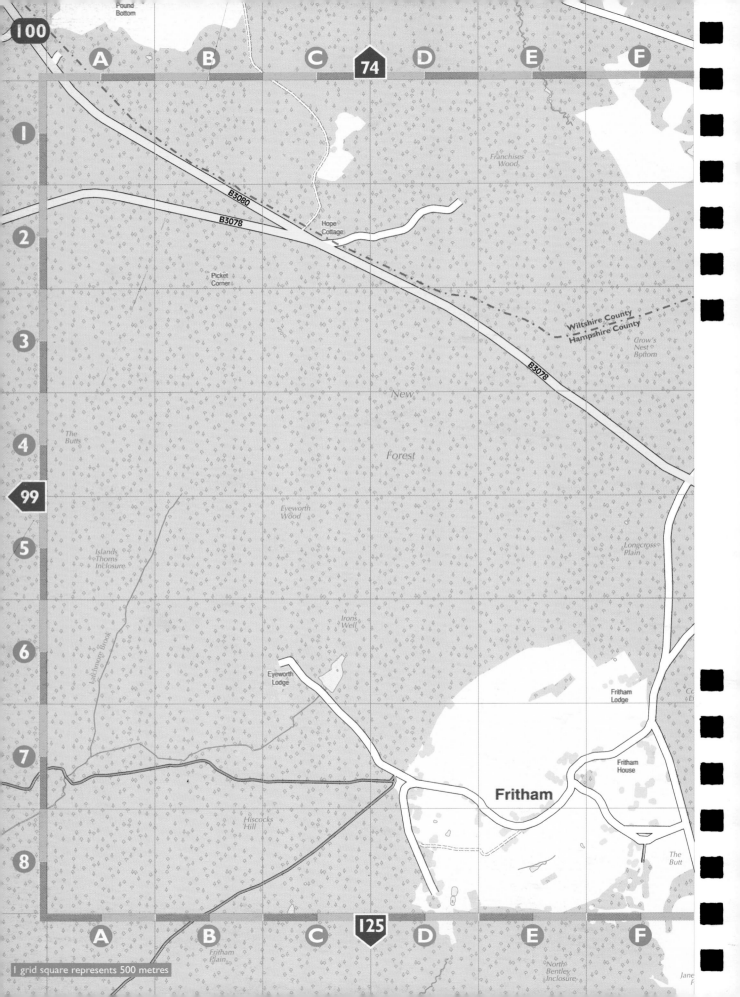

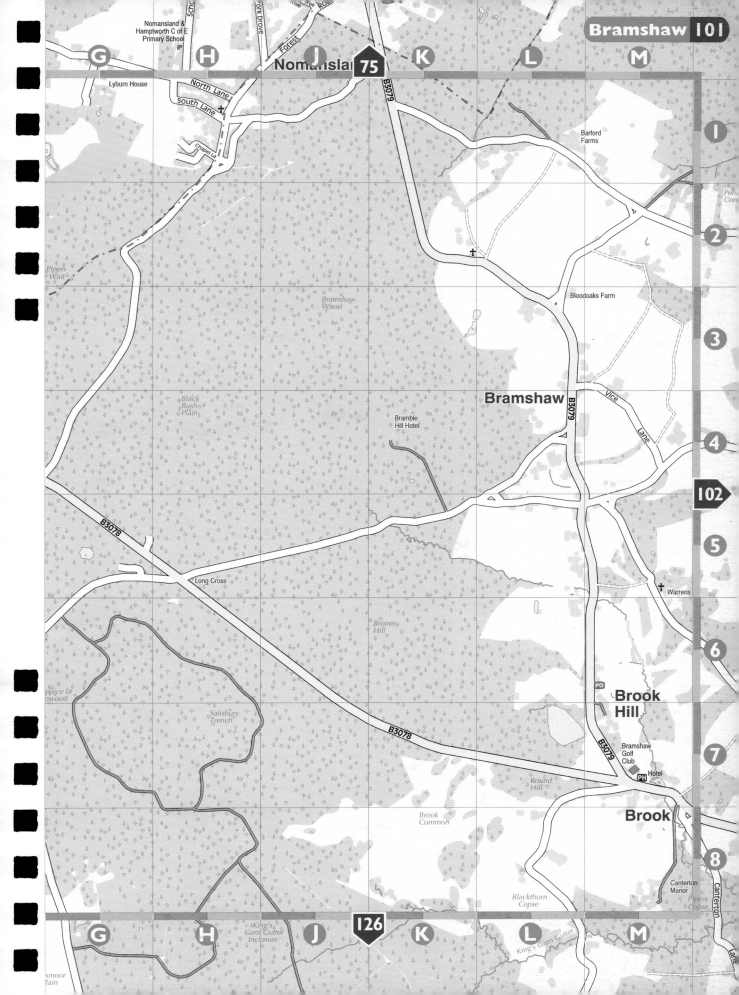

G
H
J
K
L
M

Nomansland & Hamptworth C of E Primary School

Nomanslar 75

B3079

North Lane
South Lane
Chapel La

Lyburn House

School
York Drove
Forest
Live Tree Ro

I
2
3
4
5
6
7
8

Barford Farms

Pen Con

Pipers Wait

Bramshaw Wood

Bloodoaks Farm

Bramshaw

B3079

Vice Lane

Black Bush Plain

Bramble Hill Hotel

102

B3078

Long Cross

Warrens

Broom Hill

Round Hill

ppice of nwood

Salisbury Trench

PO

Brook Hill

Bramshaw Golf Club

B3079

Hotel
PH

Brook

B3078

Brook Common

Canterton Manor

Pipers Copse

Blackthorn Copse

Canterton La

King's Garn Gutter Inclosure

King's Garn Gutter

smoor lain

G
H
J
126
K
L
M

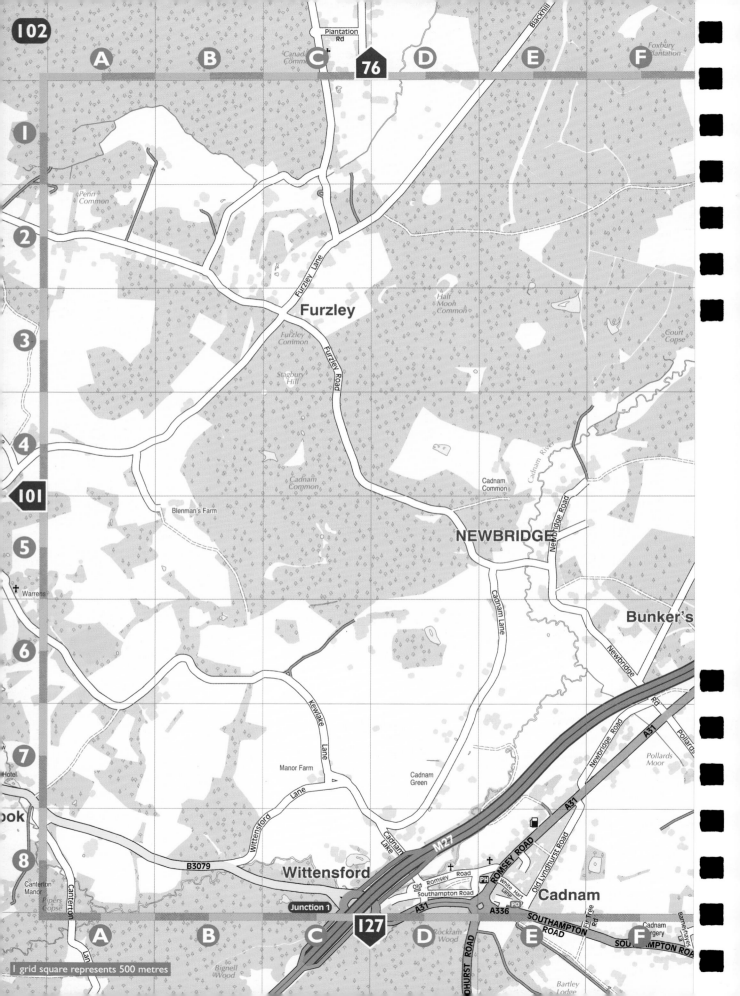

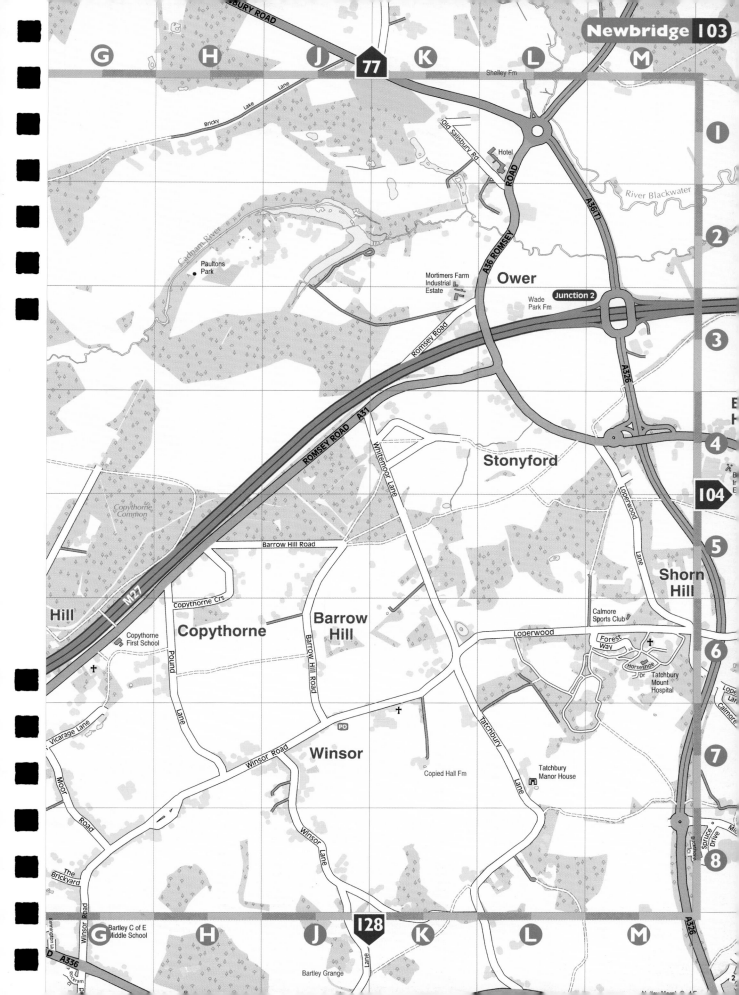

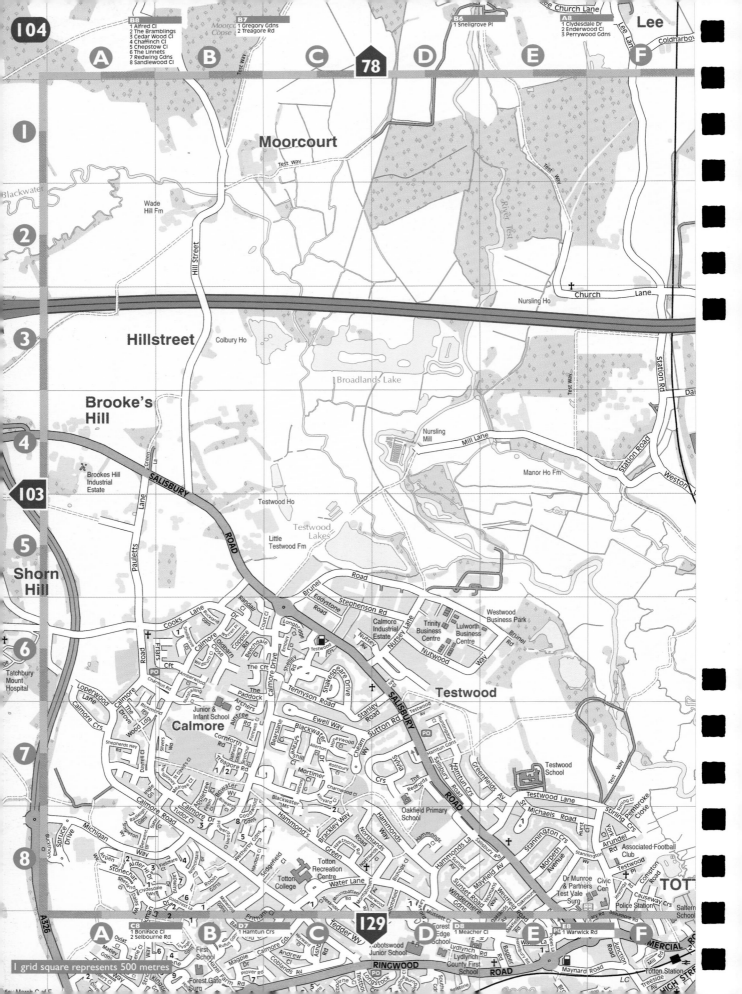

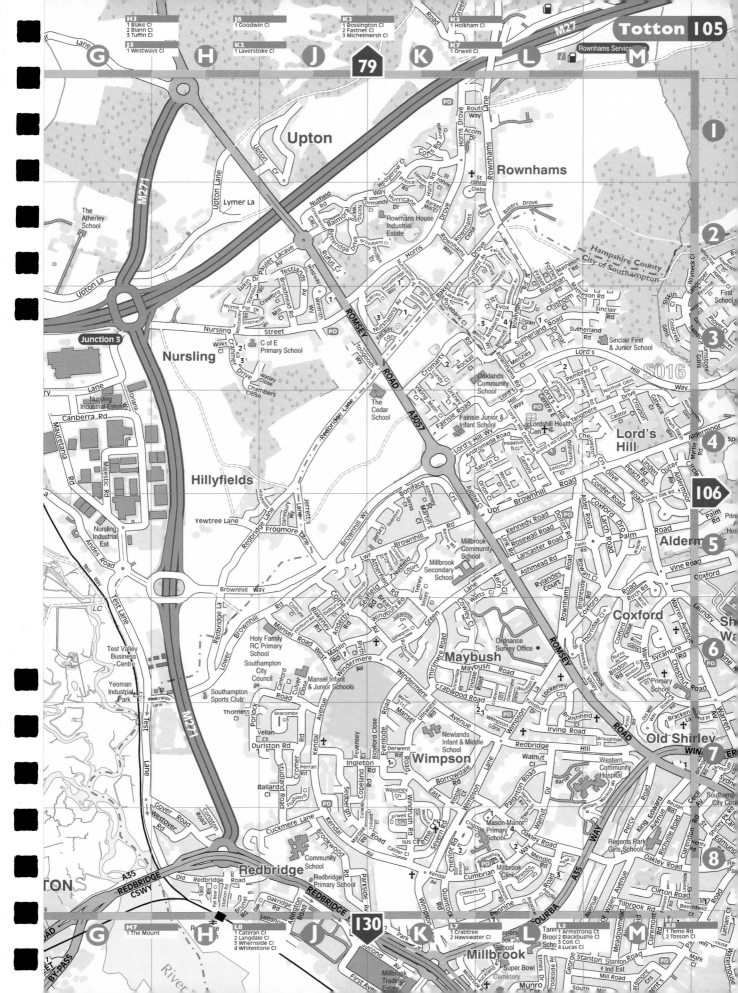

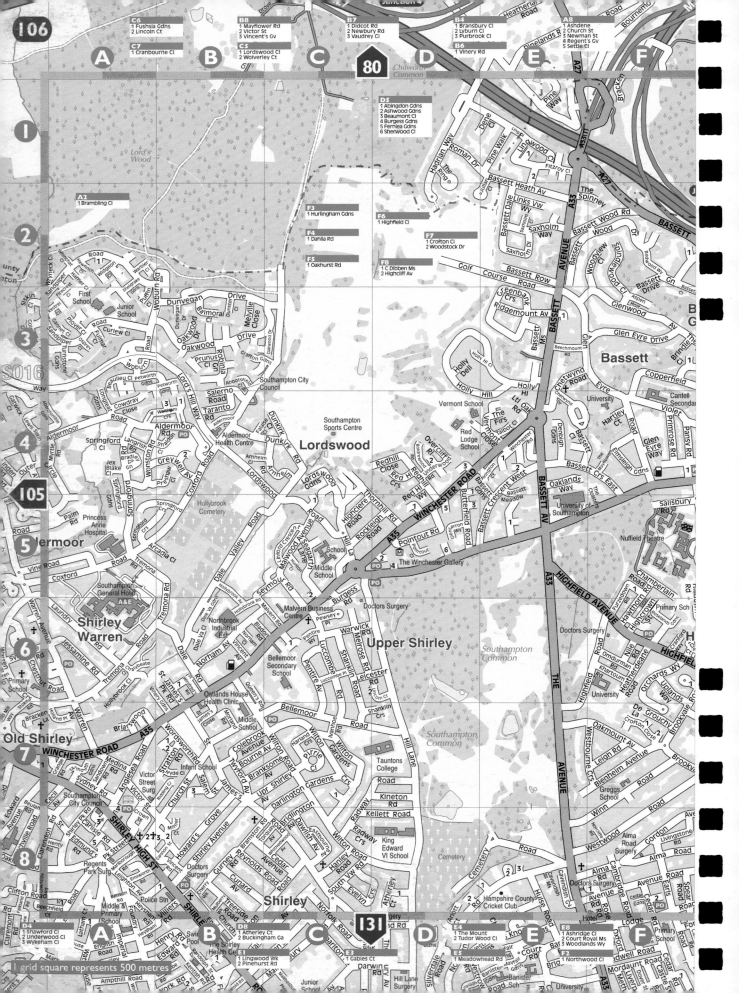

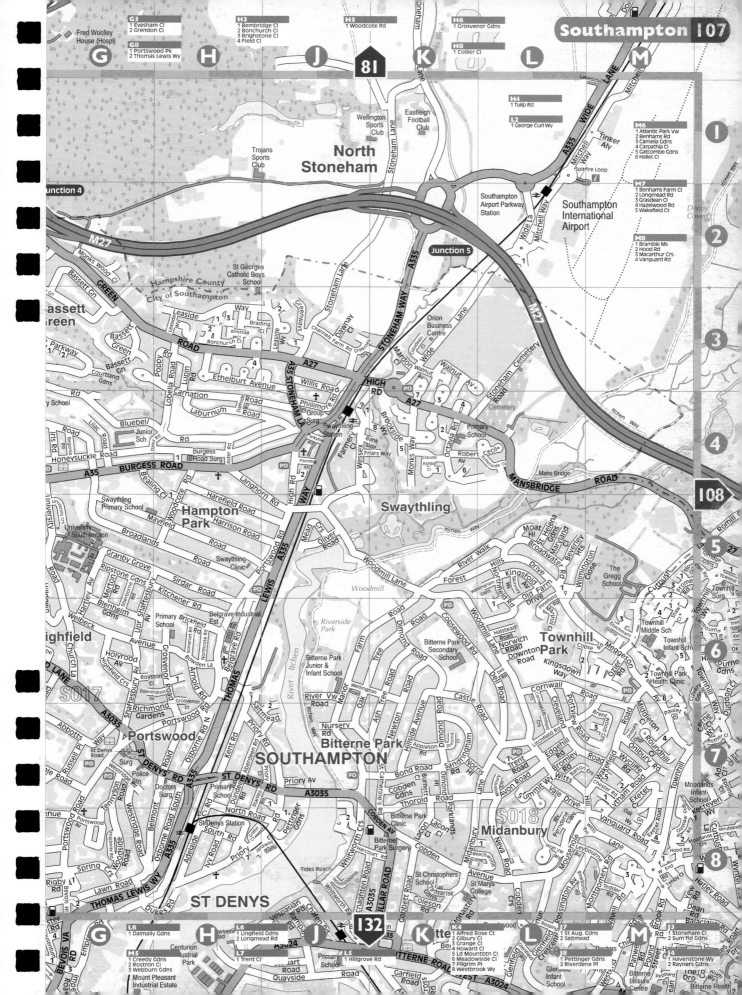

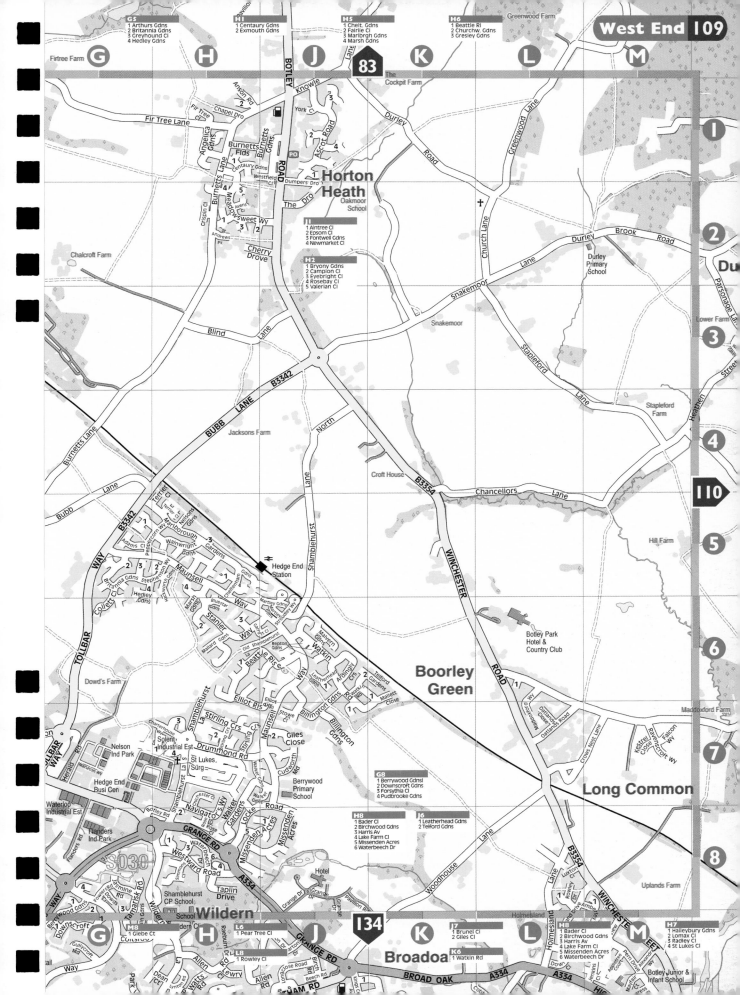

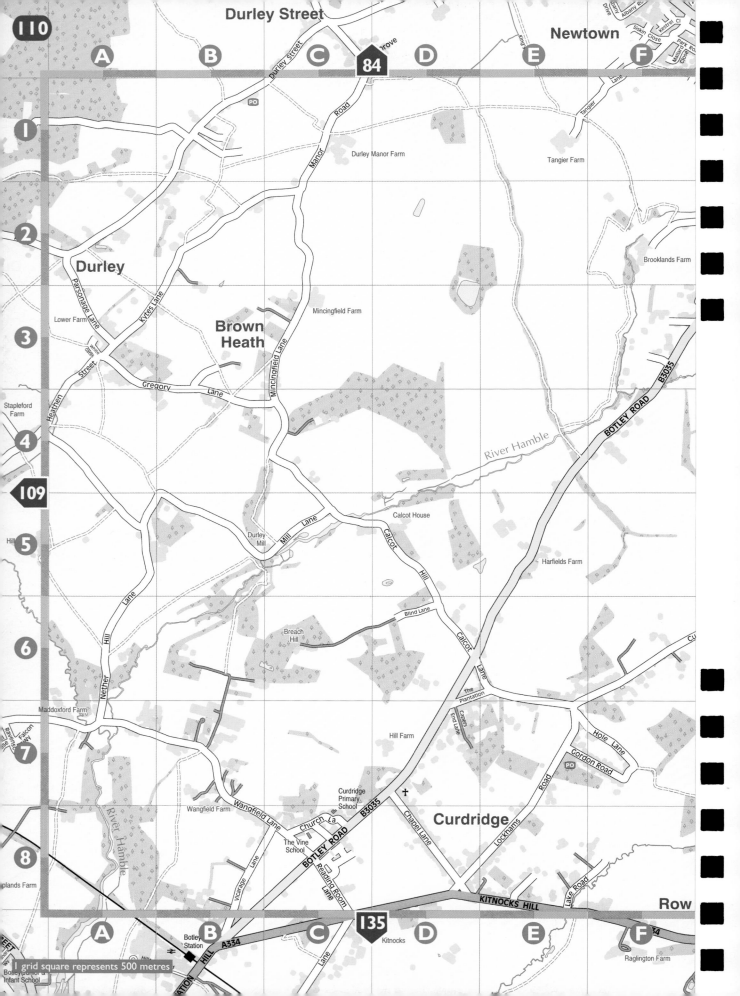

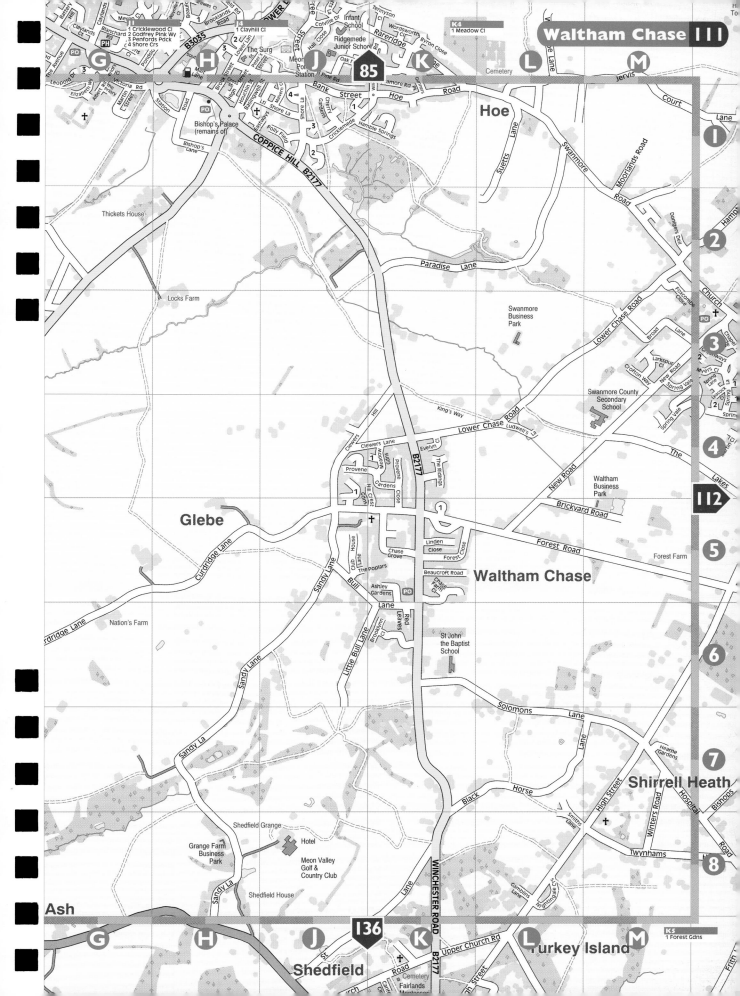

Hoe

Waltham Chase

Shirrell Heath

Glebe

Ash

Turkey Island

Shedfield

85

111

112

136

1 Cricklewood Cl
2 Godfrey Pink Wy
3 Penfords Pdck
4 Shore Crs

1 Clayhill Cl

K4
1 Meadow Cl

K5
1 Forest Gdns

Thickets House

Locks Farm

Bishop's Palace (remains of)

Bishop's Lane

COPPICE HILL B2177

Paradise Lane

Swanmore Business Park

Swanmore County Secondary School

Lower Chase Road

King's Way

Lower Chase Road

Ludwell's La

Curdridge Lane

Nation's Farm

Sandy Lane

Sandy La

Bull Lane

Little Bull Lane

Club House Lane

The Poplars

Ashley Gardens

Chase Grove

Linden Close

Forest Close

Beaucroft Road

Chase Farm Cl

Red Leaves

Brooklynn Cl

St John the Baptist School

Waltham Business Park

Brickyard Road

Forest Road

Forest Farm

New Road

The Lakes

Solomons Lane

Hearne Gardens

Black Horse Lane

Smiths Lane

High Street

Winters Road

Hospital Road

Bisnops Road

Twynhams

Grange Farm Business Park

Shedfield Grange

Hotel

Meon Valley Golf & Country Club

Shedfield House

WINCHESTER ROAD

B2177

Upper Church Rd

Cemetery

Fairlands Montessori

Swanmore Road

Moorlands Road

Church Lane

Donigers Dell

Foxcombe Close

Broad Lane

Larkspur Cl

Crofton Way

New Road

Spring Vale

Myers Cl

Greenways

Spring Lane

Suetts Lane

Ridgemede Junior School

Infant School

Rareridge Lane

Tennyson

Wordsworth

Byron Close

Cemetery

Jervis

Hamble Springs

Cricklemede

Folly Field

Victoria Rd

Station Road

Malt Lane

High Street

Bank Street

Cherry Gardens

Hoe Road

Clewers Hill

Clewers Lane

Provene

Meadow

Provene Gardens

Hill Crest Gdns

The Ridings

Evelyn

B2177

Leopold Dr

The Avenue

Claylands Ct

Merlin Cl

Blanchard

Brooklands Road

B3035

The Surg

Meon Police Station

Oak Lane

Pine Rd

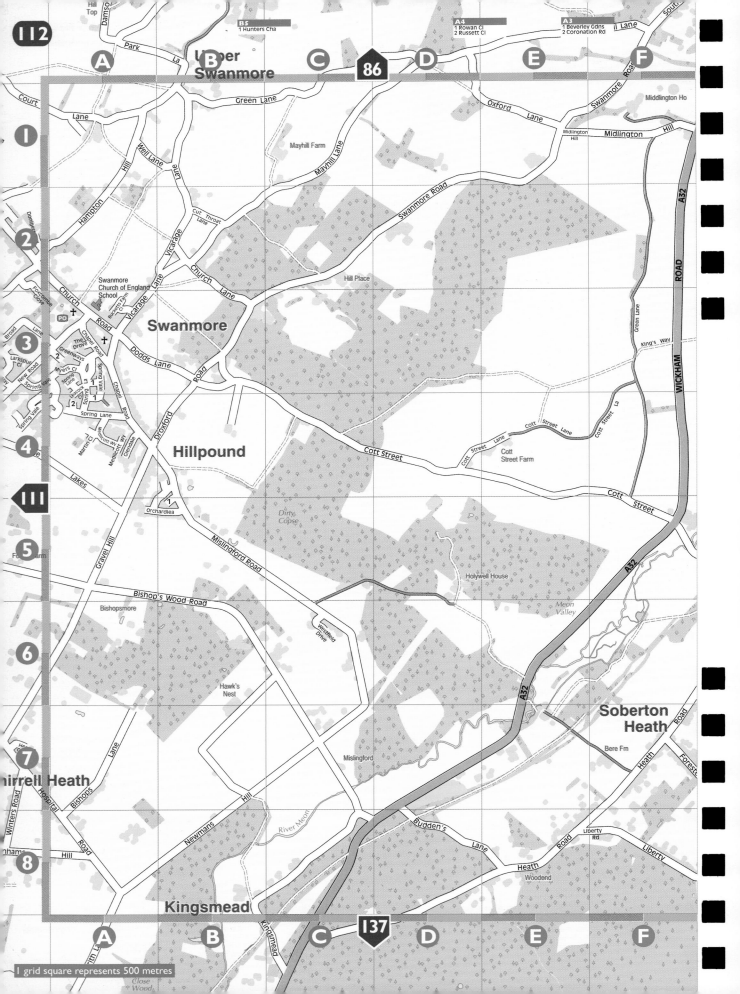

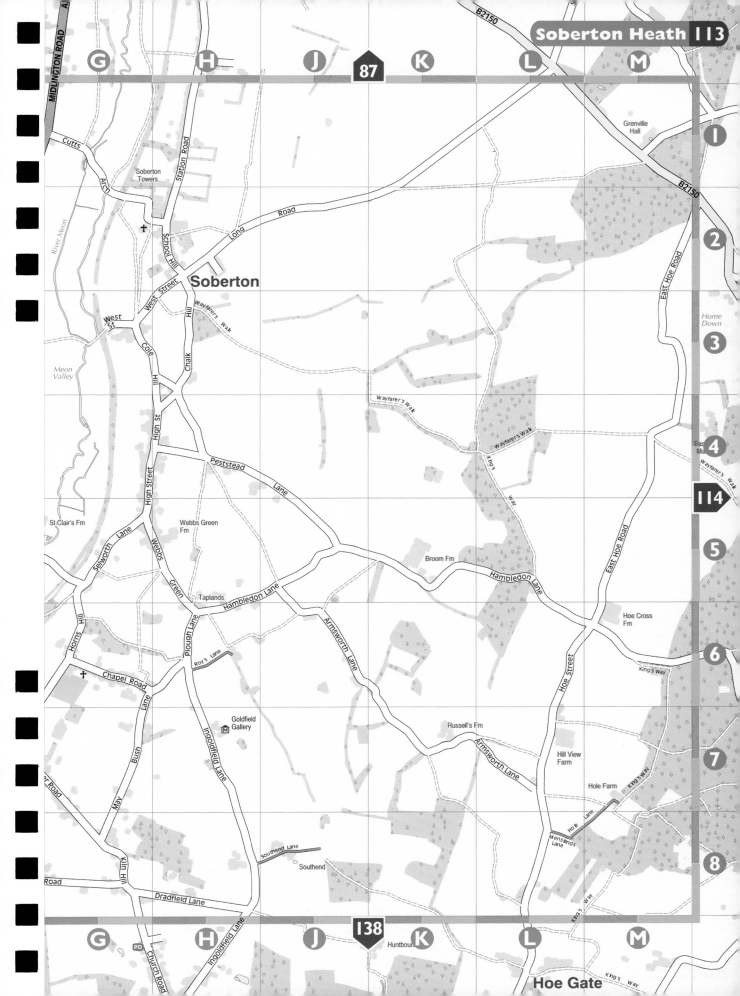

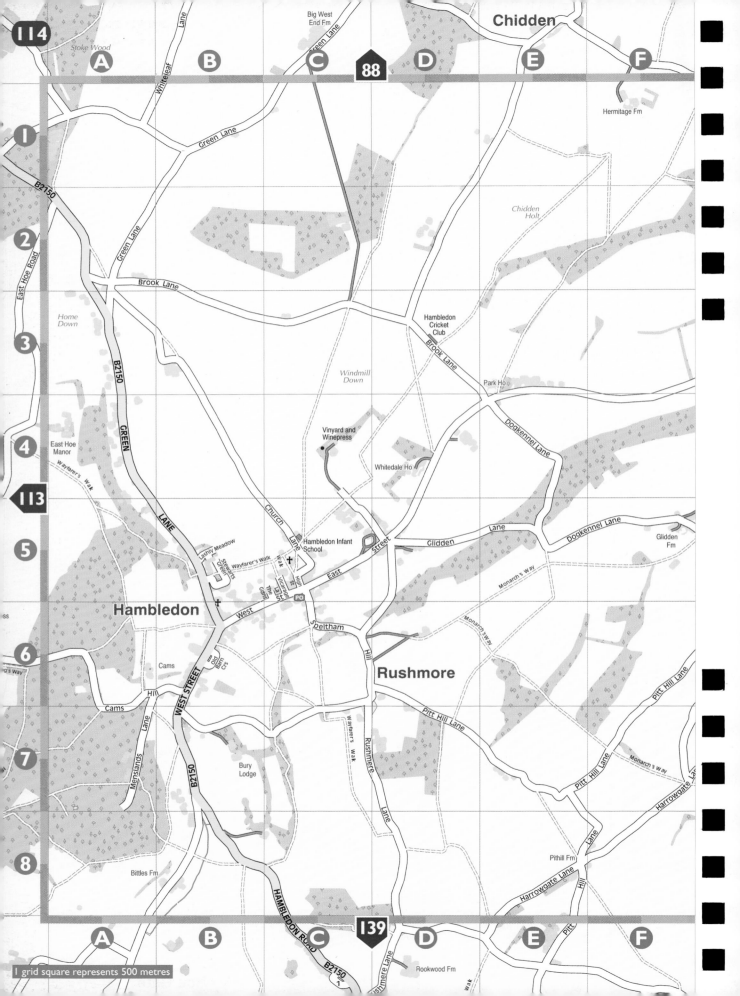

G   H   J   **89**   K   L   M

Clanfield

1

2

3

4

116

5

6

7

Catherin

8

North Fm

Stoneridge Fm

Monarch's Way

Hyden Farm Lane

Old Mill Lane

Broadhalfpenny Down

Dogkennel   Lane

Monarch's Way

Horsepost   Lane

Harrowgate Lane

Denmead Mill

Monarch's Way

Old Mill Lane

Broadway Lane

Hinton Daubnay

Monarch's Way

Loyedean Lane

Tagdell   Lane

Hinton Manor Lane

Hinton Manor Lane

Hinton Manor

Downhouse   Road

Hambledon Road

Pipers   Rd

Peak   Rd

South

Drift

Catherington Lane

Catherington Down

Catherington C of E Contr Infant School

Roads   Hill

Ham   Lane

Five

Crouch   Lane

Day   Lane

Monarch's Way

Lychgate   Drive

G   H   J   **140**   K   L   M

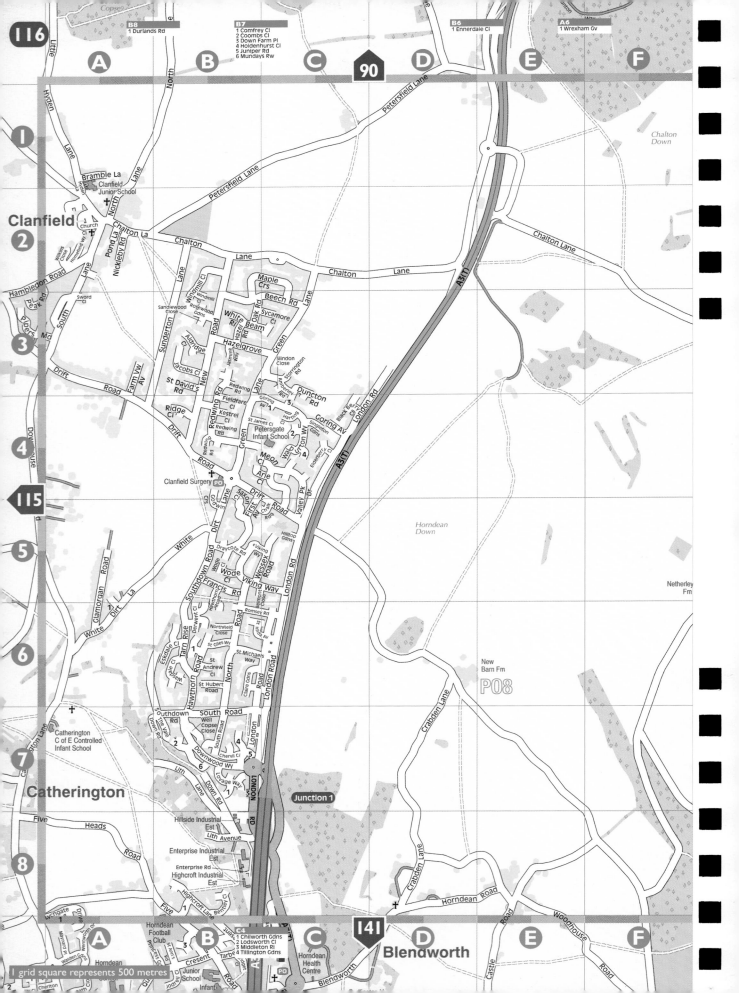

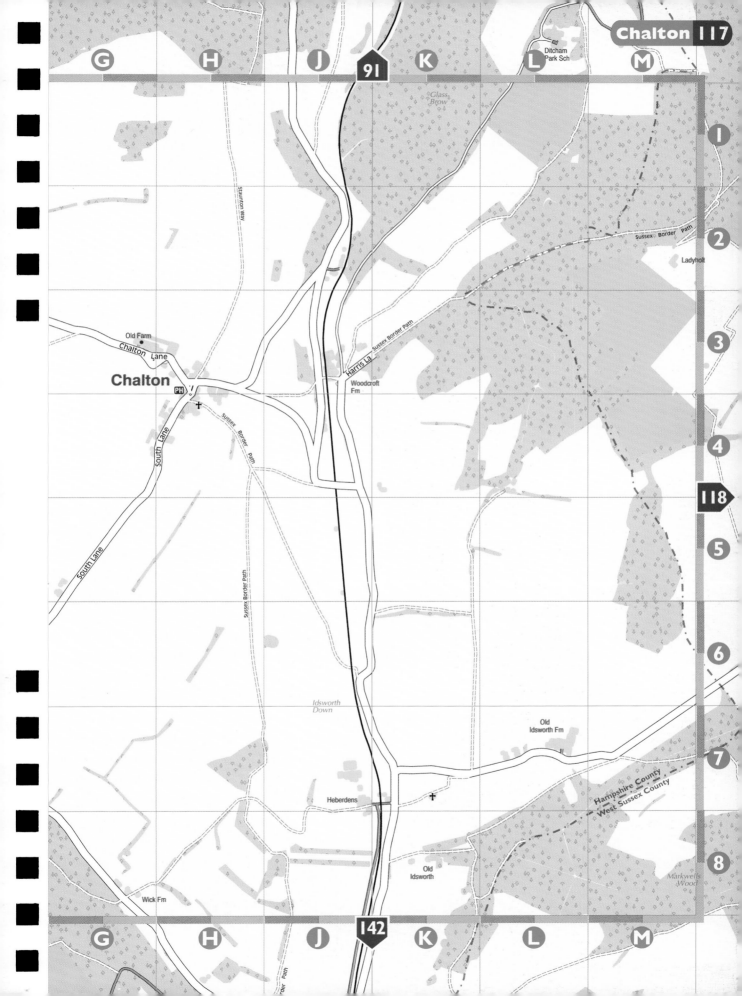

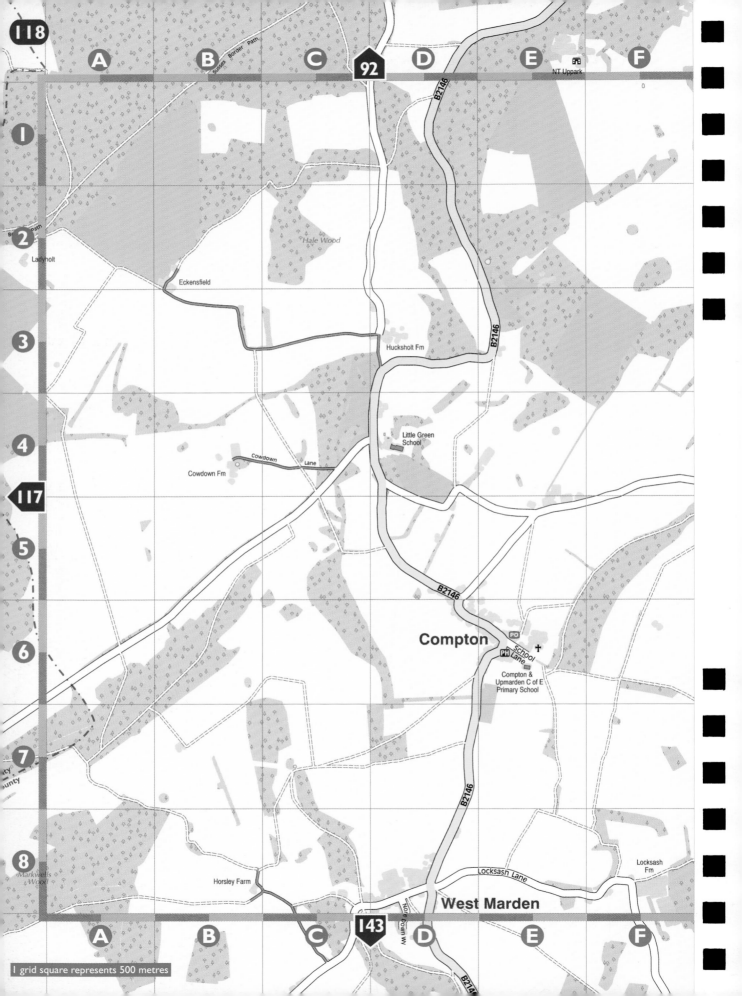

A   B   C   92   D   E   F
NT Uppark

0

1

2
Ladyholt
Hale Wood

Eckensfield

B2146

3
Hucksholt Fm

4
Little Green
School
Cowdown   Lane
Cowdown Fm

5

B2146

6
Compton
PO
PH
School Lane
Compton &
Upmarden C of E
Primary School

B2146

7
County
County

8
Markwells
Wood
Horsley Farm
Locksash Lane
Locksash
Fm
West Marden
Nore Down W
B2146

A   B   C   143   D   E   F
B2146

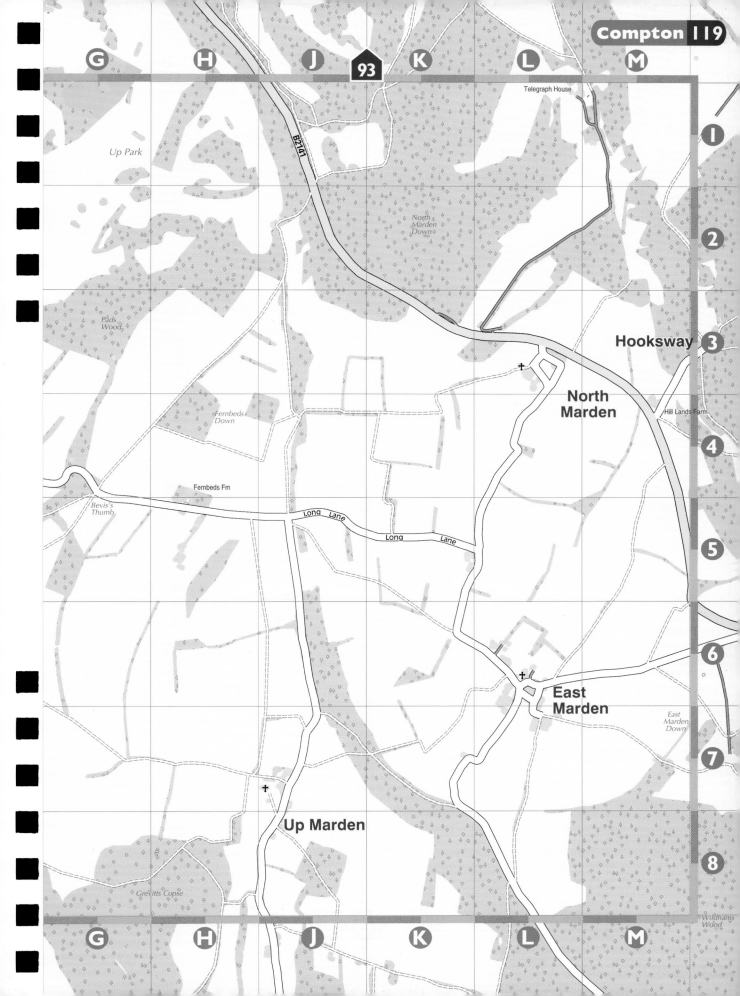

G H J K L M

93

Telegraph House

1

Up Park

2

Hooksway 3

North
Marden

Pads
Wood

North
Marden
Down

Hill Lands Farm

Fernbeds
Down

4

Bevis's
Thumb

Fernbeds Fm

Long Lane

Long Lane

5

East
Marden

6

East
Marden
Down

Up Marden

7

Grevitts Copse

8

Wildhams
Wood

G H J K L M

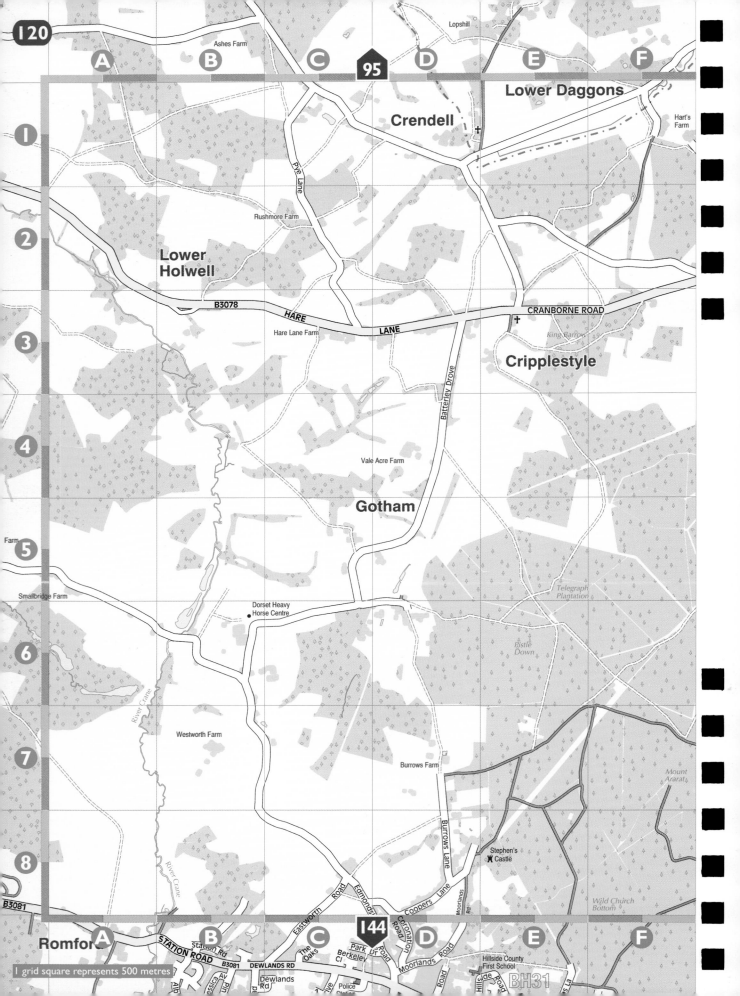

Ashes Farm

Lopshill

Lower Daggons

Crendell

Hart's Farm

A **B** **C** 95 **D** **E** **F**

1

Pye Lane

Rushmore Farm

2

Lower Holwell

B3078

HARE LANE

CRANBORNE ROAD

Hare Lane Farm

King Barrow

3

Cripplestyle

Batterley Drove

4

Vale Acre Farm

Gotham

Farm

5

Telegraph Plantation

Smallbridge Farm

Dorset Heavy Horse Centre

Pistle Down

6

River Crane

Westworth Farm

7

Burrows Farm

Mount Ararat

Burrows Lane

8

Stephen's Castle

River Crane

Eastworth Road

Edmonds Road

Coopers Lane

Moorlands Rd

Wild Church Bottom

B3081

A Romfor **B** 144 **C** **D** **E** **F**

STATION ROAD

Station Rd

B3081

DEWLANDS RD

The Oaks

Park Dr

Berkeley Cl

Road

Moorlands Road

Coronation Road

Moorlands Rd

Hillside County First School

Hillside Road

BH31

Jessica Av

Pin

Dewlands Rd

Police Station

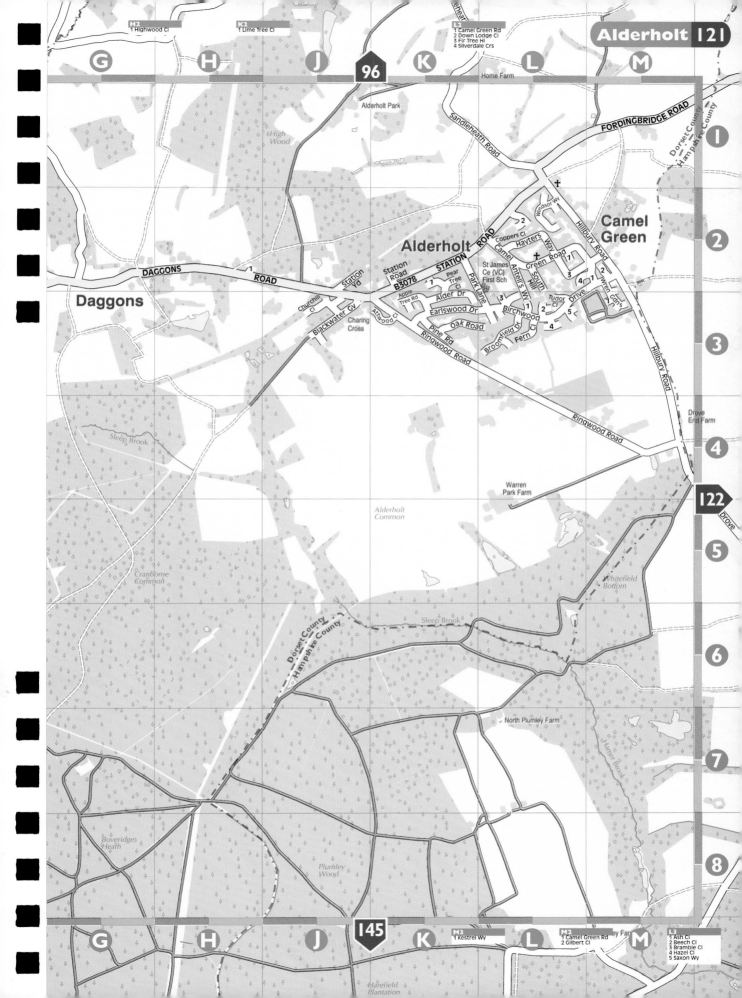

G   H   J   **96**   K   L   M

H2
1 Highwood Cl

K2
1 Lime Tree Cl

L2
1 Camel Green Rd
2 Down Lodge Cl
3 Fir Tree Hl
4 Silverdale Crs

FORDINGBRIDGE ROAD

Home Farm

Alderholt Park

High
Wood

Sandleheath Road

Dorset County
Hampshire County

I

2

Windsor Wy
Camel
Green Road
Hillbury Road

**Camel
Green**

Alderholt

Coppers Cl
Hayters Way
Anten's Wy
South Hill
Warren Gdns
Tudor Cl
Drive

STATION ROAD

St James
Ce (VC)
First Sch

DAGGONS   ROAD

Station
Yd
Station
Road
B3078

Pear
Tree
Cl
Park Lane
Apple
Tree Rd
Alder Dr
Earlswood Dr
Oak Road
Pine Rd
Birchwood
Broomfield Dr
Fern Cl

Daggons

Churchill
Cl
Blackwater Gv
Charing
Cross
Attwood
Cl

Ringwood Road

Hillbury Road

Drove
End Farm

3

Ringwood Road

4

Warren
Park Farm

Alderholt
Common

122
Drove

Sleep Brook

5

Whitefield
Bottom

Cranborne
Common

Dorset County
Hampshire County

Sleep Brook

North Plumley Farm

Hamer Brook

6

7

Boveridges
Heath

Plumley
Wood

8

M3
1 Kestrel Wy

M2
1 Camel Green Rd
2 Gilbert Cl

L3
1 Ash Cl
2 Beech Cl
3 Bramble Cl
4 Hazel Cl
5 Saxon Wy

Harefield
Plantation

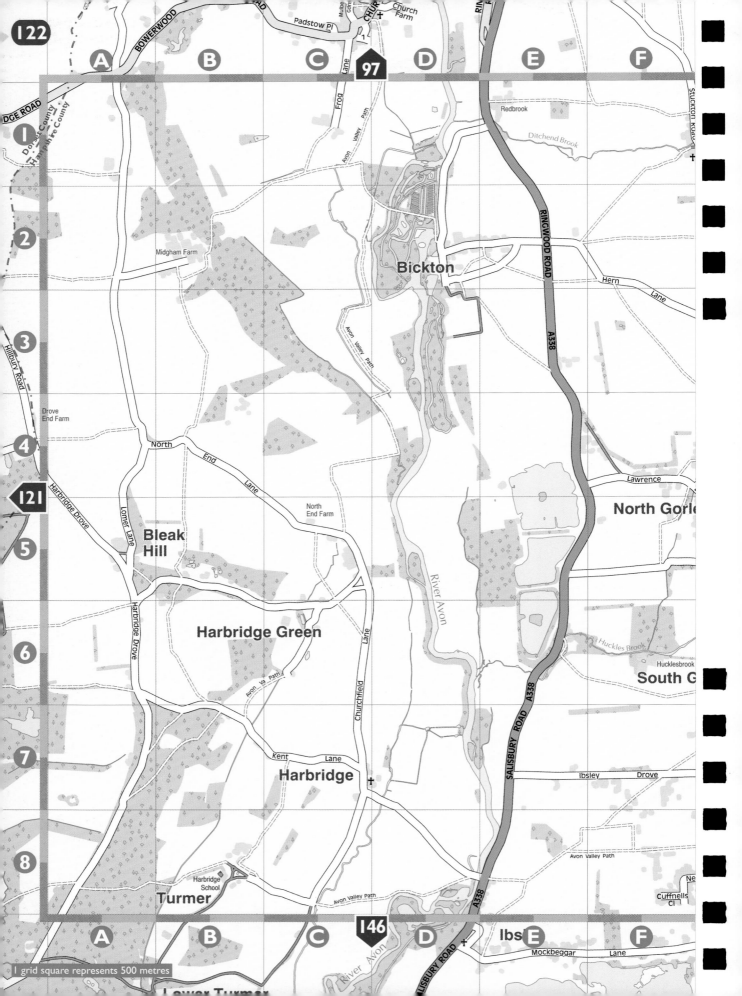

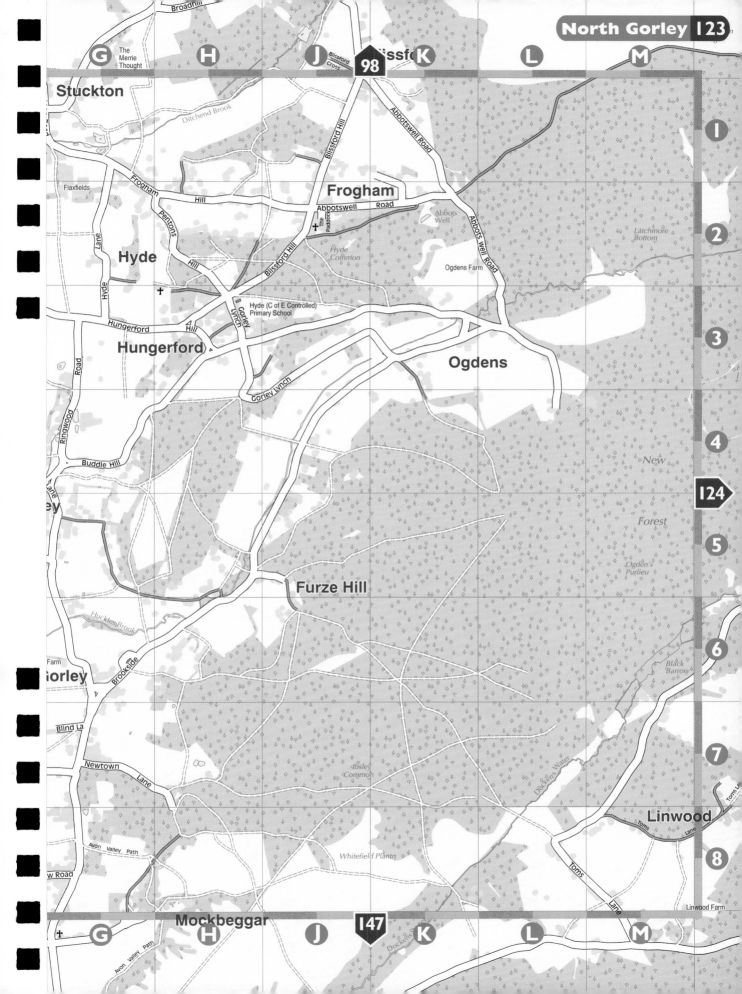

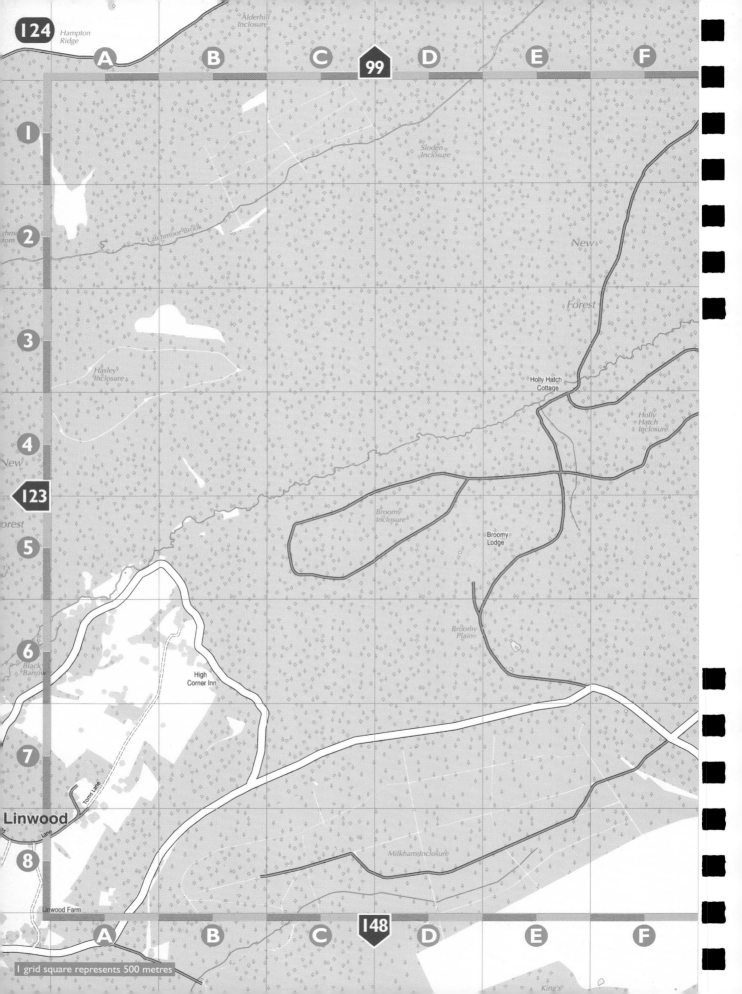

Hampton
Ridge

A   B   C   D   E   F

99

Alderhill
Inclosure

1

Sloden
Inclosure

2

Latchmoor Brook

New

3

Hasley
Inclosure

Forest

Holly Hatch
Cottage

4

New

Holly
Hatch
Inclosure

123

Forest

Broomy
Inclosure

5

Broomy
Lodge

Black
Barrow

6

High
Corner Inn

Broomy
Plain

7

Toms Lane

Linwood

Lane

8

Milkham Inclosure

Linwood Farm

A   B   C   D   E   F

King's

1 grid square represents 500 metres

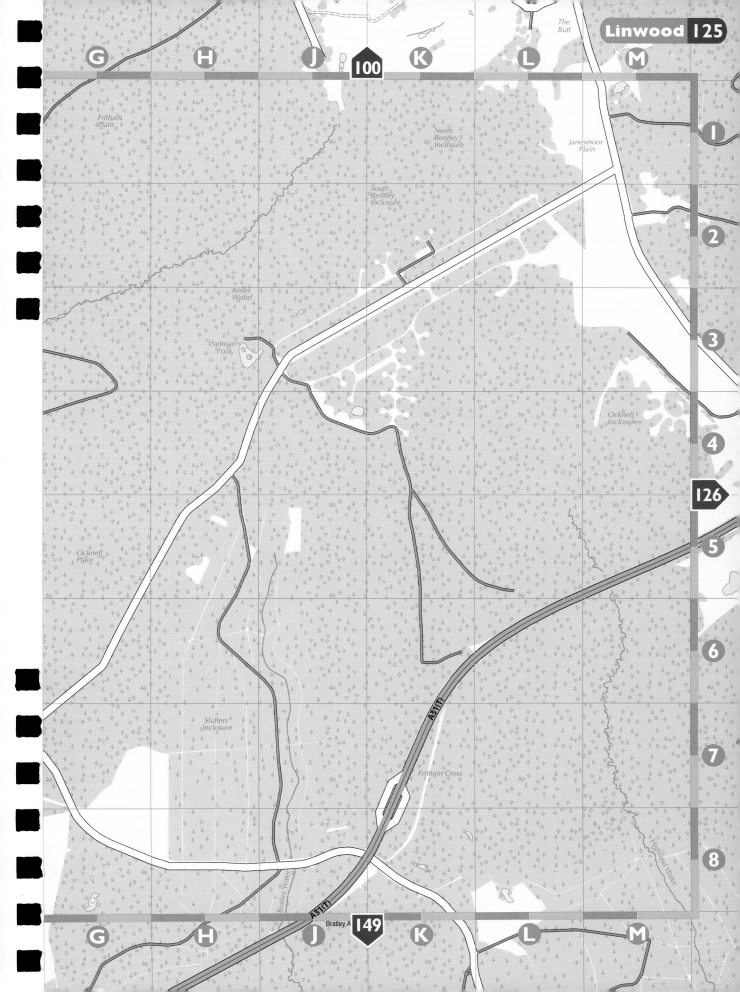

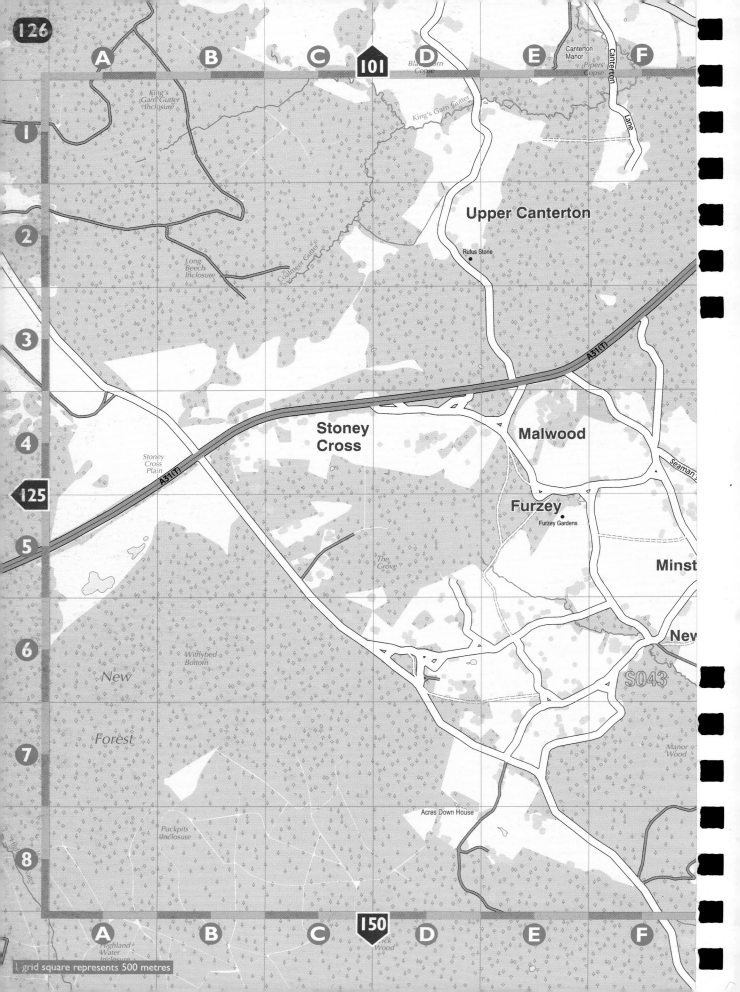

A   B   C   **101**   D   E   F

Canterton
Manor
Pipers
Copse

Canterton
Lane

Blackthorn
Copse

King's
Garn Gutter
Inclosure

King's Garn Gutter

I

Upper Canterton

2

Long
Beech
Inclosure

Coalmeer Gutter

Rufus Stone

3

A31 (t)

4

**Stoney
Cross**

Malwood

Stoney
Cross
Plain

A31 (t)

seaman

125

Furzey

Furzey Gardens

5

The
Grove

Minst

New

6

New

Withybed
Bottom

S043

7

Forest

Manor
Wood

Puckpits
Inclosure

Acres Down House

8

A   B   **150**   C   D   E   F

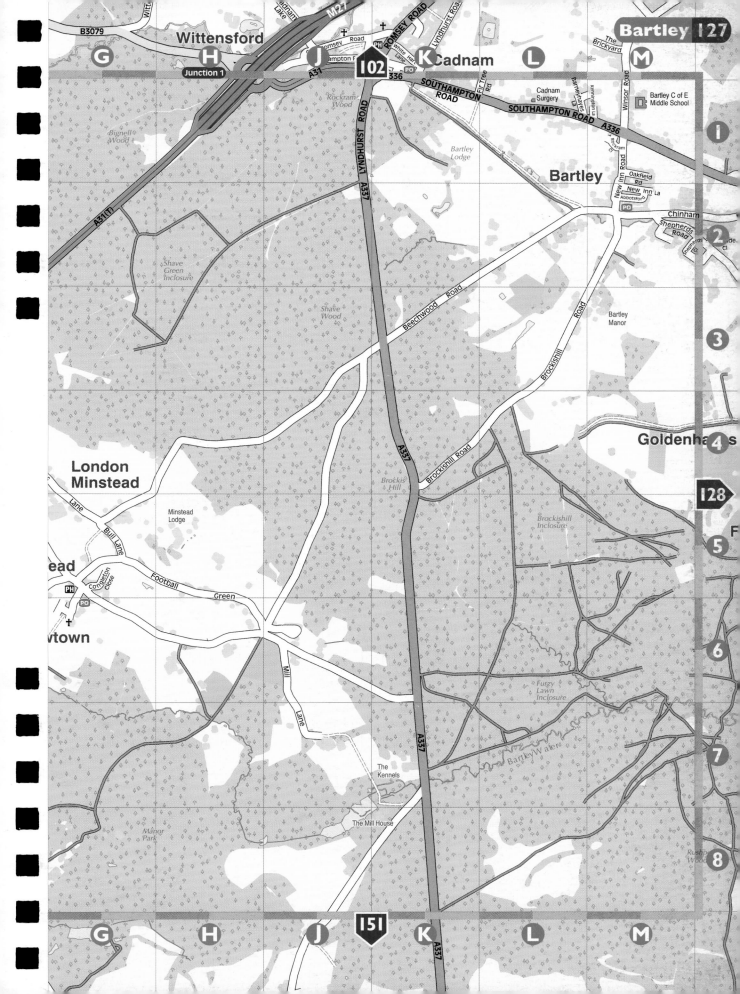

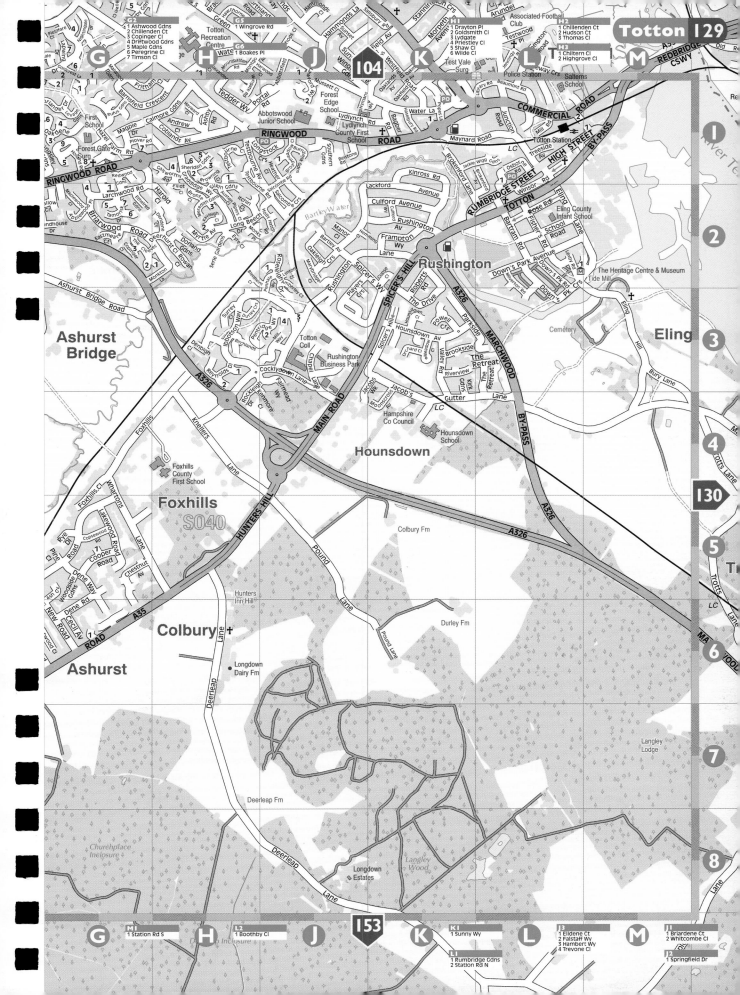

130
ASH
REDBRIDGE
CSWY

Redbridge

105

129

154

1 grid square represents 500 metres

Redbridge Station

Community School

Redbridge Primary School

Millbrook Trading Estate

Millbrook

Super Bowl

Cemetery

Trinity Ind Est

Millbrook Clinic

Tanners Brook Junior School

Tanners Brook Infant School

Westbury Road

River Test

City of Southampton Hampshire County

Bury Fm

Trotts

MARCHWOOD BY-PASS

Pooksgreen

Marchwood

Marchwood Junior School

Marchwood C of E Infant School

Pumpfield Farm

MARCHWOOD

S015

River Test

A33

Western Avenue

First Avenue

Second Av

Bury Road

Normandy Way

Maritime Av

Regents Park Girls School

Regents Park Surg

Middle & Primary School

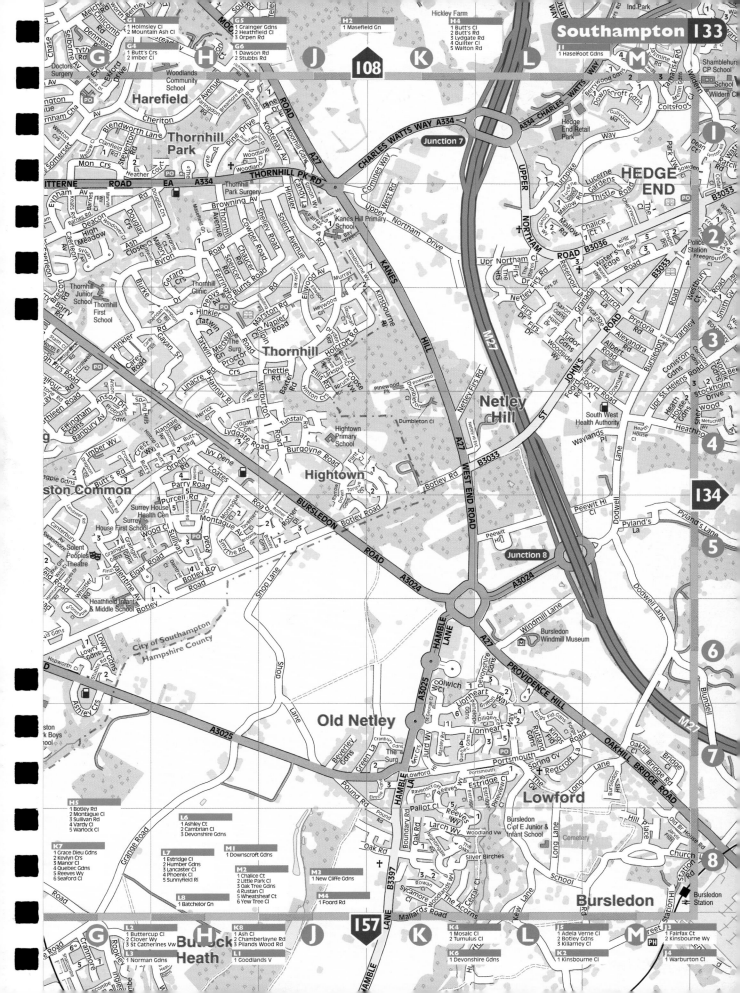

G H J 108 K L M

108

2 3 I34 5 6 7 8

HEDGE END

Harefield

Thornhill Park

Thornhill

Junction 7

Netley Hill

Hightown

South West Health Authority

Junction 8

Bursledon Windmill Museum

Old Netley

Lowford

City of Southampton Hampshire County

Bursledon

Bursledon Station

I57

Butlock Heath

G H J 157 K L M

G1
1 Holmsley Cl
2 Mountain Ash Cl

G4
1 Butt's Crs
2 Imber Cl

G5
1 Grainger Gdns
2 Heathfield Cl
3 Orpen Rd

G6
1 Dawson Rd
2 Stubbs Rd

H2
1 Masefield Gn

H4
1 Butt's Cl
2 Butt's Rd
3 Lydgate Rd
4 Quilter Cl
5 Walton Rd

L1
1 Haselfoot Gdns

H5
1 Botley Rd
2 Montague Cl
3 Sullivan Rd
4 Vardy Cl
5 Warlock Cl

K7
1 Grace Dieu Gdns
2 Kevlyn Crs
3 Manor Cl
4 Quebec Gdns
5 Reeves Wy
6 Seaford Cl

L6
1 Ashley Ct
2 Cambrian Cl
3 Devonshire Gdns

L7
1 Estridge Cl
2 Humber Gdns
3 Lancaster Cl
4 Phoenix Cl
5 Sunnyfield Ri

L8
1 Batchelor Gn

M1
1 Downscroft Gdns

M2
1 Chalice Ct
2 Little Park Cl
3 Oak Tree Gdns
4 Rustan Cl
5 Wheatsheaf Ct
6 Yew Tree Cl

M3
1 New Cliffe Gdns

M4
1 Foord Rd

G2
1 Buttercup Cl
2 Clover Wy
3 St Catherines Vw

G5
1 Norman Gdns

H3

K8
1 Ash Cl
2 Chamberlayne Rd
3 Pilands Wood Rd

L1
1 Goodlands V

K4
1 Mosaic Cl
2 Tumulus Cl

K6
1 Devonshire Gdns

K2
1 Kinsbourne Cl

L1
1 Adela Verne Cl
2 Botley Gdns
3 Killarney Cl

M1
1 Fairfax Ct
2 Kinsbourne Wy

I4
1 Warburton Cl

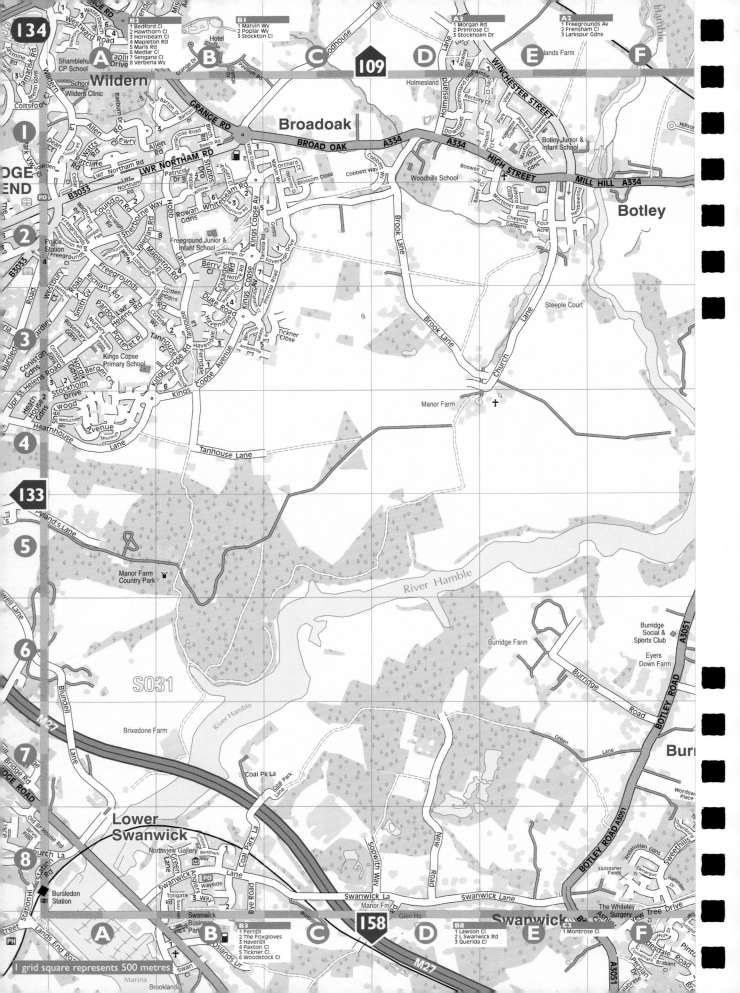

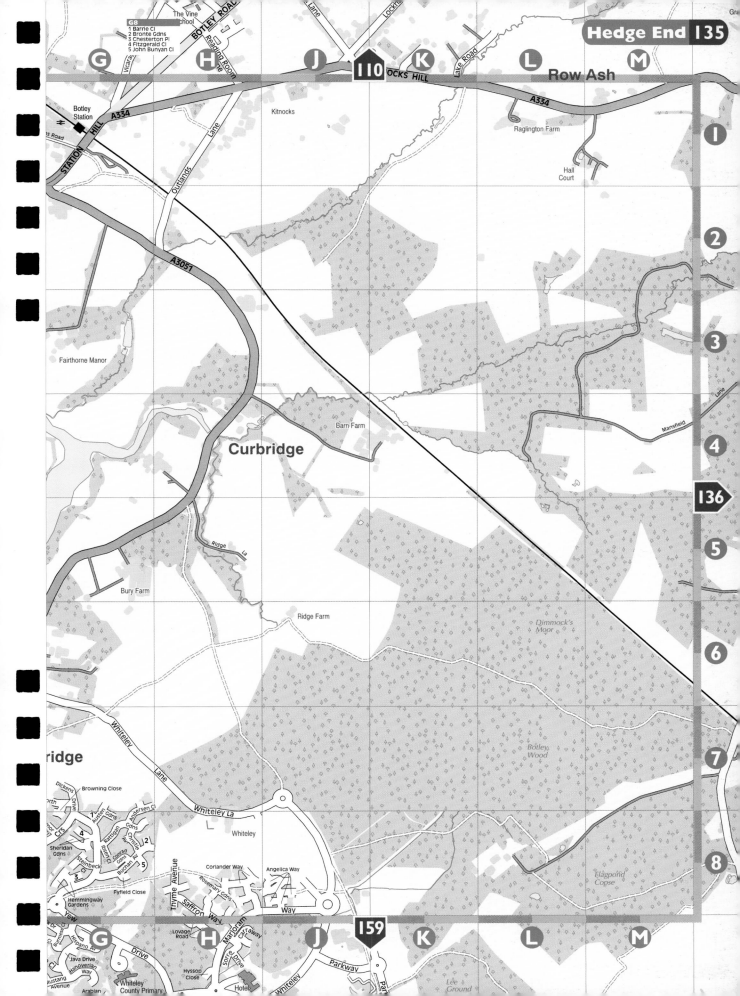

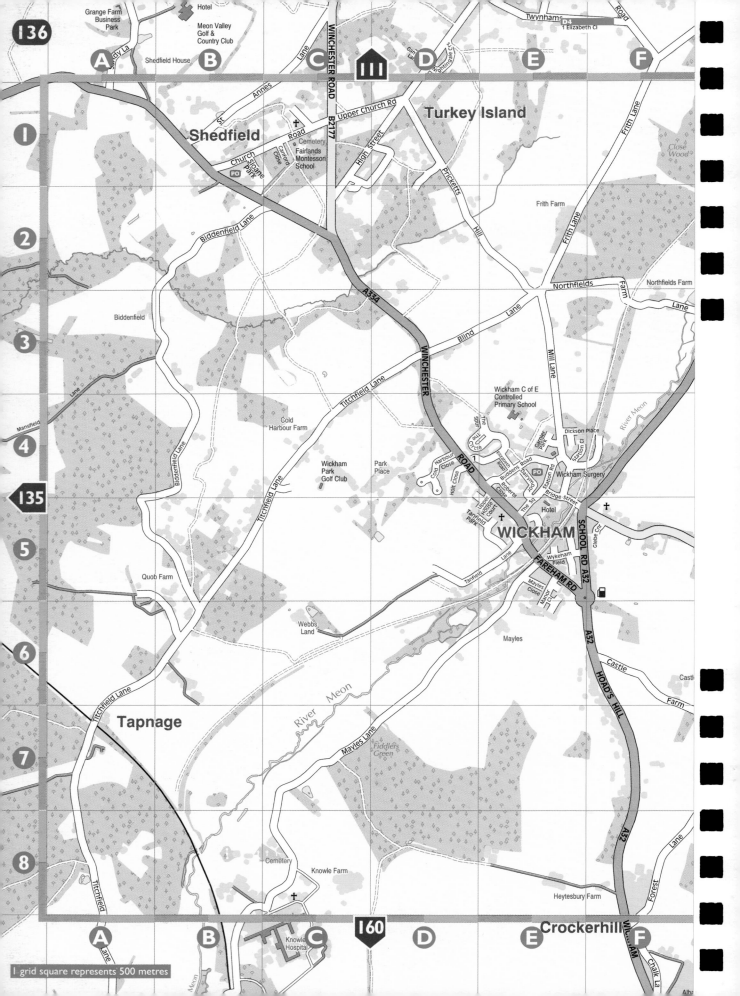

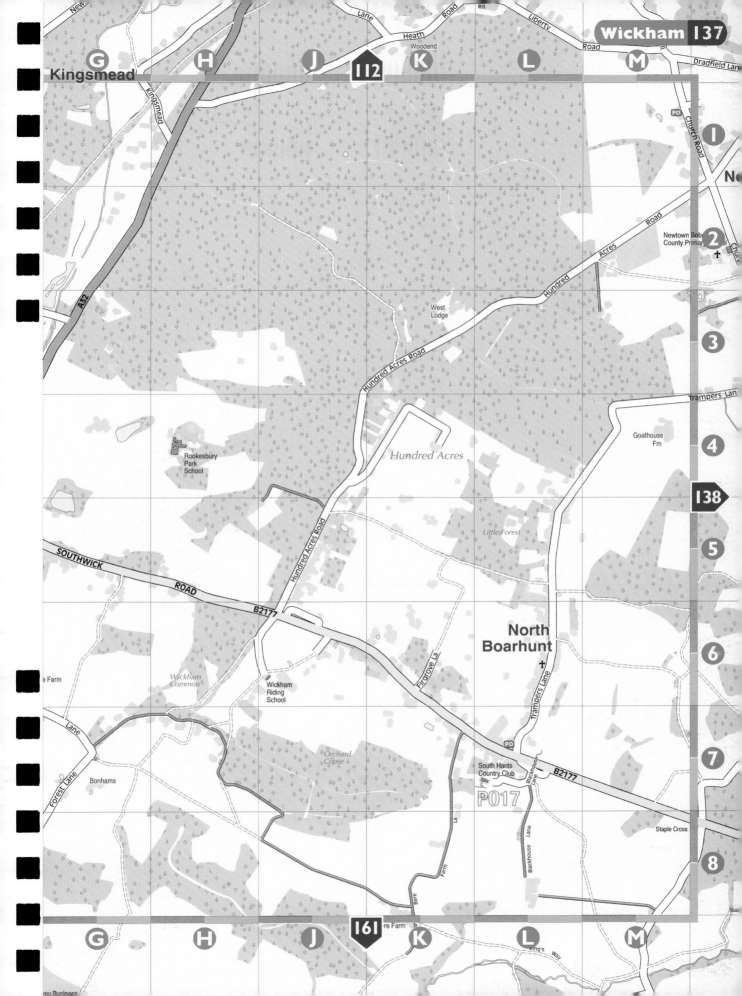

G H J K L M

Kingsmead

New

Heath

Woodend

Liberty

Road

Rd

Road

Dradfield Lan

Church Road

PO

1

Ne

2

Newtown Sob
County Primary School

Chur

Hundred

Acres

Road

3

A32

West
Lodge

Trampers Lan

Hundred Acres Road

Goathouse
Fm

4

Rookesbury
Park
School

Hundred Acres

138

Little Forest

5

SOUTHWICK

ROAD

Hundred Acres Road

B2177

6

North
Boarhunt

Firgrove La

Trampers Lane

e Farm

Wickham
Common

Wickham
Riding
School

Orchard
Copse

PO

7

Lane

Forest Lane

Bonhams

South Hants
Country Club

Blackhouse Lane

B2177

P017

Staple Cross

Blackhouse Lane

8

Bere

La

Farm

re Farm

G H J K L M

King's Way

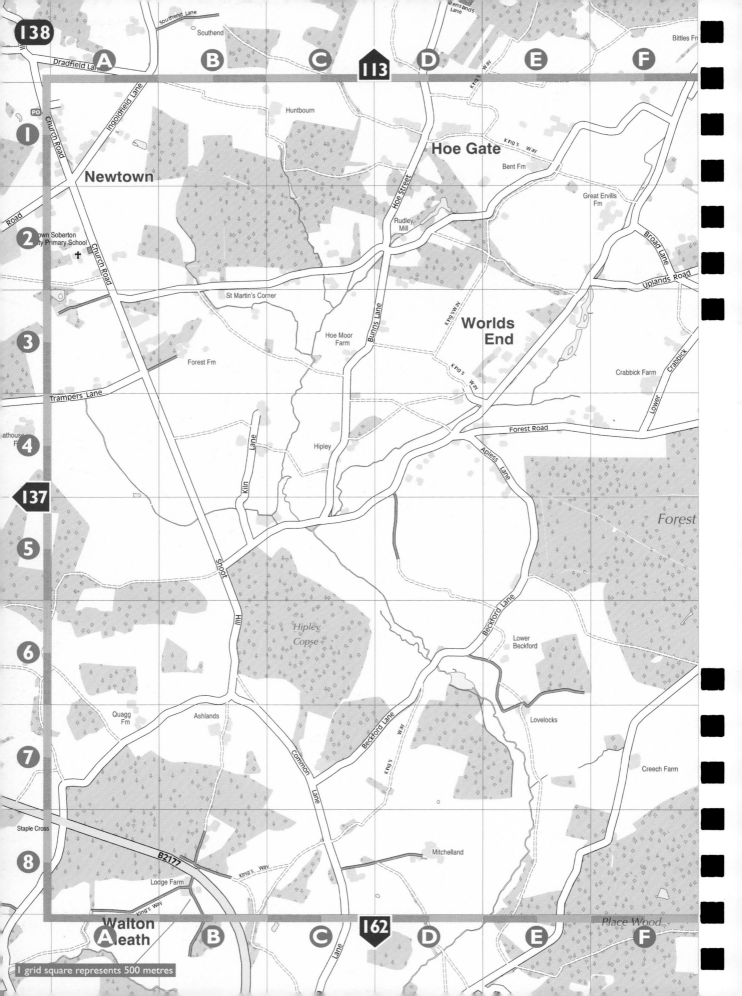

H1
1 Hambledon Rd

J4
1 Frenchies Vw
2 Furdies
3 Peakfield

J5
1 The Pastures

G   H   J   K   L   M

I

2

3

4

140

5

6

7

8

HAMBLEDON ROAD
B2150

Forest
Gate

Rushmere Lane

Rookwood Fm

Wayfarer's Wak

Kidmore Lane

The Crossways

White Lane

Horse Lane

Edneys Lane

Uplands Road

Thompsons Lane

Anthill
Common

Upr Crabbick La

Anthill Cl

Anthill Cl

HAMBLEDON ROAD

School Lane

Lane

Inhams Lane

Inhams Lane

P07

Glasspool

Harvest Road

Green Lane

B2150

Denmead Health
Centre

Cem   Cemetery La

Tanner's Lane

Park Road
PO

DENMEAD

Anmore Road

Forest Road

Hawthorn
Rd

Yew Tree Gdns

Southwick Road

Ashling Cl

Ashling Park Road

Ashling Gdns

Chestnut Cl

The Heath

Martin Avenue

Mill Road

Mill Close

Anmore

The Smithy

Windsor Road

Lovedons Rd

The Meadow

The Orchard

Bere Road

Field Wy

Brookside Cl

Denmead
Infant School

Denmead
Junior
School

Bere Rd

Dando Rd

Maple Drive

of Bere

Creech Woods

Bunkers Hill

Bunkers Hill

Forest Road

The Willows

The Liberty

Pond Place

Home Mead

Cottage Cl

The Cherry

Kilnside

Forest Md

Old River

Hilda Gdns

Little Ch

Mead End Rd

Three Acres

Great Md

B2150

Soake Road

Soake

The Spinney

Paddock End

Parklands Business
Park

Little Md

Little Md

Byngs
Business Park

HAMBLEDON ROAD

PO

Furzeley Road

Sheepwash Lane

Newlands Lane

Furzeley
Corner

Wayfarer's Wak

Closewood Road

Old Park
Farm

Westside

Belney Lane

Sheepwash Lane

Belney Farm

Closewood

Wayfarer's Wk

Newlands Lane

Pi
Wood In

Sheepwash Farm

G   H   J   K   L   M

K5
1 The Tithe

Wanstead Farm

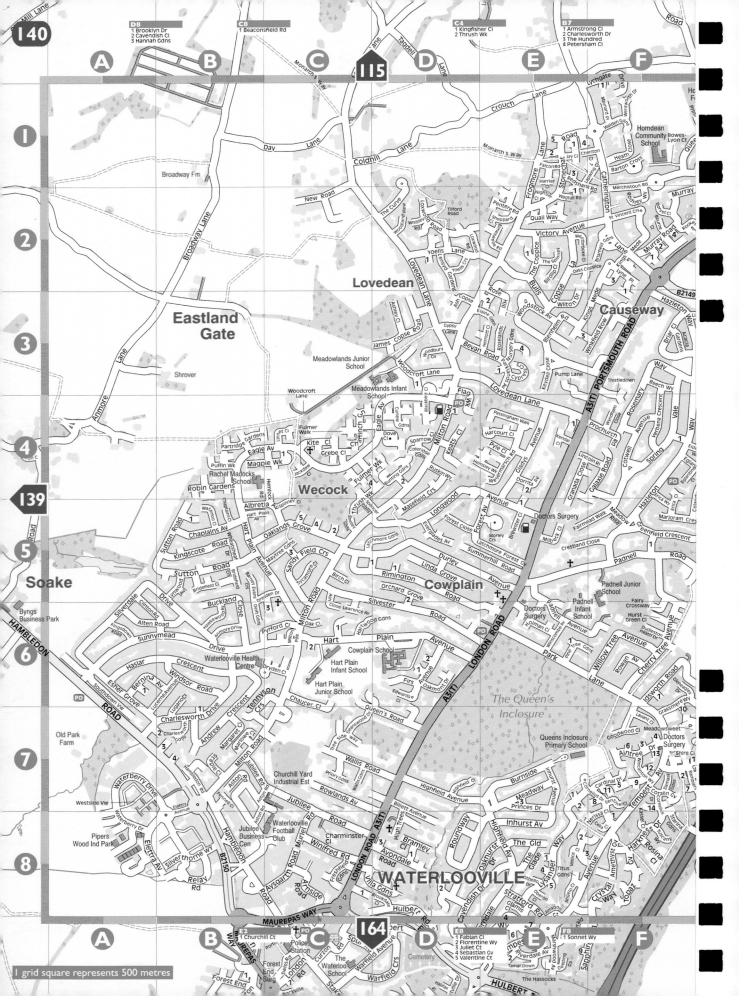

D8
1 Brooklyn Dr
2 Cavendish Cl
3 Hannah Gdns

C8
1 Beaconsfield Rd

C4
1 Kingfisher Cl
2 Thrush Wk

B7
1 Armstrong Cl
2 Charlesworth Dr
3 The Hundred
4 Petersham Cl

A   B   C   115   D   E   F

1

2

Lovedean

Eastland
Gate

3

Causeway

Shrover

Meadowlands Junior
School

Woodcroft
Lane

Meadowlands Infant
School

4

Wecock

139

Rachel Madocks
School

5

Soake

Byngs
Business Park

Cowplain

HAMBLEDON

6

Waterlooville Health
Centre

Cowplain School

Hart Plain
Infant School

The Queen's
Inclosure

Padnell Junior
School

Padnell
Infant
School

Hart Plain
Junior School

Doctors
Surgery

Old Park
Farm

Doctors
Surgery

7

Charlesworth Drive

Churchill Yard
Industrial Est

Queen's Road

Queens Inclosure
Primary School

Doctors
Surgery

Westside Vw

Churchill Yard
Industrial Est

Pipers
Wood Ind Park

Waterlooville
Football
Club

Jubilee
Business
Cen

8

WATERLOOVILLE

E2
1 Churchill Ct

E8
1 Fabian Cl
2 Florentine Wy
3 Juliet Ct
4 Sebastian Gv
5 Valentine Ct

F8
1 Sonnet Wy

Police
Station

The Waterloo
School

Cemetery

1 grid square represents 500 metres

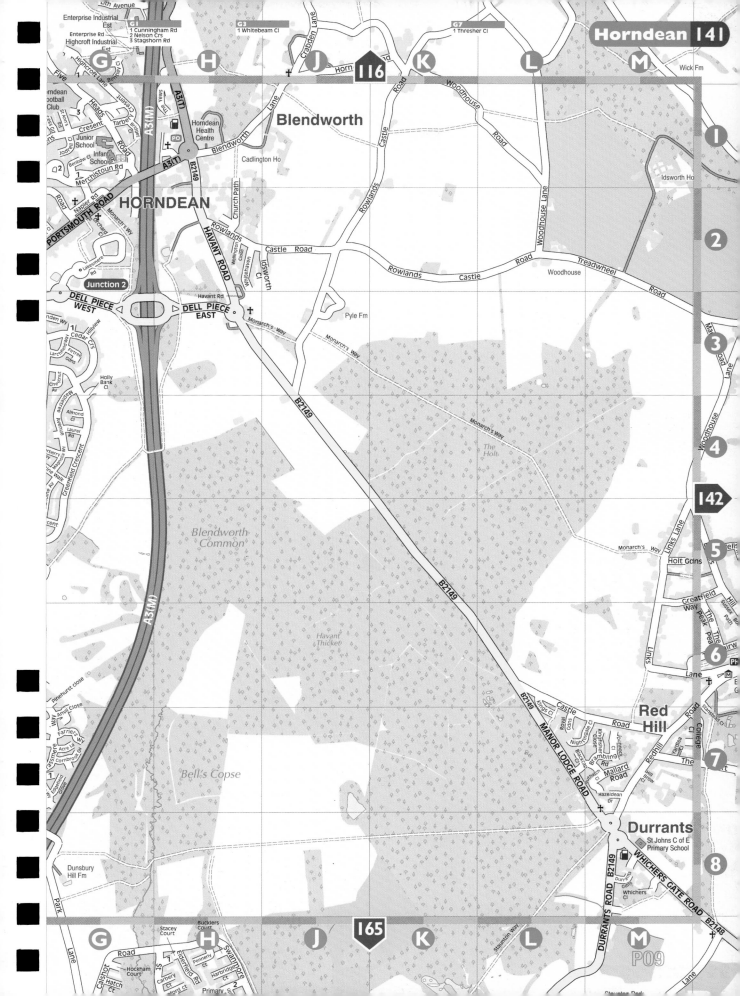

117

166

141

A B C D E F

1
2
3
4
5
6
7
8

Wick Fm

Old
Idsworth

Markwells
Wood

Idsworth Ho

Ashcroft
La

Finchdean

South
Holt Fm

Northwood
Fm

Forestside

Road

Magpie Road

Dean Lane

Finchdean Rd

Deanlane
End

Warren
Down

Woodhouse Lane

Sussex Border Path

Drews Fm

Firtree
Piece

Wellsworth

Wellsworth La

Finchdean Rd

Stansted Forest

Lane

Bowes

Wellswood Gdns.

Meadowlands

Sussex Border Path

Holt Gdns

Hare's
Warren

Greatfield Way

The The Peak

Broad Cft

Uplands Road

Hill

Rowlands/
Castle Station

Monarch's Wy

The Fairway

Doctors Surgery

PO

PH

M

PH

Finchdean Rd

Sussex Border Path

English
Gallery

Rowland's
Castle

Monarch's Way

ed
Hill

Road

College

Stansted Cl

Woodberry

Horsepasture Fm

Sussex

Border

Path

The

Drift

Glen Dl

Glen

La

rrants

St Johns C of E
Primary School

Sussex Border Path

Holme Farm

Stubbermere

HERS GATE ROAD

B2148

LC

West Hampshire County

Woodberry Lane

Park Lane

09

1 grid square represents 500 metres

121

169

146

G H J K L M

I
2
3
4
5
6
7
8

Boveridge Heath

G3
1 Lavender Cl

Plumley Wood

Plumley Farm

Harefield Plantation

Shepherds Lane

Home Farm

Nea Drive

Nea Drive

Chestnut

Ringwood Forest

...hay Rd

The Chase

Hunters Cl

Barberry Cl

Fairwood Rd

Magnolia

Laburnum

Woodlinken Wy

Acacia

Close

Wisteria Dr Av

Black Moor Rd

RINGWOOD ROAD

The Forestside

Rosebery Close

Parham Cl

Ebblake

Cemetery

Brunel Cl

Forest Cl

Bessemer Close

Ebblake Industrial Est

B3081

Hampshire County
Dorset County

Moors Valley
Country Park

Duncombe Drive

VERWOOD ROAD B3081

Baker's Hanging

Watchmo...

River Moors

Ashley Heath
Industrial Est

Watching Wood

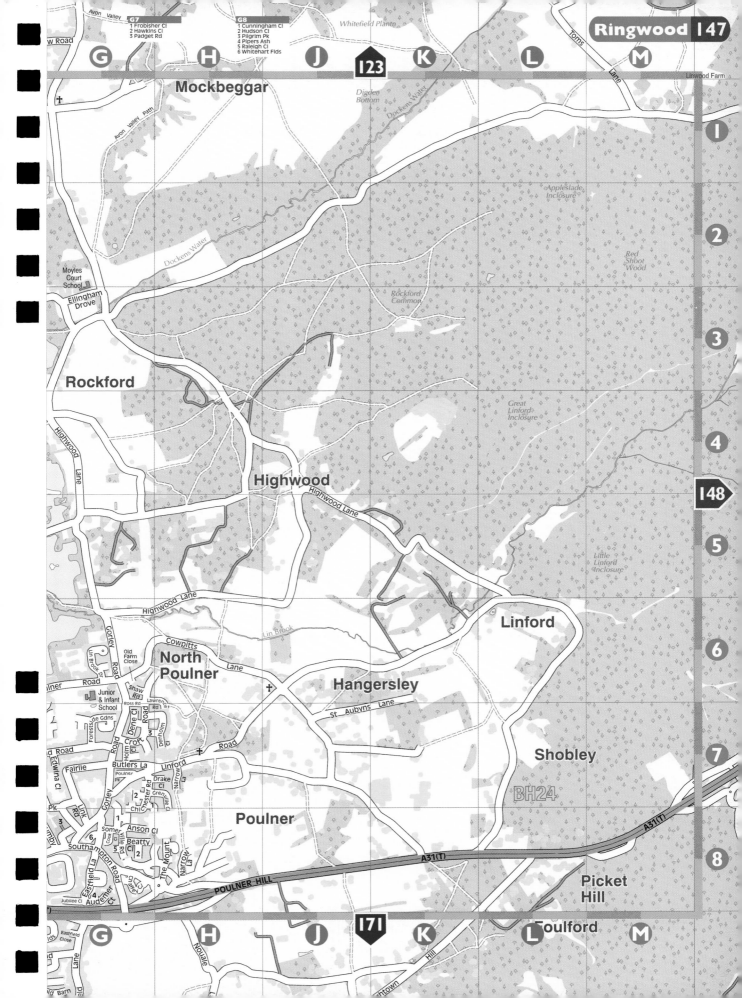

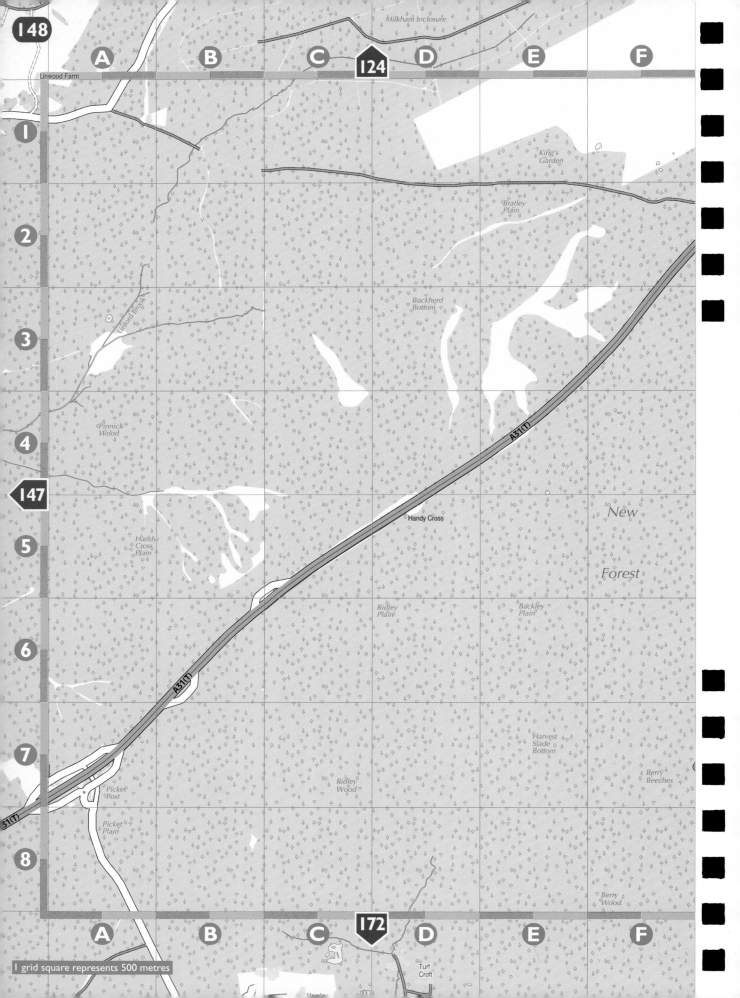

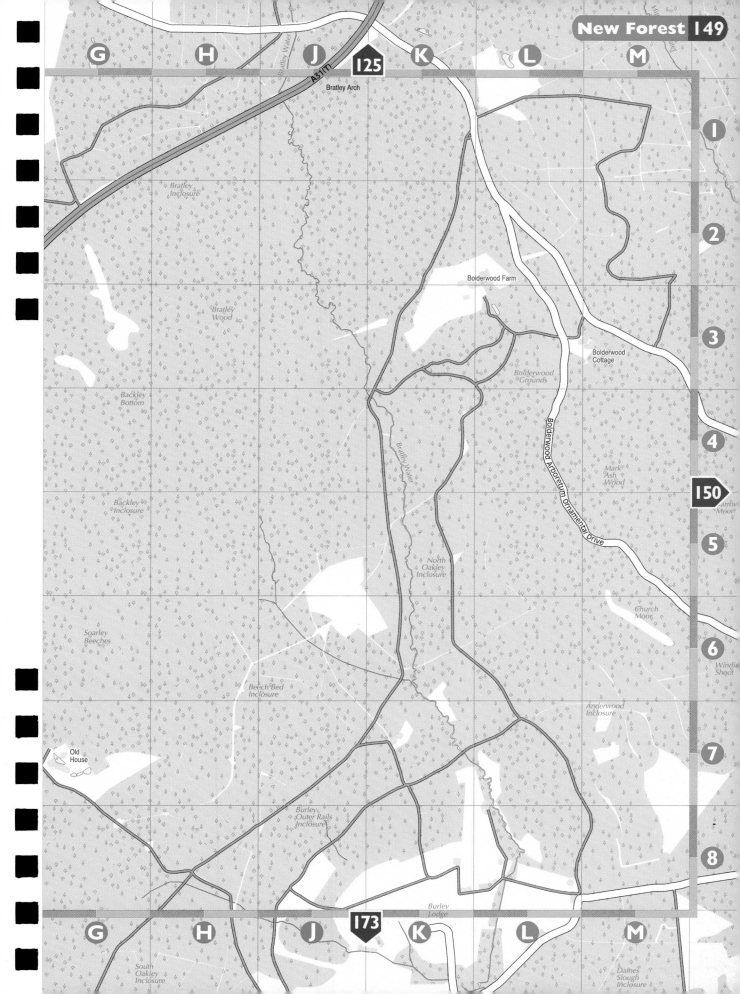

G H J 125 K L M

Bratley Water

A31 (T)

Bratley Arch

1

Bratley
Inclosure

2

Bolderwood Farm

Bratley
Wood

3

Bolderwood
Cottage

Bolderwood
Grounds

Backley
Bottom

4

Bratley Water

Mark
Ash
Wood

150

Backley
Inclosure

Bolderwood Arboretum Ornamental drive

Harrow
Moor

5

North
Oakley
Inclosure

Church
Moor

Soarley
Beeches

6

Winding
Shoot

Beech Bed
Inclosure

Anderwood
Inclosure

7

Old
House

Burley
Outer Rails
Inclosure

8

Burley
Lodge

G H J 173 K L M

South
Oakley
Inclosure

Dames
Slough
Inclosure

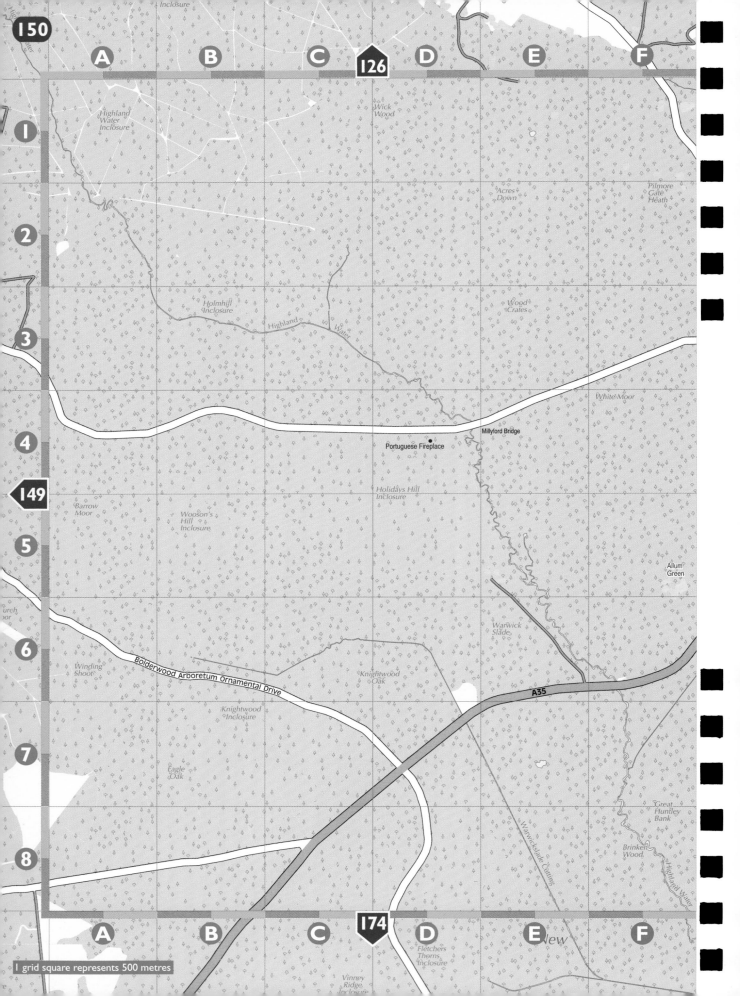

A   B   C **126** D   E   F

Inclosure

Highland
Water
Inclosure

Wick
Wood

1

Acres
Down

Pilmore
Gate
Heath

2

Holmhill
Inclosure

Highland   Water

Wood
Crates

3

White Moor

Millyford Bridge

• Portuguese Fireplace

4

◀ **149**

Barrow
Moor

Wooson's
Hill
Inclosure

Holidays Hill
Inclosure

5

Allum
Green

urch
oor

Warwick
Slade

6

Winding
Shoot

Bolderwood Arboretum Ornamental Drive

Knightwood
Oak

A35

Knightwood
Inclosure

7

Eagle
Oak

Great
Huntley
Bank

8

Warwickslade Cutting

Brinken
Wood

Highland Water

A   B   C **174** D   E *lew*   F

Fletchers
Thorns
Inclosure

1 grid square represents 500 metres

Vinney
Ridge
Inclosure

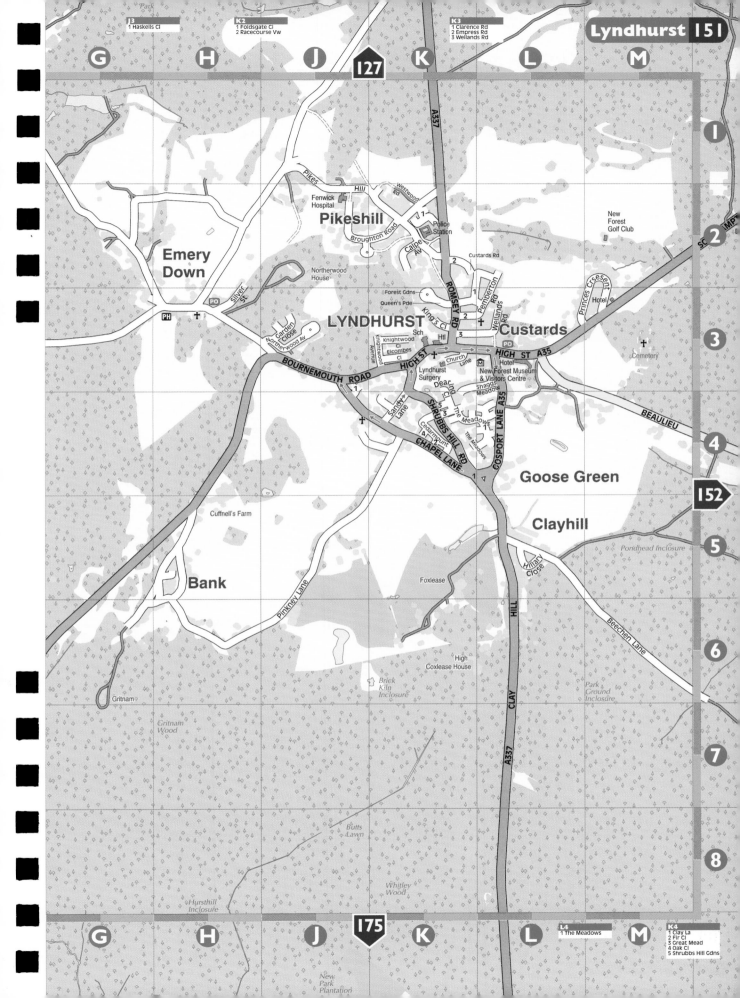

G   H   J   127   K   L   M

J3
1 Haskells Cl

K2
1 Foldsgate Cl
2 Racecourse Vw

K3
1 Clarence Rd
2 Empress Rd
3 Wellands Rd

I
2   SC IMP
3
4   152
5
6
7
8

New Forest Golf Club

Princes Crescent

Hotel

Cemetery

Custards

Custards Rd

Pemberton Rd
Wellands Rd

PO
Hotel

New Forest Museum & Visitors Centre

HIGH ST A35

BEAULIEU

Goose Green

Clayhill

Pondhead Inclosure

Park Ground Inclosure

Beechen Lane

CLAY HILL A337

Hillary Close

Foxlease

High Coxlease House

Brick Kiln Inclosure

Butts Lawn

Whitley Wood

Gritnam Wood

Gritnam

Hursthill Inclosure

Bank

Pinkney Lane

Cuffnell's Farm

BOURNEMOUTH ROAD

Emery Down

Silver St.
PO
PH   †

Garden Close
Northerwood Av.
Knightwood Avenue

Northerwood House

Pikeshill

Pikes Hill

Fenwick Hospital

Westwood Rd

Broughton Road

Calpe Av.

Police Station

ROMSEY RD A337

Custards Rd

Forest Gdns

Queen's Pde

King's Cl

LYNDHURST

Sch
Htl

Knightwood Cl
Elcombes Cl

HIGH ST
Church
Lyndhurst Surgery
Dear Cl

The Meadows

Shaggs Meadow

SHRUBBS HILL RD

CHAPEL LANE

Cesarmpunt

Sandy Lane

GOSPORT LANE A35

G   H   J   175   K   L   M

L4
1 The Meadows

K4
1 Clay La
2 Fir Cl
3 Great Mead
4 Oak Cl
5 Shrubbs Hill Gdns

New Park Plantation

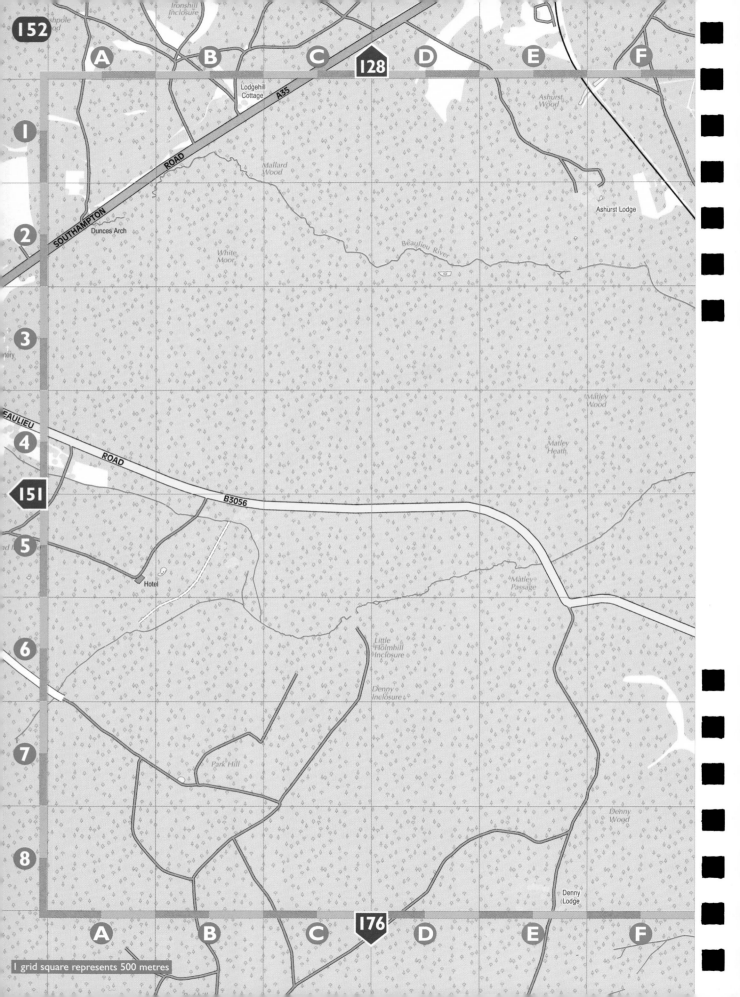

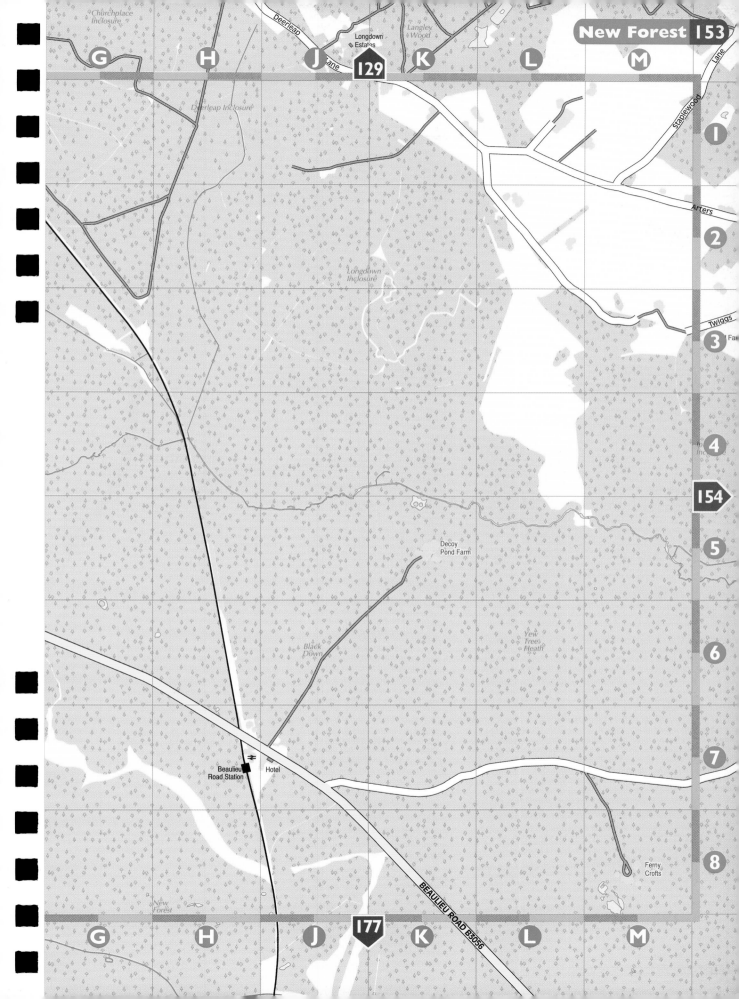

G H J K L M

129

Churchplace
Inclosure

Deerleap
Lane

Longdown
Estates

Langley
Wood

Staplewood
Lane

I

Deerleap Inclosure

Arters

2

Longdown
Inclosure

Twiggs

3 Fa

4
Inc

154

5

Decoy
Pond Farm

Yew
Tree
Heath

6

Black
Down

Beaulieu
Road Station

Hotel

7

New
Forest

Ferny
Crofts

8

BEAULIEU ROAD B3056

G H J K L M

177

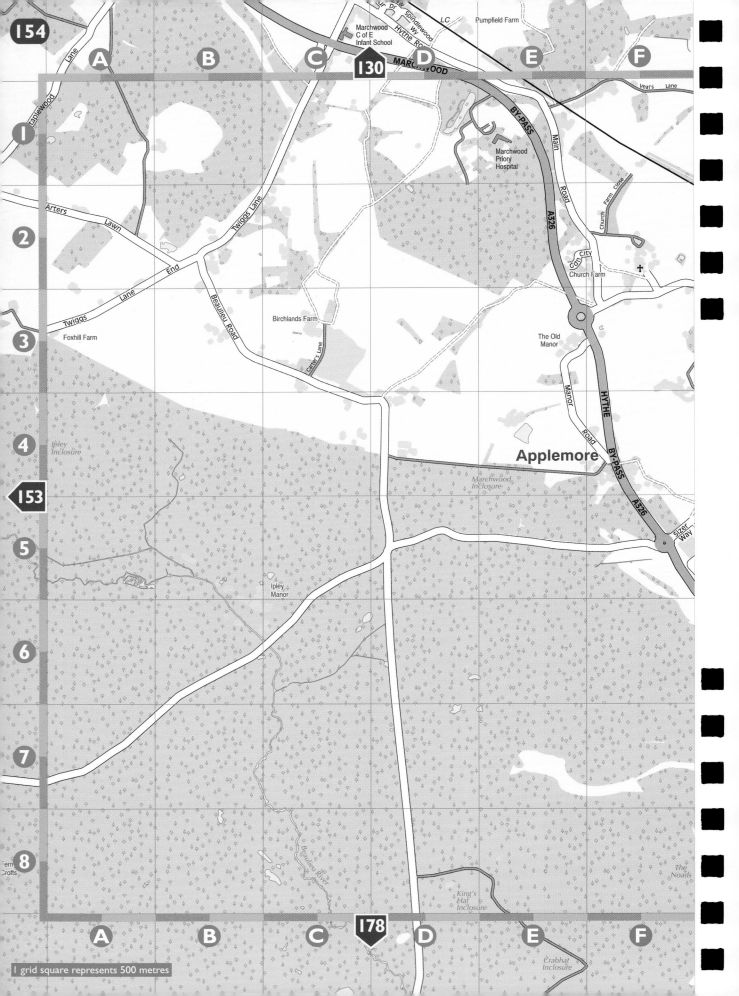

A B C 132 D E F

1

City of Southampton
Hampshire County

2

3

4

155

5

Langdown

Harvey Gdns

Solent Way

Road

Fulmar Drive

Cormorant Cl

Gannet Cl

Frost Lane

Solent Way

Hart Hill

Spinney Dl

Hardy Dr

Lane

6

Frostlane

7

West Road

East Road

Charleston Road

New Road

Hardley La

Solent Way

First Street

Second St

Avenue E

Av C

8

A B C 180 D E F

Weston Shore
First School

Sparsholt

Abbey

Kingsclere
Rd

Drayton
Ct

Fullerton
Lambeth

Tick

1 Sedgemead
F3

Woolston

NETLE

Netley
Abbey Infant
School

Grange Road

Grange Ct

Priory Road

Wykeham Road

Queens
Vw

Castle
Rd

Queens
View

Rotary
Ct

Grange
Rd

Carfield rd

Victoria
Rd

Chamberlayne
Rd

New

Mortimer Cl

Monks Rd

Road

Station

Denham
Gdns

Netley
Court
School

PO

Road

1

Southampton W

Cadland
Creek

Butlocks Heath

Hound

Bursledon

HAMBLE-LE-RICE

Netley Station

Hamble Station

Bursledon Station

Hamble County Secondary School

Hamble County Primary School

Royal Victoria Country Park

Hamblecliff House

Sidings Industrial Est

Hamble Common

Hamble Spit

Marina

River Hamble

Southampton Water

Satchell Lane

Solent Way

G1
1 Calbourne
2 Carisbrooke
3 Culver
4 Kingston
5 Nettlestone
6 Shorewell
7 Whitwell
8 Wootton

G2
1 Arreton
2 The Badgers
3 Newbridge
4 Oakhurst Cl

G3
1 Latelie Cl
2 Waverley Ct

H1
1 Old School Cl

H6
1 Westfield Common

L5
1 Coronation Pde
2 Hardwicke Wy

L6
1 Hamble House Gdns

L5
1 Oakwood Wy

L4
1 Kingfisher Cl
2 St Agatha's Rd

K6
1 College Cl
2 Pegasus Cl

K5
1 Acorn Ct

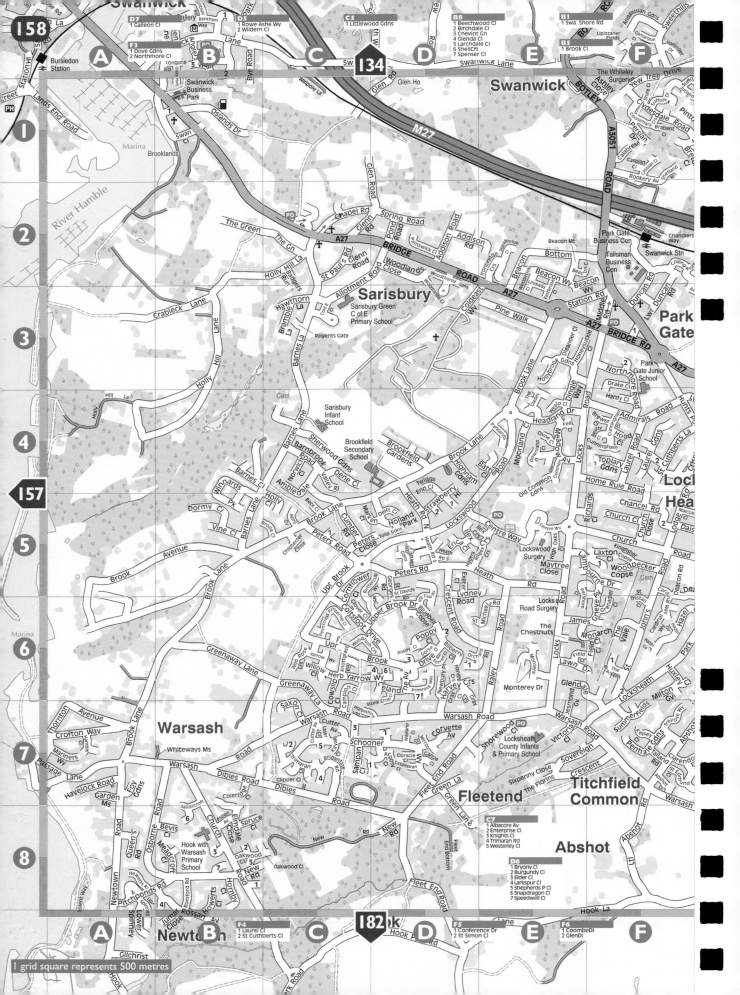

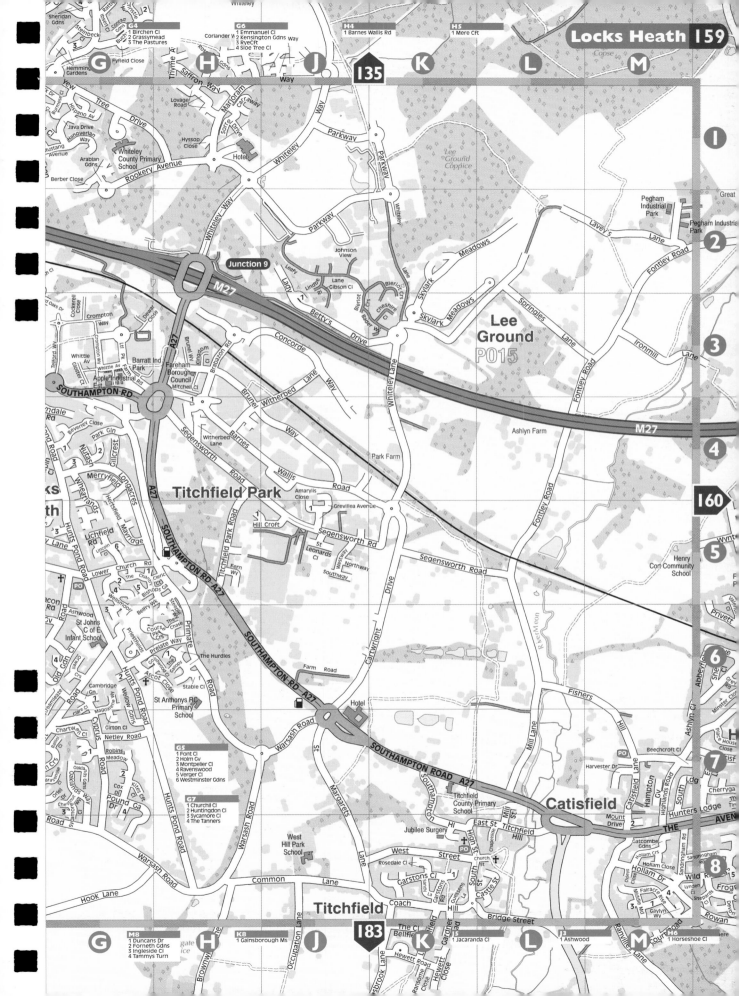

G6
1 Archery La
2 Wallington Hl

H6
1 The Maltings

H7
1 Waterside Gdns

I8
1 Goldcrest Cl
2 Partridge Cl

G H J **137** K L M

I

Blackhouse La

King's Way

Bere Farm

Portcheste

1

2

3

Boundary Oak School

Whitedell Farm

Manor Farm

Boarhunt

Ashley Down Far

3

any Business Centre

Farm

Wallington River

Whitedell Lane

Spurlings Road

North Fareham Farm

Nine Elms Lane

Boarhunt Road

Boarhunt Road

Monumen

Lane

4

162

Down Barn Farm

Swivelton Lane

King's Way

Fort Nelson

National Museum of Artillery

5

Junction 11

M27

Foxgloves

Standard Way

Wallington Way

Military Rd

Military Road

King's Way

Portsdown Hill Road

King's Way

Downend Road

Nelson Lane

6

M27

St Christophers Hospital

Ft Wallington Industrial Estate

Pinks Hill

A27

Paradise Lane

King's Way

Kilmiston Cl

Walt

Dore Ave

High

Wallington

Broadcut

North Dr

Riverside Av

Pallant Gdns

Greenbanks Gdns

Woodlands

Waterside Gdns

Causeway

Downend

Lancaster Cl

Merlin Gdns

Jute Cl

Danes Rd

Saxon Cl

7

infa Sch

WALLINGTON WAY

Wykeham House School

7

Cams Hill

The Ridgeway

Vernor Way

St Catherines Way

Alum Way

The Thicket

The Spinney

PO 16

Camelot Crs

Solent Vw

Hawthorn Cl

Red Barn

Linden

Simpso

Red Barn County Primary School

7

Quay Street

EASTERN WAY

Bath La

The Surg

Deane's Pk

Bath La (Tower)

Cams Hill

A27

The Dell

Paradise Lane

CAMS HILL

Cams Hill School

Shearwater

Rooksway Grove

Birdwood Grove

Swancote

Clew Dr

Chaffinch Wy

Teal Cl

Kingfishers

Wagtail Wy

A27 PORTCHESTER RD

Romsey Avenue

Ashtead Cl

Beaulieu

Rockingham Wy

Dore Avenue

Redwood Dr

PORTCHES

8

Upper Whf

Cams Hall Estate Golf Club

Peacock Close

Condor Avenue

Flamingo Ct

Wicor County Primary School

Quintrell Av

Wallington River

The Close

The Queensway

Kingswa

8

M8
1 Hatherley Dr
2 Rudgwick Cl
3 Stoneleigh Cl

M7
1 Boxwood Cl
2 Tudor Cl

L8
1 Severn Cl

K8
1 Cormorant Cl
2 Cygnet Ct
3 Eagle Cl
4 Falcon Cl
5 Grebe Cl
6 Lapwing Gv
7 The Linnets
8 Wren Wy

K7
1 Cams Bay Cl
2 East Cams Cl

Fareham Borough Council

Cranleigh Rd

Grove

White Hart

Westla
Medical
Centre

D7 1 Ridgeway Cl 2 Winterbourne Rd
C8 1 Elgar Cl 2 Hopkins Cl
C7 1 Rowland Rd
Mitchelland **B7** 1 Conifer Ms
A7 1 Canon's Barn Cl 2 Steep Cl

A   **B**   **C**   138   **D**   **E**   **F**

Lodge Farm

Place Wood

Walton Heath

King's Way

1

2

Portchester Lane

Common Lane

Bridge St

Fareham Road

Back Lane

Southwick
West Street
PO
Doctors Surgery
North
High St

Castle Rd
Norton Cl
Norton Rd

W
West Rd
Main
Drive
North
Road E
South Rd
East Road
Priory Rd

Boulter La
Wood Lane

Pinsley
Drive

Southwick Park
Naval Recreation Centre

3
Ashley Down Farm

Southwick Park Lake

B2177

Pitymoor Lane

4
Monum Lane

Offwell Farm

Portchester Lane

Drove Road

B2177

New Barns

161

5
Museum

Crooked Walk Lane

Portchester Lane

Portsdown Hill Road

Portsdown Hill Road

Fort Southwick

Workshop
North Rd
The Circus Road
Hilltop
South Rd

Pound Road
Eastfield Rd
Link Road
Aerial Rd
North Hl
South Sp

6
Nelson Lane
Skew Road

James Callaghan Dr

Ports Down

M27

Waltham
Kilmiston Dr
Weyhill Cl
Rogate Gdns
Hill
Anson Grove
Carlton Road
Benedict Ww

Browning Avenue

Hillsley
Kingscote Rd
Almondsbury Road

Rockrose Wy
Butterfly Drive
Chalkpit Road

Lime Gv

Leominster

7
Swan Cl
Dore Avenue
Merlin Gdns
High Vw
Harting Gdns
Froxfield Gdns
Pentland Rise
Keats Av
Chaucer Av
Shelley Av
Dryden Av
Coleridge Rd

Tintern Rd

Longdean Cl

Winchcombe Road
Elscote Rd
Tarleton Rd

Junior & Infant School
Laverock Lea
Richmond Lea
Dore Avenue
Burton Close
Leith Avenue
Pentland
Montrose Av
Seaview Av
Southwick Av
Edward Gv
Wordsworth Av
Masefield Rd
Macaulay Rd

Newbolt
Bude Cl
Falmouth Road
Severn Rd
Chedworth Crs

Beverston Road
Deerhurst Crescent
Wooferton Rd
Colesbourne Rd
Birdlip Rd

Collin
Hempsted Rd

Hill View Rd
Linden Lea
Simpson Cl
The Hillway
Portsview Gdns
Colinton Gv
Morningside Av
Raymond Rd
Hillside Crs
Truro Rd
Mousehole Rd
Heston Rd

Pemberton Rd

Rydal Cl
Portsmouth City Council

Red Barn County Primary School
The Crossway
Kelvin Grove
Portsview Avenue
Jubilee Avenue
Junior School
Saxon Shore Infant Sch
Sedgefield Close
Allaway Avenue

King Richard School

Doctors Surgery
Paulsgrove

St Pauls RC Primary School

Prima Scho

8
The Close
The Fairway
The Kingsway
Downsway
St James Wy
Portchester Station
New Town Rd
Station Rd
Portsdown Rd
Neelands Gv
Parry Cl
Sullivan Cl
Coltsmead
Beach Dr
Shorehaven
Farmlea Rd
Port Wy

Paulsgrove Cen

ORTCHESTER
Portchester Health Centre
West
Kg George Road
PO
A27
A27 SOUTHAMPTON ROAD
A27 SOUTHAMPTO

Binnacle Wy

A   **B**   **C**   **D**   **E**   **F**

Westla Medica Centre
C8 1 Delifield Cl 2 Desborough Cl 3 Rothwell Cl
E8 1 Bodmin Rd 2 Watersedge Rd
1 Camcross Cl 2 Cleeve Cl 3 Edwards Cl 4 Huntn's Cl 5 St Michaels Ct 6 Westbury Cl

grid square represents 500 metres

G · H · J **139** · K · L · M

I · 2 · 3 · 4 · **164** · 5 · 6 · 7 · 8

G7
1 Cinderford Cl
2 Dorstone Rd

H7
1 Fitzpatrick Ct
2 Sheringham Rd
3 Walsingham Cl

H8
1 Blackwater Cl
2 Bryson Cl
3 Hadleigh Rd
4 Hockley Cl
5 Maldon Rd
6 Mellor Cl
7 Parr Rd
8 Pebmarsh Rd

Wanstead Farm

wash Farm

Pitymoor Lane

Newlands Farm

Comphouse Farm

Southwick House

Purbrook Heath Road

Hookheath Farm

Purbrook Heath Road

Mill Lane

Broomfield House

Widley Walk

Purbrook
Cricket Club

Potwell

Pigeon House Lane

Wayfarer's Walk

Pigeon House Farm

Widley Farm

Mill Lane

Widley Walk

Meadow Edge

Wayfarer's Walk

New Down La

Highbank Av

Victoria Av

Lansdowne Av

LONDON

A3(T)

Hampshire County
City of Portsmouth

Geoffrey Avenue

Lily Av

Hillside Av

The Crest

SOUTHWICK ROAD B2177

James Callaghan Dr

Boundary Way

Delcrest

Hilltop Crs

B2177

B2177 SOUTHWICK HILL ROAD

PORTSDOWN HILL ROAD

Fort Widley

Drayton

Down End La

Augustine

Dormington Rd
Blakemere Crescent
Meadowsweet Way
Harleston Rd

Bredenbury Crs

Ledbury Rd

Lowestoft Rd

Mablethorpe Road

Norwich Rd

Cromer Rd

Peterborough Rd

Cavell Dr

Kintyre Rd
Shetland Rd

Orkney Rd

Jura

Chalkridge Road

Brecon Avenue

Merthyr Avenue

Carmarthen Avenue

Aberdare Av

Down End

Ludlow Rd

Rapson Rd

Harwich Rd

Colchester Rd

Maldstone Crs

Braintree Road

Queen Alexandra
A&E Hosp

Cranborne Road

Courtmount Gv

Colville Rd

Penarth Av

Lampeter Av

Abbeydore

Bromyard Rd

Hythe Road

Sudbury Rd

Clacton Rd

Whitstable

Westerham Cl

Portsmouth
City Council

Southdown Rd

St John's Road

St Colman's

Burrill Avenue

Bernard Avenue

Allaway Avenue

Rochford Rd

Stanford

Sevenoaks Rd

Sundridge Cl

Chipstead Rd

London Rd

St Matthew's Rd

Padwick Av

Lodge Av

East Cosham Rd

East Ct

Cheltenham Rd

SOUTHAMPTON ROAD

Herne Rd

Ashurst Rd

St George's

Havant Cl

Havant Road

A3

Halstead Rd

Bell Rd

Sixth Av
Fifth Av
Fourth Av
Third Av

First Av

Spur Rd

Doctors Surgery

Havant Cl

Aidsworth

Acorn
Business
Cen

Medina Rd

Freshwater Rd

Cosham Health Cen

Cosham
Primary
School

Gosham

Wymering

A27

Northarbour Rd

M27

WESTERN ROAD

Junction 12

G · **H**
1 Lordington Cl

· **J** · **187** · **K**
1 Christ. Gdns
2 Thornton Cl

· **L**
1 Mallow Cl

· **M**
1 Glebefield Gdns
2 Tankerton Cl
3 Wym'g Mnr Cl

Wayte St Albert Road

Hilary Av

Beaconsfield Avenue

Lonsdale Avenue

Mansvid Av

Gofton Av

Braemar Av

Kirton Rd

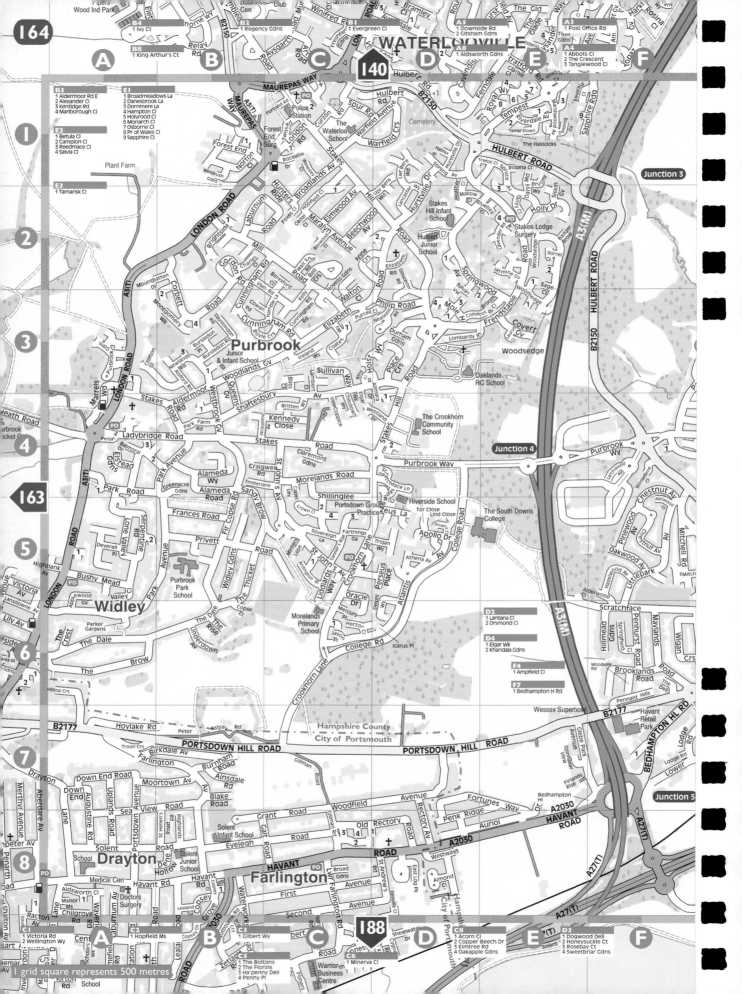

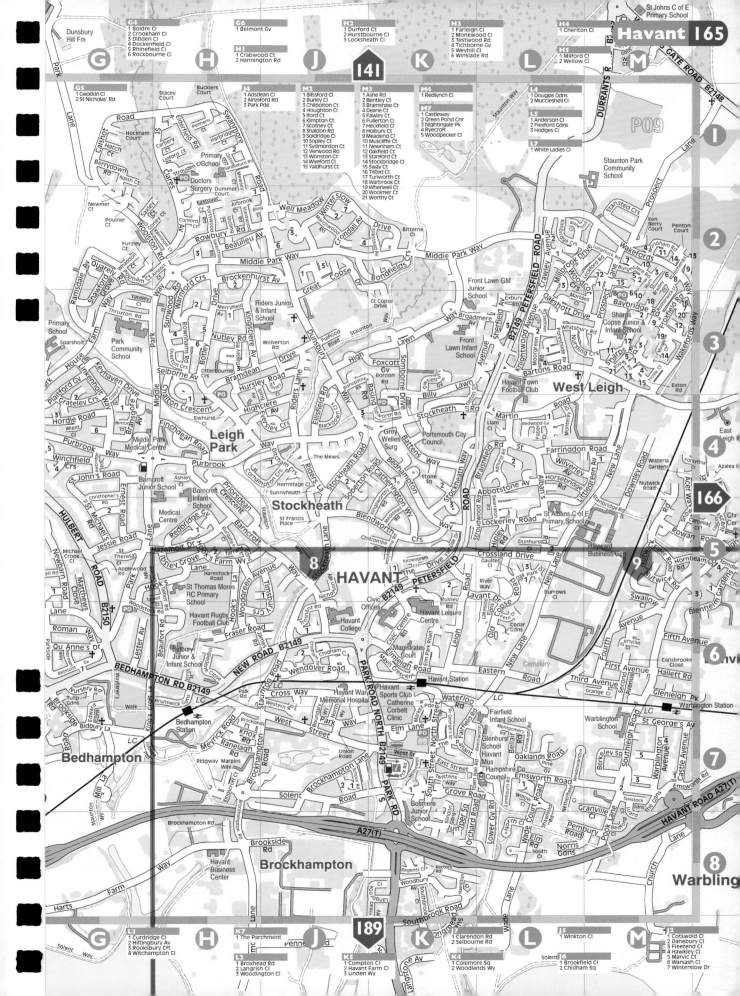

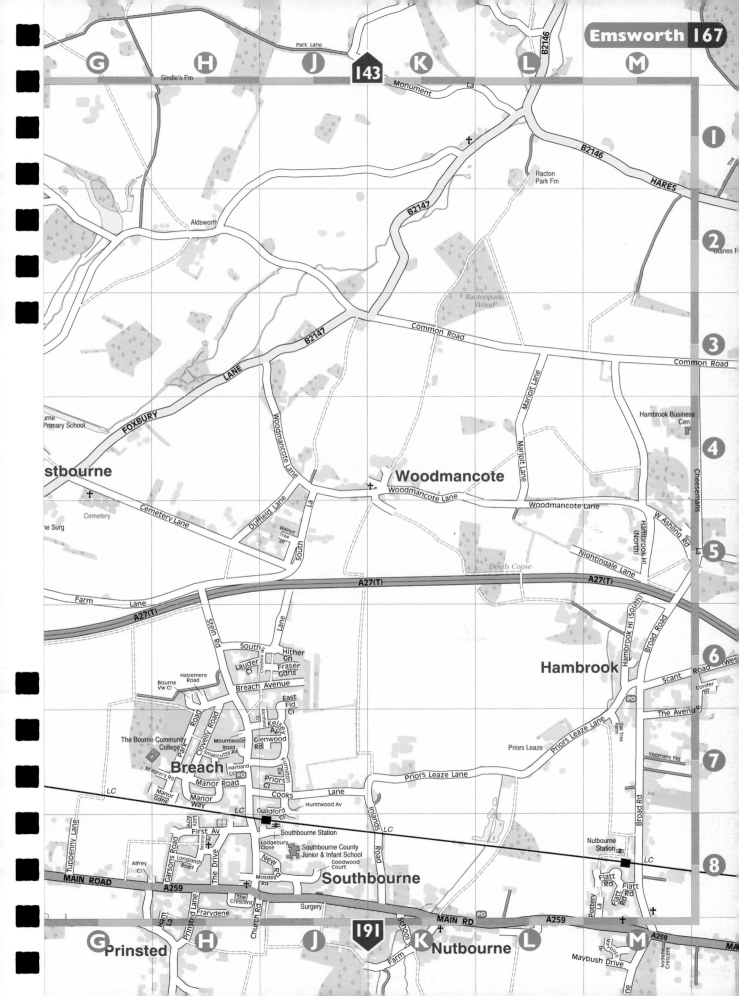

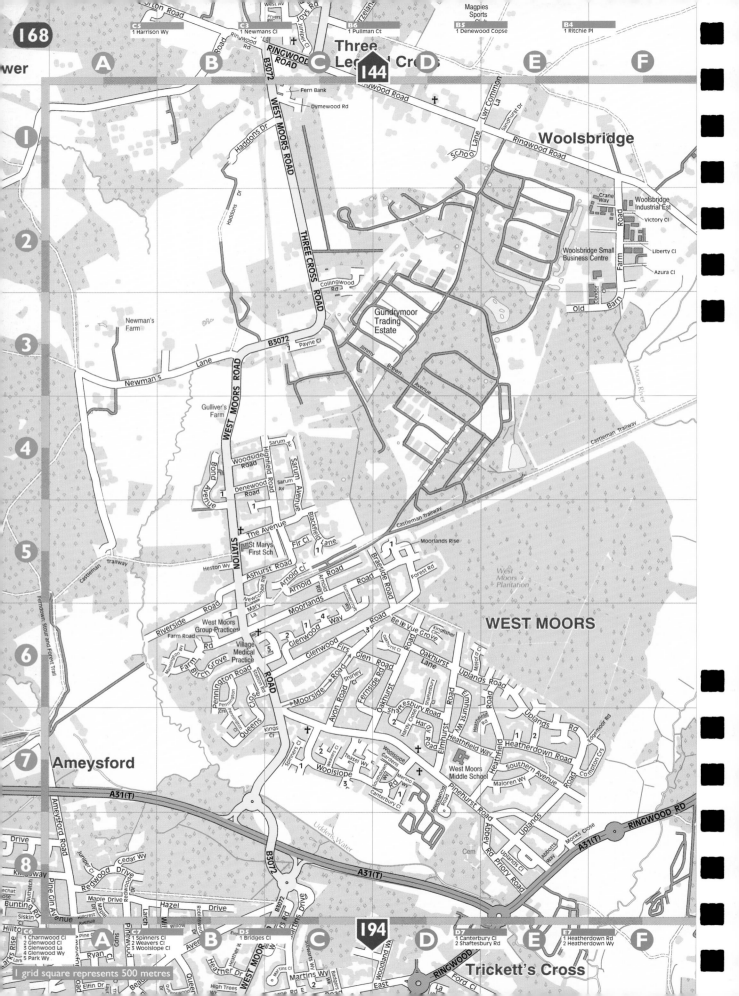

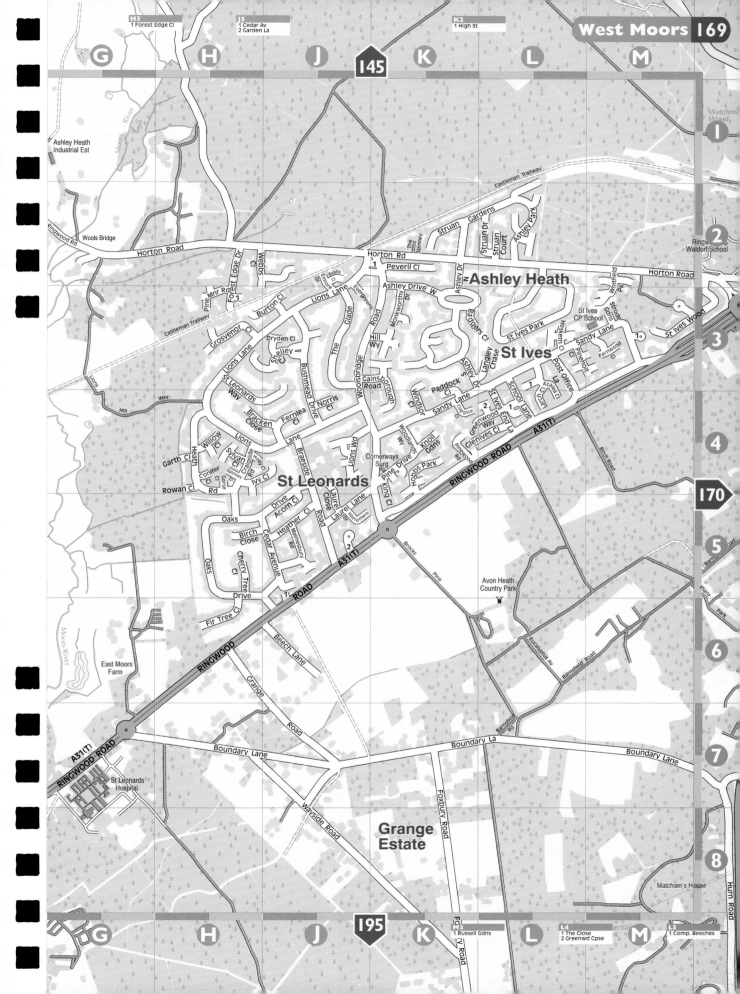

G H J 145 K L M

I

2

3

4

170

5

6

7

8

Watchm Woods

Ringw Waldorf School

Castleman Trailway

Struan Gardens

Ashley Park

Horton Rd

Peveril Cl

Ashley Heath

Horton Road

Whitfield Pk

St Ives Wood

Strode Gdns

The Spinney

Struan Dr

Struan Court

Ashley Dr

Horton Road

Wools Bridge

Ringwood Rd

Horton Road

Webbs

Pine Mnr

Forest Edge Dr

Castleman Trailway

Burton Cl

Lions Lane

The Glade

Evergreens

Woolsbridge Road

Elmore Dr

Ashley Drive

Monkworthy

Hill Wy

St Ives Park

St Ives CP School

Hesketh Cl

Sandy Lane

Fernwood

Pineholt Cl

Grosvenor Cl

Dryden Cl

Shelley

Bushmead Drive

Gainsborough Road

Badgers Cl

Langley Chase

St Ives

Post Office

Azalea Cl

Church

St Leonards Way

Lions Lane

Norris Cl

Fernlea Cl

The Glade

Paddock

Windsor

Sandy Lane

Coppice

St Ives End La

School Lane

7

Ashley Dr

Way

Hill

Lions

Willow Cl

Bracken Close

Lions Lane

Braeside

Lions Wd

St Leonards

Cornerways Surg

Pine Drive

Woodlands Wy

Knoll Gdns

Hobbs Park

2

Greenwood Way

Glenives Cl

Pinewood Cl

Garth Cl

Heath

Sylvan Cl

Conifer Cl

Gorse

Spinney

Ivy Cl

Drive

Acorn Cl

Laurel Close

Laurel Lane

King Cl

Haxelmere

Rowan Cl

Rd

Oaks

Birch Close

Cedar Avenue

Heather Cl

Malmesbury Rd

Road

2

A31(T)

RINGWOOD ROAD

A31(T)

Brocks

Pine

Avon Heath Country Park

Birch Road

Eucalyptus Av

Barnsfield Road

Oaks

Cherry Tree Cl

Fir Tree Cl

1

RINGWOOD ROAD

Beech Lane

Grange Road

Moors River

East Moors Farm

A31(T)

RINGWOOD ROAD

Boundary Lane

Wayside Road

Boundary La

Barnsfield Rd

Boundary Lane

St Leonards Hospital

Foxbury Road

Grange Estate

Matcham's House

Hurn Road

Southampton Road

H2
1 Forest Court Hills

1 The Cloisters
2 Greenfinch Wk
3 Linnet Cl
4 Lych Gate Ct
5 Old Stacks Gdns
6 Sanderlings
7 Wren Cl

A31(T)

Picket Hill

Foulford

Hightown

Hightown Road

Hightown Hill

Hightown Hill

Forest Lane

Forest Lane

Hurn Farm

Crow

Nouale Lane

Holmwood Garth
Ashburn Garth
Lakeview Dr
Ashley
Forestoke Av
Chip Dr
Lakeside
Merlin
Mdw
Pelican Rd
Views

Wood End Rd

Forest Edge Rd

Knaves Ash

Vales Meor

Crow Hill Top

Lane

Crow Lane

Lane

Streets Lane

Barrack

Lane

Green

Charles's Lane

Strodgemoor Bottom

172

Upper Kingston Farm

Lakes Farm

Charles's Lane

North Kingston

Charles's Lane

Bagnum Farm

Kingston Great Common

Cran Moo

Brixey's Farm

Sandford

Farm

Dragon Lane

Bisterne Common

147

197

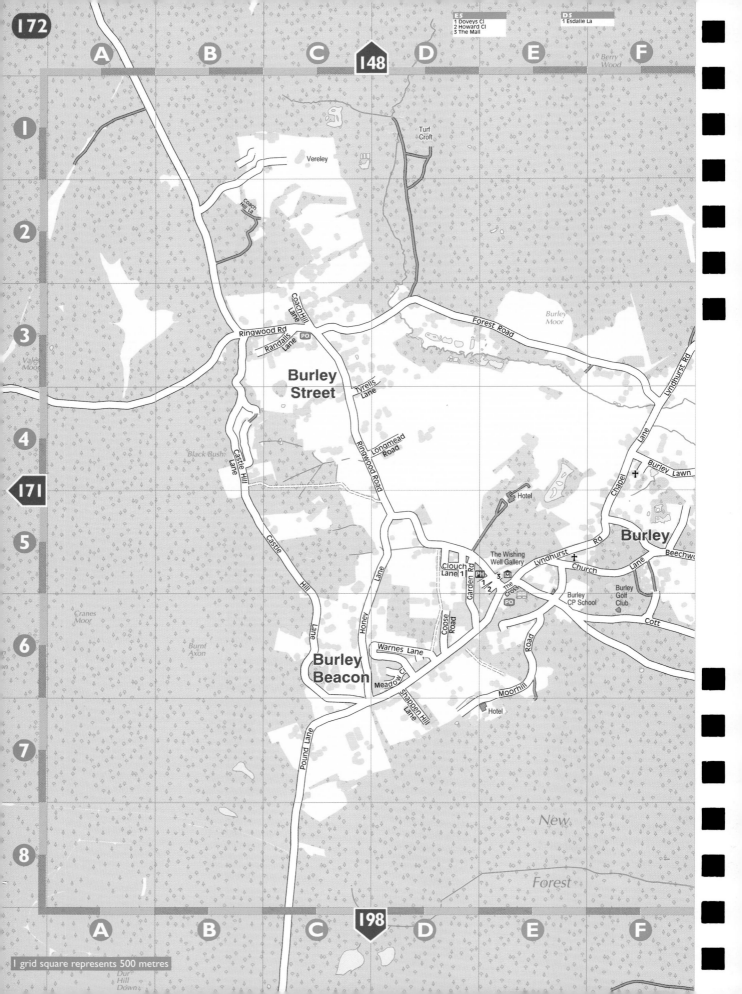

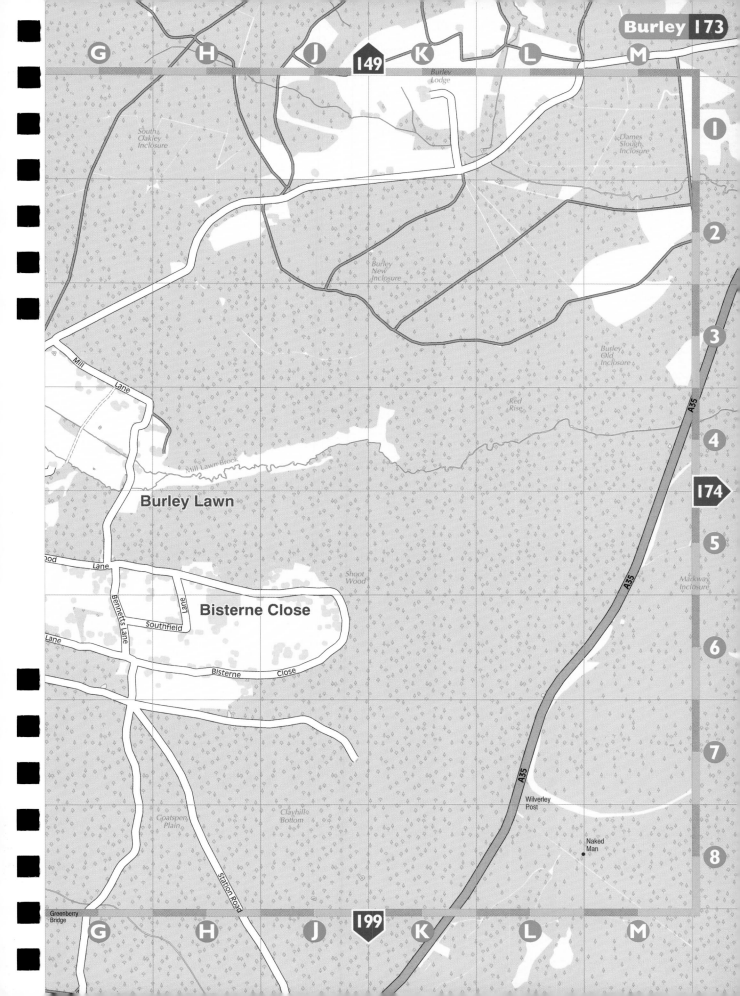

G   H   J   149   K   L   M

149

I

2

3

A35

174

5

Markway
Inclosure

6

7

8

Burley
Lodge

South
Oakley
Inclosure

Dames
Slough
Inclosure

Burley
New
Inclosure

Burley
Old
Inclosure

Red
Rise

Mill
Lane

Mill Lawn Brook

Burley Lawn

Wood   Lane

Bennetts Lane

Southfield   Lane

Bisterne Close

Lane

Bisterne   Close

Shoot
Wood

A35

A35

Wilverley
Post

Naked
Man

Goatspen
Plain

Clayhille
Bottom

Greenberry
Bridge

Station Road

G   H   J   199   K   L   M

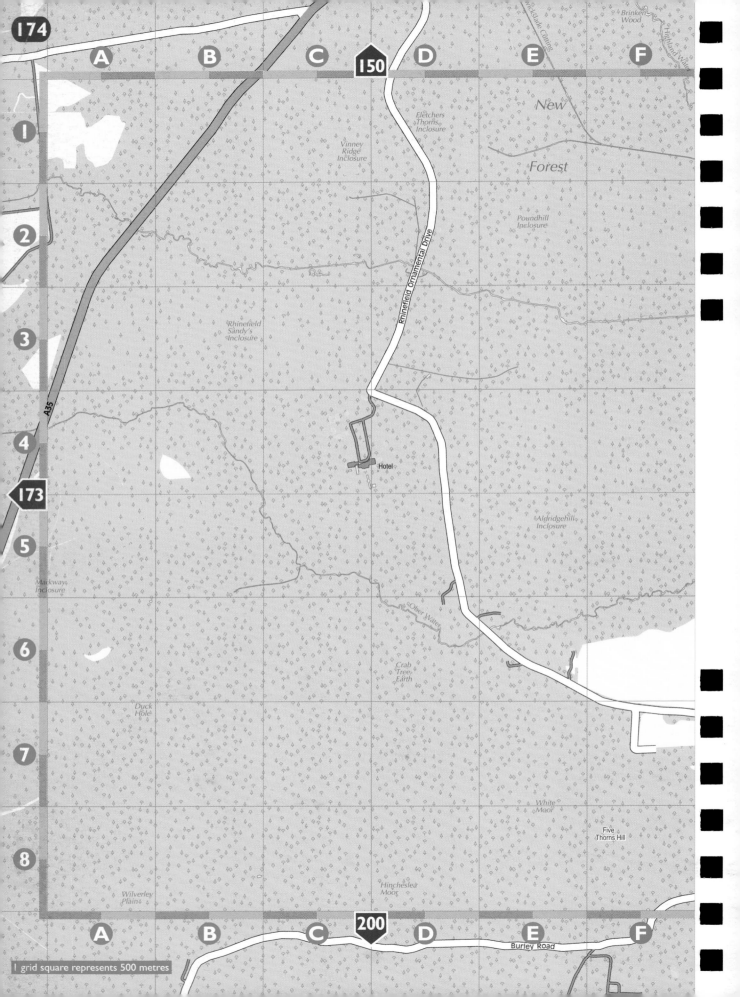

G H J 151 K L M

K7
1 Culverley Cl
2 The Paddock
3 Wide Lane Cl

L6
1 Horlock Rd
2 Waters Gn
3 Waters Green Ct

L7
1 Auckland Pl
2 Forest Hall
3 Greenways Rd
4 Sutton Pl

Whitley Wood

Hurst Hill Inclosure

I

Hollands Wood

2

Poundhill Heath

Ramnor Inclosure

Black Water

New Park

Hotel

3

Hotel

Bolderford Bridge

Ober Heath

Ober Water

Highland Water

Balmer Lawn

4

176

Black Knowl

Hotel

5

Balmerlawn

BALMER LAWN

Butts Lawn

LYNDHURST ROAD A337

Beachern Wood

Meerut Rd
Martin's Rd
Waters Gn
Park Cl
Burford La
Butts Lawn

Hotel

Brockenhurst College

6

Ober House
The Coppice
Oberfield Rd
Whitemoor Road
Moorlands Cl
Knowle Rd
New Forest Drive
Broadlands Rd
Forest Park Road
Hotel
Ober Rd
Brookside Road
Careys Cottages
Fathersfield

New Forest Dr

BROCKENHURST

Grigg Lane
Chestnut
Noel Cl
North Rd

Hotel

MILL LANE

7

Forest Glade
Forest Close
Forest Drive
Forest Vw
Armstrong Road
Armstrong Lane
Armstrong Cl
Broadlands Rd
Wilverley Road
Brookley
Filbards Road
The Rise
PO
Brookley Rd
Auckland
LC

North Weirs

North Weirs

Brockenhurst Station

Church Lane

Brockenhurst Park

Burley Road

South Weirs

Brockenhurst Primary School
Avenue Rd
E Ban Rw
Partridge Rd
Highwood Road
The Surgery
Tattenham Rd
Addison Road
Colvers Cl

SWAY ROAD

A337

8

G H J **201** K L M

South Weirs

Tilebarn Lane

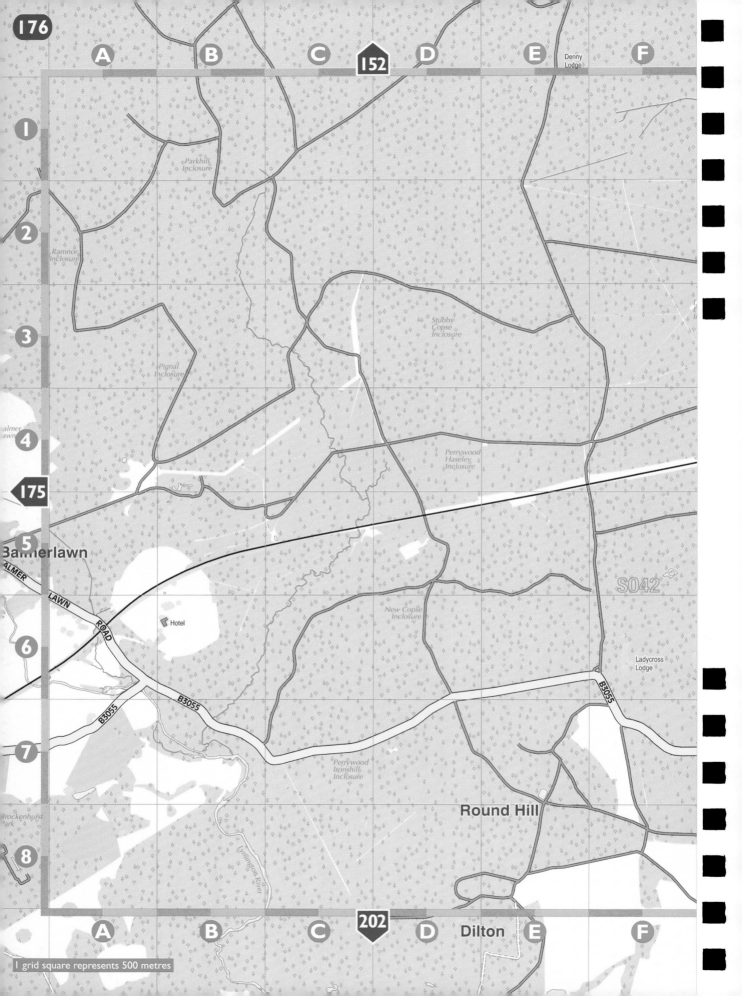

A　　　B　　　C　**152**　D　　　E　　　F

Denny
Lodge

1

Parkhill
Inclosure

2

Ramnor
Inclosure

Stubby
Copse
Inclosure

3

Pignal
Inclosure

4

Perrywood
Haseley
Inclosure

5

Bannerlawn

PALMER

LAWN

ROAD

Hotel

New Copse
Inclosure

S042

6

Ladycross
Lodge

B3055

B3055

7

B3055

B3055

Perrywood
Ironshill
Inclosure

Round Hill

Brockenhurst
Park

8

Lymington River

A　　　B　　　C　**202**　D　Dilton　E　　　F

G   H   J   **153**   K   L   M

ILIEU ROAD B3056

I

New
Forest

Pig
Bush

Culverley Farm

2

Shepton Bridge

Denny
Lodge
Inclosure

3

Rowbarrow

Tantany
Wood

LC

4

Frame
Heath
Inclosure

Stubbs
Wood

178

5

Frame
Wood

Moon
Hill

6

Hawkhill
Inclosure

**Furzey
Lodge**

7

Stockley
Inclosure

**Hatch
Gate**

Furzey

B3055

Lane

8

G   H   J   **203**   K   L   M

Masseys La

B3054

East

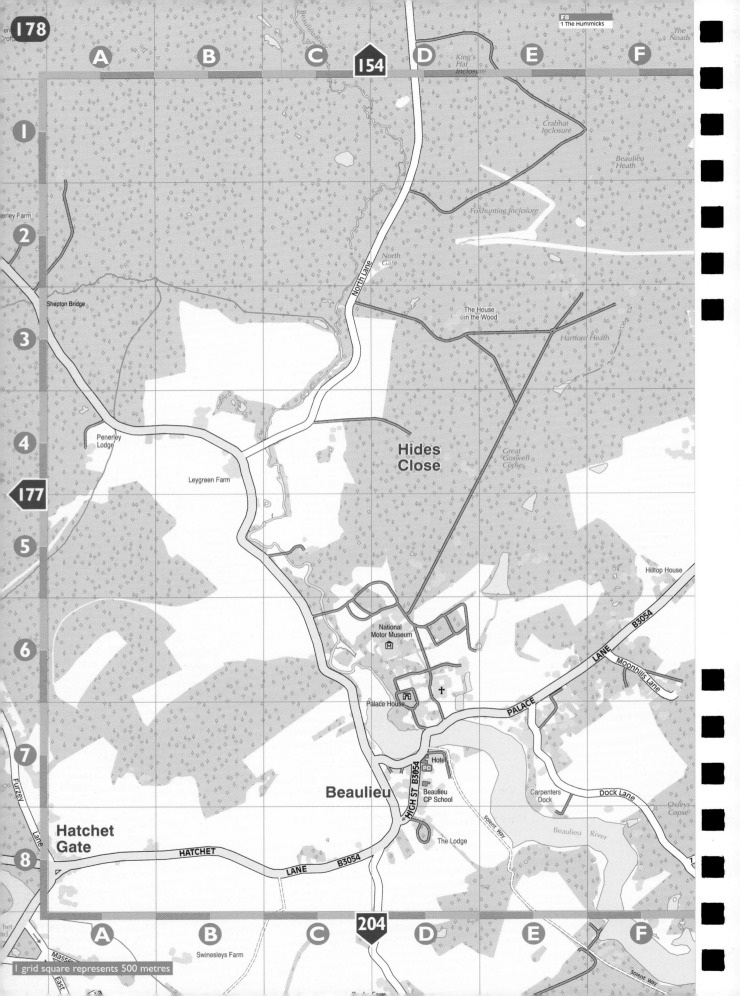

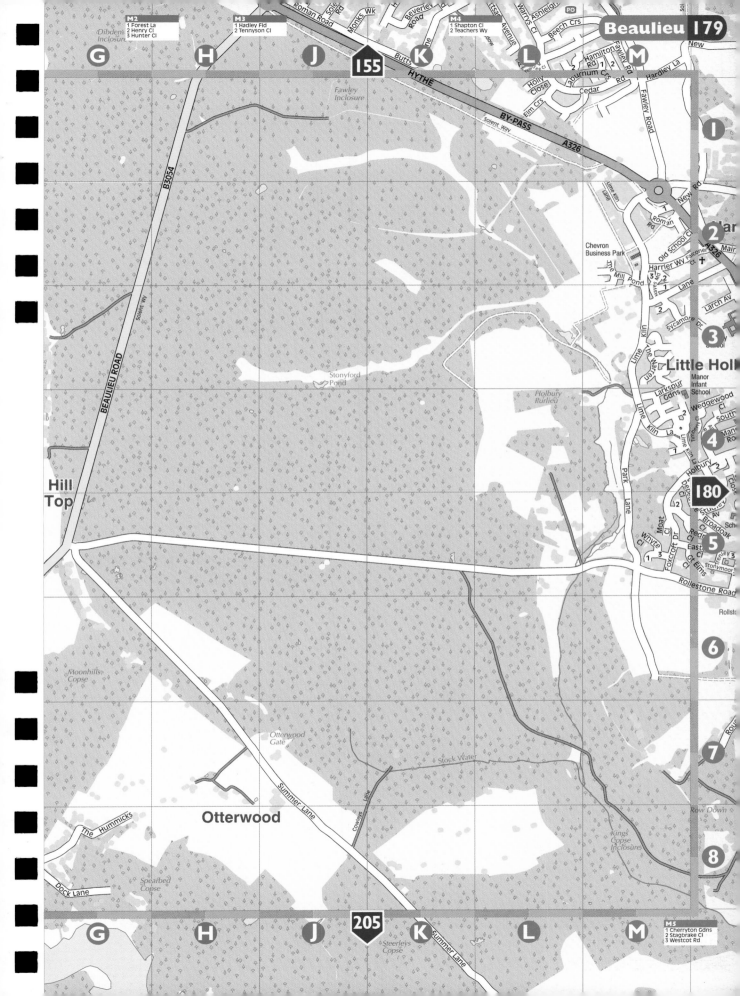

G
H
J
155
K
L
M

I

2

3

4

5

6

7

8

HYTHE BY-PASS A326

Solent Way

Fawley Inclosure

Chevron Business Park

Stonyford Pond

Holbury Purlieu

Little Holl

Manor Infant School

Larkspur Gdns

Wedgewood Cl

180

Broadoak

Rollestone Road

B3054

Solent Wy

BEAULIEU ROAD

Hill Top

Moonhills Copse

Otterwood Gate

Summer Lane

Otterwood

The Hummicks

Dock Lane

Spearbed Copse

Stock Water

Cowleys Lane

Kings Copse Inclosure

Row Down

Steerleys Copse

G
H
J
205
K
L
M

B6
1 Wentworth Gdns

B5
1 Ashleycross Cl
2 Hobson Wy

B4
1 Sloane Av
2 Sloane Ct

A5
1 Pondhead Cl
2 Roewood Cl
3 Stockley Cl

A4
1 Broadley Cl
2 Hayward Ct
3 Ridley Cl

Cadland Creek

Hardley

Cadland Road

New Road

Old School Cl

Harrier Wy

Larch Av

Hardley School

Little Holbury

Manor Infant School

Larkspur Gdns

LONG LANE

Long Lane

Main Rd

A326

Falconer

13th street

12th Street

11th Street

10th Street

9th Street

8th Street

7th Street

D Av

B Avenue

A Avenue

C

Wedgewood Cl

Southbourne Avenue

Westcourne

Ivor Close

Manor Road

Drove

Ruxley Close

Renda

Watton Rd

PO

Waltons Avenue

Stanley Rd

Springfield

Springfield

The Close

J Av

H Avenue

G

6th St

5th Street

F

E Avenue

E Avenue

7th street

6th Street

5th street

4th Street

3rd Street

2nd St

Foreshore

North

Foreshore

P.L.P.H.

Rd

Burmah Road

South

Cadland Road

Oil Refinery

Holbury

Bower Cl

Studley Av

Broadoak

Redrise

Eastcot Cl

St Elms

Moat

Foch

Whitefield

Fairtcross

Pennywood

Roewood Rd

William

Winters Cl

Hobson Cl

Raymond Cl

May Crs

Alum Cl

May Close

Wentworth Gv

Long Copse

Long Lane Close

South Avenue

7th street

S045

FAWLEY ROAD

B3053

Fawley Business Centre

Ashdown

Fawley County First School

PO

Church

Forest

Orchard

Edge

School Rd

Sheringham Lane

Marsh Ln

Salterns La

Rye Paddock La

Calmore Rd

Fawley

179

Rollestone Road

Rollstone Farm

Myvern

Crawte Avenue

Brambie

Rollestone Rd

Newlands Road

Ashdown Road

Slades Hill

The Pentagon

Blackfield Road

Chapel La

Roughdown

Lane

Page Cl

Priest Ct Dr

The Fowey

Blackfield Health Centre

Hampton Lane

Wilverley Pl

Blackfield Junior & Infant School

The Drove

Hugh's Cl

PO

Exbury Rd

Hartsgrove Close

Heather

Foresters

Thornhill Rd

Fry Cl

Trome

Smith Rd

Milliken

Glyn-Jones Cl

Hedley Cl

Furzey Cl

Heather

Dark Lane

New Rd

St Michaels Cl

Newlands Corpse

Fields Heath

Fields Farm

Row Down

King's Copse Road

Janes Cl

Hampton Lane

Wheelers Walk

Newlands Rd

Walker's Walk

Saxon Cl

Norman Rd

Wessex Cl

Viking

Dane Rd

Cedric

Saxon Lane N

Thornbury Avenue

Green Lane

Walker's Lane South

Blackfield

Tom's Down

Mopley Pond

Cem

Hampton Gdns

Hampton Lane

Northampton La

Chapel Lane

Holly Rd

Langley

Charnwood Way

Chalewood Road

St Francis Rd

Lea Road

Foxnayes

Clare Gdns

Mopley

Forest

Green Road

Badminston Common

C6
1 The Greenwich
2 Harvey Ct

C7
1 Edward Cl
2 Fields Cl
3 Pendleton Gdns

D6
1 Fourshells Cl
2 Thornhill Cl

D7
1 Valley Cl

F5
1 Admirals Cl
2 Churchfields
3 Denny Cl
4 The Lane
5 Linda Rd cont.

1 grid square represents 500 metres

Hamble
Spit

1

2

3

ISLE OF WIGHT   4

182

5

6

7

8

North Trestle Road

Burnah Road N

South   Trestle   Road

Old   Agwi   Road

Road

Flume Rd

Copthorne Lane

Ashlett Cl

Ashlett

Ashlett

Road

Coast Clinic

Ashlett Creek

FAWLEY BY-PASS

Stonehills

B3053

Stonehills

Northern Access   Road

Northern Access Rd

Badminston Lane

Badminston Farm

Badminston   Drove

Ower

B3053

Calshot

Calshot
Cl

PO

Calshot
Castle

Stanswood   Road

6 Meadow Wy
7 The Paddocks
8 Rhyme Hall Ms
9 The Square
10 Whites La

Castle
Lane

B3053

Hillhead

Abshot

A   B   158   D   E   F

Hook La

Queen Rd
Hook with
Warsash
Primary
School
Oakwood Cl
New Road
Hewett's Rd
Newtown
Meadcroft
Pitchponds Rd
Jumar Close
Rossan Av
Hornby
Romford Rd
Hook Lane

Hook

Hook Park Rd

Hook Lane

Newtown

Lower Spinney

Gilchrist Gdns

I

Hook

Solent Court

Pk Road

2

Hook Park

Solent Drive

Hook Lane

Cowes Lane

Workman's

Lane

Solent Way

3

Chilling Lane

Chilling

Workman's La

Solent Way

WIGH

4

5

Solent Way

6

Calshot Castle

7

8

1 grid square represents 500 metres

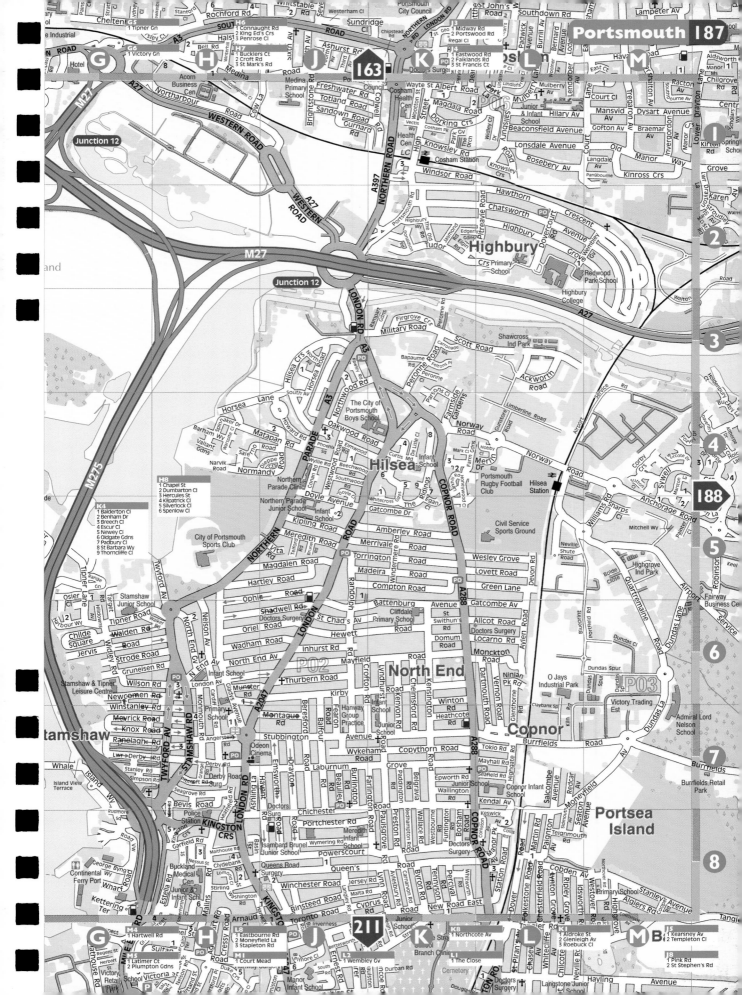

166

9

Cemetery

Solent Way

Conigar
Point

EMSWORTH

West Rd
Beach Road
Warblington Road
Western Parade
Curlew Cl
Beacon Sq
Wayfarer's Walk
Solent Way

Lane End Drive

Creek
End

The Promenade

St Peter's Sq
Swan Cl

Waters
Edge
Gdns

Roundhouse
Meadow

Heron Quay
Avocet
Quay

Mill Quay

Osprey

Quay

Sussex Border Path

Thorney Road

Thornham

Fowley
Island

Sweare

Deep

Sussex Border Path

Wickor
Point

Great Deep

Emsworth Road

Spinnaker
Grange

Northney La

Northney

189

Clovelly
Rd

Pycroft
Close

Church
Lane

St Peter's Rd

North Hayling

St Peter's Av

St Peter's Road

Hampshire County
West Sussex County

Hunter

Spartan Cl

Swift Road

Sabre Rd

Meteor

Road

Javelin Road

s Bay
N Bay

Canberra Rd

Hornet Road

Emsworth Rd

Thorney County
Primary School

Emsworth Road

Chichester Road

Tye

Cutner Lane

Woodgaston Lane

214

Marker Point

Emsworth Channel

I grid square represents 500 metres

MAIN ROAD A259

G **H** **J** **Southbourne** **167** **K** **L** **M**

MAIN RD A259 PO

Prinsted

Nutbourne

Southbourne County
Junior & Infant School

Goodwood
Court

Lodgebury
Close

Longlands
Road

Carsons Road

The Drive

New Rd

Mosdell
Rd

The Crescent

Frarydene

Church Rd

Prinsted Lane

Ham La

Tuppenny

Alfrey
Cl

Surgery

Farm

School La

Maybush Drive

Pottery La

Flatt Rd

Cot Lane

Ivydene
Crescent

Nutbourne
Station

I

2

Path

**Prinsted
Point**

Chidham Point

3

Marsh Lane

Marsh
La

PH

Str... Lane

4

Lane

Sussex Border Path

5

**Stanbury
Point**

Cobnor Fm

6

New
Barn

Thorney Island

Cobnor Ho

7

West Thorney

Thorney Island
Airfield

Smith
Lane

Church

Thorney Old Pk

**Thorney
Channel**

Victor Rd

Vulcan Road

Valiant
Road

Varsity Road

Valetta Road

Pleasant Lane

8

Sussex
Border
Path

G **H** **J** **215** **K** **L** **M**

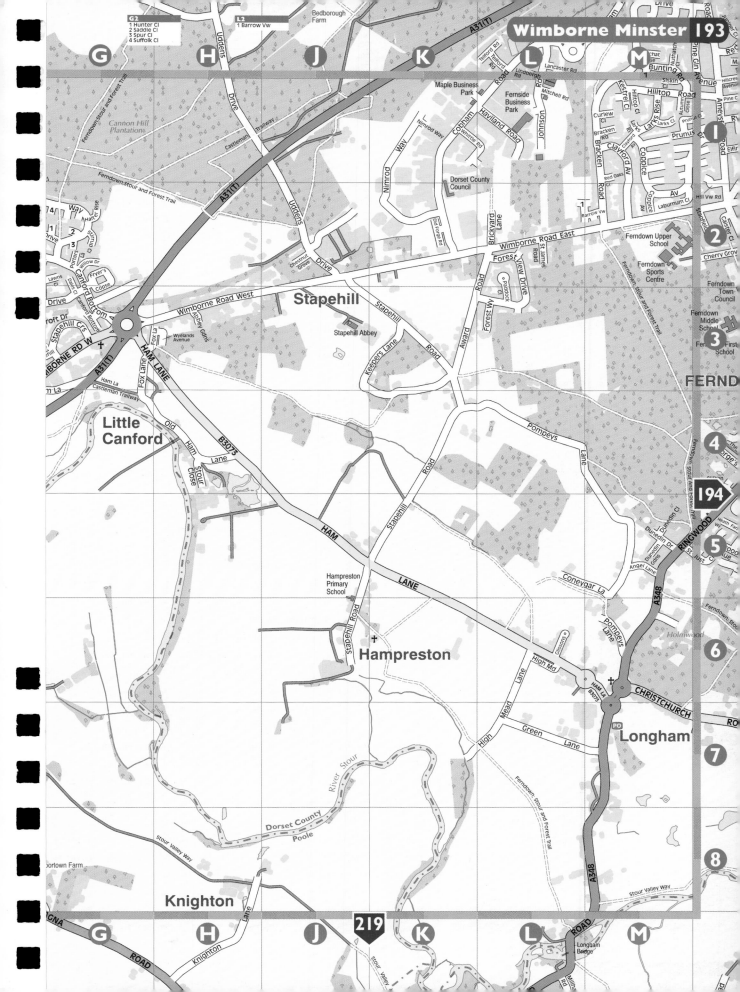

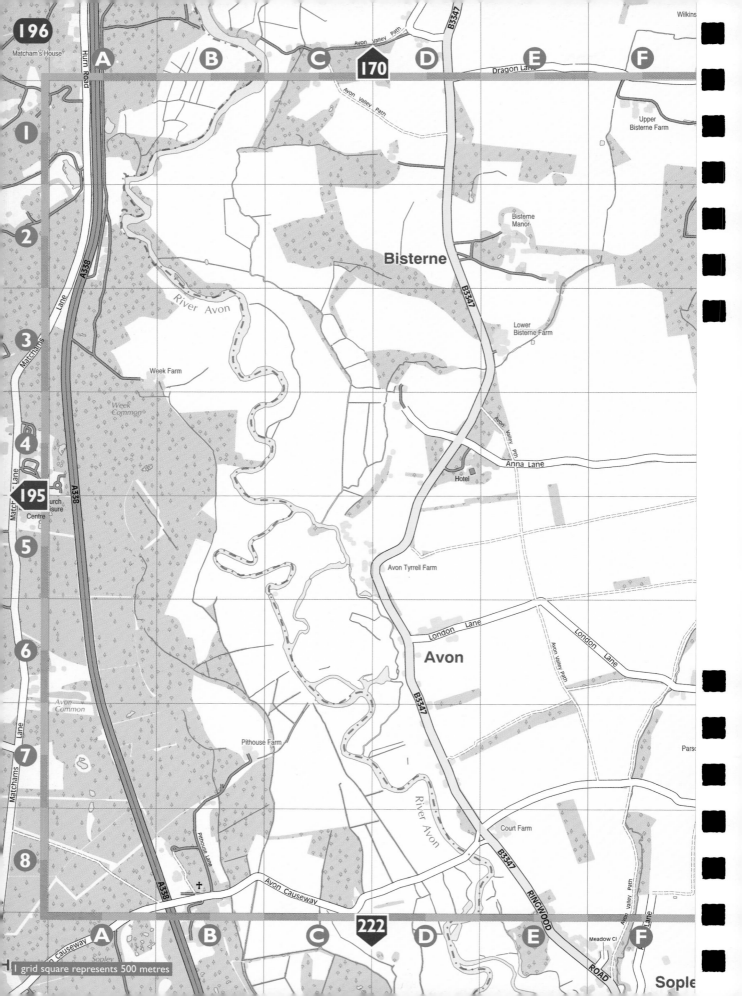

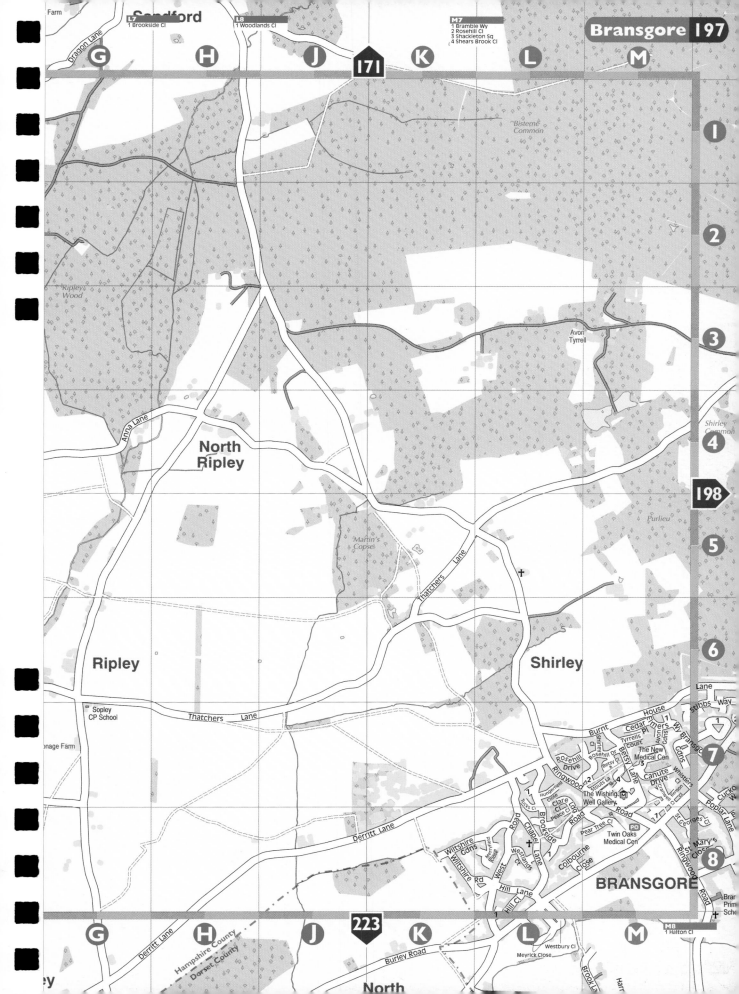

198

A   B   C   D   E   F

172

1 The Orchard   1 Mnt P'sant Dr
A8   A7 2 Wedgewd Gdns

Forest

1

Dur
Hill
Down

Holmsley
Ridge

2

Whitten
Bottom

Thorney
Hill
Holms

3

Forest Rd

Burley Rd

School Lane

School Road

Forest Road

Shirley
Common

4

Brick Lane

Valley Lane

Brick Lane

197

Thorney Hill

Whitelands

Purlieu

Willow Lane

5

Burley Road

Hill Farm

Plain
Heath

6

Dial Cl

Poors
Common

Lane

Stibbs Way

Burley Road

Forest
Lodge

House

1   2

Wy Bransgore
Gdns

A35

7

Canute Drive

Cuckoo Hill Way

Bransgore Ho

Blackbird Way

Heathfield

Poplar Lane

Lyndhurst Road

St Georges Cl

8

St Mary's Close

Ringwood Road

Poplar Cl

Beech House

Bransgore
Primary
School

North Hinton Farm

Holm

224

A   B   C   D   E   F

Harrow Road

Harrow

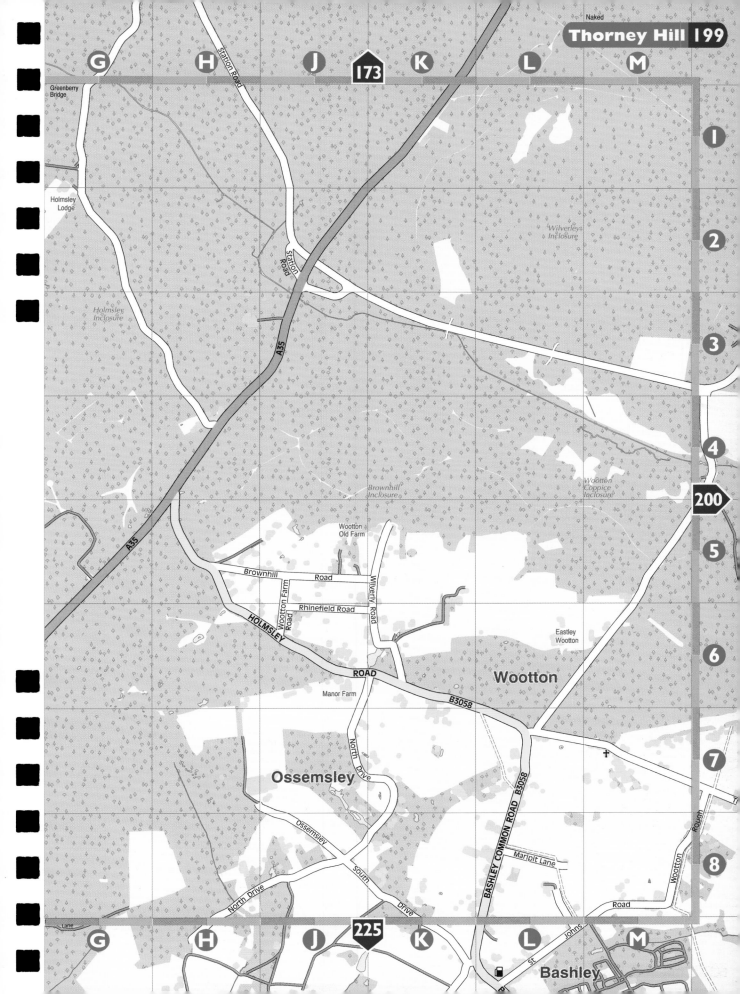

Naked

G   H   Station Road   173   K   L   M

I

2

3

4

200

5

6

7

8

Greenberry
Bridge

Holmsley
Lodge

Holmsley
Inclosure

A35

Wilverley
Inclosure

Wootton
Coppice
Inclosure

Brownhill
Inclosure

Wootton
Old Farm

Brownhill   Road

Wootton Farm Road

Rhinefield Road

Wilverly Road

Eastley
Wootton

HOLMSLEY

ROAD

B3058

Wootton

Manor Farm

North Drive

Ossemsley

Ossemsley

North Drive

South

Drive

BASHLEY COMMON ROAD

B3058

Maripit Lane

Wootton

Rough

Road

Johns St

Lane

G   H   J   225   K   L   M

Bashley

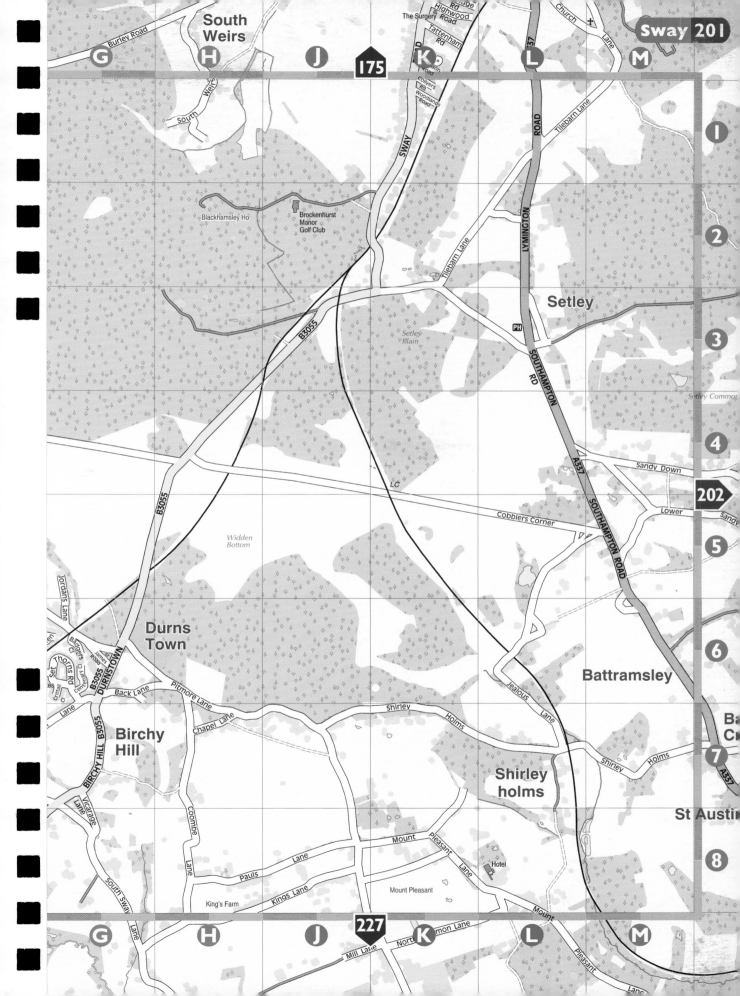

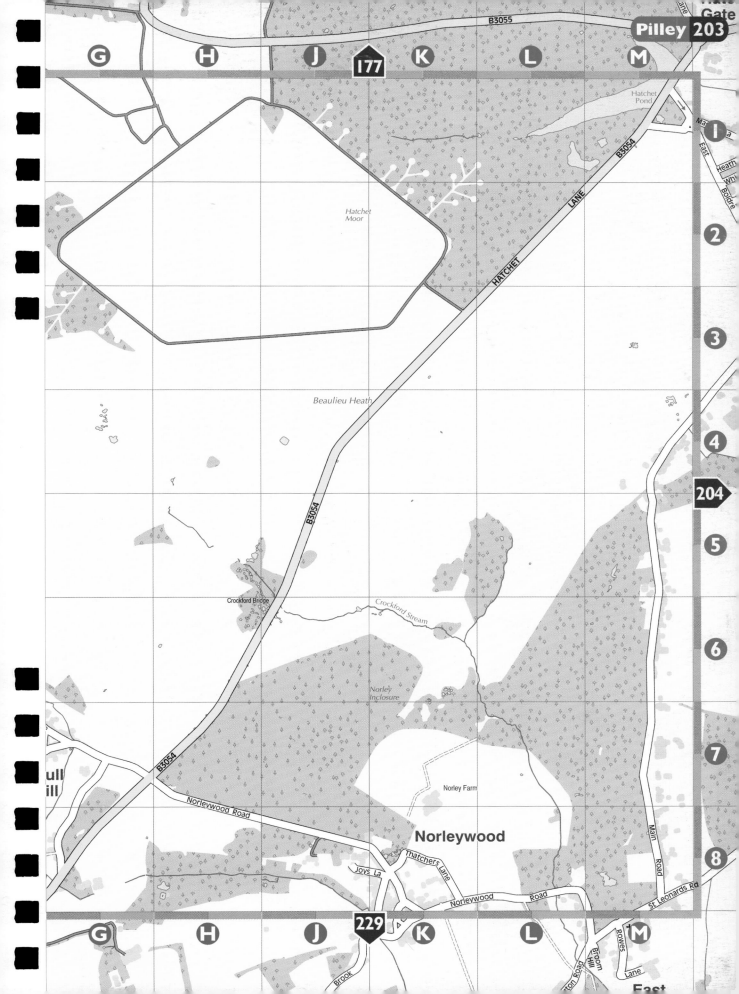

G H J **177** K L M

I

2

3

4

204

5

6

7

8

G H J **229** K L M

B3055

Hatchet
Pond

East
Heath

Whi
Boldre

HATCHET LANE

B3054

Beaulieu Heath

B3054

Crockford Bridge

Crockford Stream

Norley
Inclosure

Norley Farm

Norleywood Road

Norleywood

Thatchers Lane

Joys La

Norleywood Road

St Leonards Rd

Brook

Broom Hill

Rowes Lane

Main Road

ull
ill

Hatchet
Moor

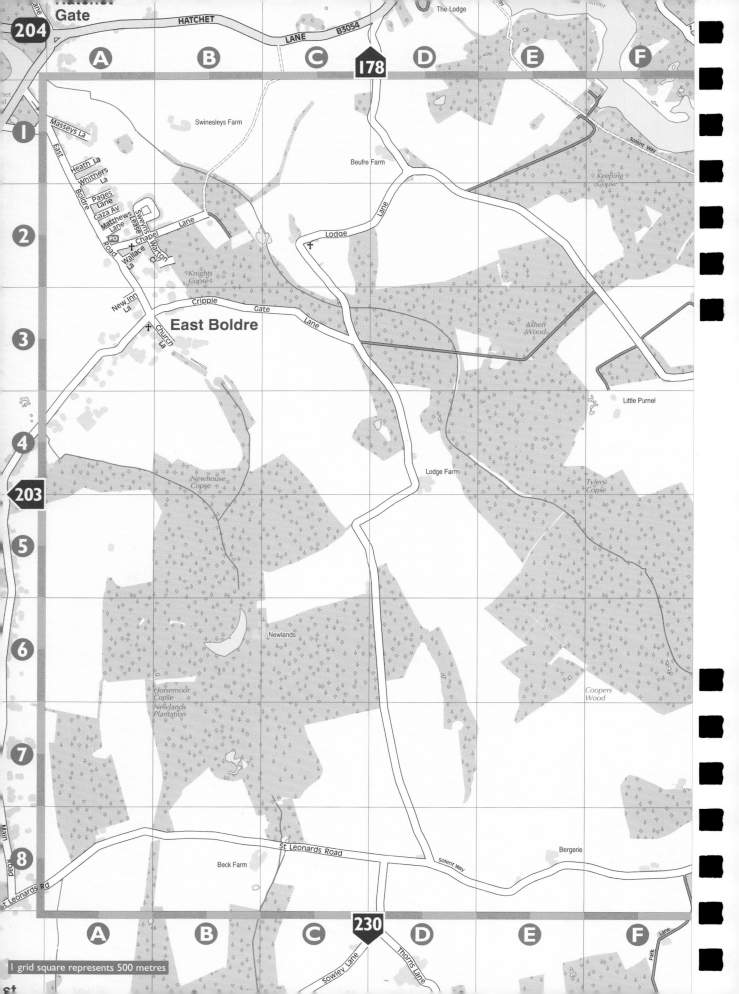

Gate

HATCHET

LANE B3054

The Lodge

River

A   B   C   178   D   E   F

Masseys La

Swinesleys Farm

Beufre Farm

Solent Way

East Heath La

Keeping Copse

Whithers La

Boldre

Pages Lane

Caza Av

Matthews Lane

Sweyns Lease

Walton

Lane

Lodge

Lane

Knights Copse

Chapel

PO

Wallace La

New Inn La

Cripple   Gate   Lane

Ashen Wood

East Boldre

Church La

Little Purnel

Lodge Farm

Newhouse Copse

203

Tylers Copse

Newlands

Coopers Wood

Horsemoor Copse

Newlands Plantation

St Leonards Road

Bergerie

solent Way

Beck Farm

St Leonards Rd

Main Road

A   B   C   230   D   E   F

Sowley Lane

Thorns Lane

Park Lane

1 grid square represents 500 metres

Blackfield

D1
1 Foxglade
2 Foxlands
3 Fox's Wk
4 Foxy Paddock
5 Langley Lg Gdn
6 The Mews

C1
1 Bowland Wy
2 St Francis Cl

Tom's Down

A   B   C   D   E   F

Blackwell
Common

Cem

Hampton Hampton
Gdns   Cl
Northampton Lane

Viking
South

180

Thornbury Avenue

Chapel
Lane

The
Glade

Lea Road

Mopley Cl

Nicholas
Rd

Clare
Gdns

Mopley

Forest

1

Langley

Charnwood Way

Chalewood
Road

St Francis
Rd

Hursley

Wychwood

Lepe Road

Foxhayes
La

Kings Ride

Foresters

7

I

W Common

Common

Homer Farm
Lane

Forge Road

Dark Water

**West
Common**

Whitefield
Farm

2

Exbury

Dark Water

3

East Hill Farm

Lepe Road

Stranswood Road

Stone Farm

4

205

Lepe Farm

Lepe Road

5

Flaxland
Pits

6

Inchmery House

Lepe

7

Needs
Ore Point

8

A   B   C   D   E   F

The Solent

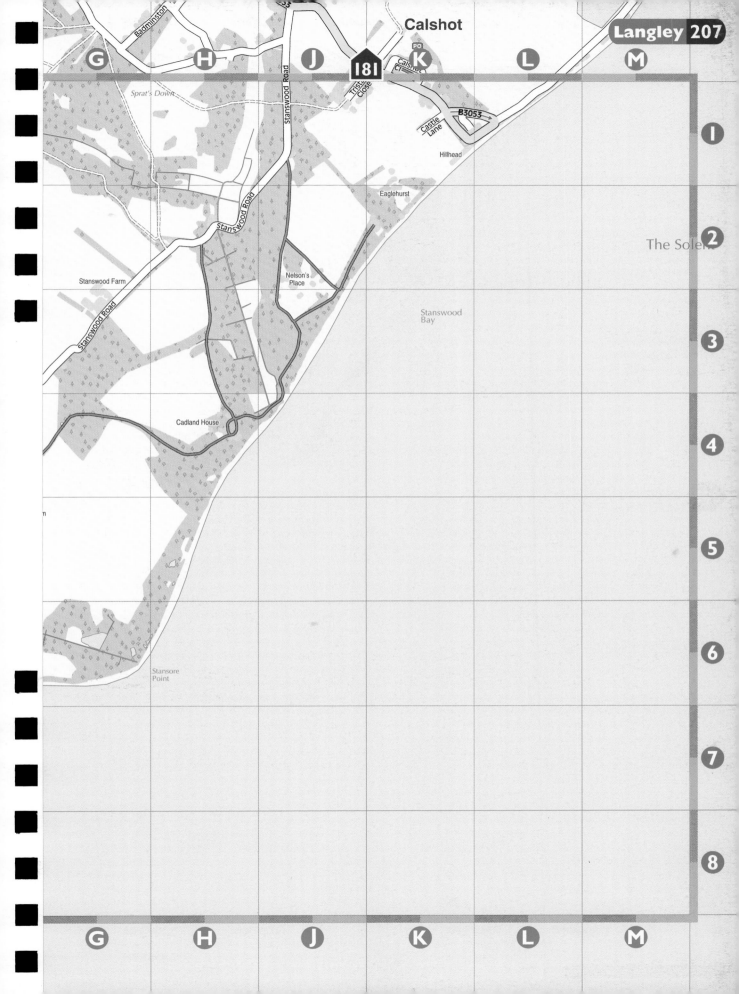

184

207

A Sea Avenue Ibbington Lane

D1 cont.
7 Sparrow Ct
8 Swallow Ct
9 Swift Cl

D1
1 Chaffinch Wy
2 Common Barn La
3 Kimpson Wk
4 Kenilworth Cl
5 Magpie La
6 Martin Cl
cont.

C2
1 Olave Cl
2 Osborne Rd
3 Queens Cl

C1
1 Inverkip Cl
2 Nottingham Pl
3 Southcliff

B1
1 Brambles Rd

Chark Lane

HMS Daedalus

Fieldhouse Dr
Parklands Close

B3385

Cherque Lane

Homer Close

Broomfield

Theseus

Drake Rd Marine Parade

Implacable Road
Ark Royal
Implacable Rd
Crs
Unicorn Rd
Hermes Rd
Vengeance Rd
King's Road
Eagle Rd

Norwich
Place
Manor
Road
Newton Pl
Eastcliff
Cl
Westcliff
Court Barn
Lane
Blackbird
Way

St Annes
School
Court Road
Ross Way
Fell Drive
Cordhill La

Richmond
Rd
Victoria
Road
Swanage Rd

Montserrat
Road
Britten
Rd
Cheltenham
Crescent
Cresent

Grove
Road
Leamington Crescent
Smeeton Rd
field Rd
Wheatcroft Road

Russell
Close
Petrie Rd
Russell Road

Broom Way

Manor Way

B3385

West Parade

LEE-ON-THE-SOLENT

Pier St
Lee-on-the-Solent
Health Cen
PO
Marine Parade East

Studland
Rd
Clanwilliam
Road
Lulworth Rd

Derwent Rd
Sea Crest
Skipper

Francis
Close

Compton Close

Spencer Drive
Cherry
Way

Sandhill Lane

River Alver

High Street

Solent Way
Avon
Close
Lee-on-
the-Solent
Infant School
Elmore
Close

Rowan
Close
Elmore Avenue

Hotel
Cambridge
Road
Junior
School

Milvil Rd B3333

Solent Way
Gosport
Road
Seymour Rd

Elmore
Road
Wooton
Road
Pennine Way

Cross Rd

Portsmouth Road

Marine Pde East
Raynes Rd
Andlesea Rd
Warwick
Close
Lancaster
Close

Queens Rd
Lakeside
South
Rd
Clifton
Rd
Ryde
Place
York Crs
Chester
Crs
Canterbury Close

PORTSMOUTH ROAD B3333

Solent Way

Browndown

Browndown
Point

Solent

A
D3
1 Cheyne Wy
2 Maple Cl

B
D2
1 Chilcomb Cl
2 Esmonde Cl
3 Gibson Cl
4 Harrier Cl
5 Headley Cl
6 Kimpton Cl
cont.

C

D
D2 cont.
7 Osprey Gdns
8 Trent Wy
9 Waveney Cl

E
E4
1 The Seagulls

E3
1 Larch Cl

F

1 grid square represents 500 metres

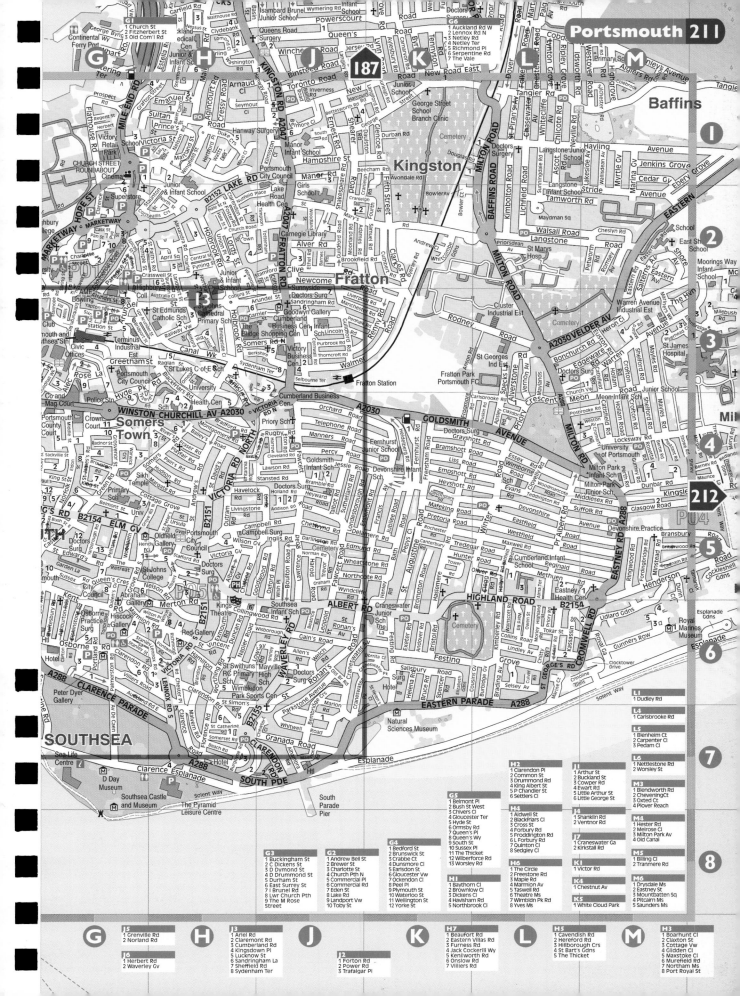

Baffins

Milton

Eastney

Langstone Channel

Sinah Lake

Hampshire County
City of Portsmouth

University of Portsmouth

Ferry Road

Sinah Common

West Winner

East Winner

Fort Cumberland

Eastney Swimming Baths

Royal Marines Museum

Esplanade

Portsmouth Sixth Form College

Tangier Road

EASTERN ROAD A2030

East Shore School

Moorings Way Infant School

Locksway Road

Fort Cumberland Road

Henderson Road

A5
1 Eastney Farm Rd

A4
1 Towpath Mead

A3
1 Brasted Ct
2 Longfield Cl
3 Redwing Ct
4 Wayfarer Cl

A2
1 Godwit Rd
2 Revenge Cl
3 Seagull Cl

B3
1 Sovereign Dr

1 grid square represents 500 metres

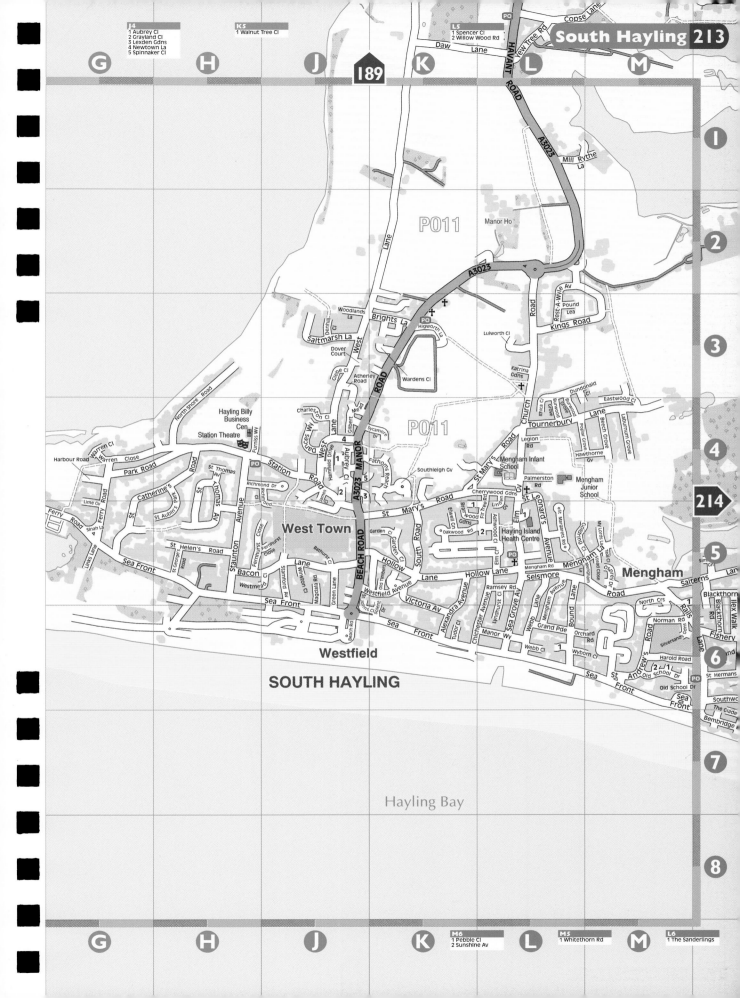

A   B   C   **190**   D   E   F

1

Mill Rithe

2

Pilsey Sand

3

Stocker's Lake

4

213

5

Simmons Gdn

Mengham Salterns

Black Point

Salterns Cl

Marine

Walk

Seaview Rd

gham

Salterns

Lane

Blackthorn Dr

Selsmore Avenue

Seaview

Road

Brackelsham Rd

Road

th Crs

Blackthorn

Dr

Ilex Walk

Kingfisher

Astrid La

Burdale Dr

Selsmore

Norman Rd

Rd

Blackthorn

Lane

1

Silversands

Fishery

Lane

Rd

6

Foreland

Ct

Fishermans

Wk

Eastoke

Avenue

Earnley

Witterings Rd

Selsey Cl

Sidlesham Cl

Road

2

St Hermans Rd

Eastoke

Rowin Close

Avenue

Birdham Rd

Haslemere Gdns

Sidlesham Cl

Pagham Cl

Itchenor Rd

Bracklesham

School Dr

PO

Bosmere Rd

Road

Old School Dr

Southwood

Culver Dr

Haven Road

Haven Road

Sea Front

The Glade

Road

Meath Cl

West Haye Road

Creek

Nutbourne Rd

Point

Road

West Sussex County

Bembridge Drive

The Strand

Burgess Cl

Sandy

Coronation Rd

Treloar Rd

Hampshire County

7

Winsor Cl

Wheatlands

1

Avenue

Treloar Rd

Road

Southwood Road

Eastoke Point

8

A   B   C   D   E   F

G H J **191** K L M

I

2

3

4

5

6

7

8

Longmere Point

Pilsey Island

Chichester Harbour

East Head

Sussex Border Path

Rookwood Lane

Rookwood Lane

Sheepwash Lane

ROOKWOOD RD

Rookwood Road

Summerfield Rd

Summerfield Road

Elmstead Park Road

Cuniffe Close

Elmstead Pk Rd

Elmstead Gdns

Locksash Cl

B2179

Royce Close

Royce Way

Elms Ride

Elms Ride

Elms Lane

Elms Wy

Meadow La

Elms Lane

Nunnington Farm

PO

West Wittering

The Byeway

Middlefield

Wellsfield

Seaward Dr.

Roman Landing

Roman Landing

Roman Landing

Roman Landing

Coastguard Lane

West Wittering Parochial School †

Ellanore Lane

Pound Rd

The Wad

West Strand

Berrybarn Lane

CAKEHAM

East Strand

ROAD

East Wittering

B2179

Howard Avenue

Jolliffe Road

Southcote

Marine Dr West

Owers

G H J K L M

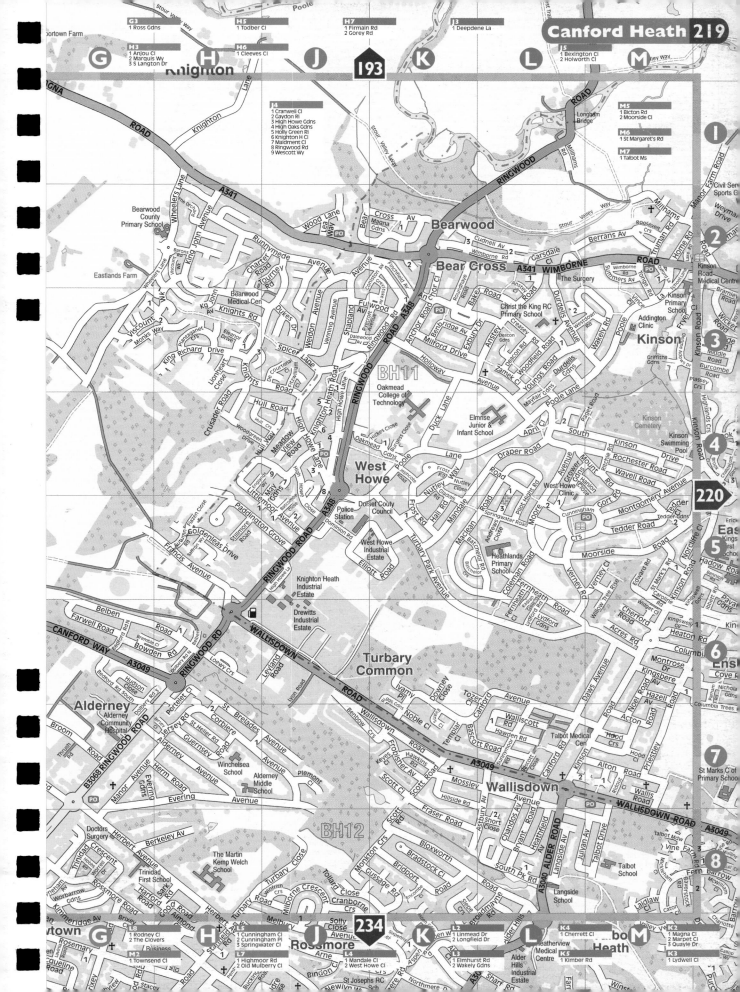

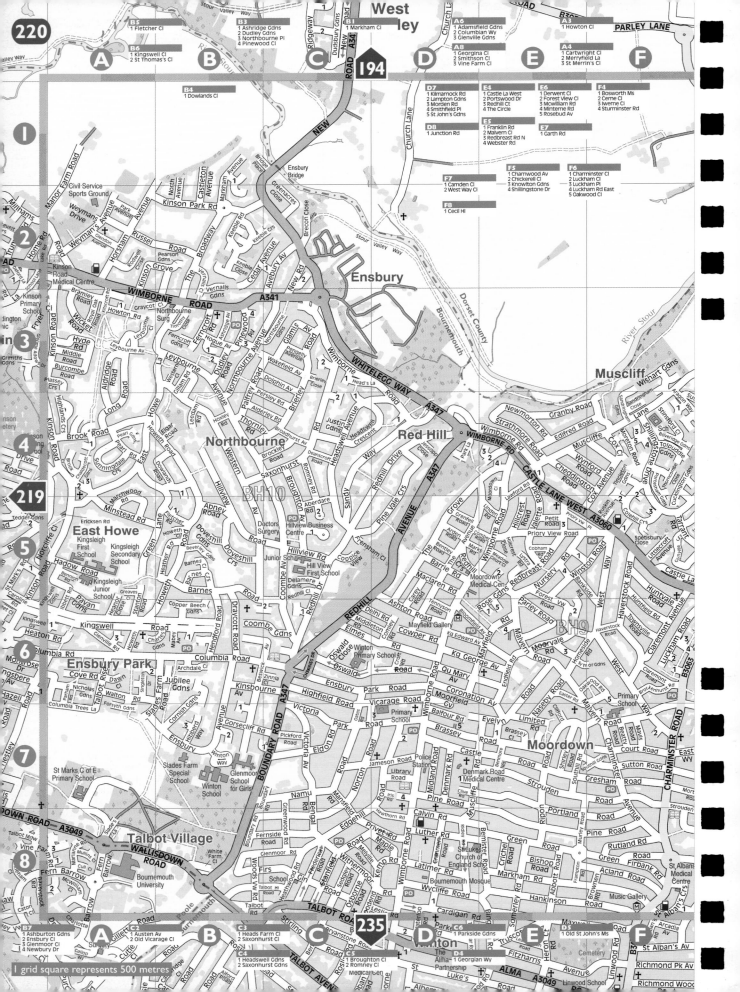

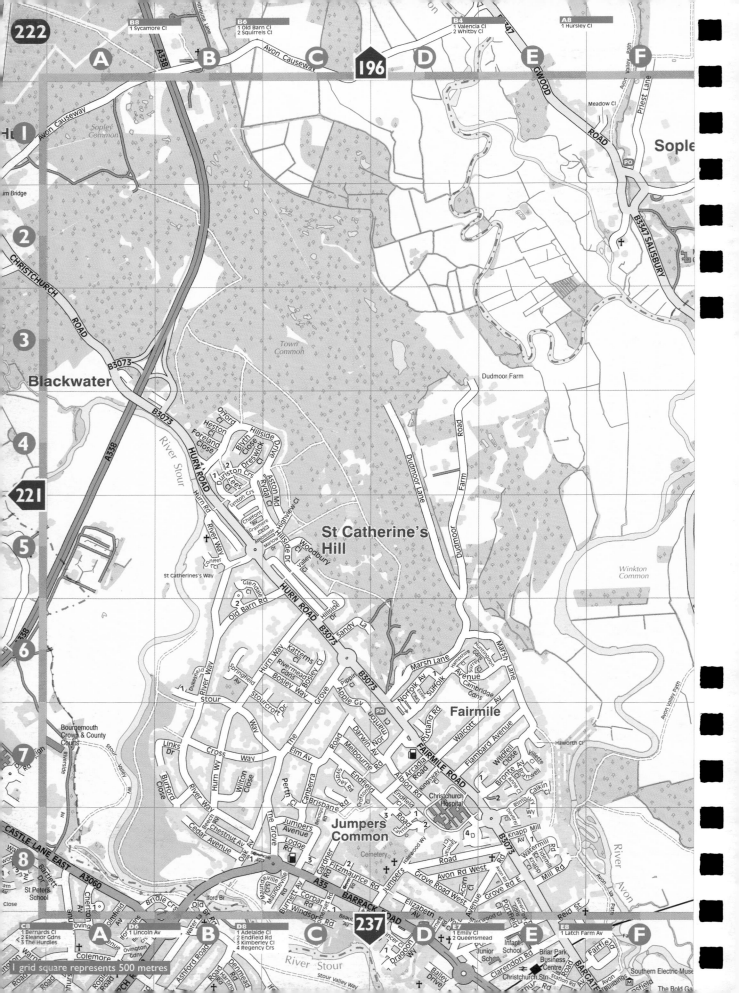

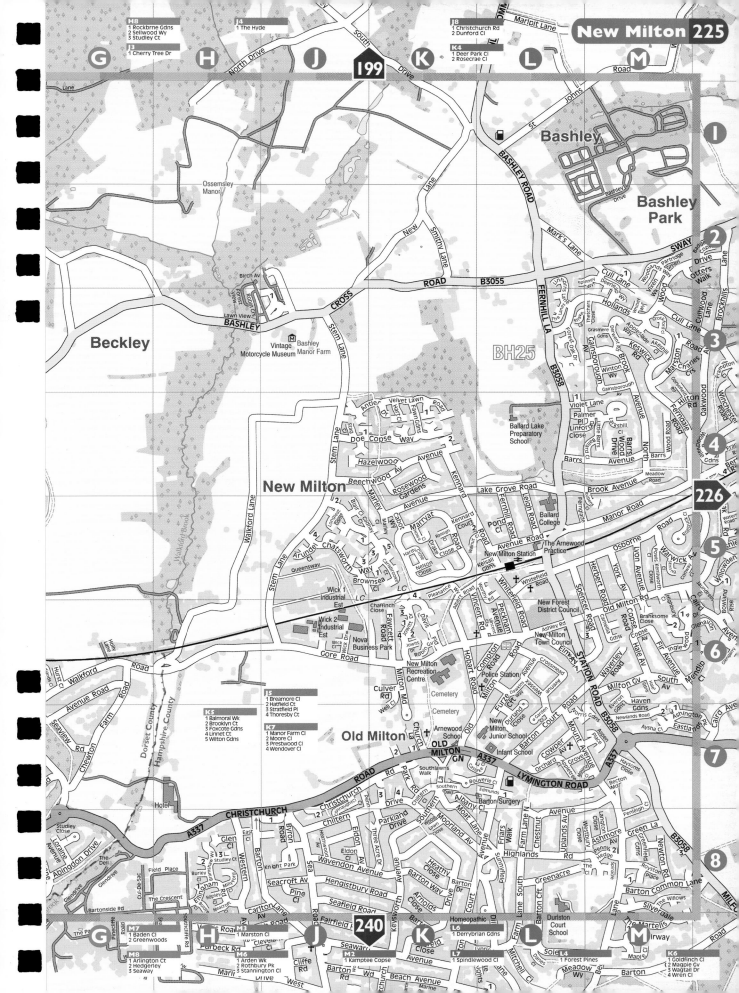

Norleywood

Thatchers Lane

Joys La

Norleywood Road

203

Brook Hill

East End

Lymington Road

Broom Hill

Rowes Lane

St Leonards Rd

Newtown Park

South Baddesley

South Baddesley
C of E Primary
School

PH

Solent Way

Snooks Farm

Solent Way

Sowley Lane

Pitts

Road

Shotts Lane

Mill Lane

Tanners Lane

Deep Lane

230

Court Road

Lisle Court

The Solent

YARMOUTH

G H J K L M

I 2 3 4 5 6 7 8

G H J K L M

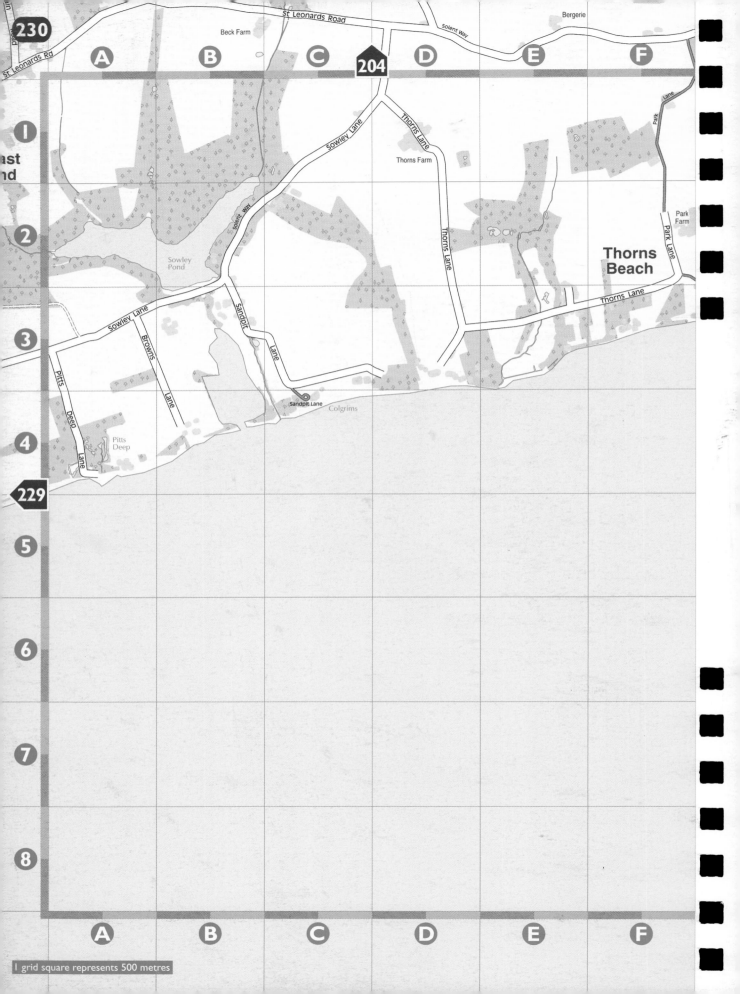

St Leonards Road

Beck Farm

solent Way

Bergerie

St Leonards Rd

ast
nd

1

Sowley Lane

Thorns Lane

Park Lane

Thorns Farm

Solent Way

2

Sowley
Pond

Thorns Lane

Thorns Beach

Park Farm

Park Lane

Sowley Lane

Sandpit Lane

3

Browns Lane

Pitts Deep Lane

Thorns Lane

Sandpit Lane   Colgrims

4

Pitts
Deep

5

6

7

8

1 grid square represents 500 metres

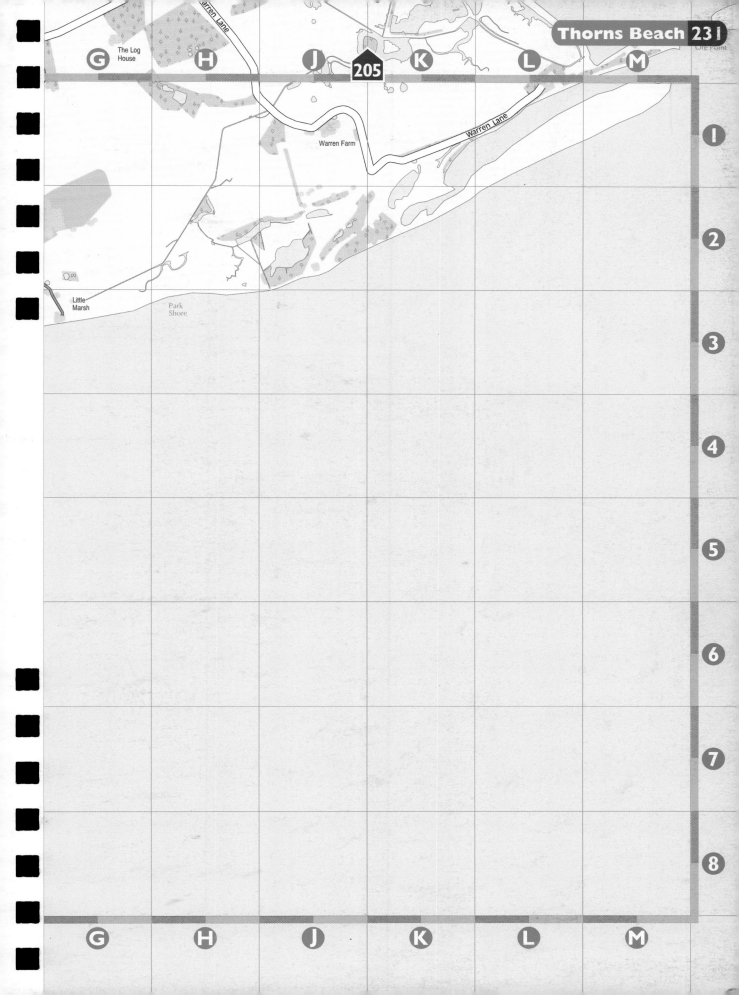

Ore Point

G The Log House

H

J 205

K

L

M

Warren Lane

Warren Farm

Warren Lane

Little Marsh

Park Shore

I

2

3

4

5

6

7

8

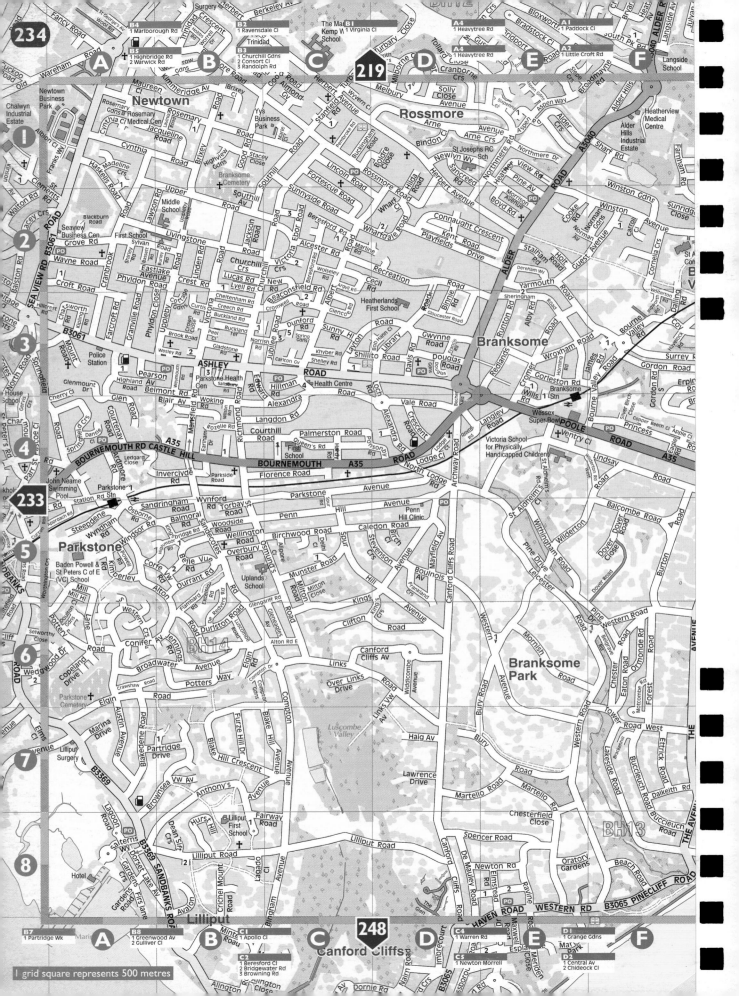

Talbot Village

Talbot Heath

Talbot Woods

BH3

Winton

Meyrick Park

Meyrick Park Golf Course

BH2

Westbourne

BH4

West Cliff

West Undercliff Promenade

Poole Bay

Alum Chine

Branksome Chine

BOURNEMOU...

G5
1 Eldon Pl
2 Seamoor La

G6
1 Drury Rd
2 Groveley Rd

H1
1 Bishop Cl

H2
1 Heatherbank Rd
2 Landseer Rd

H7
1 Crosby Rd

J4
1 Kensington Dr

J6
1 Suffolk Rd S

K4
1 Durrant Rd

E6
1 Bury Rd

E8
1 Chaucer Rd
2 Moorfields Rd

F6
1 Leicester Rd

C3
1 Carnegie Cl
2 Heatherlands Ri
3 Jubilee Crs
4 Madeira Rd
5 The Drive

E1
1 Cashmoor Cl

E3
1 Cromer Gdns
2 Thetford Rd

F2
1 Guest Cl

K6
1 Durley Rd South
2 Durley Rbt
3 Hahnemann Rd
4 Kerley Rd
5 South View Pl
6 West Cliff Gdns

D4
1 Highwood Rd

E4
1 Cardigan Rd

F1
1 Yarmouth Cl

G
M5
1 Cumnor Rd
2 St Peters Rbt

M6
1 Bath Hill Rbt

H
M3
1 Coach House Pl

M4
1 The Firs
2 Lansdowne Gdns
3 Park Rd
4 St Pauls Rbt

J
L6
1 B'mouth I C Rbt
2 Exeter Park Rd
3 South Cliff Rd

K
L4
1 St Stephen's Wy

L5
1 Albert Rd
2 Post Office Rd
3 Verulam Pl

L
L1
1 Bonham Rd
2 Crimea Rd

L2
1 Rushton Crs

M
K5
1 Mannington Pl
2 Orchard St
3 The Triangle
4 West Hill Pl

222

238

G3
1 Ashbourne Rd
2 Chilcombe Rd
3 Connaught Rd
4 Cromwell Pl
5 Hampden La
6 Seabourne Pl
7 Southville Rd
8 Stedman Pl
9 Stourvale Pl

G1
1 Petersfield Pl
2 Swanmore Cl

G2
1 Durrington Pl
2 Harewood Pl

G4
1 Seabourne Rd

G5
1 Rotherfield Rd

H1
1 Southwick Pl

H2
1 Amesbury Rd

H3
1 Appletree Cl
2 Douglas Ms

M1
1 Addiscombe Rd
2 Arthur La

M2
1 Turnberry Cl

M3
1 Magnolia Cl
2 Wickmeads Rd
3 Willow Wy

M4
1 Kingsley Av

M5
1 Stevenson Rd

G
L4
1 Twynham Rd

L5
1 Admiralty Rd
2 Shires Copse
3 Warren Edge Cl

H
L2
1 Galton Av
2 Wentworth Dr

L3
1 Riverside Rd

J

L1
1 Hussar Cl

K
K2
1 Kingfisher Cl

K5
1 Avoncliffe Rd
2 Bolton Rd

L
J3
1 Heytesbury Rd

K1
1 Bernards Cl

M
J1
1 Shakespeare Rd

J2
1 Kittiwake Cl

223

237

Grid reference indexes

D2
1 Alexander Cl
2 Buccaneers Cl
3 Groveley Rd
4 Johnstone Rd
5 Rosedale Cl
6 Stroud Gdns

C3
2 Asquith Cl

D
1 Bingham Cl
2 Court Cl
3 Wolfe Cl

C2
1 Addington Pl
2 Asquith Cl
3 Grafton Cl

A5
1 Selfridge Cl

C1
1 Amsterdam Sq
2 Cameron Rd
3 Chant Cl
4 Delft Ms
5 Haking Rd
6 Livingstone Rd
7 Utrecht Ct

D3
1 Harbour Crs

E1
1 Amethyst Rd
2 Marmion Gn
3 Southey Rd

E1
1 Amethyst Rd
2 Marmion Gn
3 Southey Rd

E2
1 Drake Cl
2 Frobisher Cl
3 The Hawthorns

E4
1 Hamilton Cl

F2
1 Ambassador Cl
2 Cunningham Cl
3 Grebe Cl
4 Lark Rd

F3
1 Anchor Cl
2 Mountbatten Cl
3 Partridge Cl

Places labelled on map

Purewell

Somerford

CHRISTCHURCH

Stanpit

Wick

Stanpit Marsh

Christchurch Harbour

Dorset County
Bournemouth

Hengistbury Head

224

240

G!
1 Beaufort Cl
2 Britannia Wy
3 Caledonian Cl
4 Sunderland Dr
5 Swordfish Dr

A3
1 Regent Wy
2 Silver St
3 Wickfield Cl

1 Roscrea Cl

G2
1 B Homage Gdns
2 Sopwith Cl
3 The Coppice

H1
1 Auckland Rd
2 Saxonford Rd

L1
1 Abbots Cl

HIGHCLIFFE

Christchurch Business
Cen

Business Cen

LYMINGTON RD

SHELLEY HL

A337

LYMINGTON RD

A337

LYMINGTON

Highcliffe
Castle
Golf Club

Highcliffe
Medical
Centre

Waterford
Gardens

Wharncliffe
Road

Friars
Cliff

Hotel

Mudeford

Wren
Cl

Highcliffe
Medical
Centre

Capesthorne

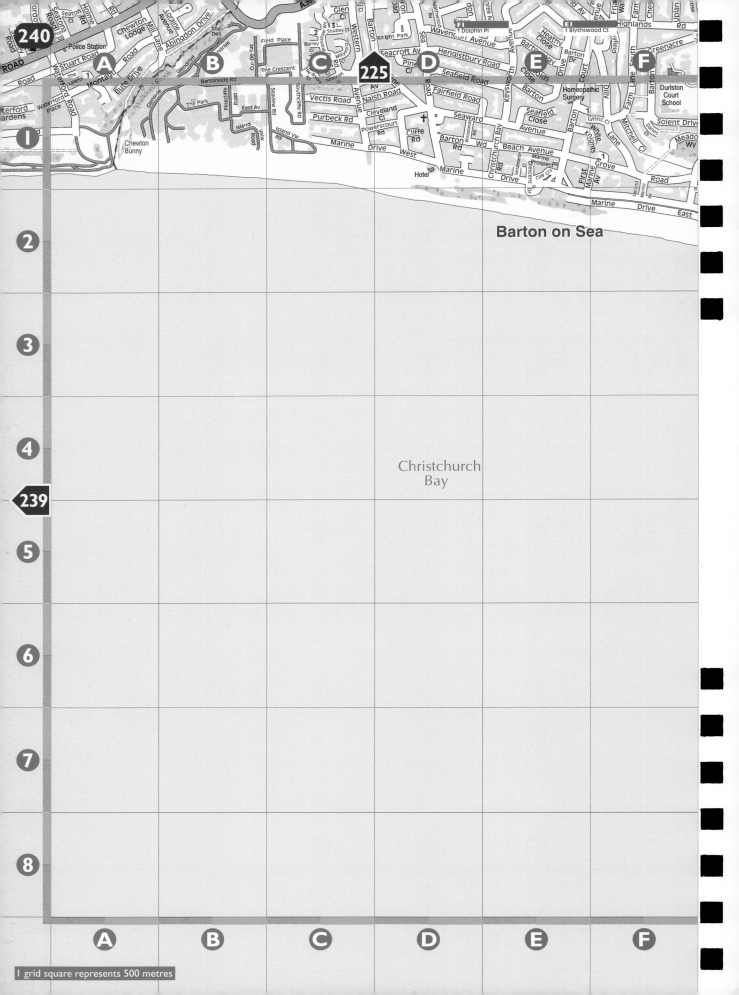

ROAD

Police Station

Chewton
Lodge

The
Dell

Field Place

The Crescent

225

Glen

1 Dolphin Pl

1 Blythswood Ct

Highlands
Rd

Durlston
Court
School

Homeopathic
Surgery

Solent Drive

Barton on Sea

Christchurch
Bay

1 grid square represents 500 metres

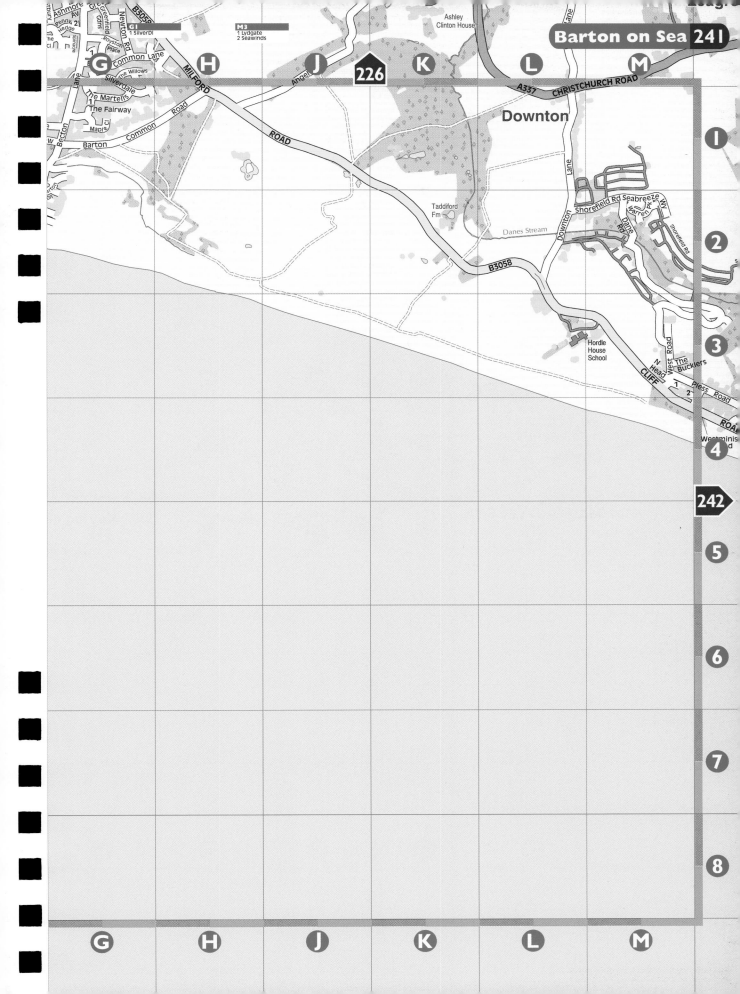

G1
1 SilverDl

M3
1 Lydgate
2 Seawinds

G Common Lane
The Willows
Silverdale
The Martell's
The Fairway
Barton Common Road
Maple Cl
Becton
Ashmore AV
Greenfield Gdns
Penn
Hedge
Spruce
Newton Rd
Royston Place
B3058

H MILFORD ROAD

J Angel

226

K

Ashley Clinton House

L A337 CHRISTCHURCH ROAD

M

Downton

Taddiford Fm

Danes Stream

B3058

Downton Lane

Shorefield Rd Seabreeze
Warren Pk
Dane Rd
Shorefield Rd
West Road
West Road
N Head
CLIFF
The Bucklers
Pless Road
ROAD
Westminis
Hordle House School

I

2

3

4

242

5

6

7

8

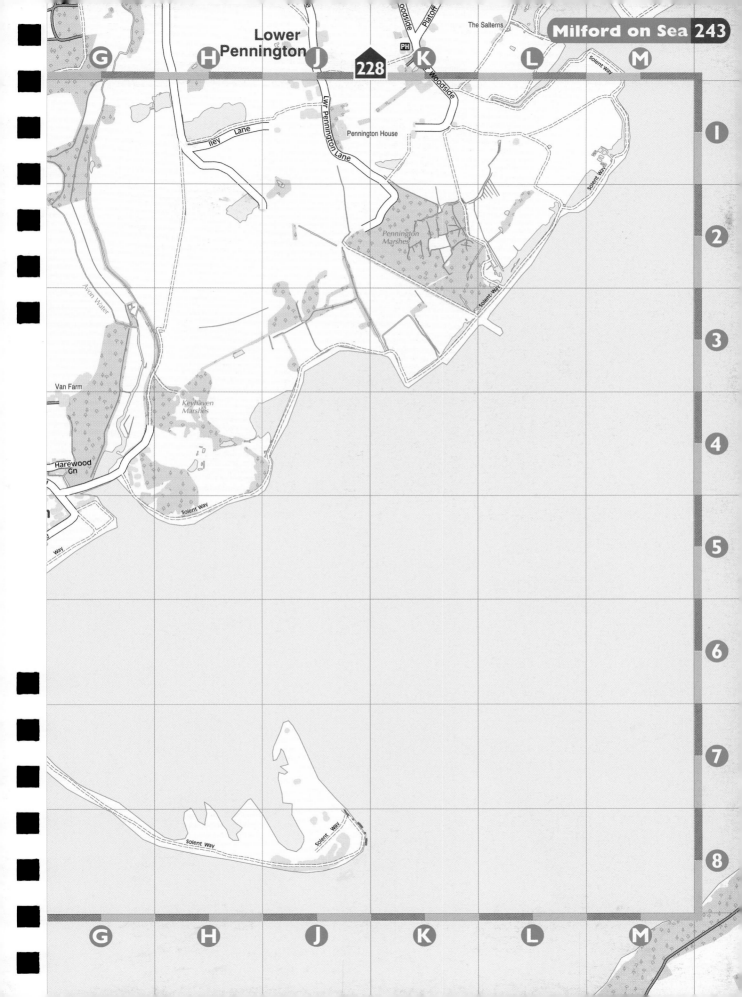

G H J 228 K L M

I
2
3
4
5
6
7
8

Lower
Pennington

PH

Woodside

Platoff

The Salterns

Iley Lane

Lwr Pennington Lane

Pennington House

Pennington
Marshes

Solent Way

Solent Way

Solent Way

Avon Water

Van Farm

Keyhaven
Marshes

Harewood
Gn

Solent Way

Way

Solent Way

Solent Way

233

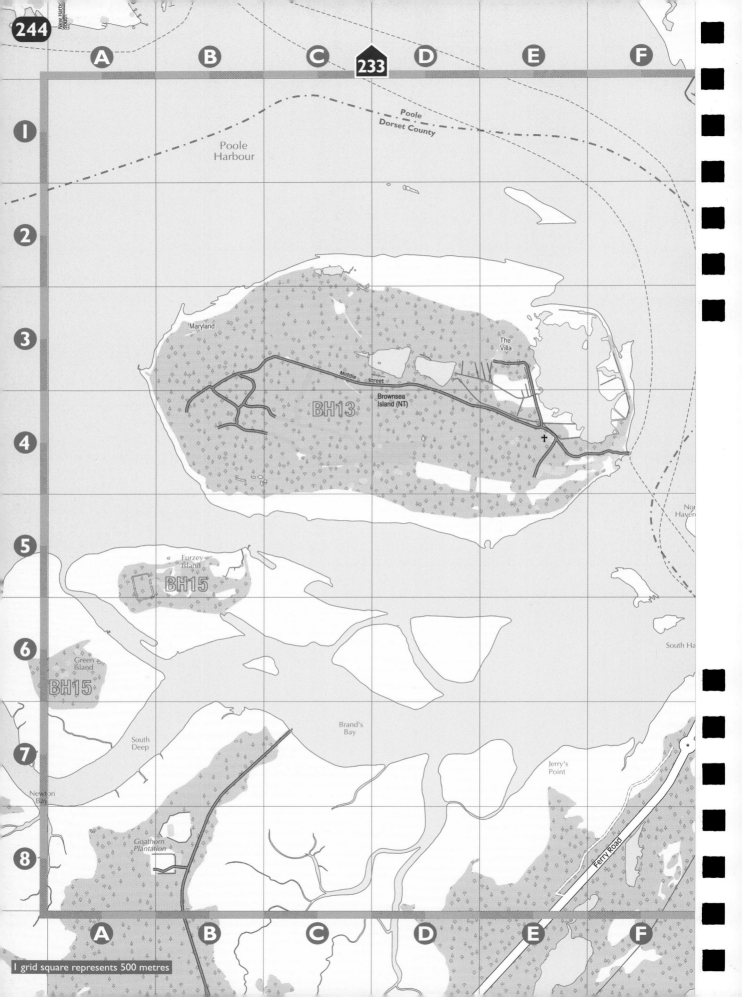

New Harbor South

Poole
Dorset County

Poole
Harbour

Maryland

The Villa

Middle Street

BH13

Brownsea
Island (NT)

†

Nor
Haven

Furzey
Island

BH15

Green
Island

BH15

South Ha

South
Deep

Brand's
Bay

Jerry's
Point

Newton
Bay

Goathern
Plantation

Ferry Road

I grid square represents 500 metres

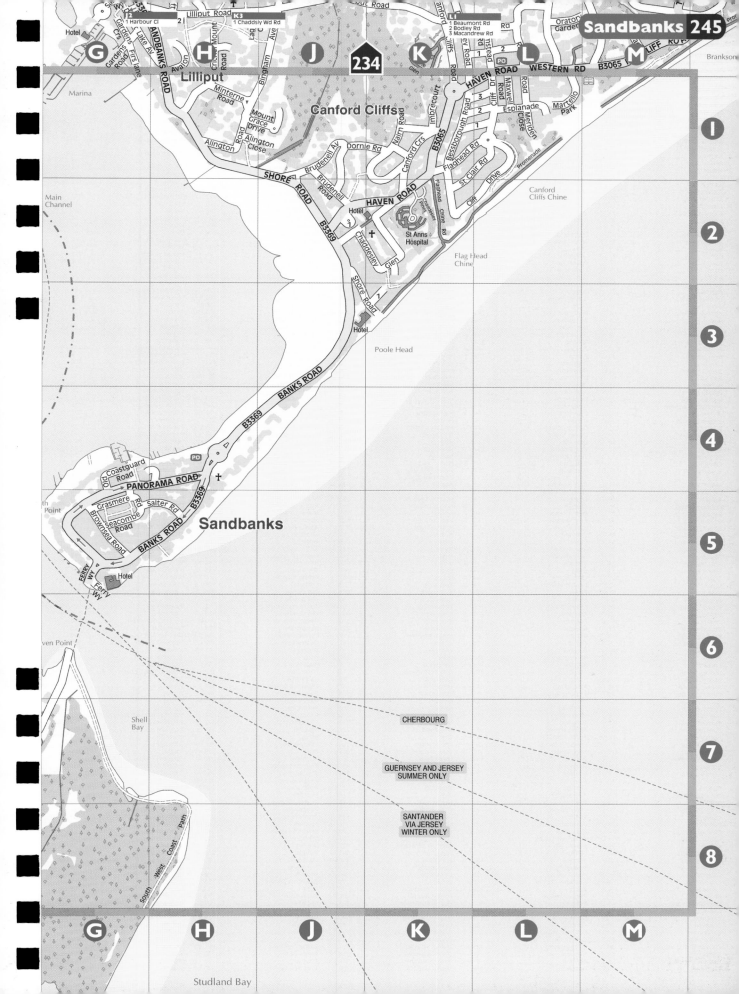

Branksome

Hotel

Marina

Main
Channel

Lilliput

Canford Cliffs

Canford
Cliffs Chine

Flag Head
Chine

St Anns
Hospital

Hotel

Hotel

Poole Head

Coastguard
Road

PANORAMA ROAD

Grasmere
Rd

Seacombe
Road

Brownsea Road

BANKS ROAD

Sandbanks

Hotel

Ferry
WY

Shell
Bay

CHERBOURG

GUERNSEY AND JERSEY
SUMMER ONLY

SANTANDER
VIA JERSEY
WINTER ONLY

Studland Bay

234

Lilliput Road

Harbour Cl
Chaddsly Wd Rd

Beaumont Rd
Bodley Rd
Macandrew Rd

ANDBANKS ROAD

SHORE ROAD

B3369

HAVEN ROAD

WESTERN RD

B3065

CLIFF ROW

Minterne
Road

Mount
Grace
Drive

Alington
Close

Alington

Brudenell Av

Brudenell
Road

Dornie Rd

Nairn Road

Canford Crs

B3065

Bessborough Road

Flaghead Rd

St Clair Rd

Cliff

Drive

Promenade

Esplanade

Meriden
Close

Martello
Park

Orator
Garden

Chaddesley
Glen Rd

Glen

Shore Road

B3369

BANKS ROAD

B3369

Salter Rd

Coast Path

South West

G H J K L M

I 2 3 4 5 6 7 8

Abbotswood 50 F5
Abbots Worthy 17 J2
Abshot 158 E8
Alderholt 121 K2
Aldermoor 105 M5
Allbrook 81 M2
Alverstoke 10 B7
Ameysford 168 A7
Ampfield 52 B5
Anchorage Park 188 A5
Anmore 139 M4
Ann's Hill 10 A1
Anthill Common 139 H2
Applemore 154 E4
Ashfield 79 G4
Ashford 97 J7
Ashlett 181 G5
Ashley 170 A3
Ashley 226 A5
Ashley Heath 169 K2
Ashton 85 G5
Ashurst 129 G6
Ashurst Bridge 129 G3
Awbridge 49 K4
Baffins 211 M1
Bailey Green 33 H5
Balmerlawn 175 M5
Bank 151 H5
Bar End 27 G2
Barrow Hill 103 J6
Barrow Hill 216 B4
Bartley 127 L1
Barton on Sea 240 E2
Bashley 225 L1
Bashley Park 225 M2
Bassett 106 F3
Bassett Green 106 F3
Battramsley 201 L6
Battramsley Cross 202 A7
Baybridge 56 B5
Beacon Hill 216 E6
Beaulieu 178 C7
Beauworth 29 M8
Beckley 225 C3
Bedhampton 165 C7
Bell Hill 63 K3
Bickton 122 D2
Birchy Hill 201 C7
Bishopstoke 82 B6
Bishop's Waltham 85 C7
Bisterne 196 D2
Bisterne Close 173 H6
Bitterne 132 C1
Bitterne Park 107 J7
Blackfield 180 E8
Blackhill 76 F7
Blashford 146 D5
Bleak Hill 122 A5
Blendworth 141 H1
Blissford 98 D8
Boarhunt 161 M3
Bohemia 73 M4
Boldre 202 B7
Boorley Green 109 K6
Borden 66 C2
Botley 134 F2
Bournemouth 15 G6
Boveridge 94 F6
Bowling Green 227 K2
Boyatt Wood 81 L3
Braishfield 51 H1
Brambridge 54 C8
Bramdean 31 H3
Bramshaw 101 L4
Breach 167 H7
Breamore 71 M7
Bridgemary 184 F5
Broad Chalke 40 A1
Broadgate 52 D6
Broadoak 134 C1
Brockbridge 87 H6
Brockenhurst 175 J7
Brockhampton 8 A7
Brockhurst 209 H2
Brook 22 B2
Brook 101 M7
Brooke's Hill 104 A4
Brook Hill 101 M6
Brown Heath 110 B3
Bucket Corner 80 B1
Buckland 228 A3
Bucklers Hard 205 G3
Bull Hill 202 F7
Bunker's Hill 102 F6
Bunstead 53 H2
Burgates 36 D2
Buriton 91 K3
Burley 172 F5
Burley Beacon 172 C6
Burley Lawn 173 G5
Burley Street 172 C3
Burridge 134 F7
Bursledon 133 L8
Butlocks Heath 157 H1
Buttsash 155 M8
Butt's Green 20 F7
Cadnam 102 E8
Calmore 104 B7
Calshot 181 K8
Camel Green 121 M2
Canada 76 C7
Canford Cliffs 245 J1
Carter's Clay 48 F2
Catherington 115 M7
Catisfield 159 L7
Causeway 63 K6
Causeway 140 F3
Chalton 117 H3
Chandler's Ford 53 J8
Charlton-All-Saints 44 E4
Cheriton 30 C3
Chidden 88 E8
Chilbolton 27 L3
Chilcomb 28 C7
Chilworth 80 C7
Chilworth Old Village 80 B6
Chithurst 66 F5
Church Common 35 G8
Clanfield 115 M2

Clayhall 11 G8
Clayhill 151 L5
Colbury 129 H6
Colden Common 54 F7
Colehill 192 D1
Compton 22 B1
Compton 54 C1
Compton 118 E6
Compton End 26 B7
Coombe 88 E2
Copnor 187 L7
Copythorne 103 H6
Corfe Mullen 217 G2
Corhampton 87 G3
Cosham 163 L8
Cowesfield Green 47 H5
Cowplain 140 D5
Coxford 105 M6
Crab Orchard 144 C6
Crampmoor 51 K7
Cranborne 94 C8
Crendell 120 D1
Criddlestyle 98 A7
Cripplestyle 120 E3
Critchell's Green 20 D8
Crockerhill 160 E1
Croucheston 40 F1
Crow 171 G4
Crowdhill 83 H3
Cupernham 50 F7
Curbridge 135 H4
Curdridge 110 D8
Custards 151 L3
Daggons 120 F3
Damerham 96 C3
Dean 85 K5
Deanlane End 142 B3
Denmead 139 K3
Denvilles 9 L2
Dewlands Common 144 B3
Dibden 155 H3
Dibden Purlieu 155 G7
Dilton 202 D1
Downton 73 G1
Downton 241 L1
Drayton 164 A3
Droxford 87 G7
Dumpford 66 D8
Dunbridge 21 H7
Dundridge 86 A7
Durleighmarsh 64 F5
Durley 110 A2
Durley Street 84 B8
Durns Town 201 G6
Durrants 141 M8
East Boldre 204 B3
East Dean 19 M6
East End 60 C3
East End 229 M1
East Grimstead 18 B4
East Harting 93 J5
Eastland Gate 140 B3
Eastleigh 82 A5
East Liss 37 G5
East Marden 119 L6
East Martin 69 H4
East Meon 61 J8
Eastney 212 A5
Easton 17 M3
East Tytherley 20 D1
East Wellow 76 F3
Ebblake 145 H4
Eling 129 M3
Ellingham 146 C3
Elmers Marsh 39 K3
Elson 185 L8
Elsted 93 M4
Emery Down 151 H2
Emsworth 190 C1
Everton 227 J7
Exbury 205 M3
Exton 87 H1
Fair Oak 83 H6
Fareham 6 F5
Farlington 164 B8
Fawley 180 F6
Ferndown 193 M3
Filmore Hill 32 F4
Finchdean 142 B2
Fisher's Pond 83 G2
Fleet 189 K8
Fleetend 158 D7
Fleetlands 185 G3
Flexford 52 E8
Flood Street 97 L1
Fordingbridge 97 M7
Forest Gate 139 H1
Forestside 142 F2
Forton 209 M2
Foulford 171 L1
Foxhills 129 H5
Foyers 128 A5
Freemantle 131 G2
The Frenches 49 G6
Frenchmoor 19 L3
Fritham 100 E7
Frogham 123 J2
Frostlane 156 A6
Froxfield Green 34 B8
Fryern Hill 81 J2
Fulflood 2 B6
Funtley 160 C3
Furzedown 23 G1
Furze Hill 123 J5
Furzeley Corner 139 K7
Furzey 126 E5
Furzey Lodge 177 M7
Furzley 102 C3
Fyning 65 M3
Glebe 111 H5
Godshill 98 D6
Goldenhayes 127 M4
Golden Hill 226 B5
Goose Green 151 L4
Gosport 11 H2
Gosport 51 M6
Gotham 120 C5

Grange Estate 169 K8
The Green 20 A1
Habin 65 L6
Hale 73 G7
Halecommon 65 K3
Halterworth 79 H1
Hambledon 114 B6
Hamble-le-Rice 157 K5
Hambrook 167 L6
Hampton Park 107 H5
Hamptworth 74 F4
Hamworthy 232 D5
Hangersley 147 J6
Harbridge 122 C7
Harbridge Green 122 B6
Hardley 180 A2
Hardway 209 M1
Harefield 133 G1
Harestock 16 B5
Hatch Bottom 108 C6
Hatchet Gate 177 M8
Hatchet Green 73 H5
Hatt Hill 21 J7
Havant 8 E1
Hawkley 35 K1
Hayling Island 189 L6
Headbourne Worthy 16 E3
Heathfield 160 A7
Hedge End 133 M1
Hensting 55 J7
Hermitage 166 E7
Hides Close 178 D4
Highbridge 82 C1
Highbury 187 K2
Highcliffe 224 E8
High Cross 34 E6
Highfield 106 F6
Hightown 133 J4
Hightown 171 H2
Highwood 147 H4
Hill Brow 37 H6
Hill Head 183 K7
Hill Park 6 A1
Hillpound 112 B4
Hill Side 36 F4
Hillstreet 104 A3
Hill Top 179 G4
Hill View 217 H4
Hillyfields 105 H4
Hilsea 187 K4
Hiltingbury 53 J6
Hinton 224 E4
Hinton Ampner 30 D4
Hocombe 53 H5
Hoe 111 L1
Hoe Gate 138 D1
Holbury 180 A5
Hook 182 C1
Hook Park 182 B2
Hooksway 119 M3
Hordle 226 E4
Horndean 141 G2
Horton Common 144 A6
Horton Heath 109 J1
Hound 157 J2
Hounsdown 129 J4
Hungerford 123 G3
Hursley 53 G1
Hyde 3 H5
Hyde 123 G2
Hythe 155 M4
Ibsley 146 E1
Iping 67 H6
Itchen 132 C5
Kents Oak 49 K3
Keyhaven 242 F5
Kilmeston 30 C7
Kimbridge 21 K8
Kingsmead 112 B8
Kingston 170 C7
Kingston 211 K1
Kings Worthy 17 H2
Knapp 52 C4
Ladwell 53 G4
Lake 232 C7
Landford 75 J4
Landfordwood 75 J1
Lane End 29 H8
Lane End 33 J1
Langdown 155 M5
Langley 37 L2
Langley 206 B1
Langrish 62 B4
Langstone 189 J2
Leagreen 226 E8
Lee 78 F8
Lee Ground 159 L3
Lee-on-the-Solent 208 A2
Leigh Park 165 H4
Lepe 206 E6
Lilliput 245 H1
Linford 147 L6
Linwood 123 M8
Liss 36 F5
Liss Forest 36 E1
Little Holbury 179 M3
Little Posbrook 183 J3
Littleton 16 A3
Lockerley 20 D7
Locks Heath 158 F4
London Minstead 127 G4
Long Common 109 L7
Lord's Hill 105 M4
Lordswood 106 C4
Lovedean 140 C2
Lover 73 L3
Lower Bordean 61 M2
Lower Brook 22 A4
Lower Buckland 228 C3
Lower Burgate 97 L4
Lower Daggons 120 E1
Lower Holwell 120 B2
Lower Pennington 228 A8
Lower Ratley 49 L5
Lower Slackstead 51 L1
Lower Swanwick 134 A8
Lower Turmer 146 B1
Lower Upham 84 C4

Lowford 133 L7
Lumley 166 E7
Lymington 228 B4
Lymore 242 E2
Lyndhurst 151 J3
Malwood 126 E4
Marchwood 130 C6
Martin 69 H5
Martin Drove End 68 B1
Maybush 105 K6
Mead End 139 L5
Mead End 200 C7
Meon 183 J5
Merry Oak 132 C3
Meyrick Park 14 C1
Michelmersh 22 B7
Midanbury 107 L8
Milford on Sea 242 A5
Milland 38 D6
Millbrook 130 C1
Milton 212 A4
Minstead 126 F5
The Mint 36 F3
Mockbeggar 147 H1
Moorcourt 104 B1
Moorgreen 108 E5
Moortown 170 E3
Morestead 27 L8
Morgan's Vale 73 H1
Mottisfont 21 K6
Mount Sorrel 40 A2
Netley 156 F2
Netley Hill 133 L4
Netley Marsh 128 E2
Newbridge 102 D5
New Brighton 166 E5
New Cheriton 30 C4
Newgrounds 98 F6
New Milton 225 J4
Newton 46 E6
Newtown 49 G4
Newtown 84 E8
Newtown 126 F6
New Town 132 E7
Newtown 138 A2
Newtown 182 B1
Nob's Crook 82 F1
No Man's Land 17 L8
Nomansland 75 J8
Norleywood 203 K8
North Baddesley 79 M4
North Boarhunt 137 L6
Northbrook 85 H7
North Charford 73 H4
North End 30 B1
North End 96 B3
North End 187 K6
Northfields 54 F1
North Gorley 122 F5
North Hayling 189 M5
North Kingston 171 G6
North Marden 119 L4
Northney 190 A4
North Poulner 147 H6
North Stoneham 107 J1
North Street 72 A6
North Weirs 175 G7
Nursling 105 H3
Nursted 92 B1
Nutbourne 191 K1
Nutburn 80 A3
Nyewood 65 K8
Oakshott 35 J4
Ocean Village 5 K7
Ogdens 123 K3
Old Milton 225 J7
Old Netley 133 J7
Old Portsmouth 12 C3
Old Shirley 105 M7
Oliver's Battery 25 M5
Ossemsley 199 J7
Otterbourne 54 A4
Otterwood 179 H8
Outwick 71 K8
Ower 103 K2
Owslebury 55 M5
Park Gate 158 F3
Paulsgrove 162 E8
Peartree Green 132 B4
Peel Common 184 D6
Pennington 228 A6
Pentridge 68 A8
Petersfield 63 J5
Picket Hill 147 L8
Pikeshill 151 J2
Pilley 202 F6
Pilley Bailey 202 D6
Pitt 25 M3
Plaitford 75 M4
Plaitford Green 48 B8
Pooksgreen 130 B6
Portchester 161 M8
Portmore 228 E1
Portsea 12 E1
Portsea Island 187 M8
Portswood 107 G7
Post Green 216 B8
Poulner 147 H8
Prince's Marsh 36 F6
Prinsted 191 C1
Privett 33 H6
Privett 209 J5
Pucknall 51 L2
Purbrook 164 B3
Pylehill 83 H5
Queen's Corner 39 H8
Rake 37 K4
Ramsdean 62 B7
Ratlake 52 D5
Redbridge 105 H8
Redford 39 K7
Red Hill 141 M7
Redlynch 73 K2
Ridge 216 D8
Ridge Common 63 H3
Ringwood 146 C8
Robins 66 F1
Rockbourne 70 D7

Rockford 147 G3
Rogate 65 K5
Romsey 78 D1
Round Hill 176 D8
Row Ash 110 F8
Rowland's Castle 142 A6
Rowner 185 G8
Rownhams 105 L1
Rushcombe Bottom 217 J1
Rushington 129 K2
Rushmore 114 D6
St Austins 201 M8
St Cross 26 E5
St Denys 107 H8
St Giles's Hill 3 K8
St Ives 169 L3
St Leonards 169 J4
Sandbanks 245 H5
Sandford 171 G8
Sandleheath 96 E6
Sandy Down 202 A4
Sarisbury 158 C3
Setley 201 L3
Shawford 54 D1
Shedfield 136 B1
Sheet 64 A3
Sherfield English 48 C7
Shirley 106 C8
Shirley Holms 201 L7
Shirley Warren 106 A6
Shirrell Heath 111 M7
Shobley 147 L7
Sholing 132 F4
Sholing Common 132 E3
Shootash 49 J7
Shorley 30 A7
Shorn Hill 103 M5
Silkstead 53 K3
Sleepers Hill 26 C2
Soake 139 M5
Soberton 113 H2
Soberton Heath 112 F7
Southampton 4 F7
South Baddesley 229 J2
Southbourne 167 J8
South Down 54 C3
South End 96 B5
South Gorley 122 F6
South Harting 92 F4
South Hayling 213 J6
South Weirs 175 H8
Southwick 162 C2
Spearywell 21 J5
Springbourne 15 M1
Stamshaw 186 F7
Standon 24 F6
Stanmore 26 C3
Stapehill 193 J3
Stedham 67 K7
Steep 63 K1
Steep Marsh 35 M7
Stockheath 165 J5
Stoke 189 L7
Stoke Common 82 B3
Stonehills 181 G6
Stoner Hill 35 C8
Stoney Cross 126 C4
Stonyford 103 L4
Stonymarsh 21 M7
Street End 85 H4
Stroud 62 F4
Stubbermere 142 E8
Stubbington 184 B5
Stuckton 123 C1
Swanmore 112 A3
Swanwick 158 E1
Sway 200 E7
Swaythling 107 K5
Tapnage 136 A7
Terwick Common 66 A3
Testwood 104 D6
Thorney Hill 198 C4
Thorney Island 191 G5
Thornhill 133 J3
Thornhill Park 133 H1
Thorns Beach 230 F2
Three Legged Cross 144 C8
Tidpit 69 J6
Timsbury 50 B1
Tipner 186 F5
Tiptoe 200 B8
Titchfield 159 J8
Titchfield Common 158 E7
Titchfield Park 159 H5
Titty Hill 39 H8
Toothill 79 K7
Tote Hill 67 K3
Totton 104 F8
Townhill Park 107 L6
Trickett's Cross 194 D1
Trotten Marsh 66 B1
Trotton 66 D7
Trotts 130 A5
Tullecombe 37 K8
Turkey Island 93 H5
Turkey Island 136 D1
Turlin Moor 232 A4
Turmer 122 B8
Twyford 54 F2
Tye 190 A7
Upham 84 E2
Up Marden 119 J8
Upper Burgate 97 M2
Upper Canterton 126 D2
Upper Pennington 227 L5
Upper Ratley 49 L4
Upper Shirley 106 C6
Upper Slackstead 23 M7
Upper Street 71 L6
Upper Swanmore 86 B8
Upper Wardley 38 F3
Upton 105 J1
Upton 232 A1
Verwood 144 D2
Walhampton 228 D3
Walkford 224 F7
Wallington 7 M4
Waltham Chase 111 K5

Walton Heath	162 A1	West Cliff	14 B8	Weston	63 C8	Wildern	134 A1	Woodlands	128 C5
Warblington	9 L6	West Common	206 C2	Weston	132 C7	Wimborne Minster	192 A3	Woodley	51 H7
Wardley	38 F4	West Dean	19 J5	Weston Common	132 F4	Wimpson	105 K7	Woodmancote	167 K4
Warnford	59 K4	West End	6 E8	West Thorney	191 H6	Winchester	3 G9	Woodmansgreen	39 K5
Warren Corner	34 F3	West End	108 D8	West Tisted	32 D1	Winnall	3 L6	Woodside	228 C7
Warsash	158 B7	West Harting	92 F1	West Wellow	76 D5	Winsor	103 J7	Woolbeding	67 L6
Waterford	228 E6	West Leigh	165 L3	Whitenap	79 H1	Wintershill	84 C7	Woolsbridge	168 E1
Waterlooville	140 D8	West Liss	36 E3	Whiteparish	46 F4	Wittensford	102 C3	Woolston	132 C6
Wecock	140 C4	West Marden	118 D8	Whitsbury	70 F5	Wick	72 B1	Wootton	199 L6
Weeke	2 B4	West Meon	60 A4	Wick	72 B1	Wickham	136 E5	Worlds End	138 D3
Wellow Wood	48 C8	West Meon Woodlands	32 B6	Wickham	136 E5	Widley	164 A6	Wymering	163 J8
Westbourne	166 F4	West Moors	168 E6	Widley	164 A6				

USING THE STREET INDEX

Street names are listed alphabetically. Each street name is followed by its postal town or area locality, the Postcode District, the page number, and the reference to the square in which the name is found.

Abbey Cl *FAWY* SO45 .... 155 L5 🔢

Some entries are followed by a number in a blue box. This number indicates the location of the street within the referenced grid square. The full street name is listed at the side of the map page.

GENERAL ABBREVIATIONS

ACC	ACCESS	CUTT	CUTTINGS	HOL	HOLLOW	NW	NORTH WEST	SKWY	SKYWAY
ALY	ALLEY	CV	COVE	HOSP	HOSPITAL	O/P	OVERPASS	SMT	SUMMIT
AP	APPROACH	CYN	CANYON	HRB	HARBOUR	OFF	OFFICE	SOC	SOCIETY
AR	ARCADE	DEPT	DEPARTMENT	HTH	HEATH	ORCH	ORCHARD	SP	SPUR
ASS	ASSOCIATION	DL	DALE	HTS	HEIGHTS	OV	OVAL	SPR	SPRING
AV	AVENUE	DM	DAM	HVN	HAVEN	PAL	PALACE	SQ	SQUARE
BCH	BEACH	DR	DRIVE	HWY	HIGHWAY	PAS	PASSAGE	ST	STREET
BLDS	BUILDINGS	DRO	DROVE	IMP	IMPERIAL	PAV	PAVILION	STN	STATION
BND	BEND	DRY	DRIVEWAY	IN	INLET	PDE	PARADE	STR	STREAM
BNK	BANK	DWGS	DWELLINGS	IND EST	INDUSTRIAL ESTATE	PH	PUBLIC HOUSE	STRD	STRAND
BR	BRIDGE	E	EAST	INF	INFIRMARY	PK	PARK	SW	SOUTH WEST
BRK	BROOK	EMB	EMBANKMENT	INFO	INFORMATION	PKWY	PARKWAY	TDG	TRADING
BTM	BOTTOM	EMBY	EMBASSY	INT	INTERCHANGE	PL	PLACE	TER	TERRACE
BUS	BUSINESS	ESP	ESPLANADE	IS	ISLAND	PLN	PLAIN	THWY	THROUGHWAY
BVD	BOULEVARD	EST	ESTATE	JCT	JUNCTION	PLNS	PLAINS	TNL	TUNNEL
BY	BYPASS	EX	EXCHANGE	JTY	JETTY	PLZ	PLAZA	TOLL	TOLLWAY
CATH	CATHEDRAL	EXPY	EXPRESSWAY	KG	KING	POL	POLICE STATION	TPK	TURNPIKE
CEM	CEMETERY	EXT	EXTENSION	KNL	KNOLL	PR	PRINCE	TR	TRACK
CEN	CENTRE	F/O	FLYOVER	L	LAKE	PREC	PRECINCT	TRL	TRAIL
CFT	CROFT	FC	FOOTBALL CLUB	LA	LANE	PREP	PREPARATORY	TWR	TOWER
CH	CHURCH	FK	FORK	LDG	LODGE	PRIM	PRIMARY	U/P	UNDERPASS
CHA	CHASE	FLD	FIELD	LGT	LIGHT	PROM	PROMENADE	UNI	UNIVERSITY
CHYD	CHURCHYARD	FLDS	FIELDS	LK	LOCK	PRS	PRINCESS	UPR	UPPER
CIR	CIRCLE	FLS	FALLS	LKS	LAKES	PRT	PORT	V	VALE
CIRC	CIRCUS	FLTS	FLATS	LNDG	LANDING	PT	POINT	VA	VALLEY
CL	CLOSE	FM	FARM	LTL	LITTLE	PTH	PATH	VIAD	VIADUCT
CLFS	CLIFFS	FT	FORT	LWR	LOWER	PZ	PIAZZA	VIL	VILLA
CMP	CAMP	FWY	FREEWAY	MAG	MAGISTRATE	QD	QUADRANT	VIS	VISTA
CNR	CORNER	FY	FERRY	MAN	MANSIONS	QU	QUEEN	VLG	VILLAGE
CO	COUNTY	GA	GATE	MD	MEAD	QY	QUAY	VLS	VILLAS
COLL	COLLEGE	GAL	GALLERY	MDW	MEADOWS	R	RIVER	VW	VIEW
COM	COMMON	GDN	GARDEN	MEM	MEMORIAL	RBT	ROUNDABOUT	W	WEST
COMM	COMMISSION	GDNS	GARDENS	MKT	MARKET	RD	ROAD	WD	WOOD
CON	CONVENT	GLD	GLADE	MKTS	MARKETS	RDG	RIDGE	WHF	WHARF
COT	COTTAGE	GLN	GLEN	ML	MALL	REP	REPUBLIC	WK	WALK
COTS	COTTAGES	GN	GREEN	ML	MILL	RES	RESERVOIR	WKS	WALKS
CP	CAPE	GND	GROUND	MNR	MANOR	RFC	RUGBY FOOTBALL CLUB	WLS	WELLS
CPS	COPSE	GRA	GRANGE	MS	MEWS	RI	RISE	WY	WAY
CR	CREEK	GRG	GARAGE	MSN	MISSION	RP	RAMP	YD	YARD
CREM	CREMATORIUM	GT	GREAT	MT	MOUNT	RW	ROW	YHA	YOUTH HOSTEL
CRS	CRESCENT	GTWY	GATEWAY	MTN	MOUNTAIN	S	SOUTH		
CSWY	CAUSEWAY	GV	GROVE	MTS	MOUNTAINS	SCH	SCHOOL		
CT	COURT	HGR	HIGHER	MUS	MUSEUM	SE	SOUTH EAST		
CTRL	CENTRAL	HL	HILL	MWY	MOTORWAY	SER	SERVICE AREA		
CTS	COURTS	HLS	HILLS	N	NORTH	SH	SHORE		
CTYD	COURTYARD	HO	HOUSE	NE	NORTH EAST	SHOP	SHOPPING		

POSTCODE TOWNS AND AREA ABBREVIATIONS

ALTN	Alton	ENEY	Eastney	ITCH	Itchen	PSEA	Portsea	TOTT	Totton
BDST	Broadstone	EPSF	Petersfield East	LIPH	Liphook	PSF	Petersfield	TWDS	Talbot Woods
BKME/WDN	Branksome/Wallisdown	FAWY	Fawley/Hythe	LISS	Liss	PSTN	Parkstone	UPTN	Upton
BMTH	Bournemouth	FBDG	Fordingbridge	LSOL/BMARY	Lee-on-the-Solent/Bridgemary	PTSW	Portswood	VWD	Verwood
BOSC	Boscombe	FERN	Ferndown/West Moors			RCCH	Rural Chichester	WBNE	Westbourne
BPWT	Bishop's Waltham	FHAM	Fareham	LTDN	Littledown	RGWD	Ringwood	WCLF	West Cliff
BROC	Brockenhurst	FHAM/PORC	Fareham/Portchester	LYMN	Lymington	ROMY	Romsey	WEND	West End
BWD	Bearwood	FHAM/STUB	Fareham/Stubbington	LYND	Lyndhurst	RWNH	Rownhams	WHAM	Wickham
CCLF	Canford Cliffs	GPORT	Gosport	MIDH	Midhurst	RSAL	Rural Salisbury	WIMB	Wimborne Minster
CFDH	Canford Heath	HASM	Haslemere	MOOR/WNTN	Moordown/Winton	RWIN	Rural Winchester	WINC	Winchester
CHAM	Cosham	HAV	Havant	NALR	New Alresford	SBNE	Southbourne	WINW	Winchester west
CHAR	Charminster	HEND	Hedge End	NBAD	North Baddesley	SELS	Selsey	WSHM	Southampton west
CHCH/BSGR	Christchurch/Bransgore	HISD	Hayling Island	NBNE	Northbourne	SHAM	Southampton	WVILLE	Waterlooville/Denmead
CHFD	Chandler's Ford	HLER	Hamble-le-Rice	NEND	North End	SSEA	Southsea		
ELGH	Eastleigh	HORN	Horndean	NMIL/BTOS	New Milton/Barton on Sea	STOK	Stockbridge		
EMRTH	Emsworth/Southbourne	HSEA	Hilsea	PLE	Poole	SWGE	Swanage		

Index - streets

10th - Ake

10th St *FAWY* SO45	180 B4	*FHAM* PO15	6 B4
11th St *FAWY* SO45	180 B3	Abbey Water *ROMY* SO51	78 D1 🔢
12th St *FAWY* SO45	180 B3	Abbotsbury Rd *BDST* BH18	217 J3
13th St *FAWY* SO45	180 B2	Abinger Rd *LTDN* BH7	236 F2
14th St *FAWY* SO45	180 A3	Abney Rd *NBNE* BH10	220 B5
1st St *FAWY* SO45	180 E5	Above Bar St *SHAM* SO14	4 F1
2nd St *FAWY* SO45	180 E4	Abraham Cl *HEND* SO30	134 B3
3rd St *FAWY* SO45	180 D4	Abshot Cl *FHAM/STUB* PO14	158 F7
4th St *FAWY* SO45	180 D4	Abshot Rd *FHAM/STUB* PO14	158 F7
5th St *FAWY* SO45	180 D3	Acacia Av *VWD* BH31	145 G4
6th St *FAWY* SO45	180 D2	Acacia Gdns *HORN* PO8	140 F3
7th St *FAWY* SO45	180 C4	Acacia Rd *ITCH* SO19	132 D3
8th St *FAWY* SO45	180 B4	Acer Wy *HAV* PO9	165 M4
9th St *FAWY* SO45	180 B4	Ackworth Rd *HSEA* PO3	187 L3
		Acland Rd *MOOR/WNTN* BH9	220 F8
A		Acorn Cl *CHAM* PO6	164 C8 🔢
		CHCH/BSGR BH23	222 D8
Aaron Cl *CFDH* BH17	233 L1	*FUFL* SO22	2 A3
Aaron Ct *TOTT* SO40	130 D6	*LSOL/BMARY* PO13	185 H7
A Av *FAWY* SO45	180 B3	*NMIL/BTOS* BH25	226 A4 🔢
Abbey Cl *FAWY* SO45	155 L5 🔢	*RGWD* BH24	169 J5
Abbeydore Rd *CHAM* PO6	163 G7	*TOTT* SO40	130 C1 🔢
Abbeyfield Dr *FHAM* PO15	160 A6	Acorn Ct *HLER* SO31	157 K5 🔢
Abbey Gdns *WIMB* BH21	193 H3	Acorn Dr *ROWN* SO16	105 M4
Abbey Hl *ITCH* SO19	132 C8	Acorn Gv *NBAD* SO52	80 E4
Abbey Hill Cl *WINC* SO23	3 G3	The Acorns *HLER* SO31	133 K8
Abbey Hill Rd *WINC* SO23	2 F3	*WIMB* BH21	192 E4
Abbey Rd *FERN* BH22	168 E8	Acorn Wy *VWD* BH31	144 E2 🔢
		Acre La *HORN* PO8	141 G7
Abbey Cl *FAWY* SO45	155 L5 🔢	Acres Rd *BWD* BH11	219 M6
Abbeydore Rd *CHAM* PO6	163 G7	Acton Rd *NBNE* BH10	219 M7
Abbeyfield Dr *FHAM* PO15	160 A6	Adair Rd *ENEY* PO4	211 L6
Abbey Gdns *WIMB* BH21	193 H3	Adames Rd *PSEA* PO1	211 J2
Abbey Hl *ITCH* SO19	132 C8	Adams Cl *HEND* SO30	109 G5
Abbey Hill Cl *WINC* SO23	3 G3	Adamsfield Gdns	
Abbey Hill Rd *WINC* SO23	2 F3	*NBNE* BH10	220 A6 🔢
Abbey Rd *FERN* BH22	168 E8	Adamson Cl *CHFD* SO53	53 J8
Abbotsfield *TOTT* SO40	129 J1	Adams Rd *FAWY* SO45	155 L6
Abbotsfield Cl *ROWN* SO16	106 B3	Adams Wood Dr *TOTT* SO40	130 D7
Abbotsford *TOTT* SO40	127 M2	Adastral Rd *CFDH* BH17	233 K1 🔢
Abbotstone Av *HAV* PO9	165 L4	Adderbury Av *EMRTH* PO10	166 D4
Abbots Wy *FHAM* PO15	6 A5	Addington Pl	
HLER SO31	157 H2	*CHCH/BSGR* BH23	238 C2 🔢
Abbots Well Rd *FBDG* SP6	123 K1	Addiscombe Rd	
Abbotswood Cl *ROMY* SO51	51 H7 🔢	*CHCH/BSGR* BH23	237 M1 🔢
Abbott Rd *MOOR/WNTN* BH9	220 F8	Addison Rd *BROC* SO42	175 K8
Abbotts Ann Rd *FUFL* SO22	16 C5	*ELGH* SO50	82 A3 🔢
Abbotts Cl *WINC* SO23	3 H2	*ENEY* PO4	13 L5
Abbotts Dro *ROMY* SO51	29 K4	*FUFL* SO22	26 B3
Abbotts Rd *ELGH* SO50	81 K7	Addison Sq *RGWD* BH24	170 D5
Abbotts Wy *FERN* BH22	168 E8	Adela Verne Cl *ITCH* SO19	133 J3 🔢
		Adela Verne Cl *ITCH* SO19	133 J3 🔢
Abercrombie Gdns		Adela Verne Cl *ITCH* SO19	133 J3 🔢
ROWN SO16	105 M4	Adeline Rd *BMTH* BH1	236 D4
Aberdare Av *CHAM* PO6	163 M7	Adey Cl *ITCH* SO19	132 F6
Aberdare Rd *NBNE* BH10	220 C5	Adhurst Rd *HAV* PO9	165 L4
Aberdeen Cl *FHAM* PO15	6 D2	Adlam's La *LYMN* SO41	200 D5
Aberdeen Rd *PTSW* SO17	107 H7	Admirals Cl *FAWY* SO45	180 F5 🔢
Abingdon Dr		Admirals Rd *HLER* SO31	158 F4
CHCH/BSGR BH23	225 G8	Admirals Wk *GPORT* PO12	10 A4
Abingdon Gdns *ROWN* SO16	106 D5 🔢	Admiralty Rd *PSEA* PO1	12 C1
Abingdon Rd *CFDH* BH17	218 B7	*SBNE* BH6	237 L5 🔢
		Admiralty Wy *TOTT* SO40	130 D5
		Adsdean Cl *HAV* PO9	165 J4 🔢
		Adstone La *HSEA* PO3	188 A4 🔢
		Adur Cl *GPORT* PO12	209 K1 🔢
		WEND SO18	108 A7
		Aerial Rd *CHAM* PO6	162 F6
		Aerodrome Rd	
		LSOL/BMARY PO13	185 H4
		Africa Dr *TOTT* SO40	130 D7
		Agars La *LYMN* SO41	226 E1
		LYMN SO41	226 F3
		Agarton La *LYMN* SO41	242 E2
		Aggis Farm Rd *VWD* BH31	144 C2
		Agitor Rd *FAWY* SO45	181 G3
		Agnew Rd *LSOL/BMARY* PO13	185 G5
		Aikman La *TOTT* SO40	128 F1
		Ailsa La *ITCH* SO19	132 B4
		Ainsdale Rd *CHAM* PO6	164 B7
		Ainsley Gdns *ELGH* SO50	81 M3
		Aintree Cl *ELGH* SO50	109 J1 🔢
		Aintree Dr *WVILLE* PO7	140 F7
		Aintree Rd *TOTT* SO40	104 B7
		Airetons Cl *BDST* BH18	218 A5
		Airfield Rd *CHCH/BSGR* BH23	238 E1
		Airfield Wy *CHCH/BSGR* BH23	238 E1
		Airport Service Rd *HSEA* PO3	187 M5
		Ajax Cl *FHAM/STUB* PO14	184 B7
		Akeshill Cl *NMIL/BTOS* BH25	225 M3

Alameda Rd *WVILLE* PO7 .... 164 B4
Alameda Wy *WVILLE* PO7 .... 164 B4
Alandale Rd *ITCH* SO19 .... 133 H4
Alan Drayton Wy *ELGH* SO50 .... 82 D6
Alan Gv *FHAM* PO15 .... 6 C4
Albacore Av *HLER* SO31 .... 158 C7 🔢
Albany Cl *NMIL/BTOS* BH25 .... 225 K7
Albany Ct *BPWT* SO32 .... 84 F8
Albany Dr *BPWT* SO32 .... 84 F8
    WIMB BH21 .... 144 C8
Albany Gdns *PLE* BH15 .... 232 E6
Albany Rd *BPWT* SO32 .... 84 F8
    FAWY SO45 .... 180 A4
    ROMY SO51 .... 78 D1
    SSEA PO5 .... 13 J6
    WSHM SO15 .... 131 G2
Albatross Wk
    LSOL/BMARY PO13 .... 184 F6
Albemarle Av *GPORT* PO12 .... 209 K7
Albemarle Rd *TWDS* BH3 .... 235 L1
Albert Cl *HLER* SO31 .... 157 G3
Albert Rd *BKME/WDN* BH12 .... 234 J2
    BMTH BH1 .... 14 E5
    BPWT SO32 .... 111 G1
    CHAM PO6 .... 187 K1
    ELGH SO50 .... 82 A3
    FERN BH22 .... 194 B3
    FHAM/STUB PO14.. .... 184 D6
    HEND SO30 .... 133 M3
    NMIL/BTOS BH25 .... 225 K6
    SSEA PO5 .... 13 K7
    WIMB BH21 .... 217 H3
Albert Rd North *SHAM* SO14 .... 5 K5
Albert Rd South *SHAM* SO14 .... 5 K6
Albert St *GPORT* PO12 .... 11 G2
Albion Cl *FHAM/PORC* PO16.. 185 M2
Albion Pl *SHAM* SO14 .... 4 F4
Albion Rd *CHCH/BSGR* BH23 222 D7
    FBDC SP6 .... 97 L6
Albion Wy *VWD* BH31 .... 144 B2
Albury Pl *CHFD* SO53 .... 53 G7 🔢
Alby Rd *BKME/WDN* BH12 .... 234 E3
Alcantara Crs *SHAM* SO14 .... 5 K6
Alcester Rd *BKME/WDN* BH12.. 234 C2
Alder Cl *CHCH/BSGR* BH23 .... 223 H7
    FAWY SO45 .... 155 G5
    ROMY SO51 .... 79 J2
    RWIN SO21 .... 54 F8
    TOTT SO40 .... 130 D6
Alder Crs *BKME/WDN* BH12 .... 234 E1
Alder Dr *FBDC* SP6 .... 121 K3
Alderfield *PSF* GU32 .... 63 K5
Alder Hill Dr *TOTT* SO40 .... 104 A8
Alder Hills *BKME/WDN* BH12 .. 234 F1
    ROWN SO16 .... 105 L5
Alderholt Rd *FBDC* SP6 .... 96 F7
Alder La *LSOL/BMARY* PO13 .... 209 H3
Alderley Rd *NBNE* BH10 .... 220 B4
Aldermoor Av *ROWN* SO16 .... 105 M4
Aldermoor Cl *ROWN* SO16 .... 106 B4
Aldermoor Rd
    LSOL/BMARY PO13 .... 209 H1
    ROWN SO16 .... 105 M4
    WVILLE PO7 .... 164 B4
Aldermoor Rd East
    WVILLE PO7 .... 164 B3 🔢
Alderney Av *BKME/WDN* BH12 .. 219 H7
Alderney Cl *ROWN* SO16 .... 105 L5
Alder Rd *BKME/WDN* BH12 .... 219 L8
    ROWN SO16 .... 105 L5
Alders Rd *FHAM/PORC* PO16 .. 184 F1
Alderwood Av *CHFD* SO53 .... 80 F2
Alderwood Cl *HAV* PO9 .... 164 K5
Aldis Gdns *PLE* BH15 .... 232 D5 🔢
Aldrich Rd *PSEA* PO1 .... 210 E2
Aldridge Cl *HORN* PO8 .... 116 B3
Aldridge Rd *FERN* BH22 .... 194 C5
    NBNE BH10 .... 220 A3
Aldroke St *CHAM* PO6 .... 187 K1 🔢
Aldsworth Cl *CHAM* PO6 .... 164 A8
Aldsworth Gdns *CHAM* PO6 .... 164 A8 🔢
Aldwell St *SSEA* PO5 .... 13 J3 🔢
Alec Rose La *PSEA* PO1 .... 13 G2
Alecto Rd *GPORT* PO12 .... 10 E6
Alencon Cl *GPORT* PO12 .... 186 A8 🔢
Alexander Cl
    CHCH/BSGR BH23 .... 238 D2 🔢
    TOTT SO40 .... 104 C8
    WVILLE PO7 .... 164 B3 🔢
Alexander Gv
    FHAM/PORC PO16 .... 7 H8
Alexandra Av *HISD* PO11 .... 213 K6
Alexandra Cl *FAWY* SO45 .... 155 L4 🔢
Alexandra Ct *CHFD* SO53.. .... 53 L8
    FAWY SO45 .... 155 L4
    FBDC SP6 .... 97 L6
    HEND SO30 .... 133 M3
    LYMN SO41 .... 228 A3
    PSEA PO1 .... 211 H2
    PSTN BH14 .... 234 D4
    SBNE BH6 .... 237 G3
    WSHM SO15 .... 131 H2
Alexandra St *GPORT* PO12 209 L2 🔢
Alexandra Ter *WINC* SO23 .... 2 E9
Alexandra Wy *HEND* SO30 .... 134 E1
Alford Rd *TWDS* BH3 .... 235 J1
Alfred Cl *TOTT* SO40 .... 104 B8 🔢
    TOTT SO40 .... 129 G1 🔢
Alfred Rd *FHAM/STUB* PO14 .. 184 B5
    PSEA PO1 .... 12 F1
Alfred Rose Ct *WEND* SO18 .. 107 K4 🔢
Alfred St *SHAM* SO14 .... 131 M2
Alfrey Cl *EMRTH* PO10 .... 167 G8
Alfriston Gdns *ITCH* SO19 .... 132 F5
Algiers Rd *HSEA* PO3 .... 187 M8
Alhambra Rd *ENEY* PO4 .... 13 L9
Alington Cl *PSTN* BH14 .... 245 H1
Alington Rd *PSTN* BH14 .... 245 H1
    TWDS BH3 .... 235 M2
Alipore Cl *PSTN* BH14 .... 234 C5
Allaway Av *CHAM* PO6 .... 162 D8
Allbrook Hill *ELGH* SO50 .... 82 A1
Allbrook Knoll *ELGH* SO50 .... 81 M1
Allbrook Wy *ELGH* SO50 .... 53 M8
Allcot Rd *HSEA* PO3 .... 187 K6

Allenby Cl *CFDH* BH17 .... 217 M6 🔢
Allenby Gv *FHAM/PORC* PO16.. 186 A1
Allenby Rd *CFDH* BH17 .... 217 M7
    GPORT PO12 .... 209 J2
Allen Ct *WIMB* BH21 .... 192 A3
Allendale Av *EMRTH* PO10 .... 166 C5
Allen Rd *HEND* SO30 .... 134 A1
    WIMB BH21 .... 192 A4
Allens La *NMIL/BTOS* BH25 .... 226 B6
Allen's Rd *SSEA* PO5 .... 13 L7
    UPTN BH16 .... 232 C3
Allenview Rd *WIMB* BH21 .... 192 A3
Allerton Cl *TOTT* SO40 .... 104 C7
The Alley *MIDH* GU29 .... 67 K7
Alliance Cl *LSOL/BMARY* PO13.. 185 H8
Allington La *HEND* SO30 .... 108 D3
Allington Rd *WSHM* SO15 .... 130 B1
Allmara Dr *WVILLE* PO7 .... 164 C3
Allotment Rd *HLER* SO31 .... 158 C3
All Saints Rd *LYMN* SO41 .... 228 C6
    PSEA PO1 .... 211 H1
Alma La *BPWT* SO32 .... 84 A1
Alma Rd *MOOR/WNTN* BH9 .. 235 M1
    ROMY SO51 .... 78 C1
    SHAM SO14 .... 106 F8
Alma St *GPORT* PO12 .... 209 L2
Almatade Rd *WEND* SO18 .... 132 E1
Almer Rd *PLE* BH15 .... 232 D5
    HORN PO8 .... 141 G4
Almond Cl *CHAM* PO6 .... 164 D8
Almond Gv *BKME/WDN* BH12 .. 234 C1
Almond Rd *WSHM* SO15 .... 131 G3
Almondsbury Rd *CHAM* PO6 .. 162 D6
Almondside
    LSOL/BMARY PO13 .... 185 J7
Alpine Cl *WEND* SO18 .... 108 A3
Alpine Rd *RGWD* BH24 .... 170 A6
    TOTT SO40 .... 128 D5
Alresford Rd *HAV* PO9 .... 165 J4 🔢
    RWIN SO21 .... 27 L1
    WINC SO23 .... 3 L8
Alsford Rd *WVILLE* PO7 .... 164 B3
Alten Rd *WVILLE* PO7 .... 140 A6
Althorpe Dr *HSEA* PO3 .... 188 A4
Alton Cl *ELGH* SO50 .... 83 G6
Alton Gv *FHAM/PORC* PO16 .. 186 A2
Alton Rd *NBNE* BH10 .... 219 M7
    PSTN BH14.. .... 234 A5
Alton Rd East *PSTN* BH14 .... 234 C6
Alum Chine Rd *WBNE* BH4 .. 235 H7
Alum Cl *FAWY* SO45 .... 180 B5
Alumdale Rd *WBNE* BH4 .... 235 H7
Alumhurst Rd *WBNE* BH4 .... 235 G6
Alum Wy *FHAM/PORC* PO16 .. 161 J7
    WEND SO18 .... 132 F1
Alvara Rd *GPORT* PO12 .... 10 D7
Alvercliffe Dr *GPORT* PO12 .... 10 B8
Alver Rd *GPORT* PO12 .... 10 F5
    PSEA PO1 .... 211 J2
Alverstone Rd *ENEY* PO4 .... 211 L4
Alverton Av *PLE* BH15 .... 233 L5
Alveston Av *FHAM/STUB* PO14.. 160 A8
Alyth Rd *TWDS* BH3.. .... 235 H2
Amarylis Cl *FHAM* PO15 .... 159 J4
Ambassador Cl
    CHCH/BSGR BH23 .... 238 F2 🔢
Amberley Cl *CHCH/BSGR* BH23.. 224 C8
    HEND SO30 .... 109 L8
    NBAD SO52 .... 79 K3
Amberley Ct *TOTT* SO40 .... 129 J2
Amberley Rd *GPORT* PO12 .... 185 L8
    HORN PO8 .... 116 C3
    NEND PO2 .... 187 K5
Amber Rd *WIMB* BH21 .... 217 G4
Amberslade Wk *FAWY* SO45.. 155 K7
Amberwood Cl *FERN* BH22 .. 194 C1 🔢
Amberwood Ct *TOTT* SO40.. .. 104 B6
Amberwood Dr
    CHCH/BSGR BH23 .... 224 E6
Amberwood Gdns
    CHCH/BSGR BH23 .... 224 E6
Ambledale *HLER* SO31 .... 158 C4
Ambleside *CHCH/BSGR* BH23 .. 222 B5
    HEND SO30 .... 134 B1
Ambleside Gdns *ITCH* SO19 .. 132 E5
Ambleside Rd *LYMN* SO41 .... 228 C6
Ambury La *CHCH/BSGR* BH23.. 223 K8
Amersham Cl *GPORT* PO12 .. 209 J4
Amesbury Rd *SBNE* BH6 .... 237 H2 🔢
Amethyst Gv *WVILLE* PO7 .... 140 F8
Amethyst Rd
    CHCH/BSGR BH23 .... 238 E1 🔢
Ameysford Rd *FERN* BH22.. .. 168 A7
Ameys La *FERN* BH22 .... 194 D1 🔢
Amoy St *WSHM* SO15 .... 131 K2
Ampfield Cl *HAV* PO9 .... 164 F4 🔢
Ampfield Rd *CHAR* BH8 .... 221 H5
Amport Cl *FUFL* SO22 .... 16 B5
Amport Ct *HAV* PO9 .... 165 H2
Ampthill Rd *WSHM* SO15 .... 130 F1
Amsterdam Sq
    CHCH/BSGR BH23 .... 238 C2 🔢
Amyas Ct *ENEY* PO4 .... 212 A4
Ancasta Rd *SHAM* SO14 .... 131 M1 🔢
Anchorage Rd *HSEA* PO3 .... 187 M5
The Anchorage *GPORT* PO12.. 11 H4
Anchor Cl *BWD* BH11 .... 219 K3
    CHCH/BSGR BH23 .... 238 F3 🔢
Anchor Ga *PSEA* PO1 .... 210 E2
Anchor La *PSEA* PO1 .... 210 E2
Anchor Ms *LYMN* SO41 .... 228 C6
Anchor Rd *BWD* BH11 .... 219 K3
Andalusian Gdns *HLER* SO31 .. 134 F8
Anderby Rd *ROWN* SO16 .... 105 J6
Andersen Cl *HLER* SO31 .... 135 G8
Anderson Cl *HAV* PO9 .... 9 G1
    ROMY SO51 .... 51 H6 🔢
Anderson's Rd *SHAM* SO14 .. 5 K5
Anderwood Dr *LYMN* SO41 .. 200 F6
Andes Cl *SHAM* SO14 .... 5 L6
Andes Rd *ROWN* SO16 .... 105 G5
Andlers Ash Rd *LISS* GU33 .... 36 C5
Andover Cl *CHCH/BSGR* BH23 .. 239 G1
Andover Rd *ENEY* PO4 .... 211 K6
    BOSC BH5 .... 236 D4
    FUFL SO22 .... 2 E2
Ariel Cl *SBNE* BH6 .... 238 A3

WSHM SO15 .... 131 H2
Andover Rd North *FUFL* SO22.. 16 B1
Andrew Bell St *PSEA* PO1 .... 211 G2 🔢
Andrew Cl *FAWY* SO45 .... 155 L7 🔢
    PSEA PO1 .... 211 K2
    TOTT SO40 .... 129 H1
Andrew Crs *WVILLE* PO7 .... 140 B7
Andrewes Cl *BPWT* SO32 .... 85 M8
Andrew La *NMIL/BTOS* BH25 .. 226 B6
Andrew Pl *FHAM/STUB* PO14.. 183 M6
Andromeda Rd *ROWN* SO16 .. 105 K4
Anfield Cl *ELGH* SO50 .... 83 H7
Angel Crs *ITCH* SO19 .... 132 D2
Angelica Gdns *ELGH* SO50 .... 109 H1
Angelica Wy *FHAM* PO15 .... 159 J8
Angeline Cl
    CHCH/BSGR BH23 .... 224 D8 🔢
Angel La *FERN* BH22 .... 193 M5
    NMIL/BTOS BH25 .... 226 B8
Angelo Cl *WVILLE* PO7 .... 140 E8
Angelus Cl *FHAM/STUB* PO14 .. 184 A6
Angerstein Rd *NEND* PO2 .... 187 H7
Anglers Wy *HLER* SO31 .... 134 B8
Anglesea Rd
    LSOL/BMARY PO13 .... 208 E4
    PSEA PO1 .... 12 F2
    WSHM SO15 .... 106 C7
Anglesea Ter *SHAM* SO14 .... 5 K5
Anglesey Arms Rd *GPORT* PO12.. 10 C8
Angus Cl *GPORT* PO12 .... 10 C8
Angus Cl *FHAM* PO15 .... 6 C2
Anjou Cl *BWD* BH11 .... 219 H3 🔢
Anjou Crs *FHAM* PO15.. .... 6 B4
Anker La *FHAM/STUB* PO14 .. 184 A4
Ankerwyke
    LSOL/BMARY PO13 .... 184 F7 🔢
Anmore Dr *WVILLE* PO7 .... 140 A4
Anmore La *WVILLE* PO7 .... 140 A4
Anmore Rd *WVILLE* PO7 .... 139 L4
Anna La *CHCH/BSGR* BH23 .... 196 E4
Anne Cl *CHCH/BSGR* BH23 .... 222 E7
Anne Crs *WVILLE* PO7 .... 164 C2
Annerley Rd *BMTH* BH1 .... 15 L4
Annet Cl *PLE* BH15 .... 232 D6
Ann's Hill Rd *GPORT* PO12 .... 10 C4
Anson Cl *CHCH/BSGR* BH23 .. 238 C2
    LSOL/BMARY PO13 .... 209 H3
    RGWD BH24 .... 147 G3
Anson Dr *ITCH* SO19 .... 133 G3
Anson Rd *ELGH* SO50 .... 109 H1
    ENEY PO4 .... 211 K3
Anstey Cl *BWD* BH11 .... 219 J3
Anstey Rd *BWD* BH11 .... 219 L3
    ROMY SO51 .... 51 G7
Antell's Wy *FBDC* SP6 .... 121 J2
Anthill Cl *WVILLE* PO7 .... 139 G2
Anthony Gv *GPORT* PO12 .... 185 K7
Anthony's Av *PSTN* BH14 .... 245 L1
Antler Dr *NMIL/BTOS* BH25 .. 225 J4
Anton Cl *ROMY* SO51 .... 79 H1
Anvil Cl *HORN* PO8 .... 141 G7
Anvil Crs *BDST* BH18 .... 217 J3
Anzac Cl *FHAM/STUB* PO14 .. 184 A4
Apless La *WVILLE* PO7 .... 138 C1
Apollo Cl *BKME/WDN* BH12 .. 234 C1 🔢
Apollo Dr *WVILLE* PO7 .... 164 D5
Apollo Rd *CHFD* SO53 .... 81 L1
Appleshaw Cl *FUFL* SO22 .... 16 C4
Appleslade Wy
    NMIL/BTOS BH25 .... 225 M3
Appleton Rd *FHAM* PO15 .... 160 A7
    HEND SO30 .... 108 E7
Apple Tree Cl *NMIL/BTOS* BH25.. 225 L7
    SBNE BH6 .... 237 H3 🔢
    TOTT SO40 .... 104 B8
Appletree Ct *HEND* SO30 .... 134 E1
Apple Tree Gv *FERN* BH22 .. 194 C3
Apple Tree Rd *FBDC* SP6 .... 121 K3
Appletree Rd *RSAL* SP5 .... 7 J4
Applewood Gdns *ITCH* SO19 ... 132 E5 🔢
Applewood Pl *WVILLE* PO7 .. 164 A6
Applewood Pl *TOTT* SO40 .... 129 G2
Applewood Rd *HAV* PO9 .... 165 G5
Approach Rd *PSTN* BH14 .... 234 A5
April Cl *BWD* BH11 .... 219 L4
    WEND SO18 .... 132 F1
April Gv *HLER* SO31 .... 158 C5
April Sq *PSEA* PO1 .... 211 H2
Apsley Crs *CFDH* BH17 .... 218 A7
Apsley Pl *CHFD* SO53 .... 53 G7 🔢
Apsley Rd *ENEY* PO4 .... 211 L4
Aquila Wy *HLER* SO31 .... 157 K6
Arabian Gdns *FHAM* PO15 .. 159 G2
Aragon Wy *MOOR/WNTN* BH9 .. 220 F3
Arcadia Av *CHAR* BH8 .... 236 A1
Arcadia Cl *ROWN* SO16 .... 106 A5
Arcadia Rd *CHCH/BSGR* BH23 .. 222 D7
Archdale Cl *NBNE* BH10 .... 220 B8
Archers Cl *TOTT* SO40 .... 104 B6
Archers Rd *ELGH* SO50 .... 81 M4
    WSHM SO15 .... 131 J1
Archery Gdns *ITCH* SO19 .... 132 D6
Archery Gv *ITCH* SO19 .... 132 C6
Archery La *FHAM/PORC* PO16.. 7 L4
    WINC SO23 .... 2 E8
Archery Rd *ITCH* SO19 .... 132 C7
Archway Rd *CCLF* BH13 .... 234 D4
Arden Cl *WEND* SO18 .... 108 A7
Arden Rd *MOOR/WNTN* BH9 .. 220 D5
Arden Wk *NMIL/BTOS* BH25.. 225 M6 🔢
Ardingly Crs *HEND* SO30 .... 109 J6
Ardington Ri *WVILLE* PO7 .... 164 C5
Ardmore Rd *PSTN* BH14 .... 234 A4
Argosy Cl *HLER* SO31 .... 158 D7
Argyle Crs *FHAM* PO15 .... 6 B3
Argyle Rd *CHCH/BSGR* BH23 .. 238 D3
    SHAM SO14 .... 5 H1
Argyll Rd *BKME/WDN* BH12 .. 234 C2
    BOSC BH5 .... 236 D4
Ariel Cl *SBNE* BH6 .... 238 A3

Ariel Dr *SBNE* BH6 .... 238 A4
Ariel Rd *PSEA* PO1 .... 13 L1
Ark Royal Crs
    LSOL/BMARY PO13 .... 208 C1
Arle Cl *HORN* PO8 .... 116 B4
Arley Rd *PSTN* BH14 .... 233 M6
Arlington Ct
    NMIL/BTOS BH25 .... 225 M8 🔢
Arliss Rd *ROWN* SO16 .... 105 M7
Arlott Ct *WSHM* SO15 .... 131 J1
Armada Cl *ROWN* SO16 .... 105 K1
Armada Dr *FAWY* SO45 .... 155 K6
Arminers Cl *GPORT* PO12 .... 10 E9
Armitage Av *FAWY* SO45 .... 155 K7
Armory La *PSEA* PO1 .... 12 D4
Armstrong Cl *BROC* SO42 .... 175 J7
    WVILLE PO7 .... 140 B7 🔢
Armstrong Ct *ROWN* SO16 .. 105 L3 🔢
Armstrong La *BROC* SO42 .... 175 J7
Armstrong Rd *BROC* SO42 .... 175 J7
Armsworth La *BPWT* SO32 .. 113 J6
Arnaud Cl *NEND* PO2 .... 211 H1
Arne Av *BKME/WDN* BH12 .. 234 D1
Arne Crs *BKME/WDN* BH12 .. 234 D1
Arnewood Bridge Rd
    LYMN SO41 .... 226 D1
Arnewood Rd *SBNE* BH6 .... 237 H3
Arnheim Cl *ROWN* SO16 .... 106 B4
Arnheim Rd *ROWN* SO16 .... 106 C4
Arnold Cl *FERN* BH22 .... 168 C5
Arnold Rd *ELGH* SO50 .... 81 M8
    FERN BH22 .... 168 C5
    PTSW SO17 .... 107 H6
Arnolds Cl *NMIL/BTOS* BH25 .. 225 K8
Arnside Rd *WVILLE* PO7 .... 140 C8
Arnwood Av *FAWY* SO45 .... 155 K8
Aron Cl *PSF* GU32 .... 63 K6
Arragon Ct *WVILLE* PO7 .... 140 C8
Arran Cl *CHAM* PO6 .... 163 K7
Arran Wy *CHCH/BSGR* BH23 .. 224 F7
Arreton *HLER* SO31 .... 157 G2 🔢
Arrow Cl *ELGH* SO50 .... 81 M4
    ITCH SO19 .... 132 B7
Arrowsmith La *WIMB* BH21 .. 218 C1
Arrowsmith Rd *WIMB* BH21 .. 218 B2
Arters Lawn *TOTT* SO40 .... 153 M2
Arthur Cl *WCLF* BH2 .... 14 F2
Arthur La *CHCH/BSGR* BH23 .. 237 M1 🔢
Arthur Rd *CHCH/BSGR* BH23 .. 237 M1
    ELGH SO50 .... 81 M4
    WINC SO23 .... 3 G4
    WSHM SO15 .... 131 H1
Arthurs Gdns *HEND* SO30 .. 109 G5 🔢
Arthur St *NEND* PO2 .... 211 J1 🔢
Artillery Cl *CHAM* PO6 .... 163 J8
Arun Cl *EPSF* GU31 .... 63 K6
Arundel Cl *NMIL/BTOS* BH25.. 225 J5
Arundel Dr *FHAM/PORC* PO16.. 7 G2
Arundel Rd *ELGH* SO50 .... 81 M2
    GPORT PO12 .... 10 B1
    TOTT SO40 .... 104 F8
Arundel St *PSEA* PO1 .... 13 K1
Arundel Wy *CHCH/BSGR* BH23 .. 239 L1
Arun Rd *WEND* SO18 .... 108 A6
Arun Wy *ROMY* SO51 .... 76 C5
Ascham Rd *CHAR* BH8 .... 15 J2
Ascot Cl *FHAM/STUB* PO14.. .. 159 G6
Ascot Rd *BDST* BH18 .... 217 L4
    ELGH SO50 .... 109 J1
    HSEA PO3 .... 211 L1
Ascupart St *SHAM* SO14 .... 5 J3
Asford Gv *ELGH* SO50 .... 82 C4
Ashburn Crs *FUFL* SO22 .... 26 C3
Ashbourne Rd *BOSC* BH5 .... 237 G3 🔢
Ashbridge Ri *CHFD* SO53 .... 52 F7
Ashburn Garth *RGWD* BH24.. 171 H2
Ashburnham Cl *ITCH* SO19 .. 132 B3 🔢
Ashburton Gdns *NBNE* BH10 .. 220 B7 🔢
Ashburton Rd *GPORT* PO12.. .. 10 B8
    SSEA PO5 .... 13 G8
Ashby Pl *SSEA* PO5 .... 13 H8
Ashby Rd *ITCH* SO19 .... 132 F5
    TOTT SO40 .... 129 H1
Ash Cl *FAWY* SO45 .... 155 L8
    FBDC SP6 .... 121 L3 🔢
    FHAM/STUB PO14.. .... 6 C7
    GPORT PO12 .... 10 E4
    HLER SO31 .... 133 K8 🔢
    HORN PO8 .... 140 C5
    ITCH SO19 .... 133 G2
    NBAD SO52 .... 79 L3
    ROMY SO51 .... 79 H2
    RWIN SO21 .... 54 F8
    UPTN BH16 .... 216 F8
Ash Copse *HORN* PO8 .... 140 D3
Ashcroft La *HORN* PO8 .... 142 B2
Ashdene *WSHM* SO15 .... 106 A8 🔢
Ashdene Cl *WIMB* BH21 .... 192 B3
Ashdene Rd *TOTT* SO40 .... 128 F6
Ashdown *FAWY* SO45 .... 180 D5
    LSOL/BMARY PO13 .... 185 H7
Ashdown Cl *CHFD* SO53 .... 53 H6
Ashdown Dr *CHFD* SO53 .... 53 H6
Ashdown Rd *CHFD* SO53 .... 53 H7
    FAWY SO45 .... 180 D6
Ashdown Wk
    NMIL/BTOS BH25 .... 226 A6 🔢
Ashdown Wy *ROMY* SO51 .... 79 G1
Ashen Cl *CHFD* SO53 .... 53 L6
Ashe Rd *HAV* PO9 .... 165 M3 🔢
Ashford Cl *CHAM* PO6 .... 163 J7
    FBDC SP6 .... 97 J3
Ashford Crs *FAWY* SO45 .... 155 M5
Ashford Rd *FBDC* SP6 .... 97 H8
    SBNE BH6 .... 237 J1
Ash Gv *LYMN* SO41 .... 227 H8
    RGWD BH24 .... 171 G1
    TOTT SO40 .... 129 G6
Ashington Cl *HORN* PO8 .... 140 C5
Ashington Pk
    NMIL/BTOS BH25 .... 225 M7
Ashlea Cl *ELGH* SO50 .... 83 J6
Ashleigh Cl *FAWY* SO45 .... 155 L8
Ashlet Gdns *NMIL/BTOS* BH25.. 226 B4
Ashlett Cl *FAWY* SO45 .... 181 G5
Ashlett Rd *FAWY* SO45 .... 181 G5
Ashley Cl *BMTH* BH1 .... 236 C2

FUFL SO22 .... 16 B5
HAV PO9 .... 165 H4
HLER SO31 .... 158 F1
HORN PO8 .... 140 D3
RGWD BH24 .... 171 H2
Ashley Common Rd
    NMIL/BTOS BH25 .... 226 A4
Ashley Ct *HLER* SO31 .... 133 L6 🔢
Ashley Crs *ITCH* SO19 .... 133 G6
Ashleycross Cl *FAWY* SO45 .. 180 B5 🔢
Ashley Dr *RGWD* BH24 .... 146 A8
Ashley Dr North *RGWD* BH24.. 169 K3
Ashley Dr South *RGWD* BH24.. 169 K3
Ashley Dr West *RGWD* BH24.. 169 K3
Ashley Gdns *BPWT* SO32 .... 111 K5
    CHFD SO53 .... 81 K3
Ashley La *LYMN* SO41 .... 228 C4
    NMIL/BTOS BH25 .... 226 B4
Ashley Mdw *ROMY* SO51 .... 50 F8
Ashley Meads
    NMIL/BTOS BH25 .... 226 B4
Ashley Pk *RGWD* BH24 .... 169 L2
Ashley Rd *LTDN* BH7 .... 236 E5 🔢
    NMIL/BTOS BH25 .... 225 L6
    PSTN BH14 .... 234 B3
Ashling Cl *CHAR* BH8 .... 221 G8
    WVILLE PO7 .... 139 K4
Ashling Gdns *WVILLE* PO7 .... 139 K4
Ashling La *NEND* PO2 .... 187 H8
Ashling Park Rd *WVILLE* PO7.. 139 K4
Ashlyn Cl *FHAM* PO15 .... 159 M7
Ashmead Rd *ROWN* SO16 .... 105 L5
Ashmeads Cl *WIMB* BH21 .... 192 E2 🔢
Ashmeads Wy *WIMB* BH21 .. 192 E2
Ashmore *WIMB* BH21 .... 192 B4
Ashmore Av *NMIL/BTOS* BH25.. 225 M8
    PLE BH15 .... 232 E7
Ashmore Cl *RSAL* SP5 .... 47 G4
Ashmore Gv *CHCH/BSGR* BH23.. 224 C7
Ashmore La *RSAL* SP5 .... 47 G3
Ashmore Rd *FUFL* SO22 .... 16 B7 🔢
Ashridge Av *NBNE* BH10 .... 220 B3
Ashridge Cl *WSHM* SO15 .... 106 C8 🔢
Ashridge Gdns *NBNE* BH10 .. 220 B3 🔢
Ash Rd *TOTT* SO40 .... 128 F6
Ashtead Cl *FHAM/PORC* PO16.. 161 L8
Ashton Cl *BPWT* SO32 .... 84 F7
Ashton Cross *ROMY* SO51 .... 76 F6
Ashton La *BPWT* SO32 .... 84 F6
Ashton Rd *MOOR/WNTN* BH9.. 220 D6
Ashton Wy *FHAM/STUB* PO14.. 184 B8
Ashtree Cl *NMIL/BTOS* BH25.. 226 B6
Ash Tree Rd *WEND* SO18 .... 107 K7
Ashurst Bridge Rd *TOTT* SO40.. 129 G2
Ashurst Cl *FUFL* SO22 .... 16 C5
    ITCH SO19 .... 132 E7
    TOTT SO40 .... 128 F6
Ashurst Rd *CHAM* PO6 .... 163 J8
    CHAR BH8 .... 221 H5
    FERN BH22 .... 168 A8
Ashwood *FHAM* PO15 .... 159 J3 🔢
    HLER SO31 .... 159 G6
Ashwood Cl *HAV* PO9 .... 164 F5
    HISD PO11 .... 213 L5
Ashwood Dr *BDST* BH18 .... 218 A4
Ashwood Gdns *ROWN* SO16 .. 106 D5 🔢
    TOTT SO40 .... 129 G2 🔢
Aspen Av *HLER* SO31 .... 158 B8
Aspen Cl *HEND* SO30 .... 134 B1
    RWIN SO21 .... 54 F8
Aspen Dr *VWD* BH31 .... 144 A3
Aspen Gdns *BKME/WDN* BH12 .. 234 E1
Aspengrove
    LSOL/BMARY PO13 .... 185 J7
Aspen Holt *ROWN* SO16 .... 106 F3
Aspen Pl *NMIL/BTOS* BH25 .. 225 M7
Aspen Rd *BKME/WDN* BH12 .. 234 E1
Aspen Wk *TOTT* SO40 .... 104 A8
Aspen Wy *BKME/WDN* BH12.. 234 E1
Asquith Cl *CHCH/BSGR* BH23 .. 238 C3 🔢
Astbury Av *BKME/WDN* BH12 .. 219 L8
Aster Rd *ROWN* SO16 .... 107 H4
Astley St *SSEA* PO5 .... 13 G4
Aston Md *CHCH/BSGR* BH23 .. 222 C4
Aston Rd *WVILLE* PO7 .... 140 B7
Astra Ct *FAWY* SO45 .... 155 L8
Astral Gdns *HLER* SO31 .... 157 K5
Astrid Cl *HISD* PO11 .... 214 A5
Asturias Wy *SHAM* SO14 .... 5 L6
Asylum Rd *WSHM* SO15 .... 131 L2
Atalanta Cl *ENEY* PO4 .... 212 A3
Atheling Rd *FAWY* SO45 .... 155 L4
Athelstan Rd *ITCH* SO19 .... 132 C1
    SBNE BH6 .... 237 K3
Athena Av *WVILLE* PO7 .... 164 D5
Athena Cl *ELGH* SO50 .... 82 C4
Atherfield Rd *ROWN* SO16 .... 105 K5
Atherley Ct *WSHM* SO15 .... 106 D8 🔢
Atherley Rd *HISD* PO11 .... 213 J3
    WSHM SO15 .... 131 H2
Atkinson Cl *GPORT* PO12 .... 10 D8
Atkins Pl *FHAM* PO15 .... 160 A5
Atlantic Cl *SHAM* SO14 .... 5 K8
Atlantic Park Vw
    WEND SO18 .... 107 M6 🔢
Atlantis Av *WVILLE* PO7 .... 164 D6
Attwood Cl *FBDC* SP6.. .... 121 K3
Attwoods Dro *RWIN* SO21 .... 26 B8
Aubrey Cl *HISD* PO11 .... 213 J4 🔢
    LYMN SO41 .... 242 E4
Auckland Pl *BROC* SO42 .... 175 L7 🔢
Auckland Rd
    CHCH/BSGR BH23 .... 239 H1 🔢
    WSHM SO15.. .... 130 D1
Auckland Rd East *SSEA* PO5 .. 13 H8
Auckland Rd West *SSEA* PO5.. 13 G8
Audemer Ct *RGWD* BH24 .... 147 G8
Audret Cl *FHAM/PORC* PO16.. 185 M2
Augustine Rd *CHAM* PO6 .... 164 A7
    SHAM SO14 .... 131 M2 🔢
Augustus Wy *CHFD* SO53 .... 81 K1
Aukland Av *BROC* SO42 .... 175 L7
Auriol Dr *CHAM* PO6 .... 164 E8
Austen Av *FUFL* SO22 .... 26 B5
    NBNE BH10 .... 220 C2 🔢
Austen Cl *TOTT* SO40.. .... 129 H2
    WINC SO23 .... 3 H2

Austen Gdns *HLER* SO31............ 135 G8
Austerberry Wy
  LSOL/BMARY PO13...... 185 H8
Auster Cl *CHCH/BSGR* BH23.... 239 C1
Austin Av *PSTN* BH14............ 234 A6
Austin Cl *BMTH* BH1............ 236 C3 ▯
Austin Ct *CHAM* PO6............ 162 F7
Australia Cl *PSEA* PO1............ 13 J1
Aust Rd *FHAM/STUB* PO14........ 6 A7
Autumn Cl *FERN* BH22............ 193 M1
Autumn Rd *BWD* BH11............ 219 H5
  TOTT SO40............ 130 E7
Avalon *PSTN* BH14............ 234 B8
Avebury Av *NBNE* BH10............ 220 C2
Avebury Gdns *CHFD* SO53........ 52 F7
Avenger Cl *SO53*............ 81 G3
Avens Cl *ELGH* SO50............ 109 H2
Avenue C *FAWY* SO45............ 156 C5
Avenue Ct *GPORT* PO12............ 10 C7
Avenue D *FAWY* SO45............ 156 C5
Avenue De Caen *SSEA* PO5........ 13 H9
Avenue E *FAWY* SO45............ 156 C5
Avenue La *WCLF* BH2............ 14 D6
Avenue Rd *BROC* SO42............ 175 G3
  CHCH/BSGR BH23.... 225 G7
  CHCH/BSGR BH23.... 237 L1
  FHAM/STUB PO14........ 6 F6
  FUFL SO22............ 2 D6
  GPORT PO12............ 11 G2
  HISD PO11............ 189 K5
  LYMN SO41............ 228 B4
  NMIL/BTOS BH25....... 225 L5
  SHAM SO14............ 106 F8
  WCLF BH2............ 14 D6
  WIMB BH21............ 192 B4
The Avenue *BPWT* SO32............ 85 G8
  CCLF BH13............ 234 F8
  EPSF GU31............ 63 L5
  FERN BH22............ 168 B5
  FHAM PO15............ 6 E6
  FHAM/STUB PO14........ 6 F6
  GPORT PO12............ 10 C7
  MOOR/WNTN BH9........ 220 D5
  PTSW SO17............ 106 E6
  RCCH PO18............ 167 M7
  RWIN SO21............ 54 F2
Avery La *GPORT* PO12............ 209 K1
Avington Cl *ELGH* SO50............ 82 C3 ▯
Avington Ct *ROWN* SO16............ 106 E4
Avocet Quay *EMRTH* PO10........ 190 E1
Avocet Wk *LSOL/BMARY* PO13... 184 E6
Avon Av *RGWD* BH24............ 170 B5
Avonborne Wy *CHFD* SO53........ 53 G2
Avon Buildings
  CHCH/BSGR BH23.... 238 A1
Avon Castle Dr *RGWD* BH24...... 170 B4
Avon Cswy *CHCH/BSGR* BH23.... 221 M1
Avoncliffe Rd *SBNE* BH6............ 237 K5 ▯
Avon Cl *BMTH* BH1............ 236 C2 ▯
  LSOL/BMARY PO13...... 208 C3
  LYMN SO41............ 228 A4
  PSF GU32............ 63 K6
Avon Crs *ROMY* SO51............ 79 H1
Avondale Rd *PSEA* PO1............ 211 K1
  WVILLE PO7............ 140 C5
Avon Gdns *CHCH/BSGR* BH23... 197 M7
Avon Gn *CHFD* SO53............ 81 J3
Avon Meade *FBDG* SP6............ 97 K6 ▯
Avon Pk *RGWD* BH24............ 170 B5
Avon Rd *CHAR* BH8............ 236 B2
  FERN BH22............ 168 C3
  WEND SO18............ 107 L7
Avon Rd East
  CHCH/BSGR BH23.... 222 E8
Avon Rd West
  CHCH/BSGR BH23.... 222 D8
Avon Run Cl *CHCH/BSGR* BH23.. 239 G3
Avon Run Rd
  CHCH/BSGR BH23.... 239 G3
  RSAL SP5............ 44 E5
Avon Vw *FBDG* SP6............ 98 C7
Avon View Rd
  CHCH/BSGR BH23.... 223 G5 ▯
Avon Wy *HEND* SO30............ 108 D6
Award Rd *WIMB* BH21............ 193 K3
Awbridge Rd *HAV* PO9............ 165 G4
Axford Cl *CHAR* BH8............ 221 H5
Aylen Rd *HSEA* PO3............ 187 L6
  NEND PO2............ 187 K8
Aylesbury Rd *BMTH* BH1............ 236 C1
Ayling Cl *LSOL/BMARY* PO13... 209 G1
Aylward St *PSEA* PO1............ 12 D1 ▯
Aysgarth Rd *WVILLE* PO7............ 140 C8
Aysha Cl *NMIL/BTOS* BH25...... 225 M7
Azalea Cl *HAV* PO9............ 166 A4
  RGWD BH24............ 169 L3

B

Back La *LYMN* SO41............ 201 G6
  ROMY SO51............ 21 J3
  WHAM PO17............ 162 C2
Back of the Walls *SHAM* SO14.... 5 G5
Back St *WINC* SO23............ 26 E4
Bacon Cl *ITCH* SO19............ 132 D7
Bacon La *HISD* PO11............ 213 H5
Badbury Cl *BDST* BH18............ 218 A3
Badbury Vw *WIMB* BH21............ 192 B3
Baddesley Cl *NBAD* SO52............ 79 L3
Baddesley Rd *CHFD* SO53............ 52 F7
Baden Cl *NMIL/BTOS* BH25..... 225 M7 ▯
Bader Cl *HEND* SO30............ 109 H8 ▯
Bader Rd *CFDH* BH17............ 218 C8
Bader Wy *FHAM* PO15............ 159 J3
Badger Brow *WVILLE* PO7............ 164 E2
Badger Cl *ELGH* SO50............ 82 E6
  FHAM PO15............ 6 A3
Badger Farm Rd *FUFL* SO22...... 26 A4
Badgers Cl *LYMN* SO41............ 201 G6
  RGWD BH24............ 169 K3
Badgers Copse
  NMIL/BTOS BH25...... 226 A2
Badgers Run *HLER* SO31............ 157 G2 ▯
The Badgers *HLER* SO31............ 157 G2 ▯
Badgers Wk *FAWY* SO45............ 155 K6 ▯

  FERN BH22............ 194 C1
Badger Wy *VWD* BH31............ 144 D3
Badminton Dro *FAWY* SO45...... 181 G8
Badminton La *FAWY* SO45...... 181 G7
Badshear La *NARL* SO24............ 30 D1
Baffins Rd *HSEA* PO3............ 211 L2
Bagber Rd *TOTT* SO40............ 129 K1
Baigent Cl *WINC* SO23............ 3 L7
Bailey Crs *PLE* BH15............ 233 H1
Bailey Dr *CHCH/BSGR* BH23.... 237 L1
Bailey's Rd *SSEA* PO5............ 13 J3
Baiter Gdns *PLE* BH15............ 233 J7 ▯
Baker Rd *BWD* BH11............ 219 K3
Bakers Dro *ROWN* SO16............ 105 K3
Bakers Farm Rd *VWD* BH31...... 144 C1 ▯
Baker St *NEND* PO2............ 211 H1
Balaclava Rd *WEND* SO18............ 132 E1
Balcombe Rd *CCLF* BH13............ 234 F5
Balderton Cl *NEND* PO2............ 187 K4 ▯
Baldwin Cl *FHAM/STUB* PO14... 159 G7
Balfour Cl *CHCH/BSGR* BH23... 224 B8
Balfour Dr *LISS* GU33............ 36 D4
Balfour Rd *ITCH* SO19............ 132 F3
Ballam Cl *UPTN* BH16............ 232 B1
Ballard Cl *NMIL/BTOS* BH25..... 225 M4
  PLE BH15............ 233 J7 ▯
  ROWN SO16............ 105 H7
Ballard Rd *PLE* BH15............ 233 J7 ▯
Balliol Cl *FHAM/STUB* PO14...... 159 G7
Balliol Rd *NEND* PO2............ 211 J1
Balmoral Av *CHAR* BH8............ 221 J7
Balmoral Cl *CHFD* SO53............ 53 G8 ▯
  LSOL/BMARY PO13...... 185 H5
  ROWN SO16............ 106 B3
Balmoral Dr *WVILLE* PO7............ 164 A4
Balmoral Rd *FHAM* PO15............ 6 D2
  PSTN BH14............ 234 B4
Balmoral Wk
  NMIL/BTOS BH25...... 225 K5 ▯
Balmoral Wy *PSF* GU32............ 63 L4
  ROWN SO16............ 105 J2
Balston Rd *PSTN* BH14............ 233 M3
Baltic Rd *HEND* SO30............ 108 D6
Banbury Av *ITCH* SO19............ 133 G4
Bangor Rd *WSHM* SO15............ 130 F2
Banister Gdns *WSHM* SO15...... 131 K1
Banister Rd *WSHM* SO15............ 131 K1
Bankhill Dr *LYMN* SO41............ 228 B3
Bankside *LYMN* SO41............ 228 B2 ▯
Bank Side *WEND* SO18............ 107 J4
Bankside Rd
  MOOR/WNTN BH9............ 220 E5
Banks Rd *CCLF* BH13............ 245 G5
The Banks *ROMY* SO51............ 48 F3
Bank St *BPWT* SO32............ 111 J1
Bankview *LYMN* SO41............ 228 B2
Bannerman Rd *PSF* GU32............ 63 L4 ▯
Banning St *ROMY* SO51............ 78 D2
Bapaume Rd *HSEA* PO3............ 187 K3
Barbe Baker Av *HEND* SO30...... 108 F1
Barberry Wy *VWD* BH31............ 145 G3
Barbers Piles *PLE* BH15............ 233 J7 ▯
Bardon Wy *FHAM/STUB* PO14.... 6 B8
Bar End Rd *WINC* SO23............ 27 G2
Barfield Cl *WINC* SO23............ 27 G2
Barfields *LYMN* SO41............ 228 C4
Barfleur Cl *FHAM* PO15............ 6 A3
Barfleur Rd *FHAM/STUB* PO14 . 184 E3
Barford Cl *CHFD* SO53............ 53 G8 ▯
Barford La *RSAL* SP5............ 44 F8
Bargates *CHCH/BSGR* BH23.... 237 M1
Bargate St *SHAM* SO14............ 4 F4
Barham Cl *GPORT* PO12............ 209 M2 ▯
Barham Rd *PSF* GU32............ 63 L5
Barham Wy *NEND* PO2............ 187 H4
Baring Rd *SBNE* BH6............ 237 M4
  WINC SO23............ 3 K9
Barker Mill Cl *ROWN* SO16............ 105 K2
Barlands Cl
  CHCH/BSGR BH23.... 223 G6 ▯
Barle Cl *WEND* SO18............ 108 A7
Barley Down Dr *FUFL* SO22...... 26 C4
Barlow Cl *FHAM/STUB* PO14.... 183 M6
Barnbrook Rd *HLER* SO31............ 158 C4
Barn Cl *EMRTH* PO10............ 166 B8
  ITCH SO19............ 133 G2
Barncroft Wy *HAV* PO9............ 165 H5
Barn End Rd *WIMB* BH21............ 192 C4
Barnes Cl *HLER* SO31............ 158 B4
  ITCH SO19............ 133 G2
Barnes Crs *NBNE* BH10............ 220 B5
  WIMB BH21............ 192 C4
Barnes La *HLER* SO31............ 158 C3
  LYMN SO41............ 227 G8
Barnes Rd *ITCH* SO19............ 133 G2
  NBNE BH10............ 220 B5
  PSEA PO1............ 211 J2
Barnes Wallis Rd
  FHAM PO15............ 159 H4 ▯
Barnes Wy *HAV* PO9............ 165 G5
Barnet Side La *PSF* GU32............ 34 C3
Barney Evans Crs *HORN* PO8...... 140 F5
Barneyhayes La *TOTT* SO40...... 102 F8
Barnfield *CHCH/BSGR* BH23.... 224 B8
Barnfield Cl *EMRTH* PO10............ 167 J6
  ITCH SO19............ 132 C7
Barnfield Ct *FHAM/STUB* PO14... 6 D8
  ITCH SO19............ 132 D7
Barnfield Dro *WIMB* BH21............ 120 D4
Barnfield Rd *EPSF* GU31............ 64 B5
  ITCH SO19............ 132 C7
Barnfield Wy *ITCH* SO19............ 132 D7
Barn Fold *HORN* PO8............ 140 F7
Barn Green Cl *WVILLE* PO7............ 139 K4
Barn Piece *NBAD* SO52............ 80 E2
Barn Rd *BDST* BH18............ 217 M5
Barnsfield Crs *TOTT* SO40............ 129 G1
Barnsfield Rd *RGWD* BH24............ 169 L7
Barnsland *HEND* SO30............ 108 B6
Barns Rd *FERN* BH22............ 194 E2

Baron Rd *HLER* SO31............ 157 K5
Barons Md *ROWN* SO16............ 105 K5
Barons Rd *BWD* BH11............ 219 H2
Barrack La *RGWD* BH24............ 171 H4
Barrack Rd *CHCH/BSGR* BH23.. 222 D5
  FERN BH22............ 194 E6
Barrie Cl *HLER* SO31............ 135 G8 ▯
Barrie Rd *MOOR/WNTN* BH9...... 220 D5
Barrington Cl *ELGH* SO50............ 81 J3
Barrow Down Gdns *ITCH* SO19.. 133 J5
Barrow Dr *CHAR* BH8............ 221 K6
Barrowgate Rd *CHAR* BH8...... 221 H4 ▯
Barrowgate Wy *CHAR* BH8...... 221 H5
Barrow Hill Rd *TOTT* SO40...... 103 J5
Barrow Rd *CHAR* BH8............ 221 K6
Barrows La *LYMN* SO41............ 226 F1
  RSAL SP5............ 75 G2
Barrow Vw *FERN* BH22............ 193 L2 ▯
Barrow Wy *CHAR* BH8............ 221 K6
Barrs Av *NMIL/BTOS* BH25...... 225 L4
Barrs Wood Dr
  NMIL/BTOS BH25...... 225 M4
Barrs Wood Rd
  NMIL/BTOS BH25...... 225 M4
Barry Gdns *BDST* BH18............ 217 K3
Barry Rd *ITCH* SO19............ 132 F6
Barters Cl *ROWN* SO16............ 105 L7
Barters La *BDST* BH18............ 217 K4
Bartlett Cl *FHAM* PO15............ 6 C2
Bartlett Dr *LTDN* BH7............ 221 M8
The Bartletts *HLER* SO31............ 157 L6
Bartley Av *TOTT* SO40............ 129 J2
Bartley Rd *TOTT* SO40............ 128 A5
Barton Cl *ROMY* SO51............ 51 G8 ▯
Barton Common La
  NMIL/BTOS BH25...... 225 M8
Barton Common Rd
  NMIL/BTOS BH25...... 241 G1
Barton Court Av
  NMIL/BTOS BH25...... 240 C1
Barton Court Rd
  NMIL/BTOS BH25...... 225 L7
Barton Crs *WEND* SO18............ 107 L7
Barton Cft *NMIL/BTOS* BH25.... 240 C1
Barton Cross *HORN* PO8............ 140 F1
Barton Dr *HEND* SO30............ 134 B1
  HLER SO31............ 157 K5
  NMIL/BTOS BH25...... 225 K8
Barton Gn *NMIL/BTOS* BH25.... 240 F2
Barton La *NMIL/BTOS* BH25..... 225 H8
Barton Rd *ELGH* SO50............ 82 B5
Bartonside Rd
  NMIL/BTOS BH25...... 225 G8
Bartons Rd *FBDG* SP6............ 97 L7
  HAV PO9............ 165 L3
The Bartons *FBDG* SP6............ 97 L7 ▯
Barton Wy *NMIL/BTOS* BH25.... 225 K8
Barton Wood Rd
  NMIL/BTOS BH25...... 240 D1
Bartram Rd *TOTT* SO40............ 129 L2
Barwell Gv *EMRTH* PO10............ 166 C5 ▯
Bascott Cl *BWD* BH11............ 219 L7
Bascott Rd *BWD* BH11............ 219 K7
Bashley Common Rd
  NMIL/BTOS BH25...... 199 L8
Bashley Cross Rd
  CHCH/BSGR BH23.... 225 H3
Bashley Dr *NMIL/BTOS* BH25... 225 M2
Bashley Rd *NMIL/BTOS* BH25... 225 L1
Basing Dean *ALTN* GU34............ 33 K3
Basing Rd *HAV* PO9............ 165 J3
Basingstoke Rd *WINC* SO23...... 17 J2
Basing Wy *CHFD* SO53............ 80 F4
Basingwell St *BPWT* SO32............ 111 H1
Basin St *NEND* PO2............ 187 H8
Bassett Av *ROWN* SO16............ 106 C4
Bassett Cl *ROWN* SO16............ 106 E4
Bassett Crs East *ROWN* SO16.... 106 E4
Bassett Crs West *ROWN* SO16.. 106 E4
Bassett Dl *ROWN* SO16............ 106 E2
Bassett Gdns *ROWN* SO16...... 106 D5
Bassett Gn Cl *ROWN* SO16...... 106 F3
Bassett Green Cl *ROWN* SO16.. 106 F3
Bassett Green Dr *ROWN* SO16.. 106 F3
Bassett Green Rd *ROWN* SO16.. 106 F2
Bassett Heath Av *ROWN* SO16.. 106 E1
Bassett Meadow *ROWN* SO16.. 106 E4
Bassett Ms *ROWN* SO16............ 106 E3
Bassett Rd *BKME/WDN* BH12.. 234 A2
Bassett Rw *ROWN* SO16............ 106 E2
Bassett Wood Dr *ROWN* SO16.. 106 E2
Bassett Wood Rd *ROWN* SO16.. 106 E2
Batcheler Cl *BWD* BH11............ 219 K5
Batchelor Gn *HLER* SO31............ 133 L8 ▯
Batchelor Rd *BWD* BH11............ 219 K5
Batcombe Cl *BWD* BH11............ 219 L5
Bath Cl *ITCH* SO19............ 132 F2
Bath Hill Rbt *BMTH* BH1............ 14 F7
Bathing La *PSEA* PO1............ 12 B4
Bath La *FHAM/PORC* PO16...... 7 M6
Bath Lane (Lower)
  FHAM/PORC PO16...... 7 M7
Bath Rd *BMTH* BH1............ 14 F7
  EMRTH PO10............ 166 D8
  ENEY PO4............ 211 K5
  ITCH SO19............ 132 F2
  LYMN SO41............ 228 D5
Bath Sq *PSEA* PO1............ 12 A5
Bath St *SHAM* SO14............ 131 L1
Bathurst Cl *HISD* PO11............ 213 J5
Battenburg Av *NEND* PO2............ 187 K6
Battenburg Rd *GPORT* PO12...... 11 G2 ▯
Batten Cl *CHCH/BSGR* BH23.... 223 H8
Batten Rd *RSAL* SP5............ 44 D8
Battens Wy *HAV* PO9............ 165 K4
Batterley Dro *WIMB* BH21............ 120 D4
Battery Cl *GPORT* PO12............ 185 K8
Battery Hl *BPWT* SO32............ 85 G8
  FUFL SO22............ 26 B2
Battery Rw *PSEA* PO1............ 12 C5
Battle Cl *HLER* SO31............ 158 D4
B Av *FAWY* SO45............ 180 B3
Baverstock Rd
  BKME/WDN BH12...... 219 M8
Baxter Rd *ITCH* SO19............ 133 J4
Baybridge Cl *BPWT* SO32............ 56 D6
Baybridge Rd *HAV* PO9............ 165 M3
Bay Cl *ITCH* SO19............ 132 E5

  UPTN BH16............ 232 A2
Bayard Rd *BMTH* BH1............ 144 C8
Bay Hog La *PLE* BH15............ 233 G6 ▯
Bayly Av *FHAM/PORC* PO16...... 183 G4
Bay Rd *GPORT* PO12............ 10 A6
  ITCH SO19............ 132 E5
Bays Rd *LYMN* SO41............ 228 A5
Baythorn Cl *NEND* PO2............ 211 H1 ▯
Bay Trees *ITCH* SO19............ 133 J2
Bay Tree Wy *CHCH/BSGR* BH23.. 224 B7
Beach Av *NMIL/BTOS* BH25...... 240 E1
Beach Dr *CHAM* PO6............ 162 D8
Beach Rd *CCLF* BH13............ 234 F8
  EMRTH PO10............ 166 C8
  HISD PO11............ 213 J5
  LSOL/BMARY PO13...... 208 C3
  SSEA PO5............ 13 K9
Beachway *FHAM/PORC* PO16.... 186 D5
Beacon Bottom *HLER* SO31...... 158 E2
Beacon Cl *HLER* SO31............ 158 D2
  LYMN SO41............ 227 H7
Beacon Ct *HLER* SO31............ 158 E2
Beacon Dr *CHCH/BSGR* BH23.. 239 L1
Beacon Gdns *BDST* BH18............ 217 J5
Beacon Hill La *BPWT* SO32...... 58 E8
  BPWT SO32............ 87 G2
  UPTN BH16............ 216 F5
Beacon Mt *HLER* SO31............ 158 D2
Beacon Park Crs *UPTN* BH16.... 216 E8
Beacon Park Rd *UPTN* BH16.... 216 E8
Beacon Rd *BDST* BH18............ 217 H5
  HEND SO30............ 108 C8
  UPTN BH16............ 232 A1
  WCLF BH2............ 14 D7
Beaconsfield Av *CHAM* PO6...... 187 L1
Beaconsfield Rd
  BKME/WDN BH12...... 234 C3
  CHCH/BSGR BH23.... 238 C1
  FHAM/PORC PO16...... 7 J3
  WVILLE PO7............ 140 C8 ▯
Beacon Sq *EMRTH* PO10............ 190 C1
Beacon Wy *BDST* BH18............ 217 J5
  HLER SO31............ 158 E2
Bealing Cl *ROWN* SO16............ 107 G4
Beamish Rd *CFDH* BH17............ 218 D8
Bear Cross Av *BWD* BH11............ 219 J2
Bearslane Cl *TOTT* SO40............ 104 C7
Beatrice Rd *ENEY* PO4............ 14 M7
  WSHM SO15............ 131 G1 ▯
Beattie Ri *HEND* SO30............ 109 H6 ▯
Beatty Cl *HLER* SO31............ 158 F4
  RGWD BH24............ 147 G8
Beatty Dr *GPORT* PO12............ 10 B7
Beatty Rd *MOOR/WNTN* BH9... 220 F7
Beauchamp Av
  LSOL/BMARY PO13...... 185 G6
Beauchamps Gdns *LTDN* BH7.... 221 L8
Beaucroft La *WIMB* BH21............ 192 C2
Beaucroft Rd *BPWT* SO32............ 111 K5
  WIMB BH21............ 192 B2
Beaufort Av *FHAM/PORC* PO16.. 6 L2
Beaufort Cl
  CHCH/BSGR BH23.... 239 G1 ▯
  WIMB BH21............ 192 A3
Beaufort Dr *BPWT* SO32............ 85 H8
  WIMB BH21............ 192 A3
Beaufort Rd *HAV* PO9............ 8 A3
  SBNE BH6............ 237 H3
  SSEA PO5............ 13 K9
  WINC SO23............ 26 E2
Beaufoys Av *FERN* BH22............ 194 A1
Beaufoys Cl *FERN* BH22............ 194 A1
Beaulieu Av *CHCH/BSGR* BH23 . 237 K1
  ELGH SO50............ 81 M4
Beaulieu Cl *FUFL* SO22............ 16 C4 ▯
  ROWN SO16............ 106 A3
Beaulieu Pl
  LSOL/BMARY PO13...... 185 G1
Beaulieu Rd *BROC* SO42............ 153 K8
  BROC SO42............ 179 G4
  CHCH/BSGR BH23.... 237 K1
  ELGH SO50............ 81 M4 ▯
  FAWY SO45............ 155 J7
  LYND SO43............ 151 M4
  NEND PO2............ 187 J2
  TOTT SO40............ 127 K3
  WBNE BH4............ 235 C7
Beaumaris Gdns *FAWY* SO45.... 155 K4
Beaumond Gn *WINC* SO23............ 2 E8
  ROWN SO16............ 106 D5 ▯
Beaumont Cl *FHAM* PO15............ 6 B1
Beaumont Ct *GPORT* PO12...... 185 L8 ▯
Beaumont Ri *FHAM* PO15............ 160 B4 ▯
Beaumont Rd *CCLF* BH13............ 245 L1 ▯
  TOTT SO40............ 129 L1
Beauworth Av *WEND* SO18............ 108 B8
Beaver Dr *ELGH* SO50............ 82 F6
Beccles Cl *PLE* BH15............ 232 E6
Becher Rd *PSTN* BH14............ 234 D4
Beck Cl *HLER* SO31............ 158 C5
Becket Gn *WHAM* PO17............ 138 C7
Beckford La *NMIL/BTOS* BH25.. 225 M7
Beckham La *PSF* GU32............ 63 J4
Beckhampton Rd *PLE* BH15.... 232 D5 ▯
Bedale Wy *PLE* BH15............ 233 L3
Bedenham La
  LSOL/BMARY PO13...... 185 J5
Bedfield La *WINC* SO23............ 17 G3
Bedford Av *ITCH* SO19............ 132 C6
Bedford Cl *FBDG* SP6............ 97 L5 ▯
  HAV PO9............ 9 J3
  HEND SO30............ 134 B2 ▯
Bedford Crs *LTDN* BH7............ 237 H1
Bedford Pl *WSHM* SO15............ 131 K2
Bedford Rd *PSF* GU32............ 63 J5
Bedford Rd North
  BKME/WDN BH12...... 219 G6
Bedford Rd South
  BKME/WDN BH12...... 219 G6
Bedford St *GPORT* PO12............ 209 L2
  SSEA PO5............ 13 G3
Bedhampton Hl *CHAM* PO6...... 164 E7
Bedhampton Hill Rd
  HAV PO9............ 164 F7 ▯

Bedhampton Rd *HAV* PO9............ 165 G6
  NEND PO2............ 187 K7
Bedhampton Wy *HAV* PO9...... 165 K4
Bedwell Cl *ROWN* SO16............ 105 L3
Beecham Rd *PSEA* PO1............ 211 J1
Beech Av *CHCH/BSGR* BH23.... 222 B8
  SBNE BH6............ 237 H4
  WEND SO18............ 132 C1
Beech Cl *BDST* BH18............ 217 H4
  CHFD SO53............ 53 J8
  FBDG SP6............ 121 L3 ▯
  FUFL SO22............ 26 A5
  HLER SO31............ 157 J6
  HORN PO8............ 140 D6
  LYMN SO41............ 227 H8 ▯
  ROMY SO51............ 79 H2
  VWD BH31............ 144 C3 ▯
Beech Copse *FUFL* SO22............ 16 A7
Beech Ct *WIMB* BH21............ 192 C4
Beech Crs *FAWY* SO45............ 155 L8
Beechcroft Cl *CHFD* SO53............ 81 J3
  FHAM PO15............ 159 M7
Beechcroft La *RGWD* BH24...... 146 F8
Beechcroft Rd *GPORT* PO12...... 10 D6
Beechcroft Wy *CHFD* SO53...... 81 J2 ▯
Beechdale Cl *TOTT* SO40............ 104 B6
Beechen La *LYND* SO43............ 151 M6
Beeches Hl *BPWT* SO32............ 85 J6
The Beeches *ELGH* SO50............ 83 J7 ▯
  LTDN BH7............ 221 L8 ▯
  ROMY SO51............ 76 C5
Beechey Rd *BMTH* BH1............ 15 H2
  CHAR BH8............ 15 H1
Beechfield Ct *WSHM* SO15...... 105 M8
Beech Gdns *HLER* SO31............ 157 J6
Beech Gra *RSAL* SP5............ 75 J6
Beech Gv *GPORT* PO12............ 10 D5
  HISD PO11............ 213 M4
  RWIN SO21............ 55 M4
Beech La *RGWD* BH24............ 169 J6
Beechmount Rd *ROWN* SO16.... 106 C3
Beech Rd *CHFD* SO53............ 53 J8
  FHAM PO15............ 6 D4
  HEND SO30............ 134 B1
  HORN PO8............ 116 C3
  TOTT SO40............ 128 C6
  WSHM SO15............ 130 F2
Beech Wy *HORN* PO8............ 140 F3
Beechwood Av *CHAM* PO6...... 187 L1
  LISS GU33............ 36 F2 ▯
Beechwood Crs *CHFD* SO53...... 52 F6
Beechwood Gdns *BOSC* BH5...... 236 F4
  WEND SO18............ 107 K8
Beechwood La *RGWD* BH24...... 172 F5
Beechwood Ri *WEND* SO18...... 108 B7
Beechwood Rd *FAWY* SO45...... 180 A5
  FERN BH22............ 168 D8
  NEND PO2............ 187 J4
  TOTT SO40............ 127 K3
Beechwood Wy *FAWY* SO45...... 155 G6
Beechworth Rd *HAV* PO9............ 9 G4
Beehive Wk *PSEA* PO1............ 12 C4 ▯
Beggar's La *WINC* SO23............ 3 J7
Begonia Rd *ROWN* SO16............ 107 G4
Behrendt Cl *GPORT* PO12............ 209 L2
Belben Cl *BKME/WDN* BH12...... 219 H6
Belben Rd *BKME/WDN* BH12.... 219 H6
Belbins *ROMY* SO51............ 50 E4
Belfield Rd *SBNE* BH6............ 237 M4
Belfry Wk *FHAM/STUB* PO14...... 159 G6
Belgrave Rd *NEND* PO2............ 187 K7
Bellair Rd *HAV* PO9............ 9 G5
Bell Crs *WVILLE* PO7............ 164 C2
Bell Davies Rd
  FHAM/STUB PO14...... 183 M7
Bellemoor Rd *WSHM* SO15...... 106 C7
Belle Vue Crs *SBNE* BH6............ 237 L4
Belle Vue Gv *FERN* BH22............ 168 B5
Belle Vue Rd *PSTN* BH14............ 234 B5
  SBNE BH6............ 237 L5
Bellevue Rd *ELGH* SO50............ 81 M5
  WSHM SO15............ 131 L2
Bellevue Ter *SSEA* PO5............ 12 E6
Belle Vue Wk *FERN* BH22............ 194 C6
Bellflower Cl
  CHCH/BSGR BH23.... 223 M8 ▯
Bellflower Wy *NBAD* SO52............ 80 E1
Bell Heather Cl *UPTN* BH16...... 216 F8 ▯
Bell Hl *PSF* GU32............ 63 J3
Bell Hill Rdg *PSF* GU32............ 63 K3
Bell Rd *CHAM* PO6............ 163 H8
Bells La *FHAM/STUB* PO14...... 184 A6
Bell St *ROMY* SO51............ 78 D1
  SHAM SO14............ 5 H5
Belmont Av *CHAR* BH8............ 221 G6
Belmont Cl *FAWY* SO45............ 155 L6
  FHAM/STUB PO14...... 184 B5 ▯
  HORN PO8............ 116 B6
  VWD BH31............ 144 E3
Belmont Gv *HAV* PO9............ 165 G1 ▯
Belmont Pl *SSEA* PO5............ 13 H5
Belmont Rd *CHFD* SO53............ 81 M5
  NMIL/BTOS BH25...... 226 A4
  PSTN BH14............ 234 A5
  PTSW SO17............ 107 G8
Belmont St *SSEA* PO5............ 13 H5
Belmore Cl *PSEA* PO1............ 211 J3
Belmore La *LYMN* SO41............ 228 C5
  RWIN SO21............ 56 C5
Belmore Rd *LYMN* SO41............ 228 B5
Belney La *WHAM* PO17............ 139 G3
Belstone Rd *TOTT* SO40............ 129 J1
Belton Rd *ITCH* SO19............ 132 F5
Belvedere Rd
  CHCH/BSGR BH23.... 237 M1
  FAWY SO45............ 155 L6
  TWDS BH3............ 235 M2
Belverdere Cl *PSF* GU32............ 63 L4 ▯

Belvidere Rd SHAM SO14 5 L2
Belvidere Ter SHAM SO14 5 L1
Belvoir Cl FHAM/PORC PO16 7 J7
Bembridge HLER SO31 157 G2
Bembridge Cl ROWN SO16 107 H3 1
Bembridge Crs ENEY PO4 13 L9
Bembridge Dr HISD PO11 214 A7
Bemister Rd
MOOR/WNTN BH9 220 E8
Benbow Cl HORN PO8 141 G1
Benbow Crs BKME/WDN BH12 219 J7
Benbow Pl PSEA PO1 12 C1 1
Benbridge Av BWD BH11 219 K3
Bendigo Rd CHCH/BSGR BH23 222 C8
Benedict Cl ROMY SO51 79 H1
Benedict Wy
FHAM/PORC PO16 162 C6
Beneficial St PSEA PO1 12 C2 1
Benellen Av WBNE BH4 235 H4
Benellen Gdns WBNE BH4 235 H4
Benellen Rd WBNE BH4 235 H3
Bengal Rd MOOR/WNTN BH9 220 C7
Benger's La ROMY SO51 21 J6
Benham Dr HSEA PO3 187 K4 2
Benham Gv FHAM/PORC PO16 186 B2
Benhams Farm Cl
WEND SO18 107 M7 1
Benhams Rd WEND SO18 107 M6 2
Benjamin Rd PLE BH15 232 D6
Ben La RSAL SP5 18 C1
Benmoor Rd CFDH BH17 217 L8
Benmore Cl NMIL/BTOS BH25 226 A6
Benmore Gdns CHFD SO53 53 G8
Benmore Rd
MOOR/WNTN BH9 220 E7
Bennett Cl RSAL SP5 73 J2 1
Bennett Rd CHAR BH8 236 B2
Bennetts La RGWD BH24 173 G6
Bennion Rd NBNE BH10 220 A5
Benridge Cl BDST BH18 217 L5
Benson Cl CHCH/BSGR BH23 197 M7
Benson Rd WSHM SO15 106 A8
Bentham Rd GPORT PO12 10 E6
Bentham Wy HLER SO31 134 B8
Bentley Cl HORN PO8 116 B8
WINC SO23 17 G2
Bentley Ct HAV PO9 165 M3 2
Bentley Crs FHAM/PORC PO16 6 F3
Bentley Gn WEND SO18 108 B8
Bentley Rd MOOR/WNTN BH9 220 D5
Bepton Down EPSF GU31 63 M5
Berber Cl FHAM PO15 159 G1
Bercote Cl FUFL SO22 16 A3
Bere Cl CFDH BH17 218 B6
CHFD SO53 52 F8
FUFL SO22 2 A3
Bere Farm La WHAM PO17 137 K8
Bere Rd WVILLE PO7 139 L4
Beresford Cl
BKME/WDN BH12 234 C2 1
CHFD SO53 81 K3 1
WVILLE PO7 164 C2
Beresford Gdns
CHCH/BSGR BH23 238 D2
CHFD SO53 81 K3 2
Beresford Rd
BKME/WDN BH12 234 C2
CHFD SO53 81 K3
FHAM/STUB PO14 184 B5
LYMN SO41 228 A4
NEND PO2 187 J6
SBNE BH6 237 G4
Bereweeke Av FUFL SO22 2 C1
Bereweeke Cl FUFL SO22 2 C4
Bereweeke Rd FUFL SO22 2 C4
Bereweeke Wy FUFL SO22 2 D3
Bergen Crs HEND SO30 134 A3
Berkeley Av BKME/WDN BH12 219 G8
Berkeley Cl FHAM/STUB PO14 183 M6
VWD BH31 144 C1
WSHM SO15 131 J1
Berkeley Gdns HEND SO30 134 A3
Berkeley Rd TWDS BH3 235 K1
Berkeley Sq HAV PO9 9 J4
Berkley Av FERN BH22 194 B6
Berkshire Cl PSEA PO1 13 K2
Bernard Av CHAM PO6 163 L8
Bernards Cl
CHCH/BSGR BH23 237 K1 1
Bernard St SHAM SO14 5 G5
Berney Rd ENEY PO4 212 A4
Bernina Av WVILLE PO7 140 A6
Bernina Cl WVILLE PO7 140 A6
Bernwood Gv FAWY SO45 206 C1
Berrans Av BWD BH11 219 M2
Berrybarn La SELS PO20 215 K8
Berry Cl HEND SO30 134 B2
Berrydown Rd HAV PO9 165 G1
Berryfield Rd LYMN SO41 226 E6
Berrylands LISS GU33 36 F1
Berry La FHAM/STUB PO14 183 L6
RWIN SO21 54 F1
Berrywood Gdns
HEND SO30 109 G8 1
HEND SO30 133 M1
Bertie Rd ENEY PO4 211 M4
Bertram Rd NMIL/BTOS BH25 226 A4
Berwick Rd TWDS BH3 235 K2
Beryl Av GPORT PO12 185 K8
Beryton Cl GPORT PO12 209 L2 2
Beryton Rd GPORT PO12 209 L2
Besomer Dro RSAL SP5 73 L4
Bessborough Rd CCLF BH13 245 K1
Beswick Av NBNE BH10 220 B6
Bethia Cl BMTH BH1 236 C2 2
Bethia Rd CHAR BH8 236 C2
Betsy Cl CHCH/BSGR BH23 197 M7
Betsy La CHCH/BSGR BH23 197 M7
Betteridge Dr ROWN SO16 105 J2
Bettesworth Rd PSEA PO1 211 J1
Bettiscombe Cl CFDH BH17 218 B6
Betula Cl WVILLE PO7 164 E2 1
Beulah Rd ROWN SO16 105 M7
Bevan Cl ITCH SO19 132 C7
Bevan Rd HORN PO8 140 D3
Beverley Cl HLER SO31 159 G4
Beverley Gdns BPWT SO32 112 A3 1
HLER SO31 133 J7
NBNE BH10 220 B5
ROMY SO51 51 H7 2
Beverley Hts WEND SO18 107 L5
Beverley Rd FAWY SO45 155 K8
FHAM/STUB PO14 184 A7
Beverly Cl LSOL/BMARY PO13 185 H6
Beverston Rd CHAM PO6 162 E7
Bevis Cl FAWY SO45 180 D6
HLER SO31 158 B8
Bevis Rd GPORT PO12 10 F2
NEND PO2 187 H7
Bevois Gdns SHAM SO14 131 L1
Bevois Hl PTSW SO17 107 G8
Bevois Valley Rd SHAM SO14 131 M1
Bexington Cl BWD BH11 219 J5 1
Beyne Rd FUFL SO22 26 A5
Bickerley Gdns RGWD BH24 170 D2
Bickerley Rd RGWD BH24 170 D2
Bicton Rd BWD BH11 219 M5 1
Bidbury La HAV PO9 165 G7
Biddenfield La WHAM PO17 136 B4
Biddlecombe Cl
LSOL/BMARY PO13 185 G8
Bideford Cl ROWN SO16 105 K7
Bilberry Cl HLER SO31 158 D6
Bilberry Dr TOTT SO40 130 C6
Billett Av WVILLE PO7 140 D7
Billing Cl ENEY PO4 211 M5 1
Billington Gdns HEND SO30 109 J7
Billy Lawn Av HAV PO9 165 K4
Bilton Wy HSEA PO3 188 A6
Bindon Cl BKME/WDN BH12 234 D1
ROWN SO16 105 M6
Bindon Rd ROWN SO16 105 M6
Bingham Av PSTN BH14 245 J1
Bingham Cl
CHCH/BSGR BH23 238 D1 1
Bingham Dr LYMN SO41 228 C5
Bingham Rd CHCH/BSGR BH23 238 D1
MOOR/WNTN BH9 220 E8
VWD BH31 144 E4
Binnacle Wy CHAM PO6 162 F8
Binness Wy CHAM PO6 188 C1
Binnie Rd BKME/WDN BH12 234 D3
Binsey Cl ROWN SO16 105 K8
Binstead Cl ROWN SO16 107 H3
Binsteed Rd NEND PO2 187 J8
Birch Av CHCH/BSGR BH23 223 G5
FERN BH22 194 D7
NMIL/BTOS BH25 225 H2
Birch Cl HORN PO8 140 C5
LISS GU33 36 F4
PSTN BH14 234 D5
RGWD BH24 169 H5
ROMY SO51 79 H2
ROWN SO16 105 M6
WIMB BH21 217 H2 1
Birch Dl FAWY SO45 155 M6
Birchdale Cl HLER SO31 158 B8 2
Birchdale Rd WIMB BH21 192 B3
Birch Dr CHAR BH8 221 L6
LSOL/BMARY PO13 185 G4
Birchen Cl HLER SO31 159 G4 1
The Birches Cl NBAD SO52 79 L3
The Birches WEND SO18 108 A8 2
Birch Gv ELGH SO50 81 L2
FERN BH22 168 B6
Birchlands TOTT SO40 129 H3
Birchmore Cl
LSOL/BMARY PO13 185 G6 2
Birch Rd HEND SO30 134 B1
RGWD BH24 169 M4
ROWN SO16 80 F8
ROWN SO16 105 M6
Birch Tree Cl EMRTH PO10 166 D4
Birch Tree Dr EMRTH PO10 166 D4
Birch Wd ITCH SO19 133 J3
Birchwood Cl
CHCH/BSGR BH23 224 C7 1
Birchwood Dr FBDG SP6 121 L3
Birchwood Gdns HEND SO30 109 H8 1
Birchwood Rd PSTN BH14 234 C5
UPTN BH16 232 A2
Birchy Hl LYMN SO41 201 G7
Birdham Rd HISD PO11 214 C6
Birdlip Cl HORN PO8 140 E2
Birdlip Rd CHAM PO6 162 F7
Bird's Hill Rd PLE BH15 233 K4
Birdwood Gv
FHAM/PORC PO16 161 K8
Birinus Rd WINC SO23 3 H5
Birkdale Av CHAM PO6 164 A7
Birkdale Ct WIMB BH21 217 L3
Birkdale Rd WIMB BH21 217 L3
Biscay Cl FHAM/STUB PO14 183 M5 1
Bishearne Gdns LISS GU33 36 D3 1
Bishop Cl BKME/WDN BH12 235 H1 1
Bishop Ct RGWD BH24 170 E1 1
Bishop Rd MOOR/WNTN BH9 220 E8
Bishops Cl LTDN BH7 236 E2
Bishops Ct ELGH SO50 82 C3
Bishops Crs ITCH SO19 132 D3
Bishopsfield Rd
FHAM/STUB PO14 6 D8
Bishops Ga FHAM/STUB PO14 159 G5
Bishop's La BPWT SO32 111 H1
BPWT SO32 112 A7
Bishops Rd ITCH SO19 132 C5
Bishopstoke La ELGH SO50 82 D2
Bishopstoke Rd ELGH SO50 82 B5
HAV PO9 165 J3
Bishop St PSEA PO1 12 D1
Bishop's Wood Rd BPWT SO32 112 A5
Bisterne Cl RGWD BH24 173 H6
Bittern Cl GPORT PO12 209 M1
Bitterne Cl HAV PO9 165 K2
Bitterne Crs ITCH SO19 132 E2 1
Bitterne Rd East WEND SO18 132 E2
Bitterne Rd West WEND SO18 132 C1
Bitterne Wy ITCH SO19 132 C2
LYMN SO41 228 B6
VWD BH31 144 E3
Black Berry Cl HORN PO8 116 C4
Blackberry La
CHCH/BSGR BH23 238 E2
Blackberry Ter SHAM SO14 131 M1 2
Blackbird Cl CFDH BH17 217 J8
HORN PO8 140 D4
Blackbird Rd ELGH SO50 81 J6
Blackbird Wy
CHCH/BSGR BH23 198 A8
LSOL/BMARY PO13 208 D1
Blackbrook House Dr
FHAM PO15 6 D5
Blackbrook Park Av FHAM PO15 6 C5
Blackbrook Rd FHAM PO15 6 D5
Blackburn Rd
BKME/WDN BH12 234 A2
Blackbushe Cl ROWN SO16 105 L3 2
Blackbush Rd LYMN SO41 242 A2
Blackcap Cl HAV PO9 141 L7
Blackdown Cl FAWY SO45 155 H6 1
Blackdown Crs HAV PO9 165 J4
Blackfield La FERN BH22 168 C5
Blackfield Rd CHAR BH8 221 H5 1
FAWY SO45 180 C7
Blackfriars Cl SSEA PO5 13 J3 2
Blackfriars Rd SSEA PO5 13 J2
Black Hl VWD BH31 144 E2
Blackhill Rd ROMY SO51 76 E8
Black Horse La BPWT SO32 111 K7
Blackhouse La WHAM PO17 137 L8
Black La RSAL SP5 73 M3
Blackmore La PSF GU32 34 D4
Blacksmith Cl WIMB BH21 217 H3
Blackthorn Cl ITCH SO19 132 D3 1
LYMN SO41 227 M6
Blackthorn Dr GPORT PO12 185 L7
HISD PO11 214 A5
Blackthorn Gn RWIN SO21 54 F8
Blackthorn Rd HISD PO11 214 A5
ITCH SO19 132 D3
Blackthorn Wy VWD BH31 144 F3
Blackwater Cl CHAM PO6 163 H8 1
Blackwater Dr TOTT SO40 104 C7
WIMB BH21 218 B1
Blackwater Gv FBDG SP6 121 J3
Blackwater Ms TOTT SO40 104 C7
Bladon Cl HAV PO9 9 L1
Bladon Rd ROWN SO16 106 B6
Blair Av PSTN BH14 234 B4
Blair Cl NMIL/BTOS BH25 225 J5
Blake Cl ROWN SO16 105 H3 1
Blakedene Rd PSTN BH14 234 A7
Blake Hill Av PSTN BH14 234 B7
Blake Hill Crs PSTN BH14 234 B7
Blakemere Crs CHAM PO6 163 G7
Blakeney Rd ROWN SO16 105 J6
Blake Rd CHAM PO6 164 B7
GPORT PO12 11 G2
Blakesley La HSEA PO3 188 A4
Blanchard Rd BPWT SO32 85 G8
Blandford Cl PLE BH15 232 E6
Blandford Rd PLE BH15 232 F7
RSAL SP5 42 C1
UPTN BH16 232 B2
Blandford Rd North
UPTN BH16 216 D5
Blaney Wy WIMB BH21 217 G2
Blankney Cl
FHAM/STUB PO14 183 M6 1
Blann Cl ROWN SO16 105 H3 2
Bleaklow Cl ROWN SO16 105 L8
Blechynden Ter WSHM SO15 4 D2
Blencowe Dr NBAD SO52 80 D3
Blendworth Crs HAV PO9 165 J5
Blendworth La HORN PO8 141 H1
WEND SO18 133 G1
Blendworth Rd ENEY PO4 211 M3 1
Blenheim Av PTSW SO17 106 F7
Blenheim Cl NBAD SO52 80 E4
TOTT SO40 129 H2
Blenheim Ct ENEY PO4 211 L5 1
Blenheim Crs LYMN SO41 226 C4
Blenheim Dr CHCH/BSGR BH23 239 G1
Blenheim Gdns FAWY SO45 155 H6
GPORT PO12 185 M8
HAV PO9 9 L2
PTSW SO17 107 G6
Blenheim Rd ELGH SO50 81 M6
HORN PO8 140 E3
Bleriot Crs FHAM PO15 159 K2
Blighmont Crs WSHM SO15 130 F2
Blind La BPWT SO32 109 H3
FBDG SP6 123 G7
WHAM PO17 136 D3
Bliss Cl WVILLE PO7 164 C3
Blissford Cl HAV PO9 165 M2 1
Blissford Cross FBDG SP6 98 D8
Blissford Hl FBDG SP6 123 J2
Blissford Rd FBDG SP6 98 C7
Bloomfield Av
MOOR/WNTN BH9 220 D6
Blossom Cl HEND SO30 134 C2
Blount Rd PSEA PO1 12 E5
Bloxworth Rd
BKME/WDN BH12 219 K8
Blue Ball Hl WINC SO23 3 J7
Bluebell Cl CHCH/BSGR BH23 223 M8
WVILLE PO7 164 D2
Bluebell Copse HLER SO31 158 D6
Bluebell La CFDH BH17 217 J7
Bluebell Rd ROWN SO16 107 G4
Bluestar Gdns HEND SO30 109 H6
Blundell La HLER SO31 134 A6
Blyth Cl CHCH/BSGR BH23 222 B4
ROWN SO16 105 J6
Blythe Rd WIMB BH21 217 H2
Blythswood Ct
NMIL/BTOS BH25 240 E1 1
Boakes Pl TOTT SO40 129 G6 1
Boarhunt Cl PSEA PO1 13 J1 1
Boarhunt Rd WHAM PO17 161 L4
Bob Hann Cl BKME/WDN BH12 234 D3
Bockhampton Rd
CHCH/BSGR BH23 223 J3
Bodley Rd CCLF BH13 245 L1 2
Bodmin Rd CHAM PO6 162 E8 1
ELGH SO50 82 D5
Bodorgan Rd WCLF BH2 14 E4
Bodowen Cl
CHCH/BSGR BH23 223 H6
Bodowen Rd
CHCH/BSGR BH23 223 H6
Bodycoats Rd CHFD SO53 81 J2
Bognor Rd BDST BH18 217 K4
Bohemia La RSAL SP5 73 L5
Boiler Rd PSEA PO1 210 D2
Bolde Cl HSEA PO3 187 M5
Boldens Rd GPORT PO12 10 E9
Bolderford Br BROC SO42 175 J3
Bolderwood Arboretum Ornamental
Dr LYND SO43 149 L4
RGWD BH24 150 A6
Bolderwood Cl ELGH SO50 82 E5
Boldre Cl BKME/WDN BH12 234 D1
HAV PO9 165 G4 1
NMIL/BTOS BH25 225 H8
Boldre La LYMN SO41 228 B1
Boldrewood Rd ROWN SO16 106 D4
Boleyn Crs MOOR/WNTN BH9 221 G4
Bolhinton Av TOTT SO40 130 B7
Bolton Crs FERN BH22 194 E2
Bolton Rd SBNE BH6 237 K5 2
The Boltons WVILLE PO7 164 C5 1
Bonchurch Cl ROWN SO16 107 H3 2
Bonchurch Rd ENEY PO4 211 L3
Bond Av FERN BH22 168 B4
Bond Cl LYMN SO41 200 F5
Bondfields Crs HAV PO9 165 K2
Bond Rd PLE BH15 233 L3
WEND SO18 107 K7
Bond St SHAM SO14 132 A2
Bones La EPSF GU31 91 J3
Bonfire Cnr PSEA PO1 210 E2
Bonham Rd TWDS BH3 235 L1 1
Boniface Cl TOTT SO40 104 C8 1
Boniface Crs ROWN SO16 105 K5
Bonington Cl
CHCH/BSGR BH23 223 J8 1
Boothby Cl TOTT SO40 129 L2 1
Bordean La PSF GU32 62 A3
Borden La LIPH GU30 66 C2
Border Dr UPTN BH16 232 B3
Border Rd UPTN BH16 232 B3
Bordon Rd HAV PO9 165 K3
Boreham Rd SBNE BH6 237 J3
Borley Rd CFDH BH17 217 L8
Borough Gv PSF GU32 63 K6
Borough Hl PSF GU32 63 K5
Borough Rd PSF GU32 63 J6
The Borough RSAL SP5 72 D1
Borrowdale Rd ROWN SO16 105 K7
Borthwick Rd BMTH BH1 236 D3
Boscobel Rd FUFL SO22 2 E4
Boscombe Cliff Rd BOSC BH5 236 D5
Boscombe Grove Rd
BMTH BH1 236 C3
Boscombe Overcliff Dr
BOSC BH5 236 E5
Boscombe Spa Rd BOSC BH5 236 C4
Bosham Rd NEND PO2 187 K8
Bosham Wk
LSOL/BMARY PO13 184 F6
Bosley Cl CHCH/BSGR BH23 222 C6
Bosley Wy CHCH/BSGR BH23 222 C6
Bosmere Gdns EMRTH PO10 166 C7
Bosmere Rd HISD PO11 214 C6
Bossington Cl ROWN SO16 105 K3 1
Boston Rd CHAM PO6 163 J7
Bosuns Cl FHAM/PORC PO16 184 F2
Bosville ELGH SO50 81 M2
Boswell Cl HEND SO30 134 D1
ITCH SO19 133 G2
Bosworth Ms
MOOR/WNTN BH9 220 F4 1
Botany Bay Rd ITCH SO19 132 E6
Botley Dr HAV PO9 165 H3
Botley Gdns ITCH SO19 133 J5 2
Botley Rd BPWT SO32 110 C8
ELGH SO50 83 J8
HEND SO30 108 E7
HEND SO30 135 H2
HLER SO31 134 E8
ITCH SO19 133 H5 1
NBAD SO52 79 L3
Bottom La ROMY SO51 76 D4
Boulnois Av PSTN BH14 234 D5
Boulter La WHAM PO17 162 E1
Boulton Rd SSEA PO5 13 L6
Boundary Cl WSHM SO15 130 D2
Boundary Dr WIMB BH21 192 B2
Boundary La RGWD BH24 169 H7
Boundary Rd HLER SO31 133 K8
MOOR/WNTN BH9 220 B8
NBNE BH10 220 B7
Boundary Wy CHAM PO6 163 M6
HAV PO9 8 D4
Bound La HISD PO11 213 L6
Boundstone FAWY SO45 155 K5 1
Boundway LYMN SO41 200 B7
Bourne Av WCLF BH2 14 C5
WSHM SO15 106 B7
Bourne Cl HORN PO8 140 F2
ROMY SO51 76 C5
RWIN SO21 54 A4
WBNE BH4 14 A5
Bourne Ct WIMB BH21 192 B3
Bournefields RWIN SO21 55 G1
Bourne La RWIN SO21 54 F1
TOTT SO40 128 B3
Bournemouth Av
GPORT PO12 209 L1
Bournemouth International Centre
Rbt
WCLF BH2 14 E7
Bournemouth Rd CHFD SO53 81 G5
LYND SO43 151 J3
PSTN BH14 234 B4
ROWN SO16 80 F8
Bournemouth Road Castle Hl
PSTN BH14 234 A4
Bournemouth Station Rbt
BMTH BH1 15 J4
Bourne Rd CHAM PO6 162 F8
TOTT SO40 128 A3
WSHM SO15 4 B1
Bourne Valley Rd
BKME/WDN BH12 234 F3
Bourne View Cl EMRTH PO10 167 H6
Bournewood Dr WBNE BH4 235 H4
Bourton Gdns LTDN BH7 221 M8 1
Bouverie Cl NMIL/BTOS BH25 225 K7
Boveridge Gdns
MOOR/WNTN BH9 220 F4
Bovington Cl CFDH BH17 218 D7
Bowater Cl TOTT SO40 104 B7
Bowater Wy TOTT SO40 104 B7
Bowcombe HLER SO31 157 G1
Bowden La PTSW SO17 107 H6
Bowden Rd BKME/WDN BH12 219 G6
Bower Cl FAWY SO45 180 A5
ITCH SO19 132 D7
Bower Rd CHAR BH8 221 H8
Bowers Cl HORN PO8 140 E4
Bowers Hl RSAL SP5 73 K1
Bowerwood Rd FBDG SP6 97 H8
Bowes Hl HAV PO9 142 A5
Bowland Ri CHFD SO53 80 F1
NMIL/BTOS BH25 226 A6
Bowland Wy FAWY SO45 206 C1 1
Bowler Av PSEA PO1 211 K2
Bowler Ct HSEA PO3 211 K2
Box Cl CFDH BH17 233 G1
Boxwood Cl
FHAM/PORC PO16 161 M7 1
WVILLE PO7 164 C2
Boyatt Crs ELGH SO50 53 M8
Boyatt La CHFD SO53 53 M7
ELGH SO50 54 A7
Boyd Cl FHAM/STUB PO14 183 M7 1
Boyd Rd BKME/WDN BH12 234 E2
LSOL/BMARY PO13 184 F5
Boyes La RWIN SO21 54 F7
Boyle Crs WVILLE PO7 164 B3
Boyne Mead Rd WINC SO23 17 G1
Boynton Cl CHFD SO53 53 G8
Brabant Cl HLER SO31 158 F1
Brabazon Dr CHCH/BSGR BH23 239 G1
Brabazon Rd FHAM PO15 159 H3
WIMB BH21 192 D7
Brabourne Av FERN BH22 194 A4
Bracken Cl NBAD SO52 79 M5
RGWD BH24 169 H4
Bracken Crs ELGH SO50 82 E6
Brackendale Ct WIMB BH21 144 B8 1
Brackendale Rd CHAR BH8 221 G8
Bracken Gln PLE BH15 233 K4
Bracken Heath HORN PO8 140 F7
Brackenhill CCLF BH13 234 F7
Brackenhill Rd WIMB BH21 192 E1
Bracken La ROWN SO16 105 M7
Bracken Pl ELGH SO50 106 F1
Bracken Rd EPSF GU31 64 B6
FERN BH22 193 M1
NBAD SO52 79 M5
SBNE BH6 237 H4
The Brackens FAWY SO45 155 H5 2
HLER SO31 158 F6
Brackens Wy LYMN SO41 228 D6 1
Bracken Wy CHCH/BSGR BH23 224 F7
Brackenway Rd CHFD SO53 53 H8
Bracklesham Cl ITCH SO19 132 D5
Bracklesham Rd HISD PO11 214 D7
LSOL/BMARY PO13 185 H8
Brackley Av ELGH SO50 83 G6
Brackley Cl CHCH/BSGR BH23 195 L8
Brackley Wy TOTT SO40 104 C8
Bradburne Rd WCLF BH2 14 C5
Bradford Rd
MOOR/WNTN BH9 221 G4
SSEA PO5 13 K3
Brading Av ENEY PO4 211 L6
LSOL/BMARY PO13 185 G6
Brading Cl ROWN SO16 107 H3
Bradley Ct HAV PO9 165 M3
Bradley Gn ROWN SO16 106 A4
Bradley Peak FUFL SO22 16 B7
Bradley Rd FUFL SO22 16 B5
Bradly Rd FHAM PO15 160 A7
Bradpole Rd CHAR BH8 221 J7
Bradshaw Cl ELGH SO50 83 K6 1
Bradstock Cl BKME/WDN BH12 219 K6
Braehead FAWY SO45 155 K6
Braemar Av CHAM PO6 187 M1
SBNE BH6 237 M4
Braemar Cl FHAM PO15 6 D1
LSOL/BMARY PO13 185 H6
SBNE BH6 237 M4
Braemar Dr
CHCH/BSGR BH23 224 D7
Braemar Rd
LSOL/BMARY PO13 185 H5
Braeside Cl FUFL SO22 26 A4
Braeside Crs ITCH SO19 132 C3 1
Braeside Rd FERN BH22 168 C5
ITCH SO19 132 C3
RGWD BH24 169 J4
Braidley Rd WCLF BH2 14 D3
Brailswood Rd PLE BH15 233 J4
Braintree Rd CHAM PO6 163 H7
Brairwood Gdns HISD PO11 213 K5
Braishfield Cl ROWN SO16 105 L7
Braishfield Gdns CHAR BH8 221 H6
Braishfield Rd HAV PO9 165 L4
ROMY SO51 51 H7
Bramber Rd GPORT PO12 209 L1
Bramble Cl ELGH SO50 82 A3 2
FAWY SO45 180 A5
FBDG SP6 121 L3 3
FHAM/STUB PO14 183 L7
Bramble Dr ROMY SO51 51 H7 3
Bramble Hl CHFD SO53 81 G2
Bramble La CHCH/BSGR BH23 224 F7
HLER SO31 158 C3
HORN PO8 116 A1
Bramble Ms WEND SO18 107 M8 1
Bramble Rd ENEY PO4 13 L4
EPSF GU31 64 B5
Brambles Cl RWIN SO21 54 F8
Brambles Rd
LSOL/BMARY PO13 208 B1 1
Bramble Wk LYMN SO41 228 A4 1
Bramble Wy
CHCH/BSGR BH23 197 M7 1
LSOL/BMARY PO13 184 E6
Brambling Cl ROWN SO16 106 A2 1
Brambling La MIDH GU29 67 L5
Brambling Rd HAV PO9 141 M7
The Bramblings TOTT SO40 104 B8 2
Bramdean Dr HAV PO9 165 H3

Bramdean Rd *WEND* SO18......... **133** H1
Bramham Moor
  FHAM/STUB PO14 ....**183** M6 ☑
Bramley Cl *LYMN* SO41 ......**228** C6 ☑
  WVILLE PO7 ....**140** D8
Bramley Crs *ITCH* SO19........**132** F6
Bramley Gdns *EMRTH* PO10.. **166** F8
  GPORT PO12 ....**209** L7
Bramley Rd *FERN* BH22 ......**194** B2 ☑
  NBNE BH10 ....**220** A3
The Bramleys *RSAL* SP5 ....**47** G5
Brampton La *HSEA* PO3 ....**188** A4
Brampton Rd *PLE* BH15 ....**233** J2 ☑
Bramshaw Cl *FUFL* SO22 ....**16** B5
Bramshaw Ct *HAV* PO9 ....**165** M3 ☑
Bramshaw Gdns *CHAR* BH8 ..**221** H5 ☑
Bramshaw Wy
  NMIL/BTOS BH25 ....**225** H8
  ITCH SO19 ....**132** D7 ☑
Bramston Rd *WSHM* SO15 ......**106** B8
Branches La *ROMY* SO51 ....**48** E6
Branders Cl *SBNE* BH6 ....**237** M4
Branders La *SBNE* BH6 ....**237** M3
Brandon Rd *SSEA* PO5 ....**13** J8
Branksea Av *PLE* BH15 ....**232** C7
Branksea Cl *PLE* BH15 ....**232** D7
Branksome Av *WSHM* SO15 ...**106** B7
Branksome Cl *FUFL* SO22 ....**26** A2
  NMIL/BTOS BH25 ....**225** M6
Branksome Dene Rd
  WBNE BH4 ....**235** G6
Branksome Hill Rd
  WBNE BH4 ....**235** G3
Branksome Towers *CCLF* BH13.. **235** G8
Branksome Wood Gdns
  WCLF BH2 ....**14** B3
Branksome Wood Rd
  WBNE BH4 ....**235** H3
Bransbury Cl *ROWN* SO16 ...**106** B4 ☑
Bransbury Rd *ENEY* PO4 .....**211** M5
Bransgore Av *HAV* PO9 ....**165** G4
Bransgore Gdns
  CHCH/BSGR BH23 ....**197** M7
Bransley Cl *ROMY* SO51 ....**76** C5
Branwell Cl *CHCH/BSGR* BH23... **222** E7
Branwood Cl *LYMN* SO41 ....**227** J7 ☑
Brasenose Cl
  FHAM/STUB PO14 ....**159** G7
Brasher Cl *ELGH* SO50..........**82** F6
Brassey Cl *MOOR/WNTN* BH9 ...**220** F7
Brassey Rd *FUFL* SO22 ....**2** E4
  MOOR/WNTN BH9 ....**220** D7
Brasted Ct *ENEY* PO4 ....**212** A3 ☑
Brazil Rd *SHAM* SO14 ....**5** J8
Breach Av *EMRTH* PO10 ....**167** H6
Breamore Cl *ELGH* SO50 ....**81** M2 ☑
  NMIL/BTOS BH25 ....**225** J5 ☑
  RSAL SP5 ....**72** C2
  WEND SO18 ....**133** H1
Brean Cl *ROWN* SO16 ....**105** K5
Brecon Av *CHAM* PO6 ....**163** M7
Brecon Cl *CHFD* SO53 ....**81** G5 ☑
  FAWY SO45 ....**155** J5
  FHAM/STUB PO14 ....**6** B7
  NBNE BH10 ....**220** C2
  NMIL/BTOS BH25 ....**226** A6
Brecon Rd *ITCH* SO19 ....**133** G3
Bredenbury Crs *CHAM* PO6 ...**163** G7
Bredy Cl *CFDH* BH17 ....**218** B7 ☑
Breech Cl *HSEA* PO3 ....**187** K4 ☑
Bremble Cl *BKME/WDN* BH12 ...**219** G6
Brenchley Cl
  FHAM/PORC PO16 ....**185** L1
Brendon Cl *CHAR* BH8 ....**221** J6 ☑
  FAWY SO45 ....**155** H6 ☑
Brendon Gn *ROWN* SO16 .....**105** L8
Brendon Rd *FHAM/STUB* PO14 .....**6** B8
Brent Ct *EMRTH* PO10 ....**166** C8
Brentwood Crs *WEND* SO18 ...**107** M7
Breton Cl *FHAM* PO15 ....**158** F1
Brewells La *LISS* GU33 ....**37** K2
Brewer Cl *HLER* SO31 ....**158** F4
Brewers La *LSOL/BMARY* PO13..**185** G6
  NARL SO24 ....**33** G1
  RWIN SO21 ....**54** E3
Brewer St *PSEA* PO1 ....**211** G2 ☑
Brewhouse Sq *GPORT* PO12 ......**11** J1
Brewster Cl *HORN* PO8.........**140** E5
Briar Cl *CHCH/BSGR* BH23 ...**238** E2
  GPORT PO12 ....**209** J5
  HORN PO8 ....**140** F3
  PLE BH15 ....**233** K3
Briardene Ct *TOTT* SO40 ....**129** J1 ☑
Briarfield Gdns *HORN* PO8.....**140** F2
Briarswood *ROWN* SO16 ....**106** A7
Briarswood Ri *FAWY* SO45 ...**155** H6
Briarswood Rd *UPTN* BH16 ..**232** B1 ☑
Briar Wy *ROMY* SO51 ....**51** H7
  WIMB BH21 ....**192** F3
Briar Wd *LISS* GU33 ....**36** F1
Briarwood Cl *FHAM/PORC* PO16...**7** J7
Briarwood Rd *TOTT* SO40 .....**129** G2
Brickfield La *CHFD* SO53........**81** G3
  LYMN SO41 ....**228** D3
Brickfield Rd *PTSW* SO17 .....**107** H6
Brick Kiln La *NARL* SO24 ....**32** E1
Brickmakers Rd *RWIN* SO21 ......**54** E8
Brickwoods *ROMY* SO51 .....**51** G8 ☑
Brickworth La *RSAL* SP5 ....**46** B4
Brickworth Rd *RSAL* SP5 ....**46** D4
Brickyard La *WIMB* BH21 .....**193** L2
Brickyard Rd *BPWT* SO32 .....**111** L5
The Brickyard *TOTT* SO40 ....**103** G8
Bricky Lake La *ROMY* SO51 ...**103** H1
Bridefield Cl *HORN* PO8 ....**140** B5
Bridefield Crs *HORN* PO8 .....**140** B5
Bridge Ap *PLE* BH15 ....**233** L2 ☑
Bridge Cl *HLER* SO31 ....**133** M7
Bridgefoot Dr
  FHAM/PORC PO16 ....**7** M5
Bridgefoot Pth *EMRTH* PO10 ..**166** D8
Bridgemary Av
  LSOL/BMARY PO13 ....**185** H5
Bridgemary Gv
  LSOL/BMARY PO13 ....**185** G4

Bridgemary Rd
  LSOL/BMARY PO13 ....**185** G3
Bridgemary Wy
  LSOL/BMARY PO13 ....**185** G3 ☑
Bridge Md *BPWT* SO32 ....**87** J3
Bridge Mdw *LISS* GU33 ....**36** E4
Bridge Pl *NBNE* BH10 ....**220** B1
Bridge Rd *EMRTH* PO10 ......**166** D7
  HLER SO31 ....**133** M7
  HLER SO31 ....**158** C2
  ITCH SO19 ....**132** B5
  LYMN SO41 ....**228** D4
  ROMY SO51 ....**78** E1
  RSAL SP5 ....**41** G1
Bridgers Cl *ROWN* SO16 ......**105** K3
Bridges Cl *ELGH* SO50............**81** L5
  FERN BH22 ....**168** D5 ☑
Bridgeside Cl *PSEA* PO1 ....**13** K1
The Bridges *RGWD* BH24 .....**170** C1
Bridge St *CHCH/BSGR* BH23... **238** B2
  FBDC SP6 ....**97** L7
  FHAM/STUB PO14.................**159** L8
  WHAM PO17 ....**136** E4
  WHAM PO17 ....**162** B2
  WINC SO23 ....**3** J8 ☑
Bridget Cl *HORN* PO8 ....**141** G1
Bridgewater Rd
  BKME/WDN BH12 ....**234** C2 ☑
Bridgewater Ct *WSHM* SO15 ....**4** A1
Bridle Cl *UPTN* BH16 ....**232** C1
Bridle Crs *LTDN* BH7 ....**222** A8
Bridle Wy *WIMB* BH21 ....**192** F2
Bridleways *WHM* WSH1 ....**144** C2
Bridlington Av *WSHM* SO15...**106** C8
Bridport Rd *BKME/WDN* BH12...**219** K8
  VWD BH31 ....**144** D2
Bridport St *PSEA* PO1 ....**13** H1
Brierley Av *FERN* BH22 ....**194** C4
Brierley Cl *NBNE* BH10 ....**220** C3
Brierley Rd *NBNE* BH10 ....**220** C3
Brigantine Rd *HLER* SO31 ....**158** C7
Brighstone Cl *ROWN* SO16 .....**107** H3 ☑
Brightlands Av *SBNE* BH6 ....**237** L4
Brighton Av *GPORT* PO12 ....**185** K8
Brighton Rd *LYMN* SO41.......**200** E5
  WSHM SO15 ....**131** K1
Bright Rd *PLE* BH15 ....**233** J2
Brightside *WVILLE* PO7 ....**164** B2
Brightside Rd *ROWN* SO16 ...**105** L6
Brights La *HISD* PO11 ....**213** K3
Brightstone Cl *CHAM* PO6 ....**187** J1
Brindle Cl *ROWN* SO16 ....**106** F3
Brinsons Cl *CHCH/BSGR* BH23 ..**223** G5
Brinton La *FAWY* SO45 ....**155** L3
Brinton's Rd *SHAM* SO14 ....**5** J3
Brinton's Ter *SHAM* SO14 ...**131** L2 ☑
Brisbane Rd
  CHCH/BSGR BH23 ....**222** C7
Bristol Rd *ENEY* PO4 ....**211** K6
Britain St *PSEA* PO1 ....**12** D2
Britannia Gdns *HEND* SO30 ...**109** C5 ☑
Britannia Rd *PSTN* BH14 ......**233** M5
  SHAM SO14 ....**5** K1
  SSEA PO5 ....**13** K4 ☑
Britannia Rd North *SSEA* PO5 ....**13** K4
Britannia Wy
  CHCH/BSGR BH23 ....**239** G1 ☑
Briton St *SHAM* SO14 ....**4** F6
Britten Rd *LSOL/BMARY* PO13...**208** C2
Britten Wy *WVILLE* PO7 ....**164** C4
Brixey Cl *BKME/WDN* BH12 ..**234** B1
Brixey Rd *BKME/WDN* BH12 .**234** B1
Broad Av *CHAR* BH8 ....**221** H8
Broadbent Cl *ROWN* SO16 ...**105** J2
Broad Chalke Down *FUFL* SO22 ..**26** B4
Broad Cft *HAV* PO9 ....**142** A6
Broadcut *FHAM/PORC* PO16 .....**7** M3
Broadfields Cl *LYMN* SO41 ...**242** C3
Broad Gdns *CHAM* PO6 ....**164** C8
Broad Gn *SHAM* SO14 ....**5** H2
Broadhill La *FBDC* SP6 ....**98** C3
Broadhurst Av *NBNE* BH10 ...**220** C4
Broadlands Av *ELGH* SO50 .....**81** M3
  SBNE BH6 ....**237** L4
  WVILLE PO7 ....**164** C2
Broadlands Cl *CHAR* BH8 ....**221** H5
  CHCH/BSGR BH23 ....**224** F6
Broadlands Rd *BROC* SO42 ...**175** A6
  PTSW SO17 ....**107** G5
Broad La *BPWT* SO32 ....**111** M3
  LYMN SO41 ....**228** D5
  NBAD SO52 ....**79** K3 ☑
  WVILLE PO7 ....**138** F2
Broadley Cl *FAWY* SO45 .....**180** A4 ☑
Broadly Cl *LYMN* SO41 ....**227** M6
Broadmayne Rd
  BKME/WDN BH12 ....**234** E1
Broadmeadow Cl
  TOTT SO40 ....**129** J1
Broadmeadows La
  WVILLE PO7 ....**164** E1 ☑
Broadmead Rd *ROWN* SO16 ...**105** J2
Broad Mead Rd *WIMB* BH21 .**144** C2
Broadmere Av *HAV* PO9 ....**165** K3
Broadmoor Rd *WIMB* BH21 ..**217** G2
Broad Oak *HEND* SO30 ....**134** C1
Broadoak Cl *FAWY* SO45 .....**180** A5
Broad Rd *RCCH* PO18 ....**167** M8
Broadsands Dr *GPORT* PO12 .**209** H5
Broadshard La *RGWD* BH24 ..**146** E2
Broadstone Wy *BDST* BH18 ..**217** K7
Broad St *PSEA* PO1 ....**12** D5
Broad View La *FUFL* SO22 ......**25** M5
Broadwater Av *PSTN* BH14 ...**234** A6
Broadwater Rd *ROMY* SO51 ....**78** D2
  WEND SO18 ....**107** L5
Broad Wy *HLER* SO31 ....**157** J3
  PSF GU32 ....**34** D3
Broadway *SBNE* BH6 ....**237** M4
Broadway La *CHAR* BH8........**221** G5
  HORN PO8 ....**140** B2
The Broadway *NBNE* BH10 ...**220** B2
  WINC SO23 ....**3** H4
Broad Woods La *ROMY* SO51 ...**76** F1
Brockenhurst Av *HAV* PO9 ...**165** H2
Brockenhurst Rd
  MOOR/WNTN BH9 ....**220** F6
Brockhampton La *HAV* PO9 .....**8** D5

Brockhampton Rd *HAV* PO9 ......**8** B5
Brockhills La *NMIL/BTOS* BH25.. **226** A3
Brockhurst Rd *GPORT* PO12 .**209** K1
Brockishill Rd *LYND* SO43.....**127** K4
  TOTT SO40 ....**127** L1
Brocklands *HAV* PO9 ....**8** A4
Brockley Rd *NBNE* BH10 .....**220** B4
Brocks Cl *FAWY* SO45 ....**155** H6
Brocks Pine *RGWD* BH24 .....**169** K5
Brockwood Bottom *NARL* SO24...**31** K7
Brodrick Av *GPORT* PO12 ....**10** D6
Brokenford Rd *TOTT* SO40 ...**129** L1
Brokenford La *TOTT* SO40 ....**129** K1
Bromley Rd *WEND* SO18 ......**107** L7
Brompton Rd *ENEY* PO4 ......**211** K6
Bromyard Crs *CHAM* PO6.....**163** G8
Bronte Av *CHCH/BSGR* BH23 .**222** E7
Bronte Cl *TOTT* SO40 ....**129** H2
Bronte Gdns *FHAM* PO15 ....**135** G8 ☑
Bronte Wy *ITCH* SO19 ....**132** C2
Brook Av North *NMIL/BTOS* BH25...**225** M3
Brook Av *HLER* SO31 ....**158** B5 ☑
  NBAD SO52 ....**79** M5
  NBNE BH10 ....**220** A4
Brookdale Cl *WIMB* BH21......**217** L4
  WVILLE PO7 ....**140** C8
Brook Dr *VWD* BH31 ....**144** F4
Brookers La
  LSOL/BMARY PO13 ....**184** E5
Brook Farm Av *FHAM* PO15.......**6** E5
Brookfield Cl *HAV* PO9 ....**8** D2
Brookfield Gdns *HLER* SO31 ..**158** D4
Brookfield Rd *ELGH* SO50 ......**83** C6
  PSEA PO1 ....**211** J2
Brookfields *ROMY* SO51 ....**76** C5
Brook Gdns *EMRTH* PO10 .....**166** B8
Brook Hl *LYMN* SO41 ....**229** J1
Brookland Cl *LYMN* SO41 ...**228** A5 ☑
Brooklands Rd *BPWT* SO32 .....**85** H8
  HAV PO9 ....**164** F6
Brook La *CHCH/BSGR* BH23 .**223** L1
  FBDC SP6 ....**98** D1
  HEND SO30 ....**134** D2
  HLER SO31 ....**158** A7
  WIMB BH21 ....**217** G2
  WVILLE PO7 ....**114** A2
Brookley Rd *BROC* SO42 ......**175** K7
Brooklyn Cl *RWIN* SO21 ....**54** B5
Brooklyn Ct
  NMIL/BTOS BH25 ....**225** K5 ☑
Brooklyn Dr *WVILLE* PO7 ...**140** D8 ☑
Brooklynn Cl *BPWT* SO32 .....**111** K6
Brookmeadow *FHAM* PO15 ......**6** E5
Brookmead Wy *HAV* PO9 ....**8** E8
Brook Rd *BKME/WDN* BH12 ..**234** B3
  ELGH SO50 ....**83** H6
  LYMN SO41 ....**228** D6
  NBNE BH10 ....**220** A4
  WEND SO18 ....**132** C1
  WIMB BH21 ....**192** C4
Brookside Cl *RGWD* BH24 ....**170** F2
Brookside *FBDC* SP6 ....**123** G6
  LSOL/BMARY PO13 ....**184** F3
  TOTT SO40 ....**129** K3
Brookside Av *WSHM* SO15 ...**130** D1
Brookside Cl
  CHCH/BSGR BH23 ....**197** L7 ☑
  WVILLE PO7 ....**139** K4
Brookside Rd *BROC* SO42......**175** K6
  CHCH/BSGR BH23 ....**235** L8
  HAV PO9 ....**8** B6
  HAV PO9 ....**165** G6
  WIMB BH21 ....**192** D4
Brookside Wy
  CHCH/BSGR BH23 ....**224** C7
  HEND SO30 ....**108** D5 ☑
  WEND SO18 ....**107** K4
Brook St *BPWT* SO32 ....**111** H1
Brook Ter *FBDC* SP6 ....**97** L8 ☑
Brookvale Rd *PTSW* SO17 ....**106** F7
Brook Va *ROWN* SO16 ....**105** M6
Brook Wy *CHCH/BSGR* BH23 .**239** H1
  ROMY SO51 ....**50** F7
Brookwood Av *ELGH* SO50 .....**81** L5
Brookwood Rd *ROWN* SO16 ..**105** J8
Broom Cl *ENEY* PO4 ....**212** B4
  WVILLE PO7 ....**164** E3
Broomfield Crs
  LSOL/BMARY PO13 ....**208** F1
Broomfield Dr *FBDC* SP6 .....**121** G8
Broomfield La *LYMN* SO41 ...**228** C4
Broom Hl *LYMN* SO41 ....**229** H1
Broomhill *RSAL* SP5 ....**75** J7
Broomhill Wy *ELGH* SO50 ......**81** L1
Broom Rd *BKME/WDN* BH12 ..**219** G7
Broomfield Crs
Brooms Gv *ITCH* SO19 ....**133** H5
Brooms Sq *ENEY* PO4 ....**212** B4
Broom Wy *LSOL/BMARY* PO13 ..**208** D1
Broomy Cl *FAWY* SO45 ....**155** G4
Brougham La *GPORT* PO12 .**209** L2 ☑
Brougham Rd *SSEA* PO5 ....**13** G4
Brougham St *GPORT* PO12 .**209** L2 ☑
Broughton Av *NBNE* BH10 ...**220** C5 ☑
Broughton Cl *NBNE* BH10 ..**220** C5 ☑
  ROWN SO16 ....**105** M7
Broughton Ct *HSEA* PO3 ....**188** A4 ☑
Broughton Rd *LYND* SO43 ...**151** J2
Browndown Rd
  LSOL/BMARY PO13 ....**209** G5
Brownen Rd
  MOOR/WNTN BH9 ....**220** F6
Brownhill Cl *CHFD* SO53 ....**81** H1
Brownhill Ct *ROWN* SO16 ....**105** K5
Brownhill Rd *CHFD* SO53 ....**81** H1
  NBAD SO52 ....**80** A4
  NMIL/BTOS BH25 ....**199** H5
Brownhill Wy *ROWN* SO16 ...**105** H5
Browning Av *BOSC* BH5 ....**236** E4
  CHAM PO6 ....**162** C7
  ITCH SO19 ....**133** H2
Browning Cl *ELGH* SO50 .....**81** G5 ☑
  HLER SO31 ....**135** G8
  TOTT SO40 ....**129** H1
Browning Dr *FUFL* SO22 ....**2** B6

Browning Rd
  BH12 ....**234** C2 ☑
Brownings Cl *LYMN* SO41 ....**227** L4
Brownlow Av *ITCH* SO19 ......**132** E2
Brownlow Cl *PSEA* PO1 ......**211** H1 ☑
Brownlow Gdns *ITCH* SO19 ..**132** E2
Brownsea Av *WIMB* BH21 .....**217** H2
Brownsea Cl *NMIL/BTOS* BH25 ..**225** J5
Brownsea Rd *CCLF* BH13 .....**245** J4
Brownsea View Av *PSTN* BH14...**234** F1
Browns La *FBDC* SP6 ....**96** A3
  LYMN SO41 ....**230** A3
Brownwich La
  FHAM/STUB PO14 ....**183** H3
The Brow *WVILLE* PO7 ....**164** A6
Broxburn Cl *CHFD* SO53 ....**53** K7
Broxhead Rd *HAV* PO9 ......**165** L2 ☑
Bruce Cl *FHAM/PORC* PO16 ....**7** H2
Bruce Rd *ENEY* PO4 ....**211** K6
Brudenell Av *CCLF* BH13 .....**245** J1
Brudenell Rd *CCLF* BH13 ....**245** J1
Brue Cl *CHFD* SO53 ....**81** G1
Brune La *LSOL/BMARY* PO13 .**184** E7
Brunel Cl *HEND* SO30 ....**109** J7 ☑
Brunel Rd *NEND* PO2 ....**187** J5
  TOTT SO40 ....**104** C5
  WSHM SO15 ....**130** A1
Brunel Wy *FHAM* PO15 ....**159** H3
Brune Wy *FERN* BH22 ....**194** B5 ☑
Brunstead Pl
  BKME/WDN BH12 ....**235** G4
Brunstead Rd
  BKME/WDN BH12 ....**234** F4
Brunswick Cl *ELGH* SO50 ...**83** G5 ☑
Brunswick Gdns *HAV* PO9 ....**8** A3
Brunswick Pl *LYMN* SO41 ....**228** C3
  WSHM SO15 ....**131** K2
Brunswick Rd *ELGH* SO50 .....**83** G5
Brunswick Sq *SHAM* SO14 ......**5** G6
Brunswick St *SSEA* PO5 .....**13** G4 ☑
Bruyn Rd *FBDC* SP6 ....**97** M7
Bryanstone Rd *TWDS* BH3 ...**235** K1
Bryanston Rd *ITCH* SO19 ....**132** B4
Bryant Rd *BKME/WDN* BH12 .**219** L8
Bryher Island *CHAM* PO6 .....**186** F1
Brympton Cl *FBDC* SP6 ....**97** H6
Bryon Rd *WIMB* BH21 ....**192** A2
Bryony Cl *BDST* BH18 ....**217** K5
  HLER SO31 ....**158** D6 ☑
Bryony Gdns *ELGH* SO50 ...**109** H2 ☑
Bryony Wy *WVILLE* PO7 ....**164** E2
Bryson Rd *CHAM* PO6 ....**163** H8 ☑
Bubb La *BPWT* SO32 ....**109** H4
  HEND SO30 ....**109** G5
Bub La *CHCH/BSGR* BH23 ...**238** D2
Buccaneers Cl
  CHCH/BSGR BH23 ....**238** D2 ☑
Buccleuch Rd *CCLF* BH13 ....**234** F7
Bucehayes Cl
  CHCH/BSGR BH23 ....**224** E8
Buchanan Av *LTDN* BH7 ......**236** D2
Buchanan Rd *ROWN* SO16 ...**105** L3
Buchan Av *FHAM* PO15 ....**135** G8
Buchan Ct *FAWY* SO45 ....**155** G6
Buckby La *HSEA* PO3 ....**188** A4
Bucketts Farm Cl *BPWT* SO32...**112** A3
Buckingham Ga *WSHM* SO15 .**106** D8 ☑
Buckingham Rd
  BKME/WDN BH12 ....**234** C1
  PSF GU32 ....**63** J5
  WVILLE PO7 ....**140** B6
Buckland Cl *ELGH* SO50 ....**81** M3
Buckland Dene *LYMN* SO41 ..**228** B3
Buckland Gdns *TOTT* SO40 ...**104** B6
Buckland Gv *CHCH/BSGR* BH23...**224** C6
Buckland Rd *BKME/WDN* BH12...**234** B3
Buckland St *NEND* PO2 ......**211** J1 ☑
Buckland Ter
  BKME/WDN BH12 ....**234** B3
Bucklers Cl *HAV* PO9 ....**187** H7 ☑
  NEND PO2 ....**187** H7
Bucklers Rd *GPORT* PO12 ....**186** A8
The Bucklers *LYMN* SO41 ....**241** M3
Bucklers Wy *CHAR* BH8 ....**221** H5
Buckmore Av *PSF* GU32 ....**63** J4
Bucksey Rd
  LSOL/BMARY PO13 ....**185** G8
Bucks Head Hl *BPWT* SO32 .....**87** H3
Buckstone Cl *LYMN* SO41 ....**227** J7
Buckthorn Cl *TOTT* SO40 .....**103** M8
  WIMB BH21 ....**217** K6 ☑
Budden's La *WHAM* PO17 ....**112** D8
Buddens Rd *WHAM* PO17 ....**136** E4
Buddle Hl *FBDC* SP6 ....**123** C4
Budds La *ROMY* SO51 ....**50** D7
Bude Cl *CHAM* PO6 ....**162** D7
Bugdens La *VWD* BH31 ....**144** D2
Bugle St *SHAM* SO14 ....**4** F6
Bulbeck Rd *HAV* PO9 ....**8** E5
Buldowne Wk *LYMN* SO41 ...**200** F5
Bullar Rd *WEND* SO18 ....**132** C1
Bullar St *SHAM* SO14 ....**131** M2
Bull Dro *WINC* SO23 ....**27** G3
Bullfinch Cl *CFDH* BH17 ......**217** K7
  TOTT SO40 ....**129** G1 ☑
Bull Hl *LISS* GU33 ....**37** K4
  LYMN SO41 ....**202** F7
Bull La *BPWT* SO32 ....**111** J5
  LYND SO43 ....**127** G5
Bullrush Cl *FAWY* SO45 ....**155** G4
Bulls Copse La *HORN* PO8 ...**140** E2
Bulls Dro *RSAL* SP5 ....**19** M2
Bulls La *RSAL* SP5 ....**40** A1
Bunkers Hl *WVILLE* PO7 ....**139** H5
Bunns La *WVILLE* PO7 ....**138** C3
Bunny La *ROMY* SO51 ....**50** E2
  RSAL SP5 ....**47** M4
Bunstead La *RWIN* SO21 ....**53** J2
Bunting Gdns *HORN* PO8 .....**140** D4
Burbidge Gv *ENEY* PO4 ....**211** L6
Burbridge Cl *CFDH* BH17 ....**218** C8 ☑
Burbush Cl *FAWY* SO45 ....**180** A5
Burcombe Rd *NBNE* BH10 ...**220** A4
Burcote Dr *HSEA* PO3 ....**187** M4
Burdale Dr *HISD* PO11 ....**214** B5
Burdock Cl *CHCH/BSGR* BH23 .**223** M7
Bure Cl *CHCH/BSGR* BH23 ...**239** G2

Bure Haven Dr
  CHCH/BSGR BH23 ....**238** F2
Bure Homage Gdns
  CHCH/BSGR BH23 ....**239** G2 ☑
Bure Homage La
  CHCH/BSGR BH23 ....**238** F2
Bure La *CHCH/BSGR* BH23 ...**239** G3
Bure Pk *CHCH/BSGR* BH23 ..**239** G2
Bure Rd *CHCH/BSGR* BH23 ..**239** G2
Burford Cl *CHCH/BSGR* BH23 .**222** B7
Burford La *BROC* SO42 ....**175** L6
Burgate Cl *HAV* PO9 ....**165** H5
Burgess Cl *BWD* BH11 ....**219** K4
  HISD PO11 ....**214** B7
Burgess Gdns *ROWN* SO16 ..**106** D5 ☑
Burgess Rd *PTSW* SO17 ....**107** G4
  WSHM SO15 ....**106** C6
Burghclere Rd *HAV* PO9 ......**165** M2
  ITCH SO19 ....**132** D8 ☑
Burgoyne Rd *ITCH* SO19 .....**133** J4
  SSEA PO5 ....**211** H7
Burgundy Cl *HLER* SO31 ....**158** D6 ☑
Buriton Rd *FHAM/PORC* PO16...**162** B7
Buriton Rd *FUFL* SO22 ....**16** C4
Buriton St *PSEA* PO1 ....**211** H2
Burke Dr *ITCH* SO19 ....**133** G2
Burleigh Rd *NEND* PO2 ....**187** K8
  SBNE BH6 ....**237** J2
Burley Cl *CHFD* SO53 ....**81** G4
  HAV PO9 ....**165** M2 ☑
  NMIL/BTOS BH25 ....**225** H8
  VWD BH31 ....**144** C3
Burley Down *CHFD* SO53 ....**81** G4
Burley Lawn *RGWD* BH24 .....**172** F4
Burley Rd *BKME/WDN* BH12 .**234** B2
  BROC SO42 ....**200** E1
  CHCH/BSGR BH23 ....**198** B3
  CHCH/BSGR BH23 ....**223** C3
  FUFL SO22 ....**16** C4
Burlington Rd *NEND* PO2 .....**187** J7
  WSHM SO15 ....**131** J2
Burmah Rd North *FAWY* SO45..**181** G2
Burmah Rd South *FAWY* SO45...**180** F3
Burma Wy *TOTT* SO40 ....**130** D8
Burmese Cl *FHAM* PO15 ......**159** G1
Burnaby Rd *PSEA* PO1 ....**12** C2
  WBNE BH4 ....**235** H7
Burnbake Rd *VWD* BH31 .....**144** D3
Burnbank Gdns *TOTT* SO40 ..**129** J1
Burnbrae Rd *FERN* BH22 .....**194** B7
Burn Cl *VWD* BH31 ....**144** F4
Burnett Av *CHCH/BSGR* BH23..**237** K1
Burnett Cl *FAWY* SO45 ....**155** M6
  FUFL SO22 ....**16** B6
  WEND SO18 ....**107** K7
Burnett Rd
  CHCH/BSGR BH23 ....**237** L1
  GPORT PO12 ....**209** K2
Burnetts Flds *ELGH* SO50 ....**109** H1
Burnetts Gdns *ELGH* SO50 ...**109** J1
Burnetts La *HEND* SO30 ......**109** G4
Burney Rd *GPORT* PO12 ......**209** J5
Burngate Rd *PLE* BH15 ....**232** D6
Burnham Beeches *CHFD* SO53...**81** C2
Burnham Cha *WEND* SO18 ...**132** F1
Burnham Dr *CHAR* BH8 ....**236** B1
Burnham Rd *CHAR* BH8 ....**164** B7
  CHCH/BSGR BH23 ....**223** C8
  FBDC SP6 ....**97** L3
Burnham Wd
  FHAM/PORC PO16 ....**7** G1
Burnleigh Gdns
  NMIL/BTOS BH25 ....**226** A4 ☑
Burns Cl *ELGH* SO50 ....**81** K7
Burnside *CHCH/BSGR* BH23 .**224** E8 ☑
  LSOL/BMARY PO13 ....**184** F3
  WVILLE PO7 ....**140** E7
Burns Pl *ROWN* SO16 ....**105** M6
Burns Rd *ELGH* SO50 ....**81** L7
  ITCH SO19 ....**133** L1
  SBNE BH6 ....**237** J1
Burnt House La
  CHCH/BSGR BH23 ....**197** M7
  FHAM/STUB PO14 ....**184** B5
  LYMN SO41 ....**202** D7
Burrard Gv *LYMN* SO41 ....**228** D6
Burr Cl *RWIN* SO21 ....**54** E8
Burrfields Rd *HSEA* PO3 ......**187** M7
Burridge Rd *HLER* SO31 ......**134** E6
Burrill Av *CHAM* PO6 ....**163** L8
Burrows Cl *HAV* PO9 ....**9** H1
Burrows La *VWD* BH31 ....**120** D8
Bursledon Hts *HLER* SO31 ...**133** M7
Bursledon Pl *WVILLE* PO7 ....**164** B3
Bursledon Rd *HEND* SO30 ...**133** M3
  ITCH SO19 ....**132** G2
  WVILLE PO7 ....**164** B3
Burtley Rd *SBNE* BH6 ....**237** K5
Burton Cl *CHCH/BSGR* BH23...**223** G7 ☑
  RGWD BH24 ....**169** H3
Burtoncroft
  CHCH/BSGR BH23 ....**223** G5
Burton Hall Pl
  CHCH/BSGR BH23 ....**223** H5 ☑
Burton Rd *CCLF* BH13 ....**234** F5
  CHCH/BSGR BH23 ....**238** D1
  WSHM SO15 ....**131** J1
Burt's Hl *WIMB* BH21 ....**192** A2
Burwood Gv *HISD* PO11 ......**213** L4
Bury Cl *GPORT* PO12 ....**10** F4
Bury Crs *GPORT* PO12 ....**10** E4
Bury Hall La *GPORT* PO12 .....**10** E5
Bury La *TOTT* SO40 ....**129** M3
Bury Rd *CCLF* BH13 ....**234** E6 ☑
  GPORT PO12 ....**10** E4
  TOTT SO40 ....**130** C6
Bushell Rd *PLE* BH15 ....**233** H4
Bushells Farm *FBDC* SP6 ....**97** M8 ☑
Bushey Rd *CHAR* BH8 ....**221** H4
Bushmead Dr *RGWD* BH24 ..**169** J3
Bush Saint West *SSEA* PO5 .**13** G5 ☑
Bush St East *SSEA* PO5 ....**13** G5
Bush St West *SSEA* PO5 ....**13** G5
Busket La *WINC* SO23 ....**3** H8
Bushy Md *WVILLE* PO7 ....**164** A5
Butcher St *PSEA* PO1 ....**12** C2
Bute Dr *CHCH/BSGR* BH23 ...**240** A1

Butlers Cl ROMY SO51 .... 20 F7
Butlers La FERN BH22 .... 147 G7
Buttercup Cl FAWY SO45 .... 155 L7
  HEND SO30 .... 133 L2
Buttercup Dr
  CHCH/BSGR BH23 .... 223 M7
Butterfield Rd ROWN SO16 .... 106 D4
Butterfly Dr CHAM PO6 .... 162 E6
Buttermere Cl ROWN SO16 .... 105 K6
The Buttery CHCH/BSGR BH23 .... 238 C1
Buttons La ROMY SO51 .... 76 D5
Buttsash Av FAWY SO45 .... 155 L8
Butts Ash Gdns FAWY SO45 .... 155 L7
Butts Ash La FAWY SO45 .... 155 L7
Buttsbridge Rd FAWY SO45 .... 155 L7
Butts Cl FUFL SO22 .... 2 B4
  ITCH SO19 .... 133 H4
Butt's Crs ITCH SO19 .... 133 G4
Butts La BPWT SO32 .... 85 J8
Butts Lawn BROC SO42 .... 175 K6
Butts Paddock BROC SO42 .... 175 K6
Butt's Rd ITCH SO19 .... 132 F5
  ITCH SO19 .... 133 H4
Butt's Sq ITCH SO19 .... 133 G4
The Butts BPWT SO32 .... 87 H2
Byerley Cl EMRTH PO10 .... 166 F3
Byerley Rd PSEA PO1 .... 211 K2
Byeways FAWY SO45 .... 155 K6
The Byeway SELS SO20 .... 215 L7
By-pass Rd ROMY SO51 .... 78 D2
Byrd Cl WVILLE PO7 .... 164 C3
Byron Av FUFL SO22 .... 2 A7
Byron Cl BPWT SO32 .... 85 K8
  FHAM/PORC PO16 .... 7 G3
Byron Rd BOSC BH5 .... 236 E4
  ELGH SO50 .... 82 A4
  ITCH SO19 .... 133 H2
  NEND PO2 .... 187 K8
  NMIL/BTOS BH25 .... 225 J8

C

Cable St SHAM SO14 .... 5 L1
Cabot Dr FAWY SO45 .... 155 L5
Cabot La CFDH BH17 .... 217 L8
Cabot Wy NMIL/BTOS BH25 .... 225 K5
Cadgwith Pl POLE PO6 .... 186 F1
Cadhay Cl NMIL/BTOS BH25 .... 225 J5
Cadland Rd FAWY SO45 .... 180 B1
Cadlands Park Est FAWY SO45 .... 180 A2
Cadnam La TOTT SO40 .... 102 C5
Cadnam Rd ENEY PO4 .... 211 M5
Cadnam Wy CHAR BH8 .... 221 H5
Cadogan Rd RGWD BH24 .... 170 F1
Caerleon Av ITCH SO19 .... 133 C2
Caerleon Dr ITCH SO19 .... 132 F2
Caernarvon Gdns CHFD SO53 .... 80 F4
Caesar's Wy WIMB BH21 .... 217 J4
Cains Cl FHAM/STUB PO14 .... 184 A3
Cairns Cl CHCH/BSGR BH23 .... 222 D8
Cairo Ter NEND PO2 .... 211 H1
Caister Cl FERN BH22 .... 194 A2
Caistor Cl ROWN SO16 .... 105 M4
Cakeham Rd SELS SO20 .... 215 L8
Calabrese HLER SO31 .... 158 F1
Calbourne HLER SO31 .... 157 G1
Calcot Hl BPWT SO32 .... 110 D5
Calcot La BPWT SO32 .... 110 D6
Calder Cl ROWN SO16 .... 105 K8
Calder Rd CFDH BH17 .... 218 D8
Calderwood Dr ITCH SO19 .... 132 E4
Caledonia Dr FAWY SO45 .... 155 H5
Caledonian Cl
  CHCH/BSGR BH23 .... 239 G1
Caledon Rd PSTN BH14 .... 234 C5
Calkin Cl CHCH/BSGR BH23 .... 222 E7
Calluna Rd BKME/WDN BH12 .... 218 F1
Calmore Cl CHAR BH8 .... 221 H5
Calmore Crs TOTT SO40 .... 104 A3
Calmore Dr TOTT SO40 .... 104 B6
Calmore Gdns TOTT SO40 .... 129 G3
Calmore Rd TOTT SO40 .... 104 A7
Calpe Av LYND SO43 .... 151 K2
Calshot Cl FAWY SO45 .... 181 K8
Calshot Dr CHFD SO53 .... 80 F4
Calshot Rd FAWY SO45 .... 180 F5
  HAV PO9 .... 165 G1
Calshot Wy
  LSOL/BMARY PO13 .... 184 F7
Calvin Rd MOOR/WNTN BH9 .... 220 D8
Camargue Cl HLER SO31 .... 134 F8
Camber Pl PSEA PO1 .... 12 B5
Cambria La RWIN SO21 .... 54 C1
Cambrian Cl HLER SO31 .... 133 L6
Cambridge Dr CHFD SO53 .... 81 H5
Cambridge Gdns
  CHCH/BSGR BH23 .... 222 D6
Cambridge Gn
  FHAM/STUB PO14 .... 159 G6
Cambridge Rd GPORT PO12 .... 209 J2
  LSOL/BMARY PO13 .... 208 D4
  PSEA PO1 .... 12 E4
  SHAM SO14 .... 106 F8
  WCLF BH2 .... 14 B3
Camcross Cl CHAM PO6 .... 162 F7
Camden Cl
  MOOR/WNTN BH9 .... 220 F7
Camden St GPORT PO12 .... 209 L2
  FBDG SP6 .... 121 L2
Camel Green Rd FBDG SP6 .... 121 M2
Camelia Ct HAV PO9 .... 165 M5
  NBAD SO52 .... 79 M3
Camelia Gdns WEND SO18 .... 107 M6
Camelia Gv ELGH SO50 .... 83 K6
Camellia Cl WIMB BH21 .... 144 C7
Camellia Gdns
  NMIL/BTOS BH25 .... 225 M6
Camelot Crs FHAM/PORC PO16 .... 161 M7
Cameron Cl
  LSOL/BMARY PO13 .... 185 G5
Cameron Rd
  CHCH/BSGR BH23 .... 238 C1

Camley Cl ITCH SO19 .... 132 C7
Cammel Rd FERN BH22 .... 194 B6
Campbell Rd BMTH BH1 .... 236 D3
  CHCH/BSGR BH23 .... 223 G5
  ELGH SO50 .... 82 A7
  SSEA PO5 .... 13 K5
Campbell St SHAM SO14 .... 132 A2
Campion Cl Wy ELGH SO50 .... 83 H6
Campion Cl ELGH SO50 .... 109 H2
  HLER SO31 .... 158 C7
  LYMN SO41 .... 228 C3
  WVILLE PO7 .... 164 E2
Campion Dr ROMY SO51 .... 51 H7
Campion Gv CHCH/BSGR BH23 .... 238 E2
Campion Wy ITCH SO19 .... 133 H3
Campion Wy LYMN SO41 .... 228 C3
Camp Rd LSOL/BMARY PO13 .... 185 H5
Cams Bay Cv
  FHAM/PORC PO16 .... 161 K7
Cams Hl FHAM/PORC PO16 .... 161 J7
  WVILLE PO7 .... 114 A7
Canada Rd ITCH SO19 .... 132 C6
Canal Cl ROMY SO51 .... 50 F7
Canal Wk ROMY SO51 .... 50 E8
  SHAM SO14 .... 5 G5
  SSEA PO5 .... 13 J2
Canberra Cl GPORT PO12 .... 10 B4
Canberra Rd CHCH/BSGR BH23 .... 222 C7
  EMRTH PO10 .... 190 E5
  ROWN SO16 .... 105 G4
Candy La WEND SO18 .... 133 J1
Canford Av BWD BH11 .... 219 K7
Canford Bottom WIMB BH21 .... 193 G2
Canford Cliffs Av PSTN BH14 .... 234 C6
Canford Cliffs Rd CCLF BH13 .... 234 D6
Canford Cl BPWT SO32 .... 136 C1
  ROWN SO16 .... 105 J6
Canford Crs CCLF BH13 .... 245 K1
Canford Heath Rd CFDH BH17 .... 218 B7
Canford Rd BWD BH11 .... 219 L7
  PLE BH15 .... 233 J4
Canford View Dr
  WIMB BH21 .... 192 F2
Canford Wy BKME/WDN BH12 .... 219 G6
Canhouse La LISS GU33 .... 37 L5
Cannon Cl BDST BH18 .... 217 K7
Cannon Hill Gdns WIMB BH21 .... 192 F1
Cannon Hill Rd WIMB BH21 .... 192 E1
Cannon St LYMN SO41 .... 228 C3
  WINC SO23 .... 106 B8
Canoe Cl HLER SO31 .... 158 D7
Canon's Barn Cl
  FHAM/PORC PO16 .... 162 A7
Canon St WINC SO23 .... 2 F9
Canterbury Cl ITCH SO19 .... 133 C3
Canterbury Cl FERN BH22 .... 168 D7
  LSOL/BMARY PO13 .... 208 F2
Canterbury Dr FAWY SO45 .... 155 G5
Canterbury Rd FHAM/STUB PO14 .... 184 A5
Canterton La LYND SO43 .... 102 A8
Canton St WSHM SO15 .... 131 K2
Canute Dr CHCH/BSGR BH23 .... 197 M7
Canute Rd SHAM SO14 .... 5 K6
  WINC SO23 .... 27 G2
Capel Ley WVILLE PO7 .... 164 C4
Capers End La BPWT SO32 .... 110 D7
Capesthorne
  CHCH/BSGR BH23 .... 239 G3
Capstone Pl CHAR BH8 .... 236 C2
Capstone Rd CHAR BH8 .... 236 B2
Captains Pl SHAM SO14 .... 5 J6
Captain's Rw LYMN SO41 .... 228 D4
  PSEA PO1 .... 12 B5
Carberry Dr FHAM/PORC PO16 .... 185 M1
Carbery Av SBNE BH6 .... 237 J4
Carbery Ct HAV PO9 .... 165 H1
Carbery Gdns SBNE BH6 .... 237 K3
Carbis Cl CHAM PO6 .... 186 E1
Cardew Rd ITCH SO19 .... 133 G3
Cardiff Rd NEND PO2 .... 187 H6
Cardigan Rd CCLF BH13 .... 234 E4
  MOOR/WNTN BH9 .... 220 D8
Cardinal Dr WVILLE PO7 .... 140 F7
Cardinal Wy HLER SO31 .... 158 F5
  MOOR/WNTN BH9 .... 220 D6
Carey Rd ITCH SO19 .... 133 G3
Careys Cottages BROC SO42 .... 175 K6
Careys Rd CHAR BH8 .... 221 H4
Carisbrooke HLER SO31 .... 157 G1
Carisbrooke Av
  FHAM/STUB PO14 .... 183 L6
Carisbrooke Cl HAV PO9 .... 9 J3
Carisbrooke Ct
  NMIL/BTOS BH25 .... 225 K5
  ROMY SO51 .... 50 F7
Carisbrooke Crs CHFD SO53 .... 81 K3
  PLE BH15 .... 232 D5
Carisbrooke Dr ITCH SO19 .... 132 D2
Carisbrooke Rd ENEY PO4 .... 211 L4
  LSOL/BMARY PO13 .... 184 F5
Carisbrooke Wy
  CHCH/BSGR BH23 .... 224 C7
Carless Cl LSOL/BMARY PO13 .... 209 H1
Carlisle Rd ROWN SO16 .... 106 A8
  SSEA PO5 .... 13 K2
Carlton Av NMIL/BTOS BH25 .... 240 C5
Carlton Crs WSHM SO15 .... 131 K2
Carlton Gv PSTN BH14 .... 234 C3
Carlton Pl WSHM SO15 .... 131 K2
Carlton Rd BMTH BH1 .... 15 M3
  FHAM/PORC PO16 .... 162 B7
  GPORT PO12 .... 11 H3
  WSHM SO15 .... 131 K1
Carlton Wy GPORT PO12 .... 11 H2
Carlyle Rd GPORT PO12 .... 10 E1
  SBNE BH6 .... 237 J2
Carlyn Dr CHFD SO53 .... 81 J1
Carmans La RWIN SO21 .... 54 C1
Carmarthen Av CHAM PO6 .... 163 M7
Carnarvon Rd BOSC BH5 .... 236 D4
  GPORT PO12 .... 10 C3
  NEND PO2 .... 187 H3
Carnation Rd ROWN SO16 .... 107 H4
Carne Cl CHFD SO53 .... 53 H6

Carnegie Cl BKME/WDN BH12 .... 234 C3
Caroline Av CHCH/BSGR BH23 .... 238 D3
Caroline Cl BWD BH11 .... 219 M5
Carolyn Cl ITCH SO19 .... 132 C6
Carpathia Cl WEND SO18 .... 107 M6
Carpenter Cl ENEY PO4 .... 211 L5
  FAWY SO45 .... 155 L4
  LYMN SO41 .... 228 B3
Carraway FHAM PO15 .... 159 H1
Carrbridge Cl FHAM BH3 .... 235 J1
Carrbridge Rd TWDS BH3 .... 235 J1
Carrick Wy NMIL/BTOS BH25 .... 226 A6
Carrington Cl LYMN SO41 .... 242 D4
Carrington Av FERN BH22 .... 194 B3
Carrington La LYMN SO41 .... 242 D3
Carroll Av FERN BH22 .... 194 B3
Carroll Cl BKME/WDN BH12 .... 234 F2
  ELGH SO50 .... 83 J7
Carronade Wk HSEA PO3 .... 187 K3
Carshalton Av CHAM PO6 .... 163 M8
Carsworth Wy CFDH BH17 .... 218 E6
Carters Av PLE BH15 .... 232 C4
Carter's Clay Rd ROMY SO51 .... 49 G3
Carter's Cl FBDG SP6 .... 73 J5
Cartersland La LIPH GU30 .... 38 E5
Carter's La PLE BH15 .... 233 H6
  TOTT SO40 .... 154 C3
Carthage Cl CHFD SO53 .... 81 L1
Cartref Cl VWD BH31 .... 144 D2
Cartwright Cl NBNE BH10 .... 220 A4
Cartwright Dr FHAM PO15 .... 159 K6
Carvers La RGWD BH24 .... 170 E1
Carysfort Rd BMTH BH1 .... 236 C4
Cashmoor Cl
  BKME/WDN BH12 .... 234 E1
Cask St PSEA PO1 .... 211 G2
Caslake Cl NMIL/BTOS BH25 .... 225 K7
Caspar John Cl
  FHAM/STUB PO14 .... 183 M7
Caspian Cl HLER SO31 .... 158 F1
Cassel Av WBNE BH4 .... 235 G7
Castle Cl CHCH/BSGR BH23 .... 224 C8
  HAV PO9 .... 9 K5
  SSEA PO5 .... 13 G5
Castle Cl LYMN SO41 .... 242 D5
Castledene Crs PSTN BH14 .... 233 M6
Castle Farm La WHAM PO17 .... 136 F6
Castle Gate Cl CHAR BH8 .... 221 G6
Castle Gv FHAM/PORC PO16 .... 186 B1
Castle Hill La RGWD BH24 .... 172 B4
Castle La CHFD SO53 .... 80 F4
  FAWY SO45 .... 207 K1
  NBAD SO52 .... 80 A4
  SHAM SO14 .... 4 F4
Castle La East LTDN BH7 .... 221 M8
Castle La West CHAR BH8 .... 221 K6
  MOOR/WNTN BH10 .... 220 E4
Castlemain Av SBNE BH6 .... 237 H3
Castlemans La HISD PO11 .... 189 L7
Castleman Trailway
  CFDH BH17 .... 217 J8
  FERN BH22 .... 168 A5
  RGWD BH24 .... 169 H3
  WIMB BH21 .... 192 E5
Castleman Wy RGWD BH24 .... 170 A3
Castlemews RGWD BH24 .... 170 A3
Castle Mws HAV PO9 .... 141 L6
  HLER SO31 .... 156 F2
  MOOR/WNTN BH9 .... 220 D7
  SSEA PO5 .... 12 F6
  WEND SO18 .... 107 K6
  WHAM PO17 .... 136 F6
Castleshaw Cl ROWN SO16 .... 130 D1
Castle Sq SHAM SO14 .... 4 F5
Castle St CHCH/BSGR BH23 .... 238 A2
  FHAM/PORC PO16 .... 186 B1
  FHAM/STUB PO14 .... 159 K8
  PLE BH15 .... 233 H7
  SHAM SO14 .... 131 L1
Castleton Av NBNE BH10 .... 220 B2
Castle Vw GPORT PO12 .... 185 M8
Castle View Rd
  FHAM/PORC PO16 .... 186 B2
Castleway HAV PO9 .... 9 K5
Castle Wy SHAM SO14 .... 4 F4
Castlewood RGWD BH24 .... 170 B3
Castle Woods RSAL SP5 .... 73 J2
Catalina Cl CHCH/BSGR BH23 .... 238 F2
Catalina Dr PLE BH15 .... 233 K7
Catamaran Cl HLER SO31 .... 158 D7
Cateran Cl ROWN SO16 .... 105 L8
Cathay Gdns FAWY SO45 .... 155 G5
Cathedral Vw WINC SO23 .... 27 G2
Catherine Cl HEND SO30 .... 108 D6
Catherine Crs RSAL SP5 .... 72 C1
Catherine Gdns HEND SO30 .... 108 D6
Catherington La HORN PO8 .... 140 F1
Catherington Wy HAV PO9 .... 165 K4
Catisfield La FHAM PO15 .... 159 M7
Catisfield Rd ENEY PO4 .... 211 M3
  FHAM PO15 .... 160 A7
Caton Cl BKME/WDN BH12 .... 219 M8
Cattistock Rd CHAR BH8 .... 221 J7
Causeway Crs TOTT SO40 .... 104 B4
Causeway Farm HORN PO8 .... 140 F3
The Causeway EPSF GU31 .... 63 K6
  FHAM/PORC PO16 .... 161 J7
  LSOL/BMARY PO13 .... 208 D1
Cavalier Cl FAWY SO45 .... 155 G5
Cavan Crs CFDH BH17 .... 217 M7
Cavanna Cl LSOL/BMARY PO13 .... 184 F5
Cavell Dr CHAM PO6 .... 162 F6
Cavendish Cl ROMY SO51 .... 51 G6
  WVILLE PO7 .... 140 D8
Cavendish Dr WVILLE PO7 .... 164 D1
Cavendish Gv WINC SO23 .... 3 J1
  WSHM SO15 .... 106 E8
Cavendish Ms WSHM SO15 .... 106 E8
Cavendish Pl BMTH BH1 .... 15 G2
Cavendish Rd BMTH BH1 .... 15 G2
  SSEA PO5 .... 13 J6
  WCLF BH2 .... 14 F2
C Av FAWY SO45 .... 180 B3
Caversham Cl HEND SO30 .... 108 C7
  ITCH SO19 .... 132 E4
  PLE BH15 .... 232 D5
Cawdor Rd CHAR BH8 .... 221 J7
Cawte Rd WSHM SO15 .... 131 G2
Caxton Av ITCH SO19 .... 132 F2

Caxton Cl CHCH/BSGR BH23 .... 238 E1
Cecil Av CHAR BH8 .... 221 G8
  ROWN SO16 .... 106 A7
  TOTT SO40 .... 129 G6
Cecil Cl WIMB BH21 .... 217 J2
Cecil Gv SSEA PO5 .... 12 F6
Cecil Hl MOOR/WNTN BH9 .... 220 F8
Cecil Pl SSEA PO5 .... 12 F6
Cecil Rd BKME/WDN BH12 .... 234 C2
  BOSC BH5 .... 236 D4
  ITCH SO19 .... 132 D5
Cedar Av CHCH/BSGR BH23 .... 222 B8
  NBNE BH10 .... 220 B2
  RGWD BH24 .... 169 J5
  WSHM SO15 .... 106 C8
Cedar Cl GPORT PO12 .... 185 L7
  HEND SO30 .... 134 A1
  HLER SO31 .... 133 L8
  UPTN BH16 .... 216 F8
  WVILLE PO7 .... 164 C2
Cedar Dr LYMN SO41 .... 227 H8
  WIMB BH21 .... 192 F3
Cedar Gdns HAV PO9 .... 9 G2
Cedar Gv HSEA PO3 .... 211 M1
Cedar Lawn ROMY SO51 .... 51 H7
Cedar Pl CHCH/BSGR BH23 .... 197 M7
Cedar Rd ELGH SO50 .... 81 K7
  FAWY SO45 .... 179 L1
  SHAM SO14 .... 106 F8
Cedars Vw RSAL SP5 .... 20 D1
Cedarwood Cl FERN BH22 .... 168 A3
Cedar Wood Cl ELGH SO50 .... 83 K6
Celia Cl WVILLE PO7 .... 140 F8
Cellars Farm Rd SBNE BH6 .... 237 M5
Cement Ter SHAM SO14 .... 4 F5
Cemetery Av PLE BH15 .... 233 J3
Cemetery La EMRTH PO10 .... 167 G5
  WVILLE PO7 .... 139 K3
Cemetery Rd WSHM SO15 .... 106 D8
Centaur St NEND PO2 .... 187 H8
Centaury Gdns ELGH SO50 .... 109 H1
Centenary Cl LYMN SO41 .... 201 G6
Centenary Wy BMTH BH1 .... 236 D3
Central Av BKME/WDN BH12 .... 234 D2
  WIMB BH21 .... 217 H1
Central Br SHAM SO14 .... 5 J5
Central Dr WCLF BH2 .... 14 D1
Central Rd CHAM PO6 .... 188 A1
  FHAM/PORC PO16 .... 185 M1
  SHAM SO14 .... 5 H7
Central Station Br WSHM SO15 .... 4 C2
Central St PSEA PO1 .... 211 H2
Centre La LYMN SO41 .... 227 J7
Centre Pl RGWD BH24 .... 170 D1
Centre Wy HLER SO31 .... 158 D5
Cerdic Ms HLER SO31 .... 157 L4
Cerne Cl MOOR/WNTN BH9 .... 220 F4
  NBAD SO52 .... 79 K4
  WEND SO18 .... 108 A7
Chadderton Gdns PSEA PO1 .... 12 E5
Chaddesley Gln CCLF BH13 .... 245 J2
Chaddesley Wood Rd
  CCLF BH13 .... 245 K3
Chadwell Av ITCH SO19 .... 132 F4
Chadwick Rd ELGH SO50 .... 81 K6
Chafen Rd WEND SO18 .... 107 J8
Chaffey Cl RGWD BH24 .... 147 G8
Chaffinch Cl CFDH BH17 .... 217 K6
  NMIL/BTOS BH25 .... 225 K6
  TOTT SO40 .... 104 B8
Chaffinch Gn HORN PO8 .... 140 C4
Chaffinch Wy
  FHAM/PORC PO16 .... 161 K8
  LSOL/BMARY PO13 .... 208 D1
Chalbury Cl CFDH BH17 .... 218 E6
Chaldecott Gdns NBNE BH10 .... 220 A4
Chaldon Rd CFDH BH17 .... 218 D6
Chale Cl LSOL/BMARY PO13 .... 185 G6
Chalewood Rd FAWY SO45 .... 206 C1
Chalfont Av CHCH/BSGR BH23 .... 222 B5
Chalice Ct HEND SO30 .... 133 M2
Chalk Hl BPWT SO32 .... 113 H3
Chalkpit Rd CHAM PO6 .... 162 F6
Chalk Rdg HORN PO8 .... 116 C5
  WINC SO23 .... 3 M9
Chalkridge Rd CHAM PO6 .... 163 J7
Chalk's Cl RSAL SP5 .... 73 J1
Chalky La BPWT SO32 .... 85 J8
Challenger Wy FAWY SO45 .... 155 H4
Challis Ct SHAM SO14 .... 5 H5
Chalmers Wy HLER SO31 .... 157 J5
Chaloner Crs FAWY SO45 .... 155 L7
Chalton Crs HAV PO9 .... 165 H3
Chalton La HORN PO8 .... 116 C2
Chalvington Rd CHFD SO53 .... 81 H3
Chalybeate Cl ROWN SO16 .... 106 A6
Chamberlain Gv
  FHAM/STUB PO14 .... 7 G8
Chamberlain Rd PTSW SO17 .... 106 F5
Chamberlayne Rd ELGH SO50 .... 81 M7
  HLER SO31 .... 133 K8
Chambers Av ROMY SO51 .... 79 G1
Chambers Cl ROWN SO16 .... 105 H3
Champion Cl LYMN SO41 .... 242 D4
Chancellors La BPWT SO32 .... 109 K5
Chancel Rd HLER SO31 .... 158 F5
Chander Cl FERN BH22 .... 194 C4
Chandlers Cl HISD PO11 .... 214 A6
  LTDN BH7 .... 221 M8
Chandlers Wy HEND SO30 .... 134 C5
Chandos Av BKME/WDN BH12 .... 219 L8
Chandos St SHAM SO14 .... 5 H5
Channels Farm Rd
  ROWN SO16 .... 107 J3
Channel Wy SHAM SO14 .... 5 K6
Chant Cl CHCH/BSGR BH23 .... 238 C1

Chantry Cl CHCH/BSGR BH23 .... 224 D7
Chantry Rd GPORT PO12 .... 209 L1
  HORN PO8 .... 140 F1
  SHAM SO14 .... 5 K5
The Chantry FHAM/STUB PO14 .... 159 G5
Chapel Cl WIMB BH21 .... 217 G2
Chapel Crs ITCH SO19 .... 132 E4
Chapel Dro ELGH SO50 .... 109 H1
  HEND SO30 .... 133 M2
Chapel La BPWT SO32 .... 110 D8
  BROC SO42 .... 204 A2
  CHCH/BSGR BH23 .... 195 G5
  CHCH/BSGR BH23 .... 197 L8
  ELGH SO50 .... 54 A7
  FAWY SO45 .... 180 C8
  FAWY SO45 .... 180 E5
  LYMN SO41 .... 201 H7
  LYND SO43 .... 151 K4
  PLE BH15 .... 233 H6
  RGWD BH24 .... 172 F5
  ROMY SO51 .... 22 C8
  ROMY SO51 .... 48 D2
  RSAL SP5 .... 41 G1
  RSAL SP5 .... 44 E3
  RSAL SP5 .... 73 K2
  RSAL SP5 .... 101 H1
  RWIN SO21 .... 17 M6
  TOTT SO40 .... 129 J3
  WIMB BH21 .... 217 G3
Chapel Ri RGWD BH24 .... 170 B6
Chapel Rd BPWT SO32 .... 87 H5
  BPWT SO32 .... 112 A3
  BPWT SO32 .... 113 G6
  HEND SO30 .... 108 D6
  HLER SO31 .... 158 C2
  PSTN BH14 .... 233 M4
  SHAM SO14 .... 5 J4
Chapelside FHAM/STUB PO14 .... 159 L8
Chapel St GPORT PO12 .... 185 M8
  NEND PO2 .... 187 H8
  PSF GU32 .... 61 J8
  PSF GU32 .... 63 L4
  SSEA PO5 .... 12 F5
Chaplains Av HORN PO8 .... 140 B5
Chaplains Rd HORN PO8 .... 140 B4
Charborough Rd BDST BH18 .... 217 M5
Charden Rd ELGH SO50 .... 82 F7
  LSOL/BMARY PO13 .... 185 H8
Charfield Cl FHAM/STUB PO14 .... 6 A7
  FUFL SO22 .... 26 D3
Charing Cl RGWD BH24 .... 170 E2
Chark La LSOL/BMARY PO13 .... 184 D8
Charlecote Dr CHFD SO53 .... 52 F8
Charlesbury Av GPORT PO12 .... 10 A4
Charles Cl WINC SO23 .... 3 H2
Charles Crs NMIL/BTOS BH25 .... 225 M3
Charles Dickens St PSEA PO1 .... 13 G2
Charles Gdns NBNE BH10 .... 220 A6
Charles Knott Gdns
  WSHM SO15 .... 131 K1
Charles Rd CHCH/BSGR BH23 .... 223 K8
  PLE BH15 .... 233 J5
Charles's La RGWD BH24 .... 171 H6
Charles St PSEA PO1 .... 211 H2
  PSF GU32 .... 63 K5
  SHAM SO14 .... 5 H5
Charleston Cl HISD PO11 .... 213 J4
Charleston Rd FAWY SO45 .... 156 B8
Charles Watts Wy HEND SO30 .... 133 J1
Charlesworth Dr
  WVILLE PO7 .... 140 F7
Charlesworth Gdns
  WVILLE PO7 .... 140 B7
Charliejoy Gdns SHAM SO14 .... 132 A2
Charlotte Cl BKME/WDN BH12 .... 235 H1
  CHCH/BSGR BH23 .... 238 F2
Charlotte Pl SHAM SO14 .... 131 L2
Charlotte St PSEA PO1 .... 211 G2
Charlton Cl LYMN SO41 .... 226 D5
  MOOR/WNTN BH9 .... 221 G4
Charlton Rd WSHM SO15 .... 131 H1
Charminster Av
  MOOR/WNTN BH9 .... 220 F7
Charminster Cl
  MOOR/WNTN BH9 .... 220 F6
  WVILLE PO7 .... 140 C8
Charminster Pl CHAR BH8 .... 221 G6
Charminster Rd CHAR BH8 .... 220 F7
Charmus Rd TOTT SO40 .... 104 A6
Charmouth Gv PSTN BH14 .... 233 M4
Charmwen Crs HEND SO30 .... 108 B6
Charnock Cl LYMN SO41 .... 226 D5
Charnwood
  LSOL/BMARY PO13 .... 185 H6
Charnwood Av
  MOOR/WNTN BH9 .... 220 F5
Charnwood Cl CHFD SO53 .... 53 H6
  FERN BH22 .... 168 C6
  TOTT SO40 .... 104 C7
Charnwood Crs CHFD SO53 .... 53 H6
Charnwood Dr FBDG SP6 .... 97 K6
Charnwood Gdns CHFD SO53 .... 53 H6
Charnwood Wy FAWY SO45 .... 206 B1
Charterhouse Wy HEND SO30 .... 109 G7
Charter Rd BWD BH11 .... 219 H2
Chartwell Cl ELGH SO50 .... 82 A2
  FHAM/STUB PO14 .... 159 G7
Chartwell Dr HAV PO9 .... 9 L1
Chase Cl LISS GU33 .... 36 F4
Chase Farm Cl BPWT SO32 .... 111 K5
Chase Gv BPWT SO32 .... 111 K5
Chase Rd LISS GU33 .... 36 F4
Chaseside LTDN BH7 .... 221 L8
The Chase FHAM/STUB PO14 .... 159 H6
  GPORT PO12 .... 10 A4
  RGWD BH24 .... 170 B3
  VWD BH31 .... 144 F2
Chasewater Av HSEA PO3 .... 211 L1
Chatburn Av HORN PO8 .... 140 C5
Chatfield Av NEND PO2 .... 186 E7
Chatfield Rd
  LSOL/BMARY PO13 .... 185 G4
Chatham Dr PSEA PO1 .... 12 E5
Chatham La FUFL SO22 .... 26 E3
Chatsworth Av NEND PO2 .... 187 G2
Chatsworth Cl FHAM PO15 .... 160 A7
Chatsworth Rd CHAR BH8 .... 236 A2

ELGH SO50 82 A2
ITCH SO19 132 E3
PSTN BH14 234 A3
Chatsworth Wy
NMIL/BTOS BH25 225 J5
Chaucer Av CHAM PO6 162 C7
Chaucer Cl FHAM/PORC PO16 6 F4
WIMB BH21 192 A2 1
WVILLE PO7 140 C6
Chaucer Dr LYMN SO41 242 C3
Chaucer Rd CCLF BH13 234 E8 1
ITCH SO19 133 H2
Chaundler Rd WINC SO23 3 H3
Chaveney Cl FAWY SO45 155 K7 1
Chawton Cl FUFL SO22 16 C4
WEND SO18 108 C8 1
Cheam Rd BDST BH18 217 K4
Cheam Wy TOTT SO40 104 C7
Cheddar Cl ITCH SO19 132 C5 1
Cheddington Rd
MOOR/WNTN BH9 220 E4
Chedington Cl CFDH BH17 218 C6
Chedworth Crs CHAM PO6 162 E7
Cheesecombe Farm La
LISS GU33 35 L2
Chelmsford Rd NEND PO2 187 K6
UPTN BH16 232 A1
Chelsea Rd SSEA PO5 13 K6
Cheltenham Crs
LSOL/BMARY PO13 208 D2
Cheltenham Gdns
HEND SO30 109 H5 1
Cheltenham Rd
BKME/WDN BH12 234 B3
CHAM PO6 163 G8
Chelveston Crs ROWN SO16 105 L4
Chene Rd WIMB BH21 192 B4
Cheping Gdns HEND SO30 134 E2
Chepstow Cl CHFD SO53 81 G2 1
TOTT SO40 104 B8 5
Chepstow Ct WVILLE PO7 140 F7
Cherbourg Rd ELGH SO50 81 L7
Cherford Rd BWD BH11 219 M6
Cherita Ct PLE BH15 233 L2
Cheriton Av LTDN BH7 222 A8
WEND SO18 133 G1
Cheriton Cl FUFL SO22 2 B5
HAV PO9 165 H4 1
HORN PO8 140 E1
Cheriton Rd ELGH SO50 81 L8
FUFL SO22 2 C5
GPORT PO12 10 B3
Cheriton Wy WIMB BH21 192 A2
Cherque La LSOL/BMARY PO13 184 E8
Cherrett Cl BWD BH11 219 K4 1
Cherries Dr MOOR/WNTN BH9 220 C6
Cherry Cl LSOL/BMARY PO13 208 D3
PSTN BH14 234 A4
Cherry Dro ELGH SO50 109 H2
Cherry Gdns BPWT SO32 111 J1
Cherrygarth Rd FHAM PO15 160 A7
Cherry Gv FERN BH22 194 A2
Cherry Hill Gv UPTN BH16 232 A2
Cherryton Gdns FAWY SO45 179 M5 1
Cherry Tree Av
FHAM/STUB PO14 6 B8
HORN PO8 140 F6
Cherry Tree Cl
LYMN SO41 227 H8 5
RGWD BH24 169 H5
Cherry Tree Dr
NMIL/BTOS BH25 225 J3 1
Cherry Wk WSHM SO15 106 B8
Cherrywood HEND SO30 133 M2
Cherrywood Gdns
TOTT SO40 129 G1 5
HISD PO11 213 K4
Chervil Cl HORN PO8 116 B7
Cherville St ROMY SO51 50 C8
Cherwell Crs ROWN SO16 105 K8
Cherwell Gdns CHFD SO53 81 J3
Cheshire Cl FHAM PO15 159 K3
Cheshire Dr CHAR BH8 221 L6
Cheshire Wy EMRTH PO10 167 J6
Chesildene Av CHAR BH8 221 H6
Chesildene Dr CHAR BH8 221 H5
Chesil St WINC SO23 3 J9
Cheslyn Rd HSEA PO3 211 M2
Chessel Av BOSC BH5 236 E4
ITCH SO19 132 C1
Chessel Crs ITCH SO19 132 C1
Chester Crs LSOL/BMARY PO13 208 F4
Chesterfield Cl CCLF BH13 234 E8
Chesterfield Rd HSEA PO3 211 L1
Chester Pl SSEA PO5 13 J7
Chester Rd CCLF BH13 234 F6
WEND SO18 107 M7
WINC SO23 3 J8
Chesterton Gdns HORN PO8 140 C5
Chesterton Pl FHAM PO15 135 G8 1
Chestnut Av CHCH/BSGR BH23 222 B8
CHFD SO53 81 H5
ELGH SO50 81 K7
ENEY PO4 211 K4 1
FUFL SO22 16 A4
HAV PO9 164 F5
HORN PO8 141 G3
NMIL/BTOS BH25 225 L8
RGWD BH24 145 M2
RWIN SO21 54 E7
SBNE BH6 237 H4
TOTT SO40 129 G5
Chestnut Cl CHFD SO53 81 H6
ROMY SO51 79 J2
WVILLE PO7 139 K4
Chestnut Gv WIMB BH21 193 J2
Chestnut Ri BPWT SO32 86 F7
ELGH SO50 81 J7 1
Chestnut Rd BROC SO42 175 L7
ROWN SO16 105 M6
The Chestnuts HLER SO31 158 E6
Chestnut Wk GPORT PO12 185 M7
Chestnut Wy
CHCH/BSGR BH23 223 G5
FHAM/STUB PO14 159 G7
Chetnole Cl CFDH BH17 218 D7
Chettle Rd ITCH SO19 133 J3
Chetwode Wy CFDH BH17 217 M6
Chetwynd Dr ROWN SO16 106 E4
Chetwynd Rd ENEY PO4 13 L5
ROWN SO16 106 E4
Chevening Ct ENEY PO4 211 M3 2
Cheviot Dr FAWY SO45 155 H5
Cheviot Gn HLER SO31 158 B8 5
Cheviot Rd ROWN SO16 105 K8
Cheviot Wy VWD BH31 144 D3
Chewter Cl SSEA PO5 13 L9
Chewton Common Rd
CHCH/BSGR BH23 224 E7
Chewton Farm Rd
CHCH/BSGR BH23 225 G7
Chewton Ldg
CHCH/BSGR BH23 224 F8
Chewton Wy
CHCH/BSGR BH23 224 F7
Cheyne Gdns WBNE BH4 235 H6
Cheyne Wy
LSOL/BMARY PO13 208 D3 1
Chichester Av HISD PO11 213 K6
Chichester Cl HEND SO30 109 H7
HLER SO31 158 C5
LSOL/BMARY PO13 184 F6
ROMY SO51 77 G6
Chichester Rd HISD PO11 190 A7
NEND PO2 187 J8
RGWD BH24 147 G8
WEND SO18 132 E1
Chichester Wk WIMB BH21 192 C7
Chickenhall La ELGH SO50 82 B6
Chickerell Cl
MOOR/WNTN BH9 220 F5 2
Chidden Cl PSF GU32 61 J7
Chidden Holt CHFD SO53 80 F3
Chideock Cl
BKME/WDN BH12 234 D2 2
Chidham Cl HAV PO9 8 D2
Chidham Dr HAV PO9 8 C2
Chidham Rd CHAM PO6 163 L7
Chidham Sq HAV PO9 8 C3
Chigwell Rd CHAR BH8 221 G7
Chilbolton Av FUFL SO22 2 A6
Chilbolton Ct HAV PO9 165 M2 5
Chilcomb Cl
LSOL/BMARY PO13 208 D2 1
Chilcombe Cl HAV PO9 165 J5
Chilcombe Rd SBNE BH6 237 G3 2
Chilcomb La RWIN SO21 27 K3
WINC SO23 27 G3
Chilcomb Rd WEND SO18 108 B8
Chilcote Rd HSEA PO3 211 L1
Childe Sq NEND PO2 187 G6
Chilfrome Cl CFDH BH17 218 A7
Chilgrove Rd CHAM PO6 164 A8
Chilham Cl ELGH SO50 81 M1 1
Chillenden Ct TOTT SO40 129 H2 1
Chillerton HLER SO31 157 G2
Chilling La HLER SO31 182 C3
Chillington Gdns CHFD SO53 53 G7 5
Chilsdown Wy WVILLE PO7 164 C3
Chiltern Cl NMIL/BTOS BH25 225 K7
TOTT SO40 129 H3 1
WBNE BH4 235 G3
Chiltern Dr NMIL/BTOS BH25 225 J8
VWD BH31 144 D2
Chiltern Gn ROWN SO16 105 K8
Chilworth Cl ROWN SO16 80 C7
Chilworth Dro ROWN SO16 80 B8
Chilworth Gdns HORN PO8 116 C4 1
Chilworth Gv GPORT PO12 10 D1
Chilworth Rd ROWN SO16 80 D7
Chine Av ITCH SO19 132 C2
Chine Cl HLER SO31 158 E4
Chine Crs WCLF BH2 14 B7
Chine Crescent Rd WBNE BH4 14 B7
The Chine LSOL/BMARY PO13 185 J7 1
Chine Wk FERN BH22 194 C7
Chinham Rd TOTT SO40 127 M2
Chipstead Rd CHAM PO6 163 K8
Chisels La CHCH/BSGR BH23 223 M2
Chisholm Cl ROWN SO16 105 L3
Chiswell Rd CFDH BH17 218 B7
Chithurst La LIPH GU30 66 E2
Chitty Rd ENEY PO4 211 L6
Chivers Cl SSEA PO5 13 H5 1
Chorley Cl PLE BH15 233 H2
Christchurch Bay Rd
NMIL/BTOS BH25 240 E1
Christchurch By-pass
CHCH/BSGR BH23 223 J8
Christchurch Gdns
CHAM PO6 163 M6 1
WINC SO23 26 D3
Christchurch Rd BMTH BH1 15 M5
BOSC BH5 236 F3
CHCH/BSGR BH23 221 M2
FERN BH22 193 M6
LYMN SO41 241 L1
NMIL/BTOS BH25 225 J8 1
RGWD BH24 170 D1
WINC SO23 26 D3
Christie Av HLER SO31 135 G8
Christopher Crs PLE BH15 233 H2
Christopher Wy EMRTH PO10 166 D6
Church Cl ELGH SO50 82 B4
HLER SO31 158 F5
HORN PO8 116 A2
NBAD SO52 79 M4
Churcher Cl GPORT PO12 209 H5
Churcher Rd EMRTH PO10 166 F4
Church Farm FBDG SP6 97 L8
Church Farm Cl FAWY SO45 154 F2
Churchfield VWD BH31 144 C2 1
Churchfield Crs PLE BH15 233 K4
Churchfield La RGWD BH24 122 C6
Churchfield Rd EPSF GU31 64 A4
PLE BH15 233 K5
Churchfields FAWY SO45 180 F5 2
Churchfields Rd RWIN SO21 54 E2
Church Hatch RSAL SP5 44 F8 1
Church Hl HEND SO30 108 B7
LYMN SO41 242 D3
RSAL SP5 73 L3
VWD BH31 144 C2
Churchill Av BPWT SO32 84 F7
Churchill Cl FBDG SP6 121 J3
FHAM/STUB PO14 159 G7 1
Churchill Ct HORN PO8 140 E2 1
Churchill Crs BKME/WDN BH12 234 B2
Churchill Dr EMRTH PO10 166 D4
Churchill Gdns
BKME/WDN BH12 234 B3 1
Churchill Rd BKME/WDN BH12 234 B3
BMTH BH1 236 C3
WIMB BH21 192 B5
Church La ALTN GU34 33 H5
BPWT SO32 109 L2
BPWT SO32 110 C8
BPWT SO32 112 B2
BROC SO42 175 L8
BROC SO42 204 B3
CHCH/BSGR BH23 238 A2
ELGH SO50 54 D8
FAWY SO45 180 E5
FBDG SP6 96 C4
FERN BH22 220 D1
HAV PO9 9 K7
HEND SO30 133 M3
HEND SO30 134 E3
HISD PO11 190 A5
HLER SO31 133 M8
LYMN SO41 200 F7
LYMN SO41 202 B5
LYMN SO41 228 C5
LYND SO43 151 K3
NARL SO24 31 H4
NMIL/BTOS BH25 225 K7
PSF GU32 60 A3
PTSW SO17 107 G6
RGWD BH24 172 E5
ROMY SO51 21 L6
ROMY SO51 48 C5
ROMY SO51 49 K4
ROMY SO51 51 H1
ROMY SO51 76 A3
ROMY SO51 78 D1
ROWN SO16 104 E3
RSAL SP5 44 D3
RWIN SO21 17 L3
RWIN SO21 26 F8
RWIN SO21 54 E8
WINC SO23 17 H2
WVILLE PO7 114 C5
Church Md LYMN SO41 228 C6
Churchmoor Rd WIMB BH21 192 E3
Church Pth EMRTH PO10 166 D8
FHAM/PORC PO16 7 L5
GPORT PO12 11 K4
HORN PO8 141 H2
Church Pth North PSEA PO1 211 G2 2
Church Rd BPWT SO32 112 A2
BPWT SO32 136 B1
ELGH SO50 82 C3
EMRTH PO10 166 D5
EMRTH PO10 191 H1
EMRTH PO10 191 H7
FERN BH22 194 A2
FHAM/PORC PO16 186 C2
GPORT PO12 10 C7
HISD PO11 213 L3
HLER SO31 158 B8
HLER SO31 158 F5
ITCH SO19 132 B7
PSF GU32 63 K1
PSTN BH14 233 M4
ROMY SO51 22 C6
ROMY SO51 78 D1
RSAL SP5 18 B1
SBNE BH6 237 L5
WHAM PO17 137 M1
WIMB BH21 144 C7
Church St BPWT SO32 84 E2
CHCH/BSGR BH23 238 A2
FBDG SP6 97 K8
FHAM/STUB PO14 159 K8
LISS GU33 36 D2
PLE BH15 233 G7
PSEA PO1 211 G1 1
PSF GU32 61 J7
ROMY SO51 78 D1
WSHM SO15 106 A8 2
Church Street Rbt PSEA PO1 211 G1
Church Vw EMRTH PO10 166 F5 1
ENEY PO4 211 L4
Church View Cl ITCH SO19 132 E5
Church Wk RSAL SP5 73 M3
Churchward Gdns HEND SO30 109 H6 2
Cinderford Cl CHAM PO6 163 G7 1
Cinnamon La PLE BH15 233 G7 2
The Circle MOOR/WNTN BH9 220 E4 5
SSEA PO5 13 J8
WHAM PO17 136 D4
Circular Rd PSEA PO1 210 F2
The Circus WVILLE PO7 162 E6
Cirrus Gdns HLER SO31 157 K6
City Rd WINC SO23 2 F6
Civic Centre Rd HAV PO9 8 E2
SHAM SO14 4 F2
Civic Wy FHAM/PORC PO16 7 L5
Clack La FBDG SP6 96 F2
Clacton Rd CHAM PO6 163 H8
Claire Gdns HORN PO8 116 B6
Clandon Dr ELGH SO50 81 L2
Clanfield Cl CHFD SO53 81 J2
Clanfield Dr CHFD SO53 81 J2
Clanfield Rd WEND SO18 133 G1
Clanfield Wy CHFD SO53 81 J2
Clanwilliam Rd
LSOL/BMARY PO13 208 C2
Clare Cl FHAM/STUB PO14 159 G7
Clare Gdns EPSF GU31 64 B5
FAWY SO45 206 D1
Clare Lodge Cl
CHCH/BSGR BH23 197 L8
Claremont Av
MOOR/WNTN BH9 220 F6
Claremont Cl ELGH SO50 81 M2 2
Claremont Crs WSHM SO15 130 E1
Claremont Gdns WVILLE PO7 164 C4
Claremont Rd
MOOR/WNTN BH9 220 F6
PSEA PO1 13 L2
WSHM SO15 130 E1
Clarence Esp SSEA PO5 12 E7
Clarence Pde SSEA PO5 12 F7
Clarence Park Rd LTDN BH7 236 F2
Clarence Rd GPORT PO12 11 K2
LYND SO43 151 K3 1
PSTN BH14 233 M5
SSEA PO5 13 J9
Clarence St PSEA PO1 211 G2
Clarendon Cl BDST BH18 217 L4
ROMY SO51 51 G7 1
Clarendon Crs
FHAM/STUB PO14 158 F7
Clarendon Pk LYMN SO41 228 B6
Clarendon Pl PSEA PO1 13 H1 1
PSEA PO1 211 H2 5
Clarendon Rd BDST BH18 217 J5
CHCH/BSGR BH23 237 M1
HAV PO9 8 D5
ROWN SO16 105 M8
SSEA PO5 13 H7
WBNE BH4 14 A7
Clarendon St PSEA PO1 211 H2
Clarendon Wy STOK SO20 24 B1
Clarkes Rd PSEA PO1 211 K2
Clark's Cl RGWD BH24 170 E1 2
Claude Ashby Cl WEND SO18 107 K4
Claudeen Cl WEND SO18 107 K3
Claudia Ct GPORT PO12 209 K2 1
Claudius Cl CHFD SO53 81 L1 1
Claudius Gdns CHFD SO53 81 L2
Clausentum Cl CHFD SO53 81 K1
Clausentum Rd SHAM SO14 131 L1
WINC SO23 26 E3
Clausen Wy LYMN SO41 228 A7
Claxton St PSEA PO1 13 J1
Claybank Sp HSEA PO3 187 L7
Claydon Av ENEY PO4 211 L4
Clayford Av FERN BH22 193 M1
Clayford Cl CFDH BH17 218 B6
Clayhall Rd GPORT PO12 10 D8
Clay Hl BROC SO42 151 L7
Clayhill Cl BPWT SO32 111 J4 1
Claylake Dr VWD BH31 144 E3
Claylands Ct BPWT SO32 85 G8
Claylands Rd BPWT SO32 85 G8 1
Clay La LYND SO43 151 K4 1
Claypit Rd ROMY SO51 52 A1
Claypits La FAWY SO45 155 G4
Claypitt La ALTN GU34 34 B2
Clay St RSAL SP5 46 F5
Cleasby Cl ROWN SO16 130 C1
Clease Wy RWIN SO21 54 B1
Clee Av FHAM/STUB PO14 6 A7
Cleethorpes Rd ITCH SO19 132 F4
Cleeve Cl CHAM PO6 162 F7 2
Cleeves Cl BKME/WDN BH12 219 H6 1
The Cleeves TOTT SO40 129 G2
Clegg Rd ENEY PO4 211 L5
Clematis Cl
CHCH/BSGR BH23 224 A8 1
Clement Attlee Wy CHAM PO6 162 F8
Clem's Wy ROMY SO51 20 F7
Cleric Ct FHAM/STUB PO14 159 H5
Cleveland Cl NMIL/BTOS BH25 240 C1
Cleveland Dr FAWY SO45 155 H6
FHAM/STUB PO14 6 B7
Cleveland Gdns BMTH BH1 15 M1
Cleveland Rd BMTH BH1 236 C3
GPORT PO12 10 F5 1
SSEA PO5 13 L4
WEND SO18 107 L6
Clevelands Cl CHFD SO53 53 G6 1
Clewers Hl BPWT SO32 111 J4
Clewers La BPWT SO32 111 J4
Cliff Crs NMIL/BTOS BH25 240 E1
Cliff Dr CCLF BH13 245 K2
CHCH/BSGR BH23 239 H2
Cliffe Av HLER SO31 157 J5
Cliffe Rd NMIL/BTOS BH25 240 D1
Clifford Dibben Ms
SHAM SO14 106 F8 1
Clifford Pl ELGH SO50 83 H6
Clifford Rd MOOR/WNTN BH9 220 E7
Clifford St SHAM SO14 5 J2
Cliff Rd FHAM/STUB PO14 183 K7
LYMN SO41 241 M3
WSHM SO15 4 A1
Cliff Wy RWIN SO21 54 C2
Clifton Crs WVILLE PO7 139 M4
Clifton Gdns FERN BH22 194 A4
WEND SO18 108 B7
Clifton Hl FUFL SO22 2 E7
Clifton Rd FUFL SO22 2 D6
LSOL/BMARY PO13 208 E4
PSTN BH14 234 C6
SBNE BH6 237 J5
SSEA PO5 13 G8
WSHM SO15 105 M8
Clifton St GPORT PO12 209 K2
PSEA PO1 211 J2
Clifton Ter FUFL SO22 2 E7
Clingan Rd SBNE BH6 237 J2
Clinkley Rd NARL SO24 32 C1
Clinton Cl CHCH/BSGR BH23 224 F6 1
Clinton Rd LYMN SO41 228 C3
WVILLE PO7 140 A5
Clipper Cl HLER SO31 158 C7
Cliveden Cl FERN BH22 194 A1
Clive Gv FHAM/PORC PO16 186 A1
Clive Rd CHCH/BSGR BH23 224 C6
MOOR/WNTN BH9 220 D7
PSEA PO1 211 J2
Clock St PSEA PO1 12 C2
Clocktower Dr ENEY PO4 211 M6
The Cloisters FHAM PO15 160 A6
RGWD BH24 171 G2 1
ROMY SO51 50 D8 1
ROWN SO16 106 F4
The Close Bellfield
FHAM/STUB PO14 183 K1
The Close BDST BH18 217 J5
CHAM PO6 187 L1 1
FAWY SO45 180 B5
FHAM/PORC PO16 162 A8
HEND SO30 133 M2
LYMN SO41 200 E6
NMIL/BTOS BH25 225 L8
PSF GU32 62 B5
RGWD BH24 169 L4 1
RGWD BH24 170 D1 2
RSAL SP5 73 J1
WEND SO18 133 H1
Closewood Rd WVILLE PO7 139 L7
Clouch La RGWD BH24 172 D5
Clough's Rd RGWD BH24 170 F1
Clovelly Rd EMRTH PO10 166 C8
EMRTH PO10 167 H7
ENEY PO4 211 L4
HISD PO11 190 A4
SHAM SO14 131 L2
Clover Cl CHCH/BSGR BH23 223 M8
HLER SO31 158 C6
LSOL/BMARY PO13 185 G6 5
Clover Ct NMIL/BTOS BH25 226 B4
Clover Dr CFDH BH17 217 K7
The Clovers
BKME/WDN BH12 219 L8 2
Clover Wy HEND SO30 133 L2 2
ROMY SO51 51 H8
Clowes Av SBNE BH6 238 A5
Club House La BPWT SO32 111 J5
Clydebank Rd NEND PO2 187 H8
Clyde Ct GPORT PO12 209 K2
Clyde Rd CFDH BH17 217 M6 2
GPORT PO12 209 K2
Clydesdale Dr TOTT SO40 104 A8 1
Clydesdale Rd HLER SO31 158 F1
Clydesdale Wy TOTT SO40 104 A8
Coach Hl FHAM/STUB PO14 159 K8
Coach Hill Cl CHFD SO53 81 G1
Coach Hill La RGWD BH24 172 B2
Coach House Pl BMTH BH1 15 H2
Coachmans Copse
WEND SO18 107 M6
Coach Rd HLER SO31 157 J6
Coal Park La HLER SO31 134 B7
Coalville Rd ITCH SO19 132 F4
Coastguard Cl GPORT PO12 10 A8
Coastguard La SELS PO20 215 J7
Coastguard Wy
CHCH/BSGR BH23 238 E4
Coates Rd ITCH SO19 133 H4
Coates Wy WVILLE PO7 164 C3
Coat Gdns FAWY SO45 155 L5 2
Cobbett Cl FUFL SO22 26 B3
Cobbett Rd WEND SO18 132 C1
Cobbett Wy HEND SO30 134 C1
Cobblers Cnr LYMN SO41 201 L5
Cobblewood EMRTH PO10 166 D5
Cobbs La PLE BH15 233 K2
Cobb's Rd WIMB BH21 192 C2
Cobden Av HSEA PO3 187 L8
WEND SO18 107 J8
Cobden Crs WEND SO18 107 L8
Cobden Gdns WEND SO18 107 K7
Cobden St GPORT PO12 10 E1
Cobham Rd MOOR/WNTN BH9 220 E5
WIMB BH21 193 K1
Cobham Wy WIMB BH21 192 C7
Coblands Av TOTT SO40 129 H1
Coburg St PSEA PO1 13 K1
SHAM SO14 132 A2
Cochrane Cl
LSOL/BMARY PO13 209 H2
Cockerell Cl WIMB BH21 192 D7
Cockleshell Gdns ENEY PO4 212 A5
Cocklydown La TOTT SO40 129 J3
Cockshott La PSF GU32 35 H6
Cogdeane Rd CFDH BH17 218 B6
Coghlan Cl FHAM/PORC PO16 7 J3
Coker Cl FUFL SO22 2 D6
Colborne Av WIMB BH21 192 D3
Colborne Cl LYMN SO41 228 C3
PLE BH15 233 J7 5
Colbourne Cl
CHCH/BSGR BH23 197 L8
Colburn Cl ROWN SO16 105 J6
Colbury Gv HAV PO9 165 G4
Colchester Av ELGH SO50 82 D4
Colchester Rd CHAM PO6 163 H7
Cold East Cl HLER SO31 158 C3
Coldeast Wy HLER SO31 158 D3
Cold Harbour Cl WHAM PO17 136 D4
Coldharbour Farm Rd
EMRTH PO10 166 D7
Coldharbour La ROWN SO16 78 F8
Coldhill La HORN PO8 140 C1
Colebrook Av HSEA PO3 211 M1
WSHM SO15 106 B7
Colebrook Pl WINC SO23 3 J9
Colebrook St WINC SO23 3 H9
Cole Hl BPWT SO32 113 G3
Colehill Crs MOOR/WNTN BH9 220 F5
Colehill La WIMB BH21 192 C1
Coleman Rd BWD BH11 219 L5
Coleman St SHAM SO14 5 J3
Colemere Gdns
CHCH/BSGR BH23 224 D7
Colemore Rd LTDN BH7 237 H1
Colemore Sq HAV PO9 165 K4 1
Colenso Rd FHAM/PORC PO16 7 H4
Coleridge Cl HLER SO31 158 B7
Coleridge Gdns HORN PO8 140 D4
Coleridge Gn
CHCH/BSGR BH23 223 K8 2
Coleridge Rd CHAM PO6 162 D7
Coles Av PLE BH15 232 D6
Colesbourne Rd CHAM PO6 162 F7
Coles Cl RWIN SO21 54 F1
Coles Gdns PLE BH15 232 D6
Coles Mede RWIN SO21 54 A5
Coleson Rd WEND SO18 107 K8
Cole's La RSAL SP5 74 D3
Coleville Av FAWY SO45 180 F5
Colin Cl WIMB BH21 217 H3
Colinton Av FHAM/PORC PO16 162 B7
Collard Wy LISS GU33 36 E4 1
College Cl HAV PO9 142 A7
HLER SO31 157 K6 1
College La PSEA PO1 12 C2 2
College Rd BOSC BH5 236 F4
ITCH SO19 132 C6
PSEA PO1 12 C1
RGWD BH24 170 E1
WVILLE PO7 164 C6
College St EPSF GU31 63 L5
PSEA PO1 12 C2
SHAM SO14 5 H5

WINC SO23 3 G9
College Wk WINC SO23 26 F2
Collett Cl HEND SO30 109 G6
Collier Cl PTSW SO17 107 H8 1
Collingbourne Av SBNE BH6 237 J2
Collingbourne Dr CHFD SO53 80 F2
Collington Crs CHAM PO6 162 F7
Collingwood Rd SSEA PO5 13 K7
WIMB BH21 168 C2
Collingworth Cl HLER SO31 158 F2
Collins Cl NBAD SO52 80 E2 1
Collins La EPSF GU31 92 E1
RGWD BH24 170 E1
RWIN SO21 53 H1
Collins Rd ENEY PO4 211 L6
Collis Rd HSEA PO3 187 L8
Collwood Cl PLE BH15 233 H1
Collyers Rd BROC SO42 175 K8
Colne Av ROWN SO16 105 J5
Colonnade Rd BOSC BH5 236 F3 1
Colpoy St SSEA PO5 12 F4
Colson Rd WINC SO23 3 K6
Colt Cl ROWN SO16 105 L3 3
WIMB BH21 192 F2
Coltsfoot Cl HEND SO30 133 M1
Coltsfoot Dr HLER SO31 158 C6
WVILLE PO7 164 D3
Coltsfoot Wk ROMY SO51 51 H7 4
Coltsmead CHAM PO6 162 D8
Colts Rd ROWN SO16 105 K1
Columbian Wy NBNE BH10 220 A6 2
Columbia Rd NBNE BH10 219 M6
Columbia Trees La NBNE BH10 220 A7
Columbine Cl
CHCH/BSGR BH23 223 M7 1
Colville Cl BOSC BH5 236 F3
Colville Dr BPWT SO32 85 J8
Colville Rd BOSC BH5 236 F3
CHAM PO6 163 L8
Colwell Cl ROWN SO16 105 J8
Colwell Rd CHAM PO6 187 K1
Combe Rd LISS GU33 37 G7
Comber Rd MOOR/WNTN BH9 220 D5
Comet Wy CHCH/BSGR BH23 238 F2
Comfrey Cl HORN PO8 116 B7 1
ROMY SO51 51 H7
Comines Wy HEND SO30 133 J2
Comley Hl HAV PO9 166 A1
Comley Rd MOOR/WNTN BH9 220 D6
Commercial Pl PSEA PO1 211 G2 5
Commercial Rd PLE BH15 233 L4
PSEA PO1 13 G1
PSEA PO1 211 G2 6
TOTT SO40 129 L1
WCLF BH2 14 C6
WSHM SO15 4 F1
Commercial St WEND SO18 132 F1
Common Barn La
LSOL/BMARY PO13 208 D1 2
Common Cl CHFD SO53 53 H8
Common Gdns CHFD SO53 53 H8
Common Hill Rd ROMY SO51 51 J2
Common La FHAM/STUB PO14 159 H8
WHAM PO17 138 C7
Common Rd CHFD SO53 53 H8
EMRTH PO10 167 K3
RSAL SP5 47 G5
Commonside EMRTH PO10 166 F3
Common St PSEA PO1 211 H2 1
Common Vw MIDH GU29 67 J7
Compass Cl
LSOL/BMARY PO13 209 H2 2
Compass Rd CHAM PO6 162 F8
Compton Av PSTN BH14 234 C6
Compton Beeches
RGWD BH24 169 L3 1
Compton Cl ELGH SO50 81 L2
FUFL SO22 26 A5
HAV PO9 8 E1
LSOL/BMARY PO13 208 E2
VWD BH31 144 D2
Compton Crs FERN BH22 168 E7
Compton Dr PSTN BH14 234 B6
Compton Gdns PSTN BH14 234 B6
Compton Rd NEND PO2 187 K5
NMIL/BTOS BH25 225 L6
TOTT SO40 104 F8
WINC SO23 2 E9
Compton's Dr ROMY SO51 75 L2
Compton St RWIN SO21 26 B8
Compton Wk SHAM SO14 5 G1
Compton Wy FUFL SO22 26 A5
Conan Rd NEND PO2 187 J4
Concorde Wy FHAM PO15 159 J3
Condor Av FHAM/PORC PO16 161 K8
Condor Cl ITCH SO19 132 B5 1
Coneygar La FERN BH22 193 L5
Conference Dr HLER SO31 158 F5 1
Conference Pl LYMN SO41 228 D6 2
Conford Ct HAV PO9 165 H2
Congleton Cl LYND SO43 127 G5
Conifer Av PSTN BH14 234 A6
Conifer Cl CHCH/BSGR BH23 222 B5
FAWY SO45 155 K5 2
FERN BH22 194 D7
FUFL SO22 2 D5
HORN PO8 140 E6
RGWD BH24 169 H4
Conifer Crs LYMN SO41 227 M5
Conifer Gv
LSOL/BMARY PO13 185 G4
Conifer Ms
FHAM/PORC PO16 162 B7 1
Conifer Rd ROWN SO16 105 M4
Conigar Rd EMRTH PO10 166 D5
Coniston Av BWD BH11 219 J3
HSEA PO3 187 L8
Coniston Cl VWD BH31 144 C3
Coniston Gdns HEND SO30 133 M3
Coniston Rd ELGH SO50 81 L6
RGWD BH24 170 F2 1
ROWN SO16 105 H8
Connaught Cl
NMIL/BTOS BH25 225 J8
Connaught Crs
BKME/WDN BH12 234 D2
Connaught Rd HAV PO9 9 G4
NEND PO2 187 H6 1
SBNE BH6 237 G3 3
Connell Rd PLE BH15 233 H3
Connemara Crs HLER SO31 158 F1
Connigar Cl
LSOL/BMARY PO13 209 G1 1
Conqueror Wy
FHAM/STUB PO14 184 B6
Conrad Gdns FHAM PO15 135 G8
Consort Cl BKME/WDN BH12 234 B3 2
Consort Rd ELGH SO50 82 A3
Constable Cl GPORT PO12 10 F9
ITCH SO19 133 G6
Constable's Ga WINC SO23 2 E8
Constantine Av CHFD SO53 81 K2
Constantine Cl CHFD SO53 81 L2 1
Constitution Hill Rd
PSTN BH14 233 L4
Convent La EMRTH PO10 166 D8
Conway Cl CHFD SO53 81 G5
NMIL/BTOS BH25 225 M5
Conways Dr PSTN BH14 233 M4 1
Cook Cl RGWD BH24 147 G8
Cooke Rd BKME/WDN BH12 234 E2
Cooks La EMRTH PO10 167 J7
RCCH PO18 143 M6
ROMY SO51 48 C1
ROMY SO51 49 M4
TOTT SO40 104 B6
Cook's Pond Rd LIPH GU30 38 D8
Cook St SHAM SO14 5 H4
Coombe Av NBNE BH10 220 C6
Coombedale HLER SO31 158 F6 1
Coombe Farm Av
FHAM/PORC PO16 7 H8
Coombe Gdns NBNE BH10 220 B6
Coombe La LYMN SO41 201 H7
PSF GU32 60 D4
ROMY SO51 49 L5
Coombe Rd GPORT PO12 209 M1
PSF GU32 61 H8
Coombs Cl HORN PO8 116 B7 2
Cooper Dean Dr CHAR BH8 221 K7
Cooper Gv FHAM/PORC PO16 186 B2
Cooper Rd HSEA PO3 211 M1
TOTT SO40 129 G5
Cooper's Cl ROMY SO51 77 G6 1
WEND SO18 108 B7
Cooper's La ITCH SO19 132 B5 2
VWD BH31 144 D1
Copeland Dr PSTN BH14 234 A6
Copeland Rd ROWN SO16 105 J7
Copinger Cl TOTT SO40 129 G2 3
Copnor Rd NEND PO2 187 K4
Copper Beech Cl
BKME/WDN BH12 234 F4
Copper Beech Dr CHAM PO6 164 C8 2
Copper Beech Gdns
NBNE BH10 220 B6
Copperfield Rd ROWN SO16 106 F3
Copperfields TOTT SO40 128 F1
Coppers Cl FBDG SP6 121 L2
Copper St SSEA PO5 12 F5
Coppice Av FERN BH22 193 M2
Coppice Cl FUFL SO22 16 B7
NMIL/BTOS BH25 226 B4
RGWD BH24 169 K4
Coppice Hl BPWT SO32 111 H1
Coppice Rd TOTT SO40 104 B6
The Coppice BROC SO42 175 H6
CHCH/BSGR BH23 239 G2 3
HORN PO8 140 E2
LSOL/BMARY PO13 185 H6 1
Coppice Vw NBNE BH10 220 C5
Coppice Wy FHAM PO15 6 A2
Coppins Gv FHAM/PORC PO16 186 A2
Copse Av NMIL/BTOS BH25 225 M6
Copse Cl EPSF GU31 64 B4
LISS GU33 36 F4
NBAD SO52 79 L4
PLE BH15 233 L5
RWIN SO21 54 B4
TOTT SO40 129 K2
WVILLE PO7 164 B6
Copse La HISD PO11 189 L8
HLER SO31 157 K6
LSOL/BMARY PO13 185 H7
ROWN SO16 80 E7
Copse Rd NMIL/BTOS BH25 225 M6
RGWD BH24 172 D6
VWD BH31 144 D2
WEND SO18 107 L6
The Copse CHFD SO53 81 K3
FHAM PO15 160 B4
Copse Vw ITCH SO19 133 J3
Copse Wy CHCH/BSGR BH23 224 C8
Copsewood Av CHAR BH8 221 J7
Copsewood Rd FAWY SO45 155 K5
TOTT SO40 129 G5
WEND SO18 107 K6
Copsey Cl CHAM PO6 164 B8
Copsey Gv CHAM PO6 164 B8
Copthorne La FAWY SO45 180 F5
Copythorne Cl CHAR BH8 221 H6 1
Copythorne Crs TOTT SO40 103 H6
Copythorn Rd NEND PO2 187 K7
Coracle Cl HLER SO31 158 D7
Coral Cl FHAM/PORC PO16 186 A2
Coralin Gv WVILLE PO7 140 F7
Coram Cl WINC SO23 3 H2
Corbar Rd CHCH/BSGR BH23 222 C8
Corbett Rd WVILLE PO7 164 B2
Corbiere Av
BKME/WDN BH12 219 H7
Corbiere Cl ROWN SO16 105 K5
Corbin Av FERN BH22 194 E2
Corbin Rd LYMN SO41 227 M6
Corbould Rd FAWY SO45 155 K8 1
Corby Crs HSEA PO3 187 M4
Cordelia Cl FAWY SO45 155 H5
Corfe Cl FHAM/STUB PO14 183 L6
Corfe Lodge Rd WIMB BH21 217 G4
Corfe View Rd PSTN BH14 234 A5
WIMB BH21 217 G3
Corfe Wy BDST BH18 217 J5
Corhampton Crs HAV PO9 165 H4
Corhampton La BPWT SO32 86 C3
Corhampton Rd SBNE BH6 237 H2
Coriander Dr TOTT SO40 128 F1
Coriander Wy FHAM PO15 135 H8
Corinna Gdns FAWY SO45 155 H5
Corinthian Rd CHFD SO53 81 K1
Cork La TOTT SO40 130 D5
Cormorant Cl
FHAM/PORC PO16 161 K8 1
Cormorant Dr FAWY SO45 155 M6
Cornaway La
FHAM/PORC PO16 185 M1
Cornbrook Gv HORN PO8 141 G7
Cornelia Crs BKME/WDN BH12 234 F2
Cornelius Dr WVILLE PO7 140 F7
Cornel Rd ITCH SO19 132 D3
Corner Md WVILLE PO7 139 K4
Cornes Cl FUFL SO22 2 A7
Cornfield FHAM/PORC PO16 160 F4
Cornfield Cl NBAD SO52 80 E2
Cornfield Rd
LSOL/BMARY PO13 208 D2
Cornflower Cl HLER SO31 158 C6
Cornflower Dr
CHCH/BSGR BH23 224 A7
Cornford Wy
CHCH/BSGR BH23 224 B8
Cornforth Rd TOTT SO40 104 B7
Cornish Gdns NBNE BH10 220 B7
Corn Market ROMY SO51 78 D1 2
Cornpits La FBDG SP6 96 B5
Cornwall Crs WEND SO18 107 L6
Cornwallis Crs PSEA PO1 211 G2
Cornwallis Rd LYMN SO41 242 A4
Cornwall Rd CHFD SO53 81 H5
PSEA PO1 13 L2
WEND SO18 107 L6
Cornwell Cl LSOL/BMARY PO13 209 H1
NEND PO2 186 F6
Coronado Rd GPORT PO12 209 M2
Coronation Av
MOOR/WNTN BH9 220 D6
UPTN BH16 232 A1 1
Coronation Pde HLER SO31 157 J5 1
Coronation Rd BPWT SO32 112 A3 2
HISD PO11 214 C7
VWD BH31 144 D1
Corporation Rd BMTH BH1 15 K3
Corsair Dr FAWY SO45 155 H4
Corscombe Cl CFDH BH17 218 C6 1
Cortina Wy HEND SO30 134 A3
Cort Wy FHAM PO15 160 A4
Corvette Av HLER SO31 158 D7
Cosford Cl ELGH SO50 82 F6 1
Cosham Park Av CHAM PO6 187 K1
Cossack Gn SHAM SO14 5 H3
Cossack La WINC SO23 3 H7
Cosworth Dr FAWY SO45 155 H5
Cotes Av PSTN BH14 233 M3
Cotlands Rd BMTH BH1 15 J4
Cot La RCCH PO18 191 M3
Cotsalls ELGH SO50 83 H7
Cotswold Cl FAWY SO45 155 H5 4
HAV PO9 165 J2 1
VWD BH31 144 D3 1
Cotswold Rd ROWN SO16 105 L8
Cottage Cl WVILLE PO7 139 K5
Cottage Gdns
BKME/WDN BH12 234 B3
Cottage Gv GPORT PO12 10 E2
SSEA PO5 13 H4
Cottage La LISS GU33 35 L4
Cottage Ms FBDG SP6 97 K6 3
RGWD BH24 170 D1 3
Cottagers La LYMN SO41 226 E5
Cottage Vw PSEA PO1 13 J1
Cottes Wy FHAM/STUB PO14 183 L7
Cottesway East
FHAM/STUB PO14 183 L7
Cott La RGWD BH24 172 F6
Cotton Cl BDST BH18 217 K3
ELGH SO50 82 D5
Cotton Dr EMRTH PO10 166 C5
Cott St BPWT SO32 112 F4
Cott Street La BPWT SO32 112 F4
Cotwell Av HORN PO8 140 F4
Coulmere Rd GPORT PO12 209 L2
Coulsdon Rd HEND SO30 134 A2
Coultas Rd CHFD SO53 53 K6
Countess Cl WIMB BH21 192 C7
Countess Gdns LTDN BH7 221 K8 1
Country Vw FHAM/STUB PO14 183 M4
ROMY SO51 76 D5
County Gdns
FHAM/STUB PO14 160 A8
Course Park Crs
FHAM/STUB PO14 159 G6
Court Barn La
LSOL/BMARY PO13 208 D1
Court Cl CHAM PO6 187 M1
CHCH/BSGR BH23 238 D1 2
LYMN SO41 228 B6
TOTT SO40 104 B6
Courtenay Dr WIMB BH21 192 A2 2
Courtenay Pl LYMN SO41 228 C6
Courtenay Rd PSTN BH14 234 A4
WINC SO23 3 G2
Court Hl FBDG SP6 96 D4
Courthill Rd PSTN BH14 234 B4
Court House Cl FAWY SO45 155 L4 3
Courtland Gdns ROWN SO16 107 G3
Court La CHAM PO6 187 M1
Court Md CHAM PO6 187 M1 1
Courtmount Gv CHAM PO6 163 L8
Court Rd LSOL/BMARY PO13 208 C1
MOOR/WNTN BH9 220 F7
WINC SO23 17 H3
WSHM SO15 131 K1
Court Royal Ms WSHM SO15 106 E8 2
The Courtyard EPSF GU31 63 L5
Cousins Gv ENEY PO4 211 L6
Covena Rd SBNE BH6 237 J2
Coventry Cl WIMB BH21 217 G4
Coventry Crs CFDH BH17 217 L7
Coventry Rd WSHM SO15 131 K2
Coverack Wy CHAM PO6 186 F1
Cove Rd NBNE BH10 220 A6
Covert Gv WVILLE PO7 164 E3
The Covert ROMY SO51 79 G2
Covington Rd EMRTH PO10 166 F3
Cowan Rd WVILLE PO7 164 B3
Coward Rd GPORT PO12 10 B8
Cowdown La RCCH PO18 118 B4
Cowdray Cl ELGH SO50 82 E6 1
ROWN SO16 106 A4
Cowdray Pk
FHAM/STUB PO14 183 L6
Cowdrey Gdns CHAR BH8 221 K6 1
Cowell Dr LTDN BH7 221 L8
Cowes La HLER SO31 182 B2
Cow La CHAM PO6 187 H1
EPSF GU31 92 F4
FHAM/PORC PO16 186 C1
Cowley Cl ROWN SO16 105 K6
Cowley Rd LYMN SO41 228 A4
Cowleys La BROC SO42 179 J8
Cowleys Rd CHCH/BSGR BH23 223 G6
Cowper Av NMIL/BTOS BH25 225 L7
Cowper Rd ITCH SO19 133 H2
MOOR/WNTN BH9 220 D6
PSEA PO1 211 J1 3
Cowpitts La RGWD BH24 147 H6
Cowslip Cl HLER SO31 158 C7
LSOL/BMARY PO13 185 G6
Cowslip Rd WIMB BH21 217 J6 1
Cox Av MOOR/WNTN BH9 220 F5
Cox Cl MOOR/WNTN BH9 220 F4
Cox Dl FHAM/STUB PO14 159 G7
Coxes Meadow PSF GU32 63 K3
Coxford Cl ROWN SO16 105 M6
Coxford Dro ROWN SO16 105 M5
Coxford Rd ROWN SO16 105 L6
Cox Rw CHFD SO53 81 J5
Cox's Dr ITCH SO19 132 F6
Coxs Hl RWIN SO21 26 F8
Coxstone La RGWD BH24 170 E2
Coy Pond Rd
BKME/WDN BH12 234 F3
Cozens Cl ITCH SO19 132 C7 1
Crabapple Cl TOTT SO40 129 G1 4
Crabbe Ct SSEA PO5 13 H4 1
Crabbs Wy TOTT SO40 128 F1
Crabbswood La LYMN SO41 200 C8
Crabden La HORN PO8 116 D8
Crableck La HLER SO31 158 A3
Crab Orchard Wy WIMB BH21 144 C6
Crabthorne Farm La
FHAM/STUB PO14 183 M5 2
Crabton Close Rd BOSC BH5 236 E3
Crabtree ROWN SO16 105 L7 1
Crabtree Cl CHCH/BSGR BH23 223 G6
Crabwood Cl ROWN SO16 105 L7
Crabwood Ct HAV PO9 165 H1 1
Crabwood Dr HEND SO30 108 D7
Crabwood Rd ROWN SO16 105 K6
Cracknore Hard TOTT SO40 131 G6
Cracknore Hard La TOTT SO40 130 F7
TOTT SO40 131 G6 1
Cracknore Rd WSHM SO15 4 A2
Craigmoor Av CHAR BH8 221 J7
Craigmoor Cl CHAR BH8 221 K7
Craigmoor Wy CHAR BH8 221 J6 2
Craigside Rd RGWD BH24 169 H4
Craigwell Rd WVILLE PO7 164 B4
Craigwood Dr FERN BH22 194 C4
Crampmoor La ROMY SO51 51 J7
Cranberry Cl TOTT SO40 130 D7
Cranborne Crs
BKME/WDN BH12 219 J8
Cranborne Gdns CHFD SO53 53 G7
Cranborne Rd CHAM PO6 163 L7
FBDG SP6 120 E3
WCLF BH2 14 D7
Cranbourne Cl WSHM SO15 106 C7 1
Cranbourne Dr RWIN SO21 54 A5
Cranbourne Rd GPORT PO12 11 G5
Cranbrook Rd
BKME/WDN BH12 234 A2
Cranbury Av SHAM SO14 131 M2
Cranbury Cl RSAL SP5 72 E2
RWIN SO21 54 A5
Cranbury Gdns HLER SO31 133 K7
Cranbury Pl SHAM SO14 131 L2
Cranbury Rd ELGH SO50 81 M6
ITCH SO19 132 D5
Crane Cl VWD BH31 144 C1
Crane Dr VWD BH31 144 C2
Cranemoor Av
CHCH/BSGR BH23 224 C6
Cranemoor Cl
CHCH/BSGR BH23 224 C6
Cranemoor Gdns
CHCH/BSGR BH23 224 D6
Cranes Ms PLE BH15 233 J5 1
Craneswater Av ENEY PO4 13 M8
Craneswater Ga ENEY PO4 13 M9 1
Craneswater Pk ENEY PO4 13 M9
Cranfield Av WIMB BH21 192 B3
Cranford Gdns CHFD SO53 53 G8
Cranford Rd PSF GU32 63 K6
Cranford Wy PTSW SO17 106 F6
Cranleigh Av PSEA PO1 211 J2
Cranleigh Cl SBNE BH6 237 K3
Cranleigh Gdns SBNE BH6 237 K3
Cranleigh Rd
FHAM/PORC PO16 185 L1
HEND SO30 134 A2
PSEA PO1 211 J2
SBNE BH6 237 J2
Cranmer Dr ROWN SO16 105 H3
Cranmer Rd MOOR/WNTN BH9 220 D8
Cranmore HLER SO31 157 G1
Crantock Gv CHAR BH8 221 K6 2
Cranwell Cl BWD BH11 219 J4 1
CHCH/BSGR BH23 197 M7
Cranworth Rd FUFL SO22 2 E5
Crasswell St PSEA PO1 211 G2
Craven Ct FHAM PO15 6 B2
Craven Rd CHFD SO53 81 J2
Craven St SHAM SO14 5 H2 1
Crawford Cl ROWN SO16 105 J3
Crawford Dr FHAM/PORC PO16 6 E1
Crawley Av HAV PO9 165 L2
Crawley Hl ROMY SO51 76 E6
Crawshaw Rd PSTN BH14 234 A6
Crawte Av FAWY SO45 180 B6
Creasey Rd BWD BH11 219 L3
Credenhill Rd CHAM PO6 163 G7
Creech Rd BKME/WDN BH12 234 B3
Creedy Gdns WEND SO18 107 M5 1
Creek End EMRTH PO10 190 D1
Creekmoor La CFDH BH17 217 K7
Creek Rd GPORT PO12 11 J3
HISD PO11 214 B6
Creighton Rd WSHM SO15 130 D2
Cremyll Cl FHAM/STUB PO14 184 A6
Crescent Cl FUFL SO22 26 A4
Crescent Dr NMIL/BTOS BH25 240 E1
Crescent Rd FHAM/PORC PO16 7 H6
GPORT PO12 10 C9
HLER SO31 158 D5
NBAD SO52 79 L3
PSTN BH14 234 D4
VWD BH31 144 E2
WCLF BH2 14 C5
WIMB BH21 192 A4
The Crescent BMTH BH1 236 D4
BPWT SO32 84 B6
ELGH SO50 81 M4
EMRTH PO10 167 H8
HLER SO31 156 F2
ITCH SO19 132 E6
NMIL/BTOS BH25 225 G8
ROMY SO51 51 G8
RWIN SO21 54 F2
TOTT SO40 128 C5
WVILLE PO7 164 A4 2
Crescent Wk FERN BH22 194 C6
Cressey Rd ROMY SO51 78 E1
Cressy Rd NEND PO2 211 H1
Cresta Gdns FERN BH22 194 C6
Crest Cl FHAM/PORC PO16 161 H7
Crestland Cl HORN PO8 140 E5
Crest Rd BKME/WDN BH12 234 B2
The Crest WVILLE PO7 164 A6
Crest Wy ITCH SO19 133 G4
Crete La FAWY SO45 155 K7
Crete Rd FAWY SO45 155 K8
Cribb Cl CFDH BH17 233 K1
Crichel Mount Rd PSTN BH14 234 B8
Crichel Rd MOOR/WNTN BH9 220 E8
Cricket Cl CHCH/BSGR BH23 238 E3
Cricket Dr HORN PO8 140 E3
Cricklemede BPWT SO32 111 J1
Cricklewood Cl BPWT SO32 111 J1 1
Crigdon Cl ROWN SO16 105 K8
Crimea Rd MOOR/WNTN BH9 235 L1 2
Cringle Av SBNE BH6 237 M4
Crinoline Gdns ENEY PO4 211 L6
Cripple Gate La BROC SO42 204 B3
Crispin Cl CHCH/BSGR BH23 224 D8
ELGH SO50 109 H2
HLER SO31 158 F4
Crispstead La WINC SO23 26 E3
Crisspyn Cl HORN PO8 140 F2
Crittall Cl LYMN SO41 201 G6
Crockford Br LYMN SO41 203 H6
Crockford Cl NMIL/BTOS BH25 225 M3
Crockford Rd EMRTH PO10 166 F4
Croft Cl WIMB BH21 217 H1
Croft Hts RSAL SP5 47 G5
Croftlands Av
FHAM/STUB PO14 184 A5
Croft La HISD PO11 189 L7
Crofton Av LSOL/BMARY PO13 184 A8
Crofton Cl CHCH/BSGR BH23 222 C8
PTSW SO17 106 F7 1
WVILLE PO7 164 A3
Crofton La FHAM/STUB PO14 183 M7
Crofton Rd ENEY PO4 211 M3
NEND PO2 187 J6
Crofton Wy BPWT SO32 111 M3
HLER SO31 158 A7
Croft Rd BKME/WDN BH12 234 A2
CHCH/BSGR BH23 223 M2
CHCH/BSGR BH23 238 E1
MOOR/WNTN BH9 220 D6
NEND PO2 187 H7 2
RGWD BH24 147 G7
The Croft CHFD SO53 81 H5 1
FHAM/STUB PO14 184 A4
TOTT SO40 104 B6
Cromarty Av ENEY PO4 211 M4
Cromarty Cl FHAM/STUB PO14 183 M5
Cromarty Rd ROWN SO16 105 K3
Crombie Cl HORN PO8 140 D4
Cromer Gdns
BKME/WDN BH12 234 E3 1
Cromer Rd BKME/WDN BH12 234 E3
CHAM PO6 163 H7
CHAR BH8 236 C1
ROWN SO16 105 J7
Cromhall Cl
FHAM/STUB PO14 160 A8 1
Crompton Wy FHAM PO15 159 G3
Cromwell Pl BOSC BH5 237 G3 4
Cromwell Rd
BKME/WDN BH12 234 C3
BOSC BH5 237 G3
ENEY PO4 211 M6
FUFL SO22 26 C2
WSHM SO15 131 K1
Crondall Av HAV PO9 165 J2
Crooked Hays Cl TOTT SO40 130 D7 1
Crooked Walk La WHAM PO17 162 C5
Crookham Cl HAV PO9 165 G4 2
Crookham Rd ITCH SO19 132 D8 2
Crookhorn La WVILLE PO7 164 C7
Crosby Rd WBNE BH4 235 H7 1
Crosfield Cl ROMY SO51 77 G6
Crossbill Cl HORN PO8 140 E1
Crosshouse Rd SHAM SO14 5 L6
Cross Keys Pas WINC SO23 3 H8 1
Crossland Cl GPORT PO12 11 G6
Crossland Dr HAV PO9 9 G1
Cross La BPWT SO32 84 F5
HORN PO8 140 E3
Crossmead Av
NMIL/BTOS BH25 225 L6
Cross Rd ITCH SO19 132 C1
LSOL/BMARY PO13 208 E4
Cross St BPWT SO32 85 H8
PSEA PO1 12 D1
SSEA PO5 13 J3 3
WINC SO23 2 F7
The Cross PSF GU32 61 J7
RGWD BH24 172 E5

RSAL SP5 .... 41 G1
Cross Wy *CHCH/BSGR* BH23 .. 222 B7
 HAV PO9 .... 8 C3
 RWIN SO21 .... 54 C3
Crossways *LYMN* SO41 .... 227 H7
The Crossways *GPORT* PO12 .. 209 M4
 UPTN BH16 .... 232 B1
The Crossway
 FHAM/PORC PO16 .... 162 A8
Crosswell Cl *ITCH* SO19 .... 133 C3
Croucher's Cft *FUFL* SO22 .... 16 A7
Croucheston Dro *RSAL* SP5 .... 41 G1
Crouch La *HORN* PO8 .... 140 E1
Crow Arch La *RGWD* BH24 .. 170 C2
Crowder Ter *FUFL* SO22 .... 2 E8
Crow La *RGWD* BH24.......... 171 G2
Crown Cl *BKME/WDN* BH12 .... 234 B5
 WVILLE PO7 .... 164 C5
Crown Md *WIMB* BH21 .... 192 A3 6
Crown St *PSEA* PO1 .... 211 H2
 WSHM SO15 .... 106 A8
Crowsbury Cl *EMRTH* PO10 .... 166 C5
Crows Nest La *BPWT* SO32 .... 109 L1
Crowsport *HISD* PO11 .... 157 L5
Crowther Cl *ITCH* SO19 .... 133 G4
Croydon Cl *ROWN* SO16 .... 105 M4
Crummock Rd *CHFD* SO53 .... 80 F1
Crumpets Dr *UPTN* BH16 ...... 216 B3
Crundles *EPSF* GU31 .... 63 H5
Crusader Rd *HEND* SO30 .... 134 B3
 WIMB BH21 .... 219 H4
Crusaders Wy *NBAD* SO52 .... 80 E2
Cruse Cl *LYMN* SO41 .... 200 F5
Crystal Wy *WVILLE* PO7 .... 140 F8
Cucklington Gdns
 MOOR/WNTN BH9 .... 220 F5
Cuckmere La *ROWN* SO16 .... 105 J8
Cuckoo Bushes La *CHFD* SO53 .. 53 G8
Cuckoo Hill Wy
 CHCH/BSGR BH23 .... 198 A7
Cuckoo La *FHAM/STUB* PO14 .. 183 M4
Cuckoo Rd *BKME/WDN* BH12 .. 218 C8
Cudnell Av *BWD* BH11 .... 219 K2
Cudworth Md *HEND* SO30 .... 109 J7
Cuffnells Cl *RGWD* BH24 ...... 122 F8
Cul-de-sac *NMIL/BTOS* BH25 .. 225 G8
Culford Av *TOTT* SO40 .... 129 K2
Culford Cl *CHAR* BH8 .... 221 K6 6
Culford Wy *TOTT* SO40 .... 129 K2
Cull Cl *BKME/WDN* BH12 ...... 220 A8
Culliford Crs *CFDH* BH17 ...... 218 C6
Cull La *NMIL/BTOS* BH25 ...... 225 M4
Culloden Cl *FHAM* PO15 .... 6 D3
Culloden Rd *FHAM/STUB* PO14.. 184 D2
Cullwood La *NMIL/BTOS* BH25 .. 226 A2
Culver *HLER* SO31 .... 157 G1 6
Culver Cl *ROWN* SO16 .... 105 J6
Culver Dr *HISD* PO11 .... 214 A7
Culverley Cl *BROC* SO42 ...... 175 K7 6
Culver Rd *ENEY* PO4 .... 211 L6
 NMIL/BTOS BH25 .... 225 K6
 WINC SO23 .... 26 C2
Culvers *EPSF* GU31 .... 93 C5
Culverwell Gdns *WINC* SO23 .... 2 F9
Culvery Gdns *WEND* SO18 ...... 107 M6
Cumberland Av *CHFD* SO53 .... 81 K3
 EMRTH PO10 .... 166 C4
Cumberland Pl *WSHM* SO15 .... 4 E1
Cumberland Rd *SSEA* PO5 .... 13 L2 6
Cumberland St *PSEA* PO1 ...... 210 F2
 SHAM SO14 .... 5 J5
Cumberland Wy *FAWY* SO45 .. 155 H5
Cumber Rd *HLER* SO31 .... 158 C5
Cumbrian Wy *ROWN* SO16 .... 105 K8
Cumnor Rd *BMTH* BH1 .... 15 C5
Cunard Av *WSHM* SO15 .... 106 B8
Cunard Rd *SHAM* SO14 .... 5 H8
Cunliffe Cl *SELS* PO20 .... 215 L6
Cunningham Av *BPWT* SO32 .. 84 F8 6
Cunningham Cl *BWD* BH11 ...... 238 F2 6
 CHCH/BSGR BH23 .... 219 L5 6
 RGWD BH24 .... 147 C8 6
Cunningham Crs *BWD* BH11 .. 219 L5
 ITCH SO19 .... 132 F4 6
Cunningham Dr *HLER* SO31 .... 158 K4
 LSOL/BMARY PO13 .... 185 H1
Cunningham Pl *BWD* BH11 ...... 219 L5 6
Cunningham Rd *HORN* PO8 .... 141 C1 6
 WVILLE PO7 .... 164 B3
Cupernham Cl *ROMY* SO51 .... 50 F8
Cupernham La *ROMY* SO51 .... 50 F5
Curdridge Cl *HAV* PO9 .... 165 L3 6
Curdridge La *BPWT* SO32 ...... 110 F5
Curlew Cl *EMRTH* PO10 .... 166 C5
 FERN BH22 .... 193 M1
 ROWN SO16 .... 106 A3
Curlew Dr *FAWY* SO45 .... 155 M6
 FHAM/PORC PO16 .... 161 K8
Curlew Gdns *HORN* PO8 .... 140 D4
Curlew Rd *CHAR* BH8 .... 221 H6
 CHCH/BSGR BH23 .... 238 F2
The Curlews *VWD* BH31 .... 144 E3
Curlieu Rd *PLE* BH15 .... 233 K2
Curtis Md *NEND* PO2 .... 187 K4
Curtis Rd *BKME/WDN* BH12 .. 234 B5
Curtiss Gdns *GPORT* PO12 .... 10 A3
The Curve *HORN* PO8 .... 140 D2
 LSOL/BMARY PO13 .... 184 F6
Curzon Howe Rd *PSEA* PO1.... 12 D1
Curzon Pl *LYMN* SO41 .... 228 B6
Curzon Rd *CHAR* BH8 .... 236 C2
 PSTN BH14 .... 233 H5
 WVILLE PO7 .... 164 C1
Custards Rd *LYND* SO43 ...... 151 K2
Cutbush La *WEND* SO18 .... 107 M5
 WEND SO18 .... 108 A8
Cuthbert Rd *PSEA* PO1 .... 211 K2
Cuthburga Rd *WIMB* BH21 .... 192 A3
Cutler Cl *BKME/WDN* BH12 .. 235 H1
 NMIL/BTOS BH25 .... 226 A5
Cutlers La *FHAM/STUB* PO14.. 184 A5
Cutlers Pl *WIMB* BH21 .... 192 E3
Cutter Av *HLER* SO31 .... 158 C7
Cut Throat La *BPWT* SO32 .... 87 C6
 BPWT SO32 .... 112 B2
Cutts Arch *BPWT* SO32 .... 113 L5
Cygnet Ct *FHAM/PORC* PO16 .. 161 K8 6

Cygnet Rd *CHAM* PO6 .... 188 D1
Cygnus Gdns *FAWY* SO45 ...... 155 G5
Cynthia Cl *BKME/WDN* BH12 .. 234 A1
Cynthia Rd *BKME/WDN* BH12 .. 234 A1
Cypress Av *ITCH* SO19 .... 132 D3
Cypress Crs *HORN* PO8 .... 140 E3
Cypress Rd *HEND* SO30 .... 134 L1
 TOTT SO40 .... 129 G1 6
Cyprus Rd *FHAM/STUB* PO14.. 159 G3
 NEND PO2 .... 187 J8
Cyril Rd *CHAR* BH8 .... 236 B2

D

Dacombe Cl *UPTN* BH16 ...... 232 B1
Dacombe Dr *UPTN* BH16 ...... 232 B1
Daffodil Rd *ROWN* SO16 .... 107 H4
Daggons Rd *FBDG* SP6 .... 121 G2
Dahlia Rd *ROWN* SO16 .... 106 F4 6
Daintree Cl *ITCH* SO19 .... 133 H5
Dairy Cl *CHCH/BSGR* BH23 .. 238 C3
 RSAL SP5 .... 73 J3
 WIMB BH21 .... 216 F4
Dairy La *ROWN* SO16 .... 104 F4
Dairymoor *WHAM* PO17 .... 136 E4
Daisy La *GPORT* PO12 .... 10 D3
 HLER SO31 .... 158 F5
Daisy Md *WVILLE* PO7 .... 164 E2
Daisy Rd *ROWN* SO16 .... 107 H4
Dale Cl *PLE* BH15 .... 233 L2
Dale Rd *FAWY* SO45 .... 155 K5
 FHAM/STUB PO14 .... 184 B5
 PLE BH15 .... 233 L2
 ROWN SO16 .... 106 B6
Dales Cl *WIMB* BH21 .... 193 G2
Dales Dr *WIMB* BH21 .... 192 F3
Dales Dr *CHCH/BSGR* BH23 .. 221 J1
Dales Wy *TOTT* SO40 .... 104 A8
The Dale *WVILLE* PO7 .... 164 A6
Dale Valley Cl *ROWN* SO16 .. 106 B6
Dale Valley Gdns *ROWN* SO16 .. 106 B6
Dale Valley Rd *PLE* BH15 ...... 233 K1
 ROWN SO16 .... 106 B5
Dalewood Av *BWD* BH11 ...... 219 J5
Dalewood Rd *FHAM* PO15 ...... 6 B5
Dalkeith Rd *CCLF* BH13 .... 234 F7
 WIMB BH21 .... 217 H4 6
Dalling Rd *BKME/WDN* BH12 .. 234 F3
Dallington Cl
 FHAM/STUB PO14 .... 184 A7 6
Dalmally Gdns *WEND* SO18 .... 107 L8 6
Dalmeny Rd *SBNE* BH6.......... 237 M5
Damask Gdns *WVILLE* PO7 .... 140 F3
Damen Cl *HEND* SO30 .... 133 M3
Damerham Rd *CHAR* BH8 ...... 221 H5
Dampier Cl *LSOL/BMARY* PO13 .. 209 G1
Damson Hl *BPWT* SO32.......... 86 A8
Danbury Ct *EMRTH* PO10 ...... 166 E6
Dances Wy *HISD* PO11 .... 213 J4
Dandelion Cl
 LSOL/BMARY PO13 .... 184 F6 6
Dando Rd *WVILLE* PO7 .... 139 L4
Dandy's Ford La *ROMY* SO51 .. 48 E8
Danebury Cl *HAV* PO9 .... 165 J2 6
Danebury Gdns *CHFD* SO53 .. 80 F1 6
Danebury Wy *ROWN* SO16 .... 105 J5
Dane Cl *FAWY* SO45 .... 180 D7
Danecourt Cl *PSTN* BH14 ...... 233 L4
Danecourt Rd *PSTN* BH14 ...... 233 L4
Danecrest Rd *LYMN* SO41 ...... 226 D5
Dane Dr *FERN* BH22 .... 194 C5
Danehurst New Rd
 LYMN SO41 .... 200 A8
Dane Rd *LYMN* SO41 .... 241 M2
Danesbrook La *WVILLE* PO7 .. 164 E1 6
Danesbury Av *SBNE* BH6 ...... 237 L4
Danes Cl *NMIL/BTOS* BH25 .. 240 F1
Danes Rd *FHAM/PORC* PO16 .. 161 M7
 ROMY SO51 .... 49 J4
 WINC SO23 .... 3 G4
Danestream Cl *LYMN* SO41 .... 242 C4 6
Daneswood Rd
 NMIL/BTOS BH25 .... 226 A5 6
Daniell's Cl *LYMN* SO41 ...... 228 C5
Daniell's Wk *LYMN* SO41 ...... 228 C6
Dansie Cl *PSTN* BH14.......... 234 A4
Dapple Pl *TOTT* SO40 .... 130 E7
Darby's Cl *PLE* BH15 .... 233 J2
Darby's La *PLE* BH15 .... 233 J2
Dark La *CHCH/BSGR* BH23 .. 224 E4
 FAWY SO45 .... 180 D7
 NARL SO24 .... 30 C3
Darley Rd *FERN* BH22.......... 194 A5
Darlington Gdns *WSHM* SO15 .. 106 C8
Darlington Rd *ENEY* PO4 ...... 13 L3
Darracott Rd *BOSC* BH5 ...... 236 F4
Darren Cl *FHAM/STUB* PO14 .. 184 B4
Dartington Rd *ELGH* SO50 .... 82 C3
Dartmouth Rd *HSEA* PO3 ...... 187 L6
Dart Rd *WEND* SO18 .... 108 A3
Darwin Av *CHCH/BSGR* BH23 .. 222 C7
Darwin Rd *ELGH* SO50 .... 82 A4
 WSHM SO15 .... 131 H1
Darwin Wy *LSOL/BMARY* PO13 .. 209 H2
Daulston Rd *PSEA* PO1 .... 211 J1
Davenport Cl
 LSOL/BMARY PO13 .... 209 G2 6
 UPTN BH16 .... 232 B1 6
Daventry La *HSEA* PO3 .... 188 A4
D Av *FAWY* SO45 .... 180 B2
David's La *RGWD* BH24.......... 170 A3
David Wy *PLE* BH15 .... 232 C6 6
Davis Cl *LSOL/BMARY* PO13 .. 185 G8 6
Davis Fld *NMIL/BTOS* BH25 .. 225 K6
Davis Rd *PSTN* BH14.......... 234 A4
Dawkins Rd *PLE* BH15 .... 232 C4
Dawkins Wy *NMIL/BTOS* BH25 .. 225 L6
Daw La *HISD* PO11 .... 189 K8
Dawlish Av *WSHM* SO15 ...... 106 C8
Dawnay Cl *ROWN* SO16 ...... 107 J3
Dawn Cl *NBNE* BH10 .... 220 A6
Dawn Gdns *FUFL* SO22 .... 26 B2
Daws Av *BWD* BH11 .... 219 M6
Dawson Rd *ITCH* SO19 .... 133 G6 6
Day La *HORN* PO8 .... 140 B1

Daylesford Cl *PSTN* BH14 ...... 233 M6 6
Dayrell Cl *TOTT* SO40 .... 104 A7
Day's Ct *WIMB* BH21 .... 192 B4
Dayshes Cl *LSOL/BMARY* PO13 .. 184 F5
Dayslondon Rd *WVILLE* PO7 .. 164 B3
Deacon Cl *ITCH* SO19 .... 132 E3
Deacon Crs *ITCH* SO19 .... 132 E2
Deacon Gdns *BWD* BH11 ...... 219 L3
Deacon Rd *BWD* BH11 .... 219 L3
 HLER SO31 .... 158 F5
 ITCH SO19 .... 132 E3
Deal Cl *FHAM/STUB* PO14 ...... 184 A4
Deal Rd *CHAM* PO6 .... 163 J7
Dean Cl *FUFL* SO22 .... 16 B6
 PLE BH15 .... 232 D5
Dean Ct *HEND* SO30 .... 133 M1
Deane Ct *HAV* PO9 .... 165 M3 6
Deane Down Dro *FUFL* SO22.. 16 A4
The Deanery *CHFD* SO53 .... 53 C8 6
Deane's Park Rd
 FHAM/PORC PO16 .... 161 H7
Deanfield Cl *HLER* SO31 ...... 157 K6
Dean La *BPWT* SO32 .... 85 K5
 HORN PO8 .... 142 B3
 RSAL SP5 .... 47 G4
Dean Park Crs *BMTH* BH1 .... 14 F4
 WCLF BH2 .... 14 F3
Dean Park Rd *BMTH* BH1 ...... 14 F4
 WCLF BH2 .... 14 F3
Dean Rd *CHAM* PO6 .... 187 K1
 ELGH SO50 .... 83 G7
 RSAL SP5 .... 18 C5
 WEND SO18 .... 132 L1
Deans Cl *PLE* BH15 .... 242 C3
Deanscroft Rd *NBNE* BH10 .... 220 C4
Deans Dell *PSF* GU32.......... 34 D7
Deans Ga *FHAM/STUB* PO14 .. 184 A7
Deans Gv *WIMB* BH21 .... 192 B1
Deansleigh Rd *LTDN* BH7 ...... 221 M7
Dean's Rd *BOSC* BH5 .... 237 G3
The Deans *BMTH* BH1 .... 14 F3
Dean St *PSEA* PO1 .... 12 D2
Dean Swift Crs *PSTN* BH14 .. 234 B8
Deanswood Dr *WVILLE* PO7 .. 140 C7
Dear Hay La *PLE* BH15 .... 233 H1
Dearing Cl *LYND* SO43 ...... 151 K3
Decies Rd *PSTN* BH14 .... 234 A3 6
De Courtenai Cl *BWD* BH11 .. 219 J3
Dee Cl *CHFD* SO53 .... 80 F3
Deepdene La *BWD* BH11 ...... 219 J3 6
Deeping Cl *ITCH* SO19 .... 132 D7 6
Deeping Ga *WVILLE* PO7 ...... 164 E1
Deerhurst Cl *TOTT* SO40 ...... 129 H2
Deerhurst Crs *CHAM* PO6 ...... 162 E7
Deer Leap *FHAM* PO15 .... 160 B3 6
Deerleap La *TOTT* SO40 ...... 129 J8
Deerleap Wy *FAWY* SO45 ...... 155 L5
 NMIL/BTOS BH25 .... 225 M2
Deer Park Cl
 NMIL/BTOS BH25 .... 225 K4 6
Dee Wy *ELGH* SO50 .... 81 L5
Defender Rd *ITCH* SO19 .... 132 B5
De Grouchy La *WINC* SO23 .. 2 E3
De Haviland Cl *WIMB* BH21 .. 192 D6
De Havilland Wy
 CHCH/BSGR BH23 .... 238 F3
Delamere Gdns *NBNE* BH10 .. 220 C5
Delamere Rd *ENEY* PO4 ...... 13 M5
De La Warr Rd *LYMN* SO41.... 242 B4
Delft Cl *HLER* SO31 .... 158 D5
Delft Gdns *WVILLE* PO7 .... 140 B6
Delft Ms *CHCH/BSGR* BH23 .. 238 C2 6
Delhi Cl *PSTN* BH14 .... 234 C5
Delhi Rd *NBNE* BH10 .... 220 C6
Delilah Rd *PLE* BH15 .... 232 C6
De Lisle Cl *NEND* PO2 .... 187 K4
De Lisle Rd *TWDS* BH3 .... 235 L1
Delius Av *ITCH* SO19 .... 133 H5
Dell Cl *BDST* BH18 .... 217 J4
 CHAM PO6 .... 163 M6
 ELGH SO50 .... 83 H7
Dellcrest Pth *CHAM* PO6 ...... 163 M7
DelField Cl *CHAM* PO6 .... 162 E7 6
Dell Piece East *HORN* PO8 .... 141 H5
Dell Piece West *HORN* PO8 .. 141 G3
Dell Quay Cl *FHAM/STUB* PO14 .. 184 E6
Dell Rd *WEND* SO18 .... 107 L6
 WINC SO23 .... 27 G2
The Dell *FHAM/PORC* PO16 .. 161 H7
 HAV PO9 .... 164 F6
 NMIL/BTOS BH25 .... 225 C8
Delme Dr *FHAM/PORC* PO16 .. 161 M6
Delphi Wy *WVILLE* PO7 .... 140 D6
Delph Rd *WIMB* BH21 .... 192 D8
Delta Cl *CHCH/BSGR* BH23 .. 238 F1
De Mauley Rd *CCLF* BH13 .... 234 D8
De Montfort Rd *WIMB* BH21 .. 192 A2
De Mowbray Wy *LYMN* SO41 .. 228 B6 6
Dempsey Cl *ITCH* SO19 ...... 132 F4
Denbigh Cl *ELGH* SO50 .... 83 L3
 TOTT SO40 .... 129 H3
Denbigh Dr *FHAM/PORC* PO16 .. 6 F3
Denbigh Gdns *ROWN* SO16 .. 106 A4
Denby Rd *PLE* BH15 .... 233 J4
Dene Cl *HLER* SO31 .... 158 C4
 RGWD BH24 .... 147 G2
 ROWN SO16 .... 106 L1
Dene Hollow *CHAM* PO6 ...... 164 B8
Dene Rd *TOTT* SO40 .... 129 G6
Deneside Copse *LYMN* SO41 .. 227 M7
Deneside Gdns *LYMN* SO41 .. 227 M6
Deneve Av *CFDH* BH17 .... 218 A5
Dene Wk *FERN* BH22 .... 194 C7
Denewood Copse
 FERN BH22 .... 168 B5 6
Denewood Rd *FERN* BH22 .... 168 B4
 WBNE BH4 .... 235 G6
Denewulf Cl *BPWT* SO32 ...... 85 H8 6
Denham Ct *FHAM/STUB* PO14 .. 183 M6
 WINC SO23 .... 2 F3
Denham Dr *CHCH/BSGR* BH23 .. 224 D7
Denham Gdns *HLER* SO31 ...... 156 F3
Denhill Cl *HISD* PO11 .... 213 J3
Denholm Cl *RGWD* BH24 ...... 147 H7

Denison Rd *CFDH* BH17 ...... 218 A7
Denmark La *PLE* BH15 .... 233 J5
Denmark Rd
 MOOR/WNTN BH9 .... 220 D7
 PLE BH15 .... 233 J5
Denmead *NMIL/BTOS* BH25 .. 226 B4 6
Denmead Rd *SBNE* BH6 ...... 237 J1
 WEND SO18 .... 108 B8
Dennis Wy *LISS* GU33 .... 36 F5
Dennistoun Av
 CHCH/BSGR BH23 .... 238 E1
Denny Cl *FAWY* SO45 .... 180 F5 6
Denville Av *FHAM/PORC* PO16 .. 186 B2
Denville Cl *CHAM* PO6 .... 164 D8
Denvilles Cl *HAV* PO9 .... 9 J2
Denzil Av *HLER* SO31 .... 157 G2
Depedene Cl *FAWY* SO45 ...... 179 M4
De Port Hts *BPWT* SO32 ...... 87 H2
Derby Rd *BMTH* BH1 .... 15 M4
 ELGH SO50 .... 81 L6
 NEND PO2 .... 187 H7
 SHAM SO14 .... 5 J1
De Redvers Rd *PSTN* BH14 .. 234 B6
Dereham Wy *BKME/WDN* BH12 .. 234 E2
Deridene Ct *TOTT* SO40 ...... 129 H2
Derlyn Rd *FHAM/PORC* PO16.. 7 H5
Derritt La *CHCH/BSGR* BH23 .. 223 C1
Derrybrian Gdns
 NMIL/BTOS BH25 .... 225 L6 6
Derwent Cl *FERN* BH22 ...... 194 C3
 FHAM/STUB PO14 .... 184 B4 6
 HORN PO8 .... 116 B6
 MOOR/WNTN BH9 .... 220 E6 6
 WEND SO18 .... 108 A7
Derwent Dr *TOTT* SO40 ...... 104 A3
Derwent Rd *LSOL/BMARY* PO13 .. 208 D3
 NMIL/BTOS BH25 .... 225 M3
 ROWN SO16 .... 105 K7
Derwentwater Rd *WIMB* BH21 .. 192 B6
Desborough Cl *CHAM* PO6 .. 162 E7 6
Desborough Rd *ELGH* SO50 .. 81 M8
Devenish Rd *FUFL* SO22 ...... 2 B1
Deverel Cl *CHCH/BSGR* BH23 .. 222 E8
Deverell Pl *WVILLE* PO7 .... 164 A5
Devine Gdns *ELGH* SO50 ...... 82 D6 6
Devon Dr *CHFD* SO53 .... 81 H5
Devon Rd *CHCH/BSGR* BH23 .. 222 C8
 HSEA PO3 .... 187 L5
 PLE BH15 .... 233 K3
Devonshire Av *ENEY* PO4 ...... 211 L5
Devonshire Gdns *FAWY* SO45 .. 155 L8 6
 HLER SO31 .... 133 K6 6
 ITCH SO19 .... 133 L6 6
Devonshire Rd *WSHM* SO15 .. 131 K2
Devonshire Sq *ENEY* PO4 ...... 211 K4
Devonshire Wy
 FHAM/STUB PO14 .... 160 A8
Dewlands Rd *VWD* BH31 ...... 144 B3
Dewlands Wy *VWD* BH31 ...... 144 B2
Dew La *ELGH* SO50 .... 81 L5
Dewlish Cl *CFDH* BH17 .... 218 E6
Dial Cl *CHCH/BSGR* BH23 .. 198 A6
Diamond Cl *FBDG* SP6 .... 97 K8 6
Diamond St *SSEA* PO5 .... 12 F5
Diana Cl *EMRTH* PO10 .... 166 C4
 GPORT PO12 .... 209 J4
Diana Wy *WIMB* BH21 .... 217 J1
Dibble Dr *NBAD* SO52 .... 79 L5
Dibden Cl *CHAR* BH8 .... 221 H5
 HAV PO9 .... 165 L4 6
Dibden Lodge Cl *FAWY* SO45 .. 155 K3
Dibles Rd *HLER* SO31 .... 158 B7
Dickens Dell *TOTT* SO40 ...... 128 F1
Dickens Dr *HLER* SO31 .... 135 C8
Dennis Cl *SBNE* BH6 .... 237 J1
Dickson Rd *WHAM* PO17 ...... 136 E4
Didcot Rd *WSHM* SO15 .... 106 B7 6
Dieppe Crs *NEND* PO2 .... 187 J4
Dieppe Gdns *GPORT* PO12 .. 10 B3 6
Diligence Cl *HLER* SO31 ...... 133 L7
Dilly La *NMIL/BTOS* BH25 .... 240 F1
Dimond Cl *WEND* SO18 .... 107 K7
Dimond Hl *WEND* SO18 .... 107 K7
Dimond Rd *WEND* SO18 .... 107 K6
Dingle Rd *BOSC* BH5 .... 237 G4
Dingle Wy *HLER* SO31 .... 158 E4
Dingley Rd *PLE* BH15 .... 233 J2
Dinham Rd *NMIL/BTOS* BH25 .. 226 B4 6
Diprose Rd *WIMB* BH21 ...... 217 J1
Discovery Cl
 FHAM/STUB PO14 .... 184 A3 6
Disraeli Rd *CHCH/BSGR* BH23 .. 238 C2
Ditcham Crs *HAV* PO9 .... 165 J4
Ditchbury *LYMN* SO41 .... 228 B2
Ditton Cl *FHAM/STUB* PO14 .. 184 A5
Dockenfield Cl *HAV* PO9 ...... 165 C4 6
Dock La *BROC* SO42 .... 178 F7
Dock Rd *BPWT* SO32 .... 111 H4
Doctor's Hl *ROMY* SO51 ...... 48 B4
Doctors La *PSF* GU32 .... 60 B3
Dodds La *BPWT* SO32 .... 112 A3
Dodgson Cl *RGWD* BH24 ...... 170 D4
Dodwell La *HLER* SO31 .... 133 M5
Doe Copse Wy
 NMIL/BTOS BH25 .... 225 J4
Dogkennel La *WVILLE* PO7 .. 114 C4
Dogwood Dell *WVILLE* PO7 .. 164 D3 6
Dogwood Rd *WIMB* BH21 ...... 217 J6
Dolbery Rd North
 BKME/WDN BH12 .... 219 H6
Dolbery Rd South
 BKME/WDN BH12 .... 219 G7
Dolman Rd *GPORT* PO12 ...... 11 C5
Dolphin Av *NBNE* BH10 .... 220 C3
Dolphin Cl *ELGH* SO50 .... 82 C6
Dolphin Ct
 FHAM/STUB PO14 .... 183 M4 6
Dolphin Crs *GPORT* PO12 ...... 10 F5
Dolphin Hl *RWIN* SO21 .... 44 A4
Dolphin Pl *NMIL/BTOS* BH25 .. 240 F1 6
Dolphin Wy *GPORT* PO12 ...... 11 H9
Dolton Rd *ROWN* SO16 .... 105 L4
Dome Aly *WINC* SO23 .... 3 G4
Dominion Rd *BWD* BH11 ...... 219 J5
Domum Rd *NEND* PO2 .... 187 K6
 WINC SO23 .... 27 G1

Domvilles Ap *NEND* PO2 ...... 186 F7
Donaldson Rd *CHAM* PO6 ...... 187 K2
Doncaster Rd *ELGH* SO50 ...... 81 M8
Donigers Dell *BPWT* SO32 .. 111 M2
Donnelly Rd *SBNE* BH6 ...... 237 L3
Donnelly St *GPORT* PO12 ...... 209 L2
Donnington Dr
 CHCH/BSGR BH23 .... 239 G1
 CHFD SO53 .... 80 F5
Donnington Gv *PTSW* SO17 .. 107 G6
Donoughmore Rd *BMTH* BH1 .. 236 C4
Dorcas Cl *WVILLE* PO7 .... 140 E7 6
Dorchester Gdns *PLE* BH15 .. 233 K3
Dorchester Rd *PLE* BH15 ...... 233 K2
Dore Av *FHAM/PORC* PO16 .. 161 M8
Dores La *ROMY* SO51 .... 24 A6
Doric Cl *CHFD* SO53 .... 81 L1
Dorking Crs *CHAM* PO6 ...... 187 K1
Dorland Gdns *TOTT* SO40 ...... 129 H2
Dormington Rd *CHAM* PO6 .. 163 G7
Dormy Cl *HLER* SO31 .... 158 B5
Dormy Wy *LSOL/BMARY* PO13 .. 184 F7
Dornie Rd *CCLF* BH13 .... 245 J1
Dornmere La *WVILLE* PO7 ...... 164 E1 6
Dorothy Dymond St
 PSEA PO1 .... 13 G2 6
Dorrien Rd *GPORT* PO12.......... 209 M1
Dorrita Av *HORN* PO8 .... 140 E4
Dorrita Cl *ENEY* PO4 .... 211 K6
The Dorrits *TOTT* SO40 .... 128 F1
Dorset Av *FERN* BH22 .... 194 B3
Dorset Cl *HORN* PO8 .... 140 F2
Dorset Lake Av *PSTN* BH14 .. 234 A8
Dorset Rd *CHCH/BSGR* BH23 .. 223 K8
 CHFD SO53 .... 81 H5 6
 WBNE BH4 .... 235 H3
Dorset St *PTSW* SO17 .... 131 H2
Dorset Wy *BKME/WDN* BH12 .. 218 C8
 PLE BH15 .... 233 J1
Dorstone Rd *CHAM* PO6 ...... 163 G7
Douglas Av *CHCH/BSGR* BH23 .. 237 L2
Douglas Cl *UPTN* BH16 .... 232 B1
Douglas Crs *ITCH* SO19 .... 133 G2
Douglas Gdns
 BKME/WDN BH12 .... 234 D3
 HAV PO9 .... 165 L4 6
Douglas Ms *SBNE* BH6 ...... 237 H3 6
Douglas Rd *BKME/WDN* BH12.. 234 D3
 PSEA PO1 .... 211 K1
 SBNE BH6 .... 237 K5
Douglas Wy *FAWY* SO45 ...... 155 J4
Doulton Gdns *PSTN* BH14 ...... 234 A6
Doussie Cl *UPTN* BH16 .... 216 E8
Dove Cl *HORN* PO8 .... 140 D4
Dove Di *ELGH* SO50 .... 81 J6
Dove Gdns *HLER* SO31 .... 158 F3 6
Dover Cl *CCLF* BH13 .... 234 F5
 FHAM/STUB PO14 .... 183 M5
Dover Ct *HISD* PO11 .... 213 J3
Dovercourt Rd *CHAM* PO6 .. 187 C2
Dover Rd *CCLF* BH13 .... 234 F5
 HSEA PO3 .... 187 L8
Dover St *SHAM* SO14 .... 131 L1
Doveshill Crs *NBNE* BH10 .... 220 B4
Doveshill Gdns *NBNE* BH10 .. 220 B5
Doves La *RSAL* SP5 .... 46 F5
Doveys Cl *RGWD* BH24 .... 172 E5 6
Dowds Cl *HEND* SO30 .... 109 G8
Dowlands Cl *NBNE* BH10 ...... 220 B4 6
Dowlands Rd *NBNE* BH10 .... 220 A4
Down End *CHAM* PO6 .... 164 A7
Down End Rd *CHAM* PO6 ...... 164 A7
Downend
 FHAM/PORC PO16 .... 161 L6
Downey Cl *BWD* BH11 .... 219 K6
Down Farm Pl *HORN* PO8 .... 116 B7 6
Downham Cl *HORN* PO8 ...... 140 D5
Downhouse Rd *HORN* PO8 .. 115 M4
Downland Cl *HEND* SO30 .... 134 D1
 HLER SO31 .... 158 E4
Downland Pl *HEND* SO30 ...... 133 M4
Downlands Cl *RSAL* SP5 ...... 72 D3
Downlands Rd *FUFL* SO22 .... 26 A4
Downley Rd *HAV* PO9 .... 165 M4
Down Lodge Cl *FBDG* SP6 .. 121 L2 6
Down Rd *HORN* PO8 .... 116 A7
Downs Cl *WVILLE* PO7 .... 164 D5
Downscroft Gdns
 HEND SO30 .... 109 G8 6
 HEND SO30 .... 133 M1 6
Downside *LSOL/BMARY* PO13 .. 185 H6
Downside Av *ITCH* SO19 .... 132 C2
Downside Rd *FUFL* SO22 ...... 16 A6
 WVILLE PO7 .... 164 A5 6
Down's Park Av *TOTT* SO40 .. 129 L2
Down's Park Crs *TOTT* SO40 .. 129 L2
Down's Park Rd *TOTT* SO40 .. 129 L2
The Downsway
 FHAM/PORC PO16 .... 162 A8
Downton Cl *CHAR* BH8 .... 221 C5
Downton Hl *RSAL* SP5 .... 73 H1
Downton La *LYMN* SO41 ...... 241 L2
Downton Rd *WEND* SO18 ...... 107 L6
Downview Rd *FBDG* SP6 ...... 97 J6
Downwood Cl *FAWY* SO45 .. 155 G6 6
 FBDG SP6 .... 97 J6
Downwood Wy *HORN* PO8 .. 116 B7 6
Doyle Av *NEND* PO2 .... 187 J4
Doyle Cl *NEND* PO2 .... 187 J4
Doyle Ct *ITCH* SO19 .... 132 D7
Doyne Rd *PSTN* BH14 .... 234 D4
Dradfield La *BPWT* SO32 ...... 113 H8
Dragon La *RGWD* BH24 .... 170 D4
Dragon St *EPSF* GU31 .... 63 L6
Dragoon Cl *ITCH* SO19 .... 133 G4
Dragoon Wy
 CHCH/BSGR BH23 .... 237 L2
Drake Cl *CHCH/BSGR* BH23 .. 238 E2 6
 HLER SO31 .... 158 F5 6
 NMIL/BTOS BH25 .... 225 K5
 RGWD BH24 .... 147 C8
 TOTT SO40 .... 130 D6
Drakeleys Cl *LIPH* GU30 .... 38 E6
Drake Rd *ELGH* SO50 .... 82 D4
 LSOL/BMARY PO13 .... 208 B1
 PLE BH15 .... 233 H7 6
Drakes Cl *FAWY* SO45 .... 155 K6 6
Draper Rd *BWD* BH11 .... 219 L4

CHCH/BSGR BH23 238 D1
Draycote Rd HORN PO8 116 B5
Draycott Rd NBNE BH10 220 B6
Drayton Cl ITCH SO19 132 D8
Drayton La CHAM PO6 163 M7
Drayton Pl TOTT SO40 129 H1 1
Drayton Rd NEND PO2 187 J7
Drayton St FUFL SO22 26 B2
Dreadnought Rd
FHAM/STUB PO14 184 C3
Dresden Dr HORN PO8 140 B6
Dreswick Cl CHCH/BSGR BH23 222 B4
Drew Cl BKME/WDN BH12 235 H1
Drift Rd FHAM/PORC PO16 7 M3
HORN PO8 116 A3
The Drift HAV PO9 141 M7
Driftwood Gdns ENEY PO4 212 A6
TOTT SO40 129 G2 4
Drill Shed Rd NEND PO2 186 F7
Drinkwater Cl ELGH SO50 81 L5
The Drive EMRTH PO10 167 H8
FHAM/PORC PO16 7 G5
HAV PO9 8 E1
HEND SO30 108 A5
LSOL/BMARY PO13 184 E6
PSTN BH14 234 C3 5
ROMY SO51 47 L7
ROMY SO51 76 F6
TOTT SO40 129 K3
Drove Cl RWIN SO21 54 E3
Drove Rd ITCH SO19 132 F4
WHAM PO17 162 E4
The Drove BPWT SO32 84 C8
BPWT SO32 112 A3
ELGH SO50 109 J2
FAWY SO45 180 C7
HEND SO30 108 E5
ROMY SO51 76 D5
RWIN SO21 54 E3
TOTT SO40 104 A7
WEND SO18 132 E1
Droxford Cl GPORT PO12 10 B3 1
Droxford Rd BPWT SO32 112 B4
LTDN BH7 237 G2
Druids Cl FERN BH22 194 B6
Druitt Rd CHCH/BSGR BH23 223 K8
Drum Md PSF GU32 63 K5
Drummond Cl FUFL SO22 26 D3 1
Drummond Rd BMTH BH1 236 C4
FAWY SO45 155 L4 4
HEND SO30 109 H7
PSEA PO1 211 H2 2
Drummond Wy CHFD SO53 53 G8 3
Drury Rd WBNE BH4 235 G6 1
Dryden Av CHAM PO6 162 C7
Dryden Cl FHAM/PORC PO16 6 F4
RGWD BH24 169 J3
WVILLE PO7 140 B6
Dryden Pl LYMN SO41 242 C3
Dryden Rd ITCH SO19 133 J3
Drysdale Ms ENEY PO4 211 M6 1
Ducking Stool La
CHCH/BSGR BH23 238 A2
Duck Island La RGWD BH24 170 E2 2
Duck La BWD BH11 219 K4
Duckmead La LISS GU33 37 G2
Duddon Cl WEND SO18 108 A7
Dudleston Heath Dr
HORN PO8 140 F6
Dudley Av FBDG SP6 97 L5
LYMN SO41 226 D6
Dudley Gdns NBNE BH10 220 B3 2
Dudley Rd HSEA PO3 211 L1 1
NBNE BH10 220 B3
Dudmoor Farm Rd
CHCH/BSGR BH23 222 D5
Dudmoor La CHCH/BSGR BH23 222 D4
Dudsbury Av FERN BH22 194 B4
Dudsbury Crs FERN BH22 194 B4
Dudsbury Gdns FERN BH22 194 C8
Dudsbury Rd FERN BH22 194 B6
Duffield La EMRTH PO10 167 H5
Dugald Drummond St
PSEA PO1 13 G2 3
Dugdell Cl FERN BH22 194 D2 1
Duisburg Wy SSEA PO5 12 E6
Duke Crs PSEA PO1 211 H1
Duke Rd HEND SO30 134 B3
Dukes Cl PSF GU32 63 J4
Dukes Dr BWD BH11 219 J3
Dukesfield CHCH/BSGR BH23 222 B6
Dukes Rd GPORT PO12 209 L2
SHAM SO14 107 G8
Duke St SHAM SO14 5 J5
Dukeswood Dr FAWY SO45 155 K7
Dulsie Rd TWDS BH3 235 H1
Dumbarton Cl NEND PO2 187 H8 2
Dumbleton Cl ITCH SO19 133 K4
Dummer Ct HAV PO9 165 H2
Dummers Rd ROMY SO51 51 J1
Dumpers Dro ELGH SO50 109 J2
Dumpford La EPSF GU31 65 L8
Dunbar Cl ROWN SO16 105 L3
Dunbar Crs CHCH/BSGR BH23 224 D6
Dunbar Rd ENEY PO4 211 M4
TWDS BH3 235 K2
Dunbridge La ROMY SO51 21 K8
Duncan Cl ITCH SO19 132 C8
Duncan Rd HLER SO31 158 F3
NMIL/BTOS BH25 226 B4
SSEA PO5 13 K7
Duncans Dr
FHAM/STUB PO14 159 M8 1
Duncliff Rd SBNE BH6 237 M4
Duncombe Dr RGWD BH24 145 M6
Duncombe Rd PSF GU32 61 J8
Duncton Rd HORN PO8 116 C3
Dundas Cl HSEA PO3 187 M6
Dundas La HSEA PO3 187 M7
Dundas Rd CFDH BH17 218 C8
Dundas Sp HSEA PO3 187 M6
Dundee Cl FHAM PO15 6 D2
Dundee Rd PTSW SO17 107 H7
Dundonald Cl HISD PO11 213 L3
ITCH SO19 132 B7 1
Dundridge La BPWT SO32 85 K7
Dundry Wy HEND SO30 134 A1
Dunedin Cl FERN BH22 193 M5
Dunedin Dr FERN BH22 193 M5
Dunedin Gdns FERN BH22 193 M5
Dunedin Gv CHCH/BSGR BH23 239 H1
Dunford Cl NMIL/BTOS BH25 225 J8 2
Dunford Rd BKME/WDN BH12 234 C3
Dunhurst Cl HAV PO9 165 L5
Dunkeld Rd GPORT PO12 209 L1
TWDS BH3 235 J2
Dunkirk Cl ROWN SO16 106 C4
Dunkirk Rd ROWN SO16 106 C4
Dunlin Cl CHCH/BSGR BH23 239 G3
ENEY PO4 212 B3
Dunn Cl ENEY PO4 211 M5
Dunnings La NBAD SO52 79 K3
Dunnock Cl HAV PO9 141 M7
Dunsbury Wy HAV PO9 165 J3
Dunsmore Cl SSEA PO5 13 H4 2
Dunstans La PSTN BH14 233 L2
Dunster Cl ROWN SO16 106 B3
Dunvegan Dr ROWN SO16 106 B3
Dunyeats Rd BDST BH18 217 M4
Durban Cl ROMY SO51 50 F7
Durban Rd PSEA PO1 211 K1
Durdells Av BWD BH11 219 L3
Durdells Gdns BWD BH11 219 L3
Durford Ct HAV PO9 165 H2 1
Durford Rd EPSF GU31 64 B5
Durham Gdns WVILLE PO7 164 D3
Durham St GPORT PO12 209 L2
PSEA PO1 13 H1
Durland Cl NMIL/BTOS BH25 225 L7
Durlands Rd HORN PO8 116 B8 1
Durley Av HORN PO8 140 D5
Durley Brook Rd BPWT SO32 109 L2
Durley Chine Rd WCLF BH2 14 B6
Durley Chine Rd South
WCLF BH2 14 B8
Durley Crs TOTT SO40 129 H3
Durley Gdns WCLF BH2 14 B8
Durley Hall La BPWT SO32 84 A7
Durley Rd ELGH SO50 109 K1
GPORT PO12 209 L2
WCLF BH2 14 C7
Durley Rd South WCLF BH2 14 C7
Durley Rbt WCLF BH2 14 B7
Durley St BPWT SO32 110 C1
Durlston Crs CHCH/BSGR BH23 222 B4
Durlston Rd PSTN BH14 234 B6
ROWN SO16 105 H7
Durnford Rd SHAM SO14 131 M2
Durngate Pl WINC SO23 3 J7
Durngate Ter WINC SO23 3 J7
Durnstown LYMN SO41 201 G6
Durrant Rd PSTN BH14 234 B5
WCLF BH2 14 D4
Durrants Gdns HAV PO9 141 M8
Durrants Rd HAV PO9 165 M1
Durrant Wy LYMN SO41 200 F6
Durrington Pl LTDN BH7 237 G2 1
Durrington Rd LTDN BH7 237 G1
Dursley Crs CHAM PO6 163 G8
Durweston Cl CHAR BH8 221 G5 1
Dutton La ELGH SO50 82 A5
Duttons Rd ROMY SO51 50 D8
Dyer Rd WSHM SO15 131 G1
Dymewood Rd WIMB BH21 168 C1
Dymoke St EMRTH PO10 166 C4
Dymott Cl WSHM SO15 4 A1
Dyram Cl ELGH SO50 81 L3
Dysart Av CHAM PO6 187 M1
Dyserth Cl ITCH SO19 132 F7
Dyson Dr WINC SO23 3 H2

E

Eadens La TOTT SO40 128 B1
Eagle Av HORN PO8 140 B4
Eagle Cl CHFD SO53 81 G4
FHAM/PORC PO16 161 K8 3
Eagle Rd BKME/WDN BH12 234 F4
LSOL/BMARY PO13 208 B1
Earle Rd WBNE BH4 235 H7
Earlham Dr PSTN BH14 234 B4
Earls Cl ELGH SO50 82 F6
Earlsdon St SSEA PO5 13 G4 2
Earlsdon Wy
CHCH/BSGR BH23 224 D8
Earls Rd FHAM/PORC PO16 7 J9
SHAM SO14 106 F8
Earlswood Dr FBDG SP6 121 K3
Earnley Rd HISD PO11 214 D6
Earthpits La RSAL SP5 68 A6
East Av NMIL/BTOS BH25 240 B1
TWDS BH3 235 H2
East Bank Rd BROC SO42 175 L8
East Boldre Rd BROC SO42 204 A1
Eastbourne Av GPORT PO12 185 L8
WSHM SO15 106 C8
Eastbourne Rd HSEA PO3 187 L8 1
Eastbrook Cl GPORT PO12 185 K8 1
HLER SO31 158 E3
East Cams Cl
FHAM/PORC PO16 161 K7 2
Eastchurch Cl ROWN SO16 105 L4
Eastcliff Cl LSOL/BMARY PO13 208 C1
East Cliff Wy
CHCH/BSGR BH23 239 H1
East Cl NMIL/BTOS BH25 225 H8
East Cosham Rd CHAM PO6 163 M8
Eastcot Cl FAWY SO45 179 M5
Eastcott Cl LTDN BH7 236 F1 2
East Ct CHAM PO6 163 M8
Eastcroft Rd GPORT PO12 10 C1
East Dean Rd ROMY SO51 20 C6
East Dr ELGH SO50 82 C4
Eastern Av HSEA PO3 211 M2
Eastern Pde ENEY PO4 211 K7
FHAM/PORC PO16 7 K9
Eastern Rd CHAM PO6 188 B2
ENEY PO4 211 M3
HAV PO9 9 G3
HEND SO30 108 C7
HSEA PO3 188 A4
LYMN SO41 228 B4
NEND PO2 186 F6
Eastern Villas Rd ENEY PO4 211 H7 2
Eastern Wy FHAM/PORC PO16 7 L6
LYMN SO41 242 E4
Easter Rd MOOR/WNTN BH9 220 E6
Eastfield Av FHAM/STUB PO14 184 D2
East Field Cl EMRTH PO10 167 J6
Eastfield Cl RGWD BH24 171 G1
Eastfield La EPSF GU31 93 K5
RGWD BH24 147 G8
Eastfield Rd CHAM PO6 162 F6
ENEY PO4 211 L5
Eastgate St SHAM SO14 5 G5
WINC SO23 3 J8
East Harting St EPSF GU31 93 J5
East Hl LYMN SO41 228 C4
WINC SO23 27 G2
East Hill Cl FHAM/PORC PO16 161 H6
East Hill Dr LISS GU33 36 F5
East Hoe Rd WVILLE PO7 113 M5
East House Av
FHAM/STUB PO14 184 B6
East Howe La NBNE BH10 220 A4
Eastlake Av BKME/WDN BH12 234 A2
Eastlake Cl EPSF GU31 64 B5
Eastlands NMIL/BTOS BH25 225 M7
East La LYMN SO41 227 J7
Eastleigh Rd ELGH SO50 83 H7
East Leigh Rd HAV PO9 166 A5
East Ldg FHAM PO15 160 A7
East Lodge Pk CHAM PO6 164 D8
Eastman Cl RSAL SP5 72 F2 1
Eastmeare Ct TOTT SO40 129 G2
Eastney Farm Rd ENEY PO4 212 A5 1
Eastney Rd ENEY PO4 211 M5
Eastney St ENEY PO4 211 M6 2
Eastoke Av HISD PO11 214 B7
Easton La RWIN SO21 17 J6
WINC SO23 3 L6
East Overcliff Dr BMTH BH1 15 H7
Eastover Ct HAV PO9 165 H2
East Park Ter SHAM SO14 5 G1
East Quay Rd PLE BH15 233 H7
East Rd FAWY SO45 156 B8
WHAM PO17 162 E2
Eastshaw La MIDH GU29 67 M4
East Strd SELS PO20 215 K8
East St EMRTH PO10 166 F5
FHAM/PORC PO16 7 M6
FHAM/STUB PO14 159 K8
HAV PO9 8 F5
PLE BH15 233 H6
PSEA PO1 12 B4
SHAM SO14 5 G4
WVILLE PO7 114 C5
East Surrey St PSEA PO1 13 H1 2
East View Rd RGWD BH24 170 F1
Eastville Rd ELGH SO50 83 H7 1
East Wy CHAR BH8 220 F7
WIMB BH21 217 H3
Eastways BPWT SO32 111 H1
Eastwood ROMY SO51 48 B7
Eastwood Av FERN BH22 194 C2
Eastwood Cl HISD PO11 213 M4
East Woodhay Rd FUFL SO22 16 C4 2
Eastwood Rd NEND PO2 187 J4 1
Eastworth Rd VWD BH31 144 C1
Eaton Rd CCLF BH13 234 F6
E Av FAWY SO45 180 C3
Ebden Rd WINC SO23 3 K6
Ebery Gv HSEA PO3 211 M2
Ebor Cl FERN BH22 194 C6
Ebor Rd BKME/WDN BH12 234 C2
Eccles Rd PLE BH15 232 F6
Ecton La HSEA PO3 188 A5
Edelvale Rd WEND SO18 108 A7
Edenbridge Rd ENEY PO4 211 M3
Eden Gv WIMB BH21 192 B5
Eden Ri FHAM/PORC PO16 7 J8
Eden Rd WEND SO18 108 A6
Eden St PSEA PO1 211 G2 7
Eden Wk CHFD SO53 80 F3
Edgar Crs FHAM/PORC PO16 186 B2
Edgar Rd WINC SO23 26 E2
Edgarton Rd CFDH BH17 218 B5
Edgecombe Crs
LSOL/BMARY PO13 185 G8
Edgefield Gv HORN PO8 141 G7
Edgehill Rd MOOR/WNTN BH9 220 C8
WEND SO18 107 L7
Edgell Rd EMRTH PO10 166 F4
Edgemoor Rd FERN BH22 168 F7
Edgerly Gdns CHAM PO6 187 K2
Edgeware Rd ENEY PO4 211 L3
Edifred Rd MOOR/WNTN BH9 220 E4
Edinburgh Rd PSEA PO1 12 F1
PSEA PO1 13 G1 1
Edington Cl BPWT SO32 85 G8 2
Edington Rd WINC SO23 3 G3
Edith Haisman Cl WSHM SO15 4 B1
Edmondsham Rd VWD BH31 120 C8
Edmund Rd ENEY PO4 13 M5
Edmunds Cl HEND SO30 134 B3
NMIL/BTOS BH25 225 L7
Edneys La WVILLE PO7 139 L3
Edward Av ELGH SO50 82 C4
Edward Cl FAWY SO45 180 C7 1
Edward Gdns HAV PO9 165 G7
Edward Gv FHAM/PORC PO16 162 C7
Edward Rd BWD BH11 219 M5
CHCH/BSGR BH23 223 K8
FAWY SO45 155 L4
PSTN BH14 234 B3
WINC SO23 26 D4
WSHM SO15 130 F1
Edwards Cl CHAM PO6 162 F7 3
WVILLE PO7 140 D6
Edwina Cl ITCH SO19 132 D2
NBAD SO52 79 M4
RGWD BH24 147 G7
Edwina Dr CFDH BH17 217 M6
Effingham Gdns ITCH SO19 133 G4
Efford Wy LYMN SO41 227 M6
Egan Cl NEND PO2 187 K5
Egbert Rd WINC SO23 3 G4
Egdon Ct UPTN BH16 232 A1 2
Egdon Dr WIMB BH21 192 C8
Egerton Gdns BMTH BH1 236 C2 3
Egerton Rd CHAR BH8 236 C2
Eglantine Cl HORN PO8 140 F4
Eglantine Wk HORN PO8 140 F4
Egmont Cl RGWD BH24 170 A6
Egmont Dr RGWD BH24 170 B6
Egmont Gdns RGWD BH24 170 B6
Egmont Rd UPTN BH16 232 A4
Eight Acres ROMY SO51 79 G1 1
Elaine Gdns HORN PO8 140 D3
Elan Cl WEND SO18 108 A7
Elcombes Cl LYND SO43 151 K3
Elderberry Cl HORN PO8 116 C4
Elderberry La
CHCH/BSGR BH23 238 E2
Elderberry Wy HORN PO8 140 F4
Elder Cl FUFL SO22 26 B4
HLER SO31 158 D6 5
TOTT SO40 130 E7
Elderfield Cl EMRTH PO10 166 E5
Elderfield Rd HAV PO9 165 H1
Elder Gn RWIN SO21 54 F8
Elder Rd HAV PO9 9 K1
Eldon Av NMIL/BTOS BH25 225 J8
Eldon Cl NMIL/BTOS BH25 225 J8
Eldon Pl WBNE BH4 235 G5 1
Eldon Rd MOOR/WNTN BH9 220 C7
STOK SO20 22 F1
Eldon St SSEA PO5 13 G4
Eldridge Gdns ROMY SO51 50 E8
Eleanor Dr BWD BH11 219 H3
Eleanor Gdns
CHCH/BSGR BH23 222 C8 2
Electron Wy CHFD SO53 81 H2
Elettra Av WVILLE PO7 140 B8
Elfin Dr FERN BH22 194 A1
Elgar Cl CHAM PO6 162 C8 1
GPORT PO12 10 B8
Elgar Rd ITCH SO19 133 G5
NBNE BH10 220 B4
Elgar Wk WVILLE PO7 164 D4 1
Elgin Cl FAWY SO45 155 L5
FHAM PO15 6 E3
Elgin Rd CHAM PO6 187 K2
PSTN BH14 234 A6
WBNE BH4 14 A1
WSHM SO15 4 A1
Eling Cl FUFL SO22 16 C5
Eling Ct HAV PO9 165 H2
Eling Hl TOTT SO40 129 M3
Eling La TOTT SO40 129 L2
Elise Cl LTDN BH7 221 M8
Elizabeth Av CHCH/BSGR BH23 222 D8
Elizabeth Cl HEND SO30 108 C7
RSAL SP5 72 C1
WHAM PO17 136 D4 1
Elizabeth Ct
FHAM/STUB PO14 184 D1 1
Elizabeth Crs LYMN SO41 226 E6
Elizabeth Gdns ENEY PO4 211 K6
FAWY SO45 155 L7
Elizabeth Rd
FHAM/STUB PO14 184 B6
PLE BH15 233 J5 2
WHAM PO17 136 E4
WIMB BH21 192 A3
WVILLE PO7 164 D2
Elizabeth Wy BPWT SO32 111 G1
Elkhams Cl LYMN SO41 227 H7
Elkstone Rd CHAM PO6 162 F7
Ellachie Gdns GPORT PO12 10 E9
Ellachie Ms GPORT PO12 10 E9
Ellachie Rd GPORT PO12 10 E9
Elland Cl ELGH SO50 83 H7
Ellanore La SELS PO20 215 K5
Elldene Ct TOTT SO40 129 J3 1
Ellen Gdns CHFD SO53 80 F3
Ellersle Cl FHAM/STUB PO14 183 L7
Ellery Gv LYMN SO41 228 C3
Ellesfield Dr FERN BH22 194 B5
Ellesmere Orch EMRTH PO10 166 F4
Ellingham Dr RGWD BH24 146 C3
Ellingham Dro RGWD BH24 146 D3
Ellingham Rd
NMIL/BTOS BH25 225 H8
Elliot Cl TOTT SO40 129 H2
Elliot Ri HEND SO30 109 H6
Elliott Rd BWD BH11 219 J5
Ellisfield Rd HAV PO9 165 J4
Ellis Rd ITCH SO19 133 J3
Ellwood Av ITCH SO19 133 J3
Ellwood Cl ITCH SO19 133 J2
Elm Av CHCH/BSGR BH23 222 C7
LYMN SO41 228 A7
NMIL/BTOS BH25 225 L6
Elm Cl HISD PO11 213 L5
Elm Crs BPWT SO32 84 D2
FAWY SO45 179 L1
Elmdale Cl HLER SO31 158 B8
Elmdale Gv ROMY SO51 76 F7
Elmers Wy CHCH/BSGR BH23 197 M7
Elmes Dr WSHM SO15 130 D1
Elmes Rd MOOR/WNTN BH9 220 C6
Elmeswelle Rd HORN PO8 140 E2
Elmfield Cl RSAL SP5 73 J3
Elm Gdns HEND SO30 108 C6
WBNE BH4 235 H3
Elmgate Dr LTDN BH7 236 E1
Elm Gv ELGH SO50 81 L6
GPORT PO12 10 F1
HISD PO11 213 L5
SSEA PO5 13 H5
Elmhurst Rd BWD BH11 219 L3 1
FERN BH22 168 D7
FHAM/PORC PO16 7 J7
GPORT PO12 11 G3
Elmhurst Wy FERN BH22 168 D6
Elm La HAV PO9 8 E4
Elmleigh Rd HAV PO9 8 E2
Elmore Av LSOL/BMARY PO13 208 D3
Elmore Cl LSOL/BMARY PO13 208 D3
Elmore Dr RGWD BH24 169 J2
Elmore Rd LSOL/BMARY PO13 208 D4
Elm Park Rd HAV PO9 8 F3
Elm Rd BPWT SO32 85 K8
FUFL SO22 2 D6
HAV PO9 9 H6
Elms Av PSTN BH14 233 M7
Elms Cl FBDG SP6 96 F6
PSTN BH14 233 M7
Elms La SELS PO20 215 L7
Elmsleigh Gdns ROWN SO16 106 F4
Elmslie Gdns HLER SO31 133 K7
Elms Ride SELS PO20 215 L7
Elms Rd FHAM/PORC PO16 7 J9
Elmstead Gdns SELS PO20 215 L6
Elmstead Park Rd SELS PO20 215 L6
Elmstead Rd CCLF BH13 234 E8
Elm St SHAM SO14 5 K4
SSEA PO5 12 F5 3
Elms Wy SBNE BH6 237 K4
SELS PO20 215 L6
Elm Ter SHAM SO14 5 K5
Elm Tree Cl TOTT SO40 128 F6
Elmtree Gdns ROMY SO51 79 H2
Elmtree Rd CHAM PO6 164 C8 3
Elm Tree Wk FERN BH22 194 C8 1
Elmwood Av FBDG SP6 97 H6
WVILLE PO7 164 C2
Elmwood Rd NEND PO2 187 J4
Elmwood Wy
CHCH/BSGR BH23 239 L1
Elphinstone Rd
CHCH/BSGR BH23 224 F8
SSEA PO5 13 G7
Elsfred Rd FHAM/STUB PO14 183 L7
Elson La GPORT PO12 185 L8
Elson Rd GPORT PO12 185 L8
Elstead Gdns WVILLE PO7 164 A4
Elstree Rd ITCH SO19 132 C4 1
Eltham Cl LTDN BH7 221 M8 3
Elvin Cl LYMN SO41 226 D4
Elwell Gn HISD PO11 213 K5
Elwyn Rd BMTH BH1 15 L2
Emanuel St NEND PO2 211 H1
Embankment Wy
RGWD BH24 170 F2
Emberley Cl FERN BH22 194 E1 1
Embley Cl TOTT SO40 104 C6
Embley La ROMY SO51 77 J2
Embsay Rd HLER SO31 134 B8
Emerald Cl ITCH SO19 132 E2
WVILLE PO7 164 E1
Emer Cl NBAD SO52 79 M3 1
Emerson Cl PLE BH15 233 H6 3
Emerson Rd PLE BH15 233 H6
Emily Cl CHCH/BSGR BH23 222 E7 1
Emmanuel Cl
FHAM/STUB PO14 159 G6 1
Emmett Rd ROWN SO16 105 L3
Emmons Cl HLER SO31 157 K7
Empress Rd LYND SO43 151 K3 2
SHAM SO14 5 J9
SHAM SO14 131 M1
Empshott Rd ENEY PO4 211 K4
Empson Wk
LSOL/BMARY PO13 208 D1 3
Emsbrook Dr EMRTH PO10 166 D6 1
Emsworth Common Rd
EMRTH PO10 166 B3
Emsworth House Cl
EMRTH PO10 166 C7
Emsworth Rd HAV PO9 9 K5
EMRTH PO10 190 F4
HAV PO9 9 G5
LYMN SO41 228 C4
NEND PO2 187 J7
WSHM SO15 106 A8
Encombe Cl BKME/WDN BH12 219 K8
Endeavour Cl GPORT PO12 11 J4
WSHM SO15 130 F1 1
Endeavour Wy FAWY SO45 155 K3
Enderwood Cl TOTT SO40 104 A8 2
Endfield Cl CHCH/BSGR BH23 222 D7
Endfield Rd
CHCH/BSGR BH23 222 D8 2
MOOR/WNTN BH9 220 E6
Endle St SHAM SO14 5 K5
Endofield Cl FHAM/STUB PO14 184 D2
Enfield Av PLE BH15 233 K2
Enfield Crs PLE BH15 233 K2
Enfield Gv ITCH SO19 132 C6
Enfield Rd PLE BH15 233 K2
Englands Wy BWD BH11 219 H4
Englefield Rd WEND SO18 132 B1
English Rd WSHM SO15 130 F1
Enmill La FUFL SO22 25 L3
Ennel Copse NBAD SO52 79 M4
Ennerdale Cl HORN PO8 116 B6 1
Ennerdale Gdns WEND SO18 108 A7 1
Ennerdale Rd
FHAM/STUB PO14 184 B4
ROWN SO16 105 K6
Ensbury Av NBNE BH10 220 B7
Ensbury Cl NBNE BH10 220 B7 2
Ensbury Park Rd
MOOR/WNTN BH9 220 C6
Ensign Dr LSOL/BMARY PO13 209 H2
Ensign Wy HLER SO31 157 J6
Enterprise Cl HLER SO31 158 C7 2
Enterprise Rd ROWN SO16 80 B7
Enterprise Wy SHAM SO14 5 J7
Epping Cl WEND SO18 108 A7
Epsom Cl ELGH SO50 109 J1 2
Epworth Rd NEND PO2 187 K7
Erica Cl HLER SO31 158 D5
HORN PO8 140 F5
Erica Dr WIMB BH21 217 H2
Erica Wy HORN PO8 140 F4
Ericksen Rd NBNE BH10 220 A5
Eric Rd FHAM/STUB PO14 184 A6
Ernest Cl EMRTH PO10 166 D7
Ernest Rd HAV PO9 165 G4
PSEA PO1 211 J1
Erpingham Rd
BKME/WDN BH12 234 F3
Erskine Rd FUFL SO22 2 D9
Escombe Rd ELGH SO50 82 C5
Escur Cl NEND PO2 187 K4 4
Esdaile La RGWD BH24 172 D5 1
Esher Gv WVILLE PO7 140 A6
Eskdale Cl HORN PO8 116 B6
Esmond Cl EMRTH PO10 166 D8
Esmonde Cl
LSOL/BMARY PO13 208 D2 2
Esmonde Wy CFDH BH17 218 D8
Esplanade CCLF BH13 245 L1
ENEY PO4 211 J7
PLE BH15 233 H5

Esplanade Gdns ENEY PO4 ...... 212 A6
The Esplanade GPORT PO12 ...... 11 M4
Essex Av CHCH/BSGR BH23 ...... 222 D6
Essex Rd ENEY PO4 ...... 211 L4
Estella Rd NEND PO2 ...... 187 H8
Estridge Cl HLER SO31 ...... 133 L7 🖪
Ethelbert Rd WIMB BH21 ...... 192 B4
Ethelburt Av ROWN SO16 ...... 107 H3
Ethelred Gdns TOTT SO40 ...... 129 G2
Ethel Rd PSEA PO1 ...... 211 J2
Eton Gdns WBNE BH4 ...... 235 G4
Eton Rd SSEA PO5 ...... 13 L3
Ettrick Rd CCLF BH13 ...... 234 F7
Eucalyptus Av RGWD BH24 ...... 169 L6
European Wy SHAM SO14 ...... 5 J8
Euryalus Rd FHAM/STUB PO14 ...... 184 D2
Euston Gv RGWD BH24 ...... 170 F2
Euston Rd ENEY PO4 ...... 211 M3
Evans Cl BWD BH11 ...... 219 K7
NEND PO2 ...... 186 F6
RGWD BH24 ...... 169 J2
Evans Rd ENEY PO4 ...... 211 L4
Evans St SHAM SO14 ...... 5 H4
Evelegh Rd CHAM PO6 ...... 164 B8
Evelyn Cl BPWT SO32 ...... 111 K4
Evelyn Crs WSHM SO15 ...... 106 C8
Evelyn Rd MOOR/WNTN BH9 ...... 220 E7
Evening Gld FERN BH22 ...... 194 C5
Evenlode Rd ROWN SO16 ...... 105 K7
Everdon La HSEA PO3 ...... 188 A4 🖪
Everest Rd CHCH/BSGR BH23 ...... 223 J8
Everglades Av HORN PO8 ...... 140 D5
Everglades Cl FERN BH22 ...... 194 B1
Evergreen Cl TOTT SO40 ...... 130 D7
WIMB BH21 ...... 144 C8 🖪
WVILLE PO7 ...... 164 B1 🖪
Evergreens RGWD BH24 ...... 169 J3
Evering Av BKME/WDN BH12 ...... 219 H7
Evering Gdns
BKME/WDN BH12 ...... 219 G7
Everlea Cl LYMN SO41 ...... 227 M1
Everon Gdns NMIL/BTOS BH25 ...... 225 M4
RGWD BH24 ...... 169 J4
Evershot Rd CHAR BH8 ...... 221 J7
Eversley Crs HAV PO9 ...... 165 H4
Eversley Pl FUFL SO22 ...... 26 C3
Everton Rd LYMN SO41 ...... 226 D4
Evesham Cl LTDN BH7 ...... 221 L8
ROWN SO16 ...... 107 G3 🖪
Ewart Ct FAWY SO45 ...... 155 L3
Ewart Rd PSEA PO1 ...... 211 J1 🖪
Ewell Wy TOTT SO40 ...... 104 C7
Ewhurst Cl HAV PO9 ...... 165 H4
Exbury Cl ELGH SO50 ...... 82 C6
Exbury Dr BWD BH11 ...... 219 K3
Exbury Rd FAWY SO45 ...... 180 C8
HAV PO9 ...... 165 L3
Excellent Rd
FHAM/STUB PO14 ...... 184 D3
Excelsior Rd PSTN BH14 ...... 234 B6
Exchange Rd PSEA PO1 ...... 12 F2 🖪
Exeter Cl ELGH SO50 ...... 81 L3
EMRTH PO10 ...... 166 D5
HLER SO31 ...... 158 D5
WEND SO18 ...... 107 M7
Exeter Crs WCLF BH2 ...... 14 E7
Exeter Park Rd WCLF BH2 ...... 14 E7
Exeter Rd ENEY PO4 ...... 211 K6
WCLF BH2 ...... 14 E6
WEND SO18 ...... 107 M8
Exford Av WEND SO18 ...... 108 B8
Exford Dr WEND SO18 ...... 108 B8
Exleigh Cl ITCH SO19 ...... 132 F2
Exmouth Gdns ELGH SO50 ...... 109 H1 🖪
Exmouth Rd GPORT PO12 ...... 185 L8
SSEA PO5 ...... 13 K7
Exton Gdns FHAM/PORC PO16 ...... 162 A7
Exton Rd HAV PO9 ...... 165 M3
SBNE BH6 ...... 237 J1
Eyebright Cl ELGH SO50 ...... 109 H2 🖪
Eyeworth Wk FAWY SO45 ...... 155 G4 🖪
Eynham Av ITCH SO19 ...... 133 G2
Eynham Cl ITCH SO19 ...... 132 F2
Eyre Cl TOTT SO40 ...... 129 H2

F

Faber Cl HAV PO9 ...... 165 L4
Fabian Cl WVILLE PO7 ...... 140 E8 🖪
Factory Rd ELGH SO50 ...... 81 M6
UPTN BH16 ...... 232 B2
Fairacre Ri FHAM/STUB PO14 ...... 159 M8
Fairbairn Wk NBAD SO52 ...... 80 E2
Fairbourne Cl HORN PO8 ...... 140 C6
Fairclose Dr FUFL SO22 ...... 16 A3
Faircross Cl FAWY SO45 ...... 180 A5
Fairdown Cl WINC SO23 ...... 3 M8
Fairfax Cl FUFL SO22 ...... 26 A3
Fairfax Ct ITCH SO19 ...... 133 J3 🖪
Fairfax Ms ITCH SO19 ...... 133 J2
Fairfield CHCH/BSGR BH23 ...... 238 A1
Fair Fld ROMY SO51 ...... 50 F7
Fairfield Av FHAM/STUB PO14 ...... 6 D9
Fairfield Cl EMRTH PO10 ...... 166 D6
FAWY SO45 ...... 155 L4 🖪
LYMN SO41 ...... 228 C5
WIMB BH21 ...... 192 C3
Fairfield Rd FUFL SO22 ...... 2 D5
HAV PO9 ...... 8 F4
NMIL/BTOS BH25 ...... 240 D1
RWIN SO21 ...... 54 C3
WIMB BH21 ...... 192 B4
Fairfield Sq CHAM PO6 ...... 163 J8
Fair Gn ITCH SO19 ...... 132 F3
Fairhome Cl GPORT PO12 ...... 209 L1
Fair Isle Cl FHAM/STUB PO14 ...... 183 M5
Fairisle Rd ROWN SO16 ...... 105 K4
Fair La RWIN SO21 ...... 17 M7
Fairlawn Cl ROWN SO16 ...... 105 L2
Fairlead Dr
LSOL/BMARY PO13 ...... 209 H2 🖪
Fairlea Rd EMRTH PO10 ...... 166 D5
LYMN SO41 ...... 228 C4
Fairlie RGWD BH24 ...... 147 G2
Fairlie Rd HEND SO30 ...... 109 H5 🖪
Fairlie Pk RGWD BH24 ...... 146 F7
Fairlight La LYMN SO41 ...... 200 B7

Fairmead Wk HORN PO8 ...... 140 F5
Fairmead Wy TOTT SO40 ...... 129 J3
Fairmile Rd CHCH/BSGR BH23 ...... 222 E8
Fair Oak HAV PO9 ...... 8 E1
Fairoak Rd ELGH SO50 ...... 82 C6
Fairthorne Gdns GPORT PO12 ...... 10 D4
Fairview Cl FAWY SO45 ...... 155 L5
ROMY SO51 ...... 51 G7
Fairview Crs WIMB BH21 ...... 217 L3
Fairview Dr FAWY SO45 ...... 155 K6
ROMY SO51 ...... 51 G8
WIMB BH21 ...... 217 L3
Fairview Pde FAWY SO45 ...... 155 L6
Fairview Rd WIMB BH21 ...... 217 L3
Fairwater Cl
LSOL/BMARY PO13 ...... 184 F7
Fairway Dr CHCH/BSGR BH23 ...... 237 L2
Fairway Gdns ROWN SO16 ...... 105 K3
Fairway Rd FAWY SO45 ...... 155 K4
PSTN BH14 ...... 234 B8
Fairways FERN BH22 ...... 194 D2
The Fairway
FHAM/PORC PO16 ...... 162 A8
HAV PO9 ...... 142 A6
LSOL/BMARY PO13 ...... 185 G7 🖪
NMIL/BTOS BH25 ...... 241 G1
Fairwood Rd VWD BH31 ...... 145 G3
Fairy Crossway HORN PO8 ...... 140 F6
Falaise Cl ROWN SO16 ...... 106 B4
Falcon Cl FHAM/PORC PO16 ...... 161 K8 🖪
Falcon Dr CHCH/BSGR BH23 ...... 239 G3
Falconer Ct FAWY SO45 ...... 179 M2
Falconer Dr PLE BH15 ...... 232 D4
Falcon Flds FAWY SO45 ...... 180 F5
Falcon Rd HORN PO8 ...... 140 F5
Falcon Sq ELGH SO50 ...... 81 J7
Falcon Vw FUFL SO22 ...... 26 A3
Falcon Wy BPWT SO32 ...... 109 M7
Falkland Rd CHFD SO53 ...... 81 H5
WSHM SO15 ...... 130 E1
Falklands Cl
LSOL/BMARY PO13 ...... 208 D1
Falklands Rd NEND PO2 ...... 187 J4 🖪
Fallow Fld FAWY SO45 ...... 26 B4
Falmouth Rd CHAM PO6 ...... 162 D7
Falstaff Wy TOTT SO40 ...... 129 J3 🖪
Fancy Rd BKME/WDN BH12 ...... 218 F8
Fanshawe St SHAM SO14 ...... 131 L3 🖪
Farcroft Rd PSTN BH14 ...... 234 A3
Fareham Rd
LSOL/BMARY PO13 ...... 185 G3
WHAM PO17 ...... 136 C5
WHAM PO17 ...... 162 C3
Faringdon Rd WEND SO18 ...... 133 H1
Farleigh Cl HAV PO9 ...... 165 H3 🖪
Farley Cl ELGH SO50 ...... 83 J7
FUFL SO22 ...... 26 A4
Farley La ROMY SO51 ...... 23 J7
Farley Mount Rd RWIN SO21 ...... 24 F2
Farlington Av CHAM PO6 ...... 164 A7
Farlington Rd NEND PO2 ...... 187 J7
Farm Cl RGWD BH24 ...... 169 K7
Farmdene Cl
CHCH/BSGR BH23 ...... 224 B8 🖪
Far Meadow Wy EMRTH PO10 ...... 166 B8
Farm Edge Rd
FHAM/STUB PO14 ...... 184 A7
Farmers Wk LYMN SO41 ...... 227 H8
Farmery Cl ELGH SO50 ...... 107 J4
Farm Gdns HSEA PO3 ...... 187 K4
Farmhouse Wy HORN PO8 ...... 140 E3
Farm La North
NMIL/BTOS BH25 ...... 225 L5
Farm La South
NMIL/BTOS BH25 ...... 240 F1
Farmlea Rd CHAM PO6 ...... 162 D8
Farmside Gdns HSEA PO3 ...... 187 K4
Farm Vw EMRTH PO10 ...... 166 D5
Farm View Av HORN PO8 ...... 116 A3
Farnham Rd BKME/WDN BH12 ...... 234 F1
LISS GU33 ...... 36 D3
PSF GU32 ...... 36 A8
Farnleys Md LYMN SO41 ...... 228 C6
Faroes Cl FHAM/STUB PO14 ...... 183 M5 🖪
Farriers Cl WIMB BH21 ...... 192 F2
Farriers Wy HORN PO8 ...... 141 G7
Farrier Wy
FHAM/PORC PO16 ...... 184 F2 🖪
Farringdon Rd HAV PO9 ...... 165 L4
Farringford Rd ITCH SO19 ...... 133 J3
Farthings Ga WVILLE PO7 ...... 164 C5
Farwell Cl CHCH/BSGR BH23 ...... 223 G5
Farwell Rd BKME/WDN BH12 ...... 219 G4
Fastnet Cl ROWN SO16 ...... 105 K3 🖪
Fastnet Wy
FHAM/STUB PO14 ...... 183 M5 🖪
Fathersfield BROC SO42 ...... 175 K7
Fathoms Reach HISD PO11 ...... 213 J4
Fawcett Rd ENEY PO4 ...... 13 L1 🖪
NMIL/BTOS BH25 ...... 225 K6
Fawley By-pass FAWY SO45 ...... 180 F5
Fawley Ct HAV PO9 ...... 165 M3 🖪
Fawley Gn CHAR BH8 ...... 221 H6
Fawley La ALTN GU34 ...... 33 G4
RWIN SO21 ...... 27 L8
Fawley Rd FAWY SO45 ...... 155 M8
FAWY SO45 ...... 180 C5
NEND PO2 ...... 187 J3
WSHM SO15 ...... 130 E2
Fawn Gdns NMIL/BTOS BH25 ...... 225 K4
Fay Cl FHAM/STUB PO14 ...... 184 A6
Fayre Rd FHAM/PORC PO16 ...... 7 H9
Fearon Rd NEND PO2 ...... 187 J6
Felix Rd GPORT PO12 ...... 209 M1
Fell Cl HLER SO31 ...... 158 C4
Fell Dr LSOL/BMARY PO13 ...... 208 D1
Felmer Dr ROMY SO51 ...... 17 H1
Feltham Cl ROMY SO51 ...... 51 H8
Felton Crs CHCH/BSGR BH23 ...... 224 D8
Felton Rd PSTN BH14 ...... 233 L7
Feltons Pl HSEA PO3 ...... 187 K3
Fen Av FHAM/PORC PO16 ...... 184 F1

Fenleigh Cl NMIL/BTOS BH25 ...... 225 M8
Fennel Gdns LYMN SO41 ...... 228 B3
Fennell Cl WVILLE PO7 ...... 140 B7
Fenton Rd SBNE BH6 ...... 237 H1
Fern Bank WIMB BH21 ...... 168 C1
Fern Barrow
BKME/WDN BH12 ...... 219 M8
Fern Cl CHCH/BSGR BH23 ...... 223 D6
EPSF GU31 ...... 64 B5
FBDG SP6 ...... 121 L3
Ferncroft Cl
FHAM/STUB PO14 ...... 184 A7 🖪
Ferncroft Gdns NBNE BH10 ...... 220 B5
Ferncroft Rd NBNE BH10 ...... 220 B5
Ferndale HEND SO30 ...... 134 B3 🖪
WVILLE PO7 ...... 164 D1
Ferndale Ms
LSOL/BMARY PO13 ...... 184 F4
Ferndale Rd NMIL/BTOS BH25 ...... 225 M4
TOTT SO40 ...... 130 D7
Ferndene Wy WEND SO18 ...... 107 L8
Ferndown, Stour & Forest Trail
FERN BH22 ...... 193 M2
FERN BH22 ...... 193 G1
Fern Dr HAV PO9 ...... 9 G2
Ferneham Rd FHAM/STUB PO15 ...... 160 A6
Fernglade NMIL/BTOS BH25 ...... 225 L5
Fernheath Cl BWD BH11 ...... 219 L6
Fernheath Rd BWD BH11 ...... 219 L5
Fernhill Cl CFDH BH17 ...... 218 E6
Fernhill La NMIL/BTOS BH25 ...... 225 L2
Fern Hill La ROMY SO51 ...... 23 J8
Fernhill Rd NMIL/BTOS BH25 ...... 225 L4
Fernhills Rd FAWY SO45 ...... 155 M7
Fernhurst Cl HISD PO11 ...... 213 J5
Fernhurst Rd ENEY PO4 ...... 211 K4
LIPH GU30 ...... 38 E5
Fernie Cl FHAM/STUB PO14 ...... 183 M6
Fernlea Av FERN BH22 ...... 194 B4
Fernlea Cl FERN BH22 ...... 194 B4
RGWD BH24 ...... 169 J4
Fernlea Gdns FERN BH22 ...... 194 B4
ROWN SO16 ...... 106 D5 🖪
Fernlea Wy FAWY SO45 ...... 155 K5
Fern Rd FAWY SO45 ...... 155 K5
ITCH SO19 ...... 132 D6 🖪
Fernside Av PSTN BH14 ...... 233 L4
Fernside Rd FERN BH22 ...... 168 C6
MOOR/WNTN BH9 ...... 220 B8
PLE BH15 ...... 233 K4
Fern Wy FHAM PO15 ...... 159 H5
Fernway Cl WIMB BH21 ...... 192 F4
Fernwood Cl RGWD BH24 ...... 169 M3
Fernyhurst Av ROWN SO16 ...... 105 L2
Ferris Av CHAR BH8 ...... 221 G6
Ferris La CHAR BH8 ...... 221 G6
Ferris Pl CHAR BH8 ...... 221 H6
Ferrol Rd GPORT PO12 ...... 210 A2
Ferry Rd ENEY PO4 ...... 212 B5
FAWY SO45 ...... 155 K5
HISD PO11 ...... 212 E4
PLE BH15 ...... 233 G7
SBNE BH6 ...... 237 L5
Ferry Wy CCLF BH13 ...... 245 L4
Festing Gv ENEY PO4 ...... 211 K6
Festing Rd ENEY PO4 ...... 211 K6
Feversham Av CHAR BH8 ...... 221 J7
Fey Rd GPORT PO12 ...... 11 G2
Fibbards Rd BROC SO42 ...... 175 K7
Field Cl HLER SO31 ...... 158 F6
LSOL/BMARY PO13 ...... 184 F3
ROMY SO51 ...... 78 F1
ROWN SO16 ...... 107 H3 🖪
RWIN SO21 ...... 54 B2
Fielden Cl NBAD SO52 ...... 79 L4
Field End WINC SO23 ...... 17 H1
Fielders Wy ROMY SO51 ...... 77 G6
Fieldfare Cl HORN PO8 ...... 116 B4
Fieldfare Ct TOTT SO40 ...... 104 B8
Fieldhouse Dr
LSOL/BMARY PO13 ...... 184 D8
Fieldmore Rd GPORT PO12 ...... 209 M1
Field Pl NMIL/BTOS BH25 ...... 225 G8
Fields Cl FAWY SO45 ...... 180 C7 🖪
Field Vw NBAD SO52 ...... 80 A2
Field Wk LYMN SO41 ...... 228 B3
Field Wy CHCH/BSGR BH23 ...... 224 B7
FBDG SP6 ...... 98 D6
RWIN SO21 ...... 54 B2
WVILLE PO7 ...... 139 K4
Fieldway RGWD BH24 ...... 146 F8
Fifth Av CHAM PO6 ...... 163 J8
HAV PO9 ...... 9 G2
Fifth St PSEA PO1 ...... 211 K1
Filmer Cl LSOL/BMARY PO13 ...... 185 H4
Filmorehill La ALTN GU34 ...... 32 E5
Filton Cl TOTT SO40 ...... 104 B8
Filton Rd LYMN SO41 ...... 228 B4
Finchdean Rd HAV PO9 ...... 142 A6
NEND PO2 ...... 165 H4
Finchfield Av BWD BH11 ...... 219 K2
Finchmead La PSF GU32 ...... 63 G4
Finch Rd ENEY PO4 ...... 212 B5
Finch's La RWIN SO21 ...... 54 E2
Findon Rd GPORT PO12 ...... 185 M8
Finisterre St
FHAM/STUB PO14 ...... 183 M4
Finzi Cl ITCH SO19 ...... 133 G5
Fiona Cl WINC SO23 ...... 3 L6
Fir Av NMIL/BTOS BH25 ...... 225 M6
Fir Cl FERN BH22 ...... 168 C5
SSEA PO5 ...... 13 K9

Firs Dr HEND SO30 ...... 133 L2
Firs Glen Rd FERN BH22 ...... 168 C6
MOOR/WNTN BH9 ...... 220 B8
VWD BH31 ...... 144 D3
Firshill CHCH/BSGR BH23 ...... 224 C7
Firside Rd WIMB BH21 ...... 217 G4
Firs La PSTN BH14 ...... 234 A8
First Av CHAM PO6 ...... 163 K8
CHAM PO6 ...... 164 C8
EMRTH PO10 ...... 167 H8
HAV PO9 ...... 9 J3
HORN PO8 ...... 116 B5
WSHM SO15 ...... 130 B1
First Marine Av
NMIL/BTOS BH25 ...... 240 E1
First St FAWY SO45 ...... 156 C1
Fir Tree Cl ELGH SO50 ...... 109 H1
RGWD BH24 ...... 169 H6
Firtree Crs LYMN SO41 ...... 226 D5
Firtree Gdns HORN PO8 ...... 141 G5
Fir Tree HI FBDG SP6 ...... 121 L2 🖪
Fir Tree La CHCH/BSGR BH23 ...... 224 B7 🖪
ELGH SO50 ...... 109 G1
Fir Tree Rd HISD PO11 ...... 213 L5
TOTT SO40 ...... 127 L1
Firtree Wy ITCH SO19 ...... 132 F3 🖪
Fir Vale Rd BMTH BH1 ...... 14 F5
Firwood Cl CHFD SO53 ...... 53 H8
Fisgard Rd GPORT PO12 ...... 209 M1
Fisher Cl FHAM/STUB PO14 ...... 183 M5 🖪
Fisherman's Av SBNE BH6 ...... 237 G4
Fishermans Rd PLE BH15 ...... 233 H7 🖪
The Fishermans
EMRTH PO10 ...... 166 E8 🖪
Fishermans Wk HISD PO11 ...... 214 C6
Fisher Rd LSOL/BMARY PO13 ...... 185 G5
Fishers Gv CHAM PO6 ...... 188 C1
Fishers HI FHAM PO15 ...... 159 L6
Fisher's Rd TOTT SO40 ...... 129 L2
Fishery Rd HISD PO11 ...... 214 A6
Fishlake Mdw ROMY SO51 ...... 50 E7
Fitzgerald Cl HLER SO31 ...... 135 G8 🖪
Fitzharris Av
MOOR/WNTN BH9 ...... 235 M1
Fitzherbert Rd CHAM PO6 ...... 188 C1
Fitzherbert Sp CHAM PO6 ...... 188 B1
Fitzherbert Rd PSEA PO1 ...... 211 G1 🖪
Fitzhugh Pl WSHM SO15 ...... 131 K1
Fitzhugh St SHAM SO14 ...... 4 E2 🖪
Fitzmaurice Rd
CHCH/BSGR BH23 ...... 222 C8
Fitzpain Cl FERN BH22 ...... 194 B6
Fitzpain Rd FERN BH22 ...... 194 B6
Fitzpatrick Ct CHAM PO6 ...... 163 H7 🖪
Fitzroy Cl ROWN SO16 ...... 106 E1
Fitzwilliam Av
FHAM/STUB PO14 ...... 183 L6 🖪
Fitzwilliam Cl BWD BH11 ...... 219 J3
Fitzworth Av UPTN BH16 ...... 232 B4
Fitzwygram Crs HAV PO9 ...... 8 E1
Five Bridges Rd WINC SO23 ...... 26 D5
Five Elms Dr ROMY SO51 ...... 79 G2
Fivefields Cl WINC SO23 ...... 3 L9
Fivefields Rd WINC SO23 ...... 3 M9
Five Heads Rd HORN PO8 ...... 115 M8
Five Post La GPORT PO12 ...... 209 K2
Flaghead Chine Rd CCLF BH13 ...... 245 K1
Flaghead Rd CCLF BH13 ...... 245 K1
Flag Staff Gn GPORT PO12 ...... 210 B2
Flag Wk HORN PO8 ...... 140 D3
Flambard Av
CHCH/BSGR BH23 ...... 222 D7
Flambard Rd PSTN BH14 ...... 234 B6
Flamborough Cl ROWN SO16 ...... 105 J6
Flamingo Ct
FHAM/PORC PO16 ...... 161 K8
Flanders Rd HEND SO30 ...... 109 G8
Flathouse Rd PSEA PO1 ...... 211 G1
Flatt Rd RCCH PO18 ...... 167 M8
Flaxfields End FBDG SP6 ...... 97 K7
Flazen Cl BWD BH11 ...... 219 H5
Fleet Cl LSOL/BMARY PO13 ...... 185 H7
Fleet End Bottom HLER SO31 ...... 158 D8
Fleetend Cl HAV PO9 ...... 165 J2 🖪
Fleet End Rd HLER SO31 ...... 158 D8
Fleets Cl PLE BH15 ...... 233 J7
Fleming Av NBAD SO52 ...... 79 M4
Fleming Pl ROMY SO51 ...... 78 E1 🖪
RWIN SO21 ...... 54 E7
Fleming Rd FUFL SO22 ...... 16 B5
ROWN SO16 ...... 107 J4
Fletcher Cl FAWY SO45 ...... 155 H5
NBNE BH10 ...... 220 B5 🖪
Fletcher Rd NBNE BH10 ...... 220 B5
Fletchwood La TOTT SO40 ...... 128 F2
Fletchwood Rd TOTT SO40 ...... 128 F2
Fleuret Cl FAWY SO45 ...... 155 L8
Flexford Cl CHFD SO53 ...... 52 F7
Flexford La LYMN SO41 ...... 227 G2
Flexford Rd NBAD SO52 ...... 80 B2
Flint Cl ITCH SO19 ...... 133 J4
Flint St SSEA PO5 ...... 12 F5
Floating Bridge Rd SHAM SO14 ...... 5 H8
Floral Farm WIMB BH21 ...... 192 E6
Florence Cl ROMY SO51 ...... 77 G6
Florence Rd BOSC BH5 ...... 236 D4
ITCH SO19 ...... 132 C6 🖪
PSTN BH14 ...... 234 B4
SSEA PO5 ...... 13 K9
Florentine Wy WVILLE PO7 ...... 140 E8 🖪
The Florins HLER SO31 ...... 158 E7
WVILLE PO7 ...... 164 C5 🖪
Floriston Gdns
NMIL/BTOS BH25 ...... 226 B5
Floud La PSF GU32 ...... 60 A3
Flowerdown Cl TOTT SO40 ...... 104 B8
Flower La ROMY SO51 ...... 76 C2
Flowers Cl HLER SO31 ...... 157 J5
Flume Rd FAWY SO45 ...... 181 G4
Flushards LYMN SO41 ...... 228 D4
Foldsgate Cl LYND SO43 ...... 151 K2 🖪
Folkestone Rd HSEA PO3 ...... 211 L1
Folly Farm La RGWD BH24 ...... 170 A2
Folly Fld BPWT SO32 ...... 111 J1
Folly La EPSF GU31 ...... 63 L5

Font Cl FHAM/STUB PO14 ...... 159 G5 🖪
Fontley Rd FHAM PO15 ...... 159 L5
Fontmell Rd BDST PO18 ...... 218 A6
Fontwell Cl TOTT SO40 ...... 104 B7
Fontwell Gdns ELGH SO50 ...... 109 J1 🖪
Fontwell Ms HORN PO8 ...... 140 F7
Fontwell Rd SSEA PO5 ...... 13 J7 🖪
SSEA PO5 ...... 13 J7 🖪
Foord Rd HEND SO30 ...... 133 M4 🖪
Football Gn LYND SO43 ...... 127 G5
Footner Cl ROMY SO51 ...... 51 H6
Footners La CHCH/BSGR BH23 ...... 223 G6
Forbes Cl ROWN SO16 ...... 105 L2
Forbury Rd SSEA PO5 ...... 13 J5
Ford Av CHFD SO53 ...... 81 J4
Ford Cl FERN BH22 ...... 194 D1
Fordingbridge Rd ENEY PO4 ...... 211 M5
FBDG SP6 ...... 121 M1
Fordington Av FUFL SO22 ...... 2 B6
Fordington Rd FUFL SO22 ...... 2 C6
Ford La FERN BH22 ...... 194 E1
Ford Rd GPORT PO12 ...... 209 K2
Foreland Cl CHCH/BSGR BH23 ...... 222 A8
Foreland Ct HISD PO11 ...... 214 A6
Foreland Rd UPTN BH16 ...... 232 A4
Foreshore North FAWY SO45 ...... 180 F2
Foreshore South FAWY SO45 ...... 180 G1
Forest Av HORN PO8 ...... 140 D5
Forest Cl BPWT SO32 ...... 111 K5
CHCH/BSGR BH23 ...... 224 B7
CHFD SO53 ...... 53 H8
HORN PO8 ...... 140 D5
NBAD SO52 ...... 79 K3
VWD BH31 ...... 145 H4
Forest Cnr LISS GU33 ...... 36 F1
Forest Court Hills
RGWD BH24 ...... 171 H2 🖪
Forest Edge FAWY SO45 ...... 180 E5
Forest Edge Cl RGWD BH24 ...... 169 H3 🖪
Forest Edge Dr RGWD BH24 ...... 169 H3
Forest Edge Rd RGWD BH24 ...... 171 J3
Forest End WVILLE PO7 ...... 164 B1
Forester Rd BPWT SO32 ...... 112 F7
Foresters Ga FAWY SO45 ...... 206 C1
Foresters Rd FAWY SO45 ...... 180 D6
Forest Front FAWY SO45 ...... 155 K8
Forest Gdns BPWT SO32 ...... 111 K5 🖪
LYND SO43 ...... 151 H2
Forest Ga FAWY SO45 ...... 206 D1
Forest Gate Gdns LYMN SO41 ...... 228 C4
Forest Glade Cl BROC SO42 ...... 175 H7
Forest Hall BROC SO42 ...... 175 L7 🖪
Forest Hills Dr WEND SO18 ...... 107 K5
Forest Hill Wy FAWY SO45 ...... 155 K6 🖪
Forestlake Av RGWD BH24 ...... 171 H2
Forest La FAWY SO45 ...... 179 M2 🖪
RGWD BH24 ...... 171 J2
VWD BH31 ...... 144 C1 🖪
WHAM PO17 ...... 136 F8
Forest Md WVILLE PO7 ...... 139 K5
Forest Meadow FAWY SO45 ...... 155 L8
Forest Oak Dr
NMIL/BTOS BH25 ...... 225 L3
Forest Park Rd BROC SO42 ...... 175 J6
Forest Pines
NMIL/BTOS BH25 ...... 225 L4 🖪
Forest Ri CHCH/BSGR BH23 ...... 224 B6
LISS GU33 ...... 36 F2
Forest Rd BPWT SO32 ...... 111 L5
CCLF BH13 ...... 234 F6
CHCH/BSGR BH23 ...... 198 C3
CHFD SO53 ...... 53 J8
FBDG SP6 ...... 73 J4
FERN BH22 ...... 168 D5
LISS GU33 ...... 36 E1
RGWD BH24 ...... 172 D3
RSAL SP5 ...... 75 J8
WVILLE PO7 ...... 138 E4
Forestside Av HAV PO9 ...... 165 L3
Forestside Gdns RGWD BH24 ...... 147 G3
The Forestside VWD BH31 ...... 145 H3
Forest Vw BROC SO42 ...... 175 H7
NMIL/BTOS BH25 ...... 225 H3
SHAM SO14 ...... 4 F1
Forest View Cl
MOOR/WNTN BH9 ...... 220 E6 🖪
Forest View Dr WIMB BH21 ...... 193 L2
Forest View Rd
MOOR/WNTN BH9 ...... 220 E5
Forest Wy CHCH/BSGR BH23 ...... 224 B7
LSOL/BMARY PO13 ...... 185 H6
LYMN SO41 ...... 227 H7
TOTT SO40 ...... 103 M6
WIMB BH21 ...... 193 L3
Forge Cl HLER SO31 ...... 133 L7
Forge Rd FAWY SO45 ...... 155 J5
Forneth Gdns FHAM PO15 ...... 159 M8 🖪
Forster Rd SHAM SO14 ...... 131 L1
Forsyth Gdns NBNE BH10 ...... 220 A4
Forsythia Cl HAV PO9 ...... 109 G8 🖪
HEND SO30 ...... 109 G8 🖪
Fort Cumberland Rd
ENEY PO4 ...... 212 B5
Fortescue Rd
BKME/WDN BH12 ...... 234 C1
TWDS BH3 ...... 235 M2
Fort Fareham Rd
FHAM/STUB PO14 ...... 184 D2
Forth Cl CHFD SO53 ...... 81 G3
FHAM/STUB PO14 ...... 183 M5 🖪
Forties Cl FHAM/STUB PO14 ...... 183 M4 🖪
Forton Rd GPORT PO12 ...... 10 E1
PSEA PO1 ...... 211 J2 🖪
Fort Gd GPORT PO12 ...... 10 C9
ITCH SO19 ...... 132 C5
Fortunes Wy CHAM PO6 ...... 164 D7
Forty Acre La EPSF GU31 ...... 92 A5
Forward Dr LYMN SO41 ...... 228 A4
Foster Cl FHAM/STUB PO14 ...... 184 A4
Foster Cl GPORT PO12 ...... 10 D5
PSEA PO1 ...... 211 H2
Founders Wy
LSOL/BMARY PO13 ...... 185 H6
Foundry La WSHM SO15 ...... 106 A8
Foundry Rd RSAL SP5 ...... 73 J1 🖪
Fountain St PSEA PO1 ...... 13 G1 🖪
Fountain Wy
CHCH/BSGR BH23 ...... 238 A2

Four Acre HEND SO30 .... 134 E2
Four Posts HI WSHM SO15 .... 4 C1
Fourshells CI FAWY SO45 ...... 180 D6
Fourth Av CHAM PO6 .... 163 J9
  HAV 9 J3
Fourth St PSEA PO1 .... 211 K2
Four Wells Rd WIMB BH21 .... 192 E1
Fowey CI CHFD SO53 ...... 81 G1
The Fowey FAWY SO45 ...... 180 C6
Fowlers Rd HEND SO30 ...... 109 G8
Fowler's Wk NBAD SO52 ...... 80 C5
Foxbury CI FAWY SO45 ...... 155 L6
Foxbury Gv FHAM/PORC PO16 .. 185 M1
Foxbury La EMRTH PO10 ...... 167 G4
  LSOL/BMARY PO13 ...... 185 H4
Foxbury Rd RGWD BH24 ...... 169 K7
Fox CI ELGH SO50 .... 82 E6
Foxcombe CI BPWT SO32 ...... 111 M2
Foxcote Gdns
  NMIL/BTOS BH25 ...... 225 K5
Foxcott CI ITCH SO19 ...... 132 D8
Foxcott Gv HAV PO9 ...... 165 K3
Foxcroft Dr FAWY SO45 ...... 179 M5
  WIMB BH21 ...... 192 F3
Foxes CI VWD BH31 .... 144 D3
  WVILLE PO7 ...... 164 C2
Foxes La ROMY SO51 ...... 76 E4
Fox Fld LYMN SO41 ...... 227 H7
Foxglade FAWY SO45 ...... 206 D1
Foxglove CI
  CHCH/BSGR BH23 ...... 224 A8
Foxglove PI
  NMIL/BTOS BH25 ...... 226 B4
Foxgloves FHAM/PORC PO16 ... 7 L1
  UPTN BH16 .... 232 A1
The Foxgloves HEND SO30 ...... 134 B3
Foxhayes La FAWY SO45 ...... 206 D1
Foxhills TOTT SO40 ...... 129 G4
  VWD BH31 .... 144 F3
Foxhills CI TOTT SO40 ...... 129 G5
Foxholes Rd PLE BH15 ...... 233 L2
  SBNE BH6 .... 237 L4
Foxlands FAWY SO45 ...... 206 D1
Foxley Dr HSEA PO3 ...... 187 M4
Fox Pond La LYMN SO41 ...... 228 A3
Fox's Wk FAWY SO45 ...... 206 D1
Foxtail Dr FAWY SO45 ...... 155 K7
Foxwood Av
  CHCH/BSGR BH23 ...... 238 E3
Foxy Paddock FAWY SO45 ...... 206 D1
Foy Gdns HLER SO31 ...... 158 A7
Foyle Rd CHFD SO53 .... 81 G2
Frampton CI NMIL/BTOS BH25 .. 226 A3
  RWIN SO21 .... 54 F1
Frampton PI RGWD BH24 ...... 170 E1
Frampton Rd
  MOOR/WNTN BH9 ...... 220 E8
Frampton Wy TOTT SO40 ...... 129 K2
  WINC SO23 .... 17 H1
Frances Rd BMTH BH1 ...... 15 K4
  WVILLE PO7 ...... 164 B5
Francis Av BWD BH11 ...... 219 H5
  ENEY PO4 ...... 211 K5
Francis CI LSOL/BMARY PO13 .... 208 C3
Francis Gdns WINC SO23 ...... 3 J2
Francis PI FHAM/STUB PO14 .... 184 B6
  HORN PO8 .... 116 B5
Francis Rd BKME/WDN BH12 .... 234 D3
  HORN PO8 .... 116 B5
Frankland Crs PSTN BH14 ...... 234 D3
Frankland Ter EMRTH PO10 .... 166 E8
Franklin Rd LSOL/BMARY PO13 .. 209 G1
  MOOR/WNTN BH9 ...... 220 E5
  NMIL/BTOS BH25 ...... 226 A4
  RWIN SO21 .... 54 F1
Franklyn Av ITCH SO19 ...... 132 E4
Franklyn CI UPTN BH16 ...... 232 A1
Frankston Rd SBNE BH6 ...... 237 H4
Frarydene EMRTH PO10 ...... 167 H8
Fraser CI ROWN SO16 ...... 105 L2
Fraser Gdns EMRTH PO10 ...... 167 J6
Fraser Rd BKME/WDN BH12 .... 219 K7
  HAV PO9 .... 8 B2
  LSOL/BMARY PO13 .... 185 G4
  NEND PO2 .... 186 F6
  SSEA PO5 .... 13 J3
Frater La GPORT PO12 ...... 185 L7
Fratton Rd PSEA PO1 ...... 211 J2
Fratton Wy ELGH SO50 .... 83 H7
Frayslea FAWY SO45 ...... 155 L6
Freda Rd CHCH/BSGR BH23 .... 237 L1
Freda Routh Gdns ELGH SO50 .. 83 J6
Frederica Rd
  MOOR/WNTN BH9 ...... 220 C8
Frederick St SHAM SO14 ...... 131 M2
Freedom CI FAWY SO45 ...... 155 L5
Freegrounds Av HEND SO30 .... 134 A2
Freegrounds CI HEND SO30 .... 134 A2
Freegrounds Rd HEND SO30 .... 134 A2
Freemans CI WIMB BH21 ...... 192 F2
Freemans La WIMB BH21 ...... 192 F3
Freemantle CI ITCH SO19 ...... 132 D3
Freemantle Common Rd
  ITCH SO19 .... 132 D3
Freemantle Rd GPORT PO12 .... 209 M1
Freestone Rd SSEA PO5 ...... 13 J8
Free St BPWT SO32 .... 85 J8
Frenches La ROMY SO51 ...... 49 G7
Frenchies Vw WVILLE PO7 .... 139 J4
Frenchmans Rd PSF GU32 ...... 63 L4
Frenchmoor La RSAL SP5 ...... 19 L5
French Rd CFDH BH17 ...... 217 M7
French St PSEA PO1 ...... 4 F6
  SHAM SO14 .... 4 F6
Frendstaple Rd WVILLE PO7 .... 140 C8
Frensham CI HEND SO30 ...... 134 A2
  NBNE BH10 .... 220 C5
Frensham Rd ENEY PO4 ...... 211 K4
Freshfield Gdns WVILLE PO7 .... 140 C8
Freshfield Rd WSHM SO15 .... 130 F1
Freshfield Sq WSHM SO15 ...... 130 F1
Freshwater Dr PLE BH15 ...... 232 C5
Freshwater Rd CHAM PO6 .... 187 J1
  CHCH/BSGR BH23 .... 239 J1

Friarsgate WINC SO23 ...... 3 H7
Friars Pond Rd FHAM PO15 .... 160 A7
Friars Rd CHCH/BSGR BH23 .... 239 G2
  ELGH SO50 .... 81 L7
Friars Wk NMIL/BTOS BH25 .... 225 L8
Friars Wy WEND SO18 ...... 107 J4
Fritham CI TOTT SO40 ...... 129 G1
Fritham Gdns CHAR BH8 ...... 221 H5
Fritham Rd WEND SO18 ...... 108 B8
Frith La WHAM PO17 ...... 136 C2
Frobisher Av
  BKME/WDN BH12 ...... 219 K7
Frobisher CI
  CHCH/BSGR BH23 ...... 238 E2
  LSOL/BMARY PO13 ...... 209 G2
Frobisher Gdns
  EMRTH PO10 ...... 166 D8
  ITCH SO19 ...... 133 G4
Frobisher Gv
  FHAM/PORC PO16 ...... 186 A1
Froddington Rd SSEA PO5 .... 13 K3
Frogham HI FBDG SP6 ...... 123 C1
Frog La FBDG SP6 ...... 122 C1
Frogmore CI FHAM/STUB PO14 .. 160 A8
  ROWN SO16 ...... 105 J5
Frogmore La HORN PO8 ...... 140 E2
Frogmore Rd ENEY PO4 ...... 211 K4
Frome CI TOTT SO40 ...... 130 C6
Frome Rd WEND SO18 ...... 107 M5
Fromond CI LYMN SO41 ...... 228 C3
Fromond Rd FUFL SO22 ...... 16 B5
Frosthole CI FHAM PO15 ...... 6 C1
Frosthole Crs FHAM PO15 ...... 6 C1
Frost La ENEY PO4 ...... 156 A6
Frost Rd BWD BH11 ...... 219 K4
Froud Wy WIMB BH21 ...... 217 G4
Froxfield Gdns
  FHAM/PORC PO16 ...... 162 A7
Froxfield Rd HAV PO9 ...... 165 M3
Froyle CI HAV PO9 .... 165 M3
Fry CI FAWY SO45 ...... 180 D6
  HLER SO31 ...... 157 L4
Fryer CI BWD BH11 ...... 219 M3
Fryern CI CHFD SO53 ...... 81 K2
Fryern Court Rd FBDG SP6 .... 97 K4
Fryern's Copse WIMB BH21 .... 193 G2
Fryers Rd WIMB BH21 ...... 144 C8
Fry's La BPWT SO32 .... 87 J4
  LYMN SO41 ...... 227 H7
Fulflood Rd HAV PO9 ...... 165 J3
Fullerton CI HAV PO9 ...... 165 M3
  ITCH SO19 ...... 132 D8
Fullerton Rd LYMN SO41 ...... 228 A4
Fulmar CI ROWN SO16 ...... 106 A3
Fulmar Dr FAWY SO45 ...... 155 M6
Fulmar Rd CHCH/BSGR BH23 .. 238 C3
Fulmer Wk HORN PO8 ...... 140 C4
Fulwood Av BWD BH11 ...... 219 J3
Funtington Rd NEND PO2 .... 187 K8
Funtley HI FHAM/PORC PO16 .. 160 C4
Funtley Rd FHAM PO15 ...... 160 B3
Furdies WVILLE PO7 ...... 139 J4
Furley CI WINC SO23 ...... 3 K7
The Furlong RGWD BH24 ...... 170 D1
Furneaux Gdns
  FHAM/PORC PO16 ...... 7 J1
Furnell Rd PLE BH15 ...... 233 J7
Furness Rd SSEA PO5 ...... 211 H7
Furniss Wy HISD PO11 ...... 213 H4
Furnston Gv EMRTH PO10 .... 167 J7
Fury Wy FHAM/STUB PO14 .... 183 M5
Furze Cft NMIL/BTOS BH25 .... 225 L7
Furzedale Gdns FAWY SO45 .... 155 M7
Furzedale Pk FAWY SO45 .... 155 M7
Furzedown Crs HAV PO9 .... 165 L3
Furzedown Ms FAWY SO45 .... 155 M7
Furzehall Av FHAM/PORC PO16 .. 7 L1
Furzelands Rd WIMB BH21 .... 144 C8
Furze La ENEY PO4 ...... 212 B3
Furzeley Rd WVILLE PO7 ...... 139 K6
Furze Meadow EPSF GU31 .... 65 K8
Furze Rd ITCH SO19 ...... 132 E3
Furze Wy HORN PO8 ...... 140 F4
Furzey CI FAWY SO45 ...... 180 D7
Furzey La BROC SO42 ...... 177 M7
Furzey Rd UPTN BH16 ...... 232 A2
Furzley CI HAV PO9 ...... 165 G2
Furzley La ROMY SO51 ...... 102 C3
Furzley Rd ROMY SO51 ...... 102 C3
Fushia CI HAV PO9 .... 166 A4
Fushsia Gdns ROWN SO16 .... 106 C6
Fyeford CI ROWN SO16 ...... 105 L2
Fyfield CI FHAM PO15 ...... 135 G8
Fyfield Wy FUFL SO22 ...... 16 A3
Fyning St PSEA PO1 ...... 211 H2

G

Gables Ct ROWN SO16 ...... 106 E3
Gage CI TOTT SO40 ...... 130 E6
Gainsborough Av
  NMIL/BTOS BH25 ...... 225 M3
Gainsborough Ms
  FHAM/STUB PO14 ...... 159 K8
Gainsborough Rd LTDN BH7 .... 236 E1
  RGWD BH24 ...... 169 J3
Gainsford Rd ITCH SO19 ...... 132 C3
Gain's Rd ENEY PO4 ...... 13 L7
Galaxie Rd HORN PO8 ...... 140 F4
Gale Moor Av GPORT PO12 .... 209 H5
Galleon CI HLER SO31 ...... 158 D7
The Gallops FHAM/STUB PO14 .. 159 H6
Gallop Wy BKME/WDN BH12 .. 235 H1
Galloway Rd PLE BH15 ...... 232 C4
Gallows Dr FERN BH22 ...... 194 B7
Galsworthy Rd TOTT SO40 .... 129 H1
Galt Rd CHAM PO6 ...... 164 B8
Gamble CI ITCH SO19 ...... 132 D4

Gambledown La ROMY SO51 .. 48 D3
Gamblins La BPWT SO32 ...... 111 L8
Ganger Farm La ROMY SO51 .... 51 H6
Ganger Rd ROMY SO51 ...... 51 H6
Gannet CI FAWY SO45 ...... 155 M6
  ROWN SO16 ...... 106 A3
The Gannets
  FHAM/STUB PO14 ...... 183 M6
Garbett Rd WINC SO23 ...... 3 L7
Garbitts La EPSF GU31 ...... 65 L5
Garden City FAWY SO45 ...... 154 E2
Garden CI HISD PO11 ...... 213 K5
  LYND SO43 ...... 151 J3
  NMIL/BTOS BH25 ...... 225 L7
Gardeners La ROMY SO51 .... 77 L2
Garden-lane RGWD BH24 .... 169 J5
Garden La SSEA PO5 ...... 13 C6
  WINC SO23 .... 3 H7
Garden Ms HLER SO31 ...... 158 A7
Garden Rd RGWD BH24 ...... 172 D6
Gardens Crs PSTN BH14 ...... 234 A8
Gardens Rd PSTN BH14 ...... 234 A8
The Gardens HAV PO9 ...... 9 K6
  WVILLE PO7 ...... 140 E8
Garden Wk FERN BH22 ...... 194 C1
Gardiner CI TOTT SO40 ...... 130 E6
Gardner Rd CHCH/BSGR BH23 .. 222 C8
  FHAM/STUB PO14 ...... 183 K1
  RGWD BH24 ...... 170 F2
Garendon CI FBDG SP6 ...... 97 K6
Garfield Av BMTH BH1 ...... 236 C3
Garfield CI BPWT SO32 .... 85 H8
Garfield Rd BPWT SO32 ...... 85 H8
  HLER SO31 ...... 156 E2
  ITCH SO19 ...... 132 C1
  NEND PO2 .... 187 H8
Garland Av EMRTH PO10 .... 166 D5
Garland Rd PLE BH15 ...... 233 J4
Garnett CI FHAM/STUB PO14 .. 184 A4
Garnier Pk WHAM PO17 ...... 136 E4
Garnier Rd WINC SO23 ...... 26 F5
Garnier St PSEA PO1 ...... 13 K1
Garnock Rd ITCH SO19 ...... 132 B6
Garratt CI HEND SO30 ...... 109 H6
Garrett CI ITCH SO19 ...... 132 E7
Garrick Gdns ITCH SO19 ...... 132 E6
Garrison HI BPWT SO32 .... 87 G6
Garrow Dr LYMN SO41 ...... 228 C3
Garsdale CI BWD BH11 ...... 219 L2
Garsons CI EMRTH PO10 ...... 167 H8
Garston CI PSF GU32 .... 61 J8
Garstons CI FHAM/STUB PO14 .. 159 K8
Garstons Rd FHAM/STUB PO14 .. 159 K8
Gar St WINC SO23 .... 2 E5
Garth CI RGWD BH24 ...... 169 H4
Garth Rd MOOR/WNTN BH9 .. 220 E7
Garton Rd ITCH SO19 ...... 132 B5
Gatcombe HLER SO31 ...... 157 C1
Gatcombe Av HSEA PO3 ...... 187 K6
Gatcombe Dr NEND PO2 ...... 187 K5
Gatcombe Gdns
  FHAM/STUB PO14 ...... 159 M8
  WEND SO18 ...... 107 M6
Gatehouse La EPSF GU31 ...... 66 C2
Gate House Rd
  FHAM/PORC PO16 ...... 185 L1
Gate Hyde WINC SO23 ...... 3 G5
Gatekeeper CI WINC SO23 .... 3 M7
Gatwick CI ROWN SO16 ...... 105 M4
Gaulter CI HAV PO9 .... 9 C1
Gavan St ITCH SO19 ...... 133 H3
G Av FAWY SO45 ...... 180 D2
Gaydon Rd BWD BH11 ...... 219 J4
Gaylyn Wy FHAM/STUB PO14 .. 159 M8
Gaza Av BROC SO42 ...... 204 A2
Gazing La ROMY SO51 ...... 76 D3
Geddes Wy EPSF GU31 .... 64 B4
Gemini CI ROWN SO16 ...... 105 L4
Geneva Av SBNE BH6 ...... 237 J3
Genoa CI LYMN SO41 ...... 228 A4
Gento CI HEND SO30 ...... 134 C2
Geoffrey Av WVILLE PO7 ...... 163 M6
Geoffrey Crs
  FHAM/PORC PO16 ...... 184 F2
George Byng Wy NEND PO2 .... 187 H4
George Curl Wy SO50 .... 107 L2
George Eyston Dr FUFL SO22 .... 26 C2
George Rd LYMN SO41 ...... 242 B3
George St ELGH SO50 .... 81 M5
  GPORT PO12 .... 11 H2
  PSEA PO1 ...... 211 J1
Georgian CI RGWD BH24 ...... 146 E8
Georgian Wy NBNE BH10 .... 220 D4
Georgina CI
  BKME/WDN BH12 ...... 220 A8
Gerald Rd TWDS BH3 ...... 235 M2
Gerard Crs ITCH SO19 ...... 133 H2
Germaine CI CHCH/BSGR BH23 .. 224 D8
Gervis Crs PSTN BH14 ...... 233 M4
Gervis PI BMTH BH1 .... 14 E6
Gervis Rd BMTH BH1 ...... 15 H4
Gibbs Rd SHAM SO14 .... 4 F2
Gibraltar CI FHAM PO15 ...... 6 A3
Gibraltar Rd ENEY PO4 ...... 212 B5
  FHAM/STUB PO14 ...... 184 D2
Gibson CI FHAM PO15 ...... 159 J2
  LSOL/BMARY PO13 ...... 208 D2
Gibson Rd CFDH BH17 ...... 233 K1
Giddylake WIMB BH21 ...... 192 A2
Gifford CI FHAM PO15 ...... 6 C2
Gilbert CI FBDG SP6 ...... 121 M2
  LSOL/BMARY PO13 ...... 185 H1
  LYMN SO41 ...... 228 B6
Gilbert Md HISD PO11 ...... 213 L5
Gilbert Rd CHAR BH8 ...... 236 C2
Gilbert Wy WVILLE PO7 ...... 164 C3
Gilbury CI WEND SO18 ...... 107 K4
Gilchrist Gdns HLER SO31 ...... 182 A1
Giles CI FHAM/PORC PO16 .... 7 K1
  GPORT PO12 ...... 209 L2
  HEND SO30 ...... 109 J7
Giles La ROMY SO51 ...... 75 M3
  RSAL SP5 .... 75 M4
Gilkicker Rd GPORT PO12 ...... 11 C9
Gillam Rd NBNE BH10 ...... 220 C4
Gillcrest FHAM PO15 ...... 159 C4
Gillett Rd BKME/WDN BH12 .. 235 H1
The Gillies FHAM/PORC PO16 .... 7 H6

Gillingham CI
  MOOR/WNTN BH9 ...... 221 G4
  WINC SO23 .... 17 H1
Gillingham Rd LYMN SO41 .... 242 C5
Gilpin CI CHAM PO6 ...... 164 C8
Gilpin CI ITCH SO19 ...... 133 K5
  LYMN SO41 ...... 202 D7
Gilpin HI LYMN SO41 ...... 200 F6
Girton CI FHAM/STUB PO14 .. 159 C7
Gitsham Gdns WVILLE PO7 .... 164 A5
Gladdis Rd BWD BH11 ...... 219 K4
Glade CI HISD PO11 ...... 213 K6
The Glade CHFD SO53 .... 53 L7
  FAWY SO45 ...... 206 C1
  FHAM PO15 ...... 160 B4
  HISD PO11 ...... 214 A6
  RGWD BH24 ...... 169 J4
  WVILLE PO7 ...... 140 E8
Gladstone Gdns
  FHAM/PORC PO16 ...... 186 A1
Gladstone Rd
  BKME/WDN BH12 ...... 234 B3
  GPORT PO12 ...... 209 J4
  ITCH SO19 ...... 132 E3
  LTDN BH7 .... 236 E3
Gladstone Rd East LTDN BH7 .... 236 E3
Gladstone Rd West BMTH BH1 .. 236 D3
Gladstone St WINC SO23 ...... 2 F6
Gladys Av HORN PO8 ...... 140 E4
  NEND PO2 .... 187 H6
Glamis Av NBNE BH10 ...... 220 C3
Glamis CI WVILLE PO7 ...... 140 E8
Glamorgan Rd HORN PO8 .... 116 A6
Glasgow Rd ENEY PO4 ...... 211 M5
Glaslaw Rd WEND SO18 ...... 107 M8
Glasspool WVILLE PO7 ...... 139 J3
Gleadowe Av
  CHCH/BSGR BH23 ...... 237 L2
Glebe CI HISD PO11 ...... 213 J3
Glebe Cnr WHAM PO17 ...... 136 F5
Glebe Ct ELGH SO50 .... 83 J6
  HEND SO30 ...... 109 M8
  PTSW SO17 .... 106 F6
Glebe Dr LSOL/BMARY PO13 .... 185 C7
Glebefield Gdns CHAM PO6 .... 163 J8
Glebefields LYMN SO41 ...... 242 C3
Glebe La RSAL SP5 .... 75 J4
Glebe Meadow RSAL SP5 .... 19 M6
Glebe Park Av CHAM PO6 .... 164 E7
Glebe Rd EPSF GU31 .... 91 J3
The Glebe FHAM/STUB PO14 .. 184 A7
Glenair Av PSTN BH14 ...... 233 M5
Glenair Rd PSTN BH14 ...... 233 M5
Glenavon NMIL/BTOS BH25 .. 225 M6
Glenavon Rd
  CHCH/BSGR BH23 ...... 224 D7
Glenbrook Wk
  FHAM/STUB PO14 ...... 160 A8
Glencarron Wy ROWN SO16 .. 106 D5
Glen CI NMIL/BTOS BH25 .... 225 H8
Glencoe Rd BKME/WDN BH12 .. 234 C3
  LTDN BH7 .... 236 E1
  PSEA PO1 ...... 211 K1
Glencoyne Gdns ROWN SO16 .. 105 L6
Glenda CI HLER SO31 ...... 158 B8
Glendale BPWT SO32 ...... 112 A3
Glen DI HAV PO9 .... 142 B7
Glendale Av FERN BH22 ...... 194 B2
Glendale CI CHCH/BSGR BH23 .. 222 B5
  WIMB BH21 ...... 192 A3
Glendale Rd SBNE BH6 ...... 237 M4
Glendon Av NBNE BH10 ...... 220 A2
Glendowan Rd CHFD SO53 .... 80 F1
Glendrive HLER SO31 ...... 158 A7
Glenesha Gdns FHAM PO15 .... 6 B3
Glen Eyre Dr ROWN SO16 .... 106 C4
Glen Eyre Rd ROWN SO16 .... 106 C3
Glen Eyre Wy ROWN SO16 .... 106 F4
Glenferness Av TWDS BH3 .... 235 J2
Glen Fern Rd BMTH BH1 ...... 15 C5
Glenfield Av WEND SO18 .... 132 D1
Glenfield Crs WEND SO18 .... 132 D1
Glenfield Wy WEND SO18 .... 132 D1
Glengariff Rd PSTN BH14 .... 234 B5
Glengarry NMIL/BTOS BH25 .. 226 A6
Glengarry Wy
  CHCH/BSGR BH23 ...... 239 H2
Glenives CI RGWD BH24 ...... 169 G2
Glenlea CI HEND SO30 ...... 108 C7
Glenlea Dr HEND SO30 ...... 108 C7
Glenleigh Av HAV PO9 ...... 187 K1
Glenleigh Pk HAV PO9 ...... 9 K3
Glenme Adows Dr BWD BH11 .. 219 M3
Glenmoor CI NBNE BH10 .... 220 B7
Glenmoor Rd FERN BH22 .... 194 B5
  MOOR/WNTN BH9 ...... 220 B7
Glenmount Dr PSTN BH14 .... 234 A3
Glenn Rd HEND SO30 ...... 108 C6
  HLER SO31 ...... 158 C2
Glen Rd BOSC BH5 ...... 236 D4
  HLER SO31 ...... 158 C1
  ITCH SO19 ...... 132 B7
  PSTN BH14 ...... 234 A4
Glenroyd Gdns SBNE BH6 .... 237 J4
Glenside FAWY SO45 ...... 155 K5
  NMIL/BTOS BH25 ...... 240 A1
Glenside Av ITCH SO19 ...... 133 H4
Glen Spey NMIL/BTOS BH25 .. 226 B6
The Glen CCLF BH13 ...... 234 D8
  LSOL/BMARY PO13 ...... 185 J7
Glenthorne CI
  FHAM/STUB PO14 ...... 184 B7
Glenthorne Meadow PSF GU32 .. 61 J8
Glenthorne Rd HSEA PO3 .... 187 L1
Glenville CI CHCH/BSGR BH23 .. 224 B5
Glenville Gdns NBNE BH10 .... 220 A6
Glenville Rd CHCH/BSGR BH23 .. 224 B5
  NBNE BH10 .... 220 A6
Glenwood Av ROWN SO16 .... 106 F3

Glenwood CI FERN BH22 ...... 168 C6
Glenwood Ct ELGH SO50 ...... 83 K6
Glenwood Gdns HORN PO8 .... 140 D5
Glenwood La FERN BH22 ...... 168 C6
Glenwood Rd EMRTH PO10 .... 167 H7
  FERN BH22 ...... 168 C6
  VWD BH31 .... 144 C3
Glenwood Wy FERN BH22 .... 168 C6
Glidden CI PSEA PO1 ...... 13 J1
Glidden La BWD BH11 ...... 114 C5
Glissons FERN BH22 ...... 193 L6
Gloucester CI PSF GU32 ...... 63 J5
Gloucester Rd
  BKME/WDN BH12 ...... 234 D3
  LTDN BH7 .... 236 E3
  PSEA PO1 ...... 210 E2
  WVILLE PO7 ...... 164 D2
Gloucester Sq SHAM SO14 .... 5 G6
Gloucester Ter SSEA PO5 ...... 13 G5
Gloucester Vw SSEA PO5 ...... 13 G5
Glyn Dr FHAM/STUB PO14 .... 184 A6
Glyn Jones CI FAWY SO45 .... 180 D6
Glynvlile CI WIMB BH21 ...... 192 E1
Glynville Rd WIMB BH21 ...... 192 E1
Glyn Wy FHAM/STUB PO14 .... 184 A6
Goathorn CI UPTN BH16 ...... 232 C4
Godfrey Pink Wy BPWT SO32 .. 111 J1
Godmanston CI CFDH BH17 .... 218 C7
Godshill CI CHAR BH8 ...... 221 H5
Godwin CI EMRTH PO10 ...... 166 C5
  FUFL SO22 .... 16 B5
Godwin Crs HORN PO8 ...... 116 B4
Godwit CI GPORT PO12 ...... 185 M8
Godwit Rd ENEY PO4 ...... 212 A2
Gofton Av CHAM PO6 ...... 187 M1
Gogg's La RSAL SP5 .... 73 L2
Goldcrest CI
  FHAM/PORC PO16 ...... 161 J8
  HORN PO8 .... 140 F3
Goldcrest La ROWN SO16 .... 105 M3
Golden Ct HEND SO30 ...... 108 E6
Golden Crs LYMN SO41 ...... 227 H7
Golden Gv SHAM SO14 .... 5 J2
Golden Hind Pk FAWY SO45 .... 155 K6
Goldenleas Dr BWD BH11 .... 219 H5
Goldfinch CI
  NMIL/BTOS BH25 ...... 225 K6
Goldfinch La
  LSOL/BMARY PO13 ...... 208 D1
Goldfinch Rd CFDH BH17 .... 217 J8
Gold Mead CI LYMN SO41 .... 228 C6
Goldring CI HISD PO11 ...... 213 L5
Goldsmith Av ENEY PO4 ...... 13 M2
Goldsmith CI TOTT SO40 ...... 129 H1
Goldsmith Rd ELGH SO50 .... 81 L7
Gold St SSEA PO5 ...... 12 F5
Golf Course Rd ROWN SO16 .... 106 D2
Golf Links Rd BDST BH18 .... 217 M3
  FERN BH22 ...... 194 C3
Goliath Rd PLE BH15 ...... 232 C6
Gomer La GPORT PO12 ...... 209 J4
Goodacre Dr NBAD SO52 .... 80 E3
The Goodens NARL SO24 ...... 30 B3
Goodison CI ELGH SO50 ...... 83 G7
Goodlands V HEND SO30 .... 133 L1
Goodleigh CI BKME/WDN BH12 .. 234 B1
Goodsell CI
  FHAM/STUB PO14 ...... 183 M6
Goodwin CI ROWN SO16 ...... 105 J6
Goodwood CI
  FHAM/STUB PO14 ...... 159 G6
  GPORT PO12 ...... 185 M8
  WVILLE PO7 ...... 140 F7
Goodwood Ct EMRTH PO10 .. 167 J8
Goodwood Gdns TOTT SO40 .. 104 B8
Goodwood Rd ELGH SO50 .... 81 K3
  SSEA PO5 ...... 13 L6
Gordon Av SHAM SO14 ...... 106 F8
  WINC SO23 .... 27 H2
Gordon Mt CHCH/BSGR BH23 .. 224 F7
Gordon Rd BKME/WDN BH12 .. 234 F3
  BMTH BH1 .... 236 C4
  BPWT SO32 ...... 110 E7
  CHCH/BSGR BH23 ...... 224 E8
  CHFD SO53 .... 53 J7
  EMRTH PO10 ...... 190 F1
  FHAM/PORC PO16 ...... 7 G5
  GPORT PO12 ...... 10 D4
  LYMN SO41 ...... 228 A5
  PSEA PO1 ...... 12 E6
  WIMB BH21 ...... 192 C4
  WINC SO23 .... 3 H5
  WVILLE PO7 ...... 164 D2
Gordon Rd South
  BKME/WDN BH12 ...... 234 F4
Gordon Ter ITCH SO19 ...... 132 E6
Gordon Vw CHCH/BSGR BH23 .. 223 C7
Gore Rd NMIL/BTOS BH25 .... 225 J6
Gorey Rd BKME/WDN BH12 .. 219 H7
Goring Av HORN PO8 ...... 116 B4
Goring Fld FUFL SO22 .... 16 B7
Gorleston Rd
  BKME/WDN BH12 ...... 234 F4
Gorley Ct HAV PO9 .... 165 G2
Gorley Lynch FBDG SP6 ...... 123 H4
Gorley Rd RGWD BH24 ...... 147 G8
Gorran Av LSOL/BMARY PO13 .. 185 G7
Gorsecliff Rd NBNE BH10 .... 220 B7
Gorse CI HLER SO31 ...... 158 D6
  NMIL/BTOS BH25 ...... 226 B4
  RGWD BH24 ...... 169 H4
Gorsefield Rd
  NMIL/BTOS BH25 ...... 225 M3
Gorse Hill CI PLE BH15 ...... 233 K3
Gorse Hill Crs PLE BH15 ...... 233 K3
Gorse Hill Rd PLE BH15 ...... 233 K3
Gorseland Ct FERN BH22 ...... 194 C5
Gorselands Rd WEND SO18 .... 108 A7
Gorselands Wy
  LSOL/BMARY PO13 ...... 185 H6
Gorse La UPTN BH16 ...... 232 B1
Gorse Rd EPSF GU31 .... 64 B5
  WIMB BH21 ...... 217 C3
Gort Crs ITCH SO19 ...... 132 F4
Gort Rd BWD BH11 ...... 219 M5
  CFDH BH17 ...... 217 L7
Gosling CI CFDH BH17 ...... 233 L1

Gosport La LYND SO43 151 L4
Gosport Rd FHAM/PORC PO16 7 K7
FHAM/STUB PO14 184 B6
LSOL/BMARY PO13 208 D3
Gosport St LYMN SO41 228 D4
Gough Crs CFDH BH17 217 M6
Gover Rd ROWN SO16 105 H7
Grace Dieu Gdns HLER SO31 133 K7 1
Grace La FBDG SP6 72 D8
Graddidge Wy TOTT SO40 129 H1
Graemar La ROMY SO51 48 B7
Grafton Cl CHCH/BSGR BH23 238 C2 3
TWDS BH3 235 M1
Grafton Gdns LYMN SO41 228 A7
ROWN SO16 106 B3
Grafton Rd TWDS BH3 235 M2
WINC SO23 26 E2
Grafton St NEND PO2 211 G1
Graham Rd ENEY PO4 13 M6
GPORT PO12 209 L2
SHAM SO14 131 M2
Graham St SHAM SO14 132 A2
Grainger Gdns ITCH SO19 133 G5 1
Granada Cl HORN PO8 140 E5
Granada Rd ENEY PO4 13 L9
HEND SO30 133 L3
Granby Gv PTSW SO17 107 G5
Granby Rd MOOR/WNTN BH9 220 E4
Grand Av SBNE BH6 237 H4
Grand Pde FUFL SO22 16 B3
HISD PO11 213 L6
PSEA PO1 12 C6
Grange Cl GPORT PO12 209 K2
HAV PO9 9 J3
LYMN SO41 227 J8
WEND SO18 107 K4 3
Grange Crs GPORT PO12 209 K2
Grange Dr HEND SO30 109 J8
Grange Gdns
BKME/WDN BH12 234 D1 1
Grange La LSOL/BMARY PO13 185 G8
Grange Ms ROMY SO51 51 H7
Grange Rd BDST BH18 217 L4
CHCH/BSGR BH23 239 G1
HEND SO30 109 H8
HLER SO31 156 E2
LSOL/BMARY PO13 209 H4
NEND PO2 187 H7
PSF GU32 63 K6
RGWD BH24 169 H6
ROWN SO16 106 A7
SBNE BH6 237 J5
WINC SO23 26 D5
The Grange LYMN SO41 227 J8
Grangewood Gdns
ELGH SO50 83 G6 1
Grantham Av HLER SO31 157 J5
Grantham Rd BMTH BH1 236 D3
ELGH SO50 81 L6
ITCH SO19 132 D2
Grantley Rd BOSC BH5 236 E4 1
Grant Rd CHAM PO6 164 B8
Grant's Av BMTH BH1 236 C2
Grants Cl BMTH BH1 236 C2
Granville Cl HAV PO9 9 H5
Granville Rd BOSC BH5 236 F3
PSTN BH14 234 A3
Granville St SHAM SO14 5 K4
Grasdean Cl WEND SO18 107 M7 3
Grasmere ELGH SO50 81 L6 1
Grasmere Cl
CHCH/BSGR BH23 222 B5
WEND SO18 108 A7 3
Grasmere Gdns
NMIL/BTOS BH25 225 M3
Grasmere Rd BOSC BH5 236 F4
CCLF BH13 245 G5
Grasmere Wy
FHAM/STUB PO14 184 B4
Grassmere Wy HORN PO8 140 F7
Grassymead FHAM PO15 159 G4 2
Grateley Crs HAV PO9 165 G4
Gravel Cl RSAL SP5 44 D8
Gravel Hl BPWT SO32 112 A5
WIMB BH21 192 B7
Gravel La RGWD BH24 146 E8
Gray Cl CFDH BH17 218 D8
HLER SO31 158 D6
Graycot Cl NBNE BH10 220 A3
Grayland Cl HISD PO11 213 J4 2
Grayling Md ROMY SO51 50 E7
Grays Av FAWY SO45 155 M5
Grays Cl ELGH SO50 54 E8
GPORT PO12 209 J5
ROMY SO51 78 F1
Grays Ct PSEA PO1 12 D4
Grayshott Cl FUFL SO22 16 C4
Grayshott Rd ENEY PO4 211 K4
GPORT PO12 10 B4
Gray's Yd PLE BH15 233 H7 3
Great Br ROMY SO51 50 D6
Greatbridge Rd ROMY SO51 50 D5
Great Copse Dr HAV PO9 165 K3
Great Elms Cl FAWY SO45 179 M5
Great Field Rd FUFL SO22 2 A1
Greatfield Wy HAV PO9 141 M6
Great Gays FHAM/STUB PO14 183 L7
Great Hanger EPSF GU31 64 A5
Great Md LYND SO43 151 K4 3
WVILLE PO7 139 L5
Great Minster St WINC SO23 3 G8
Great Southsea St SSEA PO5 13 G5
Great Well Dr ROMY SO51 50 E7
Greatwood Cl FAWY SO45 155 L6 2
Greaves Cl NBNE BH10 220 A5
Grebe Cl CFDH BH17 217 J8
CHCH/BSGR BH23 238 F2 3
FHAM/PORC PO16 161 K8 3
HORN PO8 140 C4
LYMN SO41 242 D4
Greenacre NMIL/BTOS BH25 225 L8
Greenacre Cl UPTN BH16 232 B2
Greenacre Gdns WVILLE PO7 164 B4
Greenacres RSAL SP5 72 C1
Greenacres Cl NBNE BH10 220 C1
Green Acres Cl RGWD BH24 170 B3
Greenacres Dr RWIN SO21 54 B5
Greenaway La HLER SO31 158 B6
Greenbank Crs ROWN SO16 106 E3
Greenbanks Cl LYMN SO41 242 C3
Greenbanks Gdns
FHAM/PORC PO16 161 H6
Green Bottom WIMB BH21 192 E1
Green Cl FAWY SO45 155 L4 6
RSAL SP5 47 G4
TOTT SO40 128 D4
PLE BH15 233 J7 4
Greenclose La WIMB BH21 192 B4
Green Crs LSOL/BMARY PO13 185 G7
Greendale Cl CHFD SO53 81 K2 1
The Greendale FHAM PO15 160 B4
Greenfield Crs HORN PO8 140 F5
Greenfield Gdns
NMIL/BTOS BH25 225 M8
Greenfield Ri HORN PO8 140 F5
Greenfield Rd PLE BH15 233 K2
Greenfields EPSF GU31 93 K1 1
LISS GU33 36 F4
Greenfields Av TOTT SO40 104 D7
Greenfields Cl EPSF GU31 65 K8
Greenfinch Cl CFDH BH17 217 K7
ELGH SO50 81 J7 2
Greenfinch Wk RGWD BH24 171 G2 2
Greenhayes BDST BH18 218 A6
Greenhays Ri WIMB BH21 192 A3
Greenhill Av FUFL SO22 2 C7
Greenhill Cl FUFL SO22 2 B7
WIMB BH21 192 B2
Greenhill La ROWN SO16 79 K8
WIMB BH21 192 B2
Greenhill Rd FUFL SO22 2 B7
WIMB BH21 192 B1
Greenhill Ter FUFL SO22 2 C7
Green Hollow Cl
FHAM/PORC PO16 6 D1
Green Jacket Cl FUFL SO22 26 D3
Green La BPWT SO32 112 B1
FAWY SO45 180 D8
FBDG SP6 71 H8
FERN BH22 193 L7
GPORT PO12 10 C7
HISD PO11 213 J6
HLER SO31 133 J7
HLER SO31 134 B8
HLER SO31 134 E7
HLER SO31 157 L6
HLER SO31 158 D7
HORN PO8 116 C3
HSEA PO3 187 L5
NARL SO24 32 C2
NBNE BH10 220 A5
NMIL/BTOS BH25 225 M8
PSF GU32 34 E3
RGWD BH24 170 E1
RGWD BH24 170 F5
ROMY SO51 51 K8
ROWN SO16 80 E7
ROWN SO16 105 K6
RSAL SP5 44 E8
TOTT SO40 104 A4
WVILLE PO7 113 L8
WVILLE PO7 139 J3
Greenlea Cl CHAM PO6 163 M6
Greenlea Crs ROWN SO16 107 J3
Greenlea Rd GPORT PO12 209 K1 2
Greenmead Av LYMN SO41 227 H7
Green Park Cl WINC SO23 3 J2
Green Park Rd ROWN SO16 130 C1
Green Pond Cnr HAV PO9 9 J5
Green Pond La ROMY SO51 52 B5
Green Rd FHAM/STUB PO14 184 A4
GPORT PO12 10 C7
MOOR/WNTN BH9 220 E8
PLE BH15 233 H6
SSEA PO5 13 G5
Greens Cl BPWT SO32 85 G8
ELGH SO50 82 F7
Greensleeves Av BDST BH18 217 M2
Greens Meade RSAL SP5 73 J2
Greensome Dr FERN BH22 194 D2
The Green HLER SO31 158 B2
LISS GU33 36 D3 2
ROMY SO51 51 H6 3
RSAL SP5 47 G4
Greenway Cl LYMN SO41 228 A4
Greenway La EPSF GU31 91 H2
Greenway Rd GPORT PO12 209 M2
Greenways BPWT SO32 112 A3
CHCH/BSGR BH23 224 D8
CHFD SO53 81 J2
LYMN SO41 242 B3
ROWN SO16 107 J3
Greenways Av CHAR BH8 221 G5
Greenways Rd BROC SO42 175 L7 3
The Greenwich FAWY SO45 180 C6 1
Greenwood Av CHAM PO6 163 H8
FERN BH22 194 B2
PSTN BH14 234 B8 1
ROWN SO16 105 J2
Greenwood Cl
FHAM/PORC PO16 160 E4
ROMY SO51 50 F8 1
Greenwood Copse
RGWD BH24 169 L4 2
Greenwood La BPWT SO32 83 M8
Greenwood Rd
MOOR/WNTN BH9 220 C7
Greenwoods
NMIL/BTOS BH25 225 M7 2
Greenwood Wy RGWD BH24 169 K4
Greetham St SSEA PO5 13 H2
Gregory Gdns TOTT SO40 104 B7 1
Gregory La BPWT SO32 110 A3
Gregson Cl LSOL/BMARY PO13 185 G5
Grenadier Cl HLER SO31 158 F6
Grendon Cl ROWN SO16 107 G3 2
Grenehurst Wy EPSF GU31 63 L5
Grenfell Rd MOOR/WNTN BH9 220 D5
Grenville Cl RGWD BH24 147 G7
Grenville Gdns FAWY SO45 155 L7
Grenville Rd ENEY PO4 13 L5 1
WIMB BH21 192 B4
Gresham Rd MOOR/WNTN BH9 220 E7
Gresley Gdns HEND SO30 109 H6 3
Grevillea Av FHAM PO15 159 J5
Greville Gn EMRTH PO10 166 C5
Greville Rd WSHM SO15 131 H1
Greyfriars Rd FHAM PO15 160 A6
Greyhound Cl HEND SO30 109 G5 3
Greys Farm Cl NARL SO24 30 C4
Greyshott Av
FHAM/STUB PO14 160 A8
Greystoke Av BWD BH11 219 K2
Greywell Av ROWN SO16 106 A4
Griffen Cl ELGH SO50 82 D6 2
Griffin Ct PTSW SO17 107 H8
Griffin Wk LSOL/BMARY PO13 209 G2
Griffiths Gdns BWD BH11 219 M3
Griffon Cl HLER SO31 133 L7
Grigg La BROC SO42 175 L7
Grimstead Rd RSAL SP5 18 B2
Gritanwood Rd ENEY PO4 211 M5
Grosvenor Cl PTSW SO17 107 H6
RGWD BH24 169 H3
Grosvenor Dr WINC SO23 3 J2
Grosvenor Gdns BMTH BH1 236 D4
HEND SO30 108 C7
PTSW SO17 107 H6 1
Grosvenor Rd CHFD SO53 53 K7
PTSW SO17 107 H6
WBNE BH4 235 H5
Grosvenor Sq WSHM SO15 131 K2
Grosvenor St SSEA PO5 13 H3
Grove Av FHAM/PORC PO16 186 A2
GPORT PO12 11 G2
Grove Gdns ITCH SO19 132 F7
Grovelands Rd FUFL SO22 16 A7
Grove La RSAL SP5 73 L1
Groveley Rd
CHCH/BSGR BH23 238 D2 3
WBNE BH4 235 G6 2
Grovely Av BOSC BH5 236 E4
Grovely Wy ROMY SO51 51 K7
Grove Pastures LYMN SO41 228 C5
Grove Pl ITCH SO19 132 F6
LYMN SO41 228 C5
Grove Rd BKME/WDN BH12 234 A2
BMTH BH1 15 H6
CHAM PO6 188 A1
FHAM/PORC PO16 7 G6
GPORT PO12 209 M1
HAV PO9 8 F5
LSOL/BMARY PO13 208 C2
LYMN SO41 228 D5
NMIL/BTOS BH25 240 F1
RWIN SO21 54 C3
WIMB BH21 192 A4
WSHM SO15 131 G1
Grove Rd East
CHCH/BSGR BH23 222 E8
Grove Rd North SSEA PO5 13 H5
Grove Rd South SSEA PO5 13 H6
Grove Rd West
CHCH/BSGR BH23 222 D8
Groves Down ROMY SO51 76 D4
The Grove CHCH/BSGR BH23 222 C7
EMRTH PO10 166 F5
FERN BH22 194 A4
FHAM/STUB PO14 183 M6
HLER SO31 133 L7
HLER SO31 157 H1
ITCH SO19 132 F7
MOOR/WNTN BH9 220 D5
VWD BH31 144 E3
Grower Gdns BWD BH11 219 L4
Gruneisen Rd NEND PO2 187 G6
Guardhouse Rd PSEA PO1 210 F1
Guardroom Rd NEND PO2 186 F7
Gudge Heath La FHAM PO15 6 B2
Guernsey Cl ROWN SO16 105 K5
Guernsey Rd
BKME/WDN BH12 219 H7
Guessens La FHAM/STUB PO14 159 K8
Guest Av BKME/WDN BH12 234 E2
Guest Cl BKME/WDN BH12 234 F2 1
Guest Rd ELGH SO50 82 C5
UPTN BH16 232 A1
Guildford Cl EMRTH PO10 167 H7
Guildford Dr CHFD SO53 81 G5
Guildford Rd PSEA PO1 13 M1
Guildford St SHAM SO14 5 K1 1
Guildhall Wk PSEA PO1 12 F3
Guildhill Rd SBNE BH6 237 K4
Guillemot Cl FAWY SO45 155 M5
Guillemot Gdns
LSOL/BMARY PO13 184 F5
Gull Cl LSOL/BMARY PO13 184 F6
Gulliver Cl PSTN BH14 234 B8 2
The Gulls TOTT SO40 130 D6
Gullycroft Md HEND SO30 133 M1
Gunners Pk BPWT SO32 85 K8
Gunners Rw ENEY PO4 211 M6
Gunners Wy GPORT PO12 185 K8
LSOL/BMARY PO13 185 L7
Gunville Crs MOOR/WNTN BH9 220 F5
Gunwharf Rd PSEA PO1 12 C4
Gurjun Cl UPTN BH16 216 E8 1
Gurnard Rd CHAM PO6 187 J1
Gurnays Md ROMY SO51 76 C5
Gurney Rd ENEY PO4 211 M4
WIMB BH21 217 J2
WSHM SO15 106 B8
Gussage Rd BKME/WDN BH12 219 J8
Gutner La HISD PO11 190 A7
Gwatkin Cl HAV PO9 165 G5 1
Gwenlyn Rd UPTN BH16 232 B2
Gwynne Rd BKME/WDN BH12 234 D3
Gypsy La HORN PO8 140 D3
RGWD BH24 146 F8

H

Haarlem Ms CHCH/BSGR BH23 238 C1
Habin Hl EPSF GU31 65 L4
Hack Dr RWIN SO21 54 E8
Hacketts La BPWT SO32 86 F6
Hackleys La ROMY SO51 77 G3
Hackupps La ROMY SO51 22 B7
Hackworth Gdns HEND SO30 109 H6
Hadden Rd CHAR BH8 221 H8
Haddon Cl FHAM PO15 6 D6
Haddon Dr ELGH SO50 81 M3
Haddons Dr WIMB BH21 168 B1
Hadleigh Gdns ELGH SO50 81 M3
Hadleigh Rd CHAM PO6 163 H8 3
Hadley Fld FAWY SO45 179 M3 1
Hadley Wy BDST BH18 217 J5
Hadow Rd BWD BH11 220 A5
Hadrian Cl FERN BH22 194 B6
Hadrians Cl CHFD SO53 81 K1
Hadrian Wy ROWN SO16 106 D1
Haflinger Dr HLER SO31 134 F8
Haglane Copse LYMN SO41 227 M6
Hahnemann Rd WCLF BH2 14 C7
Haig Av PSTN BH14 234 D7
Haig Rd ELGH SO50 82 F6
Haileybury Gdns HEND SO30 109 H7 1
Hainault Dr VWD BH31 144 E2
Haking Rd CHCH/BSGR BH23 238 C1 5
Halden Cl ROMY SO51 51 G7
Hale Av NMIL/BTOS BH25 225 M6
Hale Gdns NMIL/BTOS BH25 225 M6
Hale La FBDG SP6 72 E7
Hales Dr HEND SO30 133 L3
Hale St North PSEA PO1 211 H2
Hale St South PSEA PO1 211 H2
Halewood Wy
CHCH/BSGR BH23 222 D8
Halfpenny La PSEA PO1 12 D5 1
Halifax Ri WVILLE PO7 164 D1
Halifax Wy CHCH/BSGR BH23 239 G1
Hall Cl BPWT SO32 85 J8
Hallet Cl WEND SO18 107 M6 5
Hallett Rd HAV PO9 9 K3
Halletts Cl FHAM/STUB PO14 184 A5
The Halliards
FHAM/PORC PO16 184 F1
Halliday Cl GPORT PO12 10 F2
Halliday Crs ENEY PO4 212 A5
Hall Lands La ELGH SO50 83 J6
Hall Rd BWD BH11 219 K5
Halls Farm Cl FUFL SO22 16 D5
The Hall Wy FUFL SO22 16 A3
Halsey Cl GPORT PO12 10 B5
Halstead Rd CHAM PO6 163 H8
WEND SO18 107 L6
Halstock Crs CFDH BH17 218 B6
Halter Pth PLE BH15 232 D5
Halter Ri WIMB BH21 193 G2
Halterworth Cl ROMY SO51 79 G1 2
Halterworth La ROMY SO51 51 H8
Halton Cl CHCH/BSGR BH23 197 M8 1
Haltons Cl TOTT SO40 104 C7
Halyard Cl LSOL/BMARY PO13 209 H1
Hambert Wy TOTT SO40 129 J3 3
Hamble Cl HLER SO31 158 A7
Hamble Ct CHFD SO53 81 J3 1
Hambledon Cl FUFL SO22 16 C4
Hambledon Gdns SBNE BH6 237 H2
Hambledon La BPWT SO32 113 H6
Hambledon Rd HORN PO8 115 M3
LTDN BH7 237 G1
SBNE BH6 237 H2
WVILLE PO7 114 C8
WVILLE PO7 139 H1 1
Hamble House Gdns
HLER SO31 157 L6 1
Hamble La HLER SO31 133 K6
WVILLE PO7 164 C3
Hamble Rd GPORT PO12 10 B3
PLE BH15 233 L1
Hamble Springs BPWT SO32 111 J1
Hamblewood HEND SO30 134 E2
Hambrook Hl (North)
RCCH PO18 167 M5
Hambrook Hl (South)
RCCH PO18 167 M6
Hambrook Rd GPORT PO12 209 L2
Hambrook St SSEA PO5 12 F6
Hamdown Crs ROMY SO51 77 G5
Hameldon Cl ROWN SO16 130 D1 2
Hamfield Dr HISD PO11 213 J4
Hamilton Cl BMTH BH1 236 C3
CHCH/BSGR BH23 238 E4 1
HAV PO9 8 F7
PLE BH15 232 D6 1
Hamilton Ct LYMN SO41 242 B4
Hamilton Crs PLE BH15 232 D6
Hamilton Gv
LSOL/BMARY PO13 184 F7
Hamilton Ms FAWY SO45 155 M7 2
Hamilton Pk RSAL SP5 44 F8
Hamilton Rd BMTH BH1 236 C4
CHAM PO6 162 C8
ELGH SO50 82 C5
FAWY SO45 155 M8
PLE BH15 232 D6
SSEA PO5 13 J7
WIMB BH21 217 J3
Ham La EMRTH PO10 191 H1
GPORT PO12 185 L7
HORN PO8 115 L8
WIMB BH21 192 F4
Hamlet Wy GPORT PO12 185 L7
LSOL/BMARY PO13 185 K7
Hammer La MIDH GU29 67 G4
Hammond Cl FHAM PO15 6 B3
Hammond Rd FHAM PO15 6 C3
Hammonds Cl TOTT SO40 104 D8
Hammond's Gn TOTT SO40 104 C8
Hammonds La TOTT SO40 104 D8
Hammonds Wy TOTT SO40 104 D8
Hampden La SBNE BH6 237 G3 5
Hampshire Cl
CHCH/BSGR BH23 222 D6
Hampshire Hatches La
RGWD BH24 170 E4
Hampshire St PSEA PO1 211 J1
Hampshire Ter PSEA PO1 12 F4
Hampton Cl FAWY SO45 180 C8
WVILLE PO7 164 E1 1
Hampton Dr RGWD BH24 146 F7
Hampton Gdns FAWY SO45 180 C8
Hampton Gv FHAM PO15 159 M7
Hampton Hl BPWT SO32 112 A2
Hampton La FAWY SO45 180 C6
FUFL SO22 16 B7
Hamptworth Rd RSAL SP5 74 C4
Hamtun Crs TOTT SO40 104 D7 1
Hamtun Gdns TOTT SO40 104 D7
Hamtun Rd ITCH SO19 133 G6
Hamtun St SHAM SO14 4 F5
Hanbidge Crs
LSOL/BMARY PO13 185 H4
Handel Rd WSHM SO15 4 E1
Handel Ter WSHM SO15 4 D1
Handford Pl WSHM SO15 131 K2 1
Handley Rd GPORT PO12 209 K2 2
The Hangers BPWT SO32 85 M4
Hangers Wy EPSF GU31 91 H4
HORN PO8 90 F6
Hanger Wy EPSF GU31 64 A5
Hanham Rd WIMB BH21 192 A3 2
WIMB BH21 217 H3
Hankinson Rd
MOOR/WNTN BH9 220 E8
Hanley Rd WSHM SO15 106 C8
Hanlon Cl BWD BH11 219 L4
Hannah Gdns WVILLE PO7 140 D8 3
Hannay Ri ITCH SO19 133 H3
Hannington Rd HAV PO9 165 H1 2
LTDN BH7 236 F3
Hann Rd ROWN SO16 105 K2
Hanns Wy ELGH SO50 81 M6
Hanover Buildings SHAM SO14 5 G4
Hanover Gdns FHAM/PORC PO16 7 J1
Hanoverian Wy FHAM PO15 159 G1
Hanover St PSEA PO1 12 C1
Hanway Rd NEND PO2 187 H8
Ha'penny Dell WVILLE PO7 164 C5 3
Harbeck Rd CHAR BH8 221 G5
Harbour Cl CCLF BH13 245 J2 1
Harbour Crs
CHCH/BSGR BH23 238 D3 1
Harbour Hill Crs PLE BH15 233 K3
Harbour Hill Rd PLE BH15 233 K3
Harbourne Gdns WEND SO18 108 A6
Harbour Pde SHAM SO14 4 E3
WSHM SO15 4 D3
Harbour Rd GPORT PO12 11 K2
HISD PO11 213 G4
SBNE BH6 237 M5
Harbourside HAV PO9 189 K2
Harbour Vw
FHAM/PORC PO16 186 A2
Harbour View Cl PSTN BH14 233 M3
Harbour View Rd PSTN BH14 233 M3
Harbour Wy EMRTH PO10 166 E8 3
NEND PO2 187 G6
Harbridge Ct HAV PO9 165 H1
Harbridge Dro FBDG SP6 122 A4
Harcombe Cl CFDH BH17 218 C5 1
Harcourt Cl HORN PO8 140 E4
Harcourt Rd BOSC BH5 236 F3
FHAM/STUB PO14 183 M1
GPORT PO12 10 D2
PSEA PO1 211 J1
WEND SO18 107 J8
Harding La ELGH SO50 83 G5
Harding Rd GPORT PO12 209 K2
Hardley La FAWY SO45 179 M1
The Hard PSEA PO1 12 C1
Hardwicke Cl ROWN SO16 105 L6
Hardwicke Wy HLER SO31 157 J5 2
Hardwick Rd CHFD SO53 81 J2 2
Hardy Cl FERN BH22 168 D7
HLER SO31 158 F4
NMIL/BTOS BH25 225 K5
WSHM SO15 130 F2
Hardy Crs WIMB BH21 192 B4
Hardy Dr FAWY SO45 155 M7
Hardy Rd CHAM PO6 188 C1
ELGH SO50 81 L7
FERN BH22 168 D7
PSTN BH14 234 C4
Harebell Cl FHAM/PORC PO16 7 L1
Harefield Ct ROMY SO51 51 G8 3
Harefield Rd PTSW SO17 107 H5
Hare La NMIL/BTOS BH25 226 B5
RWIN SO21 54 F4
WIMB BH21 120 C3
Hares Gn LTDN BH7 221 L8
Hares La RCCH PO18 167 M1
Harestock Cl FUFL SO22 16 C3
Harestock Rd FUFL SO22 16 C4
HAV PO9 8 B1
Harewood Av LTDN BH7 236 E1
Harewood Cl ELGH SO50 81 M3
Harewood Crs LTDN BH7 236 E1
Harewood Gdns LTDN BH7 236 E1
Harewood Gn LYMN SO41 243 G4
Harewood Pl LTDN BH7 237 G2 2
Harford Cl LYMN SO41 227 M7
Harford Rd BKME/WDN BH12 219 G8
Harkness Dr WVILLE PO7 140 F8
Harkwood Dr PLE BH15 232 D4
Harland Crs WSHM SO15 106 C7
Harland Rd SBNE BH6 237 M4
Harlaxton Cl ELGH SO50 81 L3
Harlech Dr CHFD SO53 80 F4
Harlequin Gv FHAM PO15 6 D5
Harleston Rd CHAM PO6 163 H7
Harlyn Rd ROWN SO16 105 L7
Harness Cl WIMB BH21 192 F2
Harold Cl TOTT SO40 129 H2
Harold Rd EMRTH PO10 166 F4
ENEY PO4 13 M6
FHAM/STUB PO14 184 B5
HISD PO11 213 M6
WSHM SO15 131 G1
Harpway La CHCH/BSGR BH23 223 G2
The Harrage ROMY SO51 78 E1
Harrier Cl HORN PO8 140 E1
LSOL/BMARY PO13 208 D2 4
ROWN SO16 106 A2
Harrier Dr WIMB BH21 192 B6
Harriers Cl CHCH/BSGR BH23 224 B8 3
Harrier Wy EPSF GU31 64 B6
FAWY SO45 179 M2
Harriet Cl FHAM/STUB PO14 183 M6
Harris Av HEND SO30 109 H8 3
Harris La HORN PO8 117 J3
Harrison Av BMTH BH1 236 C2
Harrison Cl
CHCH/BSGR BH23 223 G5 2
Harrison Rd FHAM/PORC PO16 7 J3
PTSW SO17 107 H5
Harrison Wy FERN BH22 168 C5 1

Harris Rd *LSOL/BMARY* PO13........ **185** G5
Harrow Cl *CHCH/BSGR* BH23........ **223** M1
Harrow Down *FUFL* SO22............ **26** C4
Harrowgate La *WVILLE* PO7......... **114** E6
Harrow La *PSF* GU32................ **63** L2
Harrow Rd *CHCH/BSGR* BH23........ **223** L1
  SSEA PO5.............................. **13** L3
Harry Barrow Cl *RGWD* BH24 .. **170** E2 🗒
Hart Cl *NMIL/BTOS* BH25.......... **225** K4
Hart Hl *FAWY* SO45................ **156** A7
Harthill Dro *RSAL* SP5.............. **73** K3
Harting Cl *HORN* PO8.............. **116** C4
Harting Down *EPSF* GU31.......... **64** A5
Harting Gdns
  FHAM/PORC PO16.................. **162** A7
Harting Rd *SBNE* BH6.............. **237** J1
Hartington Rd *GPORT* PO12........ **209** G2
  SHAM SO14............................ **5** K1
Hartland Ct *EMRTH* PO10......... **167** H7
Hartland's Rd
  FHAM/PORC PO16.................... **7** K6
Hartley Av *PTSW* SO17........... **107** G6
Hartley Cl *ELGH* SO50............. **82** F7
  FAWY SO45....................... **155** L7 🗒
Hartley Ct *ROWN* SO16........... **106** F4
Hartley Rd *ELGH* SO50............. **82** F6
  NEND PO2............................ **187** H5
Hartley Wk *FAWY* SO45......... **155** K7 🗒
Hart Plain Av *HORN* PO8......... **140** C6
Hartsbourne Dr *LTDN* BH7....... **221** M8
Harts Farm Wy *HAV* PO9......... **165** G6
Hartsgrove Cl *FAWY* SO45....... **180** C8
Harts Wy *LYMN* SO41............ **227** H7
Hartwell Rd *HSEA* PO3.......... **187** M5 🗒
Hartwood Gdns *HORN* PO8....... **140** C6
Harvest Cl *FUFL* SO22.............. **26** C4
Harvester Dr *FHAM* PO15........ **159** M7
Harvester Wy *LYMN* SO41....... **228** B2
Harvesting La *PSF* GU32........... **89** M2
Harvest Rd *NBAD* SO52............ **80** E2
  WVILLE PO7.......................... **139** J4
Harvey Ct *FAWY* SO45............ **180** C6 🗒
Harvey Crs *HLER* SO31........... **158** D6
Harvey Gdns *FAWY* SO45....... **155** M5
Harvey Rd *BOSC* BH5............. **236** F8
  ELGH SO50............................ **82** D5
  WIMB BH21.......................... **192** C8
Harwich Rd *CHAM* PO6........... **163** H7
Harwood Cl
  LSOL/BMARY PO13............. **185** G4 🗒
  TOTT SO40.......................... **104** C8
Harwood Rd
  LSOL/BMARY PO13............. **185** G5
Haselbury Rd *TOTT* SO40........ **129** K1
Haselfoot Gdns *WEND* SO18 ... **133** J1 🗒
Haselworth Dr *GPORT* PO12...... **10** F9
Haskells Cl *LYND* SO43.......... **151** L8 🗒
Haskells Rd *BKME/WDN* BH12... **234** A1
Haslar Crs *WVILLE* PO7........... **140** A6
Haslar Rd *GPORT* PO12............ **11** J7
Haslemere Av
  CHCH/BSGR BH23................ **224** D8
Haslemere Gdns *HISD* PO11 ... **214** D6
Haslemere Pl
  CHCH/BSGR BH23................ **224** D8
Haslemere Rd *EMRTH* PO10.... **167** H6
  ENEY PO4........................... **211** K6
Hasler Rd *CFDH* BH17............ **218** A6
Haslop Rd *WIMB* BH21........... **192** D1
The Hassocks *WVILLE* PO7..... **164** E1
Hastings Av *GPORT* PO12....... **185** K8
Hastings Rd *CFDH* BH17........ **217** M6 🗒
  CHAR BH8............................ **221** K6
Hatch Ct *HAV* PO9................. **165** G1
Hatchers La *RWIN* SO21........... **55** L3
Hatchet Cl *FBDG* SP6.............. **73** J5
Hatchet La *BROC* SO42........... **178** B8
Hatch La *LISS* GU33................ **37** H4
Hatchley La *RWIN* SO21........... **84** A2
Hatch Md *HEND* SO30............ **108** B6
Hatch Pond Rd *CFDH* BH17 .... **218** A4
Hatfield Ct *NMIL/BTOS* BH25 .. **225** J5 🗒
Hatfield Gdns *LTDN* BH7........ **221** M8
Hatfield Rd *ENEY* PO4............ **211** L5
Hathaway Cl *ELGH* SO50.......... **82** A4
Hathaway Gdns *WVILLE* PO7... **140** F7
Hathaway Rd *SBNE* BH6......... **237** J4
Hatherden Av *PSTN* BH14...... **233** L3
Hatherell Cl *HEND* SO30......... **108** C7
Hatherley Crs
  FHAM/PORC PO16............. **185** M1
Hatherley Dr
  FHAM/PORC PO16............. **161** M8 🗒
Hatherley Rd *CHAM* PO6........ **162** F7
  FUFL SO22............................. **2** D5
Hatley Rd *WEND* SO18........... **108** A8
Hatt La *ROMY* SO51................ **21** K6
Havant Farm Cl *HAV* PO9.......... **8** F1
Havant Rd *CHAM* PO6............ **163** K8
  EMRTH PO10.......................... **9** M5
  HAV PO9................................. **9** J3
  HISD PO11.......................... **189** K5
  HORN PO8.......................... **141** H2
  NEND PO2.......................... **187** H7
Havant St *PSEA* PO1............. **12** C2 🗒
Havelock Rd
  BKME/WDN BH12................ **234** F3
  HLER SO31.......................... **158** A7
  SHAM SO14............................ **4** E1
  SSEA PO5............................. **13** K4
  WSHM SO15....................... **130** F1
Havelock Wy
  CHCH/BSGR BH23................ **224** B6
Haven Crs *FHAM/STUB* PO14... **183** K7
Havendale *HEND* SO30........... **134** B3 🗒
Haven Gdns *NMIL/BTOS* BH25.. **225** M6
Haven Rd *CCLF* BH13.............. **245** K2
  HISD PO11.......................... **214** C7
  WIMB BH21.......................... **217** G2
Havenstone Wy *WEND* SO18 ... **107** J4 🗒
The Haven *ELGH* SO50............. **82** A3
  ENEY PO4........................... **211** M3
  GPORT PO12.......................... **10** E8
H Av *FAWY* SO45................... **180** D2
Haverstock Rd
  MOOR/WNTN BH9................ **220** F6
Haviland Rd *BMTH* BH1.......... **236** E3
  WIMB BH21.......................... **193** L1

Haviland Rd East *LTDN* BH7.... **236** E3
Haviland Rd West *LTDN* BH7 ... **236** E5 🗒
Havisham Rd *NEND* PO2......... **211** H1 🗒
Hawden Rd *BWD* BH11.......... **219** L7
Hawfinch Cl *WEND* SO18....... **106** A2
Hawkchurch Gdns *CFDH* BH17.. **218** C6
Hawk Cl *FHAM/STUB* PO14..... **183** M6
  WIMB BH21.......................... **192** E1
Hawker Cl *WIMB* BH21........... **192** D7
Hawke St *PSEA* PO1................ **12** C1
Hawkeswood Rd *WEND* SO18... **132** A1
Hawkewood Av *WVILLE* PO7... **140** B6
Hawkhill *FAWY* SO45............. **155** G4
Hawkhurst Cl *ITCH* SO19........ **132** E7
Hawkley Cl *HAV* PO9............. **165** J2 🗒
Hawkley Gn *ITCH* SO19.......... **132** D8
Hawkley Rd *LISS* GU33............ **35** L1
Hawkwell *FHAM/PORC* PO16... **161** M6
Hawkwood Rd *BOSC* BH5........ **236** D4
Haworth Cl *CHCH/BSGR* BH23.. **222** E7
Hawswater Cl *ROWN* SO16..... **105** L7 🗒
Hawthorn Cl *ELGH* SO50.......... **83** H6 🗒
  FHAM/PORC PO16................ **161** M7
  HEND SO30.......................... **134** B2 🗒
  NMIL/BTOS BH25................. **226** A4 🗒
  RWIN SO21............................ **54** F8
Hawthorn Crs *CHAM* PO6....... **187** L2
Hawthorn Dr *CFDH* BH17....... **217** K7
  LYMN SO41......................... **200** F6
Hawthorne Gv *HISD* PO11...... **213** L4
Hawthorne Rd *TOTT* SO40...... **104** C8
Hawthorn La *HLER* SO31........ **158** C3
Hawthorn Rd
  CHCH/BSGR BH23................ **223** J6
  FAWY SO45........................ **155** K5 🗒
  HORN PO8.......................... **116** B6
  MOOR/WNTN BH9................ **220** D8
  PTSW SO17......................... **106** F6
  WVILLE PO7......................... **139** H4
The Hawthorns
  CHCH/BSGR BH23................ **238** C2 🗒
  ELGH SO50.......................... **81** K7 🗒
  TOTT SO40.......................... **130** E7
Hayburn Rd *ROWN* SO16....... **105** J6
Haydock Cl *TOTT* SO40.......... **104** B8
Haydock Ms *WVILLE* PO7....... **140** F7
Haydon Rd *CCLF* BH13........... **235** G7
Hayes Av *LTDN* BH7.............. **236** D2
Hayes Cl *WIMB* BH21............ **192** E4
Hayes La *WIMB* BH21............ **192** F4
Hayeswood Rd *WIMB* BH21.... **192** E2
Hayle Rd *WEND* SO18........... **108** A6
Hayley Cl *FAWY* SO45............ **155** K8
Hayling Av *HSEA* PO3............ **211** M1
Hayling Cl *FHAM/STUB* PO14...... **6** A6
Haymoor Rd *PLE* BH15.......... **233** M1
Haynes Av *PLE* BH15............. **233** J4
Haynes Wy *FAWY* SO45......... **155** J7 🗒
Haysoms Cl *NMIL/BTOS* BH25 .. **225** M7
Hay St *PSEA* PO1................... **12** C1
Hayter Gdns *ROMY* SO51........ **50** F8
Hayters Wy *FBDG* SP6........... **121** L2
Hayward Cl *TOTT* SO40......... **129** J1
Hayward Ct *FAWY* SO45........ **180** A4 🗒
Hayward Crs *VWD* BH31......... **144** C3
Haywards Farm Cl
  VWD BH31......................... **144** C3 🗒
Hayward Wy *VWD* BH31........ **144** A3
Hazelbank Cl *EPSF* GU31.......... **64** A4
Hazel Cl *CHCH/BSGR* BH23..... **224** A7
  CHFD SO53............................ **53** H8
  FBDG SP6........................ **121** L3 🗒
  RWIN SO21............................ **54** F7
Hazeldean Dr *HAV* PO9.......... **141** M7
Hazeldown Cl *ROWN* SO16..... **105** K3
Hazel Dr *FERN* BH22............. **168** B3
Hazeleigh Av *ITCH* SO19........ **132** C6
Hazeley Rd *RWIN* SO21........... **54** E7
Hazel Farm Rd *TOTT* SO40..... **129** G1
Hazel Gv *FUFL* SO22................ **26** C3
  HLER SO31.......................... **158** F6
  TOTT SO40.......................... **128** D5
Hazelgrove *HORN* PO8........... **116** B3
Hazelholt Dr *HAV* PO9.............. **8** A1
Hazell Av *NBNE* BH10............ **219** M6
Hazel Rd *HORN* PO8.............. **116** B3
  ITCH SO19.......................... **132** B5
  LYMN SO41......................... **227** L4
Hazelton Cl *LTDN* BH7........... **221** L8 🗒
Hazelwood
  FHAM/STUB PO14............... **183** M3 🗒
  NMIL/BTOS BH25................ **225** J4
Hazelwood Av *HAV* PO9......... **164** F5
Hazelwood Dr *VWD* BH31....... **144** F5
Hazelwood Rd *WEND* SO18 .... **107** M7 🗒
Hazlebury Rd *CFDH* BH17...... **233** G1
Hazlemere Dr *RGWD* BH24 .... **169** J5
Hazleton Wy *HORN* PO8......... **140** F5
Head Down *EPSF* GU31............ **64** A5
Headland Dr *HLER* SO31......... **158** A4
Headley Cl
  LSOL/BMARY PO13............. **208** D2 🗒
Headon Vw *PSF* GU32.............. **60** B3
Heads Farm Cl *NBNE* BH10.... **220** C3
Headswell Av *NBNE* BH10..... **220** C4
Headswell Crs *NBNE* BH10..... **220** C4
Headswell Gdns *NBNE* BH10 ... **220** C4 🗒
Heanor Cl *NBNE* BH10........... **220** A6
Hearne Gdns *BPWT* SO32...... **111** M7
Heath Av *PLE* BH15............... **233** J4
Heath Cl *ELGH* SO50............... **83** J7
  HORN PO8.......................... **140** F1
  WIMB BH21.......................... **192** F1
Heathcote Pl *RWIN* SO21......... **53** G1
Heathcote Rd *BMTH* BH1....... **236** E4
  BOSC BH5........................... **236** E4
  CHFD SO53............................ **81** J7
  NEND PO2.......................... **187** K7
Heathen St *BPWT* SO32......... **110** A4
Heatherbank Rd *CCLF*
  BH13................................... **235** H5 🗒
Heatherbrae Gdns
  NBAD SO52........................ **79** L4 🗒

Heatherbrae La *UPTN* BH16.... **232** A2
Heather Cha *ELGH* SO50.......... **82** F6 🗒
Heather Cl *CHAR* BH8............ **221** H4
  CHCH/BSGR BH23................ **224** E7
  LSOL/BMARY PO13............. **184** F6
  LYMN SO41......................... **226** E5
  RGWD BH24......................... **169** J5
  TOTT SO40.......................... **129** J1
  WIMB BH21......................... **217** J2 🗒
  WVILLE PO7......................... **164** D2
Heather Ct *WEND* SO18......... **133** G1
Heatherdeane Rd *PTSW* SO17... **106** F6
Heatherdell *UPTN* BH16........ **232** A2 🗒
Heatherdene Rd *CHFD* SO53.... **53** K7
Heatherdown Rd
  FERN BH22......................... **168** E7 🗒
Heatherdown Wy
  FERN BH22......................... **168** E7 🗒
Heather Dr *FERN* BH22.......... **194** B1
Heatherfield *EPSF* GU31........... **91** J3
Heather Gdns *FHAM* PO15......... **6** D7
Heatherlands Ri
  BKME/WDN BH12................ **234** C3 🗒
Heatherlands Rd *ROWN* SO16.... **80** E8
Heatherlea Rd *SBNE* BH6....... **237** J4
Heather Rd *EPSF* GU31............ **64** B5 🗒
  FAWY SO45......................... **180** D6
  NBNE BH10......................... **220** B5
Heatherstone Av *FAWY* SO45.. **155** K8
Heatherton Ms *EMRTH* PO10... **167** H6
Heatherview Rd *NBAD* SO52.... **79** L3 🗒
Heather View Rd
  BKME/WDN BH12................ **234** E1
Heather Wy *FERN* BH22......... **168** D7
Heath Farm Cl *FERN* BH22..... **194** A5 🗒
Heath Farm Rd *FERN* BH22.... **194** A5
Heath Farm Wy *FERN* BH22... **194** A5 🗒
Heathfield *FAWY* SO45......... **155** K6 🗒
Heathfield Av
  BKME/WDN BH12................ **219** L8
  FHAM PO15............................ **6** A6
Heathfield Cl *ITCH* SO19........ **133** C5 🗒
Heathfield Rd *CHFD* SO53........ **53** H6
  EPSF GU31............................ **64** B5
  FERN BH22......................... **168** A7
  ITCH SO19.......................... **132** F5
  NEND PO2.......................... **187** H8
Heathfield Wy *FERN* BH22..... **168** D7
Heath Gdns *HLER* SO31......... **157** H1
Heath House Cl *HEND* SO30.... **133** M4
Heath House Gdns *HEND* SO30.. **133** M4
Heathhouse La *HEND* SO30..... **133** M4
Heathlands Av *FERN* BH22..... **194** B6
Heathlands Cl
  CHCH/BSGR BH23............. **223** G6 🗒
  CHFD SO53............................ **53** H8
  VWD BH31......................... **144** F2 🗒
Heathlands Rd *CHFD* SO53...... **53** H8
Heath La *BROC* SO42............ **204** A1
Heath Lawns *FHAM* PO15......... **6** B6
Heath Rd *BPWT* SO32............ **112** F7
  CHCH/BSGR BH23................ **223** J6
  EPSF GU31............................ **63** M5
  HLER SO31.......................... **158** D3
  ITCH SO19.......................... **132** E3
  LYMN SO41......................... **226** D5
  NBAD SO52........................... **79** M5
  RGWD BH24......................... **169** L3
  WIMB BH21......................... **217** J2
Heath Rd East *EPSF* GU31........ **64** A6
Heath Rd North *HLER* SO31.... **158** D5
Heath Rd South *HLER* SO31.... **158** D5
Heath Rd West
  CHCH/BSGR BH23................ **195** J2
  EPSF GU31............................ **63** M6
The Heath *WVILLE* PO7......... **139** L4
Heathwood Av
  NMIL/BTOS BH25................ **225** J8
Heathwood Rd
  MOOR/WNTN BH9................ **220** C8
Heathy Cl *NMIL/BTOS* BH25.... **225** K8
Heaton Rd *GPORT* PO12........ **209** L1
  NEND PO2.......................... **219** M6
Heavytree Rd *PSTN* BH14...... **234** A4 🗒
Hebrides Cl
  FHAM/STUB PO14............... **183** M5 🗒
Heckfield Cl *HAV* PO9............ **165** M3 🗒
Heckford La *PLE* BH15............ **233** J4
Heckford Rd *PLE* BH15............ **233** J4
  WIMB BH21......................... **217** G3
Hector Cl *WVILLE* PO7........... **164** C6
Hector Rd *FHAM/STUB* PO14.. **184** E3
Hedera Rd *HLER* SO31........... **158** D5
Hedgerley *NMIL/BTOS* BH25 ... **225** M8 🗒
Hedgerow Cl *ROWN* SO16...... **105** K2
Hedgerow Dr *WEND* SO18..... **108** A2 🗒
Hedgerow Gdns
  EMRTH PO10...................... **144** D5
Hedley Cl *FAWY* SO45........... **180** C7
Hedley Gdns *HEND* SO30....... **109** G5 🗒
Heidelberg Rd *ENEY* PO4....... **211** K4
Heights Ap *UPTN* BH16......... **232** B1
Heights Rd *UPTN* BH16......... **217** G8
The Heights *FHAM/PORC* PO16.. **161** H6
  HEND SO30......................... **133** L2
Helena Rd *ENEY* PO4............ **211** K6
Helford Gdns *WEND* SO18..... **108** A6 🗒
Hellyer Rd *ENEY* PO4............ **211** L5
Helm Cl *LSOL/BMARY* PO13... **209** H2
Helsted Cl *GPORT* PO12......... **209** J4
Helston Dr *EMRTH* PO10....... **166** C5
Helston Rd *CHAM* PO6.......... **162** D7
Helvellyn Rd *ROWN* SO16...... **105** L8
Helyar Rd *CHAR* BH8............ **221** K6
Hemdean Gdns *HEND* SO30.... **108** C7
Hemlock Rd *HORN* PO8......... **140** C4
Hemlock Wy *NBAD* SO52........ **80** E3
Hemming Cl *TOTT* SO40........ **129** J2
Hemmingway Gdns
  FHAM PO15......................... **135** G8
Hempland La *ALTN* GU34........ **33** H4
Hempsted Rd *CHAM* PO6....... **162** F7
Hemsley Wk *HORN* PO8......... **140** E4
Henbury Cl *CFDH* BH17......... **218** E6 🗒
  WIMB BH21......................... **217** H2
Henbury Ri *WIMB* BH21......... **217** H2
Henbury View Rd
  WIMB BH21......................... **217** H2 🗒

Henderson Rd *ENEY* PO4........ **211** M5
Hendford Rd *NBNE* BH10....... **220** B6
Hendy Cl *SSEA* PO5................ **13** J5 🗒
Henery St *GPORT* PO12........... **11** H3 🗒
Hengistbury Rd
  NMIL/BTOS BH25................ **225** J8
  SBNE BH6........................... **237** L5
Hengist Rd *BMTH* BH1........... **236** C4 🗒
Henley Gdns *FHAM* PO15...... **160** B4
Henley Gdns *LTDN* BH7......... **236** F1 🗒
Henley Rd *ENEY* PO4............ **211** K5
Henning's Park Rd *PLE* BH15... **233** J3
Henry Cl *FAWY* SO45............ **179** M2 🗒
Henry Rd *ELGH* SO50............. **82** C4 🗒
  WSHM SO15....................... **130** F1
Henry St *WSHM* SO15............ **131** K2 🗒
Henstead Rd *WSHM* SO15..... **131** K2
Hensting La *RWIN* SO21.......... **55** K5
Henty Rd *ROWN* SO16.......... **105** M8
Henville Cl *LSOL/BMARY* PO13.. **185** H8
Henville Rd *CHAR* BH8........... **15** L1
Henwood Down *EPSF* GU31..... **63** M5 🗒
Hepworth Cl *ITCH* SO19......... **133** G6
Herbert Av *BKME/WDN* BH12.. **219** G7
Herberton Rd *SBNE* BH6........ **237** H3
Herbert Rd *ENEY* PO4............ **13** L8
  GPORT PO12.......................... **10** B2
  NMIL/BTOS BH25................. **225** M5
  RSAL SP5.............................. **73** J2
  WBNE BH4........................... **235** G6
Herbert St *PSEA* PO1............ **211** G1
Herbert Walker Av *WSHM* SO15 ... **4** F5
Hercules Rd *PLE* BH15........... **232** C5 🗒
Hercules St *NEND* PO2.......... **187** H8 🗒
Hereford Rd *SSEA* PO5............ **13** J4
Hereward Cl *ROMY* SO51........ **79** G1 🗒
Hermes Rd *LSOL/BMARY* PO13.. **208** B1
Hermitage Cl *BPWT* SO32...... **84** F8 🗒
  HAV PO9............................. **165** J4
Hermitage Rd *PSTN* BH14...... **233** M2
Herm Rd *BKME/WDN* BH12.... **219** G7
Herne Rd *CHAM* PO6............ **163** J8
  EPSF GU31............................ **63** M5
Hern La *FBDG* SP6................. **122** F2
Heron Cl *ENEY* PO4............... **211** M3
Heron Ct Rd *LYMN* SO41....... **200** F6
Heron Court Rd
  MOOR/WNTN BH9................ **235** M1
  TWDS BH3.......................... **235** M2
Heron Dr *WIMB* BH21........... **192** E3
Heron La *ROMY* SO51............. **50** C2
Heron Quay *EMRTH* PO10...... **190** A4
Herons Cl *FHAM/STUB* PO14.. **184** A4
Heron Sq *ELGH* SO50............. **81** K7
Heron Wy *LSOL/BMARY* PO13.. **184** E5
Herrick Cl *ITCH* SO19............. **133** H4
Herriott Cl *HORN* PO8............ **140** E3
Herstone Cl *CFDH* BH17........ **218** D7
Hertford Cl *FBDG* SP6............. **97** L5
Hertford Pl *PSEA* PO1............ **211** H1
Hertsfield *FHAM/STUB* PO14.. **159** G4
Hesketh Cl *RGWD* BH24........ **169** L3
Hester Rd *ENEY* PO4............ **211** M4 🗒
Hestia Rd *ROMY* SO51............ **51** H8
Heston Cl *CHCH/BSGR* BH23.. **222** B4
Heston Wy *FERN* BH22......... **168** B5
Hewett Cl *FHAM/STUB* PO14.. **183** K1
Hewett Rd *FHAM/STUB* PO14.. **183** K1
  NEND PO2.......................... **187** J6
Hewetts Ri *HLER* SO31.......... **158** A8
Hewitt Cl *GPORT* PO12......... **209** L2 🗒
Hewitt Rd *PLE* BH15.............. **232** D4
Hewitt's Rd *WSHM* SO15......... **4** B2
Heyes Dr *ITCH* SO19............. **133** G5
Heysham Rd *BDST* BH18........ **217** L5
  WSHM SO15....................... **106** A8
Heyshott Rd *ENEY* PO4........ **211** K4
Heytesbury Rd *SBNE* BH6..... **237** J3 🗒
Heyward Rd *ENEY* PO4.......... **13** L4
Heywood Gn *ITCH* SO19........ **133** J3
Hibberd Wy *NBNE* BH10....... **220** B7
Hibbs Cl *UPTN* BH16............ **232** B1
Hickes Cl *BWD* BH11............ **219** K4
Hickory Cl *UPTN* BH16......... **216** E8 🗒
Hickory Dr *FUFL* SO22............ **16** B4
Hickory Gdns *HEND* SO30..... **108** C5
Hicks Rd *FHAM/STUB* PO14... **184** B3
Hicks Wy *LSOL/BMARY* PO13.. **184** F3
Higham Gdns *SBNE* BH6........ **237** G3
Highams Cl *FAWY* SO45......... **155** H7
Highbank Av *WVILLE* PO7...... **163** M5
Highbank Gdns *FBDG* SP6....... **97** L7 🗒
Highbridge Cl *ELGH* SO50........ **82** C1
  PSTN BH14......................... **234** B5 🗒
Highbury Cl *ELGH* SO50.......... **83** H7
  NMIL/BTOS BH25................ **225** M5
Highbury Gv *CHAM* PO6........ **187** L2
Highbury St *PSEA* PO1............ **12** D4
Highbury Wy *CHAM* PO6........ **187** L2
Highclere Av *HAV* PO9........... **165** H4
Highclere Rd *ROWN* SO16..... **106** C5
Highclere Wy *CHFD* SO53........ **80** F5
Highcliff Av *SHAM* SO14........ **106** F8 🗒
Highcliffe Dr *ELGH* SO50......... **81** M1
Highcliffe Rd
  CHCH/BSGR BH23................ **223** L8
  GPORT PO12.......................... **10** B4
  WINC SO23............................ **27** G2
Highcroft La *HORN* PO8......... **116** B8
High Cross *PSF* GU32.............. **34** D6
High Cross La *PSF* GU32......... **34** D5
Highcrown St *PTSW* SO17...... **106** F6
High Dr *LSOL/BMARY* PO13... **185** G7
Higher Blandford Rd
  BDST BH18......................... **217** L3
  WIMB BH21......................... **217** K2
Highfield *LYMN* SO41............ **228** B5
  RWIN SO21............................ **54** F3
Highfield Av *FHAM/STUB* PO14..... **6** E8
  LYMN SO41......................... **228** A5
  PTSW SO17......................... **106** E5
  RGWD BH24......................... **146** E8
  RWIN SO21............................ **54** F3
  WVILLE PO7......................... **140** E8
Highfield Cl *CHFD* SO53........... **81** J2
  LYMN SO41......................... **200** F6
  PTSW SO17......................... **106** F6 🗒
  WIMB BH21......................... **217** J3
  WVILLE PO7......................... **140** D7
Highfield Crs *PTSW* SO17...... **107** G6
Highfield Gdns *LISS* GU33........ **37** G4

  LYMN SO41......................... **200** F6 🗒
  RSAL SP5.............................. **73** J3
Highfield La *PTSW* SO17....... **106** F6
  RSAL SP5.............................. **73** J3
Highfield Rd *CHFD* SO53......... **81** K2
  FERN BH22......................... **168** B4
  GPORT PO12........................ **209** K2
  LYMN SO41......................... **228** A4
  MOOR/WNTN BH9................ **220** C6
  PSEA PO1............................. **13** K1
  PSF GU32.............................. **63** L4
  PTSW SO17......................... **106** E7
  RGWD BH24......................... **146** E8
  WIMB BH21......................... **217** J3
High Firs Gdns *ROMY* SO51.... **79** H1
High Firs Rd *ITCH* SO19........ **132** F3
  ROMY SO51.......................... **51** H8
Highgate Rd *HSEA* PO3.......... **187** L7
Highgrove Cl *TOTT* SO40....... **129** H3 🗒
Highgrove Rd *HSEA* PO3........ **187** M8
High Howe Cl *BWD* BH11...... **219** J4
High Howe Gdns *BWD* BH11 ... **219** J4 🗒
High Howe La *BWD* BH11...... **219** J4
Highland Av *CHCH/BSGR* BH23.. **224** F7
Highland Cl *EMRTH* PO10...... **166** C6
Highland Rd *EMRTH* PO10..... **166** C7
  ENEY PO4........................... **211** K5
  PSTN BH14......................... **234** A3
  WIMB BH21......................... **192** B3
Highlands Cl *FAWY* SO45....... **155** L6
  NBAD SO52........................... **79** K3 🗒
Highlands Crs *NBNE* BH10.... **220** A4
Highlands Rd *CHAM* PO6....... **164** B8
  FHAM PO15............................ **6** A2
  NMIL/BTOS BH25................ **225** L8
Highland St *ENEY* PO4.......... **211** L6
Highlands Wy *FAWY* SO45..... **155** K6
  RSAL SP5.............................. **47** G4
Highland View Cl *WIMB* BH21.. **192** B3
High Lawn Wy *HAV* PO9....... **165** J3
High Md *FERN* BH22............. **193** L6
  FHAM PO15............................ **6** C1
High Mead La *FERN* BH22...... **193** L7
High Meadow *ITCH* SO19...... **133** G2
Highmoor Cl *WIMB* BH21...... **217** H3 🗒
Highmoor Rd *BWD* BH11...... **219** L7 🗒
  PSTN BH14......................... **234** B5
  WIMB BH21......................... **217** H3
Highmount Cl *WINC* SO23......... **3** K9
Highnam Gdns *HLER* SO31.... **158** D4
High Oaks Cl *HLER* SO31....... **158** E5
High Oaks Gdns *BWD* BH11 ... **219** J4 🗒
High Park Rd *BDST* BH18....... **217** J4
High Ridge Crs
  NMIL/BTOS BH25................ **226** A5
High Rd *ELGH* SO50.............. **107** J3
  ROWN SO16........................ **107** J5
High St *BPWT* SO32................ **87** G7
  BPWT SO32......................... **111** H1
  BPWT SO32......................... **113** G5
  BPWT SO32......................... **136** C1
  BROC SO42......................... **178** D8
  CHAM PO6.......................... **187** K1
  CHCH/BSGR BH23................ **238** A2
  ELGH SO50........................... **81** M7
  EMRTH PO10...................... **166** D8
  EPSF GU31............................ **63** L5
  EPSF GU31............................ **91** J3
  FAWY SO45......................... **155** L3
  FBDG SP6............................. **96** B2
  FBDG SP6............................. **97** L7
  FBDG SP6............................. **98** D1
  FHAM/PORC PO16.................. **7** L4
  FHAM/STUB PO14............... **159** K8
  GPORT PO12.......................... **11** K3
  HEND SO30......................... **108** D7 🗒
  HEND SO30......................... **134** E1
  HLER SO31.......................... **157** M1
  LSOL/BMARY PO13............. **208** C2
  LYMN SO41......................... **228** C5
  LYMN SO41......................... **242** C4
  LYND SO43......................... **151** K3
  PLE BH15........................... **233** G7
  PSEA PO1............................. **12** C5
  PSF GU32.............................. **60** B3
  PSF GU32.............................. **61** K7
  RGWD BH24......................... **169** J2 🗒
  RGWD BH24......................... **170** D1 🗒
  RWIN SO21............................ **54** F3
  SHAM SO14............................ **5** G6
  TOTT SO40.......................... **129** L1
  WHAM PO17........................ **162** D3
  WINC SO23............................ **3** G2
  WVILLE PO7......................... **114** C3
High St North *PLE* BH15....... **233** J5
Hightown Gdns *RGWD* BH24... **170** F2
Hightown Hl *RGWD* BH24...... **171** K1
Hightown Rd *RGWD* BH24..... **170** D2
Hightrees Av *CHAR* BH8........ **221** J7
High Trees Dr *FUFL* SO22........ **2** C3
High Trees *ELGH* SO50............ **83** K6
  WVILLE PO7......................... **140** D8
High Trees Wk *FERN* BH22.... **194** B1
High Vw *FHAM/PORC* PO16.... **162** A7
Highview Cl *CHCH/BSGR* BH23 .. **222** C5
Highview Gdns
  BKME/WDN BH12................ **234** B1
High View Wy *WEND* SO18.... **107** L8
High Wy *BDST* BH18............. **217** K5
Highways Rd *RWIN* SO21........ **54** E3
The Highway *RSAL* SP5........... **44** C2
Highwood Cl *FBDG* SP6........ **121** H2 🗒
Highwood La *RGWD* BH24..... **147** G6
  ROMY SO51.......................... **51** J8
Highwood Rd *BROC* SO42..... **175** K8
  LSOL/BMARY PO13............. **209** G1
  PSTN BH14......................... **234** D4 🗒
Higworth La *HISD* PO11......... **213** K3
Hilary Av *CHAM* PO6............. **187** L1
Hilary Rd *CFDH* BH17........... **218** A7
Hilda Gdns *WVILLE* PO7........ **139** L4
Hilda Rd *BKME/WDN* BH12.... **234** D2
Hiley Rd *PLE* BH15............... **233** H2
Hillary Cl *FHAM/PORC* PO16.... **6** E3
  LYND SO43......................... **151** L5
Hillborough Crs *SSEA* PO5..... **13** J6 🗒
Hillbourne Rd *CFDH* BH17..... **217** L6
Hillbrow Cl *FHAM* PO15.......... **6** B1

Hill Brow Cl HAV PO9 .... 141 M7
Hill Brow Rd LISS GU33 .... 36 E5
Hillbrow Rd SBNE BH6 .... 237 G2
Hillbury Rd FBDG SP6 .... 121 L2
Hill Cl CHCH/BSGR BH23 .... 223 L1
  ELGH SO50 .... 83 H3
Hillcrest Av CHFD SO53 .... 81 J2
  FERN BH22 .... 194 A1
Hillcrest Cl MOOR/WNTN BH9 .... 220 E5
  NBAD SO52 .... 79 J3
Hillcrest Dr CHFD SO53 .... 81 J2 [2]
Hill Crest Gdns BPWT SO32 .... 111 J4
Hillcrest Rd BKME/WDN BH12.. 233 M3
  MOOR/WNTN BH9 .... 220 E5
  WIMB BH21 .... 217 G3
Hill Cft FHAM PO15 .... 159 H5
Hilldene Wy HEND SO30 .... 108 D7 [2]
Hillditch LYMN SO41 .... 228 B2
Hilldown Rd PTSW SO17 .... 106 F5
Hilldowns Av NEND PO2 .... 187 G6
Hill Farm Rd WSHM SO15 .... 131 J2
Hillgrove Rd WEND SO18 .... 107 L5 [4]
Hill Head Rd FHAM/STUB PO14.. 183 L7
Hill Houses La NARL SO51 .... 30 A3
Hillier Wy WINC SO23 .... 3 H3
Hill La CHCH/BSGR BH23 .... 197 L8
  CHCH/BSGR BH23 .... 223 K6
  EPSF GU31 .... 93 H6
  ROWN SO16 .... 106 C5
  RWIN SO21 .... 54 E7
  WSHM SO15 .... 106 D7
Hillside Cl CHFD SO53 .... 81 J2
  FUFL SO22 .... 16 B3
  RSAL SP5 .... 19 J6
Hillside Crs CHAM PO6 .... 162 D7
Hillside Dr CHCH/BSGR BH23 .... 222 B4
Hillside Gdns WIMB BH21 .... 217 G3
Hillside Rd BKME/WDN BH12.. 219 K7
  FUFL SO22 .... 16 B1
  LYMN SO41 .... 228 A5
  VWD BH31 .... 144 E1
  WIMB BH21 .... 217 G3
Hillsley Rd CHAM PO6 .... 162 D6
Hillson Dr FHAM PO15 .... 160 A5
Hill St PLE BH15 .... 233 H6
  ROMY SO51 .... 104 B2
Hilltop FUFL SO22 .... 16 B3
Hilltop Cl FERN BH22 .... 193 M1
Hilltop Crs CHAM PO6 .... 163 H6
Hilltop Dr ITCH SO19 .... 133 C4
Hilltop Gdns HORN PO8 .... 116 C5
Hilltop Rd FERN BH22 .... 193 M1
  WIMB BH21 .... 217 J3
  WVILLE PO7 .... 162 A6
Hillview HORN PO8 .... 141 G3
Hill Vw PSF GU32 .... 61 J7
Hill View Rd FERN BH22 .... 194 A2
  FHAM/PORC PO16 .... 162 A1
  ROMY SO51 .... 22 B8
  ROMY SO51 .... 51 H2
Hillview Rd FAWY SO45 .... 155 K5
  NBNE BH10 .... 220 C5
Hill Wy RGWD BH24 .... 169 J3
The Hillway CHFD SO53 .... 81 J1
  FHAM/PORC PO16 .... 162 A8
Hilly Cl RWIN SO21 .... 56 A4
Hillyfields ROWN SO16 .... 105 H4
Hilsea Crs NEND PO2 .... 187 L1
Hiltingbury Av HAV PO9 .... 165 L3 [2]
Hiltingbury Cl CHFD SO53 .... 53 J7
Hiltingbury Rd CHFD SO53.... 53 G7
Hiltom Rd RGWD BH24 .... 170 D3
Hilton Cl PLE BH15 .... 233 M2
Hilton Rd GPORT PO12 .... 11 H3
  NMIL/BTOS BH25 .... 225 M4
Hinchliffe Rd PLE BH15 .... 232 E6 [1]
Hinkler Rd ITCH SO19 .... 133 C3
Hinton Cl HAV PO9 .... 165 C4
Hinton Crs ITCH SO19 .... 133 J3
Hinton Flds WINC SO23 .... 17 H2
Hinton HI NARL SO24 .... 30 E4
Hinton Manor La HORN PO8 .... 115 K7
Hinton Rd BMTH BH1 .... 14 F6
Hinton Wood Av
  CHCH/BSGR BH23 .... 224 C7
Hintonwood La
  CHCH/BSGR BH23 .... 224 C6
Hipley Rd HAV PO9 .... 165 C1
Hirst Rd FAWY SO45 .... 155 M5
Hispano Av FHAM PO15 .... 159 H1
Hither Gn EMRTH PO10 .... 161 J6
Hitherwood Cl HORN PO8 .... 140 F6
Hives Wy LYMN SO41 .... 228 B2 [2]
Hoadlands EPSF GU31 .... 63 M4
Hoad's HI WHAM PO17 .... 136 F6
Hobart Dr FAWY SO45 .... 155 M5
Hobart Rd NMIL/BTOS BH25 .. 225 K6
Hobb La HEND SO30 .... 134 B2
Hobbs Pk RGWD BH24 .... 169 K4
Hobbs Rd BKME/WDN BH12 .. 219 G4
Hobby Cl HSEA PO3 .... 187 L4
Hobson Wy FAWY SO45 .... 180 B5 [2]
Hoburne Gdns
  CHCH/BSGR BH23 .... 224 C7
Hoburne La CHCH/BSGR BH23 .. 223 M8
Hockham Ct HAV PO9 .... 165 G1
Hockley Cl CHAM PO6 .... 163 H8 [2]
Hockley Link RWIN SO21 .... 26 D6
Hocombe Dr CHFD SO53 .... 53 G6
Hocombe Park Cl CHFD SO53 .. 53 G6
Hocombe Rd CHFD SO53 .... 53 G6
Hocombe Wood Rd CHFD SO53 .. 52 F6
Hodder Cl CHFD SO53 .... 81 G3 [1]

Hodges Cl CFDH BH17 .... 233 K1
  HAV PO9 .... 9 G1
Hoeford Cl FHAM/PORC PO16.. 184 F2
Hoe La ROMY SO51 .... 79 H6
Hoe Rd BPWT SO32 .... 111 K1
Hoe St WVILLE PO7 .... 138 D2
The Hoe LSOL/BMARY PO13 .... 185 J7 [2]
Hogarth Cl ROMY SO51 .... 51 G7
Hoggarth Cl EPSF GU31 .... 63 M4
Hogs Lodge La HORN PO8 .... 90 C6
Hogue Av NBNE BH10 .... 220 B3
Holbein Rd FHAM/PORC PO16 .... 7 J7
  PSEA PO1 .... 13 K1
Holbury Cl CHAR BH8 .... 221 J5
Holbury Ct HAV PO9 .... 165 M3 [3]
Holbury Dro FAWY SO45 .... 179 M4
Holbury La RSAL SP5 .... 20 C1
Holcot La HSEA PO3 .... 188 A4
Holcroft Rd ITCH SO19 .... 133 J3
Holdaway Cl WINC SO23 .... 17 H1
Holdenbury Ct HSEA PO3 .... 188 A3
Holdenhurst Av LTDN BH7 .... 237 H1
Holdenhurst Cl HORN PO8 .... 116 B7 [1]
Holdenhurst Rd BMTH BH1 .... 15 J5
  CHAR BH8 .... 221 L5
  CHAR BH8 .... 236 C2
Holden La RWIN SO21 .... 57 L1
Holding La NARL SO24 .... 29 K6
Hole La BPWT SO32 .... 110 F7
  WVILLE PO7 .... 113 L8
Holes Bay Rd PLE BH15 .... 233 G4
Holes Cl LYMN SO41 .... 226 D4
Holkham Cl ROWN SO16 .... 105 K5 [1]
Hollam Cl FHAM/STUB PO14 .. 159 M8
Hollam Crs FHAM/STUB PO14.. 159 M8
Hollam Dr FHAM/STUB PO14.. 159 M8
Hollam Pk HLER SO31 .... 158 D5
Holland Pl
  LSOL/BMARY PO13 .... 185 H6 [2]
  ROWN SO16 .... 106 A7
Holland Rd ENEY PO4 .... 13 L4
  ITCH SO19 .... 132 B6
  TOTT SO40 .... 129 C2
Hollands Wood Dr
  NMIL/BTOS BH25 .... 225 M3
Holland Wy BDST BH18 .... 217 K3
Hollies Cl LYMN SO41 .... 200 F7
Hollingbourne Cl WEND SO18.. 107 J8
Hollist La EPSF GU31 .... 93 J4 [1]
Holliman Dr ROMY SO51 .... 50 C8
Holloway Av BWD BH11 .... 219 K3
Hollow La HISD PO11 .... 213 K5
Hollybank LSOL/BMARY PO13.. 208 D3
Holly Bank Rd HORN PO8 .... 141 C3
Hollybank Crs FAWY SO45 .... 155 K4
Hollybank La EMRTH PO10 .... 166 D4
Hollybank Rd FAWY SO45 .... 155 K5
Hollybrook Av ROWN SO16 .... 106 B5
Hollybrook Cl ROWN SO16 .... 106 A7
Hollybrook Gdns HLER SO31 .. 158 E3
Hollybrook Rd ROWN SO16 .... 106 B6
Holly Cl FAWY SO45 .... 179 L1
  HLER SO31 .... 158 C5
  RGWD BH24 .... 169 H4
Holly Dell ROWN SO16 .... 106 D3
Holly Dr WVILLE PO7 .... 164 E2
Holly Gdns CHCH/BSGR BH23 .. 223 H7
  HEND SO30 .... 108 C5
  LYMN SO41 .... 242 B3
Holly Green Ri BWD BH11 .... 219 J4 [2]
Holly Gv FHAM/PORC PO16 .... 160 C4
  VWD BH31 .... 144 B3
Holly Hatch Rd TOTT SO40 .... 129 J2
Holly Hedge La CFDH BH17 .... 218 A4
Holly HI ROWN SO16 .... 106 D3
Holly Hill Cl ROWN SO16 .... 106 D3
Holly Hill La HLER SO31 .... 158 A4
Holly La CHCH/BSGR BH23 .... 225 C6
  LYMN SO41 .... 202 F7
  NMIL/BTOS BH25 .... 226 A4
Holly Oak Rd ROWN SO16 .... 105 M5
Holly Rd FAWY SO45 .... 180 C8
  TOTT SO40 .... 128 F6
Holly St GPORT PO12 .... 11 H3
Hollywell Dr CHAM PO6 .... 186 F1
Hollywood Cl NBAD SO52 .... 79 L4
Hollywood La LYMN SO41 .... 228 B3
Holman Cl HORN PO8 .... 140 E6
Holm Cl RGWD BH24 .... 147 C2
Holmdale Rd GPORT PO12 .... 209 K1
Holmefield Av
  FHAM/STUB PO14 .... 184 D2
Holme Rd CHCH/BSGR BH23 .. 224 F8
Holmesland Dr HEND SO30 .. 134 D1
Holmesland La HEND SO30 .. 134 D1
Holmfield Av LTDN BH7 .... 237 H1
Holmgrove
  FHAM/STUB PO14 .... 159 G5 [2]
Holm Hill La
  CHCH/BSGR BH23 .... 224 F1
Holmhurst Av
  CHCH/BSGR BH23 .... 224 D7
Holmsley Cl LYMN SO41 .... 227 M6
  WEND SO18 .... 133 G1 [1]
Holmsley Rd
  NMIL/BTOS BH25 .... 199 H6
Holmwood Garth RGWD BH24 .. 147 C1 [3]
Holne Ct ENEY PO4 .... 212 A5
Holnest Rd CFDH BH17 .... 218 B7
Holst Wy WVILLE PO7 .... 164 D3
Holt Cl WHAM PO17 .... 136 D4
Holt Ct ITCH SO19 .... 132 C4
Holt Down EPSF GU31 .... 64 A5
Holt Gdns HAV PO9 .... 141 M5
Holt Rd BKME/WDN BH12 .... 234 E2 [2]
  WIMB BH21 .... 144 B8
  WSHM SO15 .... 131 K1
Holworth Cl BWD BH11 .... 219 J5 [1]
Holyborne Rd ROMY SO51 .... 79 C1
Holybourne Rd HAV PO9 .... 8 E1
Holyrood Av PTSW SO17 .... 107 G6
Holyrood Cl WVILLE PO7 .... 164 E1 [2]
Holywell Cl CFDH BH17 .... 218 B5
Home Farm Cl FAWY SO45 .... 155 M6
Home Farm Wy VWD BH31 .... 144 C2

Homefield ROMY SO51 .... 50 F7 [2]
Home Field Dr ROWN SO16 .. 105 H3
Homefield Rd CHAM PO6 .... 188 A1
  EMRTH PO10 .... 166 F4
Homefield Wy HORN PO8 .... 116 A2
Home Md WVILLE PO7 .... 139 K5
Homer Cl HORN PO8 .... 140 C6
  LSOL/BMARY PO13 .... 184 F8
Homer Farm La FAWY SO45.. 206 C2
Home Rd BWD BH11 .... 219 M2
Home Rule Rd HLER SO31 .... 158 E4
Homeside Rd
  MOOR/WNTN BH9 .... 220 E6
Home Wy EPSF GU31 .... 64 B5
Homewell HAV PO9 .... 8 E5
Homewood Cl
  NMIL/BTOS BH25 .... 226 A5 [2]
Honeybourne Crs SBNE BH6... 237 M4
Honeycritch La PSF GU32 .... 35 G5
Honey La FHAM PO15 .... 160 B3
  RGWD BH24 .... 172 C6
Honeysuckle Cl FUFL SO22 .... 26 C4
  HLER SO31 .... 158 E3
  LSOL/BMARY PO13 .... 184 F5 [1]
Honeysuckle Ct WVILLE PO7 .. 164 D3 [2]
Honeysuckle La CFDH BH17 .. 217 K7
Honeysuckle Rd ROWN SO16 .. 107 G4
Honeysuckle Wy
  CHCH/BSGR BH23 .... 223 M8 [2]
  NBAD SO52 .... 80 F2
Honeywood Cl HSEA PO3 .... 187 K4
Hood Cl HLER SO31 .... 158 F4
  NBNE BH10 .... 219 M7
Hood Crs NBNE BH10 .... 219 M7
Hood Rd WEND SO18 .... 107 M8 [2]
Hook Cl CHFD SO53 .... 52 F6
Hook Crs CHFD SO53 .... 52 F6
Hooke Cl CFDH BH17 .... 218 C6
Hook La HLER SO31 .... 182 E1
Hook Park Rd HLER SO31 .... 182 D5
Hook Rd ROMY SO51 .... 52 D5
Hook's La HAV PO9 .... 8 B2
Hook Water Rd CHFD SO53 .... 52 F6
Hookwood La ROMY SO51 .... 52 E6
Hope La HEND SO30 .... 108 D6
Hope St PSEA PO1 .... 211 G2
Hopfield Cl WVILLE PO7 .... 164 C1
Hopfield Ms WVILLE PO7 .... 164 C2 [1]
The Hop Gdn EPSF GU31 .... 92 F5
Hopkins Cl CHAM PO6 .... 162 C8 [2]
  CHAR BH8 .... 221 L6
Horace Rd BOSC BH5 .... 236 D4
Hordle La LYMN SO41 .... 226 D8
Hordle Rd HAV PO9 .... 165 G4
Horlock Rd BROC SO42 .... 175 L6 [1]
Hornbeam Rd HEND SO30 .... 134 B2 [3]
Hornbeam Gdns HEND SO30 .. 108 C6 [1]
Hornbeam Wy HAV PO9 .... 9 K1
  NBAD SO52 .... 80 D3
Hornby Cl HLER SO31 .... 158 B8
Hornchurch Rd ROWN SO16 .. 105 L3
Horndean Rd EMRTH PO10 .. 166 B4
  HORN PO8 .... 116 D8
Hornet Cl FHAM PO15 .... 6 A3
  GPORT PO12 .... 11 H6
Hornet Rd EMRTH PO10 .... 190 E5
  FHAM/STUB PO14 .... 184 D3
Horning Rd BKME/WDN BH12.. 234 E3
Horns Dro ROWN SO16 .... 105 K2
Horns HI BPWT SO32 .... 113 G6
Horsa Cl SBNE BH6 .... 237 H4
Horsa Ct SBNE BH6 .... 237 K4
Horsa Rd SBNE BH6 .... 237 K4
Horsea La NEND PO2 .... 187 H4
Horsea Rd NEND PO2 .... 187 J3
Horsebridge Rd HAV PO9 .... 165 L4
Horsebridge Wy ROWN SO16 .. 105 K2
Horsecroft ROMY SO51 .... 50 E8 [1]
Horsefair Cl ROMY SO51 .... 78 D1
Horsepost La WVILLE PO7 .... 115 G6
Horse Sands Cl ENEY PO4 .... 212 B5
Horseshoe Cl
  FHAM/STUB PO14 .... 159 H6 [1]
  WIMB BH21 .... 192 F2
Horseshoe Dr ROMY SO51 .... 51 H6
Horseshoe Ldg HLER SO31 .... 158 C7
Horsham Av NBNE BH10 .... 220 A2
Horton Cl MOOR/WNTN BH9 .. 221 G5
Horton Rd LSOL/BMARY PO13.. 185 G4
  RGWD BH24 .... 169 G2
Horton Wy ELGH SO50 .... 82 E7
  VWD BH31 .... 144 B3
Hosker Rd BOSC BH5 .... 237 G3
Hospital La FHAM/PORC PO16.. 186 C2
Hospital Rd BPWT SO32 .... 111 M4
Hotspur Cl FAWY SO45 .... 155 K3
Houchin St BPWT SO32 .... 111 H1
Houghton Cl HAV PO9 .... 165 M2 [3]
Houlton Rd PLE BH15 .... 233 K4
Hound Cl HLER SO31 .... 157 H3
Hound Rd HLER SO31 .... 157 H2
Hound Road Gdns HLER SO31.. 157 H3
Hounds Wy WIMB BH21 .... 192 F3
Hound Wy HLER SO31 .... 157 H2
Houndwell Pl SHAM SO14 .... 5 H4
Hounsdown Av TOTT SO40 .. 129 K3
Hounsdown Cl TOTT SO40 .. 129 K3
Hounslow Cl PLE BH15 .... 232 D6
House Cl RWIN SO21 .... 54 F7
House Farm Rd GPORT PO12.. 209 J4
Hoveton Gv CHFD SO53 .... 53 G8
Howard Cl CHCH/BSGR BH23.. 238 C2
  CHFD SO53 .... 81 J4
  ELGH SO50 .... 83 H6
  RGWD BH24 .... 172 E5 [2]
  WEND SO18 .... 107 K4 [1]
Howard Rd CHAR BH8 .... 236 B1
  NEND PO2 .... 187 J4
  VWD BH31 .... 144 D2
  WSHM SO15 .... 131 H2
Howard's Gv WSHM SO15 .... 106 B8
Howards Md LYMN SO41 .... 227 M6
Howe Cl CHCH/BSGR BH23 .. 238 C3
  NMIL/BTOS BH25 .... 225 K5
Howe La VWD BH31 .... 144 C3

Howe Rd LSOL/BMARY PO13.. 209 C2
Howerts Cl HLER SO31 .... 182 B1
Howeth Cl NBNE BH10 .... 220 B5
Howeth Rd NBNE BH10 .... 220 A4
Howgare Rd RSAL SP5 .... 40 A6
Howlett Cl LYMN SO41 .... 228 A4
Howton Cl NBNE BH10 .... 220 A3 [3]
Howton Rd NBNE BH10 .... 220 A3
Hoxley Rd NBNE BH10 .... 220 A4
Hoyal Cl PLE BH15 .... 232 C5
Hoylake Cl
  LSOL/BMARY PO13 .... 185 G7 [1]
Hoylake Rd CHAM PO6 .... 164 A7
Hoylecroft Cl FHAM PO15 .... 6 C1
Hubert Rd WINC SO23 .... 26 D4
Hudson Cl BKME/WDN BH12.. 219 G6
  LSOL/BMARY PO13 .... 209 G2 [3]
  RGWD BH24 .... 147 C2 [3]
Hudson Ct TOTT SO40 .... 129 H2 [2]
Hudson Davies Cl LYMN SO41.. 202 D7
Hudson Rd SSEA PO5 .... 13 G4
Hugh's Cl FAWY SO45 .... 180 C7
Hulbert Rd HAV PO9 .... 164 F3
  WVILLE PO7 .... 164 E1
Hull Crs BWD BH11 .... 219 H4
Hulles Wy NBAD SO52 .... 79 L4
Hull Rd BWD BH11 .... 219 H4
Hull Wy BWD BH11 .... 219 H4
Hulse Rd WSHM SO15 .... 106 E8
Hulton Cl ITCH SO19 .... 132 B7
Humber Cl
  FHAM/STUB PO14 .... 183 M5 [3]
Humber Gdns HLER SO31 .... 133 L7 [2]
Humber Rd FERN BH22 .... 194 E2
The Hummicks BROC SO42 .... 178 F8 [1]
Hundred Acres Rd
  WHAM PO17 .... 137 L3
Hundred La LYMN SO41 .... 228 D1
The Hundred ROMY SO51 .... 78 D1
  WVILLE PO7 .... 140 B7 [3]
Hungerfield Cl
  CHCH/BSGR BH23 .... 197 L7
Hungerford HLER SO31 .... 157 K1
Hungerford HI FBDG SP6 .... 123 G3
Hungerford La CHAR BH8 .... 221 H5 [1]
Hunt Av HLER SO31 .... 157 C2
Hunter Cl CHCH/BSGR BH23 .. 238 F1
  FAWY SO45 .... 179 M2 [3]
  LSOL/BMARY PO13 .... 209 H1
  WIMB BH21 .... 193 G2 [2]
Hunters Cha BPWT SO32 .... 112 B5 [1]
Hunters Cl VWD BH31 .... 145 G3
Hunters Crs ROMY SO51 .... 51 H6
  TOTT SO40 .... 128 F2
Hunters HI TOTT SO40 .... 129 H5
Hunters Ldg FHAM PO15 .... 159 M8
Hunters Ride HLER SO31 .... 164 C1
Hunters Wy ELGH SO50 .... 82 F6
Huntfield Rd
  MOOR/WNTN BH9 .... 220 F5
Huntingdon Cl
  FHAM/STUB PO14 .... 159 G7 [3]
  TOTT SO40 .... 104 D7
Huntingdon Dr WIMB BH21 .. 192 C7
Huntingdon Gdns
  CHCH/BSGR BH23 .... 222 D6
Huntley Cl CHAM PO6 .... 162 F7 [2]
Huntly Rd TWDS BH3 .... 235 J2
Huntly Wy WEND SO18 .... 132 D1
Hunton Cl ROWN SO16 .... 106 C5
Hunt Rd CHCH/BSGR BH23 .. 223 K8
  PLE BH15 .... 233 H6
Huntsbottom La LISS GU33 .... 37 G5
Hunts Pond Rd HLER SO31 .. 158 F4
Huntvale Rd
  MOOR/WNTN BH9 .... 220 F5
The Hurdles
  CHCH/BSGR BH23 .... 222 C8 [5]
  FHAM/STUB PO14 .... 159 H6
Hurdle Wy RWIN SO21 .... 26 B8
Hurlingham Gdns
  ROWN SO16 .... 106 F3 [1]
Hurn Cl RGWD BH24 .... 170 D3
Hurn Ct HAV PO9 .... 165 M2
Hurn Court La
  CHCH/BSGR BH23 .... 221 K2
Hurn La RGWD BH24 .... 170 D3
Hurn Rd CHCH/BSGR BH23.... 222 C5
  RGWD BH24 .... 170 A8
Hurn Wy CHCH/BSGR BH23 .. 222 B7
Hurricane Dr ROWN SO16 .... 105 K2
Hursley Cl LTDN BH7 .... 222 A8 [1]
Hursley Dr FAWY SO45 .... 206 C1
Hursley Rd CHFD SO53 .... 81 C1
  HAV PO9 .... 165 H3
  RWIN SO21 .... 53 C4
Hurstbourne Av
  CHCH/BSGR BH23 .... 224 C7
Hurstbourne Cl HAV PO9 .... 165 H2 [3]
Hurst Cl CHCH/BSGR BH23 .. 225 C6
  CHFD SO53 .... 80 F4
  FHAM/STUB PO14 .... 183 L7
  TOTT SO40 .... 104 E8
Hurstdene Rd CHAR BH8 .... 221 G6
Hurst Gn LSOL/BMARY PO13.. 184 F6
Hurst Green Cl HORN PO8 .. 140 F6
  ITCH SO19 .... 132 C7
Hurst HI PSTN BH14 .... 234 B8
Hurst La ALTN GU34 .... 34 A5
  RWIN SO21 .... 83 M2
Hurst Rd LYMN SO41 .... 242 D5
  RGWD BH24 .... 146 E7
Hurstville Dr WVILLE PO7 .... 164 D1
Hurstwood Av EMRTH PO10.. 167 J8
Hussar Cl CHCH/BSGR BH23 .. 237 L1 [1]
Hussey Cl WINC SO23 .... 3 H2
Hutwood Rd ROWN SO16 .... 80 F8
Huxley Cl HLER SO31 .... 158 F6
Huxley Rd FAWY SO45 .... 155 G5
Hyacinth Cl CFDH BH17 .... 217 K7
Hyde Abbey Rd WINC SO23 .... 3 G6
Hyde Church La WINC SO23 .... 3 G5
Hyde Cl LYMN SO41 .... 200 F6
  TOTT SO40 .... 128 F1
  WINC SO23 .... 2 F5

WSHM SO15 .... 106 B7
Hyden Farm La HORN PO8 .... 123 G3
Hyde Farm Cl WIMB BH21 .... 115 J2
Hyde Park Rd SSEA PO5 .... 13 H5
Hyde Rd NBNE BH10 .... 220 A3
Hyde St SSEA PO5 .... 13 G5 [2]
  WINC SO23 .... 3 G5
The Hyde NMIL/BTOS BH25 .. 225 J4 [2]
Hylton Rd PSF GU32 .... 63 L7
Hymans Wy TOTT SO40 .... 129 J1
Hynesbury Rd
  CHCH/BSGR BH23 .... 239 H2
Hyssop Cl FHAM PO15 .... 159 H1
Hythe By-pass FAWY SO45 .. 154 F4
Hythe Rd CHAM PO6 .... 163 J8
  PLE BH15 .... 233 M1
  TOTT SO40 .... 130 D8

I

Ibbertson Cl CHAR BH8 .... 221 K6
Ibbertson Rd CHAR BH8 .... 221 K7
Ibbertson Wy CHAR BH8 .... 221 K6
Ibbett Rd NBNE BH10 .... 220 A6
Ibbotson Wy TOTT SO40 .... 129 H3
Ibsen Cl HLER SO31 .... 135 G8
Ibsley Cl CHAR BH8 .... 236 B2
Ibsley Dro RGWD BH24 .... 122 E7
Ibsley Gv HAV PO9 .... 8 A1
Icarus PI WVILLE PO7 .... 164 D6
Iddesleigh Rd TWDS BH3 .... 235 L2
Idsworth Cl HORN PO8 .... 141 H2
Idsworth Rd HORN PO8 .... 140 F6
  HSEA PO3 .... 187 L8
Iford Ct HAV PO9 .... 165 M2 [3]
Iford Gdns LTDN BH7 .... 237 H1
Iford La SBNE BH6 .... 237 K1
Ilex Crs HLER SO31 .... 158 D5
Ilex Wk HISD PO11 .... 214 D5
Iley La LYMN SO41 .... 243 H1
Ilford Cl SBNE BH6 .... 237 L2
Imber Cl ITCH SO19 .... 133 G4 [2]
Imber Dr CHCH/BSGR BH23 .. 224 D8
Imber Rd WINC SO23 .... 3 L6
Imber Wy ITCH SO19 .... 133 G4
Imbrecourt CCLF BH13 .... 245 K1
Imperial Av WSHM SO15 .... 130 F1
Imperial Rd SHAM SO14 .... 131 M3
Implacable Rd
  LSOL/BMARY PO13 .... 208 D3
Ingersley Ri HEND SO30 .... 108 C7
Ingledene Cl GPORT PO12 .... 10 E4
  HAV PO9 .... 8 A3
Ingle Gln FAWY SO45 .... 155 L7 [3]
Ingle Gn TOTT SO40 .... 104 A7
  PLE BH15 .... 232 D4 [1]
Inglesham Wy PLE BH15 .... 232 D5 [1]
Ingleside HLER SO31 .... 157 G1
Ingleside Cl
  FHAM/STUB PO14 .... 159 M8 [3]
Ingleton Rd ROWN SO16 .... 105 J7
Inglewood Av CHAR BH8 .... 221 K7
Inglewood Dr
  NMIL/BTOS BH25 .... 225 M6
Inglis Rd SSEA PO5 .... 13 L5
Ingoldfield La WHAM PO17 .. 138 A1
Ingworth Rd
  BKME/WDN BH12 .... 234 F3
Inhams La WVILLE PO7 .... 139 H4
Inhurst Av WVILLE PO7 .... 140 E8
Inhurst Rd NEND PO2 .... 187 H6
Inkerman Rd ITCH SO19 .... 132 B5
Inlands Rd RCCH PO18 .... 167 K7
Inmans La PSF GU32 .... 64 A3
Insley Crs WIMB BH21 .... 217 J3
International Wy ITCH SO19 .. 132 C8
Inveravon CHCH/BSGR BH23.. 238 C4
Inverclyde Rd PSTN BH14 .... 234 B4
Invergordon Av CHAM PO6 .. 187 M1
Inverkip Cl
  LSOL/BMARY PO13 .... 208 C1 [1]
Inverleigh Rd SBNE BH6 .... 237 H2
Inverness Av FHAM PO15 .... 6 C2
Inverness Rd NEND PO2 .... 211 J1
Inwood Rd LISS GU33 .... 36 F4
Ionic Cl CHFD SO53 .... 81 L1
Iping Av HAV PO9 .... 165 H3
Iping Cl MIDH GU29 .... 67 H5
Iping Rd LIPH GU30 .... 38 E5
Ipley Wy FAWY SO45 .... 155 L6
Ipswich Rd WBNE BH4 .... 235 L4
Ireland Wy WVILLE PO7 .... 164 C3
Iris Rd MOOR/WNTN BH9 .. 220 D7
  ROWN SO16 .... 107 G4
Ironbridge Crs HLER SO31 .. 158 E2
Ironbridge La ENEY PO4 .... 212 A4
Iron Mill Cl FHAM PO15 .... 6 A1
Ironmill La FHAM PO15 .... 159 M3
Irvine Cl FHAM/PORC PO16 .... 7 J5
Irvine Wy CHCH/BSGR BH23 .. 223 J8
Irving Rd ROWN SO16 .... 105 L7
  SBNE BH6 .... 237 J3
Irwell Cl CHFD SO53 .... 80 F3
Isaacs Cl BKME/WDN BH12 .. 235 C1
Isambard Brunel Rd PSEA PO1.. 13 C4
Isis Cl ROWN SO16 .... 105 K8
Island View Av
  CHCH/BSGR BH23 .... 239 H2
Island View Cl LYMN SO41 .. 242 D5
Island View Rd
  NMIL/BTOS BH25 .... 240 C1
Island View Ter NEND PO2 .. 187 G6
Islay Gdns CHAM PO6 .... 163 K7
Itchen Av ELGH SO50 .... 82 C5
Itchen Cl PSF GU32 .... 63 K6
  ROMY SO51 .... 76 C3
Itchenor Rd HISD PO11 .... 214 D6
Itchen Rd HAV PO9 .... 165 M2 [3]
Itchenside Cl WEND SO18 .. 107 L4
Itchen Wy WEND SO18 .... 82 A2
  ITCH SO19 .... 132 B5
  RWIN SO21 .... 17 J3
  WINC SO23 .... 3 M1
Itchin Cl TOTT SO40 .... 129 H2
Ithica Cl HISD PO11 .... 213 L4

Ivamy Pl BWD BH11 — 219 K6
Ivanhoe Rd WSHM SO15 — 106 C7
Ivor Cl FAWY SO45 — 180 A4
Ivor Rd PLE BH15
  WIMB BH21 — 217 H4
Ivy Cl FUFL SO22 — 26 D3
  RGWD BH24 — 169 H4
  TOTT SO40 — 104 D6
Ivy Ct WVILLE PO7 — 164 B4
Ivy Dene ITCH SO19 — 133 H4
Ivydene Crs RCCH PO18 — 191 M1
Ivydene Gdns HORN — 140 E4
Ivy La HEND SO30 — 108 A6
  RGWD BH24 — 146 E5
Ivy Rd PTSW SO17 — 107 H8
  WIMB BH21 — 192 B8
Iwerne Cl MOOR/WNTN BH9 — 220 F4

J

Jacaranda Cl FHAM PO15 — 159 J5
Jack Cockerill Wy SSEA PO5 — 211 H7
Jackdaw Cl HORN PO8 — 140 C4
Jackdaw Ri ELGH SO50 — 81 J7
Jackie Wigg Gdns TOTT SO40 — 129 K1
Jackmans HI RWIN SO21 — 55 M1
Jackson Cl CHAM PO6 — 188 A2
Jackson Rd BKME/WDN BH12 — 234 D2
Jacobean Cl CHCH/BSGR BH23 — 224 F7
Jacobs Cl HORN PO8 — 116 B3
  ROMY SO51 — 78 F1
Jacob's Gutter La TOTT SO40 — 129 K3
Jacobs Rd PLE BH15 — 232 D6
Jacob's St PSEA PO1 — 211 G2
Jacobs Wk TOTT SO40 — 129 J4
Jacomb Pl
  LSOL/BMARY PO13 — 185 H6
Jacqueline Av WVILLE PO7 — 164 B4
Jacqueline Rd
  BKME/WDN BH12 — 234 A1
Jago Rd PSEA PO1 — 210 D2
Jamaica Cl GPORT PO12 — 11 G4
Jamaica Pl GPORT PO12 — 11 G4
Jamaica Rd GPORT PO12 — 11 G4
James Callaghan Dr — 185 K8
Jaundrells Cl NMIL/BTOS BH25 — 226 A5
Java Dr FHAM PO15 — 159 G1
Java Rd SHAM SO14 — 5 K9
Javelin Rd EMRTH PO10 — 190 E5
J Av FAWY SO45 — 180 D2
Jay Cl FHAM/STUB PO14 — 183 M4
  HORN PO8 — 140 E1
Jay's Ct CHCH/BSGR BH23 — 224 F8
Jealous La LYMN SO41 — 201 L6
Jefferson Av CHAR BH8 — 236 C2
Jeffries Cl ROWN SO16 — 105 K3
Jellicoe Av GPORT PO12 — 10 B7
Jellicoe Dr CHCH/BSGR BH23 — 238 E2
Jenkins Cl HEND SO30 — 134 C1
Jenkins Gv HSEA PO3 — 211 M1
Jenner Wy ROMY SO51 — 51 H8
Jennings Rd PSTN BH14 — 234 B6
  TOTT SO40 — 104 F8
Jephcote Rd BWD BH11 — 219 K4
Jermyns La ROMY SO51 — 51 H5
Jerome Ct ITCH SO19 — 133 H2
Jerram Cl GPORT PO12 — 10 A5
Jerrett's La ROWN SO16 — 105 J5
Jersey Cl BKME/WDN BH12 — 219 L8
  FHAM/STUB PO14 — 184 B7
  ROWN SO16 — 105 K5
Jersey Rd BKME/WDN BH12 — 219 H7
  NEND PO2 — 187 J1
Jervis Court La BPWT SO32 — 85 M8
Jervis Dr GPORT PO12 — 209 M2
Jervis Rd NEND PO2 — 187 G6
Jesmond Av CHCH/BSGR BH23 — 224 D8
Jesmond Gv HLER SO31 — 158 E7
Jessamine Rd ROWN SO16 — 106 A6
Jessica Av VWD BH31 — 194 F8
Jessica Cl WVILLE PO7 — 140 F7
Jessie Rd ENEY PO4 — 13 M4
  GPORT PO12 — 10 D4
  HAV PO9 — 165 C5
Jessop Cl FAWY SO45 — 155 H3
Jessopp Cl NBNE BH10 — 220 D4
Jessopp Rd WIMB BH21 — 192 F2
Jetty Rd FAWY SO45 — 180 F3
Jewell Rd CHAR BH8 — 221 K7
Jewry St WINC SO23 — 3 G7
Jex Blake Cl ROWN SO16 — 106 A4
Jimmy Brown Av WIMB BH21 — 168 C3
Jinny La ROMY SO51 — 50 D3
Joanna Rd RSAL SP5 — 72 C1
Jockey La ELGH SO50 — 82 D3
Jodrell Cl HORN PO8 — 141 G1
John Bunyan Cl FHAM PO15 — 135 G8
Johnson Rd WIMB BH21 — 193 L1
Johnson St SHAM SO14 — 5 H3
Johnson Vw FHAM PO15 — 159 J3
Johns Rd FHAM/PORC PO16 — 7 J9
  ITCH SO19 — 132 B5
Johnstone Rd
  CHCH/BSGR BH23 — 238 D2
Johnston Rd PLE BH15 — 233 J1
John St SHAM SO14 — 5 H6
Jolliffe Av PLE BH15 — 233 J4
Jolliffe Rd PLE BH15 — 233 J4
Jonathan Cl LYMN SO41 — 201 C5
Jonathan Cl FHAM PO15 — 6 C5
Jones La FAWY SO45 — 155 K4
Jopps Cnr CHCH/BSGR BH23 — 223 C4
Jordans La LYMN SO41 — 201 C5
Joseph St GPORT PO12 — 11 H3
Joshua Cl PLE BH15 — 232 D6
Jowitt Dr NMIL/BTOS BH25 — 225 J6
Joyce Dickson La RGWD BH24 — 170 F2
Joys La LYMN SO41 — 203 J8
Joys Rd WIMB BH21 — 144 C8
Jubilee Av CHAM PO6 — 162 C8
Jubilee Cl ELGH SO50 — 81 L7
  RGWD BH24 — 147 G8
  WIMB BH21 — 217 J1

Jubilee Ct FHAM/STUB PO14 — 184 E1
  LYMN SO41 — 200 F7
Jubilee Crs PSTN BH14 — 234 C3
Jubilee Gdns NBNE BH10 — 220 B6
  WEND SO18 — 132 E1
Jubilee Pth HAV PO9 — 165 G7
Jubilee Rd ENEY PO4 — 211 K5
  FBDG SP6 — 97 H7
  FHAM/PORC PO16 — 162 B8
  GPORT PO12 — 10 E2
  PSTN BH14 — 234 C3
  ROMY SO51 — 50 D8
  WIMB BH21 — 217 J2
  WVILLE PO7 — 140 C8
Jubilee Ter SSEA PO5 — 12 F5
Julia Cl CHCH/BSGR BH23 — 224 D8
Julian Cl ROWN SO16 — 106 C2
Julian Rd ITCH SO19 — 132 F5
Julie Av FHAM PO15 — 6 C5
Juliet Ct WVILLE PO7 — 140 E8
Julius Cl CHFD SO53 — 81 K2
Julyan Av BKME/WDN BH12 — 219 L8
Jumar Cl ITCH SO19 — 182 B1
Jumpers Av CHCH/BSGR BH23 — 222 C8
Jumpers Rd CHCH/BSGR BH23 — 222 C8
Junction Rd
  MOOR/WNTN BH9 — 220 D8
  TOTT SO40 — 129 L1
  UPTN BH16 — 232 C4
Juniper Cl FERN BH22 — 168 A4
  FUFL SO22 — 26 C3
  LYMN SO41 — 227 M6
  NBAD SO52 — 79 L3
  WIMB BH21 — 144 C8
Juniper Rd HORN PO8 — 116 B7
  WEND SO18 — 132 D1
Juniper Sq HAV PO9 — 8 F5
Jupiter Cl ROWN SO16 — 105 K4
Jura Cl FHAM PO15 — 163 K7
Jurds Lake Wy ITCH SO19 — 132 E7
Jurd Wy HLER SO31 — 133 K7
Justin Cl FHAM/STUB PO14 — 6 C6
Justin Gdns NBNE BH10 — 220 C4
Justinian Cl CHFD SO53 — 81 L1
Jute Cl FHAM/PORC PO16 — 161 M7
Jutland Cl FHAM PO15 — 158 F1

K

Kamptee Copse
  NMIL/BTOS BH25 — 225 M2
Kanes HI ITCH SO19 — 133 K2
Kangaw Pl PLE BH15 — 232 C6
Karen Av CHAM PO6 — 188 A2
Kassassin St ENEY PO4 — 211 L6
Kassel Cl WVILLE PO7 — 140 F7
Katherine Chance Cl
  CHCH/BSGR BH23 — 223 G5
Kathleen Rd ITCH SO19 — 132 F5
Katrina Gdns HISD PO11 — 213 L3
Katrine Crs CHFD SO53 — 80 F1
Katterns Cl CHCH/BSGR BH23 — 222 C6
Kayak Cl HLER SO31 — 158 C7
Kayleigh Cl TOTT SO40 — 129 H2
Kealy Rd GPORT PO12 — 209 L2
Kearsney Av NEND PO2 — 187 J5
Keats Av CHAM PO6 — 162 C7
  LYMN SO41 — 242 C3
Keats Cl FUFL SO22 — 26 B4
  HORN PO8 — 140 D4
Keats Rd WEND SO18 — 133 G2
Keble Cl CHFD SO53 — 81 H4
Keble Rd CHFD SO53 — 81 H4
Keble St FUFL SO22 — 26 B2
Keeble Cl NBNE BH10 — 220 B2
Keeble Crs NBNE BH10 — 220 B2
Keeble Rd NBNE BH10 — 220 B2
Keel Cl HSEA PO3 — 211 M1
  LSOL/BMARY PO13 — 209 H1
Keepers Cl CHFD SO53 — 81 G2
Keepers La ROMY SO51 — 21 H6
  WIMB BH21 — 193 J3
The Keep FHAM/PORC PO16 — 162 C8
  FHAM/PORC PO16 — 186 B1
Kefford Cl HORN PO8 — 140 F2
Keighley Av BDST BH18 — 217 K6
Keith Cl GPORT PO12 — 209 M2
Keith Rd TWDS BH3 — 235 H2
Kelburn Cl CHFD SO53 — 81 G1
Kellaway Rd CFDH BH17 — 218 D8
Kellett Rd WSHM SO15 — 106 C8
Kelly Cl WVILLE PO7 — 140 F7
Kelly Rd WVILLE PO7 — 164 C3
Kelmscott Gdns CHFD SO53 — 52 F7
Kelsall Gdns NMIL/BTOS BH25 — 225 L5
Kelsey Av EMRTH PO10 — 167 J7
Kelsey Cl FHAM/STUB PO14 — 158 F7
  LISS GU33 — 36 F3
Kelvin Cl FAWY SO45 — 155 L5
Kelvin Gv FHAM/PORC PO16 — 162 B8
  HLER SO31 — 157 G2
Kelvin Rd ELGH SO50 — 81 L6
Kemp Rd MOOR/WNTN BH9 — 220 D8
Kempton Pk WVILLE PO7 — 140 F7
Kemshott Cl HAV PO9 — 165 H2
Ken Berry Ct HAV PO9 — 165 M2
Kendal Av HSEA PO3 — 187 L7
  ROWN SO16 — 105 J7
Kendal Cl CHFD SO53 — 81 K1
  HORN PO8 — 140 E4
Kenilworth Cl
  LSOL/BMARY PO13 — 208 D1
  NMIL/BTOS BH25 — 225 M5
Kenilworth Dr ELGH SO50 — 81 M1
Kenilworth Gdns HEND SO30 — 108 D7
Kenilworth Rd SSEA PO5 — 13 K9
  WSHM SO15 — 131 K2
Kenmore Cl TOTT SO40 — 129 H3
Kennard Ct NMIL/BTOS BH25 — 225 K5
Kennard Rd NMIL/BTOS BH25 — 225 K4
Kennart Rd CFDH BH17 — 232 F1
Kennedy Av FHAM PO15 — 160 C4
Kennedy Cl WVILLE PO7 — 164 C4
Kennedy Crs GPORT PO12 — 209 J6
Kennedy Rd ROWN SO16 — 105 L5

Kennel Rd FUFL SO22 — 16 A4
Kennet Cl GPORT PO12 — 10 E9
  WEND SO18 — 108 A5
Kennet Rd PSF GU32 — 63 K6
Kennett Rd ROMY SO51 — 51 H8
Ken Rd SBNE BH6 — 237 K4
Kensington Cl ELGH SO50 — 82 C3
Kensington Dr WCLF BH2 — 14 B4
Kensington Flds FAWY SO45 — 155 H6
Kensington Gdns
  FHAM/STUB PO14 — 159 G6
Kensington Pk LYMN SO41 — 242 B4
Kensington Rd GPORT PO12 — 11 G5
  NEND PO2 — 187 K6
Kenson Gdns ITCH SO19 — 132 E4
Kent Gv FHAM/PORC PO16 — 186 A2
Kentidge Rd WVILLE PO7 — 164 B3
Kentish Rd WSHM SO15 — 131 G1
Kent La RGWD BH24 — 122 C7
Kent Rd BKME/WDN BH12 — 234 D2
  CHFD SO53 — 81 H5
  LSOL/BMARY PO13 — 184 F4
  PTSW SO17 — 107 H7
  SSEA PO5 — 13 G6
Kent St PSEA PO1 — 12 D2
  SHAM SO14 — 5 L1
Kenwood Rd
  FHAM/PORC PO16 — 186 B3
Kenwyn Cl WEND SO18 — 108 A6
Kenya Rd FHAM/PORC PO16 — 185 M1
Kenyon Cl PLE BH15 — 233 L1
Kenyon Rd NEND PO2 — 187 K6
  PLE BH15 — 233 K1
Keppel Cl RGWD BH24 — 170 F1
Kerley Rd WCLF BH2 — 14 D7
Kerrfield FUFL SO22 — 2 A9
Kerrfield Ms FUFL SO22 — 2 B8
Kern Cl ROWN SO16 — 105 L5
Kerry Cl CHFD SO53 — 81 H2
  LYMN SO41 — 228 A5
Kesteven Wy WEND SO18 — 107 M8
Kestrel Av BWPT SO32 — 84 F8
  BPWT SO32 — 109 M7
  FERN BH22 — 193 M1
  FHAM/STUB PO14 — 183 M4
  FUFL SO22 — 26 C4
  HORN PO8 — 116 B4
  ROWN SO16 — 106 A3
  TOTT SO40 — 130 C7
  UPTN BH16 — 216 F1
Kestrel Dr CHCH/BSGR BH23 — 238 F2
Kestrel Pl CHAM PO6 — 188 D1
Kestrel Rd ELGH SO50 — 81 K6
Kestrel Wy FBDG SP6 — 121 M3
Keswick Av HSEA PO3 — 187 L8
Keswick Rd BOSC BH5 — 236 E4
  ITCH SO19 — 132 B5
  NMIL/BTOS BH25 — 225 M3
Keswick Wy VWD BH31 — 144 C3
Kettering Ter NEND PO2 — 187 J4
Kevlyn Crs HLER SO31 — 133 K7
Kewlake La ROMY SO51 — 102 C6
Kew La HLER SO31 — 157 L1
Keydell Cl HORN PO8 — 140 E3
Keyes Cl BKME/WDN BH12 — 219 K7
  CHCH/BSGR BH23 — 238 E2
  LSOL/BMARY PO13 — 185 G4
Keyes Rd LSOL/BMARY PO13 — 185 G5
Keyhaven Cl
  LSOL/BMARY PO13 — 184 E6
Keyhaven Dr HAV PO9 — 165 G3
Keyhaven Rd LYMN SO41 — 242 D4
Keynsham Rd ITCH SO19 — 132 F2
Keysworth Av
  NMIL/BTOS BH25 — 240 E1
Keysworth Rd UPTN BH16 — 232 B4
Khandala Gdns WVILLE PO7 — 164 D4
Khartoum Rd PTSW SO17 — 106 F6
Khyber Rd BKME/WDN BH12 — 234 C3
Kidmore La WVILLE PO7 — 139 K2
Kielder Cl CHFD SO53 — 80 F1
Kielder Gv
  LSOL/BMARY PO13 — 185 H6
Kilford Ct HEND SO30 — 134 E2
Kilham La FUFL SO22 — 26 A2
Kilmarnock Rd
  MOOR/WNTN BH9 — 220 D7
Kilmeston Rd NARL SO24 — 30 C4
Kilmington Wy
  CHCH/BSGR BH23 — 224 D8
Kilmiston Cl PSEA PO1 — 211 J1
Kilmiston Dr
  FHAM/PORC PO16 — 162 A7
Kiln Cl FAWY SO45 — 155 J5
Kiln HI BPWT SO32 — 113 G8
Kiln La EPSF SO21 — 91 H4
  ROMY SO51 — 51 G2
  RSAL SP5 — 73 K1
  RWIN SO21 — 54 A6
  WVILLE PO7 — 138 B4
Kiln Rd FHAM/PORC PO16 — 160 D4
Kilnside WVILLE PO7 — 139 K5
Kilnyard Ct TOTT SO40 — 104 C7
Kilpatrick Cl NEND PO2 — 187 H8
Kilwich Wy FHAM/PORC PO16 — 185 M2
Kimberley Cl
  CHCH/BSGR BH23 — 222 D8
  ELGH SO50 — 83 J6
Kimberley Rd ENEY PO4 — 211 L6
  PSTN BH14 — 234 A5
  SBNE BH6 — 237 H2
Kimber Rd BWD BH11 — 219 K5
Kimbers PSF GU32 — 63 K4
Kimbolton Rd HSEA PO3 — 211 L1
Kimbridge Crs HAV PO9 — 165 L2
Kimbridge La ROMY SO51 — 49 L1
Kimmeridge Av
  BKME/WDN BH12 — 219 G8
Kimpton Cl
  LSOL/BMARY PO13 — 208 D2
Kimpton Ct HAV PO9 — 165 M2
Kineton Rd WSHM SO15 — 106 D7
King Albert St PSEA PO1 — 211 H2

King Alfred Pl WINC SO23 — 3 G5
King Alfred Ter WINC SO23 — 3 G5
King Arthur's Ct CHAM PO6 — 164 B8
King Charles St PSEA PO1 — 12 C4
King Cl RGWD BH24 — 169 K4
King Cup Av HLER SO31 — 158 D6
Kingcup Cl BDST BH18 — 217 J6
King Edward Av
  NEND PO2 — 187 H6
  ROWN SO16 — 105 M8
King Edward's Crs
  NEND PO2 — 187 H6
Kingfisher Cl FERN BH22 — 168 D6
  HAV PO9 — 141 M7
  HISD PO11 — 214 A6
  HLER SO31 — 157 L4
  HORN PO8 — 140 C4
  SBNE BH6 — 237 K2
Kingfisher Copse HLER SO31 — 158 D5
Kingfishers FHAM/PORC PO16 — 161 K8
The Kingfishers VWD BH31 — 144 E3
Kingfisher Wy
  CHCH/BSGR BH23 — 238 F3
  RGWD BH24 — 146 F7
  ROMY SO51 — 50 E8
  TOTT SO40 — 130 C7
King George Av EPSF GU31 — 63 L4
  MOOR/WNTN BH9 — 220 D6
King George Rd
  FHAM/PORC PO16 — 186 A1
King George's Av WSHM SO15 — 130 D2
King Henry I St PSEA PO1 — 12 F2
King John Av BWD BH11 — 219 H3
  FHAM/PORC PO16 — 185 M1
Kingland Rd PLE BH15 — 233 J6
King Richard 1 Rd PSEA PO1 — 12 F3
King Richard Dr BWD BH11 — 219 H5
Kings Arms La RGWD BH24 — 170 D1
Kings Arms Rw RGWD BH24 — 170 D1
King's Av CHCH/BSGR BH23 — 237 L2
  FUFL SO22 — 26 D3
  HLER SO31 — 157 J5
  PSTN BH14 — 234 C6
Kingsbere Av NBNE BH10 — 219 M6
Kingsbere Rd PLE BH15 — 233 K3
Kingsbridge La PSTN BH14 — 234 B5
Kingsbury's La RGWD BH24 — 170 D2
Kingsclere Av HAV PO9 — 165 H3
  ITCH SO19 — 132 D7
Kingsclere Cl ITCH SO19 — 132 D7
King's Cl CHFD SO53 — 81 J1
  FERN BH22 — 168 B7
  HAV PO9 — 141 L6
  LYND SO43 — 151 K3
  RWIN SO21 — 54 F1
Kings Copse Av HEND SO30 — 134 B1
Kings Copse Rd FAWY SO45 — 180 A8
  HEND SO30 — 134 A3
Kingscote Rd CHAM PO6 — 162 D6
  HORN PO8 — 140 B5
Kings Crs LYMN SO41 — 228 B4
  PSTN BH14 — 234 D6
Kingscroft Ct HAV PO9 — 8 B5
King's Croft La HAV PO9 — 165 G7
Kingsdown Pl PSEA PO1 — 12 D1
Kingsdown Rd WVILLE PO7 — 140 A6
Kingsdown Wy WEND SO18 — 107 L6
Kingsey Av EMRTH PO10 — 166 C8
Kingsfernsden La PSF GU32 — 63 M3
Kings Fld HLER SO31 — 133 L7
Kingsfield LYMN SO41 — 228 E6
  RGWD BH24 — 170 E1
Kings Field Gdns HLER SO31 — 133 L7
Kingsfold Av WEND SO18 — 107 L5
Kingsford Cl RSAL SP5 — 73 J3
Kingsgate St WINC SO23 — 26 E3
Kings La LYMN SO41 — 201 J8
  PSF GU32 — 34 B6
  RWIN SO21 — 27 L2
Kingsley Av SBNE BH6 — 237 M4
Kingsley Cl SBNE BH6 — 237 M4
Kingsley Gdns TOTT SO40 — 128 F1
Kingsley Pl FUFL SO22 — 26 D3
Kingsley Rd ENEY PO4 — 211 M5
  GPORT PO12 — 209 K1
  WSHM SO15 — 130 F1
Kingsmead WHAM PO17 — 137 G1
Kingsmead Av
  FHAM/STUB PO14 — 184 B7
Kings Mede HORN PO8 — 140 F2
Kingsmill Cl GPORT PO12 — 10 B4
Kingsmill Rd CFDH BH17 — 233 K1
King's Park Dr LTDN BH7 — 236 D2
King's Park Rd BMTH BH1 — 236 D2
  WSHM SO15 — 131 L2
Kings Ride FAWY SO45 — 206 C1
Kings Rd CHFD SO53 — 81 H2
  EMRTH PO10 — 166 C8
  FHAM/PORC PO16 — 7 J6
  FUFL SO22 — 26 B2
  GPORT PO12 — 10 F3
  HISD PO11 — 213 L3
  LSOL/BMARY PO13 — 208 C1
  LYMN SO41 — 228 B4
  NMIL/BTOS BH25 — 226 A4
  PSEA PO1 — 210 D2
  PSF GU32 — 63 K4
  SSEA PO5 — 12 F5
King's Saltern Rd LYMN SO41 — 228 E6
Kings Somborne Rd
  ROMY SO51 — 23 J7
King's Ter EMRTH PO10 — 166 D8
  PSEA PO1 — 12 F5
Kingston HLER SO31 — 157 G1
Kingston Crs NEND PO2 — 187 H8
Kingston Gdns FHAM PO15 — 160 B4
Kingston Pk LYMN SO41 — 228 A6
Kingston Rd GPORT PO12 — 10 B1
  NEND PO2 — 187 J8
  PLE BH15 — 233 J4
  WSHM SO15 — 131 H2
King St EMRTH PO10 — 166 F5
  GPORT PO12 — 11 K2
  SHAM SO14 — 5 H5

  SSEA PO5 — 12 F4
King's Wy BPWT SO32 — 56 D5
  BPWT SO32 — 84 D5
  BPWT SO32 — 112 F3
  FHAM/PORC PO16 — 161 K8
  RWIN SO21 — 28 C4
  WHAM PO17 — 138 D7
  WINC SO23 — 3 H4
  WVILLE PO7 — 138 D3
Kingsway CHFD SO53 — 81 J1
  HISD PO11 — 189 L5
Kingsway Cl CHCH/BSGR BH23 — 222 D7
Kingsway Gdns CHFD SO53 — 53 K8
The Kingsway
  FHAM/PORC PO16 — 162 A8
Kingswell Cl NBNE BH10 — 220 B6
Kingswell Gdns NBNE BH10 — 219 M6
Kingswell Gv NBNE BH10 — 219 M6
Kingswell Rd NBNE BH10 — 220 A6
Kingswell St PSEA PO1 — 13 G1
Kingswood TOTT SO40 — 130 C7
Kingsworthy Rd HAV PO9 — 165 K5
King William St PSEA PO1 — 210 E2
Kinnell Cl EMRTH PO10 — 166 D8
Kinross Crs CHAM PO6 — 187 M1
Kinross Rd TOTT SO40 — 129 K1
  TWDS BH3 — 235 K2
Kinsbourne Av NBNE BH10 — 220 B6
Kinsbourne Cl ITCH SO19 — 133 K2
Kinsbourne Ri ITCH SO19 — 133 K3
Kinsbourne Wy ITCH SO19 — 133 J2
Kinson Av PLE BH15 — 233 M2
Kinson Gv NBNE BH10 — 220 A3
Kinson Park Rd NBNE BH10 — 220 B2
Kinson Rd NBNE BH10 — 219 L7
Kintyre Rd FHAM/PORC PO16 — 163 K7
Kinver Cl ROMY SO51 — 51 G7
Kipling Ct ITCH SO19 — 132 D7
Kipling Rd ELGH SO50 — 81 L5
  NEND PO2 — 187 J5
  PSTN BH14 — 234 A3
Kirby Cl PLE BH15 — 233 L2
Kirby Rd NEND PO2 — 187 J6
Kirby Wy SBNE BH6 — 237 J4
Kirk Gdns TOTT SO40 — 129 K3
Kirkham Av
  CHCH/BSGR BH23 — 223 G5
Kirkstall Rd ENEY PO4 — 211 J7
Kirkway BDST BH18 — 217 M4
Kirtley Cl CHAM PO6 — 188 A2
Kirton Rd CHAM PO6 — 188 A1
Kitchener Crs CFDH BH17 — 217 M6
Kitchener Rd PTSW SO17 — 107 H5
Kitchers Cl LYMN SO41 — 200 F5
Kite Cl HORN PO8 — 140 C4
Kites Croft Cl
  FHAM/STUB PO14 — 159 G7
Kitnocks HI BPWT SO32 — 110 D8
Kitscroft Rd NBNE BH10 — 220 A3
Kittiwake Cl
  LSOL/BMARY PO13 — 184 F6
Kittiwake Cl SBNE BH6 — 237 J2
Kitt's La NARL SO24 — 32 B6
Kitwalls La LYMN SO41 — 242 B4
Kivernell Rd LYMN SO41 — 242 B4
Kiwi Cl PLE BH15 — 233 K5
Knapp Cl CHCH/BSGR BH23 — 222 E8
Knapp La ROMY SO51 — 52 C4
Knapp Mill Av
  CHCH/BSGR BH23 — 222 E8
Knapps Hard PSF GU32 — 60 A3
Knatchbull Cl ROMY SO51 — 78 C4
Knellers La TOTT SO40 — 129 H4
Knight Cl WINC SO23 — 3 G3
Knighton Heath Cl
  BWD BH11 — 219 J4
Knighton Heath Rd
  BWD BH11 — 219 J4
Knighton La BWD BH11 — 219 H1
Knighton Pk NMIL/BTOS BH25 — 225 J4
Knighton Rd ITCH SO19 — 132 D5
  RSAL SP5 — 40 C1
Knights Bank Rd
  FHAM/STUB PO14 — 183 K7
Knights Cl HLER SO31 — 158 C7
Knights Rd BWD BH11 — 219 H3
Knightstone Gra FAWY SO45 — 155 L6
Knightwood Av HAV PO9 — 165 L3
  LYND SO43 — 151 K3
Knightwood Cl
  CHCH/BSGR BH23 — 224 C8
  LYND SO43 — 151 K3
  TOTT SO40 — 128 F6
Knightwood Rd FAWY SO45 — 155 M6
  NBAD SO52 — 52 E8
Knole Gdns BMTH BH1 — 236 C4
Knole Rd BMTH BH1 — 236 C3
Knoll Gdns RGWD BH24 — 169 K4
Knoll La WIMB BH21 — 216 F1
Knottgrass Rd HLER SO31 — 158 C6
Knowland Dr LYMN SO41 — 242 C3
Knowle HI ELGH SO50 — 82 A1
Knowle La ELGH SO50 — 83 K8
Knowle Rd BROC SO42 — 175 J6
Knowles Cl CHCH/BSGR BH23 — 238 D1
Knowles Meadow LISS GU33 — 37 G7
Knowlton Gdns
  MOOR/WNTN BH9 — 220 F5
Knowlton Rd CFDH BH17 — 218 D6
Knowsley Crs CHAM PO6 — 187 L1
Knowsley Rd CHAM PO6 — 187 K1
Knox Rd HAV PO9 — 8 B4
  NEND PO2 — 187 G7
Knyght Cl ROMY SO51 — 78 F2
Knyveton Rd BMTH BH1 — 15 M4
Kootenay Av WEND SO18 — 133 J1
Kooyong Cl RSAL SP5 — 77 G6
Kynegils Rd FUFL SO22 — 2 B3
Kynon Cl GPORT PO12 — 186 A8
Kyrchil La WIMB BH21 — 192 C2
Kyrchil Wy WIMB BH21 — 192 C1
Kytes La BPWT SO32 — 110 A3

L

Labrador Dr PLE BH15 — 233 J7

Laburnum Av *CHAM* PO6 .... **188** A1
Laburnum Cl *FERN* BH22 .... **193** M2
  NBAD SO52 .... **79** M3
  VWD BH31 .... **145** G3
Laburnum Crs *FAWY* SO45 .. **155** M8 🔟
Laburnum Dr *LYMN* SO41 .... **227** J8 🔟
Laburnum Gv *ELGH* SO50 .... **81** M5 🔟
  HISD PO11 .... **213** M4
  NEND PO2 .... **187** J7
Laburnum Rd
  FHAM/PORC PO16 .... **184** F2
  HEND SO30 .... **134** B2
  ROWN SO16 .... **107** H4
  WVILLE PO7 .... **164** C2
Lacey Crs *PSTN* BH14 .... **233** M2
Lackford Av *TOTT* SO40 .... **129** L2
Lacon Cl *WEND* SO18 .... **107** K8
Lacy Cl *WIMB* BH21 .... **192** B2
Lacy Dr *WIMB* BH21 .... **192** B2
Ladram Rd *GPORT* PO12 .... **209** J4
Lady Betty's Dr *FHAM* PO15 .... **159** J4
Ladybridge Rd *WVILLE* PO7 .... **164** A4
Ladycross Rd *FAWY* SO45 .... **155** L6
Ladysmith Cl
  CHCH/BSGR BH23 .... **238** D1
Ladywood *ELGH* SO50 .... **81** L2
Lagado Cl *PSTN* BH14 .... **234** B8
Lagland St *PLE* BH15 .... **233** H7
Lagoon Rd *PSTN* BH14 .... **234** A7
Laidlaw Cl *BKME/WDN* BH12 .. **219** M8
Lainston Cl *FUFL* SO22 .... **16** B6
Lake Av *PLE* BH15 .... **232** C7
Lake Crs *PLE* BH15 .... **232** D5
Lake Dr *PLE* BH15 .... **232** C6
Lake Farm Cl *HEND* SO30 .... **109** H8 🔟
Lake Grove Rd
  NMIL/BTOS BH25 .... **225** L4
Lakeland Gdns *TOTT* SO40 .. **130** C7 🔟
Lakelands Dr *WSHM* SO15 .. **131** G2 🔟
Lake Rd *BPWT* SO32 .... **110** E8
  BWD BH11 .... **219** M2
  CHFD SO53 .... **53** K8
  ITCH SO19 .... **132** B6
  PLE BH15 .... **232** D6
  PSEA PO1 .... **211** G2 🔟
  VWD BH31 .... **144** E4
Lakeside *ELGH* SO50 .... **81** L8
  LSOL/BMARY PO13 .... **208** D4
  RGWD BH24 .... **171** G2
  WHAM PO17 .... **160** C5
Lakeside Av *HSEA* PO3 .... **211** M4
  ROWN SO16 .... **105** K3
Lakeside Gdns *HAV* PO9 .... **9** G2
Lakeside Rd *CCLF* BH13 .... **234** F7
Lakesmere Rd *HORN* PO8 .... **141** L2
The Lakes *BPWT* SO32 .... **111** M4
Lakeview Dr *RGWD* BH24 .... **171** G2
Lakewood Cl *CHFD* SO53 .... **53** J8
Lakewood Rd
  CHCH/BSGR BH23 .... **224** D7
  CHFD SO53 .... **53** J8
  TOTT SO40 .... **129** L2
Lamberhurst Cl *ITCH* SO19 .... **132** C5
Lambert Cl *FHAM/STUB* PO14 .... **6** B7
Lambourn Cl *FHAM/STUB* PO14 .... **6** B7
Lambourne Dr *HLER* SO31 .... **158** E5
Lambourne La *LIPH* GU30 .... **39** C5
Lambourne Rd *WEND* SO18 .... **108** A6
Lambourn Sq *CHFD* SO53 .... **80** F2
Lambs Cl *CFDH* BH17 .... **218** A7
Lammas Rd *FAWY* SO45 .... **155** L5
Lampeter Av *CHAM* PO6 .... **163** M8
Lampton Gdns
  MOOR/WNTN BH9 .... **220** D7 🔟
Lancaster Cl *BDST* BH18 .... **217** K3
  CHCH/BSGR BH23 .... **239** C1
  FHAM/PORC PO16 .... **161** M7
  HLER SO31 .... **133** L7 🔟
  LSOL/BMARY PO13 .... **208** F4
Lancaster Dr *BDST* BH18 .... **217** J3
  VWD BH31 .... **144** C2
Lancaster Rd *ROWN* SO16 .... **105** L5
Lancaster Wy *WVILLE* PO7 .... **164** D2
Lancer Cl *CHCH/BSGR* BH23 .... **237** L1
Lance's Hl *ITCH* SO19 .... **132** D1
Lander Cl *PLE* BH15 .... **233** J7
Landford Gdns *CHAR* BH8 .... **221** H6 🔟
Landford Wy *CHAR* BH8 .... **221** H6
Landguard Rd *WSHM* SO15 .... **131** H2
Landon Rd *LSOL/BMARY* PO13 .. **185** H8
Landport Ter *PSEA* PO1 .... **12** F4
  SSEA PO5 .... **12** F4 🔟
Landport Vw *PSEA* PO1 .... **211** G2 🔟
Landsdowne St *SSEA* PO5 .... **12** F4 🔟
The Landsdown Rbt *BMTH* BH1 .. **15** H5
Landseer Rd *CCLF* BH13 .... **235** H5 🔟
  ITCH SO19 .... **133** G5
Lands End Rd *HLER* SO31 .... **157** M1
Lane End Dr *EMRTH* PO10 .... **166** D8
Lanehays Rd *FAWY* SO45 .... **155** K5
Lanesbridge Cl *TOTT* SO40 .... **128** D3
Lanes End *FHAM/STUB* PO14 .. **184** A6
The Lanes *NMIL/BTOS* BH25 .... **225** L3
The Lane *ENEY* PO4 .... **211** K6
  FAWY SO45 .... **180** F5 🔟
  GPORT PO12 .... **10** D9
Langbar Cl *ITCH* SO19 .... **132** C2
Langbrook Cl *HAV* PO9 .... **8** E7
Langdale Av *CHAM* PO6 .... **187** M1
Langdale Rd *ROWN* SO16 .... **105** L8
Langdon Rd *PSTN* BH14 .... **234** B4
Langdown Lawn *FAWY* SO45 .. **155** L6
Langdown Lawn Cl
  FAWY SO45 .... **155** L6 🔟
Langdown Rd *FAWY* SO45 .... **155** L5
Langford La *RSAL* SP5 .... **45** L2
Langford Rd *NEND* PO2 .... **211** K1
Langham Cl *NBAD* SO52 .... **79** L1
Langhorn Rd *ROWN* SO16 .... **107** H4
Langley Cha *RGWD* BH24 .... **149** J5
Langley Gdn *FBDG* SP6 .... **97** M5
Langley Lodge Gdns
  FAWY SO45 .... **206** D1 🔟
Langley Rd *CHCH/BSGR* BH23 .. **224** C7
  NEND PO2 .... **187** J8
  PSTN BH14 .... **234** E4

WSHM SO15 .... **130** E2
Langrish Cl *HAV* PO9 .... **165** L2 🔟
Langrish Rd *ROWN* SO16 .... **106** A4
Langside Av *BKME/WDN* BH12 .. **219** L8 🔟
Langstone Av *HAV* PO9 .... **8** E8
Langstone High St *HAV* PO9 .. **189** K2 🔟
Langstone Rd *HAV* PO9 .... **8** E9
  HSEA PO3 .... **211** L2
Langstone Wk
  FHAM/STUB PO14 .... **160** A8
  LSOL/BMARY PO13 .... **184** F6
Langton Cl *FUFL* SO22 .... **2** C5
  NMIL/BTOS BH25 .... **225** M8
Langton Rd *BPWT* SO32 .... **85** G8
  LTDN BH7 .... **236** E3
Lankhills Rd *WINC* SO23 .... **2** F3
Lansdown Av
  FHAM/PORC PO16 .... **186** B2
Lansdowne Av *WINC* SO23 .... **26** E3
  WVILLE PO7 .... **163** M5
Lansdowne Cl *ROMY* SO51 .... **50** D8 🔟
Lansdowne Gdns *BMTH* BH1... **15** H3
Lansdowne Hl *SHAM* SO14 .... **4** F5 🔟
Lansdowne Rd *BMTH* BH1... **15** G1
  WSHM SO15 .... **130** E1
Lantana Cl *WVILLE* PO7 .... **164** D2 🔟
Lanyard Dr *LSOL/BMARY* PO13 .. **209** H2 🔟
Lapthorn Cl
  LSOL/BMARY PO13 .... **184** F4
Lapwing Cl *GPORT* PO12 .... **209** M1 🔟
  HORN PO8 .... **140** F1
Lapwing Dr *TOTT* SO40 .... **104** B8
Lapwing Gv
  FHAM/PORC PO16 .... **161** K8 🔟
Lapwing Rd *WIMB* BH21 .... **192** C1
Lara Cl *CHAR* BH8 .... **221** H5
Larch Av *FAWY* SO45 .... **180** A3
Larch Cl *CFDH* BH17 .... **217** J7
  HEND SO30 .... **108** C5
  LSOL/BMARY PO13 .... **208** E3 🔟
  LYMN SO41 .... **226** D5 🔟
  RGWD BH24 .... **169** L4
Larchdale Cl *HLER* SO31 .... **158** B8 🔟
Larches Gdns *FHAM* PO15 .... **160** A7
Larchfield Wy *HORN* PO8 .... **141** G3
Larch Rd *ROWN* SO16 .... **105** M5
Larch Rw *FBDG* SP6 .... **98** C6
  HLER SO31 .... **133** K8
Larchwood Av *HAV* PO9 .... **164** F4
Larchwood Rd *TOTT* SO40 .... **129** G2
Larcombe Rd *PSF* GU32 .... **63** J7
Larg Dr *FUFL* SO22 .... **16** B4
Lark Hill Ri *FUFL* SO22 .... **26** C1
Larkhill Rd *HSEA* PO3 .... **187** K4
Lark Rd *CHCH/BSGR* BH23 .. **238** F2 🔟
Larks Cl *FERN* BH22 .... **193** M1
Larksfield Av
  MOOR/WNTN BH9 .... **220** F5
Larkshill Cl *NMIL/BTOS* BH25 .. **225** M4
Larkspur Cha *ITCH* SO19 .... **133** J3
Larkspur Cl *BPWT* SO32 .... **111** M3
  HLER SO31 .... **158** D6 🔟
Larkspur Dr *TOTT* SO40 .... **130** C3
Larkspur Drive *NBAD* SO52 .... **80** E2
Larkspur Gdns *FAWY* SO45 .... **179** M4
  HEND SO30 .... **134** A2 🔟
Larks Ri *FERN* BH22 .... **193** M1
Lascelles Rd *LTDN* BH7 .... **237** G2
Laser Cl *HLER* SO31 .... **158** C7
Lashly Meadow *WVILLE* PO7 .. **114** B5
Latch Farm Av
  CHCH/BSGR BH23 .... **222** E8 🔟
Latchmore Dr *FAWY* SO45 .... **155** G4
Latchmore Forest Gv
  HORN PO8 .... **140** D5
Latchmore Gdns *HORN* PO8 .. **140** C5
Latelie Cl *HLER* SO31 .... **157** G3 🔟
Latham Cl *WSHM* SO15 .... **130** F1
Latham Rd *ELGH* SO50 .... **83** G6
  ROMY SO51 .... **50** F8 🔟
Latimer Ct *HSEA* PO3 .... **187** M4 🔟
Latimer Rd *MOOR/WNTN* BH9.... **220** D8
Latimers Cl *CHCH/BSGR* BH23 .. **224** D7
Latimer St *ROMY* SO51 .... **78** D1
  SHAM SO14 .... **5** H6
Lauder Cl *EMRTH* PO10 .... **167** H6
Launcelyn Cl *NBAD* SO52 .... **79** L5
Launceston Dr *ELGH* SO50 .... **81** L3 🔟
Laundry La *LYMN* SO41 .... **242** D4
Laundry Rd *ROWN* SO16 .... **106** A6
Laurel Cl *CHCH/BSGR* BH23 .... **224** B7
  FAWY SO45 .... **155** J5
  HLER SO31 .... **158** F4 🔟
  LYMN SO41 .... **226** C4
  RGWD BH24 .... **169** J4
  WIMB BH21 .... **217** H2
Laurel Dr *BDST* BH18 .... **217** H4
Laurel Gdns *BDST* BH18 .... **218** A4
  HLER SO31 .... **158** F4
Laurel La *RGWD* BH24 .... **169** J5
Laurel Rd *HLER* SO31 .... **158** F4
  HORN PO8 .... **141** G4
The Laurels *FERN* BH22 .... **194** A1
Lauriston Dr *CHFD* SO53 .... **53** G7 🔟
Laurus Cl *WVILLE* PO7 .... **164** E3
Lavant Cl *HORN* PO8 .... **140** F7
Lavant Dr *HAV* PO9 .... **9** G1
Lavant St *PSF* GU32 .... **63** K4
Lavender Cl *ITCH* SO19 .... **132** D3 🔟
  VWD BH31 .... **145** G3
Lavender Rd *CHAR* BH8 .... **221** H4
  LYMN SO41 .... **226** C5
  WVILLE PO7 .... **164** C2
Lavender Wy *BDST* BH18 .... **217** H5
Laverock Lea
  FHAM/PORC PO16 .... **162** A7
Laverstoke Cl *ROWN* SO16 .. **105** K2 🔟
Lavey's La *FHAM* PO15 .... **159** M2
Lavington Gdns *NBAD* SO52 .. **79** L6 🔟
Lavinia Rd *BKME/WDN* BH12.. **234** B1
  GPORT PO12 .... **10** D2
Lawford Rd *MOOR/WNTN* BH9.... **220** D5
Lawn Cl *TOTT* SO40 .... **104** D8
Lawn Cl *LSOL/BMARY* PO13 .. **185** H7 🔟
  LYMN SO41 .... **242** D4
Lawn Dr *HLER* SO31 .... **158** E6

Lawn Rd *ELGH* SO50 .... **82** A3
  FUFL SO22 .... **16** B3
  LYMN SO41 .... **227** M5
  LYMN SO41 .... **242** D4
  PTSU SO17 .... **107** G8
Lawns Cl *WIMB* BH21 .... **193** G2
Lawnside Rd *WSHM* SO15 .... **105** M8
Lawns Rd *WIMB* BH21 .... **192** F2
The Lawns *CHCH/BSGR* BH23 .. **224** F8
Lawn St *WINC* SO23 .... **3** H1
Lawnswood Cl *HORN* PO8 .... **140** D6
Lawn Vw *CHCH/BSGR* BH23 .. **225** H3
Lawrence Av *HORN* PO8 .... **140** C6
Lawrence Ct *CHAR* BH8 .... **236** B2 🔟
Lawrence Dr *PSTN* BH14 .... **234** B7
Lawrence Gv *ITCH* SO19 .... **132** D6
Lawrence La *FBDC* SP6 .... **122** F4
Lawrence Rd *FHAM* PO15 .... **6** A4
  RGWD BH24 .... **147** G6
  SSEA PO5 .... **13** L6
Lawson Cl *HLER* SO31 .... **134** B8 🔟
Lawson Rd *BKME/WDN* BH12.. **234** A2
  SSEA PO5 .... **13** L4
Laxton Cl *HLER* SO31 .... **158** F5
Layard Dr *WIMB* BH21 .... **192** B7
Layton Rd *BKME/WDN* BH12.. **234** C3
  LSOL/BMARY PO13 .... **185** G5
Lazy Acre *EMRTH* PO10 .... **167** H8
Leacock Cl *BPWT* SO32 .... **112** A4
Leafy La *FHAM* PO15 .... **159** J2
Lealand Gv *CHAM* PO6 .... **164** B8
Lealand Rd *CHAM* PO6 .... **188** D3
Leamington Crs
  LSOL/BMARY PO13 .... **208** D2
Leamington Rd
  MOOR/WNTN BH9 .... **235** M1
Lea-oak Gdns *FHAM* PO15 .... **6** A2
Leaphill Rd *LTDN* BH7 .... **236** F2
Lea Rd *FAWY* SO45 .... **206** C1
Learoyd Rd *CFDH* BH17 .... **233** J1
Lear Rd *GPORT* PO12 .... **10** F2
Leaside Wy *ROWN* SO16 .... **107** H3
The Lea *VWD* BH31 .... **144** E3
Leatherhead Gdns
  HEND SO30 .... **109** J6 🔟
Lea Wy *BWD* BH11 .... **219** J2
The Leaway *FHAM/PORC* PO16.. **162** B8
Lebanon Rd *WSHM* SO15 .... **130** B1
Lechlade Gdns *FHAM* PO15 .... **160** B4
  LTDN BH7 .... **221** L8
Leckford Cl *FHAM/PORC* PO16.. **162** A7
  WEND SO18 .... **108** C8 🔟
Leckford Rd *HAV* PO9 .... **165** M2
Ledbury Rd *CHAM* PO6 .... **163** G7
  CHCH/BSGR BH23 .... **238** E3
Lederle La *LSOL/BMARY* PO13.. **185** G5
Ledgard Ct *PSTN* BH14 .... **234** A4
Lee Church La *ROMY* SO51 .... **78** E8
Leedam Rd *NBNE* BH10 .... **220** B4
Lee Dro *ROMY* SO51 .... **78** E7
Lee La *ROMY* SO51 .... **78** F4
Leep La *GPORT* PO12 .... **10** F8
Lee Rd *GPORT* PO12 .... **209** L2
Lees Cl *CHCH/BSGR* BH23 .... **222** B4
Leesland Rd *GPORT* PO12 .... **10** C1
Lees La *GPORT* PO12 .... **10** E1
Leeson Rd *LTDN* BH7 .... **236** D1
Legg La *WIMB* BH21 .... **192** B4
Legion Cl *PLE* BH15 .... **232** D6
Legion La *WINC* SO23 .... **17** H1
Legion Rd *HISD* PO11 .... **213** L4
  PLE BH15 .... **232** D6
Leicester Rd *CCLF* BH13 .... **234** F6 🔟
Leicester Wy *WINC* SO23 .... **3** M4
Leigham Vale Rd *SBNE* BH6.... **237** J4
Leigh Common *WIMB* BH21 .. **192** C3
Leigh Gdns *WIMB* BH21 .... **192** B3
Leigh La *WIMB* BH21 .... **192** D3
Leigh Pk *LYMN* SO41 .... **228** A4
Leigh Rd *CHFD* SO53 .... **81** H4
  ELGH SO50 .... **81** K5
  ELGH SO50 .... **82** A5 🔟
  FHAM/PORC PO16 .... **7** G1
  HAV PO9 .... **8** F2
  NMIL/BTOS BH25 .... **225** L4
  PTSW SO17 .... **106** F7
  WIMB BH21 .... **192** B3
Leighton Av *WSHM* SO15 .... **106** A8
Leighton Rd *ITCH* SO19 .... **132** D1
Leith Av *FHAM/PORC* PO16.... **162** B7
Lemon Rd *WSHM* SO15 .... **130** F1
Lendorber Av *CHAM* PO6 .... **187** L1
Lennox Cl *CHFD* SO53 .... **53** K8
  GPORT PO12 .... **10** F9
  ROWN SO16 .... **105** L3
Lennox Rd South *SSEA* PO5 .. **13** J8
Lensyd Gdns *HORN* PO8 .... **140** D2
Lentham Cl *CFDH* BH17 .... **218** B7
Lentune Wy *LYMN* SO41 .... **228** B6
Leofric Ct *ENEY* PO4 .... **212** A5
Leominster Rd *CHAM* PO6 .... **162** F7
Leonard Rd *GPORT* PO12 .... **11** H2
Leopold Dr *BPWT* SO32 .... **111** G1
Leopold St *ENEY* PO4 .... **13** M7
Le Patourel Cl
  CHCH/BSGR BH23 .... **238** C1
Lepe Rd *FAWY* SO45 .... **206** D1
Lerryn Rd *LSOL/BMARY* PO13.. **185** H4
Leslie Rd *MOOR/WNTN* BH9.... **220** C8
  PSTN BH14 .... **233** M5
Lester Av *HAV* PO9 .... **165** G6
Lester Rd *GPORT* PO12 .... **10** A2
Leven Av *WBNE* BH4 .... **14** A2
Leven Cl *CHFD* SO53 .... **52** F3
  WBNE BH4 .... **14** A2
Leventhorpe Ct *GPORT* PO12 .. **11** G4 🔟
Leveson Cl *GPORT* PO12 .... **10** F6
Levet's La *PLE* BH15 .... **233** G6 🔟
Leviathan Cl *FHAM/STUB* PO14.. **184** B6
Lewens Cl *WIMB* BH21 .... **192** A4
Lewes Cl *ELGH* SO50 .... **81** M2
Lewesdon Dr *BDST* BH18 .... **217** K4
Lewin Cl *RWIN* SO21 .... **54** F8
Lewis Cl *FAWY* SO45 .... **155** G6

Lewis Rd *EMRTH* PO10 .... **166** E5
Lewis Silkin Wy *ROWN* SO16 .. **105** M4
Lewry Cl *HEND* SO30 .... **134** A1
Lexby Rd *TOTT* SO40 .... **129** L2
Lexden Gdns *HISD* PO11 .... **213** J4 🔟
Leybourne Av *NBNE* BH10 .... **220** B3
  WEND SO18 .... **107** L8
Leybourne Cl *NBNE* BH10 .... **220** A3
Leydene Av *CHAR* BH8 .... **221** K7
Leydene Cl *CHAR* BH8 .... **221** K7
Leyland Cl *GPORT* PO12 .... **10** F6
Leyland Rd *BKME/WDN* BH12 .. **219** H3
Leyside *CHCH/BSGR* BH23 .... **238** E2
Leyton Rd *SHAM* SO14 .... **132** A2
Liam Cl *HAV* PO9 .... **165** L4
Liberty Rd *BPWT* SO32 .... **112** F8
The Liberty *WVILLE* PO7 .... **139** J5
library Rd *BKME/WDN* BH12.... **234** D3
  FERN BH22 .... **194** B3
  MOOR/WNTN BH9 .... **220** D7
  TOTT SO40 .... **129** L1
Lichen Wy *TOTT* SO40 .... **108** C5
Lichfield Rd *FHAM/STUB* PO14.. **159** G5
  HSEA PO3 .... **211** L2
Liddel Wy *CHFD* SO53 .... **80** F3
Liddiards Wy *WVILLE* PO7 .... **164** C5
Lidiard Gdns *ENEY* PO4 .... **211** M6
Lilac Cl *HAV* PO9 .... **166** A5
  RGWD BH24 .... **146** F8
Lilac Rd *ROWN* SO16 .... **107** G4
Lilliput Rd *PSTN* BH14 .... **234** B8
Lily Av *WVILLE* PO7 .... **163** M6
Lime Av *ITCH* SO19 .... **132** C5
Lime Cl *FAWY* SO45 .... **155** J6
  ITCH SO19 .... **132** C5
  LISS GU33 .... **233** L2
  RWIN SO21 .... **54** F8
Lime Gdns *HEND* SO30 .... **108** C5
Lime Gv *CHAM* PO6 .... **162** F7
  HISD PO11 .... **213** G5
  LYMN SO41 .... **227** H8
Lime Kiln La *FAWY* SO45 .... **179** M4
Limekiln La *BPWT* SO32 .... **85** L5
  PSF GU32 .... **62** A8
  PSF GU32 .... **90** B1
Limes Cl *LISS* GU33 .... **36** E4
The Limes *LSOL/BMARY* PO13.. **185** H7
  TOTT SO40 .... **130** E7 🔟
Lime St *SHAM* SO14 .... **5** H5
Lime Tree Cl *FBDG* SP6 .... **121** K2 🔟
Limetree Wk *WINC* SO23 .... **3** M7
  WINC SO23 .... **17** J8 🔟
Lime Wk *FAWY* SO45 .... **155** J6
Limited Rd *MOOR/WNTN* BH9.... **220** E7
Linacre Rd *ITCH* SO19 .... **133** H4
Lin Brook Dr *RGWD* BH24 .... **147** G6
Linch Rd *HASM* GU27 .... **39** K5
  MIDH GU29 .... **67** L3
Lincoln Av *BMTH* BH1 .... **236** C2
  CHCH/BSGR BH23 .... **222** D6 🔟
Lincoln Cl *FHAM/STUB* PO14 .. **159** G5
Lincoln Ct *WSHM* SO15 .... **106** C2 🔟
Lincoln Ri *HORN* PO8 .... **140** E4
Lincoln Rd *BKME/WDN* BH12.. **234** C1
  PSEA PO1 .... **13** M1
Lincoln Ri *ELGH* SO50 .... **54** A8
Lincoln Ri *HORN* PO8 .... **140** D5
Linda Gv *HORN* PO8 .... **140** D5
Linda Rd *FAWY* SO45 .... **180** F5 🔟
Lindberg Ri *FHAM* PO15 .... **159** J2
Lind Cl *WVILLE* PO7 .... **164** D5
Linden Cl *BPWT* SO32 .... **111** K5
  FERN BH22 .... **194** B7
Linden Dr *LISS* GU33 .... **36** E4
Linden Gdns *HEND* SO30 .... **134** B3
  RGWD BH24 .... **169** J4
Linden Gv *CHFD* SO53 .... **53** H8
  GPORT PO12 .... **10** F6
  HISD PO11 .... **213** L5
Linden Lea *FHAM/PORC* PO16.. **162** A7
Linden Rd *BKME/WDN* BH12.. **234** B2
  FERN BH22 .... **194** B7
  MOOR/WNTN BH9 .... **220** E5
  ROMY SO51 .... **78** E1
  ROWN SO16 .... **105** M4
Lindens Cl *EMRTH* PO10 .... **166** D5
The Lindens *CHCH/BSGR* BH23 .. **223** L3
Linden Wk *NBAD* SO52 .... **79** L3
Linden Wy *HAV* PO9 .... **165** K5 🔟
  HORN PO8 .... **140** E7
  LYMN SO41 .... **228** A4
Lindisfarne Cl *CHAM* PO6 .... **187** L1
Lindley Av *ENEY* PO4 .... **211** L6
Lind Rd *GPORT* PO12 .... **11** G9
Lindsay Rd *CCLF* BH13 .... **234** F4
  ITCH SO19 .... **133** J2
Lindsay Wy *HLER* SO31 .... **158** E2
Lineside *CHCH/BSGR* BH23.... **223** G8
Linford Cl *NMIL/BTOS* BH25 .. **225** L4
Linford Ct *HAV* PO9 .... **165** H1
Linford Crs *ROWN* SO16 .... **106** C5
Linford Rd *RGWD* BH24 .... **147** H7
Ling Dl *ROWN* SO16 .... **106** E1
Ling Rd *BKME/WDN* BH12 .... **218** F7
Lingdale Av *SBNE* BH6 .... **237** J2
Lingfield Gdns *WEND* SO18 .. **107** L6 🔟
Lingwood Av
  CHCH/BSGR BH23 .... **238** E2
Lingwood Cl *ROWN* SO16 .... **106** C1
Lingwood Wk *ROWN* SO16 .. **106** E1 🔟
Linhorns La *NMIL/BTOS* BH25.. **225** L2
Linkenholt Wy *HAV* PO9 .... **165** G3
Link Ri *WIMB* BH21 .... **217** J2
Link Rd *CHAM* PO6 .... **162** F6
  RGWD BH24 .... **147** C7
  ROWN SO16 .... **105** J5
Links Dr *CHCH/BSGR* BH23.... **222** B7
Linkside Av *CHAR* BH8 .... **221** J8
Links La *HAV* PO9 .... **141** M5
Links Rd *FUFL* SO22 .... **2** A5
Links View Av *PSTN* BH14 .... **234** C8
Links View Wy *ROWN* SO16.... **106** D2
The Link *WVILLE* PO7 .... **140** E7 🔟
Linkway *FHAM/STUB* PO14.... **184** A7
Linmead Dr *BWD* BH11 .... **219** L2 🔟
Linnet Cl *EPSF* GU31 .... **64** B6

  HORN PO8 .... **140** C4
  RGWD BH24 .... **171** G2 🔟
Linnet Ct *NMIL/BTOS* BH25 .. **225** K5 🔟
Linnet Rd *CFDH* BH17 .... **217** J8
Linnet Sq *ELGH* SO50 .... **81** J7
The Linnets
  FHAM/PORC PO16 .... **161** K8 🔟
  TOTT SO40 .... **104** B8 🔟
Linnies La *LYMN* SO41 .... **226** E1
Linthorpe Rd *PLE* BH15 .... **233** K4
Linwood Cl *FAWY* SO45 .... **155** K4
Linwood Rd *MOOR/WNTN* BH9.. **236** A1
Lionheart Cl *BWD* BH11 .... **219** H3
Lionheart Wy *HLER* SO31 .... **133** K7
Lions Hill Wy *RGWD* BH24 .... **169** G3
Lions La *RGWD* BH24 .... **169** H4
Lion St *PSEA* PO1 .... **12** E1
Lions Wd *RGWD* BH24 .... **169** J4
Lipizzaner Flds *HLER* SO31 .. **134** A3
Lippen La *BPWT* SO32 .... **59** L5
Lisbon Rd *WSHM* SO15 .... **131** H2
Lisle Court Rd *LYMN* SO41 .... **228** F5
  LYMN SO41 .... **228** E5
Lisle Wy *EMRTH* PO10 .... **166** C5
Liss Rd *ENEY* PO4 .... **211** K4
Litchfield Crs *WEND* SO18 .... **107** L4
Litchfield Rd *FUFL* SO22 .... **16** C4
  WEND SO18 .... **107** L4
Litchford Rd *NMIL/BTOS* BH25.. **226** A4
Lith Av *HORN* PO8 .... **116** B9
Lith La *HORN* PO8 .... **116** B7
Litle Hyden La *HORN* PO8 .... **90** A8
Little Abshot Rd
  FHAM/STUB PO14 .... **158** F8
Little Anglesey Rd *GPORT* PO12.. **10** C7
Little Arthur St *NEND* PO2 .. **211** J1 🔟
Little Ashton La *BPWT* SO32 .. **85** J5
Little Barn Pl *LISS* GU33 .... **37** G4
Little Barrs Dr
  NMIL/BTOS BH25 .... **225** M4
Little Bull La *BPWT* SO32 .... **111** J6
Little Cnr *WVILLE* PO7 .... **139** K5
Littlecroft Av
  MOOR/WNTN BH9 .... **220** F5
Little Croft Rd
  BKME/WDN BH12 .... **234** A2 🔟
Little Dene Copse *LYMN* SO41.. **227** M6
Little Dewlands *VWD* BH31 .. **144** B2 🔟
Littledown Av *LTDN* BH7 .... **236** D1
Littledown Dr *LTDN* BH7 .... **236** D1
Little Dro *FBDG* SP6 .... **98** D2
Littlefield Crs *NBAD* SO52 .... **80** D2
Little Forest Rd *WBNE* BH4 .... **14** B1
Little Gays *FHAM/STUB* PO14.. **183** K6
Little George St *PSEA* PO1 .. **211** J1 🔟
Little Gn *GPORT* PO12 .... **10** C7
Littlegreen Av *HAV* PO9 .... **165** L5
Little Hambrook St *SSEA* PO5.. **12** F5 🔟
Little Hyden La *HORN* PO8.... **116** A1
Little Lance's Hl *ITCH* SO19 .. **132** D1
Little La *GPORT* PO12 .... **10** C7
Littie Md *WVILLE* PO7 .... **139** L5
Littlemead Cl *CFDH* BH17 .. **232** F1 🔟
Littlemeads *ROMY* SO51 .... **78** C1
Littlemill La *FBDG* SP6 .... **96** B3
Little Minster St *WINC* SO23 .... **3** G8
Littlemoor Av *BWD* BH11 .... **219** H4
Little Oak Rd *ROWN* SO16 .... **106** E4
Littlepark Av *HAV* PO9 .... **164** F5
Little Pk Cl *HEND* SO30 .... **133** M2 🔟
Little Park Farm Rd
  FHAM PO15 .... **159** G3
Little Quob La *HEND* SO30 .... **108** D6
Little Shore La *BPWT* SO32 .... **111** H1
Little Southsea St *SSEA* PO5 .. **12** F5 🔟
Littleton Gv *HAV* PO9 .... **165** K4
Littlewood Gdns *HEND* SO30.. **108** C7
  HLER SO31 .... **158** C5 🔟
Little Woodham La
  LSOL/BMARY PO13 .... **209** G3
Liverpool Rd *FHAM/STUB* PO14.. **184** D2
  PSEA PO1 .... **13** M1
Liverpool St *SHAM* SO14 .... **131** L1
Livery Rd *RSAL* SP5 .... **18** E2
Livingstone Rd
  BKME/WDN BH12 .... **234** B2
  BOSC BH5 .... **237** G2
  CHCH/BSGR BH23 .... **238** C1 🔟
  SHAM SO14 .... **106** D7
  SSEA PO5 .... **13** K5
  WIMB BH21 .... **192** C4
Llewellin Cl *UPTN* BH16 .... **217** G8
Lloyd Av *TOTT* SO40 .... **130** C7 🔟
Loader Cl *WINC* SO23 .... **17** H1
Loane Rd *ITCH* SO19 .... **132** D5
Lobelia Rd *ROWN* SO16 .... **107** H4
Locarno Rd *HSEA* PO3 .... **187** K6
Locke Rd *HEND* SO30 .... **109** H8
Lockhams Rd *BPWT* SO32 .... **110** D8
Locksash Cl *SELS* PO20 .... **215** K6
Locksash La *RCCH* PO18 .... **118** D8
Locksheath Cl *HAV* PO9 .. **165** H2 🔟
Locksheath Park Rd
  HLER SO31 .... **158** F7
Locksley Dr *FERN* BH22 .... **194** A3
Locksley Rd *ELGH* SO50 .... **81** K7
Locks Rd *HLER* SO31 .... **158** E4
Locksway Rd *ENEY* PO4 .... **211** M4
Lockswood Rd *HLER* SO31 .... **158** D5
Lock Vw *CHAM* PO6 .... **186** E8
Lockyers Dr *FERN* BH22 .... **194** D2
Lode HI *RSAL* SP5 .... **73** G1
Loders Cl *CFDH* BH17 .... **218** A5
Lodge Av *CHAM* PO6 .... **163** L8
Lodgebury Cl *EMRTH* PO10 .. **167** J8
Lodge Cl *PSTN* BH14 .... **234** D4
Lodge Dr *PSTN* BH14 .... **234** D4
Lodge Dr *FAWY* SO45 .... **155** K7

Lodge Dro *RSAL* SP5 .... **73** H4
Lodge Gdns *GPORT* PO12 .... **10** C5
Lodge La *BROC* SO42 .... **204** C2
  HAV PO9 .... **143** H2
Lodge Rd *CHCH/BSGR* BH23 .... **222** C8
  HAV PO9 .... **164** F7
  HLER SO31 .... **158** F5
  LYMN SO41 .... **227** M5
  SHAM SO14 .... **131** L1
Lodge V *ROMY* SO51 .... **77** G3
Lodsworth CI *HORN* PO8 .... **116** C4
Loewy Crs *BKME/WDN* BH12 .... **219** H6
Lofting CI *ELGH* SO50 .... **82** D6 [2]
Logan CI *ROWN* SO16 .... **105** L3
Lomax CI *HEND* SO30 .... **109** H7 [2]
Lombard Av *SBNE* BH6 .... **237** J3
Lombard St *PSEA* PO1 .... **12** C5 [2]
Lombardy CI
  LSOL/BMARY PO13 .... **185** J6 [2]
  VWD BH31 .... **144** F3
Lombardy Ri *WVILLE* PO7 .... **164** D3
Lomer La *RGWD* BH24 .... **122** A5
Lomond CI *NEND* PO2 .... **187** H6
Londesborough Rd *ENEY* PO4 ..... **13** M5
London Av *NEND* PO2 .... **187** H6
London La *CHCH/BSGR* BH23 ...... **196** D6
London Rd *CHAM* PO6 .... **163** K8
  EPSF GU31 .... **64** A3
  HORN PO8 .... **116** B2
  NEND PO2 .... **187** J6
  WINC SO23 .... **17** G3
  WSHM SO15 .... **131** K2
  WVILLE PO7 .... **140** C5
  WVILLE PO7 .... **164** A4
Lone Barn La *BPWT* SO32 .... **86** D1
Lone Pine Dr *FERN* BH22 .... **194** C5
Lone Pine Wy *FERN* BH22 .... **194** D6
Lone Va *WVILLE* PO7 .... **164** A5
Longacre CI *LISS* GU33 .... **36** F4
Longacres *FHAM/STUB* PO14 ...... **159** C4
Longbarrow CI *CHAR* BH8 .... **221** L7 [2]
Long Beech Dr *TOTT* SO40 .... **129** K2
Longbridge CI *TOTT* SO40 .... **104** C6
Long CI *RSAL* SP5 .... **44** D8
Longclose Rd *HEND* SO30 .... **134** B1
Long Close West *RSAL* SP5 ...... **44** D8
Long Copse *FAWY* SO45 .... **180** C5
Long Copse La *EMRTH* PO10 ...... **166** D4
Long Curtain Rd *PSEA* PO1 ...... **12** D1
Longdean CI *CHAM* PO6 .... **162** E7
Long Down *EPSF* GU31 .... **64** A4
Long Dr *HEND* SO30 .... **108** D6
  LSOL/BMARY PO13 .... **185** C7
Long Dro *RSAL* SP5 .... **18** C3
Longespee Rd *WIMB* BH22 .... **192** C8 [2]
Longfield Av *FHAM/STUB* PO14 ... **6** B9
Longfield CI *ENEY* PO4 .... **212** A3 [2]
Longfield Dr *BWD* BH11 .... **219** L2 [2]
  FERN BH22 .... **194** C8 [2]
Longfield Rd *EMRTH* PO10 .... **166** C5
  LYMN SO41 .... **226** F6
  WINC SO23 .... **17** J3
Longfleet Dr *WIMB* BH21 .... **218** E1
Longfleet Rd *PLE* BH15 .... **233** K4
Longhouse Gn *WINC* SO23 .... **3** M7
Longlands Rd *EMRTH* PO10 .... **167** H8
Long La *FAWY* SO45 .... **180** A3
  HLER SO31 .... **133** L1
  RCCH PO18 .... **119** J5
  RGWD BH24 .... **170** F4
  TOTT SO40 .... **130** B7
  WIMB BH21 .... **192** B1
Long Lane CI *FAWY* SO45 .... **180** B5
Longleat Gdns
  NMIL/BTOS BH25 .... **225** J5
  ROWN SO16 .... **106** A3
Longmead CI *LISS* GU33 .... **36** E5
Longmead Av *ELGH* SO50 .... **82** C4
Longmead Gdns *HAV* PO9 .... **8** F8
Longmeadow Gdns
  FAWY SO45 .... **155** L4
Longmeadow La *CFDH* BH17 .... **217** J7
Longmead Rd *RGWD* BH24 .... **172** E7
  WEND SO18 .... **107** L6 [2]
Longmore Av *ITCH* SO19 .... **132** B6
Longmore Crs *ITCH* SO19 .... **132** B6 [1]
Longmynd Dr
  FHAM/STUB PO14 .... **6** B8
Long Priors *PSF* GU32 .... **60** A3
Longridge Rd *HEND* SO30 .... **134** A2
Long Rd *BPWT* SO32 .... **113** H2
  NBNE BH10 .... **220** B4
  PSF GU32 .... **63** M3
Longshore Wy *ENEY* PO4 .... **212** B3
Longs La *FHAM/STUB* PO14 .... **184** A5
Longstaff Gdns
  FHAM/PORC PO16 .... **6** F2
Long Steeple La *FBDG* SP6 ...... **71** K6
Longstock CI *ITCH* SO19 .... **132** E8 [1]
Longstock Crs *TOTT* SO40 .... **129** H1
Longstock Rd *HAV* PO9 .... **165** M2
Long Wk *RWIN* SO21 .... **17** J4
Long Water Dr *GPORT* PO12 ...... **11** G9
Longwood Av *HORN* PO8 .... **140** D5
Longwood Dean La *RWIN* SO21 .... **57** H2
Longwood Rd *RWIN* SO21 .... **56** B4
Lonsdale Av *CHAM* PO6 .... **187** L1
  FHAM/PORC PO16 .... **186** B2
Lonsdale Rd *TWDS* BH3 .... **235** L1
Loperwood *TOTT* SO40 .... **103** L6
Loperwood La *TOTT* SO40 .... **103** M4
Loraine Av *CHCH/BSGR* BH23 ..... **225** G8
Lord CI *CFDH* BH17 .... **233** L1
Lordington CI *CHAM* PO6 .... **163** M8 [2]
Lord Montgomery Wy
  SSEA PO5 .... **12** F3 [2]
Lord Mountbatten CI
  WEND SO18 .... **107** K4 [2]
Lord's Hill Centre East
  ROWN SO16 .... **105** L3
Lord's Hill Centre West
  ROWN SO16 .... **105** L3
Lord's Hill Wy *ROWN* SO16 ...... **105** L3
Lords St *PSEA* PO1 .... **211** H2
Lordswood *ELGH* SO50 .... **82** D1
Lordswood CI *ROWN* SO16 .... **106** C5 [1]
Lordswood Gdns *ROWN* SO16 ...... **106** C4
Lordswood Rd *ROWN* SO16 .... **106** B4

Loreille CI *ROWN* SO16 .... **105** K1
Lorne Park Rd *BMTH* BH1 .... **15** G5
Lorne Rd *SSEA* PO5 .... **13** L4
Loughwood CI *ELGH* SO50 .... **81** M2
Lovage Gdns *TOTT* SO40 .... **129** G1
Lovage Rd *FHAM* PO15 .... **159** H1
Lovage Wy *HORN* PO8 .... **116** B7
Love La *EMTH* PO10 .... **58** A5
  EPSF GU31 .... **63** M4
  FBDG SP6 .... **72** D8
  PSF GU32 .... **60** B4
  ROMY SO51 .... **78** D1
  RWIN SO21 .... **55** G3
Lovett Rd *HSEA* PO3 .... **187** K5
Lowcay Rd *SSEA* PO5 .... **13** L7
Lowden CI *FUFL* SO22 .... **26** C4
Lower Alfred St *SHAM* SO14 ..... **131** M2
Lower Ashley Rd
  NMIL/BTOS BH25 .... **226** B5
Lower Banister St *WSHM* SO15 ... **131** K2
Lower Bartons *FBDG* SP6 .... **97** L7
Lower Baybridge La *RWIN* SO21 .. **56** A7
Lower Bellfield
  FHAM/STUB PO14 .... **183** K1
Lower Bere Wd *WVILLE* PO7 ...... **164** D1
Lower Blandford Rd
  BDST BH18 .... **217** L4 [2]
Lower Brook St *WINC* SO23 ...... **3** H7
Lower Brownhill Rd
  ROWN SO16 .... **105** H6
Lower Buckland Rd
  LYMN SO41 .... **228** B3
Lower Canal Wk *SHAM* SO14 ...... **5** C7
Lower Chase Rd *BPWT* SO32 ...... **111** M3
Lower Church Pth *PSEA* PO1 ..... **13** H1 [3]
Lower Church Rd
  WVILLE PO7 .... **138** F4
Lower Common La
  WIMB BH21 .... **168** E1
Lower Common Rd *ROMY* SO51 ..... **76** D6
Lower Crabbick La
  WVILLE PO7 .... **138** F4
Lower Densome Wd *FBDG* SP6 ..... **72** D8
Lower Derby Rd *NEND* PO2 .... **187** G7
Lower Drayton La *CHAM* PO6 ..... **188** A1
Lower Duncan Rd *HLER* SO31 ..... **158** F3
Lower Farlington Rd
  CHAM PO6 .... **164** C8
Lower Forbury Rd *SSEA* PO5 ..... **13** J3 [2]
Lower Golf Links Rd
  BDST BH18 .... **217** M3
Lower Gv *FBDG* SP6 .... **71** G6
Lower Grove Rd *HAV* PO9 .... **9** G6
Lower Heyshott *EPSF* GU31 ...... **63** M4
Lower Lamborough La
  NARL SO24 .... **30** C3
Lower La *BPWT* SO32 .... **85** J3
Lower Md *EPSF* GU31 .... **64** A5
Lower Mead End Rd
  LYMN SO41 .... **200** D8
Lower Moors Rd *RWIN* SO21 ...... **54** E7
Lower Mortimer Rd *ITCH* SO19 ... **132** B5
Lower Mullin's La *FAWY* SO45 ... **155** J4
Lower New Rd *HEND* SO30 .... **108** C7
Lower Northam Rd
  HEND SO30 .... **134** A1
Lower Pennington La
  LYMN SO41 .... **228** B7
Lower Preshaw La *BPWT* SO32 .... **57** L8
Lower Quay CI
  FHAM/PORC PO16 .... **7** J8
Lower Quay Rd
  FHAM/PORC PO16 .... **7** K8
Lower Rd *HAV* PO9 .... **164** F7
  RSAL SP5 .... **44** E4
Lower St Helens Rd
  HEND SO30 .... **134** A3
Lower Sandy Down La
  LYMN SO41 .... **201** M5
Lower Spinney *HLER* SO31 .... **182** A1
Lower St *ROMY* SO51 .... **51** G1
Lower Swanwick Rd
  HLER SO31 .... **134** B8 [2]
Lower Vicarage Rd *ITCH* SO19 ... **132** B5
Lower Wardown *EPSF* GU31 .... **64** A4
Lower Woodside *LYMN* SO41 ...... **228** C8
Lower York St *SHAM* SO14 .... **132** B2
Lowestoft Rd *CHAM* PO6 .... **163** H7
Lowford Hl *HLER* SO31 .... **133** K7
Lowland Rd *WVILLE* PO7 .... **139** J4
Lowry Gdns *ITCH* SO19 .... **133** G6
Lowther Gdns *CHAR* BH8 .... **15** L1
Lowther Rd *CHAR* BH8 .... **235** M2
Loxwood Rd *HORN* PO8 .... **140** D2
Luard Ct *HAV* PO9 .... **9** J5
Lucas CI *ROWN* SO16 .... **105** L3 [2]
Lucas Rd *BKME/WDN* BH12 .... **234** B2
Luccombe PI *WSHM* SO15 .... **106** C6
Luccombe Rd *WSHM* SO15 .... **106** C6
Lucerne Av *SBNE* BH6 .... **237** J3
  WVILLE PO7 .... **140** B6
Lucerne Gdns *HEND* SO30 .... **133** L2
Lucerne Rd *LYMN* SO41 .... **242** C4
Luckham CI
  MOOR/WNTN BH9 .... **220** F6 [2]
Luckham PI
  MOOR/WNTN BH9 .... **220** F6 [2]
Luckham Rd
  MOOR/WNTN BH9 .... **220** F6
Luckham Rd East
  MOOR/WNTN BH9 .... **220** F6 [2]
Lucknow St *PSEA* PO1 .... **13** L2
Lucky La *LYMN* SO41 .... **202** E7
Ludcombe *WVILLE* PO7 .... **139** K3
Ludlow Rd *CHAM* PO6 .... **163** G7
  ITCH SO19 .... **132** C4
Ludwell's La *BPWT* SO32 .... **111** L4
Lugano CI *WVILLE* PO7 .... **140** B7
Lukin Dr *ROWN* SO16 .... **105** H3
Lulworth Av *PLE* BH15 .... **232** D7
Lulworth CI *CHFD* SO53 .... **81** G5
  HISD PO11 .... **213** J3
  PLE BH15 .... **232** D7
  ROWN SO16 .... **105** K6
Lulworth Crs *PLE* BH15 .... **232** D7
Lulworth Gn *ROWN* SO16 .... **105** K6

Lulworth Rd
  LSOL/BMARY PO13 .... **208** C2
Lumby Dr *RGWD* BH24 .... **146** F8
Lumby Drive Pk *RGWD* BH24 ...... **146** F8 [1]
Lumley Rd *EMRTH* PO10 .... **166** F7
Lumsden Av *WSHM* SO15 .... **131** G3
Lumsden Rd *ENEY* PO4 .... **212** B5
Lundy CI *ROWN* SO16 .... **105** K3
Lunedale Rd *FAWY* SO45 .... **155** J8
Lupin Rd *ROWN* SO16 .... **107** H3
Luscombe Rd *PSTN* BH14 .... **234** B6
Luther Rd *MOOR/WNTN* BH9 .... **220** D8
Lutman St *EMRTH* PO10 .... **166** C4
Luton Rd *ITCH* SO19 .... **132** F4
Luxton CI *HEND* SO30 .... **109** L8
Luzborough La *ROMY* SO51 .... **79** G4
Lyburn CI *ROWN* SO16 .... **106** B4 [2]
Lyburn Rd *RSAL* SP5 .... **74** F6
Lych Gate Ct *RGWD* BH24 .... **171** G2 [1]
Lychgate Dr *HORN* PO8 .... **140** F1
Lychgate Gn *FHAM/STUB* PO14 .... **184** A3
Lydford Gdns *BWD* BH11 .... **219** L6
Lydford Rd *BWD* BH11 .... **219** L6
Lydgate *LYMN* SO41 .... **241** M3 [1]
  TOTT SO40 .... **129** H1 [3]
Lydgate CI *ITCH* SO19 .... **133** H4
Lydgate Gn *ITCH* SO19 .... **133** H4
Lydgate Rd *ITCH* SO19 .... **133** H4 [1]
Lydiard CI *ELGH* SO50 .... **81** M3
Lydlinch CI *FERN* BH22 .... **194** B7
Lydlynch Rd *TOTT* SO40 .... **129** J1
Lydney CI *CHAM* PO6 .... **163** G8
Lydney Rd *HLER* SO31 .... **158** D6
Lydwell Rd *BWD* BH11 .... **219** K3 [1]
Lyell Rd *BKME/WDN* BH12 .... **234** B2
Lymbourn Rd *HAV* PO9 .... **9** J5
Lyme CI *ELGH* SO50 .... **81** L3 [2]
Lyme Crs *CHCH/BSGR* BH23 .... **224** D8
Lymefields *LYMN* SO41 .... **242** C2
Lymer La *ROWN* SO16 .... **105** H2
Lymington Rd *BROC* SO42 .... **201** L2
  CHCH/BSGR BH23 .... **239** J1
  LYMN SO41 .... **229** L3
  LYMN SO41 .... **242** D1
  NMIL/BTOS BH25 .... **225** J3
Lymington Road Shelley Hl
  CHCH/BSGR BH23 .... **239** H1
Lymore La *LYMN* SO41 .... **227** J8
Lymore Va *LYMN* SO41 .... **242** D1
Lynch CI *FUFL* SO22 .... **2** C3
Lynch La *PSF* GU32 .... **60** B4
Lyndale CI *LYMN* SO41 .... **242** D3
Lyndale Rd *HLER* SO31 .... **158** F4
Lynden CI *FHAM/STUB* PO14 ...... **159** M8
Lynden Gs *ITCH* SO19 .... **132** E5 [2]
  HISD PO11 .... **213** L6
Lyndhurst CI *FUFL* SO22 .... **16** C4
Lyndhurst Rd *BROC* SO42 .... **175** L6
  CHCH/BSGR BH23 .... **198** D8
  CHCH/BSGR BH23 .... **223** M3
  GPORT PO12 .... **10** C2
  NEND PO2 .... **187** K6
  RGWD BH24 .... **172** E5
  RSAL SP5 .... **75** H5
  TOTT SO40 .... **127** J1
Lyndock CI *ITCH* SO19 .... **132** C6 [2]
Lyndock PI *ITCH* SO19 .... **132** C6
Lyndum CI *EPSF* GU31 .... **63** L5
Lyne PI *HORN* PO8 .... **140** F2
Lynes La *RGWD* BH24 .... **170** D1
Lynford Av *FUFL* SO22 .... **2** C2
Lynford Wy *FUFL* SO22 .... **2** D1
Lynn Rd *CFDH* BH17 .... **218** D8
  NEND PO2 .... **187** K8
Lynn Wy *WINC* SO23 .... **17** H2
Lynric CI *NMIL/BTOS* BH25 ...... **240** E1
Lynton CI *TOTT* SO40 .... **129** J2
Lynton Crs *CHCH/BSGR* BH23 ..... **222** B5
Lynton Gdns *FHAM/PORC* PO16 .... **6** L1
Lynton Gv *HSEA* PO3 .... **187** L8
Lynton Rd *HEND* SO30 .... **134** A1
  PSF GU32 .... **63** K4
Lynwood Av *WVILLE* PO7 .... **140** B5
Lynwood CI *FERN* BH22 .... **194** B1
Lynwood Dr *WIMB* BH21 .... **192** D7
Lynx CI *ELGH* SO50 .... **82** E6
Lyon Av *NMIL/BTOS* BH25 .... **225** M5
Lyon Rd *BKME/WDN* BH12 .... **219** J6
Lyon St *SHAM* SO14 .... **131** L2
Lysander CI *CHCH/BSGR* BH23 .... **239** G1
Lysander Wy *WVILLE* PO7 .... **140** E8
Lyster Rd *FBDG* SP6 .... **97** M6
Lystra Rd *MOOR/WNTN* BH9 .... **220** E5
Lytchett Dr *BDST* BH18 .... **217** L5
Lytchett Wy *UPTN* BH16 .... **232** A2 [2]
Lyteltane Rd *LYMN* SO41 .... **228** B6
Lytham Rd *BDST* BH18 .... **217** L5
  WEND SO18 .... **107** M8
Lythe La *PSF* GU32 .... **62** F3
Lytton Rd *BMTH* BH1 .... **15** L2
  FAWY SO45 .... **155** M6

M

Mabey Av *NBNE* BH10 .... **220** B6
Mabey CI *GPORT* PO12 .... **11** G8
Mablethorpe Rd *CHAM* PO6 .... **163** G7
Macandrew Rd *CCLF* BH13 .... **245** L1 [1]
Macarthur Crs *WEND* SO18 .... **107** M8 [2]
Macaulay Av *CHAM* PO6 .... **162** D7
Macaulay Rd *BDST* BH18 .... **217** L4
Maclaren Rd
  MOOR/WNTN BH9 .... **220** D5
Maclean Rd *BWD* BH11 .... **219** K5
Macnaghten Rd *WEND* SO18 .... **132** B1
Madden CI *GPORT* PO12 .... **10** A5
Maddison St *SHAM* SO14 .... **4** F5 [5]
Maddoxford Wy *BPWT* SO32 .... **109** L7
Madeira Rd *BMTH* BH1 .... **15** G4
  NEND PO2 .... **187** J5
  PSTN BH14 .... **234** C3 [2]
Madeline Crs
  BKME/WDN BH12 .... **234** A1
Madeline Rd *EPSF* GU31 .... **63** L4
Madison Av *BMTH* BH1 .... **236** C2

Madison CI
  LSOL/BMARY PO13 .... **185** J8 [1]
Mafeking Rd *ENEY* PO4 .... **211** K5
Magazine La *TOTT* SO40 .... **130** E5
Magdala Rd *CHAM* PO6 .... **187** K1
  HISD PO11 .... **213** J5
Magdalene Wy
  FHAM/STUB PO14 .... **159** G7
Magdalen La
  CHCH/BSGR BH23 .... **237** M2
Magdalen Rd *NEND* PO2 .... **187** J5
Magennis CI
  LSOL/BMARY PO13 .... **209** H1
Magna CI *BWD* BH11 .... **219** K2 [1]
Magna Gdns *BWD* BH11 .... **219** K2
Magna Rd *WIMB* BH21 .... **192** F8
Magnolia CI *FAWY* SO45 .... **155** G4 [1]
  FHAM/STUB PO14 .... **6** C7
  SBNE BH6 .... **237** M3 [1]
  VWD BH31 .... **145** G4
Magnolia Rd *ITCH* SO19 .... **132** D3
Magnolia Wy *HORN* PO8 .... **141** G4
Magpie CI *CHAR* BH8 .... **221** G5
Magpie Dr *TOTT* SO40 .... **129** G1
Magpie Gdns *ITCH* SO19 .... **132** F1
Magpie Gv *NMIL/BTOS* BH25 ...... **225** K6 [2]
Magpie La *ELGH* SO50 .... **81** K6
  LSOL/BMARY PO13 .... **208** D1 [3]
Magpie Rd *HORN* PO8 .... **142** A3
Magpie Wk *HORN* PO8 .... **140** B4
Mag's Barrow *FERN* BH22 .... **194** C6
Maiden La *LYMN* SO41 .... **228** D7
Maidford Gv *HSEA* PO3 .... **188** A4 [4]
Maidment CI *BWD* BH11 .... **219** J4 [7]
Maidstone Crs *CHAM* PO6 .... **163** J7
Main Dr *FAWY* SO45 .... **205** L2
  WHAM PO17 .... **162** E2
Main Rd *EMRTH* PO10 .... **167** G8
  FAWY SO45 .... **154** E1
  FAWY SO45 .... **180** A2
  LSOL/BMARY PO13 .... **185** H4
  LYMN SO41 .... **203** M8
  LYMN SO41 .... **228** B2
  PSEA PO1 .... **12** B1
  PSEA PO1 .... **210** D2
  RWIN SO21 .... **54** A6
  RWIN SO21 .... **54** E6
  RWIN SO21 .... **56** A4
  RWIN SO21 .... **83** G1
  TOTT SO40 .... **129** J4
  TOTT SO40 .... **130** D7
Mainsail Dr *FHAM/PORC* PO16 .... **7** J8
Mainstone *ROMY* SO51 .... **78** C2
Mainstream Ct *ELGH* SO50 .... **82** C5 [4]
Maisemore Gdns *EMRTH* PO10 ..... **166** B8
Maitland St *PSEA* PO1 .... **211** H1
Majestic Rd *ROWN* SO16 .... **105** G4
Malan CI *CFDH* BH17 .... **218** C8
Malcolm CI *CHFD* SO53 .... **53** K7
  HLER SO31 .... **158** F5
Malcolm Rd *CHFD* SO53 .... **53** K7
Malcroft Ms *TOTT* SO40 .... **130** E7 [5]
Maldon CI *ELGH* SO50 .... **82** C5
Maldon Rd *CHAM* PO6 .... **163** H8 [2]
  ITCH SO19 .... **132** C4
Malibres Rd *CHFD* SO53 .... **53** L8
Malin CI *FHAM/STUB* PO14 .... **183** M5
Malins Rd *NEND* PO2 .... **211** H1
Mallard CI *BPWT* SO32 .... **84** F8
  CHAR BH8 .... **221** G7
  CHCH/BSGR BH23 .... **238** F2
  LYMN SO41 .... **226** E5
  ROMY SO51 .... **50** E8
Mallard Gdns *HEND* SO30 .... **109** H6
  LSOL/BMARY PO13 .... **184** F6 [2]
Mallard Rd *CHAR* BH8 .... **221** H7
  ENEY PO4 .... **211** M3
  HAV PO9 .... **141** M7
  WIMB BH21 .... **192** E1
Mallards Rd *HLER* SO31 .... **157** K1
The Mallards *FHAM/PORC* PO16 ... **7** H7
  HAV PO9 .... **8** D8
Mallett CI *HEND* SO30 .... **109** K6
Mallory CI *CHCH/BSGR* BH23 ..... **223** K8
Mallory Crs *FHAM/PORC* PO16 .... **7** G2
Mallow CI *BDST* BH18 .... **217** J5
  CHAM PO6 .... **163** K8 [1]
  WVILLE PO7 .... **164** D2
Mallow Rd *HEND* SO30 .... **133** L2
The Mallows *NMIL/BTOS* BH25 .... **226** B4
The Mall *RGWD* BH24 .... **172** E5 [3]
Malmesbury CI *ELGH* SO50 .... **83** H6 [1]
Malmesbury Ct *CHAR* BH8 .... **236** B2 [2]
Malmesbury Gdns *FUFL* SO22 ..... **2** C8
Malmesbury Park PI *CHAR* BH8 ... **15** M1
Malmesbury Park Rd
  CHAR BH8 .... **236** A2
Malmesbury PI *WSHM* SO15 .... **131** H1
Malmesbury Rd *RGWD* BH24 .... **169** J5
  ROMY SO51 .... **50** D8
  WSHM SO15 .... **131** H1
Malorey Wy *FERN* BH22 .... **168** E7
Malory CI *ITCH* SO19 .... **133** H2
Malta Rd *NEND* PO2 .... **187** J8
Malthouse CI *PLE* BH15 .... **233** H6 [8]
Malthouse Ct *ROMY* SO51 .... **50** D8 [3]
  RWIN SO21 .... **17** L3
Malthouse Gdns *TOTT* SO40 ...... **130** D7
Malthouse La *FHAM/PORC* PO16 ... **7** J1
Malthouse Rd *NEND* PO2 .... **187** H8
The Maltings *EPSF* GU31 .... **63** L5
  FHAM/PORC PO16 .... **161** H6 [1]
Malt La *BPWT* SO32 .... **85** H8
Malus CI *CHAM* PO6 .... **184** D1
Malvern Av *FHAM/STUB* PO14 ..... **6** C8
Malvern CI *BPWT* SO32 .... **111** J1
  MOOR/WNTN BH9 .... **220** D5 [2]
Malvern Dr *FAWY* SO45 .... **155** H5
Malvern Gdns *HEND* SO30 .... **109** J6
Malvern Ms *EMRTH* PO10 .... **166** D7
Malvern Rd *GPORT* PO12 .... **10** B1
  LISS GU33 .... **37** G6
  MOOR/WNTN BH9 .... **220** D6
  ROWN SO16 .... **106** B6

  SSEA PO5 .... **13** J9
Malwood Av *ROWN* SO16 .... **106** C5
Malwood CI *HAV* PO9 .... **165** L2
Malwood Gdns *TOTT* SO40 .... **104** B8
Malwood Rd *FAWY* SO45 .... **155** K4
Malwood Rd West *FAWY* SO45 ..... **155** J4
Manchester Rd *LYMN* SO41 .... **200** F5
  PSEA PO1 .... **13** M1
Mancroft Av
  FHAM/STUB PO14 .... **184** A7
Mandale CI *BWD* BH11 .... **219** L4 [1]
Mandale Rd *BWD* BH11 .... **219** K5
Mandela Wy *WSHM* SO15 .... **4** C1
Manderley *LYMN* SO41 .... **242** D5
Manley Rd *HLER* SO31 .... **133** K7
Manners La *ENEY* PO4 .... **13** L3
Manners Rd *ENEY* PO4 .... **13** M3
Manning Av *CHCH/BSGR* BH23 ..... **224** C7
Manningford CI *WINC* SO23 ...... **3** H1
Mannings Heath Rd
  BKME/WDN BH12 .... **218** F6
Mannington PI *WCLF* BH2 .... **14** C6
Mannington Wy *FERN* BH22 .... **168** B6
Manns CI *WEND* SO18 .... **108** B6
Mannyngham Wy *ROMY* SO51 .... **50** C1
Manor Av *BKME/WDN* BH12 .... **219** G7
Manor CI *FBDG* SP6 .... **97** L7
  FERN BH22 .... **194** C3
  HLER SO31 .... **133** K7 [3]
  LYMN SO41 .... **242** C3
  TOTT SO40 .... **129** J2
  WHAM PO17 .... **136** E6
  WINC SO23 .... **3** K6
Manor Ct *RGWD* BH24 .... **144** D2 [1]
  VWD BH31 .... **144** D2 [1]
Manor Crs *CHAM* PO6 .... **187** M1
  HLER SO31 .... **133** K7
Manor Farm CI
  NMIL/BTOS BH25 .... **225** K7 [1]
  RSAL SP5 .... **40** F1
Manor Farm Gn *RWIN* SO21 .... **54** E3
Manor Farm Gv *ELGH* SO50 .... **82** D6 [2]
Manor Farm La *ROMY* SO51 .... **22** C7
Manor Farm Rd *FBDG* SP6 .... **97** H7
  NBNE BH10 .... **220** A2
  WEND SO18 .... **107** J7
Manor Gdns *EMRTH* PO10 .... **167** H7
  RGWD BH24 .... **146** D8 [1]
  VWD BH31 .... **146** D8 [1]
Manor House Av *WSHM* SO15 ...... **130** C2
Manor La *VWD* BH31 .... **144** D3
Manor Lodge Rd *HAV* PO9 .... **141** M8
Manor Ms *CHAM* PO6 .... **164** A8
Manor Park Av *HSEA* PO3 .... **187** L8
Manor Rd *BMTH* BH1 .... **15** L6
  BPWT SO32 .... **110** C1
  CHCH/BSGR BH23 .... **237** M2
  ELGH SO50 .... **82** D6
  EMRTH PO10 .... **167** H7
  FAWY SO45 .... **180** A4
  HISD PO11 .... **213** K3
  LYMN SO41 .... **242** C3
  NMIL/BTOS BH25 .... **225** M5
  PSEA PO1 .... **211** J1
  RGWD BH24 .... **170** E1
  ROWN SO16 .... **80** C7
  RSAL SP5 .... **20** D1
  RWIN SO21 .... **54** E3
  TOTT SO40 .... **154** E3
  VWD BH31 .... **144** D2
Manor Rd North *ITCH* SO19 ...... **132** C4
Manor Rd South *ITCH* SO19 ...... **132** C5
Manor Wy *EMRTH* PO10 .... **167** H7
  HISD PO11 .... **213** L6
  LSOL/BMARY PO13 .... **184** F6 [3]
  VWD BH31 .... **144** D1 [1]
Mans Br *WEND* SO18 .... **107** L4
Mansbridge Rd *ELGH* SO50 .... **81** M7
  WEND SO18 .... **107** L4
Mansel CI *BKME/WDN* BH12 .... **235** H1
Mansel CI *ROWN* SO16 .... **105** K6
Mansell CI *FAWY* SO45 .... **155** G8
Mansel Rd East *ROWN* SO16 ...... **105** K7
Mansel Rd West *ROWN* SO16 ...... **105** J6
Mansfield CI *FERN* BH22 .... **194** B6
Mansfield La *WHAM* PO17 .... **135** M4
Mansfield Rd
  LSOL/BMARY PO13 .... **185** G8
  MOOR/WNTN BH9 .... **220** C7
  PSTN BH14 .... **234** B4
  RGWD BH24 .... **170** D1
Mansion Rd *ENEY* PO4 .... **211** J7
  WSHM SO15 .... **131** G2
Mansvid Av *HSEA* PO3 .... **187** M1
Mantle CI *LSOL/BMARY* PO13 ..... **209** H1
Mantle Sq *NEND* PO2 .... **187** H6
Manton Rd *PLE* BH15 .... **232** D5 [8]
Maple CI *CHCH/BSGR* BH23 .... **239** L1
  EMRTH PO10 .... **166** D6
  FHAM PO15 .... **159** H5
  LSOL/BMARY PO13 .... **208** D3 [2]
  NMIL/BTOS BH25 .... **241** G1
  ROMY SO51 .... **79** H2
Maple Crs *HORN* PO8 .... **116** B2
Maple Dr *FERN* BH22 .... **168** A8
  WVILLE PO7 .... **139** L5
Maple Gdns *TOTT* SO40 .... **129** G2 [3]
Maple Rd *FAWY* SO45 .... **155** M8 [2]
  MOOR/WNTN BH9 .... **220** D8
  PLE BH15 .... **233** J5
  SSEA PO5 .... **13** J2
  WEND SO18 .... **107** J7
Maple Sq *ELGH* SO50 .... **81** K7 [2]
The Maples *CHFD* SO53 .... **53** H8
Mapleton Rd *HEND* SO30 .... **134** B2 [2]
Mapletree Av *HORN* PO8 .... **141** G3
Maplewood CI *TOTT* SO40 .... **129** G2
Maplin Rd *ROWN* SO16 .... **105** J6
Mapperton CI *CFDH* BH17 .... **218** E6
Marabout CI *CHCH/BSGR* BH23 .... **238** C1
Maralyn Av *WVILLE* PO7 .... **164** C2
Marathon PI *ELGH* SO50 .... **83** G6
Marbican Dr *CHFD* SO53 .... **97** H6 [1]
Marchwood By-pass
  TOTT SO40 .... **129** L3
Marchwood Rd *HAV* PO9 .... **165** J2
  NBNE BH10 .... **220** A5
  TOTT SO40 .... **130** A4

WSHM SO15.......... 130 F2
Marcus Cl ELGH SO50.......... 83 C6
Mardale Rd ROWN SO16.......... 105 J8
Marden Wy EPSF GU31.......... 63 M5
Mardon Cl ELGH SO50.......... 107 K3
Mare La RWIN SO21.......... 55 K1
Margam Av ITCH SO19.......... 132 D3
Margaret Cl WVILLE PO7.......... 140 B7
Margarita Rd FHAM PO15.......... 6 C4
Margate Rd SSEA PO5.......... 13 J4
Margery's Ct PSEA PO1.......... 12 D2
Marian Cl WIMB BH21.......... 217 C4
Marianne Rd WSHM SO15.......... 130 D2
Marianne Rd
 BKME/WDN BH12.......... 220 A8
 WIMB BH21.......... 192 E1
Marian Rd WIMB BH21.......... 217 C4
Marie Av RSAL SP5.......... 72 C1
Marie Cl BKME/WDN BH12.......... 234 C1
Marie Rd ITCH SO19.......... 133 C5
Marigold Cl FHAM PO15.......... 6 C4
Marina Cl EMRTH PO10.......... 166 E8
Marina Dr PSTN BH14.......... 234 A7
Marina Gv FHAM/PORC PO16.......... 186 A2
 HSEA PO3.......... 211 M2
The Marina BOSC BH5.......... 236 D5
Marine Ct ENEY PO4.......... 211 L4
Marine Dr NMIL/BTOS BH25.......... 240 D1
Marine Dr East
 NMIL/BTOS BH25.......... 240 F2
Marine Dr West
 NMIL/BTOS BH25.......... 240 C1
Marine Pde SHAM SO14.......... 5 K4
Marine Pde East
 LSOL/BMARY PO13.......... 208 D4
Marine Pde West
 LSOL/BMARY PO13.......... 208 B1
Marine Prospect
 NMIL/BTOS BH25.......... 240 E1
Marine Rd SBNE BH6.......... 237 J5
Mariner's Cl HLER SO31.......... 157 L4
Mariners Ms FAWY SO45.......... 155 L4
Mariners Wy GPORT PO12.......... 11 J5
 HLER SO31.......... 158 A7
Marine Wk HISD PO11.......... 214 B5
Marion Rd ENEY PO4.......... 13 M8
Maritime Av TOTT SO40.......... 130 E5
Maritime Wk SHAM SO14.......... 5 J8
Maritime Wy SHAM SO14.......... 5 H7
Marjoram Crs HORN PO8.......... 140 C5
Marjoram Wy FHAM PO15.......... 159 H1
Markall Cl NARL SO24.......... 30 C5
Mark Cl HSEA PO3.......... 187 K4
 WSHM SO15.......... 130 C1
Marken Cl HLER SO31.......... 158 C5
Market La WINC SO23.......... 3 C8
Market Pde HAV PO9.......... 8 E4
Market Pl RGWD BH24.......... 170 D1
 SHAM SO14.......... 5 C6
Market St ELGH SO50.......... 82 C6
 PLE BH15.......... 233 G7
 WINC SO23.......... 3 C8
Marketway PSEA PO1.......... 211 G2
Market Wy WIMB BH21.......... 192 B4
Markham Av NBNE BH10.......... 220 B2
Markham Cl NBNE BH10.......... 220 B1
Markham Rd
 MOOR/WNTN BH9.......... 220 E8
Mark's La NMIL/BTOS BH25.......... 225 L2
Mark's Rd FHAM/STUB SO14.......... 184 C6
 MOOR/WNTN BH9.......... 220 E8
Marks Tey Rd
 FHAM/STUB SO14.......... 184 A3
Markway Rd EMRTH PO10.......... 166 B7
Marlborough WVILLE PO7.......... 164 B5
Marlborough Ct FAWY SO45.......... 155 J6
Marlborough Gdns
 HEND SO30.......... 109 H5
Marlborough Gv
 FHAM/PORC PO16.......... 186 A1
Marlborough Pk HAV PO9.......... 9 K2
Marlborough Pl LYMN SO41.......... 228 B3
 WIMB BH21.......... 192 B3
Marlborough Rd CHFD SO53.......... 53 K7
 GPORT PO12.......... 209 K2
 PSTN BH14.......... 234 B4
 WBNE BH4.......... 235 H5
 WSHM SO15.......... 106 A4
Marlborough Rw PSEA PO1.......... 210 E2
Marldell Cl HAV PO9.......... 165 L3
Marles Cl LSOL/BMARY PO13.......... 209 H1
Marley Av NMIL/BTOS BH25.......... 225 K5
Marley Cl NMIL/BTOS BH25.......... 225 K5
Marley Mt LYMN SO41.......... 200 C7
Marlhill Cl WEND SO18.......... 107 L6
Marlin Cl LSOL/BMARY PO13.......... 209 H2
Marline Rd BKME/WDN BH12.......... 234 C2
Marl La FBDG SP6.......... 97 L6
Marlott Rd PLE BH15.......... 233 H5
Marlow Cl FHAM PO15.......... 160 C4
Marlow Dr CHCH/BSGR BH23.......... 222 C5
Marlowe Ct WVILLE PO7.......... 140 B7
Marlow Rd BPWT SO32.......... 84 F7
Marlpit Dr CHCH/BSGR BH23.......... 224 E6
Marlpit La EMRTH PO10.......... 167 L4
 NMIL/BTOS BH25.......... 199 L8
Marls Rd HEND SO30.......... 134 B2
Marmion Gn
 CHCH/BSGR BH23.......... 238 E1
Marmion Rd SSEA PO5.......... 13 H7
Marne Rd WEND SO18.......... 132 E1
Marnhull Rd PLE BH15.......... 233 J4
Marpet Cl BWD BH11.......... 219 K2
Marples Wy HAV PO9.......... 8 B5
Marquis Wy BWD BH11.......... 219 H3
Marram Cl LYMN SO41.......... 228 C2
Marrels Wd WVILLE PO7.......... 164 A4
Marryat Rd NMIL/BTOS BH25.......... 225 K5
Marsden Rd CHAM PO6.......... 162 F8
Marshall Rd HISD PO11.......... 214 C4
Marshal Rd CFDH BH17.......... 217 M7
Marsh Cl CHAM PO6.......... 182 A1
Marshfield WIMB BH21.......... 192 D1

Marshfield Cl TOTT SO40.......... 130 B7
Marsh Gdns HEND SO30.......... 109 H5
Marshlands Rd CHAM PO6.......... 188 B1
Marsh La CHCH/BSGR BH23.......... 222 D6
 FAWY SO45.......... 180 F4
 FBDG SP6.......... 71 M8
 LYMN SO41.......... 228 C2
 RCCH PO18.......... 191 L4
 SHAM SO14.......... 5 H5
Marston Cl NMIL/BTOS BH25.......... 225 M3
Marston Gv CHCH/BSGR BH23.......... 224 C7
Marston La HSEA PO3.......... 187 M4
Marston Rd ITCH SO19.......... 133 H3
 NMIL/BTOS BH25.......... 225 M3
 PLE BH15.......... 233 G6
Martello Cl GPORT PO12.......... 209 H5
Martello Pk CCLF BH13.......... 245 L1
Martello Rd CCLF BH13.......... 234 E7
The Martells NMIL/BTOS BH25.......... 241 C1
Martin Av FHAM/STUB SO14.......... 184 B6
 WVILLE PO7.......... 139 L4
Martin Cl BPWT SO32.......... 112 A4
 CFDH BH17.......... 232 D1
 LSOL/BMARY PO13.......... 208 D1
Martindale Av WIMB BH21.......... 192 F3
Martin Dro End FBDG SP6.......... 68 F3
Martingale Cl UPTN BH16.......... 232 C1
Martin Rd FHAM/STUB SO14.......... 184 B6
 HAV PO9.......... 165 L4
 HSEA PO3.......... 187 L8
Martins Cl FERN BH22.......... 194 C1
Martins Dr FERN BH22.......... 194 C1
Martins Flds RWIN SO21.......... 26 B7
Martins Hill Cl
 CHCH/BSGR BH23.......... 223 G7
Martins Hill La
 CHCH/BSGR BH23.......... 223 H7
Martin's Rd BROC SO42.......... 175 L6
The Martins ELGH SO50.......... 83 J7
Martin St BPWT SO32.......... 111 G1
Martley Gdns HEND SO30.......... 109 J6
Marvic Ct HAV PO9.......... 165 J2
Marvin Wy HEND SO30.......... 134 B1
 WEND SO18.......... 133 G2
Marwell Cl LTDN BH7.......... 236 F1
Marybridge Cl TOTT SO40.......... 129 J2
Maryfield SHAM SO14.......... 5 J4
Maryland Cl WEND SO18.......... 107 L5
Maryland Gdns LYMN SO41.......... 242 A4
Maryland Rd UPTN BH16.......... 232 B4
Mary La FERN BH22.......... 168 B6
Mary Rose Cl FHAM PO15.......... 6 C1
The Mary Rose St PSEA PO1.......... 13 G2
Masefield Av CHAM PO6.......... 162 D7
Masefield Cl ELGH SO50.......... 81 L5
Masefield Crs HORN PO8.......... 140 D5
Masefield Gn ITCH SO19.......... 133 H2
Masseys La BROC SO42.......... 204 A1
Masten Crs
 LSOL/BMARY PO13.......... 185 G8
Matapan Rd NEND PO2.......... 187 H4
Matchams La
 CHCH/BSGR BH23.......... 221 M1
 RGWD BH24.......... 195 M3
Matheson Rd ROWN SO16.......... 105 L2
Matley Gdns TOTT SO40.......... 128 F1
Matlock Rd FERN BH22.......... 194 A5
Matthews Cl HAV PO9.......... 165 G5
Matthews La BROC SO42.......... 204 A2
Maturin Cl LYMN SO41.......... 228 B5
Maundeville Crs
 CHCH/BSGR BH23.......... 222 C8
Maundeville Rd
 CHCH/BSGR BH23.......... 222 C8
Maunsell Wy HEND SO30.......... 109 H5
Maureen Cl BKME/WDN BH12.......... 218 F8
Maurepas Wy WVILLE PO7.......... 164 B1
Mauretania Rd ROWN SO16.......... 105 G4
Maurice Rd ENEY PO4.......... 212 A4
Maurys La ROMY SO51.......... 76 C5
Mavis Crs HAV PO9.......... 8 E3
Mavis Rd MOOR/WNTN BH9.......... 220 F7
Maxstoke Cl SSEA PO5.......... 13 J2
Maxwell Rd BDST BH18.......... 217 H5
 CCLF BH13.......... 245 L1
 ENEY PO4.......... 211 L5
 ITCH SO19.......... 132 E5
 MOOR/WNTN BH9.......... 235 M1
May Av LYMN SO41.......... 228 B3
Maybray King Wy ITCH SO19.......... 132 E1
Maybush Dr RCCH PO18.......... 191 M1
May Bush La BPWT SO32.......... 113 G7
Maybush Rd ROWN SO16.......... 105 K6
May Cl FAWY SO45.......... 180 B5
May Copse FAWY SO45.......... 180 B5
May Crs FAWY SO45.......... 180 B5
Maydman Sq HSEA PO3.......... 211 L2
Mayfair Ct HEND SO30.......... 134 E1
Mayfair Gdns BWD BH11.......... 219 L4
 WSHM SO15.......... 131 K1
Mayfield Av PSTN BH14.......... 234 D5
 TOTT SO40.......... 104 D8
Mayfield Cl FERN BH22.......... 194 A4
 FHAM/STUB SO14.......... 184 B5
Mayfield Dr FERN BH22.......... 194 A4
Mayfield Rd FBDG SP6.......... 97 H6
 GPORT PO12.......... 10 C5
 MOOR/WNTN BH9.......... 220 E6
 NEND PO2.......... 187 J6
 PTSW SO17.......... 107 G5
Mayfield Wy FERN BH22.......... 194 A4
Mayflower Cl CHFD SO53.......... 81 K3
Mayflower Dr FERN BH22.......... 194 A4
 FHAM/STUB SO14.......... 184 A7
 LYMN SO41.......... 228 E5
Mayflower Rd WSHM SO15.......... 106 B8
Mayflower Rbt WSHM SO15.......... 4 E6
The Mayflowers ROWN SO16.......... 106 F4
Mayfly Cl FBDG SP6.......... 97 L6
Mayford Rd BKME/WDN BH12.......... 235 G2
May Gdns BWD BH11.......... 219 J5
Mayhall Rd HSEA PO3.......... 187 L7
Mayhill La BPWT SO32.......... 86 F8
 BPWT SO32.......... 112 C1

Maylands Av ENEY PO4.......... 211 L4
Maylands Rd HAV PO9.......... 164 F6
May La LYMN SO41.......... 202 E7
Mayles Cl WHAM PO17.......... 136 E5
Mayles La WHAM PO17.......... 136 C7
Mayles Rd ENEY PO4.......... 211 M3
Maylings Farm Rd
 FHAM/PORC PO16.......... 6 F2
Maylyn Rd LSOL/BMARY PO13.......... 216 D6
Maynard Cl LSOL/BMARY PO13.......... 185 C4
Maynard Pl HORN PO8.......... 140 F1
Maynard Rd TOTT SO40.......... 129 K1
Mayo Cl PSEA PO1.......... 211 H1
Mayridge FHAM/STUB SO14.......... 159 C5
May Rd WSHM SO15.......... 131 G1
Mays Firs FBDG SP6.......... 73 L6
May's La FHAM/STUB SO14.......... 184 B4
May Tree Cl FUFL SO22.......... 26 B4
Maytree Cl SELS SO31.......... 158 C5
Maytree Gdns HORN PO8.......... 140 C5
Maytree Rd CHFD SO53.......... 53 H6
 FHAM/PORC PO16.......... 7 C6
 HORN PO8.......... 140 C5
Mayvale Cl TOTT SO40.......... 130 D7
Mcintyre Rd CHCH/BSGR BH23.......... 195 K8
Mckinley Rd WBNE BH4.......... 235 H6
Mcwilliam Cl BKME/WDN BH12.......... 220 A8
Mcwilliam Rd
 MOOR/WNTN BH9.......... 220 E6
Meacher Cl HLER SO31.......... 158 C4
Meadbrook Gdns CHFD SO53.......... 81 H2
Mead Cl CFDH BH17.......... 217 L7
 ROMY SO51.......... 79 G1
Mead Crs WEND SO18.......... 107 J5
Meadcroft Cl HLER SO31.......... 158 B8
Meadend Cl HAV PO9.......... 165 M3
Mead End Rd LYMN SO41.......... 200 D7
 WVILLE PO7.......... 139 L5
Mead Hawks LISS GU33.......... 36 D3
Meadow Av HLER SO31.......... 158 C4
Meadow Cl BPWT SO32.......... 111 K4
 CHCH/BSGR BH23.......... 222 F1
 CHCH/BSGR BH23.......... 223 L1
 FBDG SP6.......... 97 K6
 FERN BH22.......... 194 B7
 HEND SO30.......... 108 D6
 HISD PO11.......... 189 K5
 NBAD SO52.......... 79 M5
 RGWD BH24.......... 146 F7
 RGWD BH24.......... 172 D6
 TOTT SO40.......... 129 K3
Meadow Ct RSAL SP5.......... 47 H4
Meadow Court Cl
 MOOR/WNTN BH9.......... 220 E5
Meadowcroft Cl RWIN SO21.......... 54 B5
Meadow Edge WVILLE PO7.......... 163 L6
Meadow Gdns BPWT SO32.......... 111 K4
Meadow Gv VWD BH31.......... 144 F3
Meadowhead Rd
 ROWN SO16.......... 106 E5
Meadowland
 CHCH/BSGR BH23.......... 238 D2
 WINC SO23.......... 17 G1
Meadowlands HAV PO9.......... 9 H5
 HAV PO9.......... 142 A5
 LYMN SO41.......... 228 A4
Meadow La CHCH/BSGR BH23.......... 223 C6
 HLER SO31.......... 157 L6
 SELS SO20.......... 215 M4
Meadowmead Av WSHM SO15.......... 130 C1
Meadow Ri BDST BH18.......... 217 K3
 HORN PO8.......... 140 F5
Meadow Rd LYMN SO41.......... 228 A6
 NMIL/BTOS BH25.......... 225 M4
 RGWD BH24.......... 146 F7
Meadows Cl UPTN BH16.......... 217 C8
Meadows Dr UPTN BH16.......... 232 B1
Meadowside WEND SO18.......... 107 K4
The Meadows
 FHAM/PORC PO16.......... 7 L1
 LYND SO43.......... 151 L4
Meadow St SSEA PO5.......... 12 F5
Meadowsweet WVILLE PO7.......... 140 F7
Meadowsweet Rd CFDH BH17.......... 217 J8
Meadowsweet Wy CHAM PO6.......... 163 H7
 ELGH SO50.......... 79 K4
The Meadow ROMY SO51.......... 50 E7
 WVILLE PO7.......... 139 K4
Meadow View Rd BWD BH11.......... 219 J4
Meadow Wk LISS GU33.......... 36 E4
 LSOL/BMARY PO13.......... 184 F3
Meadow Wy FAWY SO45.......... 180 F5
 FUFL SO22.......... 26 B4
 NMIL/BTOS BH25.......... 240 F1
 RGWD BH24.......... 146 F8
 VWD BH31.......... 144 F4
Mead Rd CHFD SO53.......... 81 H2
 LYMN SO41.......... 227 M6
 WINC SO23.......... 26 D4
Mead Wy FHAM/PORC PO16.......... 7 J2
Meadway WVILLE PO7.......... 140 E7
The Meadway
 CHCH/BSGR BH23.......... 224 B6
Mears Rd ELGH SO50.......... 83 J6
Meath Cl HISD PO11.......... 214 A7
Medina Cl CHFD SO53.......... 81 K3
Medina Rd CHAM PO6.......... 163 H8
 WSHM SO15.......... 106 A4
Medina Wy CHCH/BSGR BH23.......... 239 H2
Medlar Cl CHCH/BSGR BH23.......... 223 H7
 HEND SO30.......... 134 B2
Medlicott Wy BPWT SO32.......... 112 A4
Medstead Rd HAV PO9.......... 165 K5
Medwall Gn ITCH SO19.......... 133 H3
Medway Dr CHFD SO53.......... 52 F8
Medway Rd FERN BH22.......... 194 E2
Meerut Rd BROC SO42.......... 175 K6
Meeting House La
 RGWD BH24.......... 170 D1
Megana Wy ROMY SO51.......... 51 H3
Megan Rd HEND SO30.......... 108 C6

Meggeson Av WEND SO18.......... 107 M6
Melbourne Pl SSEA PO5.......... 12 F3
Melbourne Rd CHAR BH8.......... 236 M1
 CHCH/BSGR BH23.......... 222 C7
 MOOR/WNTN BH9.......... 134 A2
Melbourne St SHAM SO14.......... 5 K4
Melbury Av BKME/WDN BH12.......... 234 D1
Melbury Cl FERN BH22.......... 194 B4
 LYMN SO41.......... 228 B5
Melchet Cl ROMY SO51.......... 48 A7
Melchet Rd WEND SO18.......... 108 B8
Melick Cl TOTT SO40.......... 130 D6
Mellor Cl CHAM PO6.......... 163 H8
Mellstock Rd PLE BH15.......... 233 H3
Melrose Av ENEY PO4.......... 211 M4
Melrose Cl NMIL/BTOS BH25.......... 226 A5
 TOTT SO40.......... 104 B7
Melrose Gdns GPORT PO12.......... 209 K1
 WSHM SO15.......... 106 C6
Melrose Rd ROWN SO16.......... 105 L8
Melverley Gdns WIMB BH21.......... 192 B5
Melville Cl ROWN SO16.......... 106 B3
Melville Rd ENEY PO4.......... 212 A6
 GPORT PO12.......... 209 L1
 MOOR/WNTN BH9.......... 220 C8
Mendip Cl NMIL/BTOS BH25.......... 225 M6
 VWD BH31.......... 144 D3
Mendip Gdns FAWY SO45.......... 155 H6
Mendip Rd ROWN SO16.......... 105 L8
 VWD BH31.......... 144 D2
Mendips Rd FHAM/STUB SO14.......... 6 B8
Mendips Wk FHAM/STUB SO14.......... 6 B8
Mengham La HISD PO11.......... 213 L6
Mengham Rd HISD PO11.......... 213 L5
Menslands La WVILLE PO7.......... 113 L6
Mentone Rd HAV PO9.......... 233 M5
Menzies Cl ROWN SO16.......... 105 L3
Meon Cl HORN PO8.......... 116 B4
 LSOL/BMARY PO13.......... 184 F6
 PSF GU32.......... 63 K4
 ROMY SO51.......... 79 H1
Meon Crs CHFD SO53.......... 81 J2
Meon Rd ENEY PO4.......... 211 M4
 ROMY SO51.......... 79 H1
Meonwara Crs PSF GU32.......... 60 C3
Mercer Wy ROMY SO51.......... 50 F8
Merchants Pl WINC SO23.......... 3 H7
Merchistoun Rd HORN PO8.......... 140 F1
Mercury Cl ROWN SO16.......... 105 L4
Mercury Gdns HLER SO31.......... 157 L4
Merdon Av CHFD SO53.......... 53 J8
Merdon Cl CHFD SO53.......... 53 J8
Mere Cft FHAM PO15.......... 159 H5
Meredith Cl CHCH/BSGR BH23.......... 238 C1
Meredith Gdns TOTT SO40.......... 129 H2
Meredith Rd NEND PO2.......... 187 J3
Meredun Cl RWIN SO21.......... 53 C1
Merepond La ALTN GU34.......... 33 K5
Meriden Cl CCLF BH13.......... 245 L1
Meriden Ct SSEA PO5.......... 12 F3
The Meridians
 CHCH/BSGR BH23.......... 237 L3
Merino Wy FERN BH22.......... 168 D7
Merlewood Cl WCLF BH2.......... 14 E2
Merley Dr CHCH/BSGR BH23.......... 224 E8
Merley Gdns WIMB BH21.......... 192 B7
Merley La WIMB BH21.......... 192 B7
Merley Park Rd WIMB BH21.......... 192 B7
Merley Ways WIMB BH21.......... 192 B5
Merlin Cl BPWT SO32.......... 85 G8
 RGWD BH24.......... 171 G2
Merlin Dr HSEA PO3.......... 187 K4
Merlin Gdns FHAM/PORC PO16.......... 161 M7
 HEND SO30.......... 133 M1
Merlin Wy CHCH/BSGR BH23.......... 238 F3
Mermaid Rd FHAM/STUB SO14.......... 184 D8
Mermaid Wy SHAM SO14.......... 5 J7
Merrick Wy CHFD SO53.......... 52 E8
Merridale Rd ITCH SO19.......... 132 C4
Merriefield Av BDST BH18.......... 218 A2
Merriefield Dr BDST BH18.......... 217 M2
Merrieleas Cl CHFD SO53.......... 81 H1
Merrieleas Dr CHFD SO53.......... 81 H1
Merriemeade Cl FAWY SO45.......... 155 J7
Merrifield WIMB BH21.......... 192 C1
Merrifield Cl BDST BH18.......... 217 M2
Merrifield Cl
 CHCH/BSGR BH23.......... 197 L8
Merrivale Av SBNE BH6.......... 237 K3
Merrivale Cl FAWY SO45.......... 155 J5
Merrivale Rd NEND PO2.......... 187 J3
Merrow Av BKME/WDN BH12.......... 235 G2
Merryfield La NBNE BH10.......... 220 A4
Merryfield Rd EPSF GU31.......... 64 A4
Merry Gdns NBAD SO52.......... 79 M3
Merryoak Gn ITCH SO19.......... 132 D3
Merryoak Rd ITCH SO19.......... 132 D4
Mersea Gdns ITCH SO19.......... 132 E4
Mersham Gdns WEND SO18.......... 132 E1
Merstone Rd
 LSOL/BMARY PO13.......... 185 C6
Merthyr Av CHAM PO6.......... 163 M7
Merton Av FHAM/PORC PO16.......... 186 B2
Merton Cl FBDG SP6.......... 97 L5
Merton Crs FHAM/PORC PO16.......... 186 B2
Merton Rd PTSW SO17.......... 107 C6
 SSEA PO5.......... 13 H7
Meryl Rd ENEY PO4.......... 212 A4
Mesh Pond RSAL SP5.......... 44 C8
Mesh Rd ROMY SO51.......... 22 B6
Meteor Rd EMRTH PO10.......... 190 C5
Methuen Cl CHAR BH8.......... 15 L2
Methuen Rd CFDH BH17.......... 217 M6
 CHAR BH8.......... 15 J1
 ENEY PO4.......... 211 L5
Methuen St SHAM SO14.......... 131 L1
Metuchen Wy HEND SO30.......... 134 A4
Mews La FUFL SO22.......... 2 D8

The Mews FAWY SO45.......... 206 D1
 HAV PO9.......... 165 L4
 ROWN SO16.......... 105 L2
Mey Cl WVILLE PO7.......... 164 D1
Meynell Cl ELGH SO50.......... 81 L5
Meyrick Cl CHCH/BSGR BH23.......... 223 L1
Meyrick Park Crs TWDS BH3.......... 235 L2
Meyrick Rd BMTH BH1.......... 15 J5
 HAV PO9.......... 8 B4
 NEND PO2.......... 187 G4
Michael Crook Cl HAV PO9.......... 165 G5
Michaels Wy ELGH SO50.......... 83 J6
 FAWY SO45.......... 155 K4
Michelgrove Rd BOSC BH5.......... 236 D5
Michelmersh Cl ROWN SO16.......... 105 K3
Michelmersh Gn CHAR BH8.......... 221 H6
Michigan Wy TOTT SO40.......... 104 A8
Mickleham Cl
 BKME/WDN BH12.......... 219 M8
Midanbury Crs WEND SO18.......... 107 L7
Midanbury La WEND SO18.......... 107 K8
Middlebere Crs UPTN BH16.......... 232 B4
Middlebridge St ROMY SO51.......... 78 D2
Middlebrook BPWT SO32.......... 85 H8
Middle Brook St WINC SO23.......... 3 H7
Middle Common Rd
 LYMN SO41.......... 227 K5
Middlecroft La GPORT PO12.......... 209 K2
Middlefield SELS SO20.......... 215 L1
Middlehill Dr WIMB BH21.......... 192 F2
Middlehill Rd WIMB BH21.......... 192 E1
Middle La RGWD BH24.......... 170 E1
Middle Md FHAM/STUB SO14.......... 159 M8
Middle Meadow LISS GU33.......... 36 F4
Middle Park Wy HAV PO9.......... 165 H2
Middle Rd FUFL SO22.......... 2 D6
 HLER SO31.......... 158 F3
 ITCH SO19.......... 132 C5
 LYMN SO41.......... 200 B8
 LYMN SO41.......... 200 F6
 LYMN SO41.......... 228 B5
 NBAD SO52.......... 79 M3
 NBNE BH10.......... 220 A3
 PLE BH15.......... 233 K2
Middlesex Rd ENEY PO4.......... 211 L5
Middle St CCLF BH13.......... 244 C3
 SHAM SO14.......... 131 L1
 SSEA PO5.......... 13 C1
Middleton Cl FHAM/STUB SO14.......... 6 C9
 WEND SO18.......... 107 K8
Middleton Ri HORN PO8.......... 116 C4
Middleton Rd NBNE BH10.......... 220 C6
 RGWD BH24.......... 146 E6
Midfield Cl FHAM/STUB SO14.......... 184 D1
Midland Rd MOOR/WNTN BH9.......... 220 D7
Midlands Est HEND SO30.......... 108 B6
Midlington Hl BPWT SO32.......... 112 F1
Midlington Rd BPWT SO32.......... 112 F1
Midway FAWY SO45.......... 155 K5
Midway Rd NEND PO2.......... 187 J3
Midways FHAM/STUB SO14.......... 184 A7
Midwood Av CHAR BH8.......... 221 K7
Milbeck Cl HORN PO8.......... 140 E2
Milborne Crs BKME/WDN BH12.......... 234 D1
Milbourne Rd FERN BH22.......... 194 A2
Milburn Cl WBNE BH4.......... 235 H4
Milburn Rd WBNE BH4.......... 235 H4
The Milburns ROMY SO51.......... 50 C1
Milbury Crs ITCH SO19.......... 132 E2
Mildmay St FUFL SO22.......... 26 C3
Milebush Rd ENEY PO4.......... 212 A3
Mile End Rd PSEA PO1.......... 211 G1
Miles's La RSAL SP5.......... 47 J4
Milestone Rd PLE BH15.......... 233 J2
Milford Ct FERN BH22.......... 168 D6
 HAV PO9.......... 165 H5
Milford Cl LYMN SO41.......... 242 D4
Milford Crs LYMN SO41.......... 242 D4
Milford Dr BWD BH11.......... 219 K3
Milford Gdns CHFD SO53.......... 81 K2
Milford Rd LYMN SO41.......... 227 K7
 NMIL/BTOS BH25.......... 226 A4
 PSEA PO1.......... 13 J1
Military Rd FHAM/PORC PO16.......... 161 H6
 GPORT PO12.......... 209 J3
 GPORT PO12.......... 209 M8
 GPORT PO12.......... 210 A7
 HSEA PO3.......... 187 K3
 PSEA PO1.......... 211 J1
Milkwood Ct TOTT SO40.......... 129 G1
Millais Rd ITCH SO19.......... 132 C5
Milland La LIPH GU30.......... 38 D5
Milland Rd LIPH GU30.......... 38 E6
 WINC SO23.......... 27 G2
Millbank St SHAM SO14.......... 5 L1
Millbridge Gdns ITCH SO19.......... 132 F4
Millbrook Cl CHFD SO53.......... 81 J3
 LISS GU33.......... 36 F4
Millbrook Dr HAV PO9.......... 165 L2
Millbrook Point Rd
 WSHM SO15.......... 130 A2
Millbrook Rd East
 WSHM SO15.......... 131 G3
Millbrook Rd West
 WSHM SO15.......... 130 C1
Mill Cl HISD PO11.......... 189 K6
 ROWN SO16.......... 105 K6
 WVILLE PO7.......... 139 M4
Mill Ct FBDG SP6.......... 97 K7
Mill End EMRTH PO10.......... 166 F8
 FBDG SP6.......... 96 C4
Miller Cl NMIL/BTOS BH25.......... 226 A4
Miller Dr FHAM/PORC PO16.......... 6 F2
Miller Rd CHCH/BSGR BH23.......... 238 C1
Millers La FUFL SO22.......... 25 L5
Millfield CFDH BH17.......... 232 F1
Millhams Rd NBNE BH10.......... 219 L4
Millhams St CHCH/BSGR BH23.......... 238 A24
Millhams St North
 CHCH/BSGR BH23.......... 238 A2
Mill Hl HEND SO30.......... 134 B1
Mill Hill Cl PSTN BH14.......... 234 A5
Milliken Cl FAWY SO45.......... 180 D6
Mill La BPWT SO32.......... 87 H6
 BPWT SO32.......... 110 C5
 BROC SO42.......... 175 M4
 CHCH/BSGR BH23.......... 221 M2
 CHCH/BSGR BH23.......... 224 F8

EMRTH PO10 .... 166 F6
EPSF GU31 .... 66 C8
EPSF GU31 .... 93 C5
FHAM PO15 .... 159 L7
GPORT PO12 .... 209 M2
HAV PO9 .... 165 C7
HAV PO9 .... 189 J2
LYMN SO41 .... 227 J1
LYMN SO41 .... 228 D4
LYMN SO41 .... 229 K3
LYND SO43 .... 127 J6
MIDH GU29 .... 67 K6
PSEA PO1 .... 211 C1
PSF GU32 .... 35 K8
PSF GU32 .... 64 A2
PSTN BH14 .... 234 A5
RGWD BH24 .... 173 C3
ROMY SO51 .... 48 D8
ROMY SO51 .... 78 C1
ROWN SO16 .... 104 D4
WHAM PO17 .... 136 C6
WVILLE PO7 .... 163 J4
Mill Meadow LYMN SO41 .... 242 B3
Mill Pond Rd GPORT PO12 .... 209 M2
The Mill Pond FAWY SO45 .... 179 M2
Mill Quay EMRTH PO10 .... 190 E1
Mill Ri ROMY SO51 .... 21 J8
Mill Rd CHCH/BSGR BH23 .... 222 E8
EMRTH PO10 .... 166 F4
FHAM/PORC PO16 .... 7 J8
GPORT PO12 .... 209 L2
LISS GU33 .... 36 F3
TOTT SO40 .... 129 L1
WSHM SO15 .... 130 E1
WVILLE PO7 .... 139 L4
WVILLE PO7 .... 164 B2
Mill Rd (North) CHAR BH8 .... 221 H5
Mill Rd (South) CHAR BH8 .... 221 H6
Mill Rythe La HISD PO11 .... 213 L1
Mills Rd NEND PO2 .... 187 H8
Millstream Cl CFDH BH17 .... 232 F1
WIMB BH21 .... 192 A4
Millstream Ri ROMY SO51 .... 78 C1
Mill St FHAM/STUB PO14 .... 159 L8
Mill Vale Mdw LIPH GU30 .... 38 E5
Millvina Cl TOTT SO40 .... 128 D4
Mill Wy TOTT SO40 .... 129 J3
Millyford Cl NMIL/BTOS BH25 .... 225 H8
Milne Cl FAWY SO45 .... 155 G6
Milner Ct WSHM SO15 .... 106 B8
Milne Rd CFDH BH17 .... 217 M7
Milner Pl FUFL SO22 .... 26 D2
Milner Rd WBNE BH4 .... 235 H6
Milnthorpe La FUFL SO22 .... 2 C9
Milton Cl PSTN BH14 .... 234 C5
Milton Gv HLER SO31 .... 158 F7
NMIL/BTOS BH25 .... 225 M6
Milton Md NMIL/BTOS BH25 .... 225 K6
Milton Pde HLER SO31 .... 140 C6
Milton Park Av ENEY PO4 .... 211 M4
Milton Rd CHAR BH8 .... 15 H1
ELGH SO50 .... 82 A3
ENEY PO4 .... 211 L4
HSEA PO3 .... 211 L1
PSTN BH14 .... 234 C5
WIMB BH21 .... 192 A2
WSHM SO15 .... 131 J2
WVILLE PO7 .... 140 B7
Milverton Cl
CHCH/BSGR BH23 .... 224 C7
Milverton Rd FUFL SO22 .... 2 C6
TOTT SO40 .... 129 L2
Milvil Rd LSOL/BMARY PO13 .... 208 C3
Mimosa Av WIMB BH21 .... 192 B8
Mimosa Dr ELGH SO50 .... 83 K6
Mincingfield La BPWT SO32 .... 110 C4
Minden Wy FUFL SO22 .... 26 B3
Minerva Cl WVILLE PO7 .... 164 C6
Minley Ct HAV PO9 .... 165 M3
Minnitt Rd GPORT PO12 .... 11 J3
Minstead Av WEND SO18 .... 108 B8
Minstead Cl FUFL SO22 .... 16 C4
Minstead Rd ENEY PO4 .... 211 M5
NBNE BH10 .... 220 A5
Minsted Rd MIDH GU29 .... 67 J8
Minster Cl FHAM PO15 .... 160 A7
Minster La WINC SO23 .... 3 G8
Minster Vw WIMB BH21 .... 192 A3
Minster Wy UPTN BH16 .... 232 K1
Mintern Cl ELGH SO50 .... 82 C3
Minterne Rd CHCH/BSGR BH23 .... 238 D3
MOOR/WNTN BH9 .... 220 E6
PSTN BH14 .... 245 H1
Minters Lepe WVILLE PO7 .... 164 C5
Mint Rd LISS GU33 .... 37 G2
Mirror Cl HLER SO31 .... 158 D7
Mislingford Rd BPWT SO32 .... 112 B5
Missenden Acres
HEND SO30 .... 109 H8
Mission Rd BDST BH18 .... 217 L6
Misslebrook La NBAD SO52 .... 80 C4
Mitchell Cl NMIL/BTOS BH25 .... 240 F1
Mitchell Dr ELGH SO50 .... 83 K7
Mitchell Rd CFDH BH17 .... 218 D8
ELGH SO50 .... 82 A6
HAV PO9 .... 164 F5
WIMB BH21 .... 193 L4
Mitchells Cl ROMY SO51 .... 78 E1
RSAL SP5 .... 73 J2
Mitchell Wy ELGH SO50 .... 107 M1
HSEA PO3 .... 211 L1
Mitre Copse ELGH SO50 .... 82 E6
Mizen Wy
LSOL/BMARY PO13 .... 209 H2
Moat Cl FAWY SO45 .... 179 M5
Moat Dr GPORT PO12 .... 209 H5
Moat Hi WEND SO18 .... 107 L5
Moat La NMIL/BTOS BH25 .... 225 K7
Mockbeggar La RGWD BH24 .... 146 E1
Moffat Rd CHCH/BSGR BH23 .... 238 C1
Moggs Md EPSF GU31 .... 63 M5
Mole Hl WVILLE PO7 .... 164 D1
Molesworth Rd GPORT PO12 .... 11 G4
Molyneux Rd
NMIL/BTOS BH25 .... 226 B5
Momford Rd FUFL SO22 .... 26 A5
Monarch Cl HLER SO31 .... 158 E6
WVILLE PO7 .... 164 E1

Monarch's Wy BPWT SO32 .... 84 B1
HAV PO9 .... 142 D7
HORN PO8 .... 141 H5
ROMY SO51 .... 21 L8
WVILLE PO7 .... 88 F7
Monarch Wy FUFL SO22 .... 26 B2
HEND SO30 .... 108 D6
Monastery Rd WEND SO18 .... 132 C1
Monckton Rd GPORT PO12 .... 209 M7
HSEA PO3 .... 187 K6
Mon Crs WEND SO18 .... 133 G1
Moneyfield La HSEA PO3 .... 187 L8
Moneyfield La HSEA PO3 .... 187 L8
Moneyfly Rd VWD BH31 .... 144 F3
Monks Brook Cl ELGH SO50 .... 81 K7
Monks Cl FERN BH22 .... 168 B8
Monk's Hl EMRTH PO10 .... 166 E2
Monkshood Cl
CHCH/BSGR BH23 .... 223 M7
Monks Orch PSF GU32 .... 63 L3
Monks Pl TOTT SO40 .... 129 H2
Monks Rd HLER SO31 .... 156 F2
WINC SO23 .... 3 G5
Monks Wk FAWY SO45 .... 155 J8
Monks Wood Cl ELGH SO50 .... 107 G2
Monkton Cl FERN BH22 .... 194 B2
Monkton Crs BKME/WDN BH12 .... 219 J8
Monkton La TOTT SO40 .... 129 G2
Monkwood Cl HAV PO9 .... 165 H3
Monkworthy Dr RGWD BH24 .... 169 K3
Monmouth Cl CHFD SO53 .... 81 G2
VWD BH31 .... 144 F4
Monmouth Dr VWD BH31 .... 144 F4
Monmouth Rd NEND PO2 .... 187 H6
Monmouth Sq FUFL SO22 .... 26 A2
Monnow Gdns WEND SO18 .... 108 A7
Monroe Cl GPORT PO12 .... 209 J5
Monsal Av FERN BH22 .... 194 A4
Montacute Wy WIMB BH21 .... 192 C8
Montague Av ITCH SO19 .... 133 H5
Montague Gdns EPSF GU31 .... 64 B5
Montague Rd BOSC BH5 .... 237 G4
HEND SO30 .... 134 A3
Montagu Rd CHCH/BSGR BH23 .... 240 A1
Monteray Dr LYMN SO41 .... 226 D4
Monterey Dr HAV PO9 .... 165 L4
HLER SO31 .... 158 E6
Montfort Cl ROMY SO51 .... 79 H1
Montfort Hts ROMY SO51 .... 79 H1
Montfort Rd ROMY SO51 .... 79 H2
Montgomerie Rd SSEA PO5 .... 13 J3
Montgomery Av BWD BH11 .... 219 M5
Montgomery Rd HAV PO9 .... 9 G4
LSOL/BMARY PO13 .... 185 G4
WEND SO18 .... 107 M8
Montgomery Wk WVILLE PO7 .... 164 A3
Montgomery Wy CHFD SO53 .... 81 G5
Montpelier Cl HLER SO31 .... 159 G5
Montrose Av
FHAM/PORC PO16 .... 162 C7
Montrose Cl HEND SO30 .... 134 C2
VWD BH31 .... 144 D2
Montrose Dr NBNE BH10 .... 219 M6
Monserrat Rd
LSOL/BMARY PO13 .... 208 C2
Monument La LYMN SO41 .... 228 E3
RCCH PO18 .... 167 K1
WHAM PO17 .... 161 M4
Moody Rd FHAM/STUB PO14 .... 183 M7
Moody's Hl RSAL SP5 .... 19 H6
Moonhills La BROC SO42 .... 178 F6
Moonrakers Wy
CHCH/BSGR BH23 .... 224 C7
Moonscross Av TOTT SO40 .... 129 K4
Moorcroft Av
CHCH/BSGR BH23 .... 223 G6
Moordown Cl
MOOR/WNTN BH9 .... 220 E5
Moore Av BWD BH11 .... 219 L5
Moore Cl NMIL/BTOS BH25 .... 225 K7
Moore Crs HLER SO31 .... 156 F2
Moore Gdns GPORT PO12 .... 10 A3
Moorfield Gv
MOOR/WNTN BH9 .... 220 D6
Moorfields Rd CCLF BH13 .... 234 E8
Moorgreen Rd HAV PO9 .... 165 L3
HEND SO30 .... 108 D7
Moorhill Gdns WEND SO18 .... 133 J1
Moorhill Rd HEND SO30 .... 108 C8
RGWD BH24 .... 172 E6
Moorhouse La MIDH GU29 .... 66 F2
The Moorings
FHAM/PORC PO16 .... 184 F1
Moorings Wy ENEY PO4 .... 212 A2
Moorland Av NMIL/BTOS BH25 .... 225 K8
Moorland Cl FAWY SO45 .... 155 H5
HLER SO31 .... 158 E4
Moorland Crs UPTN BH16 .... 232 A1
Moorland Ga RGWD BH24 .... 170 E3
Moorland Rd BMTH BH1 .... 236 C4
PSEA PO1 .... 211 J2
Moorlands Cl BROC SO42 .... 175 H7
Moorlands Crs WEND SO18 .... 107 M8
Moorlands Ri FERN BH22 .... 168 D5
Moorlands Rd BPWT SO32 .... 111 M2
FERN BH22 .... 168 C6
VWD BH31 .... 144 D1
Moorland Wy UPTN BH16 .... 232 A1
Moor La RSAL SP5 .... 46 D7
Moor Pk HORN PO8 .... 140 F7
Moor Rd BDST BH18 .... 217 M3
Moors Cl CHCH/BSGR BH23 .... 221 M1
RWIN SO21 .... 54 E7
Moorside Cl BWD BH11 .... 219 M5
Moorside Rd BWD BH11 .... 219 L5
FERN BH22 .... 168 C6
WIMB BH21 .... 217 H3
WIMB BH21 .... 217 H3
Moortown Av CHAM PO6 .... 164 A7

Moortown Dr WIMB BH21 .... 192 F7
Moortown La RGWD BH24 .... 170 F4
Moorvale Rd
MOOR/WNTN BH9 .... 220 E6
Moor View Rd PLE BH15 .... 233 K2
Moot Cl RSAL SP5 .... 72 C2
Moot Gdns RSAL SP5 .... 72 C2
Moot La FBDG SP6 .... 72 C6
RSAL SP5 .... 72 C2
Mopley FAWY SO45 .... 206 D1
Mopley Cl FAWY SO45 .... 206 D1
Morant Rd RGWD BH24 .... 146 F7
Moraunt Cl GPORT PO12 .... 185 M8
Moraunt Dr FHAM/PORC PO16 .... 185 M2
Mordaunt Rd SHAM SO14 .... 131 L1
Morden Av FERN BH22 .... 194 A4
Morden Rd
MOOR/WNTN BH9 .... 220 D7
Moreland Rd GPORT PO12 .... 10 E2
Morelands Rd WVILLE PO7 .... 164 C4
Morestead Rd RWIN SO21 .... 27 G3
Moreton Rd MOOR/WNTN BH9 .... 220 F4
Morgan Rd ENEY PO4 .... 212 A4
Morgans Dr FHAM/STUB PO14 .... 184 A3
Morgans Rise Rd RSAL SP5 .... 73 J1
Morgans Vale Rd RSAL SP5 .... 73 J2
Morland Rd WSHM SO15 .... 106 B7
Morley Cl BOSC BH5 .... 236 F3
CHCH/BSGR BH23 .... 223 G5
ITCH SO19 .... 132 D2
Morley Crs HORN PO8 .... 140 C5
Morley Dr BPWT SO32 .... 85 H8
Morley Rd BOSC BH5 .... 236 F3
ENEY PO4 .... 211 L6
Morningside Av
FHAM/PORC PO16 .... 162 B7
Mornington Dr FUFL SO22 .... 16 B6
Mornish Rd CCLF BH13 .... 234 E6
Morpeth Av TOTT SO40 .... 104 E8
Morris Cl FAWY SO45 .... 155 H4
LSOL/BMARY PO13 .... 185 G4
Morris Rd WSHM SO15 .... 4 D1
Morrison Av BKME/WDN BH12 .... 234 C2
Morshead Crs FHAM/PORC PO16 .... 6 F7
Mortimer Cl CHCH/BSGR BH23 .... 238 F2
HLER SO31 .... 156 F2
TOTT SO40 .... 104 C7
WINC SO23 .... 17 G2
Mortimer Rd CHAM PO6 .... 163 G7
CHAR BH8 .... 220 F7
HEND SO30 .... 134 C2
ITCH SO19 .... 132 C4
Mortimers Dr ELGH SO50 .... 83 J6
Mortimers La ELGH SO50 .... 83 J6
Mortimer Wy NBAD SO52 .... 79 J5
Mortimore Rd GPORT PO12 .... 209 K2
Mosaic Cl ITCH SO19 .... 133 K4
Mosdell Rd EMRTH PO10 .... 167 H8
Moss Cl LISS GU33 .... 36 F4
Moss Dr TOTT SO40 .... 130 D6
Mossleigh Av ROWN SO16 .... 105 L3
Mossley Av BKME/WDN BH12 .... 219 K7
Moss Rd WINC SO23 .... 3 K7
Motcombe Rd CCLF BH13 .... 244 F7
Mottisfont Cl WSHM SO15 .... 130 E2
Mottisfont Rd ELGH SO50 .... 81 M4
Mound Cl GPORT PO12 .... 10 C5
Mountain Ash Cl WEND SO18 .... 133 G1
Mount Av NMIL/BTOS BH25 .... 225 L7
Mountbatten Av ROMY SO51 .... 78 E1
Mountbatten Cl
CHCH/BSGR BH23 .... 238 F3
LSOL/BMARY PO13 .... 185 G4
Mountbatten Ct FUFL SO22 .... 2 C1
Mountbatten Dr FERN BH22 .... 194 A3
WVILLE PO7 .... 164 A2
Mountbatten Rd CCLF BH13 .... 235 G7
CHAR BH8 .... 221 K6
ELGH SO50 .... 81 M3
TOTT SO40 .... 104 C8
Mountbatten Sq ENEY PO4 .... 211 M6
Mount Cl FUFL SO22 .... 2 C1
NMIL/BTOS BH25 .... 225 L7
Mount Dr CHFD SO53 .... 81 K4
FHAM PO15 .... 159 M8
Mountfield GPORT PO12 .... 10 E7
Mount Grace Dr PSTN BH14 .... 245 H1
Mount House Cl FAWY SO45 .... 155 L3
Mountjoy Cl WIMB BH21 .... 192 D6
Mount La ROMY SO51 .... 48 E1
Mount Pleasant RGWD BH24 .... 170 E1
WINC SO23 .... 17 G2
Mount Pleasant Dr CHAR BH8 .... 221 K7
CHCH/BSGR BH23 .... 198 A7
Mount Pleasant La
LYMN SO41 .... 201 K8
Mount Pleasant Rd
GPORT PO12 .... 10 E7
PLE BH15 .... 233 J6
SHAM SO14 .... 131 M1
Mount Rd BWD BH11 .... 219 L4
PSTN BH14 .... 234 A3
Mount Temple ROMY SO51 .... 78 F1
The Mount
LSOL/BMARY PO13 .... 185 J7
RGWD BH24 .... 147 H8
ROWN SO16 .... 105 M7
ROWN SO16 .... 106 A4
Mount Vw ELGH SO50 .... 82 A4
Mountview Av
FHAM/PORC PO16 .... 162 C7
Mountwood Rd EMRTH PO10 .... 167 H7
Mousehole La FAWY SO45 .... 155 L5
WEND SO18 .... 107 L8
Mousehole Rd CHAM PO6 .... 162 D7
Mowbray Rd ITCH SO19 .... 132 F4
Moxhams FBDG SP6 .... 97 L7
Muccleshell Cl HAV PO9 .... 165 L4
Muddyford Rd RSAL SP5 .... 45 J7
Mudeford CHCH/BSGR BH23 .... 238 E3
Mudeford Green Cl
CHCH/BSGR BH23 .... 238 E3
Mudeford La
CHCH/BSGR BH23 .... 238 C2
Mude Gdns CHCH/BSGR BH23 .... 238 F3
Mulberry Av CHAM PO6 .... 187 L1
FHAM/STUB PO14 .... 184 A1

Mulberry Cl GPORT PO12 .... 10 E4
Mulberry Gdns FBDG SP6 .... 97 K8
Mulberry La CHAM PO6 .... 187 L1
Mulberry Rd TOTT SO40 .... 130 D7
Mulberry Wk WSHM SO15 .... 106 B8
Mullen Cl ITCH SO19 .... 132 C4
Mullins Cl BKME/WDN BH12 .... 220 A8
Mullin's La FAWY SO45 .... 155 K6
Mullion Cl CHAM PO6 .... 186 F1
Mumby Rd GPORT PO12 .... 11 K2
Mundays Rw HORN PO8 .... 116 B7
Munro Crs WSHM SO15 .... 130 C1
Munster Rd NEND PO2 .... 187 H6
PSTN BH14 .... 234 C5
Murefield Rd PSEA PO1 .... 13 K1
Muriel Rd WVILLE PO7 .... 140 C8
Murley Rd MOOR/WNTN BH9 .... 220 E8
Murray Cl FHAM PO15 .... 6 D4
ITCH SO19 .... 133 J2
Murray Rd HORN PO8 .... 140 F2
Murray's La PSEA PO1 .... 210 D2
Muscliffe Cl HAV PO9 .... 165 M3
Muscliffe La
MOOR/WNTN BH9 .... 220 E4
Muscliffe Pk
MOOR/WNTN BH9 .... 220 D8
Muscliffe Rd
MOOR/WNTN BH9 .... 220 D8
Museum Rd PSEA PO1 .... 12 E4
Mussett Cl TOTT SO40 .... 129 J1
Mustang Av FHAM PO15 .... 158 F1
Myers Cl BPWT SO32 .... 112 A3
My Lords La HISD PO11 .... 213 M5
Myrtle Av FHAM/PORC PO16 .... 186 B1
TOTT SO40 .... 129 H2
Myrtle Cl LSOL/BMARY PO13 .... 184 F5
LYMN SO41 .... 226 D4
Myrtle Gv HSEA PO3 .... 211 M2
Myrtle Rd CHAR BH8 .... 236 B2
ROWN SO16 .... 106 A4
Myvern Cl FAWY SO45 .... 180 A5

N

Nada Rd CHCH/BSGR BH23 .... 224 B7
Nailsworth Rd CHAM PO6 .... 162 F7
Nairn Rd CCLF BH13 .... 245 K1
TWDS BH3 .... 235 K2
Naish Ct HAV PO9 .... 165 G1
Naish Dr GPORT PO12 .... 185 L7
Naish Rd NMIL/BTOS BH25 .... 240 C1
Namu Rd MOOR/WNTN BH9 .... 220 C7
Nansen Av PLE BH15 .... 233 J3
Napier Crs FHAM PO15 .... 160 A7
Napier Rd HORN PO8 .... 141 G2
ITCH SO19 .... 133 J3
PLE BH15 .... 232 B5
SSEA PO5 .... 13 K7
Narrow La RGWD BH24 .... 147 H7
ROMY SO51 .... 78 D1
Narvik Rd NEND PO2 .... 187 H4
Naseby Rd MOOR/WNTN BH9 .... 220 E7
Nash Cl FAWY SO45 .... 155 H6
Nashe Cl FHAM PO15 .... 6 A2
Nashe Wy FHAM PO15 .... 160 A6
Nash Rd FAWY SO45 .... 155 H7
Nasmith Cl LSOL/BMARY PO13 .... 209 H4
Nathen Gdns PLE BH15 .... 232 C5
Nations Hl WINC SO23 .... 17 G1
Navigator's Wy HEND SO30 .... 109 H8
Navy Rd PSEA PO1 .... 210 E2
Nea Cl CHCH/BSGR BH23 .... 224 B8
Neacroft Cl NMIL/BTOS BH25 .... 225 H8
Nea Dr RGWD BH24 .... 145 J3
Nea Rd CHCH/BSGR BH23 .... 224 C8
Neath Wy CHFD SO53 .... 80 F3
Needles Point LYMN SO41 .... 242 C4
Neelands Gv CHAM PO6 .... 162 C8
Neilson Cl CHFD SO53 .... 81 H1
Nelson Av FHAM/PORC PO16 .... 185 M1
NEND PO2 .... 187 H6
Nelson Cl FAWY SO45 .... 180 A5
NMIL/BTOS BH25 .... 225 K5
ROMY SO51 .... 50 E8
ROMY SO51 .... 50 F8
Nelson Ct FHAM/STUB PO14 .... 184 D2
Nelson Crs HORN PO8 .... 141 G1
Nelson Dr CHCH/BSGR BH23 .... 238 E2
Nelson La WHAM PO17 .... 162 A5
Nelson Pl LYMN SO41 .... 228 D5
Nelson Rd BKME/WDN BH12 .... 235 G4
ELGH SO50 .... 82 C4
GPORT PO12 .... 10 F4
PSEA PO1 .... 211 H1
SSEA PO5 .... 13 H6
WINC SO23 .... 3 L9
WSHM SO15 .... 131 G2
Nelsons Gdns HEND SO30 .... 109 H5
Nepean Cl GPORT PO12 .... 10 E9
Neptune Rd FHAM PO15 .... 160 A6
FHAM/STUB PO14 .... 184 D3
Neptune Wy SHAM SO14 .... 5 J7
Nerissa Cl WVILLE PO7 .... 140 F8
Nerquis Cl ROMY SO51 .... 50 E8
Nesbitt Cl LSOL/BMARY PO13 .... 184 F5
Nessus St NEND PO2 .... 187 H8
Netherfield Cl HAV PO9 .... 9 H6
Netherhall Gdns WBNE BH4 .... 235 H5
Nether Hill La BPWT SO32 .... 110 A6
Netherton Rd GPORT PO12 .... 209 K1
Netley Cl CHFD SO53 .... 81 G5
PLE BH15 .... 233 M1
Netley Firs Rd ITCH SO19 .... 133 K4
Netley Hill Est ITCH SO19 .... 133 K4
Netley Lodge Cl HLER SO31 .... 157 G3
Netley Rd FHAM/STUB PO14 .... 159 J2
SSEA PO5 .... 13 G8
Netley Ter SSEA PO5 .... 13 G8
Nettlecombe Av ENEY PO4 .... 13 J4
Nettlestone HLER SO31 .... 157 G1
Nettlestone Rd ENEY PO4 .... 211 L6
Nettleton Cl CFDH BH17 .... 233 K1
Neva Rd WEND SO18 .... 107 L8
Neville Av FHAM/PORC PO16 .... 186 D2
Neville Gdns EMRTH PO10 .... 166 C5

Neville Rd HSEA PO3 .... 211 L1
Neville Shute Rd HSEA PO3 .... 187 L5
Newbarn La RCCH PO18 .... 143 K8
Newbarn Rd EPSF GU31 .... 91 H5
HAV PO9 .... 165 G5
Newbolt Cl HORN PO8 .... 140 C5
Newbolt Rd CHAM PO6 .... 162 D7
New Borough Rd WIMB BH21 .... 192 A5
Newbridge HLER SO31 .... 157 G2
Newbridge Rd TOTT SO40 .... 102 E5
Newbridge Wy LYMN SO41 .... 228 A7
New Brighton Rd
EMRTH PO10 .... 166 D5
Newbroke Rd
LSOL/BMARY PO13 .... 185 J8
Newbury Cl ELGH SO50 .... 83 G6
Newbury Dr NBNE BH10 .... 220 B7
Newbury Pl HLER SO31 .... 158 D6
Newbury Rd WSHM SO15 .... 106 B7
New Cliffe Gdns HEND SO30 .... 133 M3
Newcombe Rd FERN BH22 .... 168 B5
SBNE BH6 .... 237 K2
WSHM SO15 .... 131 J2
Newcomen Rd NEND PO2 .... 187 G6
Newcome Rd PSEA PO1 .... 211 J2
Newcroft Gdns
CHCH/BSGR BH23 .... 222 E8
New Cut HISD PO11 .... 189 K5
New Down La WVILLE PO7 .... 163 L6
Newenham Rd LYMN SO41 .... 228 C6
Newfield Rd LISS GU33 .... 36 F2
New Forest Dr BROC SO42 .... 175 H7
Newfoundland Dr PLE BH15 .... 233 J7
Newgate La FHAM/STUB PO14 .... 184 C2
New Harbour Rd South
PLE BH15 .... 233 G7
New Inn La BROC SO42 .... 204 A3
TOTT SO40 .... 127 M2
New Inn Rd TOTT SO40 .... 127 M2
Newland Av GPORT PO12 .... 10 C3
Newlands Av WSHM SO15 .... 131 G1
Newlands Cl FAWY SO45 .... 180 C8
NBAD SO52 .... 80 D3
Newlands Copse FAWY SO45 .... 180 D7
Newlands La WVILLE PO7 .... 139 L8
Newlands Rd
CHCH/BSGR BH23 .... 238 E1
FAWY SO45 .... 180 C6
LTDN BH7 .... 236 F2
NMIL/BTOS BH25 .... 225 M7
WVILLE PO7 .... 164 B3
Newlands Wy BDST BH18 .... 217 H5
New La EPSF GU31 .... 93 G6
HAV PO9 .... 9 G3
LYMN SO41 .... 242 E5
NMIL/BTOS BH25 .... 225 K2
Newlease Rd WVILLE PO7 .... 164 D3
Newlyn Wk ROMY SO51 .... 50 F7
Newlyn Wy BKME/WDN BH12 .... 234 D1
CHAM PO6 .... 162 C8
Newmans Cl WIMB BH21 .... 168 C3
Newmans Hl WHAM PO17 .... 112 B8
Newman's La FERN BH22 .... 168 A3
Newman St ROWN SO16 .... 106 A8
Newmarket Cl ELGH SO50 .... 109 J1
Newmer Ct HAV PO9 .... 165 H5
New Merrifield WIMB BH21 .... 192 D1
Newmorton Rd
MOOR/WNTN BH9 .... 220 E4
Newney Cl NEND PO2 .... 187 K4
Newnham Ct HAV PO9 .... 165 M3
New Orch PLE BH15 .... 233 G6
New Park Rd SBNE BH6 .... 237 H4
Newport Cl CHFD SO53 .... 80 F4
Newport La ROMY SO51 .... 51 G2
Newport Rd GPORT PO12 .... 10 A1
New Quay Rd PLE BH15 .... 232 F7
New Rd BKME/WDN BH12 .... 234 C2
BPWT SO32 .... 85 J6
BPWT SO32 .... 87 J5
BPWT SO32 .... 111 L4
ELGH SO50 .... 83 G6
EMRTH PO10 .... 166 F5
EMRTH PO10 .... 167 J8
FAWY SO45 .... 179 M2
FAWY SO45 .... 180 C7
FBDG SP6 .... 70 D7
FERN BH22 .... 194 B3
FERN BH22 .... 220 C1
FHAM/PORC PO16 .... 7 H5
FUFL SO22 .... 16 A2
HAV PO9 .... 8 D7
HLER SO31 .... 134 D8
HLER SO31 .... 156 F2
HLER SO31 .... 158 D8
HORN PO8 .... 116 B3
HORN PO8 .... 140 C2
LYMN SO41 .... 242 F4
NBNE BH10 .... 220 C3
NEND PO2 .... 211 J1
RGWD BH24 .... 122 F8
ROMY SO51 .... 50 C1
ROMY SO51 .... 50 F8
RSAL SP5 .... 75 K7
RWIN SO21 .... 54 E7
SHAM SO14 .... 5 G2
TOTT SO40 .... 129 G6
New Rd East NEND PO2 .... 187 K8
Newstead Rd SBNE BH6 .... 237 J4
New St LYMN SO41 .... 228 C4
PLE BH15 .... 233 G7
RGWD BH24 .... 170 E2
Newton Cl FHAM/STUB PO14 .... 184 A4
RSAL SP5 .... 46 F5
Newton La ROMY SO51 .... 78 D1
RSAL SP5 .... 46 C8
Newton Morrell PSTN BH14 .... 234 C5
Newton Pl LSOL/BMARY PO13 .... 208 C2
Newton Rd CCLF BH13 .... 234 D8
NMIL/BTOS BH25 .... 225 M8
RWIN SO21 .... 54 F1
WEND SO18 .... 107 K7
New Town FHAM/PORC PO16 .... 162 B8
Newtown La HISD PO11 .... 213 J4
RGWD BH24 .... 123 G7
Newtown Rd ELGH SO50 .... 81 M4
HLER SO31 .... 158 A8

ITCH SO19 .... 132 F8
ROMY SO51 .... 49 G5
VWD BH31 .... 144 A3
New Valley Rd LYMN SO41 .... 242 B4
Nicholas Cl
  CHCH/BSGR BH23 .... 224 F6
Nicholas Crs FHAM SO15 .... 6 E4
Nicholas Rd NBNE BH10 .... 220 A6
Nicholas Rd FAWY SO45 .... 206 C1
Nicholl Pl LSOL/BMARY SO13 .... 185 G6
Nichol Rd CHFD SO53 .... 53 J7
Nicholson Cl CFDH BH17 .... 218 C3
Nicholson Wk ROWN SO16 .... 105 J2
Nicholson Wy HAV PO9 .... 8 D1
Nichols Rd SHAM SO14 .... 5 K1
Nickel Cl WINC SO23 .... 3 K6
Nickel St SSEA PO5 .... 12 F5
Nickleby Gdns TOTT SO40 .... 128 F1
Nickleby Rd HORN PO8 .... 116 A2
Nickson Cl CHFD SO53 .... 53 C8
Nightingale Av ELGH SO50 .... 81 J6
Nightingale La FUFL SO22 .... 26 A2
  GPORT PO12 .... 209 K2
  HAV PO9 .... 141 L7
  ROMY SO51 .... 79 C1
  VWD BH31 .... 144 E3
Nightingale Crs BPWT SO32 .... 111 L8
Nightingale Dr TOTT SO40 .... 104 B8
Nightingale Gv WSHM SO15 .... 131 C1
Nightingale La RCCH PO18 .... 167 L5
Nightingale Pk HAV PO9 .... 9 J5
Nightingale Rd HLER SO31 .... 133 K8
  PSF GU32 .... 63 J6
  SSEA PO5 .... 12 F7
Nightingale Wk HLER SO31 .... 157 C4
Nightjar Cl CFDH BH17 .... 217 J8
  HORN PO8 .... 140 E2
Nile Rd PTSW SO17 .... 106 F6
Nile St EMRTH PO10 .... 166 D8
Nimrod Dr LSOL/BMARY SO13 .... 209 H2
Nimrod Wy BH21 .... 193 K2
Nine Elms La WHAM PO17 .... 161 J4
Ninian Cl ELGH SO50 .... 83 H7
Ninian Park Rd HSEA PO3 .... 187 L6
Niton Cl LSOL/BMARY SO13 .... 185 J2
Noads Cl FAWY SO45 .... 155 K6
Noads Wy FAWY SO45 .... 155 J7
Nobbs La PSEA PO1 .... 12 D4
Nobes Av LSOL/BMARY SO13 .... 185 C5
Nobes Cl LSOL/BMARY SO13 .... 185 H6
Noble Cl BWD BH11 .... 219 K7
Noble Rd HEND SO30 .... 134 B2
Nob's Crook RWIN SO21 .... 82 F1
Noel Cl BROC SO42 .... 175 L7
Noel Rd NBNE BH10 .... 219 M7
Nogarth Cl ROMY SO51 .... 51 G7
Nomad Cl WEND SO18 .... 108 A7
The Nook ELGH SO50 .... 82 A3
  LSOL/BMARY SO13 .... 185 J7
Noon Gdns VWD BH31 .... 144 F3
Noon Hill Dr VWD BH31 .... 144 F2
Noon Hill Rd VWD BH31 .... 144 F2
Norbury Cl CHFD SO53 .... 81 C1
Norbury Gdns HLER SO31 .... 157 J6
Norcliffe Cl BWD BH11 .... 219 M5
Norcliffe Rd PTSW SO17 .... 106 F8
Nordik Gdns HEND SO30 .... 134 A3
Nore Crs EMRTH PO10 .... 166 B7
Nore Down Wy RCCH PO18 .... 118 D8
Nore Farm Av EMRTH PO10 .... 166 B7
Noreuil Rd PSF GU32 .... 63 J5
Norfolk Cl CHCH/BSGR BH23 .... 222 D7
  WSHM SO15 .... 106 C8
Norfolk Rd GPORT PO12 .... 209 K1
Norfolk St SSEA PO5 .... 13 C5
Norgett Wy FHAM/PORC PO16 .... 185 M2
Norham Av ROWN SO16 .... 106 B6
Norham Cl ROWN SO16 .... 106 B6
Norland Rd ENEY PO4 .... 13 L5
Norlands Dr RWIN SO21 .... 54 B4
Norley Cl HAV PO9 .... 165 J3
Norleywood
  CHCH/BSGR BH23 .... 224 D8
Norleywood Rd LYMN SO41 .... 203 H1
Norman Av BKME/WDN BH12 .... 234 E1
Norman Cl FHAM/PORC PO16 .... 186 B2
Normandy Cl LYMN SO41 .... 200 E6
  ROWN SO16 .... 105 J2
Normandy Dr
  CHCH/BSGR BH23 .... 238 C1
Normandy Gdns GPORT PO12 .... 10 B3
Normandy La LYMN SO41 .... 228 D6
Normandy Rd NEND PO2 .... 187 H4
Normandy Wy FBDG SP6 .... 97 K6
  PLE BH15 .... 232 C6
  TOTT SO40 .... 130 D5
Norman Gdns
  BKME/WDN BH12 .... 234 F2
  HEND SO30 .... 133 L3
Normanhurst Av CHAR BH8 .... 221 H7
Norman Rd ENEY PO4 .... 13 L6
  FAWY SO45 .... 180 D8
  GPORT PO12 .... 10 C1
  HISD PO11 .... 213 M6
  WINC SO23 .... 26 E2
Normanton Cl
  CHCH/BSGR BH23 .... 222 D7
Norman Wy HAV PO9 .... 165 C6
Norris Cl RGWD BH24 .... 51 H6
  ROMY SO51 .... 9 H6
Norris Gdns HAV PO9 .... 9 H6
  NMIL/BTOS BH25 .... 225 L7
Norris Hl WEND SO18 .... 107 K7
Norrish Rd BKME/WDN BH12 .... 234 B3
Norset Rd FHAM PO15 .... 160 A6
Northam Br SHAM SO14 .... 132 A4
Northam Ms PSEA PO1 .... 13 J1
Northampton La FAWY SO45 .... 180 C8
Northam Rd SHAM SO14 .... 5 J3
Northam St PSEA PO1 .... 13 K1
  PSEA PO1 .... 211 H2
Northarbour Rd CHAM PO6 .... 187 H1
North Av NBNE BH10 .... 220 B2
  NEND PO2 .... 187 J3
North Battery Rd NEND PO2 .... 186 F6
North Bay EMRTH PO10 .... 190 E5
Northbourne Av NBNE BH10 .... 220 B4
Northbourne Cl FAWY SO45 .... 155 L7

Northbourne Gdns
  NBNE BH10 .... 220 C3
Northbourne Pl NBNE BH10 .... 220 B3
Northbrook Av WINC SO23 .... 3 K8
Northbrook Cl PSEA PO1 .... 211 H1
  WINC SO23 .... 3 L8
Northbrook Rd BDST BH18 .... 217 L6
Northcote Av NEND PO2 .... 187 K8
Northcote Rd BMTH BH1 .... 15 L2
  ENEY PO4 .... 13 M6
  PTSW SO17 .... 107 H6
North Crs HISD PO11 .... 213 M5
Northcroft St GPORT PO12 .... 209 K2
North Cross St GPORT PO12 .... 11 K3
Northdene Rd CHFD SO53 .... 81 H3
North Dr FUFL SO22 .... 16 A3
  NMIL/BTOS BH25 .... 199 J7
North East Cl ITCH SO19 .... 132 F3
North East Rd ITCH SO19 .... 132 E4
North End Av NEND PO2 .... 187 H6
North End Cl CHFD SO53 .... 81 H4
North End Gv NEND PO2 .... 187 H6
Northend La BPWT SO32 .... 86 F6
North End La FBDG SP6 .... 122 A4
NARL SO24 .... 30 C1
Northern Access Rd
  FAWY SO45 .... 181 H6
Northern Anchorage ITCH SO19 .... 5 M5
Northern Pde NEND PO2 .... 187 H5
Northern Rd CHAM PO6 .... 187 K2
Northerwood Av LYND SO43 .... 151 J3
Northerwood Cl NBAD SO52 .... 79 L4
North Fld SBNE BH6 .... 237 K2
Northfield Av
  FHAM/STUB SO14 .... 184 D1
Northfield Cl BPWT SO32 .... 84 F7
  HORN PO8 .... 116 B6
Northfield Rd LYMN SO41 .... 242 D3
  RGWD BH24 .... 146 E2
  WEND SO18 .... 107 L5
Northfields Farm La
  WHAM PO17 .... 136 E3
North Front SHAM SO14 .... 5 H2
North Greenlands LYMN SO41 .... 228 A6
North Head LYMN SO41 .... 241 M3
North Hl CHAM PO6 .... 162 F6
  FHAM/PORC PO16 .... 7 J1
North Hill Cl FUFL SO22 .... 2 F1
Northlands Cl TOTT SO40 .... 104 C8
Northlands Dr WINC SO23 .... 3 G3
Northlands Gdns WSHM SO15 .... 131 J1
Northlands Rd ELGH SO50 .... 81 M5
  ROMY SO51 .... 79 H2
  TOTT SO40 .... 104 C8
  WINC SO23 .... 131 J1
North La BROC SO42 .... 178 C3
  EPSF GU31 .... 91 K3
  EPSF GU31 .... 93 G4
  HORN PO8 .... 90 A7
  HORN PO8 .... 116 A2
  RSAL SP5 .... 101 H1
North Leigh La WIMB BH21 .... 192 C4
North Lodge Rd PSTN BH14 .... 234 D4
Northmead Dr CFDH BH17 .... 217 K8
Northmere Dr
  BKME/WDN BH12 .... 234 E1
Northmere Rd
  BKME/WDN BH12 .... 234 E1
Northmore Cl HLER SO31 .... 158 F3
Northmore Rd HLER SO31 .... 158 F3
Northney La HISD PO11 .... 190 A4
Northney Rd HISD PO11 .... 189 M4
Northover La LYMN SO41 .... 226 C1
North Poulner Rd RGWD BH24 .... 146 F7
North Rd BROC SO42 .... 175 L7
  FAWY SO45 .... 155 H6
  HORN PO8 .... 116 B6
  LTDN BH7 .... 236 D3
  PLE BH15 .... 232 F6
  PSF GU32 .... 63 L4
  PSTN BH14 .... 233 M4
  PTSW SO17 .... 107 H8
  WVILLE PO7 .... 162 E6
North Rd East WHAM PO17 .... 162 E2
North Rd West WHAM PO17 .... 162 D2
North Shore Rd HISD PO11 .... 213 H4
North St EMRTH PO10 .... 166 D7
  EMRTH PO10 .... 166 F4
  HAV PO9 .... 8 A3
  HAV PO9 .... 8 F4
  LYMN SO41 .... 228 A6
  PLE BH15 .... 233 H6
  PSEA PO1 .... 12 D1
  PSEA PO1 .... 211 H2
North Stroud La PSF GU32 .... 62 D6
North Town RWIN SO21 .... 54 F1
North Trestle Rd FAWY SO45 .... 180 F2
Northumberland Rd
  PSEA PO1 .... 13 J3
  SHAM SO14 .... 5 K1
  SHAM SO14 .... 131 M2
  SSEA PO5 .... 13 L2
North Wallington
  FHAM/PORC PO16 .... 7 M3
North Walls WINC SO23 .... 3 H6
Northway FHAM PO15 .... 159 J5
North Wy HAV PO9 .... 8 D4
Northways FHAM/STUB SO14 .... 184 B6
North Weirs BROC SO42 .... 175 H7
Northwood Cl ROWN SO16 .... 106 F2
Northwood La HISD PO11 .... 189 L7
Northwood Rd NEND PO2 .... 187 J4
Nortoft Rd CHAR BH8 .... 236 B2
Norton Cl CHCH/BSGR BH23 .... 238 C1
Norton Rd MOOR/WNTN BH9 .... 220 C7

WHAM PO17 .... 162 D2
WVILLE PO7 .... 164 B1
Norton Dr FHAM/PORC PO16 .... 7 H3
Norton Rd MOOR/WNTN BH9 .... 220 C7
  WHAM PO17 .... 162 D2
Norton Welch Cl NBAD SO52 .... 80 A4
Norway Rd HSEA PO3 .... 187 K4
Norwich Av WCLF BH2 .... 14 B5
Norwich Av West WBNE BH4 .... 14 A5
Norwich Cl HLER SO31 .... 158 C4
Norwich Pl LSOL/BMARY SO13 .... 208 C1
Norwich Rd CHAM PO6 .... 163 H7
  WCLF BH2 .... 14 C6
  WEND SO18 .... 107 L6
Norwood Pl BOSC BH5 .... 237 G3
Nottingham Pl
  LSOL/BMARY SO13 .... 208 C1
Nouale La RGWD BH24 .... 171 H1
Novello Gdns WVILLE PO7 .... 164 C1
Noyce Dr ELGH SO50 .... 83 J7
Noyce Gdns CHAR BH8 .... 221 M6
Nuffield Rd CFDH BH17 .... 218 B8
Nugent Rd SBNE BH6 .... 237 L4
Nunns Pk RSAL SP5 .... 47 C4
Nuns Rd WINC SO23 .... 3 H1
Nuns Wk WINC SO23 .... 3 J2
Nunton Dro RSAL SP5 .... 43 J1
Nursery Cl EMRTH PO10 .... 166 D5
  LSOL/BMARY SO13 .... 184 F5
Nursery Fld LISS GU33 .... 36 D5
Nursery Gdns CHFD SO53 .... 81 H5
  FUFL SO22 .... 2 B7
  HORN PO8 .... 140 E3
  ITCH SO19 .... 132 F2
  ROMY SO51 .... 78 F1
Nursery Gv HEND SO30 .... 134 A3
Nursery La FHAM/STUB SO14 .... 184 A7
Nursery Rd HAV PO9 .... 165 G6
  MOOR/WNTN BH9 .... 220 E5
  RGWD BH24 .... 170 E2
  WEND SO18 .... 107 J7
Nursling Crs HAV PO9 .... 165 L3
Nursling Gn CHAR BH8 .... 221 H6
Nursling St ROWN SO16 .... 105 H3
Nutash FHAM SO15 .... 159 G4
Nutbeem Rd ELGH SO50 .... 81 M6
Nutbourne Rd CHAM PO6 .... 188 D1
  HISD PO11 .... 214 C2
Nutburn Rd NBAD SO52 .... 80 A3
Nutfield Ct ROWN SO16 .... 105 K5
Nutfield Pl PSEA PO1 .... 211 H2
Nutfield Rd ROWN SO16 .... 105 J2
Nuthatch Cl ITCH SO19 .... 232 E1
  HAV PO9 .... 141 M7
Nutley Cl BWD BH11 .... 219 K4
Nutley Rd HAV PO9 .... 165 H3
Nutley Wy BWD BH11 .... 219 K5
Nutsey Av TOTT SO40 .... 104 C6
Nutsey La TOTT SO40 .... 104 D6
Nutshalling Av ROWN SO16 .... 105 K3
Nutshalling Cl TOTT SO40 .... 104 B7
Nutwick Rd HAV PO9 .... 9 K1
Nutwood Wy TOTT SO40 .... 104 D6
Nyewood Av
  FHAM/PORC PO16 .... 162 B7
Nyria Wy GPORT PO12 .... 11 J4

Oakapple Gdns CHAM PO6 .... 164 C8
Oak Av CHCH/BSGR BH23 .... 222 B8
Oakbank Rd ELGH SO50 .... 82 B5
  ITCH SO19 .... 132 B5
Oak Cl BPWT SO32 .... 84 E3
  FAWY SO45 .... 155 J7
  FERN BH22 .... 194 C7
  HORN PO8 .... 140 E2
  LYND SO43 .... 151 K4
  RSAL SP5 .... 18 B1
  WIMB BH21 .... 217 G3
  WSHM SO15 .... 130 A1
Oak Coppice Cl WIMB BH21 .... 192 C7
Oakcroft La FHAM/STUB SO14 .... 184 A3
Oakdale Rd PLE BH15 .... 233 K2
Oakdene LSOL/BMARY SO13 .... 185 H7
Oakdene Cl WIMB BH21 .... 192 B3
Oakdown Rd
  FHAM/STUB SO14 .... 184 B5
Oak Dr ELGH SO50 .... 83 H6
Oakenbrow FAWY SO45 .... 155 H6
  LYMN SO41 .... 200 C5
The Oakes FHAM/STUB SO14 .... 183 M4
Oakfield Ct HAV PO9 .... 165 M3
Oakfield Rd PLE BH15 .... 233 H2
  TOTT SO40 .... 127 M1
  TOTT SO40 .... 129 K1
Oakfields ELGH SO50 .... 81 M1
Oak Gdns LYMN SO41 .... 227 H8
Oak Green Wy WEND SO18 .... 107 M8
Oakgrove Rd ELGH SO50 .... 82 D6
Oakhill HLER SO31 .... 133 K4
Oakhill Cl CHFD SO53 .... 81 K3
  HLER SO31 .... 133 K4
Oakhurst Cl FERN BH22 .... 168 D6
  HLER SO31 .... 157 G2
Oakhurst Dr WVILLE PO7 .... 140 E8
Oakhurst Gdns CHAM PO6 .... 163 M6
Oakhurst La FERN BH22 .... 168 D6
Oakhurst Rd FERN BH22 .... 168 D7
  PTSW SO17 .... 106 F5
Oakhurst Wy HLER SO31 .... 157 G2
Oakland Dr WVILLE PO7 .... 130 D7
Oaklands LYMN SO41 .... 228 D6
Oaklands Av TOTT SO40 .... 104 C8
Oaklands Cl FBDG SP6 .... 97 K6
  FUFL SO22 .... 26 A2
  VWD BH31 .... 144 C2
Oaklands Gdns
  FHAM/STUB SO14 .... 159 G7
Oaklands Gv HORN PO8 .... 140 C5
Oaklands Rd HAV PO9 .... 9 H4
  PSF GU32 .... 63 H4
The Oaklands CHFD SO53 .... 81 H5
Oaklands Wy FAWY SO45 .... 155 G6
  FHAM/STUB SO14 .... 159 G7

ROWN SO16 .... 106 E4
Oakland Wk FERN BH22 .... 194 C7
Oak La RGWD BH24 .... 146 F6
Oakleigh Crs TOTT SO40 .... 129 J2
Oakleigh Dr RSAL SP5 .... 75 J7
Oakleigh Gdns ROMY SO51 .... 78 F1
Oakley Cl FAWY SO45 .... 180 A4
Oakley Hl WIMB BH21 .... 192 B4
Oakley La WIMB BH21 .... 192 B6
Oakley Rd HAV PO9 .... 165 H3
  ROMY SO51 .... 21 K6
  ROWN SO16 .... 105 L8
Oakley Straight WIMB BH21 .... 192 C7
Oakmead Gdns BWD BH11 .... 219 K4
Oakmeadow Cl EMRTH PO10 .... 166 C5
Oakmead Rd CFDH BH17 .... 232 F1
Oakmount Av CHFD SO53 .... 78 F1
  PTSW SO17 .... 106 F7
  TOTT SO40 .... 104 E8
Oakmount Rd CHFD SO53 .... 81 J4
Oak Pk Dr HAV PO9 .... 9 G1
Oakridge Rd WSHM SO15 .... 105 J8
Oak Rd BPWT SO32 .... 85 J8
  CHAR BH8 .... 236 B2
  FAWY SO45 .... 155 J7
  FBDG SP6 .... 121 K3
  FHAM PO15 .... 6 A4
  HLER SO31 .... 133 J8
  HORN PO8 .... 116 B3
  ITCH SO19 .... 132 B6
  NMIL/BTOS BH25 .... 226 A4
  PLE BH15 .... 232 B2
Oaks Coppice HORN PO8 .... 140 E2
Oak Dr RGWD BH24 .... 169 H5
Oakshott Dr HAV PO9 .... 165 L3
Oaks Md VWD BH31 .... 144 E2
Oak Tree Cl RWIN SO21 .... 54 E8
Oak Tree Dr EMRTH PO10 .... 166 C4
  LISS GU33 .... 36 F4
Oak Tree Farm RCCH PO18 .... 167 M7
Oak Tree Gdns HEND SO30 .... 133 M2
Oak Tree Rd WEND SO18 .... 107 J7
Oak Tree Wy ELGH SO50 .... 81 M3
Oak V HEND SO30 .... 108 A5
Oakwood Av HAV PO9 .... 164 F5
  NMIL/BTOS BH25 .... 226 A4
  RWIN SO21 .... 54 B5
Oakwood Cl HLER SO31 .... 158 B8
  MOOR/WNTN BH9 .... 220 F6
  ROMY SO51 .... 51 H7
  RWIN SO21 .... 54 B4
Oakwood Ct HEND SO30 .... 108 D6
Oakwood Dr ROWN SO16 .... 106 A3
Oakwood Rd
  CHCH/BSGR BH23 .... 224 C7
  CHFD SO53 .... 53 J8
  HISD PO11 .... 213 K5
  MOOR/WNTN BH9 .... 220 E6
  NEND PO2 .... 187 J4
Oakwood Wy HLER SO31 .... 157 L5
Oates Rd MOOR/WNTN BH9 .... 220 C7
Oatfield Gdns TOTT SO40 .... 126 B7
Oatlands ROMY SO51 .... 50 E8
Oatlands Cl BPWT SO32 .... 109 L7
Oatlands Rd BPWT SO32 .... 109 L7
Oban Rd TWDS BH3 .... 235 K1
Obelisk Rd ITCH SO19 .... 132 B6
Oberfield Rd BROC SO42 .... 175 H6
Oberon Cl WVILLE PO7 .... 140 E8
Ober Rd BROC SO42 .... 175 J6
Occupation La
  FHAM/STUB SO14 .... 183 J1
Ocean Cl FHAM PO15 .... 6 B3
Ocean Rd FHAM/STUB SO14 .... 184 D3
Ocean Wy SHAM SO14 .... 9 J5
Ockendon Cl SSEA PO5 .... 13 H4
Ocknell Gv FAWY SO45 .... 155 C5
O'connell Rd ELGH SO50 .... 81 K6
Octavia Gdns CHFD SO53 .... 81 L1
Octavia Hl FUFL SO22 .... 26 C1
Octavia Rd WEND SO18 .... 107 K4
Octavius Ct WVILLE PO7 .... 140 E7
Odell Cl FHAM/PORC PO16 .... 6 E1
Odiham Cl ROWN SO16 .... 105 L4
Odstock Rd RSAL SP5 .... 43 K1
Oglander Rd WINC SO23 .... 3 H3
Ogle Rd SHAM SO14 .... 4 F3
Okeford Rd BDST BH18 .... 217 H6
Okement Cl WEND SO18 .... 108 A6
Old Agwi Rd FAWY SO45 .... 181 C3
Old Barn Cl
  CHCH/BSGR BH23 .... 222 B6
  RGWD BH24 .... 170 F1
Oldbarn Cl TOTT SO40 .... 104 B6
Old Barn Crs WVILLE PO7 .... 114 B6
Old Barn Farm Rd WIMB BH21 .... 168 E3
Old Barn Rd CHCH/BSGR BH23 .... 222 B6
Old Bound Rd UPTN BH16 .... 232 B2
Old Brickyard Rd FBDG SP6 .... 97 G6
Old Bridge House Rd
  HLER SO31 .... 133 M8
Old Bridge Rd ENEY PO4 .... 13 M8
  LTDN BH7 .... 222 B8
Oldbury Ct ROWN SO16 .... 105 J6
Oldbury Wy FHAM/STUB SO14 .... 160 A8
Old Canal ENEY PO4 .... 211 M4
Old Christchurch Rd BMTH BH1 .... 15 J4
  LYMN SO41 .... 227 H7
Old Coastguard Rd CCLF BH13 .... 245 G4
Old Commercial Rd
  PSEA PO1 .... 211 G1
Old Common HLER SO31 .... 158 E4
Old Common Gdns HLER SO31 .... 158 E5
Old Copse Rd HAV PO9 .... 8 F7
Old Cracknore Cl TOTT SO40 .... 130 D6
Old Down RWIN SO21 .... 56 A1
Oldenburg HLER SO31 .... 134 F8
Old Farm Cl RGWD BH24 .... 147 G6

Old Farm Dr WEND SO18 .... 107 L6
Old Farm La EMRTH PO10 .... 166 F5
  FHAM/STUB SO14 .... 184 A7
Old Farm Rd PLE BH15 .... 233 K2
Old Farm Wk LYMN SO41 .... 228 B5
Old Farm Wy CHAM PO6 .... 188 C1
Old Forge La WIMB BH21 .... 193 K2
Old Garden Cl
  FHAM/STUB SO14 .... 159 G6
Old Gdns FUFL SO22 .... 2 B7
Oldgate Gdns NEND PO2 .... 187 K4
Old Gosport Rd
  FHAM/PORC PO16 .... 7 K8
Old Ham La FUFL SO22 .... 193 H4
Old Hillside Rd FUFL SO22 .... 16 B1
Oldhouse La HAV PO9 .... 143 H2
  ROMY SO51 .... 76 D1
Old Ivy La WEND SO18 .... 108 A6
Old Kennels Cl FUFL SO22 .... 25 M5
Old Kennels La RWIN SO21 .... 25 K7
Old Kiln Rd UPTN BH16 .... 232 B1
Old Litten La PSF GU32 .... 35 H5
Old Lyndhurst Rd TOTT SO40 .... 102 E8
Old Magazine Cl TOTT SO40 .... 130 D6
Old Manor Cl WIMB BH21 .... 192 C4
Old Manor Wy CHAM PO6 .... 187 M1
Old Market Rd WIMB BH21 .... 216 C1
Old Mill La EPSF GU31 .... 64 A3
  HORN PO8 .... 115 C8
Old Mill Wy ROWN SO16 .... 105 M7
Old Milton Gn
  NMIL/BTOS BH25 .... 225 K7
Old Milton Rd
  NMIL/BTOS BH25 .... 225 K7
Old Mulberry Cl NBNE BH10 .... 219 L7
Old Orch PLE BH15 .... 233 H7
Old Orchards LYMN SO41 .... 228 D6
Old Parsonage Ct RWIN SO21 .... 54 E5
Old Pines Cl FERN BH22 .... 194 C4
Old Priory Cl HLER SO31 .... 157 L6
Old Priory Rd SBNE BH6 .... 237 L4
Old Rectory Cl EMRTH PO10 .... 166 F5
Old Rectory Gdns WINC SO23 .... 17 J2
Old Rectory La RWIN SO21 .... 54 F1
Old Rectory Rd CHAM PO6 .... 188 C2
Old Redbridge Rd WSHM SO15 .... 105 H8
Old Reservoir Rd CHAM PO6 .... 188 B1
Old River WVILLE PO7 .... 139 K5
Old Rd GPORT PO12 .... 11 H5
  ROMY SO51 .... 50 F8
  SHAM SO14 .... 5 J7
The Old Rd CHAM PO6 .... 187 K2
Old Romsey Rd TOTT SO40 .... 102 D8
The Old Rope Wk PLE BH15 .... 232 E5
Old Salisbury La ROMY SO51 .... 49 K7
Old Salisbury Rd ROMY SO51 .... 103 K1
Old Sawmill Cl VWD BH31 .... 144 C2
Old School Cl FAWY SO45 .... 179 M2
  FERN BH22 .... 194 A3
  HLER SO31 .... 157 H1
Old School Dr HISD PO11 .... 213 M6
Old School Gdns HEND SO30 .... 108 D6
Old School Rd LISS GU33 .... 36 E4
Old Shamblehurst La
  HEND SO30 .... 110 H6
Old Stacks Gdns RGWD BH24 .... 171 G2
Old Star PSEA PO1 .... 12 C1
Old Station Ap WINC SO23 .... 3 K8
Old St John's Ms NBNE BH10 .... 220 D5
Old St FHAM/STUB SO14 .... 183 M5
Old Timbers HISD PO11 .... 213 K5
Old Tpk FHAM/PORC PO16 .... 7 J2
Old Vicarage Cl NBNE BH10 .... 220 C2
The Old Vineries FBDG SP6 .... 97 J7
Old Wareham Rd
  BKME/WDN BH12 .... 233 M1
  UPTN BH16 .... 216 E6
The Old Well Cl ITCH SO19 .... 133 C5
Old Winchester Hill La
  BPWT SO32 .... 59 L5
  PSF GU32 .... 60 B5
Old Wymering La CHAM PO6 .... 163 J8
Oleander Cl HLER SO31 .... 158 E3
Olive Crs FHAM/PORC PO16 .... 186 B2
Olive Rd ROWN SO16 .... 105 M4
Oliver Rd ENEY PO4 .... 211 K5
  LYMN SO41 .... 228 C5
  WEND SO18 .... 107 K4
Oliver's Battery Crs FUFL SO22 .... 26 A4
Oliver's Battery Gdns
  FUFL SO22 .... 26 A5
Oliver's Battery Rd North
  FUFL SO22 .... 26 A3
Oliver's Battery Rd South
  FUFL SO22 .... 26 A5
Olivers Cl TOTT SO40 .... 128 F1
Olivers Rd WIMB BH21 .... 192 E2
Olivers Wy WIMB BH21 .... 192 E2
Olivia Cl WVILLE PO7 .... 140 E7
Olympic Wy ELGH SO50 .... 82 E5
  ELGH SO50 .... 83 G5
Omdurman Rd PTSW SO17 .... 106 F6
Omega St SSEA PO5 .... 13 J2
Onibury Cl WEND SO18 .... 107 M7
Onibury Rd WEND SO18 .... 107 M7
Onslow Gdns WIMB BH21 .... 192 B2
Onslow Rd SHAM SO14 .... 131 L2
  SSEA PO5 .... 13 K9
Ophir Gdns BMTH BH1 .... 15 K2
Ophir Rd CHAR BH8 .... 15 J1
  NEND PO2 .... 187 H6
Oracle Dr WVILLE PO7 .... 164 C5
Orange Gv
  LSOL/BMARY SO13 .... 185 H7
Orange Rw EMRTH PO10 .... 166 D8
Oratory Gdns CCLF BH13 .... 234 E8
Orchard Av ELGH SO50 .... 82 E7
  PSTN BH14 .... 233 L6
Orchard Cl CHCH/BSGR BH23 .... 237 M2
  EPSF GU31 .... 93 K4
  FAWY SO45 .... 180 F5
  FBDG SP6 .... 97 L6
  FERN BH22 .... 194 C3
  GPORT PO12 .... 185 L7
  HORN PO8 .... 141 G2
  NBAD SO52 .... 79 L3
  RGWD BH24 .... 146 E8
  RWIN SO21 .... 54 E7

TOTT SO40 .... 129 K3
WIMB BH21 .... 217 H1
Orchard Ct HEND SO30 .... 134 C1
VWD BH31 .... 144 E3 3
Orchard Gdns FBDG SP6 .... 97 L7 2
Orchard Gv FHAM/PORC PO16 .. 185 L1
HORN PO8 .... 140 D5
NMIL/BTOS BH25 .... 225 L7
Orchard La EMRTH PO10 .... 166 E8
ROMY SO51 .... 78 D1
SHAM SO14 .... 5 H5
WIMB BH21 .... 217 H1
Orchardlea BPWT SO32 .... 112 A5
Orchard Pl SO14 .... 5 H7
Orchard Rd ELGH SO50 .... 83 H6
ENEY PO4 .... 13 M3
GPORT PO12 .... 210 B2
HAV PO9 .... 8 F6
HISD PO11 .... 213 L6
HLER SO31 .... 158 D6
RSAL SP5 .... 73 J1
Orchard St WCLF BH2 .... 14 D6
The Orchards BWD BH11 .... 219 H2
CHAM PO6 .... 187 K1
CHCH/BSGR BH23 .... 198 A3 8
LYMN SO41 .... 242 C4
ROWN SO16 .... 80 D7
WVILLE PO7 .... 139 K4
Orchard Wy FAWY SO45 .... 155 K6
Orcheston Rd CHAR BH8 .... 236 B2
Ordnance Rd GPORT PO12.. .... 11 J3
WSHM SO15 .... 131 L2
Ordnance Rw PSEA PO1 .... 12 C2
Ordnance Wy TOTT SO40 .... 130 E5
Oregon Cl ITCH SO19 .... 132 E4
Orford Cl CHCH/BSGR BH23 .... 222 B4
Oriel Dr FHAM/STUB PO14 .... 159 G7
Oriel Rd NEND PO2 .... 187 H6
Orient Dr FUFL SO22 .... 16 B5
Orion Cl FHAM/STUB PO14 .... 184 B6 8
ROWN SO16 .... 105 L4
Orkney Cl ROWN SO16 .... 105 K4
Orkney Rd CHAM PO6 .... 163 K7
Ormesby Dr CHFD SO53 .... 53 C8
Ormond Cl ELGH SO50 .... 83 C5
Ormonde Rd CCLF BH13 .... 234 F6
Ormsby Rd SSEA PO5 .... 13 H6 6
Orpen Rd ITCH SO19 .... 133 G5 8
Orsmond Cl WVILLE PO7 .... 164 D2 2
Orwell Cl ROWN SO16 .... 105 K7 8
Orwell Crs FHAM/STUB PO14.. .... 159 C6
Orwell Rd PSF GU32 .... 63 K6
Osborn Crs
LSOL/BMARY PO13 .... 184 F4
Osborne Cl WVILLE PO7 .... 164 E1 7
Osborne Dr CHFD SO53 .... 81 K3
Osborne Gdns ELGH SO50 .... 83 J7 6
Osborne Rd GPORT PO12 .... 11 J1
HLER SO31 .... 158 A8
LSOL/BMARY PO13 .... 208 C2 2
MOOR/WNTN BH9 .... 220 C8
NMIL/BTOS BH25 .... 225 M5
PSF GU32 .... 63 L4
PSTN BH14 .... 234 A5
SSEA PO5 .... 12 F7
TOTT SO40 .... 129 L1
WIMB BH21 .... 192 B4
Osborne Rd North PTSW SO17 .. 107 H7
Osborne Rd South PTSW SO17 .. 107 H8
Osborne View Rd
FHAM/STUB PO14.. .... 183 L7
Osborn Rd FHAM/PORC PO16 .. 7 K5
Osborn Rd South
FHAM/PORC PO16 .... 7 J5
Osier Cl NEND PO2 .... 187 G6
Oslands Dr HLER SO31 .... 158 B1
Osprey Cl CHCH/BSGR BH23 .... 238 F3
ROWN SO16 .... 105 L4
TOTT SO40 .... 130 C7
Osprey Dr HISD PO11 .... 213 M5
Osprey Gdns
LSOL/BMARY PO13 .... 208 D2 7
Osprey Quay EMRTH PO10 .... 190 F1
Ossemsley South Dr
NMIL/BTOS BH25 .... 199 J8
Osterley Cl HEND SO30 .... 134 C1
Osterly Rd ITCH SO19 .... 132 C4 8
Oswald Cl MOOR/WNTN BH9 .... 220 C6
Oswald Rd MOOR/WNTN BH9 .. 220 C6
Othello Dr WVILLE PO7 .... 140 E8
Otterbourne Crs HAV PO9 .... 165 H3
Otterbourne Hl CHFD SO53 .... 53 M7
Otterbourne Rd RWIN SO21 .... 54 B4
Otter Cl ELGH SO50 .... 82 F6
UPTN BH16 .... 232 A2
VWD BH31 .... 144 E3
Otter Rd PLE BH15 .... 233 L2
Otters Wk NMIL/BTOS BH25 .... 226 A2
Ouse Cl CHFD SO53 .... 52 F8
Outer Cir ROWN SO16 .... 105 M4
Outlands La HEND SO30 .... 135 H2
Outram Rd SSEA PO5 .... 13 K5
Oval Gdns GPORT PO12 .... 10 A4
Oval Rd ROMY SO51 .... 20 E8
The Oval LISS GU33 .... 36 E4
Overbrook FAWY SO45 .... 155 K6
Overbrook Wy NBAD SO52 .... 79 K3 8
Overbury Rd PSTN BH14 .... 234 B5
Overcliff Ri ROWN SO16 .... 106 D4
Overcombe Cl CFDH BH17 .... 218 C6
Over Links Dr PSTN BH14 .... 234 C6
Overstand Crs LYMN SO41 .... 242 C5
Overton Crs HAV PO9 .... 165 H3
Oviat Cl TOTT SO40 .... 128 F1
Ovington Av LTDN BH7 .... 237 H1
Ovington Gdns LTDN BH7 .... 237 H1
Owen Cl LSOL/BMARY PO13.. 209 C1
Owen Rd ELGH SO50 .... 81 L6
Owen's Rd FUFL SO22 .... 2 E4
Owen St ENEY PO4 .... 211 L1
Owls Rd BOSC BH5 .... 236 D5
VWD BH31 .... 144 E3
Owslebury Bottom
RWIN SO21.. .... 55 M3
Owslebury Gv HAV PO9 .... 165 K3
Oxburgh Cl ELGH SO50 .... 81 L3

Oxford Av SBNE BH6 .... 237 C3
SHAM SO14 .... 5 H1
Oxford Cl FHAM/PORC PO16 .. 6 F3
Oxford Ct FHAM/STUB PO32 .. 112 L1
BWD BH11 .... 219 M2
Oxford Rd BMTH BH1 .... 15 J4
GPORT PO12 .... 10 A1
SHAM SO14 .... 131 L1
SSEA PO5 .... 13 L6
Oxford St SHAM SO14 .... 5 H6
Oxlease Cl ROMY SO51 .... 50 F7
Oxleys Cl FHAM/STUB PO14.. 159 M8
Oxted Ct ENEY PO4 .... 211 M3 3
Oyster Ms PSEA PO1 .... 12 C5 3
Oyster Quay CHAM PO6 .... 186 F2
Oyster St PSEA PO1 .... 12 C5
Ozier Rd WEND SO18 .... 107 M6

P

Pacific Cl SHAM SO14 .... 5 K8
Packridge La ROMY SO51 .... 79 L7
Padbury Cl NEND PO2 .... 187 K4 2
Paddington Gv BWD BH11 .... 219 H5
Paddington Rd NEND PO2.. .... 187 K7
Paddock Cl
BKME/WDN BH12 .... 234 A1 6
RGWD BH24 .... 169 K4
WIMB BH21 .... 193 L2
Paddock End WVILLE PO7 .... 139 K5
Paddock Gdns LYMN SO41 .... 228 B3
Paddock Gv VWD BH31 .... 144 E3
The Paddocks FAWY SO45 .... 180 F5 2
ELGH SO50 .... 82 A3 8
FBDG SP6 .... 123 J2
FHAM/STUB PO14 .... 184 A4 8
GPORT PO12 .... 10 C5
TOTT SO40 .... 104 B6
WINC SO23 .... 17 H2
Paddock Wy PSF GU32 .... 63 J6
Padfield Cl SBNE BH6 .... 237 K2
Padget Rd RGWD BH24 .... 147 G2 3
Padnell Av HORN PO8 .... 140 E6
WVILLE PO7 .... 113 L8
Padnell Rd HORN PO8 .... 140 E5
Padstow Pl FBDG SP6 .... 97 K8
Padwell Rd SHAM SO14 .... 131 L1
Padwick Av CHAM PO6 .... 163 L8
Paffard Cl LSOL/BMARY PO13.. 209 G1
Page Cl WIMB BH21 .... 192 E1
Pages La BROC SO42 .... 204 A2
Paget Cl WIMB BH21 .... 192 E1 1
GPORT PO12 .... 10 C8
Paget St SHAM SO14 .... 5 K5
Pagham Cl EMRTH PO10 .... 166 E8
Pagham Gdns HISD PO11 .... 214 D6
Paignton Av HSEA PO3 .... 187 L8
Paignton Rd ROWN SO16 .... 105 L8
Pain's Rd SSEA PO5 .... 13 J4
Painswick Cl CHAM PO6 .... 163 G8
HLER SO31 .... 158 D2
Paisley Rd SBNE BH6 .... 237 H3
Palace La BROC SO42 .... 178 E7
Palfrey Rd NBNE BH10 .... 220 B4
Palk Rd HAV PO9 .... 8 A1
Pallant Gdns
FHAM/PORC PO16 .... 161 H6
The Pallant HAV PO9 .... 8 F4
Pallet Cl RWIN SO21 .... 54 E3
Pallot Cl HLER SO31.. .... 133 K8
Palmer Pl NMIL/BTOS BH25 .... 225 L4
Palmer Rd PLE BH15 .... 233 H3
Palmers Cl ELGH SO50 .... 83 J6 8
Palmer's Rd EMRTH PO10 .... 166 D7
Palmerston Av
CHCH/BSGR BH23 .... 238 C2
FHAM/PORC PO16 .... 7 K5
Palmerston Cl UPTN BH16 .... 232 C1 8
Palmerston Dr
FHAM/STUB PO14 .... 184 E1
HISD PO11 .... 213 L4
PSTN BH14 .... 234 C4
SHAM SO14 .... 5 G2
SSEA PO5 .... 13 H8
UPTN BH16 .... 232 B1
Palmerston Ms BMTH BH1 .... 236 D3 8
Palmerston Rd BOSC BH5 .... 236 D4 7
HISD PO11 .... 213 L4
PSTN BH14 .... 234 C4
SHAM SO14 .... 5 G1
SSEA PO5 .... 13 H8
UPTN BH16 .... 232 B1
Palmerston St ROMY SO51 .... 78 D1 3
ROMY SO51 .... 78 E1 8
Palmerston Wy GPORT PO12 .. 209 G4
Palm Hall Cl WINC SO23 .... 3 L8
Palm Rd ROWN SO16 .... 105 L3
Palmyra Rd GPORT PO12 .... 209 L1
Pamela Av CHAM PO6 .... 162 D8
Pamplyn Cl LYMN SO41 .... 228 A4
Pangbourne Av CHAM PO6 .... 187 M1
Pangbourne Cl ITCH SO19 .... 132 E4
Pannall Rd GPORT PO12 .... 209 L1
Panorama Rd CCLF BH13 .... 245 G4
Pan St PSEA PO1 .... 211 G2
Pansy Rd ROWN SO16 .... 106 F4
Pantheon Rd CHFD SO53 .... 81 L1
The Pantiles FBDG SP6 .... 97 J7 2
Panton Cl EMRTH PO10 .... 166 C5 2
Panwell Rd WEND SO18 .... 132 E1
The Parade PSEA PO1 .... 210 E2
Paradise La BPWT SO32 .... 111 K2
EMRTH PO10 .... 166 F4
FHAM/PORC PO16 .... 161 J6
TOTT SO40 .... 128 B2
Paradise St PLE BH15 .... 233 G7 6
PSEA PO1 .... 13 H1
Parchment St WINC SO23 .... 3 G7
The Parchment HAV PO9 .... 8 F5
Pardoe Cl HEND SO30 .... 134 A3
Parham Dr ELGH SO50 .... 81 L4
Parham Rd GPORT PO12 .... 210 A2
NBNE BH10 .... 220 A6
Parish Rd PLE BH15 .... 233 K5
Park Av LYMN SO41 .... 228 B4
NBNE BH10 .... 220 A2
WINC SO23 .... 3 H6
WVILLE PO7 .... 164 A5
Park Cl BROC SO42 .... 175 L6

CHCH/BSGR BH23 .... 223 C5
FAWY SO45 .... 155 M4
GPORT PO12 .... 209 K2
LYMN SO41 .... 242 D3
NMIL/BTOS BH25 .... 226 A3
TOTT SO40 .... 130 B7
WINC SO23 .... 3 G2
Park Crs EMRTH PO10 .... 166 B7
Park Dr VWD BH31 .... 144 A3
Parker Cl GPORT PO12 .... 185 L7
Parker Gdns WVILLE PO7 .... 164 A6
Parker Rd MOOR/WNTN BH9 .. 235 L1
Park Farm Av FHAM PO15 .... 160 A4
Park Farm Cl FHAM PO15 .... 6 A1
Park Farm Rd WVILLE PO7 .... 164 B6
Park Gv FHAM PO15 .... 187 K1
Park Hill Cl FAWY SO45 .... 180 A5
Park Homer Dr WIMB BH21 .... 192 D2
Park Homer Rd WIMB BH21 .. 192 D1 6
Park House Farm Wy HAV PO9.. 164 F3
Park Lake Rd PLE BH15 .... 233 K6
Parkland Cl VWD BH31 .... 145 H4
Parkland Dr NMIL/BTOS BH25.. 225 K8
Parklands HLER SO31 .... 158 E4
WEND SO18 .... 107 K7
Parklands Av HORN PO8 .... 140 E3
Parklands Cl CHFD SO53 .... 81 H1
GPORT PO12 .... 209 M2
Park La BPWT SO32 .... 86 B7
BPWT SO32 .... 87 G7
CHAM PO6 .... 187 L8
ELGH SO50 .... 54 A8
EMRTH PO10 .... 142 F8
FAWY SO45 .... 179 M4
FBDG SP6 .... 121 K2
FHAM/PORC PO16 .... 7 H3
HAV PO9 .... 141 G8
HAV PO9 .... 165 G5
HORN PO8 .... 140 E6
LYMN SO41 .... 230 F2
LYMN SO41 .... 242 B4
NBNE BH10 .... 220 D4
RWIN SO21 .... 17 J2
RWIN SO21 .... 54 F7
TOTT SO40 .... 130 A6
WIMB BH21 .... 192 A4
Park Pde HAV PO9 .... 165 J4 2
Park Rd BMTH BH1 .... 15 H3
BPWT SO32 .... 84 F8
CHFD SO53 .... 53 H8
EMRTH PO10 .... 167 H7
FBDG SP6 .... 97 L6
FUFL SO22 .... 2 F7
GPORT PO12 .... 10 F7
HISD PO11 .... 213 C4
LYMN SO41 .... 228 B4
LYMN SO41 .... 242 D4
NMIL/BTOS BH25 .... 225 K7
NMIL/BTOS BH25 .... 226 A3
PLE BH15 .... 233 L5
PSEA PO1 .... 12 D2
PSF GU32 .... 63 L5
WSHM SO15 .... 131 C2
WVILLE PO7 .... 139 K3
WVILLE PO7 .... 164 A4
Park Rd North HAV PO9 .... 8 D3
Park Rd South HAV PO9 .... 8 E5
Parkside CHCH/BSGR BH23 .... 224 B7
RGWD BH24 .... 170 D2
TOTT SO40 .... 129 K3
Parkside Av ROWN SO16 .... 105 G8
Parkside Gdns NBNE BH10 .. 220 C6 8
Parkside Rd PSTN BH14 .... 234 B4
Parkstone Av ENEY PO4 .... 13 L9
PSTN BH14 .... 234 F4
Parkstone Hts PSTN BH14 .... 233 L3
Parkstone Rd PLE BH15 .... 233 L3
Park St GPORT PO12 .... 10 F2
ROWN SO16 .... 106 A8
SSEA PO5 .... 12 F4
The Park BPWT SO32 .... 86 F7
NMIL/BTOS BH25 .... 225 M4
Park Vw HEND SO30 .... 133 M1
HEND SO30 .... 134 E1
Parkville Rd ROWN SO16 .... 107 J4
Park Wk SHAM SO14 .... 5 C2
Parkwater Rd RSAL SP5 .... 47 H7
Park Wy FERN BH22 .... 168 C6 8
HAV PO9 .... 8 D4
Parkway FHAM PO15 .... 159 K1
Parkway Dr CHAR BH8 .... 237 J5
Parkway Gdns CHFD SO53 .... 81 H1
The Parkway
LSOL/BMARY PO13 .... 184 F6
ROWN SO16 .... 106 F3
Parkwood Rd BOSC BH5 .... 236 F4
WIMB BH21 .... 192 A4
Parley Cl FERN BH22 .... 194 D3
Parley La CHCH/BSGR BH23 .. 194 F8
Parley Rd MOOR/WNTN BH9 .. 220 E6
Parliament Pl FUFL SO22 .... 26 B4
Parmiter Dr WIMB BH21 .... 192 C4
Parmiter Rd WIMB BH21 .... 192 C4
Parmiter Wy WIMB BH21 .... 192 C4
Parnell La ROMY SO51 .... 22 F6
Parnell Rd ELGH SO50 .... 81 L6
Parr Rd CHAM PO6 .... 163 H8 7
Parr St PSTN BH14 .... 233 M4
Parry Cl ITCH SO19 .... 132 C8
Parry Rd ITCH SO19 .... 133 H4
Parsonage Barn La
RGWD BH24 .... 146 E8
Parsonage Cl EPSF GU31 .... 64 A3
Parsonage Est EPSF GU31 .... 65 K4
Parsonage Hl RSAL SP5 .... 18 A1
Parsonage La BPWT SO32 .... 110 A2
Parsonage Park Dr FBDG SP6.. 97 M6
Parsonage Rd BMTH BH1 .... 15 C6
SHAM SO14 .... 131 M2
Parsons Cl HSEA PO3 .... 187 K4
Partridge
CHCH/BSGR BH23 .... 238 F3 8
FHAM/PORC PO16 .... 161 J8 2
Partridge Down FUFL SO22.. .... 26 A5

Partridge Dr PSTN BH14 .... 234 A7
Partridge Gdns HORN PO8 .... 140 B4
Partridge Gn
NMIL/BTOS BH25 .... 225 M2
Partridge Hl RSAL SP5 .... 75 M5
Partridge Rd BROC SO42 .... 175 K8
FAWY SO45 .... 155 K7
Partridge Wk PSTN BH14 .... 234 B7 8
Partry Cl CHFD SO53 .... 52 F8
Pascoe Cl PSTN BH14 .... 233 M4
Passage La HLER SO31 .... 157 M7
Passfield Av ELGH SO50 .... 81 K6
Passfield Cl ELGH SO50 .... 81 K6 8
Passford Hl LYMN SO41 .... 228 B1
Passingham Wk HORN PO8 .... 140 E4
The Pastures
FHAM/STUB PO14 .... 159 G4 8
NARL SO24 .... 30 B2
WVILLE PO7 .... 139 J5 6
Pat Bear Cl WSHM SO15 .... 105 H8
Patchins Rd UPTN BH16 .... 232 A4
Patchway Dr
FHAM/STUB PO14 .... 160 A8
Paternoster Rw WINC SO23 .... 3 H8
Patricia Cl HEND SO30 .... 108 C6
Patricia Dr HEND SO30 .... 134 B1
Patrick's Cl LISS GU33 .... 36 F4
Paulet Cl WEND SO18 .... 107 M7
Paulet Lacave Av ROWN SO16 .. 105 J2
Paulet Pl FUFL SO22 .... 26 D3
Pauletts La TOTT SO40 .... 104 A5
Paulsgrove Rd NEND PO2 .... 187 K8
Pauls La HAV PO9 .... 201 L8 8
Paulson Cl CHFD SO53 .... 53 H8
Pauncefoot Hl ROMY SO51 .... 78 B3
Pauncefote Rd BOSC BH5 .... 236 F3 8
Pauntley Rd CHCH/BSGR BH23.. 238 D3
Pavan Gdns NBNE BH10 .... 220 A4
Pavilion Cl ELGH SO50 .... 83 H8
Pavilion Rd HEND SO30 .... 109 J8
Paxton Cl HEND SO30 .... 134 B3 8
Paxton Rd FHAM/STUB PO14 .. 6 F6
Payne Cl WIMB BH21 .... 168 C3 8
Paynes Hay Rd ROMY SO51 .... 23 G8
Payne's Rd WSHM SO15 .... 130 F2
Peace Cl CHCH/BSGR BH23 .... 197 L8
Peach Rd ROWN SO16 .... 105 M4
Peacock Cl FHAM/PORC PO16.. 161 G8
Peacock La PSEA PO1 .... 12 C5
Peacock Pl WINC SO23 .... 3 M7
Peak Cl ROWN SO16 .... 105 L8
Peak Dr FHAM/STUB PO14.. .... 6 A7
Peak New Rd BPWT SO32 .... 59 L8
Peakfield WVILLE PO7 .... 139 J4 8
Peak La BPWT SO32 .... 84 F3
FHAM/STUB PO14.. .... 6 A8
Peak Rd HORN PO8 .... 115 M3
Pealsham Gdns FBDG SP6 .... 97 K6 8
Pearce Av PSTN BH14 .... 233 M7
Pearce Ct GPORT PO12 .... 11 H2
Pear Cl BKME/WDN BH12 .... 235 G4
Pearl Gdns NBNE BH10 .... 220 A4
Pearl Rd NBNE BH10 .... 220 A4
Pearson Av PSTN BH14 .... 234 A3
Pearson Gdns NBNE BH10 .... 220 B2
Peartree LYMN SO41 .... 228 C6 8
Peartree Av ITCH SO19 .... 132 C4
Pear Tree Cl BPWT SO32 .... 109 L6 8
CHCH/BSGR BH23 .... 197 L8
FBDG SP6 .... 121 K2
Peartree Cl
FHAM/STUB PO14 .... 184 B5 8
ITCH SO19 .... 132 B4 8
Peartree Ct LYMN SO41 .... 228 C6 8
Pear Tree Dr RSAL SP5 .... 75 J8
Peartree Rd FAWY SO45 .... 155 J6
ITCH SO19 .... 132 B4
Pease Cft EPSF GU31 .... 93 G5
Pebble Cl HISD PO11 .... 213 M6 8
Pebble Ct TOTT SO40 .... 130 D6 8
Pebmarsh Rd CHAM PO6 .... 163 H8 8
Peckham Av
NMIL/BTOS BH25 .... 225 L6
Pedam Cl ENEY PO4 .... 211 L5 8
Pedula Wy ELGH SO50 .... 82 D3
Peel Cl BKME/WDN BH12 .... 234 B3
ROMY SO51 .... 51 H7
Peel Pl SSEA PO5 .... 13 G4
Peel Rd GPORT PO12 .... 11 H2
Peel St SHAM SO14 .... 5 L1
Peewit Hl HLER SO31 .... 133 L5
Peewit Hill Cl HLER SO31 .... 133 L5
Pegasus Av LYMN SO41 .... 226 E6
Pegasus Cl HLER SO31 .... 157 K6 8
ROWN SO16 .... 105 L4
Pelham Cl CHCH/BSGR BH23 .. 238 C2
Pelham Rd GPORT PO12.. .... 10 E2
SSEA PO5 .... 13 H6
Pelham Ter EMRTH PO10 .... 166 E8 8
Pelican Cl FHAM PO15 .... 6 A3
Pelican Md RGWD BH24 .... 171 G2
Pelican Rd FHAM/STUB PO14 .. 184 D3
Pembers Cl ELGH SO50 .... 83 J6
Pemberton Rd LYND SO43 .... 151 L3
Pembrey Cl ROWN SO16 .... 105 L3
Pembridge Rd FBDG SP6 .... 97 M5
Pembroke Cl ELGH SO50 .... 81 L3
PSEA PO1 .... 12 D6 2
ROMY SO51 .... 78 E1 6
TOTT SO40 .... 104 F8
Pembroke Crs
FHAM/STUB PO14 .... 183 L7
Pembroke Rd
BKME/WDN BH12 .... 234 C1
FUFL SO22 .... 16 B3
ITCH SO19 .... 132 F4
PSEA PO1 .... 12 E4
WBNE BH4 .... 235 C6
Pembury Rd
FHAM/STUB PO14 .... 184 B4
HAV PO9 .... 9 H6
Pemerton Rd FUFL SO22 .... 2 B1
Penarth Av CHAM PO6 .... 163 M8
Pendennis Rd CHAM PO6.. .... 162 D8
Pendle Cl ROWN SO16 .... 105 L3
Pendle Gn ROMY SO51 .... 20 E7
Pendleton Gdns FAWY SO45 .. 180 C7 8

Penelope Gdns HLER SO31 .... 133 K6
Penfords Paddock
BPWT SO32 .... 111 J1 8
Pengelly Av NBNE BH10 .... 220 C3
Penhale Gdns
FHAM/STUB PO14 .... 158 F7
Penhale Rd PSEA PO1 .... 13 M1
Penhale Wy TOTT SO40 .... 129 J3
Penhurst Rd HAV PO9 .... 164 F6
Peninsula Rd FUFL SO22 .... 2 D9
Penistone Cl ITCH SO19 .... 132 F7
Penjar Av WVILLE PO7 .... 164 A4
Penk Rdg CHAM PO6 .... 164 D8
Pennant Hills HAV PO9 .... 164 F6
Pennant Wy CHCH/BSGR BH23.. 238 E1
Pennard Wy CHFD SO53 .... 80 F4
Penn Cl NMIL/BTOS BH25 .... 225 J7
Pennels Cl LIPH GU30 .... 38 C6
Pennerly Ct HAV PO9 .... 165 H1
Penner Rd HAV PO9 .... 8 C8
Penn Hill Av PSTN BH14 .... 234 C5
Pennine Gdns FAWY SO45 .... 155 H6
Pennine Rd ROWN SO16 .... 130 D1
Pennine Wy CHFD SO53 .... 81 J4
LSOL/BMARY PO13 .... 208 C4 3
VWD BH31 .... 144 D2 8
Pennington Cl ELGH SO50 .... 54 E8
FERN BH22 .... 168 B7
LYMN SO41 .... 228 A2
Pennington Crs FERN BH22.. .... 168 B6
Pennington Ov LYMN SO41 .... 227 M6
Pennington Pl FERN BH22 .... 168 B7
Pennington Wy FHAM PO15 .... 6 B1
Penns Pl EPSF GU31 .... 64 C5
Penns Rd PSF GU32 .... 63 K4
Penn Wy GPORT PO12 .... 209 J5
Pennycress HLER SO31 .... 158 C6
Penny Hedge
NMIL/BTOS BH25 .... 225 M8
Penny La EMRTH PO10 .... 166 F8
Penny Pl WVILLE PO7 .... 164 C5 8
Penny's Cl FBDG SP6 .... 97 L5
Penny's Crs FBDG SP6 .... 97 L5
Pennys La FBDG SP6 .... 97 L6
RSAL SP5 .... 18 B1
Penny St PSEA PO1 .... 12 C6
Pennywell Gdns
NMIL/BTOS BH25 .... 226 B4
Penrhyn Cl ELGH SO50 .... 81 L3
Penrith Cl VWD BH31 .... 144 C3
Penrith Rd BOSC BH5 .... 236 F4
Penrose Cl NEND PO2 .... 187 H6 8
Penrose Rd FERN BH22 .... 194 B2
Penshurst Wy ELGH SO50 .... 81 M2
The Pentagon FAWY SO45 .... 180 E6
Pentere Rd HORN PO8 .... 140 E2
Pentire Av WSHM SO15 .... 106 C6
Pentire Wy WSHM SO15 .... 106 C6
Pentland Cl FAWY SO45 .... 155 H6 8
Pentland Ri FHAM/PORC PO16.. 162 B7
Penton Ct HAV PO9 .... 165 M2
Penton Rd RWIN SO21 .... 54 F1 8
Pentons Hl FBDG SP6 .... 123 H2
Pentridge Wy TOTT SO40 .... 129 H3
Peper Harow HORN PO8 .... 140 F2
Peppard Cl WEND SO18 .... 132 C1
Peppercorn Wy HEND SO30 .... 109 G5
Pepys Av ITCH SO19 .... 133 H3
Pepys Cl ENEY PO4 .... 211 K5
GPORT PO12 .... 209 M7
Percival Rd NEND PO2 .... 187 K8
Percy Chandler St PSEA PO1 .. 211 H2 8
Percy Cl FAWY SO45 .... 155 K3
Percy Rd BOSC BH5 .... 236 D5
ENEY PO4 .... 13 L4
GPORT PO12 .... 11 C3
ROWN SO16 .... 105 M8
Peregrine Cl TOTT SO40 .... 129 G2 8
Peregrine Rd
CHCH/BSGR BH23 .... 238 F2
The Peregrines
FHAM/PORC PO16 .... 161 K8
Pergin Crs CFDH BH17 .... 233 G1
Pergin Wy CFDH BH17 .... 233 G1
Pern Dr HEND SO30 .... 134 E1
Peronne Cl HSEA PO3 .... 187 K3
Peronne Rd HSEA PO3 .... 187 K3
Perran Rd ROWN SO16 .... 105 J7
Perryfield Gdns LTDN BH7 .... 221 M8 8
Perry Gdns PLE BH15 .... 233 H7
Perryvale Rd NBAD SO52 .... 80 E3
Perrywood Cl FAWY SO45 .... 180 A5
Perrywood Gdns TOTT SO40 .. 104 A8 8
Perseus Pl WVILLE PO7 .... 164 D5
Pershore Cl HLER SO31 .... 158 C6
Persian Dr HLER SO31 .... 158 F1
Persley Rd NBNE BH10 .... 220 B4
Perth Cl CHCH/BSGR BH23 .... 222 C7
Perth Rd ENEY PO4 .... 211 M4
LSOL/BMARY PO13 .... 185 H5
Pervin Cl HAV PO9 .... 187 K1
Peststead La BPWT SO32 .... 113 H4
Peter Ashley Rd CHAM PO6 .... 164 B7
Peterborough Rd CHAM PO6 .. 163 J7
Peter Grant Wy FERN BH22 .. 194 A3
Peters Cl HLER SO31 .... 158 C5
UPTN BH16 .... 232 B2
Peterscroft Av TOTT SO40 .... 128 E2
Petersfield La HORN PO8 .... 116 A2
Petersfield Pl LTDN BH7 .... 237 G1 8
Petersfield Rd EPSF GU31 .... 91 J3
HAV PO9 .... 8 F1
LTDN BH7 .... 236 F2
NARL SO24 .... 30 C4
RWIN SO21 .... 27 M2
WINC SO23 .... 3 L9
Petersham Cl WVILLE PO7 .... 140 B7 8
Petersham Cl CFDH BH17 .... 217 K8
Peters Rd HLER SO31 .... 158 C5
Petit Rd MOOR/WNTN BH9 .... 220 E5
Petrel Wk LSOL/BMARY PO13 .. 184 F6
Petrie Rd LSOL/BMARY PO13.. 208 D2
Petticoat La RSAL SP5 .... 73 K1
Pettinger Gdns PTSW SO17 .... 107 J8 8
Petty Cl ROMY SO51 .... 78 F2 8
Pettycot Crs
LSOL/BMARY PO13 .... 184 F5
Petworth Gdns ELGH SO50 .... 81 M3 8

ROWN SO16 .... 106 A3
Petworth Rd HSEA PO3 ...... 211 M2
Petwyn Cl FERN BH22 .... 194 E2
Pevensey Cl ROWN SO16 ...... 105 J7
Peverells Rd ROWN SO16 ...... 107 J4
Peverells Rd CHFD SO53 .... 81 K2
Peverells Wood Av CHFD SO53 .. 81 L1
Peverells Wood Cl CHFD SO53 .. 81 L1
Peveril Cl RGWD BH24 .... 169 K2
Peveril Rd ITCH SO19 .... 132 C4
Pewsey Pl WSHM SO15 .... 106 C6
Phelipps Rd WIMB BH21 ...... 217 H1
Pheonix Wy
  LSOL/BMARY PO13 .... 185 G7
Philip Rd WVILLE PO7 .... 164 D3
Phillimore Rd ROWN SO16 ...... 107 J4
Phillips Cl ROWN SO16 .... 105 J4
Philpott Dr TOTT SO40 .... 130 D7
Phoenix Cl HLER SO31 .... 133 L7
Phoenix Sq NEND PO2 .... 187 J4
Phyldon Cl BKME/WDN BH12 ... 234 A3
Phyldon Rd BKME/WDN BH12 ... 234 A3
Pickard Rd FERN BH22 .... 194 D1
Pickering Cl BDST BH18 .... 217 L6
Picket Cl FBDG SP6 .... 97 L6
Pickford Rd MOOR/WNTN BH9 .. 220 C7
Pickwick Cl TOTT SO40 .... 128 F1
Pier Head Rd NEND PO2 .... 186 F8
Pier Rd PSEA PO1 .... 12 E7
  SSEA PO5 .... 12 E7
Pier St LSOL/BMARY PO13 ..... 208 C2
Pigeon House La WVILLE PO7 ... 163 H5
Pig Shoot La CHCH/BSGR BH23 . 221 K4
Pikes HI LYND SO43 .... 151 J1
Pilands Wood Rd HLER SO31 ... 133 K8
Pilchards Av ELGH SO50 .... 83 G5
Pilford Heath Rd WIMB BH21 ... 192 E1
Pilgrim Cl NMIL/BTOS BH25 .... 226 A4
Pilgrim Pk RGWD BH24 .... 147 G8
Pilgrim Pl WEND SO18 .... 107 K4
Pilgrims Cl NBAD SO52 .... 80 E3
Pilgrims Ga FUFL SO22 .... 2 C5
Pilgrims Wy CFDH BH17 .... 232 F1
  FHAM/STUB PO14 .... 183 M7
Pilley Bailey LYMN SO41 .... 202 E6
Pilley HI LYMN SO41 .... 202 E7
Pilley St LYMN SO41 .... 202 E6
Pill HI RSAL SP5 .... 46 F4
Pilning Cl FHAM/STUB PO14 .... 160 A8
Pilot Hight Rd BWD BH11 ...... 219 L5
Pilsdon Dr CFDH BH17 .... 218 C6
Pimpern Cl CFDH BH17 .... 218 C6
Pimpernel Cl HLER SO31 .... 158 C6
Pine Av BKME/WDN BH12 ...... 234 E1
  SBNE BH6 .... 237 H4
Pinecliffe Av SBNE BH6 .... 237 H4
Pinecliffe Rd NMIL/BTOS BH25 .. 240 E1
Pinecliff Rd CCLF BH13 .... 234 F8
Pine Cl FAWY SO45 .... 155 K6
  FERN BH22 .... 194 A1
  FUFL SO22 .... 26 A5
  NBAD SO52 .... 79 L3
  NMIL/BTOS BH25 .... 225 J8
  RSAL SP5 .... 75 J6
  TOTT SO40 .... 129 C5
Pine Crs CHCH/BSGR BH23 ..... 224 C8
  CHFD SO53 .... 53 H8
Pine Dr CCLF BH13 .... 234 E5
  RGWD BH24 .... 169 K4
  WEND SO18 .... 133 H1
Pine Dr East WEND SO18 ...... 133 J1
Pinefield Rd WEND SO18 ...... 107 L6
Pine Gv HAV PO9 .... 9 H5
Pinegrove Rd ITCH SO19 ...... 132 D5
Pineholt Cl RGWD BH24 .... 169 L3
Pinehurst Av
  CHCH/BSGR BH23 .... 238 E3
Pinehurst Cl HORN PO8 .... 141 G6
Pinehurst Rd FERN BH22 ...... 168 D7
  ROWN SO16 .... 106 E3
Pinelands Rd ROWN SO16 ...... 80 E8
Pine Manor Rd RGWD BH24 .... 169 K4
Pine Rd BPWT SO32 .... 85 J8
  CHFD SO53 .... 53 H7
  FBDG SP6 .... 121 K3
  MOOR/WNTN BH9 .... 220 D7
  ROMY SO51 .... 79 H2
Pinesprings Dr BDST BH18 ..... 217 J6
The Pines FBDG SP6 .... 98 D6
  FHAM/PORC PO16 .... 161 L7
Pinetops Cl LYMN SO41 .... 227 L5
Pine Tree Cl WIMB BH21 .... 192 B3
Pine Tree Gdns HORN PO8 ...... 140 E6
Pine Tree Gln WBNE BH4 ...... 235 H5
Pine Trees Cl FHAM/STUB PO14 .. 6 A4
Pinetree Wk CFDH BH17 ...... 217 K8
Pine Vale Crs NBNE BH10 ...... 220 D5
Pineview Cl HLER SO31 .... 133 L7
  RSAL SP5 .... 73 J4
Pine View Cl UPTN BH16 ...... 232 B2
Pine View Rd VWD BH31 .... 144 B1
Pine Wk HLER SO31 .... 158 B1
  LISS GU33 .... 36 F2
  ROWN SO16 .... 106 E1
  VWD BH31 .... 144 F3
Pine Wy ROWN SO16 .... 106 E1
Pinewood LSOL/BMARY PO13 ... 185 J7
Pinewood Av HAV PO9 .... 164 C5
  NBNE BH10 .... 220 B3
Pinewood Cl CHCH/BSGR BH23 .. 224 C7
  FHAM/STUB PO14 .... 184 B4
  NBNE BH10 .... 220 B3
  ROMY SO51 .... 51 H7
Pinewood Crs FAWY SO45 ..... 155 M6
Pinewood Dr FAWY SO45 ...... 155 M6
Pinewood Gdns FERN BH22 .... 194 B1
Pinewood Pk ITCH SO19 .... 133 K3
Pinewood Rd CCLF BH13 ...... 235 G7
  CHCH/BSGR BH23 .... 224 D7
  FERN BH22 .... 194 A1
  LYMN SO41 .... 228 D5
  RGWD BH24 .... 169 K4
Pinkney La LYND SO43 .... 151 J4
Pink Rd NEND PO2 .... 187 J8
Pinks HI FHAM/PORC PO16 ..... 161 H6
Pinsley Dr WHAM PO17 .... 162 E2
Pinto Cl FHAM PO15 .... 158 F1
Pipers Ash RGWD BH24 .... 147 G8

Pipers Cl TOTT SO40 .... 129 H2
Pipers Cl CHCH/BSGR BH23 .... 238 F1
Pipers Md HORN PO8 .... 115 M3
Piping Cl RWIN SO21 .... 54 E8
Piping Rd RWIN SO21 .... 54 E8
Pipit Cl GPORT PO12 .... 209 M1
Pippin Cl CHCH/BSGR BH23 .... 222 C6
  LYMN SO41 .... 228 C6
Pirelli St SHAM SO14 .... 4 E3
  WSHM SO15 .... 4 E3
Pirrie Cl WSHM SO15 .... 106 C7
Pitcairn Ms ENEY PO4 .... 211 M6
Pitchponds Rd HLER SO31 ..... 158 A3
Pitcot La RWIN SO21 .... 56 A5
Pitcroft La EPSF GU31 .... 91 L3
Pitcroft Rd NEND PO2 .... 187 H7
Pithouse La CHCH/BSGR BH23 .. 196 B8
Pitmore Cl ELGH SO50 .... 54 A8
Pitmore La LYMN SO41 .... 201 H6
Pitmore Rd ELGH SO50 .... 54 A8
Pitreavie Rd CHAM PO6 ...... 187 L2
Pitter Cl FUFL SO22 .... 16 A3
Pitt Hill La WVILLE PO7 .... 114 D7
Pittmore Rd
  CHCH/BSGR BH23 .... 223 C5
Pitt Rd WSHM SO15 .... 131 G2
Pitts Deep La LYMN SO41 ..... 230 A3
Pitts Pl NMIL/BTOS BH25 ...... 226 B6
Pitwines Cl PLE BH15 .... 233 J6
Pitymoor La WHAM PO17 ...... 162 F4
Place Crs WVILLE PO7 .... 164 D3
Place House Cl FHAM PO15 .... 160 A7
Place La RWIN SO21 .... 26 C8
Plaitford Gv HAV PO9 .... 165 G4
Plantaganet Crs BWD BH11 .... 219 H3
Plantation Dr
  CHCH/BSGR BH23 .... 224 C6
  TOTT SO40 .... 130 C7
Plantation Rd CFDH BH17 ..... 218 A7
  CHCH/BSGR BH23 .... 195 M4
  LISS GU33 .... 37 G6
  ROMY SO51 .... 76 C8
The Plantation BPWT SO32 .... 110 C6
Plant Park Rd RGWD BH24 ..... 170 A5
Plants Cl ROMY SO51 .... 77 G6
Plassey Crs BWD BH11 .... 219 M3
Platform Rd SHAM SO14 ...... 5 G7
Platoff Rd LYMN SO41 .... 228 C8
Player Cl FBDG SP6 .... 97 L5
Players Crs TOTT SO40 .... 129 J3
Playfair Rd SSEA PO5 .... 13 J4
Playfields Dr
  BKME/WDN BH12 .... 234 D2
Pleasance Wy
  NMIL/BTOS BH25 .... 225 K5
Pleasant La EMRTH PO10 ...... 191 H7
Pleasant Rd ENEY PO4 .... 211 M4
Plecy Cl FERN BH22 .... 194 B5
Plemont Cl BKME/WDN BH12 ... 219 J7
Pless Rd LYMN SO41 .... 241 M3
Plough La BPWT SO32 .... 113 H6
Plough Wy FUFL SO22 .... 26 C4
Plover Cl FHAM/STUB PO14 .... 183 M6
  ROWN SO16 .... 106 A3
Plover Dr LYMN SO41 .... 242 E4
Plover Reach ENEY PO4 .... 211 M3
Plover Rd TOTT SO40 .... 129 G1
Plovers Down FUFL SO22 ...... 26 A5
Plovers Rd HORN PO8 .... 140 E2
P.l.p.h. Rd FAWY SO45 ...... 180 F3
Plumer Rd CFDH BH17 .... 217 L7
Plumpton Gdns HSEA PO3 .... 187 M5
Plumpton Gv WVILLE PO7 .... 140 F7
Plymouth Dr
  FHAM/STUB PO14 .... 183 M6
Plymouth St SSEA PO5 .... 13 H3
Pococks La BPWT SO32 ...... 87 G7
Poets Wy FUFL SO22 .... 2 B1
Pointout Cl ROWN SO16 ...... 106 D5
Pointout Rd ROWN SO16 ..... 106 D5
Polesden Cl CHFD SO53 ...... 53 G8
Poles La LYMN SO41 .... 228 C7
  RWIN SO21 .... 53 G2
Police Station La BPWT SO32 .. 87 G7
Pollards Moor Rd TOTT SO40 .. 102 F7
The Polygon WSHM SO15 .... 4 E1
Pomona Cl FERN BH22 .... 194 B2
Pompeys La FERN BH22 ...... 193 L4
Pond Cl NMIL/BTOS BH25 ..... 225 L5
  TOTT SO40 .... 129 K1
Pondhead Cl FAWY SO45 .... 180 A5
Ponda La HORN PO8 .... 116 A2
Pond Piece WVILLE PO7 ..... 139 K5
Pond Rd HLER SO31 .... 158 D2
Pondside La BPWT SO32 ..... 85 H7
Ponsonby Rd PSTN BH14 ..... 234 C4
Pony Dr UPTN BH16 .... 232 C1
Pook La HAV PO9 .... 9 J6
  WHAM PO17 .... 160 F4
Pooksgreen TOTT SO40 ..... 130 B6
Poole La HORN PO8 .... 116 A2
Poole La BWD BH11 .... 219 K4
Poole Rd CCLF BH13 .... 234 E4
  ITCH SO19 .... 132 C4
  UPTN BH16 .... 232 B1
  WBNE BH4 .... 235 G5
  WCLF BH2 .... 14 B6
  WIMB BH21 .... 192 A4
Popes La BPWT SO32 ...... 84 B4
  TOTT SO40 .... 129 K1
Popes Rd PLE BH15 .... 233 J2
Popham Ct HAV PO9 .... 165 G2
Poplar Cl FHAM/STUB PO14 ... 6 A4
  CHCH/BSGR BH23 .... 224 A8
  WIMB BH21 .... 192 B3
Poplar Crs RGWD BH24 ...... 170 F1
Poplar Dr FHAM/STUB PO14 .. 6 A4
  TOTT SO40 .... 130 B7
Poplar Gv HISD PO11 ...... 213 L4
Poplar La CHCH/BSGR BH23 .. 198 A4
Poplar Rd ITCH SO19 ...... 132 D2
  NMIL/BTOS BH25 .... 226 B4
The Poplars BPWT SO32 .... 111 J5
Poplar Wy HEND SO30 ..... 134 B7
  NBAD SO52 .... 79 L3
  RGWD BH24 .... 170 F1
Poppy Cl CHCH/BSGR BH23 .. 223 M8
  HLER SO31 .... 158 D6

Poppyfields NBAD SO52 ...... 80 F2
Poppy Rd ROWN SO16 .... 107 H3
Porchester Rd ITCH SO19 ..... 132 C5
Porlock Rd ROWN SO16 ...... 105 H7
Portal Rd ELGH SO50 .... 82 C5
  ITCH SO19 .... 132 F4
  LSOL/BMARY PO13 .... 185 G5
  TOTT SO40 .... 129 H1
  WINC SO23 .... 27 G2
Portarlington Cl WBNE BH4 ... 14 A7
Portarlington Rd WBNE BH4 ... 235 H5
Portchester Ct BMTH BH1 ..... 15 K2
Portchester Pl BMTH BH1 ..... 15 K2
Portchester Ri ELGH SO50 ..... 81 M1
Portchester Rd CHAR BH8 ..... 15 H1
  FHAM/PORC PO16 .... 161 L8
  NEND PO2 .... 187 J8
Portelet Cl BKME/WDN BH12 .. 219 H7
Portelet Pl BKME/WDN BH12 .. 234 A3
Porteous Crs CHFD SO53 ..... 81 C2
Porter Rd CFDH BH17 ...... 233 G1
Portersbridge St ROMY SO51 .. 78 D1
Porter's La SHAM SO14 ...... 4 F6
  WIMB BH21 .... 193 G2
Portesham Gdns
  MOOR/WNTN BH9 .... 220 F4
Portesham Wy CFDH BH17 ... 218 C5
Portfield Cl CHCH/BSGR BH23 .. 222 E8
Portfield Rd CHCH/BSGR BH23 .. 237 L1
Portland Dr GPORT PO12 ..... 209 H5
Portland Rd MOOR/WNTN BH9 .. 220 E8
  SSEA PO5 .... 13 H7
  WVILLE PO7 .... 164 C1
Portland's Cl PSF GU32 ..... 64 A3
Portland Sq LISS GU33 ..... 36 F3
Portland St FHAM/PORC PO16 .. 7 K6
  PSEA PO1 .... 12 E1
  SHAM SO14 .... 4 F3
Portland Ter SHAM SO14 ..... 4 F3
Port La RWIN SO21 .... 53 C1
Portman Crs SBNE BH6 ..... 237 C5
Portman Rd LTDN BH7 ..... 236 E3
Portmore Cl BDST BH18 ..... 218 A2
Portobello Gv
  FHAM/PORC PO16 .... 162 B7
Port Royal St SSEA PO5 .... 13 K2
Portsdown Av CHAM PO6 .... 164 A8
Portsdown Hill Rd CHAM PO6 .. 163 K7
  WHAM PO17 .... 161 L6
Portsdown Rd CHAM PO6 ..... 162 C8
Portview Av
  FHAM/PORC PO16 ...... 162 B8
Portsview Gdns
  FHAM/PORC PO16 ...... 162 B7
Portswood Av PTSW SO17 .... 107 G8
Portswood Dr
  MOOR/WNTN BH9 .... 220 E4
Portswood Pk PTSW SO17 .... 107 G8
Portswood Rd HAV PO9 ..... 165 H2
  NEND PO2 .... 187 J3
  PTSW SO17 .... 107 G8
Portview Rd WEND SO18 ..... 107 L6
Port Wy CHAM PO6 .... 162 E8
Portway Cl WEND SO18 .... 132 C1
Posbrooke La
  FHAM/STUB PO14 .... 183 K1
Postern Cl FHAM/PORC PO16 .. 162 B8
Post Green Rd UPTN BH16 ... 216 B8
Post Office La RGWD BH24 ... 169 J3
Post Office La WCLF BH2 ... 14 E6
  WVILLE PO7 .... 164 A3
The Potteries FHAM/PORC PO16 .. 7 K2
Potterne Wy FHAM/PORC PO16 .. 160 E4
Potters Fld LISS GU33 ..... 36 F3
Potters Heron Cl ROMY SO51 .. 52 D5
Potters Heron La ROMY SO51 .. 52 D5
Potters Wy PSTN BH14 ..... 234 B6
Pottery La RCCH PO18 ..... 191 M1
Pottery Rd PSTN BH14 ..... 233 M6
Poulner Cl ITCH SO19 ..... 132 E7
Poulner Ct HAV PO9 .... 165 G2
Poulner HI RGWD BH24 ..... 147 L6
Poulner Pk RGWD BH24 .... 147 G7
Pound Cl LSOL/BMARY PO13 .. 185 H8
  PSTN BH14 .... 233 L3
  RGWD BH24 .... 146 E8
Pound Cottages BPWT SO32 .. 87 H3
Pound Gate Dr
  FHAM/STUB PO14 .... 159 G7
Pound HI ROMY SO51 ..... 76 B3
Pound La BPWT SO32 ..... 87 J3
  FBDG SP6 .... 96 A3
  PLE BH15 .... 233 K3
  RGWD BH24 .... 172 C7
  ROMY SO51 .... 52 A6
  ROMY SO51 .... 76 B3
  TOTT SO40 .... 103 H6
  TOTT SO40 .... 129 J5
Pound Lea HISD PO11 .... 213 L3
Pound Rd CHAM PO6 .... 162 F6
  HLER SO31 .... 133 K8
  LYMN SO41 .... 227 M5
  SELS SO20 .... 215 K7
Pound St WEND SO18 .... 132 C1
Pound Tree Rd SHAM SO14 .. 5 G3
Powell Crs TOTT SO40 .... 129 K3
Powell Rd PSTN BH14 ..... 234 A4
Powerscourt Rd NEND PO2 .. 187 J8
  NMIL/BTOS BH25 .... 240 C1
Powis Cl NMIL/BTOS BH25 ... 225 M5
Poyner Cl FHAM/PORC PO16 .. 7 J3
Poynings Pl PSEA PO1 .... 12 E5
Precosa Rd HEND SO30 ... 134 C3
Prelate Wy FHAM/STUB PO14 .. 159 G6
Preshaw Cl ROWN SO16 .... 106 A4
Preston Cl UPTN BH16 .... 232 B1

Preston La CHCH/BSGR BH23 .. 223 H5
Preston Rd NEND PO2 ...... 187 K7
  PLE BH15 .... 233 H2
Preston Wy CHCH/BSGR BH23 .. 224 B8
Prestwood Cl
  NMIL/BTOS BH25 .... 225 K7
Prestwood Rd HEND SO30 .. 134 A3
Pretoria Rd ENEY PO4 ..... 211 K5
  HEND SO30 .... 133 M3
Pricketts HI FHAM/STUB PO32 .. 136 D1
Prideaux-brune Av
  LSOL/BMARY PO13 .... 185 G4
Priest Croft Dr FAWY SO45 ... 180 G6
Priestfields FHAM/STUB PO14 .. 159 G6
Priestlands ROMY SO51 .... 50 D8
Priestlands Cl LYMN SO41 .. 228 A5
Priestlands La LYMN SO41 .. 228 A5
Priestlands Rd LYMN SO41 .. 228 A5
Priest La CHCH/BSGR BH23 .. 222 F1
Priestley Cl TOTT SO40 .... 129 H1
Priestley Rd NBNE BH10 .... 219 M7
Priestwood Cl WEND SO18 .. 133 H1
Primate Rd FHAM/STUB PO14 .. 159 H6
Primrose Cl HEND SO30 ... 134 A3
  LSOL/BMARY PO13 .... 185 G3
  NBAD SO52 .... 80 E4
Primrose Gdns CFDH BH17 .. 217 K7
Primrose La LISS GU33 .... 37 J4
  RSAL SP5 .... 73 H2
Primrose Rd ROWN SO16 ... 106 F4
Primrose Wy
  CHCH/BSGR BH23 .... 224 A8
  HLER SO31 .... 158 D6
  ROMY SO51 .... 51 H7
  WIMB BH21 .... 217 J1
Prince Albert Rd ENEY PO4 .. 211 L5
Prince Alfred St GPORT PO12 .. 10 E5
Prince George's St HAV PO9 .. 8 F4
Prince George St PSEA PO1 .. 12 C1
Prince of Wales Av
  WSHM SO15 .... 130 C1
Prince of Wales Cl
  WVILLE PO7 .... 164 E1
Prince of Wales Rd
  GPORT PO12 .... 11 H3
  WBNE BH4 .... 235 G4
Prince Rd FHAM/STUB PO14 .. 184 D2
  ROWN SO16 .... 105 K1
Princes Cl BPWT SO32 .... 85 G8
  RSAL SP5 .... 73 K1
Princes Ct SHAM SO14 ... 132 A2
Princes Crs LYND SO43 ... 151 L3
Princes HI RSAL SP5 ..... 73 K1
Princes Pl FUFL SO22 .... 26 D3
  NMIL/BTOS BH25 .... 226 A4
Princes Rd FERN BH22 ... 194 B2
  PSF GU32 .... 63 J4
  ROMY SO51 .... 52 F4
  WSHM SO15 .... 131 H2
Princess Av CHCH/BSGR BH23 .. 238 A2
Princess Cl HEND SO30 ... 108 D6
Princess Gdns HORN PO8 ... 140 F1
Princess Rd BKME/WDN BH12 .. 234 F4
  TOTT SO40 .... 128 F6
  WBNE BH4 .... 235 G4
Prince's St PSEA PO1 .... 211 H1
  SHAM SO14 .... 132 A2
Pringles Cl FERN BH22 ... 194 C3
Pringles Dr FERN BH22 ... 194 C3
Prinstead Cl WINC SO23 .. 27 G2
Prinstead Crs CHAM PO6 .. 188 B1
Prinsted La EMRTH PO10 .. 191 H1
Priors Barton WINC SO23 .. 26 E3
Priors Cl CHCH/BSGR BH23 .. 239 H1
Priorsdean Av HSEA PO3 .. 211 L2
Priorsdean Crs HAV PO9 .. 165 H4
Priors Dean Rd FUFL SO22 .. 16 C4
Priors Leaze La RCCH PO18 .. 167 K7
Priors Rd CFDH BH17 .... 217 K8
Priors Wy FUFL SO22 .... 26 A5
Priory Cl BPWT SO32 .... 85 G8
  PTSW SO17 .... 107 J7
Priory Crs ENEY PO4 .... 211 L4
Priory Gdns FHAM/PORC PO16 .. 162 A8
  WVILLE PO7 .... 140 C7
Priory Rd ELGH SO50 .... 81 L7
  ENEY PO4 .... 211 L6
  FERN BH22 .... 168 E8
  FHAM PO15 .... 6 A4
  HLER SO31 .... 156 F2
  PTSW SO17 .... 107 H8
  WCLF BH2 .... 14 E7
  WHAM PO17 .... 162 E2
The Priory BPWT SO32 ... 111 G1
Priory View Pl
  MOOR/WNTN BH9 ...... 220 E5
Priory View Rd
  CHCH/BSGR BH23 ...... 223 G6
  MOOR/WNTN BH9 ...... 220 E5
Privet Rd MOOR/WNTN BH9 .. 220 C8
Privett Pl GPORT PO12 ... 209 J4
Privett Rd FHAM PO15 ... 160 A6
  GPORT PO12 .... 209 J4
  LSOL/BMARY PO13 ..... 209 G5
  PSF GU32 .... 34 C6
  WVILLE PO7 .... 164 B5
Prochurch Rd HORN PO8 .. 140 F4
Proctor Cl ITCH SO19 ... 133 H3
Proctor Dr NBAD SO52 ... 79 L5
Proctor La PSEA PO1 .... 211 K3
Promenade CCLF BH13 ... 235 G8
The Promenade EMRTH PO10 .. 190 D1
  FAWY SO45 .... 155 L3
Propserous Rd PLE BH15 .. 233 H7
Prospect La HAV PO9 ... 165 M3
Prospect Cl CHFD SO53 .. 81 K2
  FAWY SO45 .... 155 L3
Prospect Rd NEND PO2 .. 211 G1
  NMIL/BTOS BH25 ...... 240 C1
Provene Cl BPWT SO32 ... 111 K4
Provene Gdns BPWT SO32 .. 111 J4
Providence HI HLER SO31 .. 133 L6
Provost St FBDG SP6 .... 97 L8
Pruetts La LISS GU33 ... 36 E7
Prunus Cl FERN BH22 ... 193 M1
  ROWN SO16 .... 106 B3

Prunus Dr FERN BH22 ...... 193 M1
Pudbrooke Gdns
  HEND SO30 .... 109 G8
Pudding La HAV PO9 ...... 17 G4
Puddleslosh La FBDG SP6 .. 97 J3
Puddletown Crs CFDH BH17 .. 218 D6
Puffin Cl ROWN SO16 ..... 106 A3
Puffin Crs FHAM/STUB PO14 .. 183 M4
Puffin Gdns
  LSOL/BMARY PO13 ...... 184 F5
Puffin Wk HORN PO8 ..... 140 B4
Pug's Hole RSAL SP5 .... 19 M1
Pulens Crs EPSF GU31 ... 64 A4
Pulens La EPSF GU31 .... 64 A4
Pullman Ct FERN BH22 ... 168 B6
Pullman Wy RGWD BH24 .. 170 C2
Pump La HORN PO8 ..... 140 E3
  LSOL/BMARY PO13 ..... 185 G7
Punsholt La NARL SO24 .. 32 D5
Purbeck Av PLE BH15 .... 232 D7
Purbeck Cl UPTN BH16 ... 232 A1
Purbeck Dr FHAM/STUB PO14 .. 6 A8
  VWD BH31 .... 144 D3
Purbeck Rd NMIL/BTOS BH25 .. 240 C1
  WCLF BH2 .... 14 C6
Purbeck St PSEA PO1 .... 12 E2
Purbrook Cl ROWN SO16 .. 106 B4
Purbrook Gdns WVILLE PO7 .. 164 A3
Purbrook Heath Rd
  WVILLE PO7 .... 163 K3
Purbrook Rd PSEA PO1 ... 13 M2
Purbrook Wy HAV PO9 ... 164 C4
  WVILLE PO7 .... 164 D4
Purcell Cl WVILLE PO7 .. 164 C3
Purcell Rd ITCH SO19 ... 133 H5
Purchase Rd BKME/WDN BH12 .. 235 H1
Purewell CHCH/BSGR BH23 .. 238 C2
Purewell Cl CHCH/BSGR BH23 .. 238 D1
Purewell Cross Rd
  CHCH/BSGR BH23 ...... 238 C1
Purkess Cl CHFD SO53 ... 81 J1
Purkiss Cl TOTT SO40 ... 128 A3
Purley Wy ROMY SO51 ... 76 A5
The Purrocks PSF GU32 .. 63 J3
Purvis Gdns ITCH SO19 .. 132 F6
Pussex La CHCH/BSGR BH23 .. 195 L8
Putmans La EPSF GU31 .. 92 E2
Pycroft Cl HISD PO11 ... 190 A5
  ITCH SO19 .... 132 D3
Pye Cl WIMB BH21 ..... 217 H1
Pye La WIMB BH21 ..... 120 C1
Pye St PSEA PO1 ...... 211 G2
Pyland's La HLER SO31 .. 133 M5
Pyle Cl HORN PO8 ..... 140 E4
Pylewell Rd FAWY SO45 .. 155 L3
Pyrford Cl GPORT PO12 .. 209 J5
  WVILLE PO7 .... 140 B6
Pyrford Ms LYMN SO41 .. 228 C5
Pytchley Cl FHAM/STUB PO14 .. 183 L6

Q

The Quadrangle ELGH SO50 .... 81 M4
Quail Wy HORN PO8 ...... 140 E2
Quantock Rd ROWN SO16 .. 105 K8
The Quantocks FAWY SO45 .. 155 H6
Quarely Rd HAV PO9 ..... 165 G2
Quarry Rd WIMB BH21 ... 192 E1
  WINC SO23 .... 3 K9
Quarterdeck Av NEND PO2 .. 186 F7
Quartremaine Rd HSEA PO3 .. 187 M5
Quavey Rd RSAL SP5 .... 73 K2
Quay Hvn HLER SO31 ... 134 B8
Quay La GPORT PO12 ... 185 M7
Quayle Dr BWD BH11 ... 219 K2
Quay Rd CHCH/BSGR BH23 .. 238 A3
Quayside Rd WEND SO18 .. 132 C1
Quayside Wk TOTT SO40 .. 130 D5
Quay St FHAM/PORC PO16 .. 7 J7
  LYMN SO41 .... 228 D4
The Quay PLE BH15 .... 233 H7
Quebec Gdns HISD PO11 .. 133 K7
Queen Anne Dr WIMB BH21 .. 218 C5
Queen Anne's Dr HAV PO9 .. 165 G3
Queen Elizabeth Av
  LYMN SO41 .... 228 B4
Queen Katherine Rd
  LYMN SO41 .... 228 D5
Queen Mary Av
  MOOR/WNTN BH9 ...... 220 D6
Queen Mary Rd
  FHAM/PORC PO16 .... 186 B1
Queen Rd FHAM/STUB PO14 .. 184 D2
Queen's Av CHCH/BSGR BH23 .. 238 A3
Queens Cl FAWY SO45 ... 155 L5
  FERN BH22 .... 168 B7
  LSOL/BMARY PO13 .... 208 C3
Queens Crs FHAM/STUB PO14 .. 184 D5
  HORN PO8 .... 140 F1
  SSEA PO5 .... 13 H7
Queens Gdns FBDG SP6 .. 97 L6
  WBNE BH4 .... 14 A4
Queens Gv NMIL/BTOS BH25 .. 226 A4
  WVILLE PO7 .... 164 B3
  SSEA PO5 .... 13 H7
Queensland Rd LTDN BH7 .. 236 F1
Queensmead
  CHCH/BSGR BH23 ..... 222 E7
Queens Md FUFL SO22 .. 26 B2
Queen's Pde LYND SO43 .. 151 K9
Queen's Park Av CHAR BH8 .. 221 G8
Queen's Park Gdns CHAR BH8 .. 236 C1
Queen's Park Rd CHAR BH8 .. 236 C1
Queen's Park South Dr
  CHAR BH8 .... 236 C1
Queen's Park West Dr
  CHAR BH8 .... 236 D1
Queen's Pl SSEA PO5 ... 13 H6
Queens Ride NBAD SO52 .. 79 K4
Queen's Rd CHCH/BSGR BH23 .. 238 C2
  CHFD SO53 .... 53 J7
  FERN BH22 .... 194 B1
  FHAM/PORC PO16 .... 7 J6
  GPORT PO12 .... 11 G2
  HLER SO31 .... 158 A8
  LSOL/BMARY PO13 .... 208 D4

NEND PO2 187 J8
PSEA PO1 210 D2
PSF GU32 63 J4
PSTN BH14 234 C4
WBNE BH4 14 A5
WIMB BH21 217 H3
WSHM SO15 106 B6
WVILLE PO7 140 C7
Queens St MIDH GU29 67 K6
Queen's Ter SHAM SO14 5 H6
Queenstown Rd
WSHM SO15 131 H2 2
Queen St EMRTH PO10 166 E8
FBDG SP6 73 G7
PSEA PO1 12 C1
RWIN SO21 54 E3
Queens Vw HLER SO31 156 F2
Queensway HISD PO11 189 L5
RGWD BH24 170 F1
Queen's Wy SHAM SO14 5 G6
SSEA PO5 13 H6 8
The Queensway
FHAM/PORC PO16 161 M8
Queenswood Av CHAR BH8 221 J7
Queenswood Dr FERN BH22 194 B1
Querida Cl HLER SO31 134 B8 5
Quilter Cl ITCH SO19 133 H4 4
Quince La WIMB BH21 192 B2
Quintin Cl CHCH/BSGR BH23 224 D8
Quinton Cl SSEA PO5 13 J3 6
Quintrell Av FHAM/PORC PO16 161 L8
Quob Farm Cl HEND SO30 108 D5
Quob La HEND SO30 108 D5
The Quomp RGWD BH24 170 E1 6

R

Racecourse Vw LYND SO43 151 K2 2
Rachel Cl ELGH SO50 83 G6
Racton Av CHAM PO6 187 M1
Racton Rd EMRTH PO10 166 D5
Radclyffe Rd FHAM/PORC PO16 7 M3
Radipole Rd CFDH BH17 218 D6
Radleigh Gdns TOTT SO40 104 A8
Radley Cl HEND SO30 109 H7 5
Radnor St SSEA PO5 13 H3
Radstock Rd ITCH SO19 132 C5
Radway Crs WSHM SO15 106 C8
Radway Rd WSHM SO15 106 C8
Raebarn Cl NARL SO24 30 C3
Raeburn Dr HEND SO30 134 A1
Raglan Cl CHFD SO53 80 E4
Raglan Gdns BWD BH11 219 L6
Raglan St SSEA PO5 13 J2
Ragmore La PSF GU32 34 D3
Rails La HISD PO11 213 M6
Railway Vw PSEA PO1 13 J1
Rake Rd LIPH GU30 38 C6
LISS GU33 36 F4
Raleigh Cl CHCH/BSGR BH23 238 E3
NMIL/BTOS BH25 225 K5
RGWD BH24 147 G8 5
Raley Rd HLER SO31 158 E6
Ralph Rd WIMB BH21 217 J1
Ramalley La CHFD SO53 81 G1
Rambler Dr LSOL/BMARY PO13 209 G2
Ramblers Wy HORN PO8 140 F7
Ramley Rd LYMN SO41 227 K3
Rampart Gdns HSEA PO3 187 K3
Rampart Rd WEND SO18 132 B1
The Rampart LYMN SO41 228 B3
Ramsay Pl
LSOL/BMARY PO13 185 G6 6
Ramsay Rd WINC SO23 17 H1
Ramsdale Av HAV PO9 165 G3
Ramsdean Rd PSF GU32 62 C7
Ramsey Rd HISD PO11 213 L5
Ramshill EPSF GU31 63 M4
Rances Wy FUFL SO22 26 D3
Randall Cl TOTT SO40 104 B6
Randall Rd CHFD SO53 53 J6
Randalls Hl UPTN BH16 216 D8
Randalls La RGWD BH24 172 B3
Randolph Rd BOSC BH5 234 B3 3
NEND PO2 187 J5
PSTN BH14 236 D4 3
Randolph St WSHM SO15 131 G1
Ranelagh Gdns WSHM SO15 131 J1
Ranelagh Rd
CHCH/BSGR BH23 239 L1
HAV PO9 8 B4
NEND PO2 187 G7
WINC SO23 26 D2
Ranfurly Gdns FAWY SO45 155 J6
Range Gdns ITCH SO19 132 F5
Range Gn NEND PO2 187 G5
Rannoch Cl FHAM PO15 6 C2
Ransome Cl FHAM/STUB PO14 183 K1
Ranvilles La FHAM/STUB PO14 183 M1
Rapson Cl CHAM PO6 163 G7
Rareridge La BPWT SO32 85 K8
Ratcliffe Rd FAWY SO45 155 K7 4
HEND SO30 134 A1
Ratlake La ROMY SO51 52 E4
Rattigan Gdns HLER SO31 135 G8
Raven Cl LSOL/BMARY PO13 209 G2
Raven Rd SHAM SO14 131 M2
Ravens Cl FHAM/STUB PO14 184 B5
Ravenscourt Rd LYMN SO41 228 B5
SBNE BH6 237 H3
Ravenscroft Cl HLER SO31 133 K7
Ravenscroft Wy BPWT SO32 109 M7
Ravensdale Cl
BKME/WDN BH12 234 B2 1
Raven Sq ELGH SO50 81 J6 1
Ravens Wy LYMN SO41 242 C4
Ravenswood
FHAM/STUB PO14 159 G5 4
Raven Wy CHCH/BSGR BH23 238 F3
Ravine Rd BOSC BH5 237 G4
CCLF BH13 234 E8
Raymond Cl FAWY SO45 180 B5
HEND SO30 108 E5
VWD BH31 144 F2
Raymond Rd CHAM PO6 162 C7
WSHM SO15 131 H1
Rayners Gdns ROWN SO16 107 J4 2
Raynes Rd LSOL/BMARY PO13 208 D4
Reading Room La BPWT SO32 110 C8
Readon Cl EPSF GU31 63 M4
Rebbeck Rd LTDN BH7 236 F3
The Recess ELGH SO50 82 A3
Record Rd EMRTH PO10 166 C7
Recreation Rd
BKME/WDN BH12 234 D2
Rectory Av CHAM PO6 164 D7
Rectory Cl FHAM/STUB PO14 184 A5
GPORT PO12 10 D7
Rectory Ct HEND SO30 134 D1
Rectory Hl RSAL SP5 19 J5
Rectory La BPWT SO32 87 H3
FBDG SP6 72 A7
Rectory Rd HAV PO9 8 E6
PLE BH15 233 H2
Redan Cl CHCH/BSGR BH23 239 L1
The Redan GPORT PO12 11 H9
Red Barn Av
FHAM/PORC PO16 162 A7
Red Barn La FHAM PO15 160 C4
Redbreast Rd
MOOR/WNTN BH9 220 E5
Redbreast Rd North
MOOR/WNTN BH9 220 E5 3
Redbridge Cswy WSHM SO15 105 G8
Redbridge Gv HAV PO9 165 H5
Redbridge Hl ROWN SO16 105 L7
Redbridge La ROWN SO16 105 G6
Redbridge Rd WSHM SO15 105 J8
Redcar Av HSEA PO3 187 L7
Redcliffe Cl CHCH/BSGR BH23 223 G6
Redcote Cl WEND SO18 132 F1 1
Redcroft La HLER SO31 133 L7
The Redfords TOTT SO40 104 D7
Redhill ROWN SO16 106 D4
Redhill Av NBNE BH10 220 C6
Redhill Cl NBNE BH10 220 C6
ROWN SO16 106 D4
Redhill Ct MOOR/WNTN BH9 220 E4 3
Redhill Crs MOOR/WNTN BH9 220 D5
Red Hill Crs ROWN SO16 106 D4
Redhill Dr NBNE BH10 220 C6
Redhill Rd HAV PO9 141 M7
Red Hill Wy ROWN SO16 106 D5
Redhoave Rd CFDH BH17 218 B6
Redhorn Cl UPTN BH16 232 B4 1
Red House Ct EPSF GU31 65 L4
Redhouse Park Gdns
LSOL/BMARY PO13 209 J1
Redlands BKME/WDN BH12 234 E3
Redlands Dr ITCH SO19 132 D2
Redlands Gv ENEY PO4 212 A4
Redlands La EMRTH PO10 166 D4
FHAM/STUB PO14 6 F6
Red La RSAL SP5 19 M1
Red Leaves BPWT SO32 111 K6
Red Ldg CHFD SO53 81 G5
Redlynch Cl HAV PO9 165 M4 1
Redmans Vw VWD BH31 144 B2
Redmoor Cl ITCH SO19 132 C2
Red Oaks Cl FERN BH22 193 M1
Red Oaks Dr FHAM PO15 158 F3
Redrise Cl FAWY SO45 179 M5
Redshank Cl CFDH BH17 217 K7
Redshank Rd HORN PO8 140 E1
Redvers Rd CHCH/BSGR BH23 238 D1
Redward Rd ROWN SO16 105 L3
Redwing Ct ENEY PO4 212 A3 3
Redwing Gdns TOTT SO40 104 B8 7
Redwing Rd HORN PO8 116 B3
Redwood Cl FAWY SO45 155 H5
HEND SO30 108 B6
LYMN SO41 228 A3
RGWD BH24 170 F1
Redwood Dr FERN BH22 168 A8
FHAM/PORC PO16 161 M8
Redwood Gdns TOTT SO40 129 G1
Redwood Gv HAV PO9 165 L4
Redwood Rd UPTN BH16 216 E8
Redwood Wy ROWN SO16 106 F2
Reed Dr TOTT SO40 130 D6
Reedmace Cl WVILLE PO7 164 E2 3
Reeds La LISS GU33 37 J2
Reed's Pl GPORT PO12 10 D1
Reeds Rd GPORT PO12 209 M1
Reeves Cl ROMY SO51 76 D5
Reeves Wy HLER SO31 133 K7 5
Regal Cl CHAM PO6 163 K8
Regency Crs
CHCH/BSGR BH23 222 D8 4
Regency Gdns WVILLE PO7 164 B2 1
Regency Pl FHAM PO15 6 C5
Regent Cl RWIN SO21 54 B4
Regent Dr LTDN BH7 221 K8
Regent Pl SSEA PO5 12 F6 2
Regent Rd CHFD SO53 81 J2
Regents Ct HAV PO9 8 E7
Regents Ga HLER SO31 158 C3
Regent's Gv WSHM SO15 106 A8 4
Regent's Park Gdns
WSHM SO15 130 F1 2
Regent's Park Rd WSHM SO15 130 E1
Regent St PSEA PO1 211 G1
SHAM SO14 4 F3
Regent Wy
CHCH/BSGR BH23 238 A2 1
Reginald Rd ENEY PO4 211 L5
Reid St CHCH/BSGR BH23 237 M1
Relay Rd WVILLE PO7 140 B8
Reliant Cl CHFD SO53 81 G4 1
Rempstone Rd WIMB BH21 192 B7
Renault Dr BDST BH18 217 L7
Renda Rd FAWY SO45 180 A4
Renny Rd PSEA PO1 13 M2
Renouf Cl LYMN SO41 228 A5
Renown Cl CHFD SO53 81 G3
Renown Gdns HORN PO8 140 D3
Repton Cl GPORT PO12 209 J4
Repton Gdns HEND SO30 109 J6
Reservoir La HEND SO30 133 L2
PSF GU32 63 L3
Rest-a-wyle Av HISD PO11 213 L3
Retreat Rd WIMB BH21 192 B4
The Retreat ELGH SO50 82 A4
SSEA PO5 13 H6
TOTT SO40 129 K3
Reuben Dr PLE BH15 232 C6
Revenge Cl ENEY PO4 212 A2 2
Rewlands Dr FUFL SO22 16 B4
Reynolds Dl TOTT SO40 129 H3
Reynolds Rd ELGH SO50 83 J7
WSHM SO15 106 B8
Rhinefield Cl BROC SO42 175 J6
ELGH SO50 82 E6 2
HAV PO9 165 G4 5
Rhinefield Ornamental Dr
BROC SO42 174 D3
Rhinefield Rd
NMIL/BTOS BH25 199 J6
Rhiners Cl LYMN SO41 200 F5
Rhyme Hall Ms FAWY SO45 180 F5 8
Ribble Cl BDST BH18 217 L6
CHFD SO53 81 J3
Ribble Ct ROWN SO16 105 K7
Ricardo Crs CHCH/BSGR BH23 238 F2
Rice Gdns UPTN BH16 232 C4
Richard Cl UPTN BH16 232 A1 5
Richard Gv GPORT PO12 185 L7
Richards Cl HLER SO31 158 F5
Richlans Rd HEND SO30 134 A2
Richmond Cl CHFD SO53 53 G7
HISD PO11 213 J4
TOTT SO40 104 A7
Richmond Dr HISD PO11 213 H4
Richmond Gdns PTSW SO17 107 G7
WCLF BH2 14 E5
Richmond Hl WCLF BH2 14 E5
Richmond Hill Dr WCLF BH2 14 E5
Richmond Hill Rbt WCLF BH2 14 E4
Richmond La ROMY SO51 50 F7
Richmond Pk RWIN SO21 54 C4
Richmond Park Av CHAR BH8 236 A1
Richmond Park Cl
BMTH BH1 236 C2 4
Richmond Park Crs
CHAR BH8 236 B1
Richmond Park Rd
BMTH BH1 236 C2 5
Richmond Pl PSEA PO1 12 E2
SSEA PO5 13 H7 1
Richmond Ri
FHAM/PORC PO16 162 A7
Richmond Rd GPORT PO12 10 C4
LSOL/BMARY PO13 208 B2
PSTN BH14 234 B4
WSHM SO15 131 G2
Richmond St SHAM SO14 5 H5
Richmond Wood Rd
CHAR BH8 236 A1
Richville Rd ROWN SO16 105 M8
Ridding Cl WSHM SO15 106 A8
Riders La HAV PO9 165 J4
Ridge Cl HORN PO8 116 B4
Ridge Common La PSF GU32 63 H2
Ridgefield Gdns
CHCH/BSGR BH23 224 B8
Ridge La HEND SO30 135 H5
ROMY SO51 78 A7
Ridgemount Av ROWN SO16 106 E3
Ridgemount Gdns PLE BH15 232 D5 6
The Ridge RSAL SP5 73 J4
Ridge Top La PSF GU32 62 F1
Ridgeway BDST BH18 217 M4
FERN BH22 194 C8
FUFL SO22 26 B3
Ridgeway Cl CHAM PO6 162 D7 1
CHFD SO53 81 K3
ELGH SO50 83 H5 1
Ridgeway La LYMN SO41 228 B6
The Ridgeway
FHAM/PORC PO16 161 J7
Ridgewood Cl FAWY SO45 155 G5 1
Ridgway HAV PO9 8 A5
The Ridings BPWT SO32 111 K4
ELGH SO50 82 F6
LISS GU33 37 G4
NEND PO2 187 K5
Ridley Cl FAWY SO45 180 A4 3
Ridley Rd MOOR/WNTN BH9 220 D8
Ridout Cl NBNE BH10 219 M7
Rigby Rd SHAM SO14 107 G8
Riggs Gdns BWD BH11 219 K6
Rigler Rd PLE BH15 232 F7
Rimbury Wy CHCH/BSGR BH23 222 E8
Rimington Rd HORN PO8 140 D5
Ringbury LYMN SO41 228 B2
Ringlet Wy WINC SO23 3 M7
Ringsgreen La PSF GU32 34 F5
The Ring ROWN SO16 106 D1
Ringwood Dr NBAD SO52 79 K3
Ringwood Rd
BKME/WDN BH12 219 H6
BWD BH11 219 L2
BWD BH11 219 J4 8
CHCH/BSGR BH23 196 E8
CHCH/BSGR BH23 224 A2
ENEY PO4 211 M5
FBDG SP6 97 M8
FBDG SP6 121 K3
FERN BH22 168 F8
PSTN BH14 233 L2
RGWD BH24 169 K4
RGWD BH24 172 B3
TOTT SO40 128 E1
VWD BH31 144 D1
WIMB BH21 144 C8
WIMB BH21 168 F2
Ripley Gv HSEA PO3 187 L8
Ripon Gdns WVILLE PO7 140 F7
Ripon Rd MOOR/WNTN BH9 220 E8
Ripplewood TOTT SO40 130 E7 4
Ripstone Gdns PTSW SO17 107 G5
The Rise BROC SO42 175 K7
WVILLE PO7 164 B6
Ritchie Ct ITCH SO19 132 F4
Ritchie Pl FERN BH22 168 B4 1
Ritchie Rd BWD BH11 219 M4
Rival Moor Rd EPSF GU31 64 A6
River Cl WIMB BH21 192 A2
Riverdale Av WVILLE PO7 164 E1
Riverdale Cl FBDG SP6 97 L6
Riverdale La CHCH/BSGR BH23 237 M2
Riverdene Pl WEND SO18 107 J8 2
River Gdns LYMN SO41 242 D4
River Gn HLER SO31 157 L6
Riverhead Cl ENEY PO4 211 M3
River La FHAM PO15 160 A2
Riverlea Rd CHCH/BSGR BH23 237 M2
Rivermead Cl ROMY SO51 78 C1
Rivermead Gdns
CHCH/BSGR BH23 222 C6
Riversdale Cl ITCH SO19 132 C8 2
Riversdale Rd SBNE BH6 237 M4
Riverside ELGH SO50 82 C5
RGWD BH24 170 D2
Riverside Av
FHAM/PORC PO16 161 H5
LTDN BH7 222 A7
Riverside Cl LISS GU33 36 E4
TOTT SO40 128 A2
Riverside Gdns ROMY SO51 78 D2
Riverside La SBNE BH6 237 L3
Riverside Rd FERN BH22 168 B6
SBNE BH6 237 L3 1
River's St SSEA PO5 13 J3
River St EMRTH PO10 166 F4
Riverview TOTT SO40 129 K3
River View Rd WEND SO18 107 J6
River Wk WEND SO18 107 K5
River Wy CHCH/BSGR BH23 222 B6
HAV PO9 9 G1
R L Stevenson Av WBNE BH4 235 G5
Roads Hl HORN PO8 115 L7
Road Vw NEND PO2 187 G8
Robert Cecil Av WEND SO18 107 K4
Roberts Cl LYMN SO41 227 J7
WHAM PO17 136 E4
Roberts La CFDH BH17 232 F1
Roberts Rd CFDH BH17 217 M7
FAWY SO45 155 K4
GPORT PO12 209 K2 4
LTDN BH7 236 F2
TOTT SO40 129 K3
WSHM SO15 4 B1
Robert Whitworth Dr
ROMY SO51 50 E7
Robina Cl WVILLE PO7 164 E1
Robin Crs NMIL/BTOS BH25 225 H3
Robin Gdns HORN PO8 140 B4
TOTT SO40 104 B8
Robin Gv NMIL/BTOS BH25 225 K6
Robinia Gn ROWN SO16 106 B3
Robins Cl FHAM/STUB PO14 184 A5
Robins La MIDH GU29 67 G1
Robins Meadow
FHAM/STUB PO14 159 G7
Robinson Rd
FHAM/STUB PO14 183 M7
Robinson Wy HSEA PO3 188 A5
Robin Sq ELGH SO50 81 H7
Robins Wy CHCH/BSGR BH23 239 G3
Robinswood Dr FERN BH22 168 B8
Rochester Rd BWD BH11 219 M4
ENEY PO4 211 K5
Rochester St SHAM SO14 5 L2
Rochford Rd CHAM PO6 163 H8
Rockall Cl ROWN SO16 105 K3
Rockbourne Cl HAV PO9 165 G4 6
Rockbourne Gdns
NMIL/BTOS BH25 225 H8 1
Rockbourne La FBDG SP6 96 D1
Rockbourne Rd FUFL SO22 16 C4
Rockery Cl FAWY SO45 155 G4
Rockford Cl SBNE BH6 237 L5
Rockingham Wy
FHAM/PORC PO16 161 M8
Rockleigh Dr TOTT SO40 129 H4
Rockleigh Rd ROWN SO16 106 C5
Rockley Rd PLE BH15 232 D6
Rockram Cl TOTT SO40 127 M1
Rockram Gdns FAWY SO45 155 G5 2
Rockrose Wy CHAM PO6 162 E6
Rockstone La SHAM SO14 131 L2
Rockstone Pl WSHM SO15 131 K2
Rockville Dr WVILLE PO7 164 C1
Rodbourne Cl LYMN SO41 227 H7
Rodfield La RWIN SO21 29 G5
Rodlease La LYMN SO41 202 C6
Rodney Cl BKME/WDN BH12 219 L8 1
LSOL/BMARY PO13 209 G2
Rodney Dr CHCH/BSGR BH23 238 E2
Rodney Rd ENEY PO4 211 K3
Rodney Wy HORN PO8 140 F2
Rodway WIMB BH21 192 A4
Rodwell Cl NBNE BH10 220 A2
Roebuck Av FHAM PO15 160 B3
Roebuck Cl CHAM PO6 187 K1 3
NMIL/BTOS BH25 225 M5
Roeshot Crs CHCH/BSGR BH23 224 C7
Roewood Cl FAWY SO45 180 A5 2
Roewood Rd FAWY SO45 180 A5
Rogate Gdns
FHAM/PORC PO16 162 A7
Roger Penny Wy FBDG SP6 98 F5
Rogers Cl ELGH SO50 82 D4
GPORT PO12 209 M2
Rogers Md HISD PO11 189 K5
Rogers Rd ELGH SO50 82 D4
Roker Wy ELGH SO50 83 G7
Roland Cl HORN PO8 140 F2
Rollestone Rd FAWY SO45 179 M5
Rolls Dr SBNE BH6 238 A4
Roman Cl CHFD SO53 81 K1
Roman Dr ROWN SO16 106 D1
Roman Gdns FAWY SO45 155 H7 1
Roman Gv FHAM/PORC PO16 186 B2
Roman Landing SELS PO20 215 J6
Roman Rd BDST BH18 217 J4
FAWY SO45 155 G6
FAWY SO45 179 M2
ROWN SO16 80 D7
RWIN SO21 54 F3
Romans' Rd WINC SO23 26 E2
Roman Wy FAWY SO45 155 H7
HAV PO9 165 G6
Romford Rd HLER SO31 158 B8
Romill Cl WEND SO18 108 A5
Romney Cl NBNE BH10 220 C5 2
Romney Rd NBNE BH10 220 C4
Romsey Av FHAM/PORC PO16 161 L8
HSEA PO3 211 M2
Romsey Cl ELGH SO50 81 M5
Romsey Rd ELGH SO50 81 M5
FUFL SO22 2 C8
HORN PO8 116 B6
LYND SO43 151 K2
ROMY SO51 76 D4
ROMY SO51 103 K3
ROWN SO16 105 J3
RSAL SP5 47 G4
TOTT SO40 102 E8
Romyns Ct FHAM/STUB PO14 6 E6
Rookcliff Wy LYMN SO41 242 B4
Rookery Av FHAM PO15 159 G1
HLER SO31 158 F1
Rookery La FBDG SP6 71 L7
The Rookery EMRTH PO10 166 E7
Rookes Cl HORN PO8 140 F2
Rookes La LYMN SO41 228 B6
Rook Hill Rd CHCH/BSGR BH23 239 G2
Rookley HLER SO31 157 G1
Rooksbridge FAWY SO45 155 G5 3
Rooksbury Cft HAV PO9 165 L3 3
Rooks Down Rd FUFL SO22 26 C3
Rooksway Gv
FHAM/PORC PO16 161 J8
Rookwood Cl ELGH SO50 82 A2 2
Rookwood La SELS PO20 215 L4
Rookwood Rd SELS PO20 215 L6
Rookwood Vw WVILLE PO7 139 K3
Roosevelt Crs BWD BH11 219 M2
Rope Hl LYMN SO41 202 B7
Ropers La UPTN BH16 232 C1
Ropley Cl ITCH SO19 132 E8 2
Ropley Rd HAV PO9 165 M3
LTDN BH7 237 H1
Rosamund Av WIMB BH21 192 C7
Roscrea Cl SBNE BH6 238 A4 1
Roscrea Dr SBNE BH6 238 A4
Rosebank Cl ROWN SO16 105 K3
Rosebay Cl ELGH SO50 109 H2 4
Rosebay Ct WVILLE PO7 164 D3 3
Rosebery Av CHAM PO6 187 L1
Rosebery Cl VWD BH31 145 G3
Rosebery Crs ELGH SO50 82 A2
Rosebery Rd BOSC BH5 236 F3 4
Rosebud Av
MOOR/WNTN BH9 220 E6 5
Rosebury Av FAWY SO45 155 L7
Rose Cl FAWY SO45 155 L6 5
HEND SO30 109 H8
Rosecrae Cl
NMIL/BTOS BH25 225 K4 2
Rose Crs PLE BH15 233 L2
Rosedale Av ROMY SO51 78 F1
Rosedale Cl
CHCH/BSGR BH23 238 D2 5
FHAM/STUB PO14 159 K8
Rose Gdns MOOR/WNTN BH9 220 E6
Rose Hl HORN PO8 140 E2
Rosehill Cl CHCH/BSGR BH23 197 M7 2
Rosehill Dr CHCH/BSGR BH23 197 M7
Roselands HEND SO30 108 C8 3
HORN PO8 140 E3
Roselands Cl ELGH SO50 83 G5
Roselands Gdns PTSW SO17 106 F6
Roseleigh Dr TOTT SO40 129 J2
Rosemary Gdns
BKME/WDN BH12 234 A1
FHAM PO15 135 H8
HEND SO30 134 A3
Rosemary La PSEA PO1 12 C2 4
Rosemary Rd
BKME/WDN BH12 234 B1
Rosemary Wy HORN PO8 140 F4
Rosemoor Gv CHFD SO53 53 G7
Rosemount Rd WBNE BH4 235 G6
Rosendale Rd CHFD SO53 81 J4 1
Rose Rd SHAM SO14 106 F8
TOTT SO40 129 L2
The Rosery GPORT PO12 10 E9
Rosetta Rd ENEY PO4 211 M4
Rosewall Rd ROWN SO16 105 L5
Rosewarne Ct WINC SO23 2 F5
Rosewood LSOL/BMARY PO13 185 J7
Rosewood Gdns HORN PO8 116 B3
NMIL/BTOS BH25 225 K4
TOTT SO40 130 E7
Rosina Cl WVILLE PO7 140 F8
Roslin Rd TWDS BH3 235 K1
Roslin Rd South TWDS BH3 235 J1
Rosoman Rd ITCH SO19 132 D4
Rossan Av HLER SO31 182 B1
Ross Gdns ROWN SO16 105 M6
WIMB BH21 219 G3 1
Rossington Av WEND SO18 132 D1
Rossington Wy WEND SO18 132 D1
Rossley Cl CHCH/BSGR BH23 224 C6
Rosslyn Cl NBAD SO52 79 M4
Rossmore Rd
BKME/WDN BH12 219 G8
Ross Rd RGWD BH24 147 G7
Ross Wy LSOL/BMARY PO13 208 D1
Rostron Cl WEND SO18 107 M5 2
Rosyth Rd WEND SO18 132 D1
Rotary Cl WIMB BH21 192 D1
Rotary Ct HLER SO31 156 F2
Rothbury Cl ITCH SO19 132 E4 1
TOTT SO40 104 C7
Rothbury Pk
NMIL/BTOS BH25 225 M6 2
Rotherbank Farm La LISS GU33 36 E2
Rother Cl EPSF GU31 64 B4
WEND SO18 108 A7
Rothercombe La PSF GU32 62 F3
Rother Dl ITCH SO19 133 J5
Rotherfield Rd
CHCH/BSGR BH23 224 E7
SBNE BH6 237 G5 1
Rother La EPSF GU31 66 D7
Rotherwick Cl HAV PO9 165 M3
Rothesay Dr CHCH/BSGR BH23 239 K1
Rothesay Rd GPORT PO12 209 L1
TWDS BH3 235 H2
Rothsbury Dr CHFD SO53 81 G2
Rothschild Cl ITCH SO19 132 C8
Rothville Pl CHFD SO53 53 G6 2
Rothwell Cl CHAM PO6 162 E7 3

Rotterdam Dr
CHCH/BSGR BH23 .... **238** C1
Roughdown La *FAWY* SO45 .... **180** A7
Roumelia La *BOSC* BH5 .... **236** D4
The Roundabouts *LISS* GU33 .... **36** F3 🔲
Roundcopse *FAWY* SO45 .... **155** G5 🔲
Round Hl *FBDG* SP6 .... **97** L7 🔲
Roundhaye Rd *BWD* BH11 .... **219** K3
Roundhill Cl *WEND* SO18 ...... **107** M7
Roundhouse Dr *TOTT* SO40 .... **128** F2
Roundhouse Meadow
   EMRTH PO10 .... **190** E1
Roundhuts Ri *WINC* SO23 .... **3** M7
Roundway *WVILLE* PO7 .... **140** D8
Routs Wy *ROWN* SO16 .... **105** K1
Rowallan Av
   LSOL/BMARY PO13 .... **184** F7
Rowan Av *HORN* PO08 .... **140** F6
Rowan Cl *BPWT* SO32 .... **112** A4 🔲
   CHCH/BSGR BH23 .... **224** B8
   HLER SO31 .... **133** K8
   LSOL/BMARY PO13 .... **208** D3
   LYMN SO41 .... **200** F7
   RGWD BH24 .... **169** H4
   ROMY SO51 .... **79** H2
   ROWN SO16 .... **105** L5
   TOTT SO40 .... **129** H2
Rowan Dr *CFDH* BH17 .... **217** J7
   CHCH/BSGR BH23 .... **224** B8
   VWD BH31 .... **144** F4
Rowan Gdns *HEND* SO30 ...... **134** B2
Rowan Rd *HAV* PO9 .... **165** M5
Rowans Pk *LYMN* SO41 .... **228** B5
The Rowans *TOTT* SO40 .... **130** D7
Rowan Wy *FHAM/STUB* PO14 .. **160** A8
   RGWD BH24 .... **169** H4
Rowbarrow Cl *CFDH* BH17 .... **218** C6
Rowborough Rd *WEND* SO18 .. **107** L8
Rowbury Rd *HAV* PO9 .... **165** H2
Rowden Cl *ROMY* SO51 .... **76** D6
Rowe Ashe Wy *HLER* SO31 .... **158** D5 🔲
Rowena Rd *SBNE* BH6 .... **237** L3
Rowes La *LYMN* SO41 .... **229** M1
Rowhay La *BPWT* SO32 .... **84** B3
Rowhill Dr *FAWY* SO45 .... **155** G5
Rowin Cl *HISD* PO11 .... **214** B6
Rowland Av *PLE* BH15 .... **233** K3
Rowland Rd *CHAM* PO6 .... **162** C7 🔲
   FHAM PO15 .... **6** A1
Rowlands Av *WVILLE* PO7 .... **140** C7
Rowlands Castle Rd
   HORN PO8 .... **141** K2
Rowlands Cl *CHFD* SO53 .... **80** F4
Rowlands Hl *WIMB* BH21 ...... **192** A3
Rowlett Rd *LYMN* SO41 .... **228** C5
Rowley Cl *HEND* SO30 .... **109** L8 🔲
Rowley Dr *HEND* SO30 .... **109** L8
Rowlings Rd *FUFL* SO22 .... **16** C5
Rowner Cl *LSOL/BMARY* PO13 .. **185** G7
Rowner La *LSOL/BMARY* PO13 .. **185** G6
Rowner Rd *LSOL/BMARY* PO13 .. **184** F7
Rownhams Cl *ROWN* SO16 .... **105** K2
Rownhams La *NBAD* SO52 ...... **79** L3
   ROWN SO16 .... **105** L1
Rownhams Rd *CHAR* BH8 ...... **221** G5
   HAV PO9 .... **165** H3
   NBAD SO52 .... **79** M5
   ROWN SO16 .... **105** L6
Rownhams Rd North
   ROWN SO16 .... **105** L3
Rownhams Wy *ROWN* SO16 .. **105** K2
Rowse Cl *ROMY* SO51 .... **50** E7 🔲
The Row *RSAL* SP5 .... **73** K1
Row Wood La
   LSOL/BMARY PO13 .... **184** F7
Royal Crescent Rd *SHAM* SO14 .. **5** L4
Royal Gdns *HAV* PO9 .... **141** L7
Royal Ga *ENEY* PO4 .... **211** M6
Royal Oak Rd *NBNE* BH10 .... **220** A3
Royal Sovereign Av
   FHAM/STUB PO14 .... **184** D3
Royal Wy *WVILLE* PO7 .... **164** C1
Royce Cl *SELS* PO20 .... **215** L7
Royce Wy *SELS* PO20 .... **215** L7
Royden La *LYMN* SO41 .... **202** B5
Roydon Cl *FUFL* SO22 .... **26** C3
Roy's La *BPWT* SO32 .... **113** H6
Royster Cl *CFDH* BH17 .... **218** A7
Royston Av *ELGH* SO50 .... **81** M3
Royston Cl *PTSW* SO17 .... **107** G6
Royston Dr *WIMB* BH21 .... **192** B3 🔲
Royston Pl *NMIL/BTOS* BH25 .. **225** M8
Rozelle Rd *PSTN* BH14 .... **234** B4
Rubens Cl *NMIL/BTOS* BH25 .. **225** L4
Ruby Rd *ITCH* SO19 .... **132** C2
Rudd La *ROMY* SO51 .... **50** F1
Rudgwick Cl
   FHAM/PORC PO16 .... **161** M8 🔲
Rudmore Sq *NEND* PO2 .... **187** G8
Ruffield Cl *FUFL* SO22 .... **16** B6
Rufford Cl *ELGH* SO50 .... **81** M2
Rufford Gdns *SBNE* BH6 ...... **237** H1
Rufus Cl *CHFD* SO53 .... **55** K8
   ROWN SO16 .... **105** J2
Rufus Gdns *TOTT* SO40 .... **129** G1
Rugby Rd *CFDH* BH17 .... **217** L7
   SSEA PO5 .... **13** L3
Rumbridge Gdns *TOTT* SO40 .. **129** L1 🔲
Rumbridge St *TOTT* SO40 .... **129** K2
Runnymede *FHAM* PO15 ...... **160** B4
   HEND SO30 .... **108** C2 🔲
Runnymede Av *BWD* BH11 .. **219** H2
Runton Rd *BKME/WDN* BH12 .. **234** E3
The Runway *CHCH/BSGR* BH23 .. **239** G1
Rushall La *WIMB* BH21 .... **216** E4
Rushcombe Wy *WIMB* BH21 .. **217** H2 🔲
Rushes Rd *PSF* GU32 .... **63** K4
The Rushes *TOTT* SO40 .... **130** D6
Rushfield Rd *LISS* GU33 .... **36** E5
Rushford Warren
   CHCH/BSGR BH23 .... **238** C3
Rushington Av *TOTT* SO40 .... **129** H3
Rushington La *TOTT* SO40 .... **129** J3
Rushmere La *WVILLE* PO7 .... **139** H1
Rushmere Rd *SBNE* BH6 ...... **237** H1
Rushton Crs *TWDS* BH3 .... **235** L2 🔲
Ruskin Av *MOOR/WNTN* BH9 .. **220** F5
Ruskin Rd *ELGH* SO50 .... **81** M3

   ENEY PO4 .... **211** L4
Ruskin Wy *HORN* PO08 .... **140** D4
Rusland Cl *CHFD* SO53 .... **81** G1
Russell Cl *LSOL/BMARY* PO13 .. **208** D2
Russell Cotes Rd *BMTH* BH1 .. **15** G7
Russell Dr *CHCH/BSGR* BH23 .. **238** C2
   ROMY SO51 .... **21** J8
Russell Gdns *RGWD* BH24 .... **169** M3 🔲
   UPTN BH16 .... **232** B4
Russell Pl *FHAM/PORC* PO16 .... **7** J5
   PTSW SO17 .... **107** G7
Russell Rd *HAV* PO9 .... **8** F1
   LSOL/BMARY PO13 .... **208** D3
   WINC SO23 .... **3** H3
Russel St *GPORT* PO12 .... **209** L2
   SHAM SO14 .... **5** H5
Russell Wy *EPSF* GU31 .... **63** M6
Russel Rd *NBNE* BH10 .... **220** A2
Russet Cl *FERN* BH22 .... **194** B2
   LYMN SO41 .... **228** D6
Russet Gdns *EMRTH* PO10 .... **166** F8
Russett Cl *BPWT* SO32 .... **112** A4 🔲
Rustan Cl *ELGH* SO50 .... **81** L8
   HEND SO30 .... **133** M2 🔲
Rutland Gdns *HLER* SO31 ...... **133** L7
Rutland Rd *CHCH/BSGR* BH23 .. **222** D7
   MOOR/WNTN BH9 .... **220** F8
Rutland Wy *WEND* SO18 ...... **107** M7
Ruxley Cl *FAWY* SO45 .... **180** A4
Ryall Dr *CFDH* BH17 .... **218** B7
Ryan Cl *FERN* BH22 .... **194** A1
Ryan Gdns *FERN* BH22 .... **194** A1
Rydal Cl *CHAM* PO6 .... **162** F7
   CHCH/BSGR BH23 .... **222** B4
Rydal Rd *GPORT* PO12 .... **185** L8
Ryde Pl *LSOL/BMARY* PO13 .. **208** E4
Ryde Ter *SHAM* SO14 .... **5** K5
Rye Cl *NBAD* SO52 .... **80** D7
Ryecroft *FHAM/STUB* PO14 .. **159** G6 🔲
   HAV PO9 .... **9** K4
Ryecroft Av *BWD* BH11 .... **219** J3
Rye Dl *TOTT* SO40 .... **129** G5
Ryedown La *ROMY* SO51 .... **77** H4
Ryefield Cl *EPSF* GU31 .... **64** B5
Rye Paddock La *FAWY* SO45 .. **180** F4
Rylandes Ct *ROWN* SO16 ...... **105** L5

S

Sabre Rd *EMRTH* PO10 .... **190** E5
Sackville St *SSEA* PO5 .... **13** G4
Saddle Cl *WIMB* BH21 .... **193** G2 🔲
Saddlers Cl *ELGH* SO50 .... **81** M2
Sadlers La *FAWY* SO45 .... **155** L7
Sadlers Wk *EMRTH* PO10 ...... **166** E8
Saffron Dr *CHCH/BSGR* BH23 .. **223** M8
Saffron Wy *BWD* BH11 .... **219** H5
   FHAM PO15 .... **135** H8
Sage Cl *WVILLE* PO7 .... **164** C2
Sages La *ALTN* GU34 .... **33** H3
Sailor's La *BPWT* SO32 .... **86** B1
St Agatha's Rd *HLER* SO31 .... **157** L4 🔲
St Alban's Av *CHAR* BH8 ...... **236** A1
St Alban's Crs *CHAR* BH8 ...... **236** A1
St Alban's Rd *CHAR* BH8 ...... **236** A1
   HAV PO9 .... **165** L4
   SHAM SO14 .... **5** K1 🔲
St Aldhelm's Cl *CCLF* BH13 .... **234** E5
St Aldhelm's Rd *CCLF* BH13 .. **234** E4
St Andrew Cl *HORN* PO08 .... **116** B6
St Andrews Cl *NBAD* SO52 .... **79** K3
   ROMY SO51 .... **50** C2
St Andrews Pk *ELGH* SO50 .... **109** H2
St Andrew's Rd *CHAM* PO6 .. **164** D8
   GPORT PO12 .... **10** A1
   SHAM SO14 .... **5** H1
   SSEA PO5 .... **13** J5
   WIMB BH21 .... **217** L3
St Anne's Av *SBNE* BH6 .... **237** K3
St Annes Cl *FUFL* SO22 .... **26** B3
St Anne's Gdns *ITCH* SO19 .... **132** C6
   LYMN SO41 .... **228** B5
St Anne's Gv
   FHAM/STUB PO14 .... **184** D1
St Annes La *BPWT* SO32 .... **136** B1
St Anne's Rd *ITCH* SO19 .... **132** C6
   UPTN BH16 .... **232** A1
St Ann's Crs *GPORT* PO12 .... **209** L2
St Ann's Rd *HORN* PO08 ...... **141** L1
St Anthony's Rd *WCLF* BH2 .. **14** E2
St Aubin's Av *ITCH* SO19 ...... **132** E3
St Aubin's Pk *HISD* PO11 ...... **213** H5
St Aubyns Ct *PLE* BH15 .... **233** G6 🔲
St Aubyns La *RGWD* BH24 .... **147** J7
St Augustine Gdns
   PTSW SO17 .... **107** J7 🔲
St Augustine Rd *ENEY* PO4 .. **211** K5
St Augustin's Rd *WCLF* BH2 .. **14** E1
St Austell Cl *ELGH* SO50 .... **82** D5 🔲
St Barbara Wy *NEND* PO2 .... **187** K4 🔲
St Barbe Cl *ROMY* SO51 .... **78** F2 🔲
St Bartholomew's Gdns
   SSEA PO5 .... **13** K5 🔲
St Blaize Rd *ROMY* SO51 .... **51** G8 🔲
St Bonnet Dr *BPWT* SO32 .... **85** H8 🔲
St Brelades Av
   BKME/WDN BH12 .... **219** H7
St Catherines *WIMB* BH21 .... **192** A4
St Catherine's Rd *ELGH* SO50 .. **81** M3
   HISD PO11 .... **213** G5
   SBNE BH6 .... **237** K5
   WEND SO18 .... **107** K7
   WINC SO23 .... **3** J3
St Catherines Vw
   HEND SO30 .... **133** L2 🔲
St Catherines Wy
   FHAM/PORC PO16 .... **7** K2
St Chad's Av *NEND* PO2 .... **187** J6
St Christopher Av
   FHAM/PORC PO16 .... **7** K2
St Christophers Cl *NBAD* SO52 .. **79** L4
St Christopher's Rd *HAV* PO9 .. **165** G5
St Clair Rd *CCLF* BH13 .... **245** K2

St Clares Av *HAV* PO9 .... **165** H1
St Clements Cl *ROMY* SO51 .. **50** D8 🔲
St Clements Gdns *BMTH* BH1 .. **236** C3
St Clement's Rd *BMTH* BH1 .. **236** C3
   PLE BH15 .... **234** A1
St Clement St *WINC* SO23 .... **2** F8
St Colman's Av *CHAM* PO6 .. **163** L8
St Cross Rd *WINC* SO23 .... **26** D5
St Cuthberts Cl *HLER* SO31 .. **158** F4 🔲
St Cuthberts La *HLER* SO31 .. **158** F4
St David's Cl *TOTT* SO40 ...... **104** B7
St Davids Rd *HLER* SO31 ...... **158** D5
   HORN PO08 .... **116** B3
   SSEA PO5 .... **13** K4
   UPTN BH16 .... **232** A1
St Denys Rd *PTSW* SO17 ...... **107** G7
   PTSW SO17 .... **107** G7
St Edmund Cl
   FHAM/STUB PO14 .... **158** F7
St Edmund's Rd *ROWN* SO16 .. **106** A8
St Edward's Rd *GPORT* PO12 .. **10** F4
   HLER SO31 .... **156** F1
   SSEA PO5 .... **13** G6
St Elizabeth's Av *WEND* SO18 .. **132** Y1
St Evox Cl *ROWN* SO16 .... **105** L3
St Faith's Cl *GPORT* PO12 ...... **10** C2
St Faith's Rd *PSEA* PO1 .... **211** H2
   WINC SO23 .... **26** E3
St Francis Av *WEND* SO18 .... **108** A8
St Francis Cl *FAWY* SO45 ...... **206** C1 🔲
St Francis Ct *NEND* PO2 .... **187** J4 🔲
St Francis Pl *HAV* PO9 .... **165** J5
St Francis Rd *FAWY* SO45 .... **206** C1
   GPORT PO12 .... **11** G9
St Gabriel's Rd *WEND* SO18 .. **132** F1
St George Cl *HLER* SO31 .... **133** K7
St Georges Av *CHAR* BH8 .... **236** B1
   BKME/WDN BH12 .... **218** F8
   HAV PO9 .... **9** K4
St Georges Cl
   CHCH/BSGR BH23 .... **197** M8
   CHAR BH8 .... **221** G8
   CHCH/BSGR BH23 .... **224** B8
St Georges Crs *FBDG* SP6 .... **97** L6 🔲
St George's Dr *FERN* BH22 .. **194** A4
St George's Rd *CHAM* PO6 .. **163** K8
   ENEY PO4 .... **211** L6
   FBDG SP6 .... **97** L6
   HISD PO11 .... **213** H5
   HLER SO31 .... **158** D5
   PSEA PO1 .... **12** C3
St Georges Sq *PSEA* PO1 ...... **12** D2 🔲
St Georges St *SHAM* SO14 ...... **5** G4
   WINC SO23 .... **3** G4
St George's Wy *PSEA* PO1 .... **12** D2
St Giles Cl *WINC* SO23 .... **3** K9
St Giles Wy *HORN* PO8 .... **116** B6
St Helena Rd *WEND* SO18 .... **107** L5
St Helena Wy
   FHAM/PORC PO16 .... **162** B8
St Helen's Cl *ENEY* PO4 .... **211** K6
St Helen's Pde *ENEY* PO4 ...... **13** M9
St Helens Rd *GPORT* PO12 .... **209** J5
   HISD PO11 .... **213** H5
St Helier Rd *BKME/WDN* BH12 .. **219** H7
St Hellen's Rd *CHAM* PO6 .... **164** B8
St Hermans Rd *HISD* PO11 .... **214** A6
St Hilda Av *HORN* PO08 .... **116** B6
St Hubert Rd *HORN* PO08 .... **116** B6
St Ives End La *RGWD* BH24 .. **169** L3
St Ives Gdns *WCLF* BH2 .... **14** F2
St Ives Pk *RGWD* BH24 .... **169** L3
St Ives Wd *RGWD* BH24 .... **169** M3
St James Cl *HORN* PO08 .... **116** B4
   PLE BH15 .... **233** G7 🔲
St James' La *FUFL* SO22 .... **2** D8
St James' Rd *EMRTH* PO10 .. **166** D8
   HEND SO30 .... **108** C6
   LYMN SO41 .... **201** G6
   WIMB BH21 .... **193** L2
St James's Cl *WSHM* SO15 .... **106** B7
St James's Park Rd
   ROWN SO16 .... **106** B6
St James's Rd *SSEA* PO5 .... **13** G4
   WSHM SO15 .... **106** B7
St James's Sq *BOSC* BH5 ...... **236** F3 🔲
St James's St *PSEA* PO1 .... **12** E1 🔲
St James' Ter *FUFL* SO22 .... **2** E8
St James' Vls *WINC* SO23 .... **2** E9
St James Wy
   FHAM/PORC PO16 .... **162** B8
St John's Av *WVILLE* PO7 .... **164** C4
St John's Cl *GPORT* PO12 ...... **10** E1
   HISD PO11 .... **213** L1
   ROWN SO16 .... **105** K1
   WIMB BH21 .... **192** B4
St Johns Ct *TOTT* SO40 .... **130** D7 🔲
St Johns Dr *TOTT* SO40 .... **130** C7
St John's Gdns
   MOOR/WNTN BH9 .... **220** D7 🔲
St Johns Gdns *ROMY* SO51 .. **50** E8 🔲
St Johns Glebe *ROWN* SO16 .. **105** L1
St John's Hl *WIMB* BH21 ...... **192** B3
St John's Rd *BOSC* BH5 .... **236** C4
   CHAM PO6 .... **163** L8
   CHCH/BSGR BH23 .... **237** M2
   ELGH SO50 .... **82** A4
   EMRTH PO10 .... **167** G7
   HAV PO9 .... **165** G4
   HEND SO30 .... **133** L4
   HLER SO31 .... **158** F6
   NMIL/BTOS BH25 .... **225** L1
   PLE BH15 .... **233** J4
   WINC SO23 .... **3** K7
St John's St *FAWY* SO45 .... **155** L4
   WINC SO23 .... **3** J8
St Just Cl *FERN* BH22 .... **193** M5
St Lawrence Rd *ELGH* SO50 .. **81** M4
   SHAM SO14 .... **5** J6
St Ledger's Pl *BMTH* BH1 ...... **236** C2 🔲
St Ledger's Rd *CHAR* BH8 .... **236** C1
St Leonard's Av *HISD* PO11 .. **213** L5
St Leonard's Cl *FHAM* PO15 .. **159** J5
St Leonard's Rd *CHAR* BH8 .. **236** A2
   LYMN SO41 .... **203** M8
St Leonards Wy *RGWD* BH24 .. **169** H3
St Lukes Cl *HEND* SO30 .... **109** H7 🔲
St Luke's Rd *GPORT* PO12 .... **209** L2

TWDS BH3 .... **235** L1
St Margaret's Av
   CHCH/BSGR BH23 .... **237** M2
St Margaret's Cl *WEND* SO18 .. **132** F1
St Margarets La
   FHAM/STUB PO14 .... **159** J7
St Margarets Rd *HISD* PO11 .. **213** L5
   NBNE BH10 .... **219** M6 🔲
St Mark's Cl *LYMN* SO41 ...... **227** M5
St Marks Rd *LYMN* SO41 ...... **227** M5
   BWD BH11 .... **219** M5
   GPORT PO12 .... **10** D9
   NEND PO2 .... **187** H7 🔲
St Martin's Cl *ROWN* SO16 .. **105** K5
   WINC SO23 .... **3** E7
St Mary Gv *LYMN* SO41 ...... **226** E6
St Mary's Av *GPORT* PO12 .... **10** D7
St Mary's Cl
   CHCH/BSGR BH23 .... **197** M8
   RSAL SP5 .... **73** L3
   WINC SO23 .... **17** H3
St Mary's Pl *SHAM* SO14 .... **5** H3
St Mary's Rd *CHAR* BH8 ...... **236** C2
   ELGH SO50 .... **82** C4
   FERN BH22 .... **194** C3
   FHAM/STUB PO14 .... **184** A4
   HISD PO11 .... **213** K5
   HLER SO31 .... **157** G2
   LISS GU33 .... **36** E4
   PLE BH15 .... **233** K4
   PSEA PO1 .... **211** J2
   SHAM SO14 .... **5** H1
   SHAM SO14 .... **131** G7
St Mary's Ter *RWIN* SO21 .... **54** F2 🔲
St Mary St *FUFL* SO22 .... **26** C3
St Matthews Cl *SHAM* SO14 .. **5** H1
St Matthew's Rd *CHAM* PO6 .. **163** K8
   FUFL SO22 .... **2** B2
St Merrin's Cl *NBNE* BH10 .... **220** A4 🔲
St Michaels Cl *FAWY* SO45 .. **180** C1
   PLE BH15 .... **232** D5 🔲
   VWD BH31 .... **144** D3 🔲
St Michaels Gdns *WINC* SO23 .. **2** F9
St Michael's Gv
   FHAM/STUB PO14 .... **6** F8
   FHAM/STUB PO14 .... **184** D1
St Michael's Rd *HAV* PO9 .... **165** G5
   HLER SO31 .... **158** D6
   PSEA PO1 .... **12** F5
   TOTT SO40 .... **104** E7
   VWD BH31 .... **144** C6
   WCLF BH2 .... **14** C6
   WINC SO23 .... **26** E2
St Michael's St *SHAM* SO14 .. **4** F5
St Michaels Wy *HORN* PO08 .. **116** B6
St Monica Rd *ITCH* SO19 ...... **132** C5
St Nicholas Av *WINC* SO23 .. **17** G2
St Nicholas Av
   LSOL/BMARY PO13 .... **209** L1
St Nicholas' Rd *HAV* PO9 .... **165** G5 🔲
St Nicholas St *PSEA* PO1 .... **12** D5
St Osmund's Rd *PSTN* BH14 .. **234** B5
St Patrick's La *LISS* GU33 ...... **37** H3
St Paul's La *BMTH* BH1 .... **15** J4
St Paul's Pl *BMTH* BH1 .... **15** J4
St Pauls Rd *BMTH* BH1 .... **15** J4
   HLER SO31 .... **158** C2
   SSEA PO5 .... **12** F3
St Pauls Rbt *BMTH* BH1 .... **15** J4
St Paul's Sq *SSEA* PO5 .... **12** F4 🔲
St Peter's Av *HISD* PO11 ...... **190** A6
St Peter's Gv *SSEA* PO5 .... **13** H5
St Peter's Rd *BMTH* BH1 .... **14** F5
   HISD PO11 .... **190** A6
   PSF GU32 .... **63** L5
   PSTN BH14 .... **233** M4
St Peters Rbt *BMTH* BH1 ...... **15** G6
St Peter's Sq *EMRTH* PO10 .. **166** D8
St Peter's St *BPWT* SO32 ...... **85** H8
St Peter St *WINC* SO23 .... **3** G3
St Philip's Wy *WEND* SO18 .. **132** F1 🔲
St Piran's Av *HSEA* PO3 .... **211** L1
St Ronan's Av *ENEY* PO4 ...... **13** M7
St Ronan's Rd *ENEY* PO4 ...... **13** M7
St Sebastian Crs
   FHAM/PORC PO16 .... **7** K1
St Simon Cl *HLER* SO31 .... **158** F5 🔲
St Simon's Rd *SSEA* PO5 .... **13** K8
St Stephens La *VWD* BH31 .. **144** E2
St Stephen's Rd *FUFL* SO22 .... **2** B3
   NEND PO2 .... **187** J8 🔲
   WCLF BH2 .... **14** C4
St Stephen's Wy *WCLF* BH2 .. **14** C4
St Swithin Cl *BPWT* SO32 .... **85** G8 🔲
St Swithun's Cl *ROMY* SO51 .. **51** J7 🔲
St Swithun's Rd *BMTH* BH1 .. **15** K3
   NEND PO2 .... **187** K6
St Swithun's Rd South
   BMTH BH1 .... **15** K4
St Swithun St *WINC* SO23 .... **2** F9
St Theresas Cl *HAV* PO9 ...... **165** G5
St Thomas Av *HISD* PO11 .... **213** K5
St Thomas Cl *FHAM/PORC* PO16 .. **7** L3
St Thomas Pk *LYMN* SO41 .. **228** B4
St Thomas's Cl *NBNE* BH10 .. **220** B8
St Thomas's Rd *GPORT* PO12 .. **185** M8
St Thomas's St *LYMN* SO41 .. **228** B5
   PSEA PO1 .... **12** C5
St Thomas St *WINC* SO23 .... **2** F9
St Tristan Cl *HLER* SO31 .... **158** F5
St Ursula Gv *SSEA* PO5 .... **13** J5 🔲
St Valerie Rd *GPORT* PO12 .... **10** F6
   WCLF BH2 .... **14** E2
St Vigor Wy *RWIN* SO21 ...... **54** F2
St Vincent Crs *HORN* PO08 .. **140** F2
St Vincent Rd *GPORT* PO12 .. **209** M2
   SSEA PO5 .... **13** J7
St Vincent St *SSEA* PO5 .... **12** F3
St Winifred's Rd *ROWN* SO16 .. **106** B6
Salcombe Av *HSEA* PO3 ...... **187** L7
Salcombe Cl *CHFD* SO53 .... **81** G4
Salcombe Crs *TOTT* SO40 .... **129** J2
Salcombe Rd *TOTT* SO40 .... **129** J2

WSHM SO15 .... **130** F1
Salcot Rd *WINC* SO23 .... **3** C1
Salem St *WSHM* SO15 .... **106** B7
Salerno Dr *ELGH* SO50 .... **82** D3
Salerno Pl *PLE* BH15 .... **232** C6 🔲
Salerno Rd *NEND* PO2 .... **187** H4
   ROWN SO16 .... **106** B4
Salet Wy *WVILLE* PO7 .... **140** F7
Salisbury Cl *ELGH* SO50 .... **82** A4 🔲
Salisbury Rd *BOSC* BH5 .... **236** D4 🔲
   CHAM PO6 .... **187** L1
   CHCH/BSGR BH23 .... **222** F7
   ENEY PO4 .... **211** K6
   FBDG SP6 .... **97** M6
   PSTN BH14 .... **234** B3
   PTSW SO17 .... **106** F5
   RGWD BH24 .... **122** E7
   ROMY SO51 .... **49** K8
   RSAL SP5 .... **44** D7
   TOTT SO40 .... **104** D7
Salisbury St *FBDG* SP6 .... **97** L7
   WIMB BH21 .... **94** D8
Salisbury Ter
   LSOL/BMARY PO13 .... **208** D3
Salmon Dr *ELGH* SO50 .... **82** E6
Salterns Av *ENEY* PO4 .... **211** M3
Salterns Cl *HISD* PO11 .... **214** A5
Salterns Est *FHAM/PORC* PO16 .. **7** K9
Salterns La *FAWY* SO45 .... **180** F4
   FHAM/PORC PO16 .... **184** F1
   HISD PO11 .... **213** M5
   HLER SO31 .... **157** L2
Salterns Rd *FHAM/STUB* PO14 .. **183** M8
   PSTN BH14 .... **233** M5
Salterns Wy *PSTN* BH14 ...... **234** A8
Salter Rd *CCLF* BH13 .... **245** G5
Salters Acres *FUFL* SO22 ...... **16** B6
Saltgrass La *LYMN* SO41 ...... **242** F6
Saltings Rd *UPTN* BH16 .... **232** A2
The Saltings *CHAM* PO6 .... **188** C1
   HAV PO9 .... **189** K2
Salt La *BPWT* SO32 .... **57** K5
Saltmarsh La *HISD* PO11 ...... **213** J3
Saltmarsh Rd *SHAM* SO14 ...... **5** K6
Saltmead *PTSW* SO17 .... **107** J7 🔲
Salt Meat La *GPORT* PO12 .... **210** B2
Salvia Cl *WVILLE* PO7 .... **164** E2 🔲
Salwey Rd *HEND* SO30 .... **134** B3
Samber Cl *LYMN* SO41 .... **228** A4
Sampan Cl *HLER* SO31 .... **158** C7
Samples Wy *CFDH* BH17 ...... **218** D8 🔲
Sampson Rd
   FHAM/STUB PO14 .... **184** D1
   PSEA PO1 .... **210** D2
Samson Cl *LSOL/BMARY* PO13 .. **209** H1
Samson Rd *PLE* BH15 .... **232** C5
Samuel Rd *PSEA* PO1 .... **211** K2
Sancreed Rd *BKME/WDN* BH12 .. **234** C1
Sandbanks Rd *PLE* BH15 ...... **233** L5
   PSTN BH14 .... **233** M5
Sandbourne Rd *CCLF* BH13 .. **235** G7
   PLE BH15 .... **233** J4
   WBNE BH4 .... **235** H7
Sandcroft Cl *GPORT* PO12 .... **209** J5 🔲
Sandecotes Rd *PSTN* BH14 .. **234** B5
Sanderling Rd *ENEY* PO4 ...... **212** A3
Sanderlings *RGWD* BH24 ...... **171** G2 🔲
The Sanderlings *HISD* PO11 .. **213** L6 🔲
Sandford Av *GPORT* PO12 .... **209** H4
Sandford Cl *MOOR/WNTN* BH9 .. **221** G5
Sandford Wy *BDST* BH18 .... **217** K5
Sandhill La *LSOL/BMARY* PO13 .. **208** E1
Sandhills Cl *CFDH* BH17 .... **218** B6
Sandhurst Dr *WIMB* BH21 .... **168** E1
Sandhurst Rd *WSHM* SO15 .. **131** K2
San Diego Rd *GPORT* PO12 .. **209** H4
Sandisplatt
   FHAM/STUB PO14 .... **160** A8 🔲
Sandle Copse *FBDG* SP6 .... **97** G7
Sandleford Rd *HAV* PO9 .... **165** H1
Sandleheath Rd *FBDG* SP6 .... **96** E8
Sandlewood Cl *HORN* PO08 .. **116** B3
   TOTT SO40 .... **104** B8 🔲
Sandmartin Cl
   NMIL/BTOS BH25 .... **240** E1
Sandown Cl *GPORT* PO12 .... **209** H5 🔲
Sandown Rd *CHAM* PO6 ...... **187** J1
   CHCH/BSGR BH23 .... **238** C2
   WSHM SO15 .... **106** A7
Sandpiper Cl *CFDH* BH17 ...... **217** K7
   HORN PO8 .... **140** E1
   TOTT SO40 .... **130** C7
Sandpiper Rd *ROWN* SO16 .. **105** M3
Sandpit La *LYMN* SO41 .... **230** C4
Sandport Gv
   FHAM/PORC PO16 .... **185** M1
Sandringham Cl
   MOOR/WNTN BH9 .... **220** F4
   NBAD SO52 .... **80** E4
Sandringham Gdns
   MOOR/WNTN BH9 .... **220** F4
Sandringham La *PSEA* PO1 .. **13** L1 🔲
Sandringham Rd
   FHAM/STUB PO14 .... **159** M8
   PSEA PO1 .... **13** L1
   PSF GU32 .... **63** L4
   PSTN BH14 .... **234** A5
   WEND SO18 .... **107** K7
Sandsbury La *PSF* GU32 .... **63** G3
Sandy Brow *WVILLE* PO7 .... **164** B4
Sandy Cl *EPSF* GU31 .... **64** B5
Sandycroft *HLER* SO31 .... **158** B8
Sandy Down *LYMN* SO41 .... **201** M4
Sandy Field Crs *HORN* PO8 .. **140** C5
Sandyhurst Cl *CFDH* BH17 .... **218** A7
Sandy La *BPWT* SO32 .... **111** H7
   CHCH/BSGR BH23 .... **222** A6
   ELGH SO50 .... **83** G6
   FHAM/STUB PO14 .... **159** K8
   LISS GU33 .... **37** K5
   LYND SO43 .... **151** K4
   MIDH GU29 .... **37** K2
   NBAD SO52 .... **80** A3 🔲
   RGWD BH24 .... **169** K4
   ROMY SO51 .... **50** F5
   RSAL SP5 .... **73** K1
   SBNE BH6 .... **237** G3
   UPTN BH16 .... **216** A2

VWD BH31 .... 144 E2
WIMB BH21 .... 144 C6
Sandy Mead Rd CHAR BH8 .... 221 K7
Sandy Plot CHCH/BSGR BH23 ... 228 F7
Sandy Point Rd HISD PO11 .... 214 C7
Sandy Wy NBNE BH10 .... 220 C5
Sanross Cl FHAM/STUB PO14 ... 183 L7
Sapphire Cl WVILLE PO7 ...... 164 E1 ⁴
Sapphire Rdg WVILLE PO7 ..... 164 E1
Saracen Cl LYMN SO41 .... 228 A7 ⁴
Saracens Rd CHFD SO53 .... 81 L1
Sarah Cl LTDN BH7 .... 221 M8
Sarah Sands Cl
  CHCH/BSGR BH23 .... 223 H8 ⁵
Sark Rd BKME/WDN BH12 ...... 219 H8
Sarnia Ct ROWN SO16 .... 105 K5
Sarum Av FERN BH22 .... 168 C4
Sarum Cl FUFL SO22 .... 26 B1
Sarum Rd CHFD SO53 .... 81 K2
  FUFL SO22 .... 2 A8
  FUFL SO22 .... 25 J1
Sarum St PLE BH15 .... 233 G7 ⁶
Sarum Vw FUFL SO22 .... 26 A2
Sarum Wk LYMN SO41 .... 228 B2 ⁵
Satchell La HLER SO31 .... 157 L5
Saturn Cl ROWN SO16 .... 105 L4
Saulfland Dr
  CHCH/BSGR BH23 .... 224 B8
Saulfland Pl
  CHCH/BSGR BH23 .... 224 B8 ⁴
Saunders La ROMY SO51 .... 49 K3
Saunders Ms ENEY PO4 .... 211 M6 ⁶
Savernake Cl
  LSOL/BMARY PO13 .... 185 H6 ⁵
  ROMY SO51 .... 51 G7 ⁵
Saville Cl ELGH SO50 .... 82 C3
  GPORT PO12 .... 185 K7
Saville Gdns FHAM/PORC PO16. 6 F1
Sawyer Cl FUFL SO22 .... 16 B7 ⁵
Saxholm Cl ROWN SO16 .... 106 E2
Saxholm Dl ROWN SO16 .... 106 E2
Saxholm Wy ROWN SO16 .... 106 E2
Saxley Ct HAV PO9 .... 165 G2
Saxonbury Rd SBNE BH6 .... 237 K2
Saxon Cl FHAM/PORC PO16 .... 161 M7
  HLER SO31 .... 158 C7
  HORN PO8 .... 116 B4
Saxonford Rd
  CHCH/BSGR BH23 .... 239 H1 ²
Saxon Gdns HEND SO30 .... 133 L3
Saxonhurst RSAL SP5 .... 72 F1
Saxonhurst Cl NBNE BH10 .... 220 C3 ²
Saxonhurst Gdns
  NBNE BH10 .... 220 C4 ²
Saxonhurst Rd NBNE BH10 .... 220 B4
Saxon King Gdns SBNE BH6 .... 238 A4
Saxon Pl LYMN SO41 .... 228 B2
Saxon Rd FAWY SO45 .... 180 D7
  WINC SO23 .... 3 G5
  WSHM SO15 .... 4 A2
Saxon Wy FBDG SP6 .... 121 L3 ⁶
  ROMY SO51 .... 79 G1
Sayers Rd ELGH SO50 .... 82 C6
Scafell Av FHAM/STUB PO14 ... 6 A8
Scallows La ROMY SO51 .... 76 C3
Scantabout Av CHFD SO53 .... 81 K1
Scant Road (West) RCCH PO18. 167 M6
Scarf Rd CFDH BH17 .... 233 L1
Scholars' Wk CHAM PO6 ...... 188 A1
School Cl CHFD SO53 .... 81 G3
  LYMN SO41 .... 228 A6
School Hl BPWT SO32 .... 113 H2
School La BWD BH11 .... 219 M3
  CHCH/BSGR BH23 .... 198 C4
  CHFD SO53 .... 80 F4
  EMRTH PO10 .... 166 F3
  HLER SO31 .... 157 L7
  LISS GU33 .... 36 E4
  LYMN SO41 .... 202 D8
  LYMN SO41 .... 228 C4
  LYMN SO41 .... 242 D2
  MIDH GU29 .... 67 J7
  PLE BH15 .... 233 H3
  PSF GU32 .... 63 M2
  RCCH PO18 .... 118 C4
  RCCH PO18 .... 191 K1
  RGWD BH24 .... 169 L3
  WIMB BH21 .... 168 D1
  WINC SO23 .... 17 G3
  WVILLE PO7 .... 139 H3
School Rd BPWT SO32 .... 112 G4
  CHCH/BSGR BH23 .... 198 C4
  FAWY SO45 .... 180 E5
  GPORT PO12 .... 185 K7
  HAV PO9 .... 8 D5
  HLER SO31 .... 133 L8
  ROMY SO51 .... 51 H7
  ROMY SO51 .... 76 B3
  RSAL SP5 .... 73 L4
  RSAL SP5 .... 75 H8
  RWIN SO21 .... 54 E2
  TOTT SO40 .... 129 L2
  WHAM PO17 .... 136 E5
Schooner Wy HLER SO31 ...... 158 C7
  HSEA PO3 .... 212 A2
The Scimitars
  FHAM/STUB PO14 .... 183 M5 ⁴
Scivier's La BPWT SO32 ...... 84 B6
Scotland Cl ELGH SO50 .... 83 K6
Scotland La RSAL SP5 .... 74 F1
Scotney Ct HAV PO9 .... 165 M2 ⁷
Scott Cl BKME/WDN BH12 ..... 219 K8
  FHAM/STUB PO14 .... 184 A4
  RWIN SO21 .... 54 F8
Scotter Rd ELGH SO50 .... 82 C5
  LTDN BH7 .... 237 G3
Scott Rd BKME/WDN BH12 .... 219 K8
  ELGH SO50 .... 81 L6
  HSEA PO3 .... 187 K3
  ITCH SO19 .... 132 D7
Scott's Gn CHCH/BSGR BH23 .. 223 H8
Scotts Hills La
  CHCH/BSGR BH23 .... 238 C2
Scratchface La HAV PO9 ...... 164 F6
  WVILLE PO7 .... 164 D4
Scullards La SHAM SO14 ...... 4 F3
Seabird Wy FHAM/PORC PO16 .. 7 K9

Seabourne Pl BOSC BH5 ...... 237 G3 ³
Seabourne Rd BOSC BH5 ...... 237 G4 ⁵
Seabreeze Wy LYMN SO41 ..... 241 M2
Seacombe Gn ROWN SO16 ..... 105 J7
Seacombe Rd CCLF BH13 ...... 245 G5
Sea Crest Rd
  LSOL/BMARY PO13 .... 208 D3
Seacroft Av NMIL/BTOS BH25 . 225 J8
Seafield Cl NMIL/BTOS BH25 . 240 E1
Seafield Dr SBNE BH6 .... 237 K2
Seafield Park Rd
  FHAM/STUB PO14 .... 183 M7 ⁴
Seafield Rd CHCH/BSGR BH23 . 239 H2
  FHAM/PORC PO16 .... 185 M1
  HSEA PO3 .... 187 L7
  NMIL/BTOS BH25 .... 225 J8
  ROWN SO16 .... 105 J6
  SBNE BH6 .... 237 J4
Seafields EMRTH PO10 .... 166 C8
Sea Front HISD PO11 .... 213 K6
Seagarth La ROWN SO16 ...... 106 C5
Seager's Ct PSEA PO1 .... 12 B5 ¹
Sea Grove Av HISD PO11 ..... 213 L6
Seagrove Rd NEND PO2 .... 187 H2
Seagull La EMRTH PO10 ...... 166 D7
Seagull Ln CHAR BH8 .... 221 G7
The Seagulls
  LSOL/BMARY PO13 .... 208 E4 ¹
Sea Kings FHAM/STUB PO14 ... 183 M6 ⁵
Sea La LSOL/BMARY PO13 ..... 184 A8
Seaman's La LYND SO43 ...... 126 F4
Seamead FHAM/STUB PO14 .... 184 A8
Seamoor La CCLF BH13 .... 235 G5 ⁷
Seamoor Rd CCLF BH13 .... 235 G5
  WBNE BH4 .... 235 G5
Searles Hl RWIN SO21 .... 54 F2
Sea Rd BOSC BH5 .... 236 D4
  ITCH SO19 .... 132 B4
  LYMN SO41 .... 242 D4
  NMIL/BTOS BH25 .... 225 J8
  SBNE BH6 .... 237 L5
Seaton Av HSEA PO3 .... 187 L8
Seaton Cl CHCH/BSGR BH23 ... 224 F8
  FHAM/STUB PO14 .... 184 A6
  LYMN SO41 .... 228 C3 ²
  WEND SO18 .... 108 B7
Seaton Rd CHCH/BSGR BH23 ... 224 F8
Seatown Cl CFDH BH17 .... 218 E7
Seaview Av FHAM/PORC PO16 .. 162 C7
Sea View Rd BKME/WDN BH12. 233 M3
  CHAM PO6 .... 164 A8
Seaview Rd CHCH/BSGR BH23 . 225 G7
  HISD PO11 .... 214 A5
  NMIL/BTOS BH25 .... 240 C1
  SBNE BH6 .... 237 G4
Seaward Av NMIL/BTOS BH25 . 240 D1
  SBNE BH6 .... 237 H4
Seaward Dr SELS SO20 .... 215 L7
Seaward Rd FAWY SO45 .... 155 M5
  ITCH SO19 .... 132 C4
Seaway NMIL/BTOS BH25 ..... 225 M8 ³
Seaway Av CHCH/BSGR BH23 .. 239 H2
Seaway Crs ENEY PO4 .... 212 A4
Seaway Gv FHAM/PORC PO16 .. 186 A2
Seawinds LYMN SO41 .... 241 M3 ²
Sebastian Gv WVILLE PO7 .... 140 E8 ⁴
Second Av CHAM PO6 .... 188 C1
  EMRTH PO10 .... 167 H8
  HAV PO9 .... 9 J3
  WSHM SO15 .... 130 B1
Second Marine Av
  NMIL/BTOS BH25 .... 240 F2
Second St FAWY SO45 .... 156 C8
Sedbergh Rd ROWN SO16 ..... 105 J7
Sedgefield Cl CHAM PO6 ..... 162 D8
  TOTT SO40 .... 104 B8
Sedgeley Gv GPORT PO12 ..... 185 K7
Sedgemead HLER SO31 .... 156 F3 ¹
Sedgewick Cl
  LSOL/BMARY PO13 .... 185 H8 ¹
Sedgewick Rd ELGH SO50 ..... 82 C5
  ITCH SO19 .... 133 G3
Sedgley Cl SSEA PO5 .... 18 C3
Sedgley Rd MOOR/WNTN BH9 .. 220 C8
Segars La RWIN SO21 .... 54 E3
Segensworth Rd FHAM PO15 .. 159 K5
Selangor Av EMRTH PO10 ..... 166 B7
Selborne Av HAV PO9 .... 165 L3
  WEND SO18 .... 108 B8
Selborne Cl PSF GU32 .... 63 M3
Selborne Gdns GPORT PO12 ... 10 B3
Selborne Pl FUFL SO22 ...... 26 C3 ¹
Selborne Ter PSEA PO1 ...... 13 M2
Selby Cl BDST BH18 .... 217 L5
Seldon Cl FUFL SO22 .... 26 C3
Seldown PLE BH15 .... 233 J5 ³
Seldown Br PLE BH15 .... 233 J6
Seldown La PLE BH15 .... 233 J5
Seldown Rd PLE BH15 .... 233 J5
Selfridge Av SBNE BH6 ...... 238 A5
Selfridge Cl SBNE BH6 ...... 238 A5 ⁶
Selhurst Wy ELGH SO50 ...... 83 H7
Seliot Cl PLE BH15 .... 233 J3
Selkirk Cl WIMB BH21 .... 192 C7
Sellwood Rd HLER SO31 ...... 157 G2
Sellwood Wy
  NMIL/BTOS BH25 .... 225 H8 ³
Selsdon Av ROMY SO51 .... 51 G8
Selsey Av ENEY PO4 .... 211 L6
  GPORT PO12 .... 185 K8
Selsey Cl HISD PO11 .... 214 D6
  ROWN SO16 .... 105 K6
Selsmore Av HISD PO11 ...... 214 A6
Selsmore Rd HISD PO11 ...... 213 L5
Selworth La BPWT SO32 ...... 113 G5
Selworthy Cl PSTN BH14 ..... 233 M6
Selwyn Gdns ELGH SO50 ...... 134 B2 ⁷
Sengana Cl HEND SO30 .... 134 B2
Senlac Rd ROMY SO51 .... 79 G1
Sennen Cl CHAM PO6 .... 186 E1
Sentinel Cl WVILLE PO7 ..... 140 F7
Seps 4 BPWT SO32 .... 180 F4
September Cl HEND SO30 ..... 108 C7
Serle Rd TOTT SO40 .... 128 F1

Serle Gdns TOTT SO40 .... 129 H2
Sermon Rd FUFL SO22 .... 16 A7
Serpentine Rd
  FHAM/PORC PO16 .... 7 J2
  PLE BH15 .... 233 H5
  SSEA PO5 .... 12 F8
  SSEA PO5 .... 13 C7 ⁸
  WVILLE PO7 .... 164 A5
Setley Gdns CHAR BH8 .... 221 J5
Setters Cl RWIN SO21 .... 54 E8
Set Thorns Rd LYMN SO41 .... 201 G6
Settle Cl ROWN SO16 .... 106 A3 ⁸
Settlers Dr LTDN BH7 .... 221 L8
Settlers Rd PSEA PO1 .... 211 H2 ³
Sevenoaks Dr LTDN BH7 ...... 221 L8
Sevenoaks Rd CHAM PO6 ..... 163 J8
Severals Rd MIDH GU29 ...... 67 L8
Severn Cl CHAM PO6 .... 162 F7
  FHAM/PORC PO16 .... 161 L8 ³
Severn Rd FERN BH22 .... 194 E2 ⁴
  ROWN SO16 .... 105 K8
Severn Wy HEND SO30 .... 108 C7 ⁵
Seward Ri ROMY SO51 .... 51 H8 ³
Seymour Cl CHFD SO53 .... 81 K3
  NEND PO2 .... 211 H1
  TOTT SO40 .... 104 B7
Seymour La NBAD SO52 ...... 79 L4
Seymour Rd
  LSOL/BMARY PO13 .... 208 D4
  RGWD BH24 .... 146 F2
  ROWN SO16 .... 106 B5
Shackleton Rd
  LSOL/BMARY PO13 .... 185 H8
Shackleton Sq
  CHCH/BSGR BH23 .... 197 M7 ⁸
Shadwell Rd NEND PO2 .... 187 J6
Shaftesbury Av CHFD SO53 ... 81 H4
  PTSW SO17 .... 107 G7
  WVILLE PO7 .... 164 B4
Shaftesbury Cl FERN BH22 ... 168 D6
  FERN BH22 .... 168 D7 ³
  PLE BH15 .... 233 J5 ⁶
  SSEA PO5 .... 13 G7
Shaftesbury Rd CHAR BH8 .... 236 D7
Shaftsbury Rd GPORT PO12 ... 11 G4 ³
Shaggs Meadow LYND SO43 ... 151 K3
Shakespeare Dr TOTT SO40 ... 104 C6
Shakespeare Gdns HORN PO8 . 140 C5
Shakespeare Rd ELGH SO50 ... 81 L3
  PSEA PO1 .... 211 J2
  SBNE BH6 .... 237 J1 ⁸
  WIMB BH21 .... 192 A2
Shalbourne Rd GPORT PO12 .. 209 L1
Shalcombe HLER SO31 .... 157 G1
Shaldon Cl ROWN SO16 ...... 106 A4
Shaldon Rd HAV PO9 .... 165 M2 ⁸
Shales Rd WEND SO18 .... 132 F1
Shallow La LYMN SO41 .... 202 B8
The Shallows FBDC SP6 ...... 98 B1
Shamblehurst La HEND SO30 . 109 H7
Shamblehurst La
  North BPWT SO32 .... 109 H8
Shamblehurst La South
  HEND SO30 .... 109 H8
Shamrock Cl GPORT PO12 .... 11 J4
Shamrock Rd ITCH SO19 ...... 132 B5 ⁶
Shamrock Wy FAWY SO45 ..... 155 L3
Shanklin Crs WSHM SO15 .... 106 C6
Shanklin Rd ENEY PO4 .... 13 M4 ⁸
  WSHM SO15 .... 106 C6
Shannon Cl FHAM PO15 ...... 6 A3
Shannon Rd
  FHAM/STUB PO14 .... 183 M4 ⁸
  FHAM/STUB PO14 .... 184 D3
Shannon Wy CHFD SO53 ...... 81 G2
Shapland Av BWD BH11 ...... 219 J3
Shappen Hill La RGWD BH24 . 172 D6
Shapton Cl FAWY SO45 ...... 179 M4 ⁸
Shapwick Rd PLE BH15 ...... 232 F7
Shard Cl VWD BH31 .... 144 E2
Sharf Rd BKME/WDN BH12 ... 234 F1
Sharlands Cl BDST BH18 ..... 217 M5
Sharon Rd HEND SO30 .... 108 B6
Sharpley Cl FBDG SP6 .... 97 K5
Sharpness Cl
  FHAM/STUB PO14 .... 160 A8 ⁴
Sharps Cl HSEA PO3 .... 187 M5
Sharps Rd HAV PO9 .... 165 M3
Sharvells Rd LYMN SO41 ..... 242 B3
Shavard La BPWT SO32 .... 87 J3
Shaves La NMIL/BTOS BH25 ... 225 L3
Shaw Cl TOTT SO40 .... 129 H1 ⁸
  WEND SO18 .... 107 M6
Shawfield Rd HAV PO9 .... 9 H6
Shawford Cl ROWN SO16 ..... 106 D4 ⁸
  TOTT SO40 .... 128 F1 ²
Shawford Gdns CHAR BH8 .... 221 H6 ⁶
Shawford Gv HAV PO9 .... 165 G3
Shawford Rd CHAR BH8 ...... 221 H5
  RWIN SO21 .... 54 E2
Shaw Rd RGWD BH24 .... 147 G6
Sheardley La BPWT SO32 ..... 87 L8
Shearer Rd PSEA PO1 .... 211 J1
Shear Hl EPSF GU31 .... 64 A3
Shears Brook Cl
  CHCH/BSGR BH23 .... 197 M7 ⁴
Shears Rd ELGH SO50 .... 82 D5
Shearwater Av
  FHAM/PORC PO16 .... 161 J8
Shearwater Cl
  LSOL/BMARY PO13 .... 185 H6
Shearwater Dr CHAM PO6 .... 188 D1
Sheep Pond La BPWT SO32 ... 86 F5
Sheep St PSF GU32 .... 63 L5
Sheepwash La SELS SO20 .... 215 M5
  WVILLE PO7 .... 139 H7
Sheffield Cl ELGH SO50 ..... 82 C3
Sheffield Rd PSEA PO1 ...... 13 L1
Shelbourne Cl CHAR BH8 .... 236 D2 ⁸
Shelbourne Rd CHAR BH8 .... 236 D2
Sheldrake Gdns LYMN SO41 .. 226 F4
  ROWN SO16 .... 106 A3
Sheldrake Rd
  CHCH/BSGR BH23 .... 238 F3
Shelford Rd ENEY PO4 .... 211 M3
Shellcroft HLER SO31 .... 158 B8 ⁸
Shelley Av CHAM PO6 .... 162 F7
Shelley Rd BMTH BH1 .... 236 D3 ⁸

CHCH/BSGR BH23 .... 239 H1
  FUFL SO22 .... 2 A6
  RGWD BH24 .... 169 J3
Shelley Gdns BMTH BH1 ..... 236 D3
  HORN PO8 .... 140 C5
Shelley La ROMY SO51 ...... 77 K7
Shelley Rd BMTH BH1 .... 236 D3
  ELGH SO50 .... 81 L7
  ITCH SO19 .... 133 H2
  PSTN BH14 .... 234 C3
  TOTT SO40 .... 104 C6
Shelley Rd East BMTH BH1 .. 236 D3
Shelton Rd SBNE BH6 .... 237 H2
Shenley Cl FHAM PO15 ...... 160 A6
Shepards Cl FHAM/STUB PO14. 160 A8
Shepherd Cl CHCH/BSGR BH23. 224 D7
Shepherds Cl FUFL SO22 .... 26 A4
  TOTT SO40 .... 127 M2
Shepherds Hey Rd TOTT SO40. 104 A7
Shepherds Hl RGWD BH24 .... 146 A2
Shepherds La RGWD BH24 .... 145 L2
  RWIN SO21 .... 53 L2
Shepherds Purse Cl
  HLER SO31 .... 158 D6 ⁸
Shepherds Rd TOTT SO40 .... 127 M2
  WINC SO23 .... 3 M7
  ROWN SO16 .... 105 H3
Sheppard Cl HORN PO8 ...... 140 C2
Shepton Br BROC SO42 ...... 177 M3
Sherborn Crs CFDH BH17 .... 218 D7
Sherborne Dr FERN BH22 .... 194 B4
Sherborne Rd NEND SO30 .... 134 A2
Sherfield Av HAV PO9 .... 165 L3
Sherfield English La
  ROMY SO51 .... 76 B2
  RSAL SP5 .... 76 A3
Sherfield English Rd RSAL SP5. 76 A1
Sheridan Cl FUFL SO22 ..... 26 B3
  ITCH SO19 .... 133 G3
Sheridan Gdns HLER SO31 ... 135 G8
  TOTT SO40 .... 129 H1
Sheringham Rd
  BKME/WDN BH12 .... 234 E3
  CHAM PO6 .... 163 H7 ⁸
Shermin's Bank
  CHCH/BSGR BH23 .... 238 D3
Sherrin Cl PLE BH15 .... 233 J3
Sherringham Cl CHAM PO6 ... 186 E1
Sherwood Av FERN BH22 ..... 194 A5
  HEND SO30 .... 134 A4
  PSTN BH14 .... 233 L6
Sherwood Cl
  CHCH/BSGR BH23 .... 237 L1
  LISS GU33 .... 36 F1
  ROWN SO16 .... 106 D5 ⁸
Sherwood Dr VWD BH31 ...... 144 F2
Sherwood Gdns HLER SO31 ... 158 C4
Sherwood Rd CHFD SO53 ..... 53 K7
  GPORT PO12 .... 10 D3
Sherwood Wy FAWY SO45 .... 206 C1
Shetland Cl CHAM PO6 ...... 163 K7
  TOTT SO40 .... 104 A8
Shetland Ri HLER SO31 ..... 158 F2
Shillinglee WVILLE PO7 ..... 164 C5
Shillingstone Dr
  MOOR/WNTN BH9 .... 220 F5 ⁸
Shillito Rd BKME/WDN BH12 . 234 C3
Shingle Bank Dr LYMN SO41 . 242 C4
Shipbuilding Rd PSEA PO1 ... 210 D1
Shipcote La BPWT SO32 ..... 85 H6
Ship Leopard St PSEA PO1 ... 12 C2 ⁸
Shipley Rd RWIN SO21 ...... 54 F1
Shipstal Cl UPTN BH16 ..... 232 B4
Shire Cl HLER SO31 .... 158 F1
  HORN PO8 .... 140 F7
Shires Cl RGWD BH24 .... 170 E4
Shires Copse SBNE BH6 ..... 237 L5 ⁸
Shires Md VWD BH31 .... 144 E2 ⁸
The Shires HEND SO30 ...... 133 L2
Shirley Av ENEY PO4 .... 212 A4
  WSHM SO15 .... 106 B8
Shirley Cl CHCH/BSGR BH23 . 197 M7
  FERN BH22 .... 168 C6
Shirley High St ROWN SO16 . 106 A8
Shirley Holms LYMN SO41 ... 201 K7
Shirley Park Rd ROWN SO16 . 106 A8
Shirley Rd BKME/WDN BH12 . 234 A2
  MOOR/WNTN BH9 .... 220 E7
  SSEA PO5 .... 13 L8
  WSHM SO15 .... 106 B8
Shoe La BPWT SO32 .... 84 D1
Sholing Ct HAV PO9 .... 165 H2
Sholing Rd ITCH SO19 ...... 132 C4
Shooters Hill Cl ITCH SO19 . 132 F5
Shoot Hl WHAM PO17 .... 138 B5
Shoot La LSOL/BMARY PO13 .. 184 D4
Shop La HLER SO31 .... 133 J5
Shore Av HSEA PO3 .... 211 M2
  UPTN BH16 .... 232 B2
Shore Cl UPTN BH16 .... 232 B2
Shore Crs BPWT SO32 ...... 111 J1 ⁸
Shorefield Crs LYMN SO41 .. 242 A3
Shorefield Rd LYMN SO41 ... 241 M2
  TOTT SO40 .... 130 D6
Shorefield Wy LYMN SO41 ... 242 B3
Shore Gdns UPTN BH16 ..... 232 A2 ⁸
Shorehaven CHAM PO6 ...... 162 D8
Shore La BPWT SO32 .... 111 J1
  UPTN BH16 .... 232 A3
Shore Rd CCLF BH13 .... 245 J2
  FAWY SO45 .... 155 M4
  PSTN BH14 .... 245 J1
Shorewell HLER SO31 .... 157 G1 ⁸
Shorewood Cl HLER SO31 ... 158 E7
Short Cl BKME/WDN BH12 ... 219 L8
Short Hl ROMY SO51 .... 51 H7
Short Rd FHAM/STUB PO14 .. 183 L6
Short Rw PSEA PO1 .... 210 E2
Shorts Cl CHCH/BSGR BH23 . 223 G7
Shorts Rd ELGH SO50 ...... 83 G6
Shotterfield Ter LISS GU33 . 36 E4
Shottsford Rd PLE BH15 .... 233 H3
Shotts La LYMN SO41 ...... 229 G4
Shraveshill Cl TOTT SO40 .. 104 C7

Shrubbery Cl
  FHAM/PORC PO16 .... 186 A1
The Shrubbery GPORT PO12 .. 209 K1
Shrubb's Av LYMN SO41 ..... 228 C4
Shrubs Hill Gdns
  LYND SO43 .... 151 K4 ⁸
Shrubs Hill Rd LYND SO43 .. 151 K4
Shrubland Cl WEND SO18 .... 108 A8
Sibland Cl FHAM/STUB PO14 . 6 A8
The Sidings HLER SO31 ..... 157 H3
  RSAL SP5 .... 44 F8
Sidlesham Cl HISD PO11 .... 214 D6
Sidmouth Av HSEA PO3 ...... 187 L8
Silchester Cl WCLF BH2 .... 14 C3
Silchester Rd HSEA PO3 .... 211 M1
Silkin Gdns TOTT SO40 ..... 129 H2
Silkstead Av HAV PO9 ...... 165 K2
Silkstead La RWIN SO21 .... 53 L3
Sillen La FBDG SP6 .... 68 F5
Silver Birch Av
  FHAM/STUB PO14 .... 6 C7
Silver Birch Cl
  BKME/WDN BH12 .... 234 F4
  LISS GU33 .... 36 F4
Silver Birches HLER SO31 ... 133 K8
Silverdale NMIL/BTOS BH25 . 225 M8
  NMIL/BTOS BH25 .... 241 G1 ⁸
Silverdale Cl BDST BH18 .... 217 J4
Silverdale Crs FBDG SP6 .... 121 L2 ⁸
Silverdale Dr WVILLE PO7 ... 140 A6
Silverdale Rd WSHM SO15 ... 131 J1
Silver Hl WINC SO23 .... 3 H8
Silverlock Cl NEND PO2 .... 187 H8
Silversands Gdns HISD PO11 . 213 M6
Silvers End FAWY SO45 ..... 155 L7 ⁸
Silver St CHCH/BSGR BH23 .. 238 A2 ⁸
  LYMN SO41 .... 226 D4
  LYND SO43 .... 151 H3
  SSEA PO5 .... 12 F5
Silvers Wd TOTT SO40 ...... 104 B7
Silverthorne Wy WVILLE PO7 . 140 B8
Silvertrees EMRTH PO10 .... 166 D6
Silver Wy CHCH/BSGR BH23 .. 224 C8
Silverwood Cl FUFL SO22 ... 26 C3
  WIMB BH21 .... 192 B6
Silvester Rd HORN PO8 ..... 140 C6
Silwood Cl FUFL SO22 ...... 26 C3
Simmonds Cl PLE BH15 ...... 233 J3 ⁸
Simmons Cl HEND SO30 ..... 109 H8
Simmons Gn HISD PO11 ..... 214 A5
Simnel St SHAM SO14 ...... 4 F5 ⁸
Simon Wy WEND SO18 .... 133 J1
Simpson Cl FHAM/PORC PO16. 162 A8
Simpson Rd NEND PO2 ...... 187 G7
Sinah La HISD PO11 .... 213 G5
Sinclair Rd ROWN SO16 ..... 105 M3
Singleton Dr NBNE BH10 .... 220 A6
Singleton Gdns HORN PO8 ... 116 C4
Singleton Wy TOTT SO40 .... 104 A8
Sir Christopher Cl
  FAWY SO45 .... 155 M4 ⁸
Sirdar Rd PTSW SO17 ...... 107 H5
Sir Galahad Rd NBAD SO52 .. 80 E2 ²
Sir George's Rd WSHM SO15 . 131 H2
Sir Lancelot Cl NBAD SO52 .. 80 E2
Siskin Cl BPWT SO32 .... 84 F8
  FERN BH22 .... 193 M1
  ROWN SO16 .... 105 M3
Siskin Gv WVILLE PO7 ...... 164 E2
Sissinghurst Cl ITCH SO19 .. 132 E7
Sissinghurst Rd
  FHAM/PORC PO16 .... 185 M1 ⁸
Six Oaks Rd NBAD SO52 .... 79 M3
Sixpenny Cl
  BKME/WDN BH12 .... 234 E1
  PSEA PO1 .... 158 E7
Sixth Av CHAM PO6 .... 163 J8
Sizer Wy FAWY SO45 .... 154 F5
Skew Rd WHAM PO17 .... 162 A6
Skinner St PLE BH15 ...... 233 H7
Skipper Wy LSOL/BMARY PO13. 208 D3
Skipton Cl BDST BH18 ..... 217 L6
Skipton Rd CHFD SO53 ..... 81 J4
Sky End La LYMN SO41 ..... 226 E6
Skylark Mdw FHAM PO15 .... 159 K3
Skys Wood Rd NBAD SO52 ... 80 E1
Slab La ROMY SO51 .... 76 C5
  RSAL SP5 .... 72 F1
Slade Cl LYMN SO41 .... 226 E5
Slade La EPSF GU31 .... 65 H4
Slades Farm Rd NBNE BH10 . 220 A7
Slades Hl FAWY SO45 ...... 180 D6
Slade's La NBNE BH10 ..... 220 A8
Slater Cl TOTT SO40 ...... 104 A8
Sleepbrook Cl VWD BH31 ... 144 C2
Sleepers Delle Gdns FUFL SO22. 26 D2
Sleepers Hl FUFL SO22 .... 26 C2
  FUFL SO22 .... 26 C2 ⁸
Sleepers Hill Gdns FUFL SO22. 26 C2 ⁸
Slepe Crs BKME/WDN BH12 .. 219 K8
Slindon Cl HORN PO8 ...... 116 C3
Slindon St PSEA PO1 ...... 13 H1 ⁸
Slingsby Cl PSEA PO1 ..... 12 F5 ¹⁰
Slinn Rd CHCH/BSGR BH23 .. 238 D1
Slip Wy PLE BH15 .... 233 G6
Sloane Av FAWY SO45 ...... 180 B4 ¹
Sloane Ct FAWY SO45 ...... 180 B4 ²
Sloane Pk BPWT SO32 ...... 236 B1
Sloe Tree Cl HLER SO31 ... 159 G6 ⁸
Smallcutts Av EMRTH PO10 .. 167 H7
Smeaton St NEND PO2 ...... 187 G6 ⁸
Smeeton Rd
  LSOL/BMARY PO13 .... 208 D2
Smith Cl FAWY SO45 .... 180 D6
Smithe Cl ELGH SO50 ...... 81 M5 ⁸
Smithfield Pl
  MOOR/WNTN BH9 .... 220 D7 ⁸
Smith Gv HEND SO30 .... 134 A3
Smith La EMRTH PO10 ...... 191 G7
Smith's Fld ROMY SO51 .... 50 F7 ³
Smiths Cl BPWT SO32 ...... 111 L8
Smithson Cl
  BKME/WDN BH12 .... 220 A8 ⁸
Smith St GPORT PO12 ...... 10 D3
Smithy La NMIL/BTOS BH25 . 225 K2
The Smithy WVILLE PO7 .... 139 J4

Smugglers La North
CHCH/BSGR BH23 .... 224 A8
Smugglers La South
CHCH/BSGR BH23 .... 224 C8
Smugglers Wood Rd
CHCH/BSGR BH23 .... 224 A7
Smythe Rd ITCH SO19 .... 133 H5
Snailing La LISS GU33 .... 36 A2
Snakemoor La BPWT SO32 .... 109 K3
Snapdragon Cl HLER SO31 .... 158 D6 ⑥
Snape Cl LSOL/BMARY PO13 .... 185 G8 ⑧
Snellgrove Cl TOTT SO40 .... 104 B6
Snellgrove Pl TOTT SO40 .... 104 B6 ⑤
Snooks La LYMN SO41 .... 228 F2
Snowberry Crs HAV PO9 .... 165 M5
Snowdon Dr FHAM/STUB PO14 .... 6 C8
Snowdon Rd WBNE BH4 .... 235 H4
Snowdrop Gdns
CHCH/BSGR BH23 .... 223 M7
Soake Rd WVILLE PO7 .... 139 M5
Soalwood La PSF GU32 .... 34 E7
Soberton Rd CHAR BH8 .... 236 C1
HAV PO9 .... 165 J5
Soldridge Cl HAV PO9 .... 165 M2 ⑥
Solent Av ITCH SO19 .... 133 J2
LYMN SO41 .... 228 D5
Solent Cl CHFD SO53 .... 81 K2
LYMN SO41 .... 228 D5
Solent Dr FAWY SO45 .... 155 K4
HISD PO11 .... 213 K6
HLER SO31 .... 182 B2
NMIL/BTOS BH25 .... 240 F1
Solent Mdw HLER SO31 .... 157 J7
Solent Rd CHAM PO6 .... 164 A8
CHCH/BSGR BH23 .... 224 F6
FAWY SO45 .... 155 J8
FHAM/STUB PO14 .... 183 L7
HAV PO9 .... 8 C5
SBNE BH6 .... 237 M5
Solent Vw FHAM/PORC PO16 .... 161 M7
Solent Wy BROC SO42 .... 179 G3
BROC SO42 .... 204 F1
FHAM/STUB PO14 .... 183 L7
GPORT PO12 .... 11 J7
GPORT PO12 .... 209 J5
HAV PO9 .... 8 A7
HSEA PO3 .... 212 B2
LSOL/BMARY PO13 .... 208 L5
LYMN SO41 .... 242 E6
PSEA PO1 .... 12 D2 ⑥
SHAM SO14 .... 5 G7
Solly Cl BKME/WDN BH12 .... 234 D1
Solomons La BPWT SO32 .... 111 L6
Solomon Wy PLE BH15 .... 232 C6
Solona Cl CHFD SO53 .... 81 L1 ⑥
Somborne Dr HAV PO9 .... 165 K3
Somerby Rd PLE BH15 .... 233 J2
Somerford Av
CHCH/BSGR BH23 .... 223 M8
Somerford Cl ITCH SO19 .... 132 E2 ⑥
Somerford Rd
CHCH/BSGR BH23 .... 238 E1
Somerford Wy
CHCH/BSGR BH23 .... 238 D1
Somerley Rd
MOOR/WNTN BH9 .... 235 M1
Somerley Vw RGWD BH24 .... 146 E8 ⑥
Somers Cl FUFL SO22 .... 26 C1
Somerset Av WEND SO18 .... 133 G1
Somerset Crs CHFD SO53 .... 81 H5
Somerset Rd
CHCH/BSGR BH23 .... 237 K1
LTDN BH7 .... 236 E3
PTSW SO17 .... 107 H6
SSEA PO5 .... 13 K9
Somerset Ter WSHM SO15 .... 130 F2
Somers Rd SSEA PO5 .... 13 K5
Somers Rd North PSEA PO1 .... 13 K2
Somerton Av WEND SO18 .... 132 F1
Somerton Cl
NMIL/BTOS BH25 .... 226 B5 ⑥
Somervell Cl GPORT PO12 .... 10 D8
Somervell Dr FHAM/PORC PO16 .... 7 G2
Somerville Rd RGWD BH24 .... 147 G8
WCLF BH2 .... 14 B6
Sonnet Wy WVILLE PO7 .... 140 F8 ⑥
Sopers La CFDH BH17 .... 217 L7
CHCH/BSGR BH23 .... 237 M2
Sopley Cl NMIL/BTOS BH25 .... 225 H8
Sopley Ct HAV PO9 .... 165 M2 ⑩
Sopwith Cl
CHCH/BSGR BH23 .... 239 G2 ⑦
Sopwith Crs WIMB BH21 .... 192 C6
Sopwith Wy HLER SO31 .... 134 C8
Sorrel Cl ROMY SO51 .... 51 H7
WVILLE PO7 .... 164 C2
Sorrel Dr FHAM PO15 .... 159 H1
Sorrel Gdns WIMB BH21 .... 217 K6
Sorrell Cl HLER SO31 .... 158 D6
Sorrell Wy CHCH/BSGR BH23 .... 223 M8
South Acre EPSF GU31 .... 93 G3
Southampton Hl
FHAM/STUB PO14 .... 159 K7
Southampton Rd BROC SO42 .... 201 L3
CHAM PO6 .... 162 D8
ELGH SO50 .... 81 M8
FAWY SO45 .... 155 L5
FBDG SP6 .... 98 A7
FHAM PO15 .... 159 J4
FHAM/PORC PO16 .... 7 J4
FHAM/STUB PO14 .... 159 H6
LYMN SO41 .... 228 B3
LYND SO43 .... 152 A2
RGWD BH24 .... 146 E8
ROMY SO51 .... 78 C7
TOTT SO40 .... 127 M1
Southampton St
WSHM SO15 .... 131 K2 ⑥
South Av FAWY SO45 .... 180 C5
NEND PO2 .... 187 J4
NMIL/BTOS BH25 .... 225 M6
South Baddesey Rd
LYMN SO41 .... 228 F4
South Bay EMRTH PO10 .... 190 E5
Southbourne Av CHAM PO6 .... 187 M1
EMRTH PO10 .... 166 F8
FAWY SO45 .... 180 A4

Southbourne Coast Rd
SBNE BH6 .... 237 K5
Southbourne Gv SBNE BH6 .... 237 G4
Southbourne Overcliff Dr
SBNE BH6 .... 237 H5
Southbourne Rd LYMN SO41 .... 237 G3
SBNE BH6 .... 237 G3
Southbrook Cl CFDH BH17 .... 218 E6
HAV PO9 .... 8 E7
Southbrook Rd HAV PO9 .... 8 E8
South Charford Dro FBDG SP6 .... 71 M4
Southcliff
LSOL/BMARY PO13 .... 208 C1 ⑧
Southcliffe Rd
CHCH/BSGR BH23 .... 239 G2
NMIL/BTOS BH25 .... 225 H8
Southcliff Rd SHAM SO14 .... 131 L1
South Cliff Wd WCLF BH2 .... 14 E8
South Cl GPORT PO12 .... 10 B7
HAV PO9 .... 9 G6
ROMY SO51 .... 51 H7 ⑦
Southcote Rd BMTH BH1 .... 15 L3
South Ct HLER SO31 .... 157 J6
Southcroft Rd GPORT PO12 .... 10 A1
South Cross St GPORT PO12 .... 11 K3
Southdene Rd CHFD SO53 .... 81 H3
Southdown Rd CHAM PO6 .... 163 L8
HORN PO8 .... 116 B5
RWIN SO21 .... 54 C2
South Downs Wy BPWT SO32 .... 58 F8
EPSF GU31 .... 93 K7
HORN PO8 .... 90 B5
NARL SO24 .... 29 J4
PSF GU32 .... 88 D1
RWIN SO21 .... 27 J2
WVILLE PO7 .... 113 M4
Southdown Vw WVILLE PO7 .... 140 A6
Southdown Wy FERN BH22 .... 168 D7
South Dr ROMY SO51 .... 50 A5
South East Crs ITCH SO19 .... 132 E4
South East Rd ITCH SO19 .... 132 E4
Southend La BPWT SO32 .... 113 J8
Southern Av FERN BH22 .... 168 D7
Southern Gdns TOTT SO40 .... 129 J1
Southernhay Rd VWD BH31 .... 144 F2
Southern La NMIL/BTOS BH25 .... 225 K8
Southern Oaks
NMIL/BTOS BH25 .... 225 K7
Southern Rd HEND SO30 .... 108 C8
LYMN SO41 .... 228 B4
SBNE BH6 .... 237 H4
WSHM SO15 .... 4 C3
Southey Rd
CHCH/BSGR BH23 .... 223 K8
Southfield RGWD BH24 .... 170 E2 ⑥
Southfield La RGWD BH24 .... 173 G6
Southfield Ms RGWD BH24 .... 170 E2 ⑥
Southfields Cl BPWT SO32 .... 85 H8
South Front SHAM SO14 .... 5 H3
Southgate St WINC SO23 .... 2 F8
South Gv LYMN SO41 .... 228 D5
South Haven Cl UPTN BH16 .... 232 A4
South Hl BPWT SO32 .... 86 F8
South Kinson Dr BWD BH11 .... 219 L4
Southlands LYMN SO41 .... 228 A6
Southlands Av SBNE BH6 .... 237 L4
WIMB BH21 .... 217 H2
South Ldg FHAM PO15 .... 159 M7
Southmead Rd FHAM PO15 .... 6 B5
South Millers Dl CHFD SO53 .... 81 G1
South Mill Rd WSHM SO15 .... 130 D1
Southmoor La HAV PO9 .... 8 B8
South Pde ENEY PO4 .... 211 H7
South Park Rd
BKME/WDN BH12 .... 219 L8
South Pl LSOL/BMARY PO13 .... 208 E4
South Rd BMTH BH1 .... 236 D3
CHAM PO6 .... 162 E6
CHAM PO6 .... 188 B1
HISD PO11 .... 213 K5
HORN PO8 .... 116 B7
PSEA PO1 .... 211 J1
PTSW SO17 .... 107 H8
WHAM PO17 .... 162 E2
WIMB BH21 .... 217 H1
Southsea Ter SSEA PO5 .... 12 F6
South Sp CHAM PO6 .... 162 F6
South St ELGH SO50 .... 81 M8
EMRTH PO10 .... 166 D8
FAWY SO45 .... 155 L5
FHAM/STUB PO14 .... 159 K8
GPORT PO12 .... 11 J4
HAV PO9 .... 8 F6
LYMN SO41 .... 228 A6
RSAL SP5 .... 40 A3
SSEA PO5 .... 12 F5 ⑪
South Sway La LYMN SO41 .... 201 G8
South Ter PSEA PO1 .... 12 C1 ⑥
PSEA PO1 .... 210 E2
South Trestle Rd FAWY SO45 .... 181 G3
South Vw FUFL SO22 .... 2 D7
South View Pl WCLF BH2 .... 14 C7
South View Rd
CHCH/BSGR BH23 .... 237 M2
FUFL SO22 .... 26 A5
WSHM SO15 .... 106 C8
Southville Rd BOSC BH5 .... 237 G3 ⑦
Southway WHAM PO15 .... 159 J5
Southways FHAM/STUB PO14 .... 184 B6
South Weirs BROC SO42 .... 201 H1

South West Coast Pth
SWGE BH19 .... 245 G8
South Western Crs
PSTN BH14 .... 234 A5
Southwick Av
FHAM/PORC PO16 .... 162 C7
Southwick Cl FUFL SO22 .... 16 C4 ⑥
Southwick Ct
FHAM/STUB PO14 .... 184 E2 ⑥
Southwick Hill Rd CHAM PO6 .... 163 J7
Southwick Pl SBNE BH6 .... 237 H1 ⑥
Southwick Rd CHAM PO6 .... 163 G6
SBNE BH6 .... 237 H2
WHAM PO17 .... 137 G5
WVILLE PO7 .... 139 J4
Southwood Av
CHCH/BSGR BH23 .... 224 E7
SBNE BH6 .... 237 H4
Southwood Cl
CHCH/BSGR BH23 .... 224 E7
FERN BH22 .... 194 A3
South Wood Gdns HLER SO31 .... 158 D5
Southwood Rd HISD PO11 .... 214 A6
NEND PO2 .... 187 J4
Sovereign Cl LTDN BH7 .... 221 K8 ⑥
Sovereign Crs
FHAM/STUB PO14 .... 158 E7
HEND SO30 .... 134 B2
Sovereign Dr ENEY PO4 .... 212 B3 ⑥
HEND SO30 .... 134 B2
Sovereign La WVILLE PO7 .... 164 C5
Sovereign Wy ELGH SO50 .... 81 L2
Sowden Cl HEND SO30 .... 133 M1
Sowley La LYMN SO41 .... 229 L3
The Spain PSF GU32 .... 63 K5
Spalding Rd ITCH SO19 .... 133 H3
Spaniard's La ROMY SO51 .... 78 E5
Sparkford Cl FUFL SO22 .... 26 D2
LTDN BH7 .... 221 M8 ⑥
Sparkford Rd FUFL SO22 .... 26 D2
Spa Rd SHAM SO14 .... 4 F4
Sparrow Cl HORN PO8 .... 140 D4
Sparrow Ct
LSOL/BMARY PO13 .... 208 C1 ⑦
Sparrowgrove RWIN SO21 .... 54 B4
Sparrow Sq ELGH SO50 .... 81 J6
Sparsholt Cl HAV PO9 .... 165 G3
Sparsholt Rd ITCH SO19 .... 132 D8
RWIN SO21 .... 25 G5
Spartan Cl EMRTH PO10 .... 190 E4
FHAM/STUB PO14 .... 184 A3
Spartina Dr LYMN SO41 .... 228 C2
Speakers Corner Rbt
SHAM SO14 .... 5 G4
Spear Rd SHAM SO14 .... 106 F8
Specks La ENEY PO4 .... 211 L4
Speedwell Cl HLER SO31 .... 158 D6 ⑦
Speedwell Dr
CHCH/BSGR BH23 .... 223 M8 ⑥
Speggs Wk HEND SO30 .... 134 B2
Speltham Hl WVILLE PO7 .... 114 C6
Spencer Cl HISD PO11 .... 213 L5 ⑥
Spencer Ct FHAM/STUB PO14 .... 184 C6
Spencer Dr LSOL/BMARY PO13 .. 208 D3
Spencer Gdns HORN PO8 .... 140 C5
Spencer Rd BMTH BH1 .... 15 M3
CCLF BH13 .... 234 D8
ELGH SO50 .... 81 K6
EMRTH PO10 .... 166 C4
ENEY PO4 .... 211 K6
ITCH SO19 .... 133 H2
NMIL/BTOS BH25 .... 225 L5
Spenlow Cl NEND PO2 .... 187 H8 ⑥
Spenser Cl HLER SO31 .... 158 B8 ⑦
Spetisbury Cl
MOOR/WNTN BH9 .... 220 F5
Spicer La BWD BH11 .... 219 J3
Spicer's Hl TOTT SO40 .... 129 K3
Spicer St PSEA PO1 .... 211 G2
Spicer's Wy TOTT SO40 .... 129 J2
Spicewood FHAM PO15 .... 6 C4
Spinacre NMIL/BTOS BH25 .... 225 M8
Spindle Cl HAV PO9 .... 9 L1
WIMB BH21 .... 217 K6
Spindle Warren HAV PO9 .... 9 L1
Spindlewood Cl
NMIL/BTOS BH25 .... 225 L7 ⑥
ROWN SO16 .... 106 F2
Spindlewood Wy TOTT SO40 .... 130 D8
Spinnaker Cl HISD PO11 .... 213 J4 ⑥
LSOL/BMARY PO13 .... 209 H1 ⑦
Spinnaker Dr NEND PO2 .... 187 H4
Spinnaker Gra HISD PO11 .... 190 A4
Spinnaker Vw CHAM PO6 .... 146 F7
Spinners Cl FERN BH22 .... 168 C7 ⑥
Spinney Cl HORN PO8 .... 140 C5
RGWD BH24 .... 169 H4
Spinney Dl FAWY SO45 .... 155 M6 ⑥
Spinney Gdns FAWY SO45 .... 155 M6 ⑥
Spinneys La FERN BH22 .... 194 B3
The Spinney ELGH SO50 .... 82 F6
FHAM/PORC PO16 .... 161 K7
HORN PO8 .... 140 E2
LSOL/BMARY PO13 .... 185 H7 ⑥
NARL SO24 .... 31 H3
RGWD BH24 .... 169 K2
ROWN SO16 .... 106 C2
RWIN SO21 .... 54 B1
TOTT SO40 .... 104 B7
WVILLE PO7 .... 139 K5
Spinney Wk WEND SO18 .... 107 L5
Spinney Wy NMIL/BTOS BH25 .... 225 L2
Spitfire End WINC SO23 .... 17 J8 ⑥
Spitfire Loop ELGH SO50 .... 107 L1
Spitfire Wy HLER SO31 .... 157 K6
Spithead Av GPORT PO12 .... 210 A7
Spittlefields RGWD BH24 .... 170 F1
Spouts La ROMY SO51 .... 76 C2
Springbank Rd LTDN BH7 .... 221 K8
Spring Cl ELGH SO50 .... 83 H6
ITCH SO19 .... 132 D4
VWD BH31 .... 144 D3
Spring Crs PTSW SO17 .... 107 G8
Springcroft
LSOL/BMARY PO13 .... 184 F3

Springfield Av
CHCH/BSGR BH23 .... 222 B6
FAWY SO45 .... 180 B4
SBNE BH6 .... 237 M4
Springfield Cl HAV PO9 .... 164 F6
LYMN SO41 .... 228 E5
VWD BH31 .... 144 D3
Springfield Crs PSTN BH14 .... 234 A4
RSAL SP5 .... 73 J3
Springfield Dr TOTT SO40 .... 129 J2 ⑥
Springfield Gdns
NMIL/BTOS BH25 .... 226 B6 ⑥
Springfield Gv FAWY SO45 .... 180 B4
Springfield Rd PSTN BH14 .... 233 M3
VWD BH31 .... 144 D3
Springfields Cl RWIN SO21 .... 54 E7
Springfield Wy
FHAM/STUB PO14 .... 184 A7
Springford Cl ROWN SO16 .... 106 A4
Springford Crs ROWN SO16 .... 106 A5
Springford Gdns ROWN SO16 .... 106 A4
Springford Rd ROWN SO16 .... 106 A5
Spring Garden La GPORT PO12 .... 11 H2
Spring Gdns BKME/WDN BH12 .. 234 C3
EMRTH PO10 .... 166 D8
NBAD SO52 .... 79 J3
PSEA PO1 .... 12 F2 ⑦
Spring Gv HLER SO31 .... 133 L7
Springhill Rd CHFD SO53 .... 81 H2
Spring Hills ITCH SO19 .... 133 H4
Spring La BPWT SO32 .... 112 A3
ELGH SO50 .... 82 C5
NMIL/BTOS BH25 .... 226 B6
RWIN SO21 .... 54 E7
Springles La FHAM PO15 .... 159 L3
Spring Pl ROMY SO51 .... 78 D1 ⑥
Spring Rd BMTH BH1 .... 15 M2
FAWY SO45 .... 155 K4
HLER SO31 .... 158 D2
ITCH SO19 .... 132 D2
LYMN SO41 .... 228 E5
Spring St PSEA PO1 .... 13 J1
The Spring WVILLE PO7 .... 139 K5
Spring V BPWT SO32 .... 111 M4
HORN PO8 .... 140 F4
Springvale Av LTDN BH7 .... 221 K8
WINC SO23 .... 17 G2
Springvale Rd WINC SO23 .... 17 G2
Springwater Cl BWD BH11 .... 219 L5 ⑥
Springwater Rd BWD BH11 .... 219 L5
Springwood Av WVILLE PO7 .... 164 D2
Spruce Av WVILLE PO7 .... 164 C1
Spruce Cl CFDH BH17 .... 217 J7
HLER SO31 .... 158 B8
Spruce Dr ITCH SO19 .... 133 J3
TOTT SO40 .... 104 A8
Spur Cl WIMB BH21 .... 193 G2 ⑥
Spurgeon Rd LTDN BH7 .... 237 G2
Spur Hill Av PSTN BH14 .... 234 C5
Spurlings Rd WHAM PO17 .... 161 H4
Spur Rd CHAM PO6 .... 163 K8
PSTN BH14 .... 234 C4
WVILLE PO7 .... 164 C1
The Spur GPORT PO12 .... 10 A8
WHAM PO17 .... 136 E5
The Square EMRTH PO10 .... 166 F5 ⑥
EPSF GU31 .... 93 J4
FAWY SO45 .... 180 F5 ⑥
GPORT PO12 .... 185 M8
LYMN SO41 .... 228 A5
PSF GU32 .... 63 L5
ROMY SO51 .... 49 G4
WHAM PO17 .... 136 E5
WINC SO23 .... 3 G8
Squarey Cl RSAL SP5 .... 72 C2
Squires Wk ITCH SO19 .... 132 C7
Squirrel Cl ELGH SO50 .... 82 E6 ⑥
Squirrel Dr ITCH SO19 .... 132 E5
Squirrels Cl
CHCH/BSGR BH23 .... 222 B6 ⑥
Squirrels Wk FAWY SO45 .... 155 K6
Stable Cl FHAM/STUB PO14 .... 159 H6
Stacey Cl BKME/WDN BH12 .... 234 C4
Stacey Ct HAV PO9 .... 165 H1
Stacey Gdns CHAR BH8 .... 221 K6
Stafford Rd BMTH BH1 .... 15 H5
PSF GU32 .... 63 L3
SSEA PO5 .... 12 E6
WSHM SO15 .... 131 H1
Staff Rd ROMY SO51 .... 22 A8
Stagbrake Cl FAWY SO45 .... 179 M5 ⑦
Stag Cl ELGH SO50 .... 82 E6
Stagshorn Rd HORN PO8 .... 141 G3 ⑥
Stags La RWIN SO21 .... 55 M3
Stagswood VWD BH31 .... 144 B2
Stag Wy FHAM PO15 .... 160 B3
Stainer Cl ITCH SO19 .... 133 H3
Staith Cl ITCH SO19 .... 133 G3
Stakes Hill Rd WVILLE PO7 .... 164 C1
Stakes La BPWT SO32 .... 84 D6
BPWT SO32 .... 85 L1
Stakes Rd WVILLE PO7 .... 164 B4
Stalbridge Dr FERN BH22 .... 194 B4
Stalbridge Rd CFDH BH17 .... 232 F1
Stalham Rd BKME/WDN BH12 .. 234 E2
Stallard Ct EMRTH PO10 .... 166 C7
Stallards La RGWD BH24 .... 170 E2
Stalybridge Cl HLER SO31 .... 158 E2
Stamford Av HISD PO11 .... 213 H5
Stamford Rd SBNE BH6 .... 237 J3
Stamford St PSEA PO1 .... 211 H2
Stamford Wy ELGH SO50 .... 83 H7 ⑦
Stamshaw Rd NEND PO2 .... 187 H4
Stanbridge La ROMY SO51 .... 50 A5
Stanbridge Rd HAV PO9 .... 165 M4
Standard Wy FHAM/PORC PO16 .. 7 M1
Standen Rd ROWN SO16 .... 105 J3
Standford St SHAM SO14 .... 5 K4 ⑥
Stanfield Rd BKME/WDN BH12 .. 234 C1
FERN BH22 .... 194 A2
MOOR/WNTN BH9 .... 220 C4
Stanford Ct CHAM PO6 .... 163 H8
Stanford Ct HAV PO9 .... 165 M3 ⑥
Stanford Ri LYMN SO41 .... 200 F6
Stanhope Rd PSEA PO1 .... 13 G1
Stanier Wy HEND SO30 .... 109 H6
Stanley Av HSEA PO3 .... 187 M8

Stanley Cl FHAM PO15 .... 6 C5
GPORT PO12 .... 185 L7
VWD BH31 .... 144 E3
Stanley Green Rd PLE BH15 .... 233 H3
Stanley La SSEA PO5 .... 13 H7
Stanley Rd BMTH BH1 .... 15 L2
CHCH/BSGR BH23 .... 224 E8
EMRTH PO10 .... 166 E8
FAWY SO45 .... 180 B4
LYMN SO41 .... 228 D6
NEND PO2 .... 187 G2
PLE BH15 .... 233 H7
PTSW SO17 .... 107 H7
TOTT SO40 .... 104 C7
Stanley St SSEA PO5 .... 13 H7
Stanmore La FUFL SO22 .... 26 B2
Stannington Cl
NMIL/BTOS BH25 .... 225 M6 ⑥
Stannington Crs TOTT SO40 .... 104 E8
Stannington Wy TOTT SO40 .... 104 E8
Stanpit CHCH/BSGR BH23 .... 238 D3
Stansted Cl HAV PO9 .... 142 A6
Stansted Rd ELGH SO50 .... 81 L4
SSEA PO5 .... 13 K6
Stansted Crs HAV PO9 .... 165 M2
Stansted Rd SSEA PO5 .... 13 K4
Stanswood Rd FAWY SO45 .... 206 F4
HAV PO9 .... 165 H2
Stanton Rd NBNE BH10 .... 220 A6
PSF GU32 .... 63 K4
WSHM SO15 .... 130 D1
Stanwarth La MIDH GU29 .... 67 H4
Stapehill Crs WIMB BH21 .... 192 F3
Stapehill Rd WIMB BH21 .... 193 K3
Staple Ash La PSF GU32 .... 62 B1
Staple Cl WVILLE PO7 .... 140 B7
Staple Close La PLE BH15 .... 233 H2
Staplecross La
CHCH/BSGR BH23 .... 223 H8
Stapleford Av FERN BH22 .... 194 D2
Stapleford Cl ROMY SO51 .... 51 G6
Stapleford La BPWT SO32 .... 109 L3
Staple Gdns WINC SO23 .... 2 F7
Staplehurst Cl ITCH SO19 .... 132 F4
Staplers Reach
LSOL/BMARY PO13 .... 184 F7
Stapleton Rd HSEA PO3 .... 187 L8 ⑦
Staplewood La TOTT SO40 .... 130 B7
Stares Cl LSOL/BMARY PO13 .... 209 G1
Starina Gdns WVILLE PO7 .... 140 F8
Starlight Farm Cl VWD BH31 .... 144 E1 ⑥
Starling Sq ELGH SO50 .... 81 J6 ②
Station Ap BDST BH18 .... 217 L4
PSEA PO1 .... 12 C2
Station Cl WHAM PO17 .... 136 E4
Station Hl ELGH SO50 .... 82 A5
HEND SO30 .... 135 C1
HLER SO31 .... 157 M1
WINC SO23 .... 2 F6 ⑦
Station La CHFD SO53 .... 81 H2
Station Rd BPWT SO32 .... 111 H1
BPWT SO32 .... 113 H4
CHAM PO6 .... 188 A2
CHCH/BSGR BH23 .... 224 C5
CHCH/BSGR BH23 .... 237 M1
EPSF GU31 .... 63 L4
FBDG SP6 .... 121 K2
FERN BH22 .... 168 B5
FHAM/PORC PO16 .... 162 B8
GPORT PO12 .... 209 K1
HISD PO11 .... 213 J4
HLER SO31 .... 156 F3
HSEA PO3 .... 187 L8
ITCH SO19 .... 132 E5
LISS GU33 .... 36 E4
LYMN SO41 .... 200 F6
NMIL/BTOS BH25 .... 225 L6
PSF GU32 .... 60 B4
PSF GU32 .... 63 K4
PSTN BH14 .... 234 A5
RGWD BH24 .... 199 J2
ROMY SO51 .... 78 D1
ROWN SO16 .... 104 F3
VWD BH31 .... 144 B1
WHAM PO17 .... 136 E4
WIMB BH21 .... 192 B5
WINC SO23 .... 2 E6
WSHM SO15 .... 105 H8
Station Rd North TOTT SO40 .... 129 L1 ⑥
Station Rd South
TOTT SO40 .... 129 M1 ⑥
Station St LYMN SO41 .... 228 D4
PSEA PO1 .... 13 G1
Station Ter WIMB BH21 .... 192 B4
Station Yd FBDG SP6 .... 121 J2
Staunton Av HISD PO11 .... 213 H5
Staunton Rd HAV PO9 .... 8 D3
Staunton St PSEA PO1 .... 211 G2
Staunton Wy HAV PO9 .... 8 C2
HAV PO9 .... 165 J3
HORN PO8 .... 90 E8
Stead Cl HISD PO11 .... 213 M5
Stedham La MIDH GU29 .... 67 K5
Stedman Rd BOSC BH5 .... 237 G3 ⑦
Steele Cl CHFD SO53 .... 81 J4
Steels Dro FBDG SP6 .... 98 D1
Steels La FBDG SP6 .... 96 B4
Steel St SSEA PO5 .... 12 F7
Steep Cl FHAM/PORC PO16 .... 162 A7 ⑦
Steepdene PSTN BH14 .... 234 A5
Steeple Cl CFDH BH17 .... 218 B5
Steepleton Rd BDST BH18 .... 217 J4
Steeple Wy FHAM/STUB PO14 .. 159 H5
Steerforth Cl NEND PO2 .... 211 H1
Steinbeck Cl FHAM PO15 .... 135 G8
Stein Rd EMRTH PO10 .... 167 H6
Stem La NMIL/BTOS BH25 .... 225 J3
Stenbury Wy HLER SO31 .... 157 G1
Stenhurst Rd PLE BH15 .... 233 K2 ⑥
Stephen Cl HORN PO8 .... 140 C7
Stephen Langton Dr
BWD BH11 .... 219 H3 ⑥
Stephen Martin Gdns
FBDG SP6 .... 97 K6 ⑥
Stephen Rd FHAM PO15 .... 6 F5
Stephenson Cl GPORT PO12 .... 10 C8 ⑦
Stephenson Rd TOTT SO40 .... 104 C6
Stephenson Wy HEND SO30 .... 109 H5
Steplake Rd ROMY SO51 .... 76 C1

Step Ter *FUFL* SO22 **2** D7
Sterte Av *PLE* BH15 **233** G4
Sterte Cl *PLE* BH15 **233** H4
Sterte Rd *PLE* BH15 **233** H4
Steuart Rd *WEND* SO18 **132** B1
Stevenson Crs *PSTN* BH14 **234** C5
Stevenson Rd *SBNE* BH6 **237** M5 1
Stevensons Cl *WIMB* BH21 **192** A4
Steventon Rd *WEND* SO18 **133** G1
Stewart Cl *CHAR* BH8 **15** M1
Stewart Rd *CHAR* BH8 **236** A2
Stewarts Gn *WVILLE* PO7 **114** B5
Stewarts Wy *FERN* BH22 **194** C1
Stibbs Wy *CHCH/BSGR* BH23 **198** A7
Stillmore Rd *BWD* BH11 **219** H5
Stinchar Dr *CHFD* SO53 **80** F3
Stinsford Cl *MOOR/WNTN* BH9 **220** F4
Stinsford Rd *CFDH* BH17 **218** B7
Stirling Av *WVILLE* PO7 **164** D1
Stirling Cl *NMIL/BTOS* BH25 **225** M5
TOTT SO40 **104** F8
Stirling Crs *HEND* SO30 **109** H7
TOTT SO40 **104** F8
Stirling Rd *MOOR/WNTN* BH9 **235** K1
Stirling St *NEND* PO2 **187** H8
Stirling Wy *CHCH/BSGR* BH23 **239** G2
Stirrup Cl *UPTN* BH16 **232** C1
WIMB BH21 **193** G2
Stoborough Dr *BDST* BH18 **217** L6 1
Stockbridge Cl *CFDH* BH17 **218** F6 1
HAV PO9 **165** M3 14
Stockbridge Rd *FUFL* SO22 **2** C5
ROMY SO51 **50** B1
Stocker Pl
LSOL/BMARY PO13 **185** H6 6
Stockers Av *FUFL* SO22 **2** A3
Stockheath La *HAV* PO9 **8** C2
Stockheath Rd *HAV* PO9 **165** K4
Stockheath Wy *HAV* PO9 **165** K5
Stockholm Dr *HEND* SO30 **134** A3 3
Stock La *RSAL* SP5 **75** K3
Stockley Cl *FAWY* SO45 **180** A5 3
Stocks La *ALTN* GU34 **32** F7
BPWT SO32 **87** M4
Stockton Cl *HEND* SO30 **134** B1 3
Stoddart Av *ITCH* SO19 **132** D2
Stodham La *EPSF* GU31 **36** D8
LISS GU33 **36** D6
Stoke Common Rd *ELGH* SO50 **82** D3
Stoke Gdns *GPORT* PO12 **10** F4
Stoke Hts *ELGH* SO50 **83** G5
Stoke Park Rd *ELGH* SO50 **82** D4
Stoke Rd *GPORT* PO12 **10** F4
ROWN SO16 **105** M7
WINC SO23 **3** H1
Stokes Av *PLE* BH15 **233** H4
Stokesay Cl *FAWY* SO45 **155** L8 2
Stokes Bay Rd *GPORT* PO12 **209** H6
Stoke Wood Cl *ELGH* SO50 **83** G6 3
Stoke Wood Rd *TWDS* BH3 **235** L1
Stonechat Cl *EPSF* GU31 **64** B6
Stonechat Dr *TOTT* SO40 **104** A8
Stonechat Rd *HORN* PO8 **140** E2
Stone Crop Cl *HLER* SO31 **158** C7
Stonecrop Cl *WIMB* BH21 **217** J6 2
Stone Gdns *CHAR* BH8 **221** L6
Stoneham Cemetery Rd
WEND SO18 **107** L4
Stoneham Cl *PSF* GU32 **63** J4
ROWN SO16 **107** J3 1
Stoneham La *ELGH* SO50 **81** K8
ROWN SO16 **107** J3
Stoneham Pk *PSF* GU32 **63** J4
Stoneham Wy *ELGH* SO50 **107** K3
Stonehills *FAWY* SO45 **181** G6
GPORT PO12 **10** F4 2
Stone La *GPORT* PO12 **10** F5 2
Stoneleigh Av *LYMN* SO41 **226** D4
Stoneleigh Cl
FHAM/PORC PO16 **161** M8 3
Stoners Cl *LSOL/BMARY* PO13 **184** F5
Stone Sq *HAV* PO9 **165** K4
Stone St *SSEA* PO5 **12** F5
Stoney La *FUFL* SO22 **2** A2
Stony La *CHCH/BSGR* BH23 **222** F6
FBDG SP6 **95** M4
PSEA PO1 **210** E2
Stony La South
CHCH/BSGR BH23 **238** B2
Stonymoor Cl *FAWY* SO45 **180** A5
Stopples La *LYMN* SO41 **226** D4
Storrington Rd *HORN* PO8 **116** C3
Story La *BDST* BH18 **217** M4
Stourbank Rd
CHCH/BSGR BH23 **237** M2
Stourcliffe Av *SBNE* BH6 **237** H4
Stour Cl *PSF* GU32 **63** K6
WEND SO18 **107** M5
WIMB BH21 **193** H4
Stourcroft Dr
CHCH/BSGR BH23 **222** B6
Stourfield Rd *BOSC* BH5 **237** G4
Stourpaine Rd *CFDH* BH17 **218** B6
Stour Rd *CHAR* BH8 **236** C2
CHCH/BSGR BH23 **237** M1
Stourvale Av
CHCH/BSGR BH23 **222** B8
Stourvale Gdns *CHFD* SO53 **81** J3
Stourvale Pl *BOSC* BH5 **237** G3 9
Stourvale Rd *SBNE* BH6 **237** G3
Stour Valley Wy *FERN* BH22 **194** B8
MOOR/WNTN BH9 **221** G2
SBNE BH6 **237** K1
WIMB BH21 **192** A4
Stour Wy *CHCH/BSGR* BH23 **222** B6
Stourwood Av *SBNE* BH6 **237** H4
Stourwood Rd *SBNE* BH6 **237** J4
Stouts La *CHCH/BSGR* BH23 **197** M7
Stowe Cl *HEND* SO30 **109** J7
Stowe Rd *ENEY* PO4 **211** M4
Stradbrook *LSOL/BMARY* PO13 **184** F7
Stragwyne Cl *NBAD* SO52 **79** L2 1
The Straight Mile *ROMY* SO51 **51** K7
Strand *SHAM* SO14 **5** G4
Strand St *PLE* BH15 **233** G7
The Strand *HISD* PO11 **214** A7
Stratfield Dr *CHFD* SO53 **53** G7 5
Stratfield Pl
NMIL/BTOS BH25 **225** J5 3
Stratford Pl *ELGH* SO50 **82** A4 2
LYMN SO41 **228** B3
Stratford Rd *WVILLE* PO7 **140** E8
Strathmore Dr *VWD* BH31 **144** F2
Strathmore Rd *GPORT* PO12 **11** H3
NBNE BH10 **220** E4
Stratton Cl *CHAM* PO6 **163** G8
Stratton Rd *MOOR/WNTN* BH9 **221** G4
WINC SO23 **3** K9
WSHM SO15 **106** B7
Strawberry Hl *HLER* SO31 **158** D5
Streamleaze
FHAM/STUB PO14 **159** G7
Street End *NBAD* SO52 **80** A3
Streets La *RGWD* BH24 **171** G4
The Street *MIDH* GU29 **67** K7
RSAL SP5 **46** F4
Strettons Copse *LIPH* GU30 **38** E5
Stride Av *HSEA* PO3 **211** M2
Strides La *RGWD* BH24 **170** D1
Strides Wy *TOTT* SO40 **128** F1
Strode Gdns *RGWD* BH24 **169** M3
Strode Rd *NEND* PO2 **187** G6
Strongs Cl *ROMY* SO51 **51** G8 6
Stroud Cl *WIMB* BH21 **192** E2
Strouden Av *CHAR* BH8 **220** F7
Strouden Ct *HAV* PO9 **165** H1
Stroud End *PSF* GU32 **63** G4
Strouden Rd
MOOR/WNTN BH9 **220** E7
Stroud Gdns
CHCH/BSGR BH23 **238** D2 6
Stroud La *CHCH/BSGR* BH23 **238** D2
Stroudley Av *CHAM* PO6 **188** A2
Stroudley Wy *HEND* SO30 **109** J6
Stroud Park Av
CHCH/BSGR BH23 **238** D1
Stroudwood La *BPWT* SO32 **83** M5
RWIN SO21 **83** M3
Stroudwood Rd *HAV* PO9 **165** L5
Struan Ct *RGWD* BH24 **169** L2
Struan Dr *RGWD* BH24 **169** L2
Struan Gdns *RGWD* BH24 **169** K2
Stuart Cl *FHAM/STUB* PO14 **184** A6
UPTN BH16 **232** A1
Stuart Crs *FUFL* SO22 **26** D3
Stuart Rd *CHCH/BSGR* BH23 **224** F8
Stubbington Av *NEND* PO2 **187** J7
Stubbington Gn
FHAM/STUB PO14 **184** A5
Stubbington La
FHAM/STUB PO14 **184** A8
Stubbington Wy *ELGH* SO50 **83** J7
Stubbs Dro *HEND* SO30 **134** B1
Stubbs Rd *ITCH* SO19 **133** G6 2
Stuckton Rd *FBDG* SP6 **97** M8
Studland Cl *ROWN* SO16 **105** J7
Studland Dr *LYMN* SO41 **242** A3
Studland Rd
LSOL/BMARY PO13 **208** C2
ROWN SO16 **105** J7
WBNE BH4 **235** H7
Studley Av *FAWY* SO45 **180** A5
Studley Cl *CHCH/BSGR* BH23 **225** G8
Studley Ct *NMIL/BTOS* BH25 **225** H8 3
Sturminster Rd
MOOR/WNTN BH9 **220** F4 4
Sudbury Rd *CHAM* PO6 **163** H8
Suetts La *BPWT* SO32 **111** L1
Suffolk Av *CHCH/BSGR* BH23 **222** D6
WSHM SO15 **131** H1
Suffolk Cl *CHFD* SO53 **81** H6
WIMB BH21 **193** G2 4
Suffolk Dr *CHFD* SO53 **81** H6
FHAM PO15 **158** F1
HLER SO31 **158** F1
Suffolk Rd *ENEY* PO4 **211** L5
WCLF BH2 **14** A5
Suffolk Rd South *WBNE* BH4 **14** A4
Sullivan Cl *CHAM* PO6 **162** C8
Sullivan Rd *ITCH* SO19 **133** H5 3
Sullivan Wy *WVILLE* PO7 **164** C3
Sultan Rd *EMRTH* PO10 **166** D7
NEND PO2 **211** G1
Sumar Cl *FHAM/STUB* PO14 **184** B3
Summercroft Wy *FERN* BH22 **168** C5
Summer Fld *WIMB* BH21 **192** E4
Summerfield Cl
CHCH/BSGR BH23 **223** G6 2
Summerfield Gdns
ROWN SO16 **107** J3 2
Summerfield Rd *SELS* PO20 **215** L6
Summerfields
FHAM/STUB PO14 **158** F7
LTDN BH7 **236** E1
Summer Flds *VWD* BH31 **144** D4
Summerhill Rd *HORN* PO8 **140** D5
Summerlands Rd *ELGH* SO50 **83** H6
Summer La *BROC* SO42 **179** J7
Summerleigh Wk
FHAM/STUB PO14 **184** B3 1
Summers Av *BWD* BH11 **219** M2
Summers La *CHCH/BSGR* BH23 **223** H7
Summers St *SHAM* SO14 **131** M2
Summertrees Ct
NMIL/BTOS BH25 **226** B4
Summit Wy *WEND* SO18 **107** L7
Sumner Rd *EPSF* GU31 **91** J3
Sunbeam Wy *GPORT* PO12 **10** F6
Sunbury Ct *FHAM* PO15 **160** C4
Sunderland Dr
CHCH/BSGR BH23 **239** G1 4
Sunderton La *HORN* PO8 **116** A4
Sundew Cl *CHCH/BSGR* BH23 **224** A7
NMIL/BTOS BH25 **226** B4 5
Sundew Rd *WIMB* BH21 **217** J6
Sundridge Cl *CHAM* PO6 **163** J8
Sunningdale *FAWY* SO45 **155** K6
Sunningdale Cl *ELGH* SO50 **82** E6 4
LSOL/BMARY PO13 **185** G7 3
Sunningdale Crs *NBNE* BH10 **220** A4
Sunningdale Gdns
WEND SO18 **132** F1 3
Sunningdale Rd
FHAM/PORC PO16 **186** B1
HSEA PO3 **211** L2
Sunnybank Rd *WIMB* BH21 **192** F2
Sunnydown Rd *FUFL* SO22 **25** M5
Sunnyfield Ri *HLER* SO31 **133** L7 5
Sunnyfield Rd
NMIL/BTOS BH25 **225** L8
Sunnyheath *HAV* PO9 **165** J4
Sunny Hill Rd
BKME/WDN BH12 **234** C3
Sunnyhill Rd *SBNE* BH6 **237** G3
Sunnylands Av *SBNE* BH6 **237** L4
Sunnymead Dr *WVILLE* PO7 **140** A6
Sunnymoor Rd *BWD* BH11 **219** L7
Sunnyside Rd
BKME/WDN BH12 **234** C2
Sunny Wk *PSEA* PO1 **12** B1
Sunny Wy *TOTT* SO40 **129** K1 1
Sunridge Cl *BKME/WDN* BH12 **234** F2
Sunset Av *TOTT* SO40 **104** D8
Sunset Rd *TOTT* SO40 **104** D8
Sunshine Av *HISD* PO11 **213** M6 2
Sun St *PSEA* PO1 **12** D2 5
Sunvale Cl *ITCH* SO19 **132** F5
Sunwood Rd *HAV* PO9 **165** H3
Surbiton Rd *ELGH* SO50 **82** A3
Surrey Cl *CHCH/BSGR* BH23 **222** D6
TOTT SO40 **129** H3
Surrey Gdns *WBNE* BH4 **235** H4
Surrey Rd *BKME/WDN* BH12 **234** F3
CHFD SO53 **81** H5
ITCH SO19 **132** B6
WBNE BH4 **235** H4
Surrey Rd South *WBNE* BH4 **235** H4
Surrey St *PSEA* PO1 **13** G1
Sussex Border Pth
EMRTH PO10 **190** D5
EPSF GU31 **92** E3
HAV PO9 **142** B4
HORN PO8 **117** H4
LISS GU33 **37** L2
Sussex Cl *MOOR/WNTN* BH9 **220** F4
Sussex Gdns *EPSF* GU31 **63** L6
Sussex Pl *SSEA* PO5 **13** G6 1
Sussex Rd *CHFD* SO53 **81** J5
EPSF GU31 **63** M6
SHAM SO14 **5** G3
SSEA PO5 **13** G6
Sussex St *WINC* SO23 **2** F7
Sutherland Av *BDST* BH18 **217** J3
Sutherland Cl *ROMY* SO51 **51** G7 4
Sutherland Rd *ENEY* PO4 **13** M5
ROWN SO16 **105** L3
Sutherlands Ct *CHFD* SO53 **81** H2 2
Sutherlands Wy *CHFD* SO53 **81** G1
Sutton Cl *CFDH* BH17 **218** E6
HORN PO8 **140** B5
HSEA PO3 **187** M4
Sutton Gdns *WINC* SO23 **3** G7
Sutton Pl *BROC* SO42 **175** L7 4
Sutton Rd *HORN* PO8 **140** B5
MOOR/WNTN BH9 **220** F7
TOTT SO40 **104** C7
Swale Dr *CHFD* SO53 **80** F1
Swallow Cl *CFDH* BH17 **217** K8
HAV PO9 **9** J1
TOTT SO40 **128** F2
Swallow Ct
LSOL/BMARY PO13 **208** D1 8
Swallow Dr *LYMN* SO41 **242** E4
Swallow Sq *ELGH* SO50 **81** J6 3
Swanage Cl *ITCH* SO19 **132** C5
Swanage Rd
LSOL/BMARY PO13 **208** C2
Swan Cl *EMRTH* PO10 **166** E8
HLER SO31 **158** B1
Swancote *FHAM/PORC* PO16 **161** K8
Swan La *WINC* SO23 **2** F6
Swanley Cl *ELGH* SO50 **81** M3
Swan Md *RGWD* BH24 **171** G2
Swanmore Av *ITCH* SO19 **132** F5
Swanmore Cl *FUFL* SO22 **16** C4
LTDN BH7 **237** G1 2
Swanmore Rd *BPWT* SO32 **111** L1
HAV PO9 **165** H1
LTDN BH7 **237** G2
Swansbury Dr *CHAR* BH8 **221** L6
Swan St *PSF* GU32 **63** K5
Swanton Gdns *CHFD* SO53 **81** G1
Swanwick La *HLER* SO31 **134** B8
Swanwick Shore Rd
HLER SO31 **158** B1 1
Swarraton Rd *HAV* PO9 **165** L4
Sway Ct *HAV* PO9 **165** M3 15
Sway Gdns *CHAR* BH8 **221** H6
Sway Rd *BROC* SO42 **201** K1
LYMN SO41 **227** J3
NMIL/BTOS BH25 **225** M2
Swaythling Rd *HAV* PO9 **165** H2
HEND SO30 **108** A6
The Sweep *RGWD* BH24 **170** D1 7
Sweetbriar Gdns
WVILLE PO7 **164** D3 4
Sweethills Crs *HLER* SO31 **134** F8
Sweyns Lease *BROC* SO42 **204** A2
Swift Cl *CFDH* BH17 **217** K8
ELGH SO50 **81** J6
FUFL SO22 **26** C3
HORN PO8 **140** E1
LSOL/BMARY PO13 **208** D1 9
Swift Gdns *ITCH* SO19 **132** B7
Swift Hollow *ITCH* SO19 **132** B7 2
Swift Rd *EMRTH* PO10 **190** E5
ITCH SO19 **132** B7
Swinburn Gdns *HORN* PO8 **140** D4
Swincombe Ri *WEND* SO18 **108** A7
Swiss Rd *WVILLE* PO7 **164** C1
Swivelton La *WHAM* PO17 **161** L5
Sword Cl *GPORT* PO12 **209** J6
HORN PO8 **116** A3
Swordfish Dr
CHCH/BSGR BH23 **239** G1 5
Sword Sands Rd *HSEA* PO3 **212** A1
Sycamore Av *CHFD* SO53 **53** H7
Sycamore Cl *CFDH* BH17 **217** K7
CHCH/BSGR BH23 **222** B8 1
FHAM/STUB PO14 **159** G7 3
HLER SO31 **133** K8
HORN PO8 **140** C5
LSOL/BMARY PO13 **185** J7 5
LYMN SO41 **242** B3
NBAD SO52 **79** L3
ROMY SO51 **79** H2
Sycamore Dr *FAWY* SO45 **179** M3
HISD PO11 **213** J4
Sycamore Rd *BPWT* SO32 **85** K8
FAWY SO45 **155** K5
LYMN SO41 **226** D4
ROWN SO16 **105** M6
Sydenham Ter *PSEA* PO1 **13** K2
Sydling Cl *CFDH* BH17 **218** F6
Sydmanton Cl *ROMY* SO51 **78** F2 3
Sydmonton Ct *HAV* PO9 **165** M2 11
Sydney Av *HLER* SO31 **157** J5
Sydney Rd *BDST* BH18 **217** L5
CHCH/BSGR BH23 **222** C7
ELGH SO50 **82** C4
GPORT PO12 **10** F3
WSHM SO15 **106** A7
Syers Rd *LISS* GU33 **36** E4
Sylmor Gdns
MOOR/WNTN BH9 **220** E6
Sylvan Av *ITCH* SO19 **133** G2
Sylvan Cl *LYMN* SO41 **226** F6
RGWD BH24 **169** H4
Sylvan Dr *NBAD* SO52 **79** L4
Sylvan La *HLER* SO31 **157** L6
Sylvan Rd *BKME/WDN* BH12 **234** A2
The Sylvans *FAWY* SO45 **155** H5 6
Sylvan Vw *WVILLE* PO7 **164** D2
Sylvia Crs *TOTT* SO40 **104** D7
Symes Rd *PLE* BH15 **232** C4
ROMY SO51 **79** G1
Symonds Cl *CHFD* SO53 **81** J4
Symonds St *WINC* SO23 **3** G9
Sywell Crs *HSEA* PO3 **187** M4

T

Tadburn Cl *CHFD* SO53 **81** J3
ROMY SO51 **78** F1 4
Tadburn Rd *ROMY* SO51 **78** F2
Tadden Wk *BDST* BH18 **217** K6
Tadfield Rd *ROMY* SO51 **78** F1
Tagdell La *HORN* PO8 **115** L8
Tait Cl *CFDH* BH17 **233** K1
Tait Pl *LSOL/BMARY* PO13 **185** H7
Talbot Ct *SHAM* SO14 **5** K1 4
Talbot Av *TWDS* BH3 **235** K1
Talbot Cl *HAV* PO9 **165** G5
ROWN SO16 **106** E4
Talbot Dr *BKME/WDN* BH12 **219** M8
CHCH/BSGR BH23 **224** D6
Talbot Hill Rd
MOOR/WNTN BH9 **220** B8
Talbot Mdw
BKME/WDN BH12 **219** M8
Talbot Ms *NBNE* BH10 **219** M7 1
Talbot Ri *NBNE* BH10 **220** A7
Talbot Rd *ENEY* PO4 **13** M4
FAWY SO45 **155** H7
HAV PO9 **8** A1
MOOR/WNTN BH9 **220** B8
Talland Rd *FHAM/STUB* PO14 **158** F7
Tamar Cl *FERN* BH22 **194** E3
FHAM/PORC PO16 **161** L7
Tamar Down *WVILLE* PO7 **164** E1
Tamar Gv *FAWY* SO45 **155** J5
Tamarisk Cl *ENEY* PO4 **212** A5
FHAM/STUB PO14 **184** A7 4
WVILLE PO7 **164** E3 1
Tamarisk Gdns *WEND* SO18 **107** K8
Tamarisk Rd *HEND* SO30 **133** M1
Tamella Rd *HEND* SO30 **134** C2
Tammys Turn
FHAM/STUB PO14 **159** M8 4
Tamorisk Dr *TOTT* SO40 **129** G2
Tamworth Rd *HSEA* PO3 **211** L2
LTDN BH7 **236** E3 3
Tanfield La *WHAM* PO17 **136** D5
Tanfield Pk *WHAM* PO17 **136** D5
Tangier La *BPWT* SO32 **110** E1
Tangier Rd *HSEA* PO3 **211** L1
Tanglewood
FHAM/PORC PO16 **7** G1
TOTT SO40 **130** E7 5
Tanglewood Cl *WVILLE* PO7 **164** A4 3
Tangmere Cl
CHCH/BSGR BH23 **239** G2
Tangmere Dr *ROWN* SO16 **105** L4
Tangyes Cl *FHAM/STUB* PO14 **184** B5
Tanhouse Cl *HEND* SO30 **134** A3
Tanhouse La *HEND* SO30 **134** B3
Tan Howse Cl *LTDN* BH7 **221** M8
Tankerdale La *PSF* GU32 **36** B8
Tankerton Cl *CHAM* PO6 **163** J8 2
Tankerville Rd *ITCH* SO19 **132** B5
Tanner's Brook Wy
WSHM SO15 **130** D2
Tanners La *FBDG* SP6 **96** E5
FHAM/STUB PO14 **184** C2
LYMN SO41 **229** L4
ROMY SO51 **49** J8
WVILLE PO7 **139** K3
Tanner's Rdg *WVILLE* PO7 **164** C5
Tanners Rd *NBAD* SO52 **79** M4
The Tanners
FHAM/STUB PO14 **159** G7 4
Tanner St *WINC* SO23 **3** H8
Tansy Cl *WVILLE* PO7 **164** E2
Tansy Meadow *NBAD* SO52 **80** E4 2
The Tanyards *CHFD* SO53 **53** G7 6
Taplin Dr *HEND* SO30 **109** H8
Taplings Cl *FUFL* SO22 **2** A1
FUFL SO22 **16** C5
Taplings Rd *FUFL* SO22 **2** A1
Taranto Rd *ROWN* SO16 **106** B4
Tarbery Crs *HORN* PO8 **141** G1
Target Rd *NEND* PO2 **187** G5
Tarius Cl *LSOL/BMARY* PO13 **185** H6
Tarleton Rd *CHAM* PO6 **162** F7
Tarn Dr *CFDH* BH17 **217** K7
Tarn Ri *HORN* PO8 **116** B6
Tarrant Cl *CFDH* BH17 **218** C6
Tarrant Gdns *HAV* PO9 **8** B1
Tarrant Rd *MOOR/WNTN* BH9 **220** F5
Tasman Cl *CHCH/BSGR* BH23 **222** D8
SHAM SO14 **5** K8
Taswell Rd *SSEA* PO5 **13** K8
Tatchbury La *TOTT* SO40 **103** L7
Tate Rd *WSHM* SO15 **105** H8
FAWY SO45 **155** M5 1
Tates Rd *FAWY* SO45 **155** M6 3
Tatnam Rd *PLE* BH15 **233** H4
Tattenham Rd *BROC* SO42 **175** K8
Tattershall Crs
FHAM/PORC PO16 **185** M1
Tatwin Cl *ITCH* SO19 **133** H3
Tatwin Crs *ITCH* SO19 **133** H3
Taunton Dr *WEND* SO18 **132** F1
Tavells Cl *TOTT* SO40 **130** C7
Tavell's La *TOTT* SO40 **130** C7
Taverner Cl *PLE* BH15 **233** J6 1
Taverners Cl *ITCH* SO19 **133** H5
Tavistock Cl *ROMY* SO51 **51** G7 5
Tavistock Gdns *HAV* PO9 **9** J5
Tavy Cl *CHFD* SO53 **81** G2
Taw Dr *CHFD* SO53 **81** G1
Tawny Owl Cl
FHAM/STUB PO14 **183** M4 4
Taylor Dr *CHAR* BH8 **221** H4
Taylor's Buildings *PLE* BH15 **233** H7 5
Teachers Wy *FAWY* SO45 **179** M4 2
Teal Cl *FHAM/PORC* PO16 **161** K8
HISD PO11 **213** M5
TOTT SO40 **129** G1 7
Teasel Wy *FERN* BH22 **168** C7
Teazle Cl *EPSF* GU31 **64** B6
Tebourba Dr *GPORT* PO12 **10** C6
Tebourba Wy *WSHM* SO15 **130** D1
Tedder Cl *BWD* BH11 **219** M5
Tedder Gdns *BWD* BH11 **219** M5
Tedder Rd *BWD* BH11 **219** M5
LSOL/BMARY PO13 **185** H5
WEND SO18 **107** M8
Tedder Wy *TOTT* SO40 **129** H1
Teddington Rd *ENEY* PO4 **211** L4
Tees Cl *CHFD* SO53 **80** F1
Teg Down Meads *FUFL* SO22 **16** A7
Teignmouth Rd *GPORT* PO12 **209** K1
HSEA PO3 **187** L8
Telegraph La *EPSF* GU31 **93** K6
Telegraph Rd *HEND* SO30 **108** D8
Telephone Rd *ENEY* PO4 **13** M3
Telford Gdns *HEND* SO30 **109** J6 2
Telford Rd *NEND* PO2 **187** J5
Teme Crs *ROWN* SO16 **105** K8
Teme Rd *ROWN* SO16 **105** K8 1
Tempest Av *WVILLE* PO7 **140** E8
Templar Cl *BKME/WDN* BH12 **219** K7
Templars Mede *CHFD* SO53 **81** G5
Templars Wy *NBAD* SO52 **80** E4
Templecombe Rd *ELGH* SO50 **82** E7
Temple Gdns *ITCH* SO19 **132** D6 2
Temple La *PSF* GU32 **61** J8
Templemere
FHAM/STUB PO14 **184** A1
Temple Rd *ITCH* SO19 **132** D6
LISS GU33 **36** F2
Temple St *PSEA* PO1 **211** G2
Templeton Cl *NEND* PO2 **187** J5 2
Tenby Cl *WEND* SO18 **107** M8
Tenby Dr *CHFD* SO53 **80** F4
Tench Wy *ROMY* SO51 **50** E8
Tennyson Cl *BPWT* SO32 **85** K8
FAWY SO45 **179** M3 2
Tennyson Crs *WVILLE* PO7 **140** B7
Tennyson Gdns
FHAM/PORC PO16 **7** G4
Tennyson Rd *ELGH* SO50 **81** L6
MOOR/WNTN BH9 **220** D6
NEND PO2 **187** K8
PSTN BH14 **233** M5
PTSW SO17 **107** G8
TOTT SO40 **104** C6
WIMB BH21 **192** A2
Tensing Cl *FHAM/PORC* PO16 **7** G1
Tensing Rd *CHCH/BSGR* BH23 **238** D1
Tenterton Av *ITCH* SO19 **132** F7
Terence Av *CFDH* BH17 **218** A7 1
Terence Rd *WIMB* BH21 **217** G3
Terminus Ter *SHAM* SO14 **5** J6
Tern Cl *FAWY* SO45 **155** M6
Tern Ct *SBNE* BH6 **237** J2
Terrace Rd *WCLF* BH2 **14** D6
Terrier Cl *HEND* SO30 **109** H5
Terrington Av
CHCH/BSGR BH23 **224** C7
Terriote Cl *CHFD* SO53 **81** H1
Terwick La *EPSF* GU31 **66** D8
Testbourne Av *TOTT* SO40 **129** H1
Testbourne Cl *TOTT* SO40 **129** H1
Testbourne Rd *TOTT* SO40 **129** H1
Test Cl *PSF* GU32 **63** K7
Testcombe Rd *GPORT* PO12 **10** D6
Testlands Av *ROWN* SO16 **105** J2
Test La *ROWN* SO16 **105** G7
Test Rd *SHAM* SO14 **131** M8
Test Wy *ROMY* SO51 **49** M6
TOTT SO40 **104** F7
Testwood Av *TOTT* SO40 **104** D7
Testwood Crs *TOTT* SO40 **104** C6
Testwood La *TOTT* SO40 **104** E7
Testwood Pl *TOTT* SO40 **104** F8
Testwood Rd *HAV* PO9 **165** H3 3
WSHM SO15 **130** F2
Tethering Dro *FBDG* SP6 **73** J5
Tetney Cl *ROWN* SO16 **105** K5
Teviot Rd *CHFD* SO53 **80** F3
Tewkesbury Av *FHAM* PO15 **160** A5
GPORT PO12 **209** L1
Tewkesbury Cl *CHAM* PO6 **163** H8
Texas Dr *FUFL* SO22 **26** A6
Thackeray Rd *PTSW* SO17 **107** G8
Thames Cl *FERN* BH22 **194** E2
WEND SO18 **108** A6
Thames Dr *FHAM* PO15 **160** B4
Thamesmead Cl
GPORT PO12 **209** K1 3
Thames Ms *PLE* BH15 **233** G7 7
Thames St *PLE* BH15 **233** G7
Thatchers La
CHCH/BSGR BH23 **197** K6
LYMN SO41 **203** K8

Theatre Ms *SSEA* PO5 .... **13** K7 ◻
The Itchen Br *ITCH* SO19 .... **5** M6
Theobold Rd
  CHCH/BSGR BH23 .... **195** L8
Thetchers Cl
  NMIL/BTOS BH25 .... **225** M3
Thetford Gdns *CHFD* SO53 ...... **80** F1
Thetford Rd
  BKME/WDN BH12 .... **234** E3 ◻
The Thicket
  FHAM/PORC PO16 .... **161** L8
  LSOL/BMARY PO13 .... **185** J7 ◻
  ROMY SO51 .... **79** H2 ◻
  SSEA PO5 .... **13** J6 ◻
  WVILLE PO7 .... **164** B6
Third Av *CHAM* PO6 .... **163** J8
  HAV PO9 .... **9** H3
  WSHM SO15 .... **130** D2
Thirlmere *ELGH* SO50 .... **81** L6 ◻
Thirlmere Cl
  FHAM/STUB PO14 .... **184** B4 ◻
Thirlmere Rd *ROWN* SO16 ...... **105** K6
Thirlstane Firs *CHFD* SO53 ...... **81** C4 ◻
Thistlebarrow Rd *LTDN* BH7 .. **236** D2
Thistledown *HORN* PO8 .... **140** T3
Thistledowne Gdns
  EMRTH PO10 .... **166** F8
Thistle Rd *HEND* SO30 .... **133** M2
  NBAD SO52 .... **80** E3
Thomas Cl *TOTT* SO40 .... **129** H2 ◻
Thomas Lewis Wy
  PTSW SO17 .... **107** G8 ◻
Thomas Rd *NBAD* SO52 .... **79** M4
Thompson's La *RWIN* SO21 .... **83** L1
  WVILLE PO7 .... **139** D3
Thoresby Ct
  NMIL/BTOS BH25 .... **225** J5 ◻
Thornbrake Rd *GPORT* PO12 .. **11** H5 ◻
  WSHM SO15 .... **131** J1
Thornbury Av *FAWY* SO45 .... **180** C8
  WSHM SO15 .... **131** J1
Thornbury Cl
  FHAM/STUB PO14 .... **160** A8 ◻
Thornbury Hts *CHFD* SO53 .... **53** L8
Thornbury Rd *SBNE* BH6 ..... **237** M4
Thornbury Wd *CHFD* SO53 .... **53** L7
Thorncliffe Cl *NEND* PO2 ...... **187** K4 ◻
Thorn Cl *ELGH* SO50 .... **81** M3 ◻
  EPSF GU31 .... **64** B6
Thorncombe Cl *CHFD* BH17 ... **218** C6
Thorncroft Rd *PSEA* PO1 ...... **13** M2
Thorndike Cl *ROWN* SO16 ..... **105** M6
Thorndike Rd *ROWN* SO16 .... **105** K6
Thorne Cl *VWD* BH31 .... **144** C1
Thorness Cl *ROWN* SO16 ...... **105** K7
Thorney Cl *FHAM/STUB* PO14 .. **6** A8
Thorney Old Pk *EMRTH* PO10 .. **191** H4
Thorney Rd *EMRTH* PO10 ...... **190** F3
Thornfield Dr
  CHCH/BSGR BH23 .... **224** D7
Thorngate Wy *GPORT* PO12 .. **11** K3 ◻
Thornham La *EMRTH* PO10 ... **190** F2
Thornham Rd
  NMIL/BTOS BH25 .... **226** B5
Thornhill Av *ITCH* SO19 .... **133** H2
Thornhill Park Rd *WEND* SO18 .. **133** H1
Thornhill Rd *FAWY* SO45 ..... **180** D6
  ROWN SO16 .... **106** C4
Thorni Av *FHAM* PO15 .... **160** A5
Thornleigh Rd *ITCH* SO19 ..... **132** C6
Thornley Rd *NBNE* BH10 ...... **220** B4
Thorn Rd *CHFD* BH17 .... **218** A5
Thorns La *LYMN* SO41 .... **230** D1
Thornton Av *HLER* SO31 ...... **158** A7
Thornton Cl *CHAM* PO6 .... **163** M6 ◻
  WIMB BH21 .... **217** G3 ◻
Thornton Rd *GPORT* PO12 .... **185** M8
Thornycroft Av *ITCH* SO19 .... **132** B6
Thorold Rd *CHFD* SO53 .... **53** K7
  WEND SO18 .... **107** K7
Three Acre Dr
  NMIL/BTOS BH25 .... **225** K8
Three Acres *WVILLE* PO7 ..... **139** L5
Three Castles Pth *RWIN* SO21 . **17** H4
Three Cross Rd *WIMB* BH21 ... **168** C2
Threefield La *SHAM* SO14 ..... **5** H5
Three Horse Shoes La
  ALTN GU34 .... **32** D6
Three Oaks *ITCH* SO19 .... **133** J1
Three Tun Cl *PSEA* PO1 ...... **12** D2
Thresher Cl *HORN* PO8 .... **141** G7 ◻
Throop Cl *CHAR* BH8 .... **221** L7
Throop Rd *CHAR* BH8 .... **221** J4
Throopside Av
  MOOR/WNTN BH9 ...... **221** H4
Thrush Rd *BKME/WDN* BH12 .. **219** G7
Thrush Wk *HORN* PO8 .... **140** C4 ◻
Thruxton Rd *HAV* PO9 .... **165** G3
Thurbern Rd *NEND* PO2 ...... **187** J6
Thurmell Cl *HEND* SO30 ...... **134** A4
Thurmond Crs *FUFL* SO22 .... **26** B2
Thurmond Rd *FUFL* SO22 ..... **26** B2
Thursby Rd *CHCH/BSGR* BH23 .. **224** D6
Thurston Cl *CHFD* SO53 ...... **81** J1
Thwaite Rd *BKME/WDN* BH12 .. **235** G3
Thyme Av *FHAM* PO15 .... **135** H8
Tides Reach *WEND* SO18 ..... **107** J8
Tichborne Gv *HAV* PO9 .... **165** H3 ◻
Tichborne Rd *ELGH* SO50 ..... **81** L8
  WEND SO18 .... **108** C7
Tichborne Wy
  LSOL/BMARY PO13 ...... **185** H7
Tickleford Dr *ITCH* SO19 ...... **132** C7
Tickner Rd *HEND* SO30 .... **134** B3 ◻
Ticonderoga Gdns *ITCH* SO19 . **132** C7
Tides Wy *TOTT* SO40 .... **130** D6
Tideway Gdns *ENEY* PO4 ..... **212** A4
Tidworth Rd *HAV* PO9 .... **165** K4
Tiffany Cl *LYMN* SO41 .... **226** D4 ◻
Tiffield Cl *HSEA* PO3 .... **188** A4
Tilbrook Rd *WSHM* SO15 ..... **105** M8
Tilburg Rd *CHCH/BSGR* BH23 .. **238** C1
Tilden Rd *RWIN* SO21 .... **54** B3
Tilebarn La *BROC* SO42 ...... **201** K2
Tilford Rd *HORN* PO8 .... **140** D2
Tillington Gdns *HORN* PO8 .... **116** C4 ◻
Tilmore Gdns *PSF* GU32 ...... **63** L3

Tilmore Rd *PSF* GU32 .... **63** L3
Timberlane *WVILLE* PO7 ...... **164** B4
Timberley La *RSAL* SP5 .... **73** M2
Timberly Cl *FAWY* SO45 ...... **180** A4
The Timbers *FHAM* PO15 ..... **160** A7
Timor Cl *HLER* SO31 .... **134** F8
Timothy Cl *NBNE* BH10 ...... **220** B3
Timpson Rd *PSEA* PO1 .... **211** J2
Timsbury Dr *ROWN* SO16 .... **105** L6
Timson Cl *TOTT* SO40 .... **129** G2 ◻
Tincleton Gdns
  MOOR/WNTN BH9 ...... **220** F4
Tindale Rd *ROWN* SO16 ...... **105** K6
Tinker Aly *ELGH* SO50 .... **107** M1
Tinneys Cl *RSAL* SP5 .... **73** J4
Tintagel Wy *CHAM* PO6 ...... **186** F1
Tintern Cl *CHAM* PO6 .... **162** D7
Tintern Gv *WSHM* SO15 ...... **4** C1
Tintern Rd *GPORT* PO12 ...... **10** D3
Tipner Gn *NEND* PO2 .... **187** G5 ◻
Tipner La *NEND* PO2 .... **186** F5
Tipner Rd *NEND* PO2 .... **187** G6
Tipper La *EPSF* GU31 .... **93** G5
Tiptoe Rd *NMIL/BTOS* BH25 ... **200** A7
Tiptree Cl *ELGH* SO50 .... **81** M3
Tisted Ct *FAWY* SO45 .... **165** M3 ◻◻
Titchfield Hl *FHAM/STUB* PO14 . **159** L8
Titchfield La *FHAM* PO15 .... **136** A8
  WHAM PO17 .... **136** A7
Titchfield Park Rd *FHAM* PO15 . **159** H5
Titchfield Rd
  FHAM/STUB PO14 .... **183** L1
Tithe Barn *LYMN* SO41 ...... **228** C3
Tithelands La *NARL* SO24 .... **31** L4
The Tithe *WVILLE* PO7 .... **139** K5 ◻
Tithewood Cl *CHFD* SO53 .... **53** G6 ◻
Titus Gdns *WVILLE* PO7 ...... **140** E8
Tivoli Cl *CHFD* SO53 .... **81** H6
Toby St *PSEA* PO1 .... **211** G2 ◻◻
Todber Cl *BWD* BH11 .... **219** H5 ◻
Tokar St *ENEY* PO4 .... **211** L6
Tokio Rd *HSEA* PO3 .... **187** L7
Tolefrey Gdns *NBAD* SO52 .... **80** E2 ◻
Tollard Cl *BKME/WDN* BH12 ... **219** J8
Tollbar Wy *HEND* SO30 .... **108** F8
Tollerford Rd *CHFD* BH17 .... **218** B6
Tollgate *CHFD* SO53 .... **81** H6
Tollgate Rd *HLER* SO31 ...... **134** B8
Tolpuddle Gdns
  MOOR/WNTN BH9 ...... **220** F4
Tolstoi Rd *PSTN* BH14 .... **233** M2
Toms La *RGWD* BH24 .... **123** L8
Tonbridge St *SSEA* PO5 ...... **13** H7
Tonge Rd *BWD* BH11 .... **219** M2
Tonnant Cl
  FHAM/STUB PO14 .... **184** B7 ◻
Toogoods Wy *ROWN* SO16 ... **105** J3
Toomer Cl *FAWY* SO45 ...... **180** C6
Toothill Rd *ROMY* SO51 ...... **79** H7
Topaz Gr *WVILLE* PO7 .... **140** F8
Topiary Gdns *HLER* SO31 ..... **158** F4
Top La *RGWD* BH24 .... **170** E1
Torbay Rd *PSTN* BH14 .... **234** B5
Torberry Dr *EPSF* GU31 ...... **64** A6
Torch Cl *ELGH* SO50 .... **83** G6 ◻
Tor Cl *FHAM/PORC* PO16 .... **161** J7
Torcross Cl *ITCH* SO19 ...... **132** C6 ◻
Torfrida Ct *ENEY* PO4 .... **212** A3
Tornay Gv *NBAD* SO52 .... **79** L4
Toronto Pl *GPORT* PO12 ..... **10** F2
Toronto Rd *NEND* PO2 .... **211** J1
Torquay Av *GPORT* PO12 .... **185** L8
  WSHM SO15 .... **106** B8
Torque Cl *ITCH* SO19 .... **133** J4
Torre Cl *ELGH* SO50 .... **81** M2
Torridge Gdns *WEND* SO18 ... **108** A5 ◻
Torrington Cl *ITCH* SO19 .... **132** E4 ◻
Torrington Rd *NEND* PO2 .... **187** J5
Tortworth Cl *FHAM/STUB* PO14 . **6** A8
Tor Wy *EPSF* GU31 .... **64** A6
Torwood Gdns *ELGH* SO50 ... **82** E6
Tosson Cl *ROWN* SO16 ...... **105** K8 ◻
Tote La *MIDH* GU29 .... **67** K2
Totland Cl *ROWN* SO16 ...... **105** K8
Totland Rd *CHAM* PO6 ...... **187** J1
  LSOL/BMARY PO13 ..... **185** G6
Totmel Rd *CHFD* BH17 ...... **218** E6
Totnes Cl *ELGH* SO50 .... **81** L3
Tottehale Cl *NBAD* SO52 ..... **79** L5
Tottenham Rd *PSEA* PO1 .... **211** J2
Totton By-pass *TOTT* SO40 ... **129** L2
Tournerbury La *HISD* PO11 ... **213** L4
Tourney Rd *BWD* BH11 ...... **219** H2
Tower Gdns *GPORT* PO12 ... **209** H5
Tower Gdns *HAV* PO9 .... **189** K2
Tower La *ELGH* SO50 .... **82** B6
  WIMB BH21 .... **192** B2
Tower Pl *HEND* SO30 .... **108** C7
Tower Rd *BMTH* BH1 .... **236** D3
  CCLF BH13 .... **235** G4
  ENEY PO4 .... **211** K5
  WINC SO23 .... **2** F6
Tower Rd West *CCLF* BH13 .. **234** F7
Towers Farm *WIMB* BH21 ... **217** H1 ◻
Tower St *EMRTH* PO10 ...... **166** B8
  PSEA PO1 .... **12** B5
  WINC SO23 .... **2** F7
Towers Wy *WIMB* BH21 ..... **217** H1
Towngate Br *PLE* BH15 ...... **233** H6
Town Hall Rd *HAV* PO9 ...... **8** F5
Townhill Wy *WEND* SO18 .... **107** M7
Town La *EPSF* GU31 .... **64** A3
Town Quay *SHAM* SO14 ..... **4** F7
Townsend Cl *BWD* BH11 .... **219** M2 ◻
Townsend La *FBDG* SP6 ..... **68** D2
Townsville Rd
  MOOR/WNTN BH9 ...... **220** F6
Towpath Md *ENEY* PO4 ...... **212** A4 ◻
Toynbee Cl *ELGH* SO50 ...... **81** M5
Toynbee Rd *ELGH* SO50 ..... **81** M5
Tozer Cl *BWD* BH11 .... **219** K6
Trafalgar Cl *CHFD* SO53 ..... **81** G3 ◻
Trafalgar Ct *FHAM/STUB* PO14 . **184** D1
Trafalgar Rd
  MOOR/WNTN BH9 ...... **235** L1

Trafalgar Sq *GPORT* PO12 .... **10** E1
Trafalgar St *WINC* SO23 ...... **2** F8
Trafalgar Wy *FAWY* SO45 .... **155** M7
Trafford Wy *ELGH* SO50 ...... **83** G7
Trampers La *WHAM* PO17 .... **137** L7
Tranby Rd *ITCH* SO19 .... **132** C4
Tranmere Cl *LYMN* SO41 .... **228** D6
Tranmere Rd *ENEY* PO4 ..... **211** M5 ◻
Treadwheel Rd *HORN* PO8 ... **141** L2
Treagore Rd *TOTT* SO40 ..... **104** B7 ◻
Trearnan Cl *ROWN* SO16 .... **105** L8
Treble Cl *FUFL* SO22 .... **26** A4
Tredegar Rd *ENEY* PO4 ..... **211** K5
Treebys Cl *CHCH/BSGR* BH23 . **223** H7
Treeside Cl *CHCH/BSGR* BH23 . **224** A6
Treeside Av *TOTT* SO40 ...... **129** L1
Treeside Rd *WSHM* SO15 .... **106** B8
Tree Side Wy *WVILLE* PO7 ... **140** C7
Trefoil Cl *WVILLE* PO7 .... **164** D1
Trefoil Wy *CHCH/BSGR* BH23 . **224** A5
Tregaron Av *CHAM* PO6 ..... **187** M1
Tregonwell Rd *WCLF* BH2 .... **14** D6
Treloar Rd *HISD* PO11 .... **214** C7
Treloyhan Cl *CHFD* SO53 .... **81** J4
Tremona Rd *ROWN* SO16 .... **106** A5
Trenley Cl *FAWY* SO45 .... **180** A5
Trent Cl *WEND* SO18 .... **107** L7 ◻
Trentham Av *LTDN* BH7 ...... **221** M8
Trentham Cl *LTDN* BH7 ...... **221** M8
Trent Rd *WEND* SO18 .... **107** L7
Trent Wy *FERN* BH22 .... **194** E2
Tresillian Gdns *WEND* SO18 .. **108** A6 ◻
Tresillian Wy
  CHCH/BSGR BH23 ...... **224** F6
Trevis Rd *ENEY* PO4 .... **212** A4
Trevone Cl *TOTT* SO40 ...... **129** J3 ◻
Trevor Rd *ENEY* PO4 .... **211** K6
Trevose Cl *CHFD* SO53 ...... **81** J4 ◻
  LSOL/BMARY PO13 ..... **185** G7
Trevose Crs *CHFD* SO53 ..... **81** J3
Trevose Wy *FHAM/STUB* PO14 . **158** F7
Triangle La *FHAM/STUB* PO14 . **183** J4
The Triangle *RSAL* SP5 ...... **47** G4 ◻
  WCLF BH2 .... **14** C6
Tribe Rd *GPORT* PO12 .... **10** D2
Tricketts La *FERN* BH22 ...... **194** D2
Trigon Rd *PLE* BH15 .... **233** J1
Trimaran Cl *HLER* SO31 ..... **158** C7
Trimaran Rd *HLER* SO31 ..... **158** C7 ◻
Trimm's Dro *FBDG* SP6 ...... **72** D8
Trinidad Crs
  BKME/WDN BH12 ...... **219** G8
Trinity Cl *GPORT* PO12 ...... **11** K4
Trinity Gn *GPORT* PO12 ..... **11** L4
Trinity Rd *BMTH* BH1 .... **15** H4
  SHAM SO14 .... **5** H1
Trinity St *FHAM/PORC* PO16 .. **7** J5
Tristan Cl *FAWY* SO45 ...... **207** J1
Triumph Cl *FHAM* PO15 ..... **6** B3
Triumph Rd *FHAM/STUB* PO14 . **184** D3
Troak Cl *CHCH/BSGR* BH23 .. **223** J8
Trojan Wy *WVILLE* PO7 ...... **164** D5
Troon Crs *CHAM* PO6 .... **164** A7
Troon Rd *WIMB* BH21 ...... **217** L3
Trosnant Rd *HAV* PO9 ...... **8** C2
Trotton Rd *EPSF* GU31 ...... **66** C8
Trotts La *TOTT* SO40 .... **130** A4
Trowbridge Cl *ROWN* SO16 .. **105** K2
Truman Rd *BWD* BH11 ...... **219** M4
Truro Ri *ELGH* SO50 .... **82** D5
Truro Rd *CHAM* PO6 .... **162** D8
Truscott Av
  MOOR/WNTN BH9 ...... **235** M1
Trussell Cl *FUFL* SO22 ...... **2** A1
Trussell Crs *FUFL* SO22 ..... **2** A1
Tuckers La *PLE* BH15 .... **232** E7
Tucks Cl *CHCH/BSGR* BH23 .. **197** L7
Tuckton Cl *SBNE* BH6 ...... **237** J4
Tuckton Rd *SBNE* BH6 ...... **237** J4
Tudor Av *EMRTH* PO10 ..... **166** C4
Tudor Cl *FBDG* SP6 .... **121** L3
  FHAM/PORC PO16 ..... **161** M7 ◻
  HISD PO11 .... **213** K6
  LSOL/BMARY PO13 .... **185** H8 ◻
  TOTT SO40 .... **104** B8
Tudor Ct *FHAM/STUB* PO14 .. **184** D1 ◻
  PLE BH15 .... **233** K2
Tudor Crs *CHAM* PO6 .... **187** K2
Tudor Gdns *HEND* SO30 .... **133** L3
Tudor Rd *BDST* BH18 .... **217** M4
Tudor Wood Cl *ROWN* SO16 . **106** E4 ◻
Tuffin Cl *ROWN* SO16 ...... **105** H3 ◻
Tukes Av *LSOL/BMARY* PO13 . **184** F4
Tulip Gdns *HAV* PO9 .... **165** G6
  HLER SO31 .... **158** D5
Tulip Rd *ROWN* SO16 ...... **107** H4 ◻
Tumulus Cl *ITCH* SO19 ..... **133** K4 ◻
Tunstall Rd *CHAM* PO6 ..... **163** H7
  ITCH SO19 .... **133** J4
Tunworth Ct *HAV* PO9 ..... **165** M3 ◻◻
Tuppenny La *EMRTH* PO10 .. **167** G8
Turbary Cl *BKME/WDN* BH12 . **219** J8
Turbary Ct *UPTN* BH16 ..... **217** G8 ◻
Turbary Park Av *BWD* BH11 . **219** K5
Turbary Rd *BKME/WDN* BH12 . **234** C1
  FERN BH22 .... **194** D1
Turks La *PSTN* BH14 .... **233** M7
Turlin Rd *UPTN* BH16 ...... **232** B4
Turnberry Cl
  CHCH/BSGR BH23 ..... **237** M2 ◻
Turner Av *LSOL/BMARY* PO13 . **185** J7
Turners Farm Crs
  LYMN SO41 .... **226** E6 ◻
Turnpike Down *WINC* SO23 .. **3** M7
Turnpike Wy *HEND* SO30 ... **133** L2
Turnstone Gdns *ROWN* SO16 . **106** A3
Turnworth Cl *BDST* BH18 ... **218** A5
Turtle Cl *FHAM/STUB* PO14 .. **183** M4
Tuscan Wk *CHFD* SO53 ..... **81** K2
Tuscany Wy *WVILLE* PO7 .... **140** F8
The Tussocks *TOTT* SO40 ... **130** D6
Tutland Rd *NBAD* SO52 ..... **79** L4 ◻
Tutor Cl *HLER* SO31 .... **157** K5
Tutts La *WVILLE* SO51 ..... **76** D1
Tweedale Rd
  MOOR/WNTN BH9 ...... **221** G5

Tweed Cl *CHFD* SO53 .... **80** F1
Tweed La *LYMN* SO41 .... **202** B8
Twemlow Av *PSTN* BH14 .... **233** L6
Twiggs End Cl *HLER* SO31 ... **158** D4
Twiggs La *MINS* SO40 ...... **154** A3
Twiggs Lane End *TOTT* SO40 . **154** A1
Twin Oaks Cl *BDST* BH18 ... **217** M5
Twyford Av *NEND* PO2 ...... **187** H7
  WSHM SO15 .... **106** B7
Twyford Cl *CHAR* BH8 ...... **221** H6
Twyford Rd *ELGH* SO50 ..... **82** A2
Twyford St *WINC* SO23 ..... **3** G7
Twynham Av
  CHCH/BSGR BH23 ..... **237** M2
Twynham Rd *RSAL* SP5 ..... **72** E2
Twyneham Av *BKME/WDN* BH12 . **218** F8
Twyneham Rd *SBNE* BH6 .... **237** L4 ◻
Twynhams Hl *BPWT* SO32 ... **111** M8
Tylers Cl *LYMN* SO41 .... **228** B3
The Tyleshades *ROMY* SO51 . **78** F2 ◻
Tyne Cl *CHFD* SO53 .... **80** F3
Tynedale Cl *GPORT* PO12 ... **185** K8 ◻
  MOOR/WNTN BH9 ...... **221** G4
Tyneham Av *BKME/WDN* BH12 . **218** F8
Tyne Wy *HEND* SO30 .... **108** D6
Tyrell Rd *CHFD* SO53 .... **81** H1
Tyrells La *RGWD* BH24 ..... **172** C4
Tyrrell Gdns *CHAR* BH8 ..... **221** L6
Tyrrells Ct *CHCH/BSGR* BH23 . **197** M7
Tyseley Rd *SSEA* PO5 ...... **13** H3
Tytherley Gn *CHAR* BH8 .... **221** H6
Tytherley Rd *WEND* SO18 ... **108** B8

U

Uddens Dr *WIMB* BH21 ..... **193** J2
Ullswater Av *WEND* SO18 ... **108** A7
Ullswater Rd *ROWN* SO16 ... **105** K7
  WIMB BH21 .... **192** A6
Undercliff Rd *BMTH* BH1 .... **15** H7
Undercliff Rd *BOSC* BH5 .... **236** C5
Underdown Av *WVILLE* PO7 .. **164** B4
Undershore *LYMN* SO41 .... **228** E4
Underwood Cl *CHFD* BH17 .. **217** M7 ◻
  ROWN SO16 .... **106** D4 ◻
Underwood Rd *ELGH* SO50 .. **82** C4
  ROWN SO16 .... **106** D4 ◻
Unicorn Rd *LSOL/BMARY* PO13 . **208** B1
  PSEA PO1 .... **210** F2
Union Pl *PSEA* PO1 .... **211** H2
Union Rd *HAV* PO9 .... **8** D4
  SHAM SO14 .... **131** M2
Union St *FHAM/PORC* PO16 .. **7** M6
  PSEA PO1 .... **12** D1
  WINC SO23 .... **3** J7
University Crs *PTSW* SO17 .. **107** G5
University Pkwy *ROWN* SO16 . **80** B7
University Rd *PTSW* SO17 ... **106** F5
Unwin Cl *ITCH* SO19 ...... **132** B7
Upham St *BPWT* SO32 ..... **84** B4
Uphill Rd *FUFL* SO22 ...... **16** A3
Upland La *LISS* GU33 ...... **35** M1
Uplands Av *NMIL/BTOS* BH25 . **225** L8
Uplands Crs *FERN* BH22 .... **168** E8
Uplands Crs *FHAM/PORC* PO16 . **7** J3
Uplands Rd *CHAM* PO6 .... **164** A7
  CHAR BH8 .... **221** G6
  FERN BH22 .... **168** D4
  FUFL SO22 .... **2** C1
  HAV PO9 .... **142** A6
  WVILLE PO7 .... **138** F2
Uplands Wy *PTSW* SO17 ... **106** F6
Uplyme Cl *CHFD* BH17 .... **218** E6
Upper Arundel St *PSEA* PO1 . **13** H1
Upper Banister St
  WSHM SO15 .... **131** K2 ◻
Upper Barn Copse *ELGH* SO50 . **83** G5
Upper Bere Wd *WVILLE* PO7 . **164** D2
Upper Brook Dr *HLER* SO31 . **158** C5
Upper Brook St *WINC* SO23 . **3** G7
Upper Brownhill Rd
  ROWN SO16 .... **105** L5
Upper Bugle St *SHAM* SO14 . **4** F5
Upper Church Rd *BPWT* SO32 . **136** C1
Upper Common Rd
  LYMN SO41 .... **227** K4 ◻
Upper Cornaway La
  FHAM/PORC PO16 .... **161** M8
Upper Crabbick La *WVILLE* PO7 . **139** G3
Upper Crescent Rd *NBAD* SO52 . **79** L4
Upper Deacon Rd *ITCH* SO19 . **132** F2
Upper Golf Links Rd
  BDST BH18 .... **217** M3
Upper Gordon Rd
  CHCH/BSGR BH23 .... **224** E7
Upper Heyshott *EPSF* GU31 .. **63** M5
Upper High St *FUFL* SO22 .. **2** E6
Upper Hinton Rd *BMTH* BH1 . **14** F6
Upper House St *WHAM* PO17 . **136** E5
Upper Lamborough La
  NARL SO24 .... **30** D2
Upper Market St *ELGH* SO50 . **82** A5
Upper Mead Cl *ELGH* SO50 . **83** J6 ◻
Upper Moors Rd *ELGH* SO50 . **54** E7
  RWIN SO21 .... **54** E7
Upper Mt *LISS* GU33 ...... **36** D5
Upper Mullin's La *FAWY* SO45 . **155** J5
Upper New Rd *HEND* SO30 . **108** C7
Upper Northam Cl
  HEND SO30 .... **133** L2
Upper Northam Dr
  HEND SO30 .... **133** J2
Upper Northam Rd
  HEND SO30 .... **133** L1
Upper Norwich Rd *WCLF* BH2 . **14** B6
Upper Old St
  FHAM/STUB PO14 .... **183** M4
Upper Piece *WVILLE* PO7 ... **139** L5
Upper St Helens Rd
  HEND SO30 .... **133** M4
Upper Shaftesbury Av
  PTSW SO17 .... **107** G6
Upper Shirley Av *WSHM* SO15 . **106** B7
Upper Spinney *HLER* SO31 .. **158** A8
Upper Terrace Rd *WCLF* BH2 . **14** D6

Upper Toothill Rd *ROWN* SO16 . **79** K7
Upper Wardown *EPSF* GU31 .. **64** A4
Upper Weston La *ITCH* SO19 . **132** E6
Upper Whf *FHAM/PORC* PO16.. **7** L7
Uppleby Rd *BKME/WDN* BH12 . **234** B3 ◻
Upton Cl *HAV* PO9 .... **165** H1
  UPTN BH16 .... **232** A1
Upton Ct *UPTN* BH16 ...... **232** B1 ◻
Upton Crs *ROWN* SO16 ..... **105** H1
Upton Grey Cl *FUFL* SO22 ... **16** C5
Upton Heath Est *UPTN* BH16 . **232** C1
Upton La *ROWN* SO16 ...... **105** G3
Upton Rd *CHFD* BH17 ...... **232** D1
Upton Wy *BDST* BH18 ...... **217** J5
Upwey Av *PLE* BH15 .... **232** D5
Utrecht Ct *CHCH/BSGR* BH23 . **238** C1 ◻

V

Vadne Gdns *GPORT* PO12 ... **209** M2 ◻
Vaggs La *LYMN* SO41 ...... **226** C2
Vale Dr *WEND* SO18 .... **107** L7
Vale Gv *GPORT* PO12 ...... **209** L1
Valencia Cl
  CHCH/BSGR BH23 .... **222** B4 ◻
Valentine Av *ITCH* SO19 ... **133** G5
Valentine Cl *FHAM* PO15 ... **160** A5
Valentine Ct *WVILLE* PO7 .. **140** E8 ◻
Valerian Cl *ELGH* SO50 .... **109** H2 ◻
Valerian Rd *HEND* SO30 ... **134** A2
Vale Rd *BMTH* BH1 .... **236** C4
  PSTN BH14 .... **234** D4
  RSAL SP5 .... **73** J2
  WINC SO23 .... **27** G2
The Vale *FAWY* SO45 ...... **155** K5
  HLER SO31 .... **158** F4
  HORN PO8 .... **116** B7
  SSEA PO5 .... **13** H8
Valetta Pk *EMRTH* PO10 ... **166** C8
Valetta Rd *EMRTH* PO10 ... **191** H7
Valette Rd *MOOR/WNTN* BH9 . **220** D5
Valiant Gdns *NEND* PO2 .... **187** H4
Valiant Rd *EMRTH* PO10 .... **191** H7
Valley Cl *CHCH/BSGR* BH23 . **239** G1
Valley Cl *CHCH/BSGR* BH23 . **222** C5
  FAWY SO45 .... **180** C5 ◻
  RSAL SP5 .... **73** J2
  RWIN SO21 .... **54** E8
  WVILLE PO7 .... **164** A5
Valleydene *FAWY* SO45 .... **155** K6
Valley Hl *FUFL* SO22 ...... **16** B3
Valley La *CHCH/BSGR* BH23 . **198** C4
Valley Park Dr *HORN* PO8 .. **116** C5
Valley Ri *HLER* SO31 ...... **158** C4
Valley Rd *CHAR* BH8 ...... **221** K5
  CHFD SO53 .... **81** K1
  FUFL SO22 .... **16** A3
  TOTT SO40 .... **129** K3
The Valley *FUFL* SO22 ..... **26** C2
Valley Vw *BKME/WDN* BH12 . **235** G1
Valley Wk *BPWT* SO32 ..... **57** H6
Vallis Cl *PLE* BH15 .... **233** J7
Valsheba Dr *FHAM/STUB* PO14 . **183** M7
Vanburgh Wy *CHFD* SO53 ... **53** C7
Vanguard Hl *BPWT* SO32 ... **16** B2
Vanguard Rd *CHAR* BH8 ... **221** J7
  PLE BH15 .... **233** H6 ◻
  WEND SO18 .... **107** M8 ◻
Vanstone Rd
  LSOL/BMARY PO13 ... **185** H8
Vardy Cl *ITCH* SO19 ...... **133** H5 ◻
Varna Rd *WSHM* SO15 .... **131** G3
Varos Cl *GPORT* PO12 ..... **209** L2
Varsity Rd *EMRTH* PO10 ... **191** H7
Vaudrey Cl *WSHM* SO15 ... **106** B7 ◻
Vaughan Cl *ITCH* SO19 .... **133** J3
Vaughan Rd *FAWY* SO45 ... **155** G4 ◻
Vauxhall Wy *PSF* GU32 .... **63** K5
Veal's La *TOTT* SO40 ...... **154** F2
Vear's La *RWIN* SO21 ..... **54** F8
Vecta Cl *CHCH/BSGR* BH23 . **239** F7
Vectis Rd *GPORT* PO12 .... **209** J5
  NMIL/BTOS BH25 .... **240** C1
Vectis Wy *CHAM* PO6 ..... **187** K1
Velder Av *ENEY* PO4 ...... **211** L3
Vellan Ct *ROWN* SO16 ..... **105** H7
Velmore Rd *CHFD* SO53 ... **81** G4
Velsheda Ct *FAWY* SO45 ... **155** G4
Velvet Lawn Rd
  NMIL/BTOS BH25 .... **225** K4
Venator Pl *WIMB* BH21 .... **192** A2
Venerable Rd
  FHAM/STUB PO14 .... **184** E3
Vengeance Rd
  LSOL/BMARY PO13 ... **208** C1
Venice Cl *WVILLE* PO7 .... **140** E8
Venning Av *BWD* BH11 .... **219** H3
Ventnor Rd *ENEY* PO4 ..... **13** M4 ◻
  LSOL/BMARY PO13 ... **184** F5
Ventnor Wy *FHAM/PORC* PO16.. **161** J7
Ventry Cl *CHFD* BH17 ..... **234** E4
Ventura Pl *UPTN* BH16 .... **232** C2
Venture Rd *ROWN* SO16 ... **80** C7
Verbena Crs *HORN* PO8 ... **140** F8
Verbena Wy *HEND* SO30 ... **134** B2 ◻
Verdon Av *HLER* SO31 ..... **157** J5
Verger Cl *FHAM/STUB* PO14 . **159** G5 ◻
Verity Crs *CHFD* BH17 ..... **218** E7
Vermont Cl *ROWN* SO16 ... **106** E4
Vernalls Cl *NBNE* BH10 .... **220** B4
Vernalls Gdns *NBNE* BH10 .. **220** B3
Verne Rd *VWD* BH31 ...... **144** E3
Verney Cl *BWD* BH11 ..... **219** M5
Verney Rd *BWD* BH11 ..... **219** L5
Vernham Rd *FUFL* SO22 ... **2** D4
Verno La *CHCH/BSGR* BH23 . **224** A6
Vernon Av *ENEY* PO4 ..... **211** L4
Vernon Cl *GPORT* PO12 ... **10** D2
Vernon Hl *BPWT* SO32 .... **85** H6
Vernon Rd *GPORT* PO12 ... **10** D2
  HSEA PO3 .... **187** L6
Verona Av *SBNE* BH6 ..... **237** J5
Verona Rd *CHFD* SO53 .... **81** K1
Verulam Pl *BMTH* BH1 .... **14** F5
Verulam Rd *PLE* BH15 .... **233** L7
  SHAM SO14 .... **131** M1 ◻

Verwood Crs SBNE BH6 .... 237 M4
Verwood Rd HAV PO9 ...... 165 M2 [13]
  RCWD BH24 .... 145 L7
  WIMB BH21 .... 144 D7
Veryan FHAM PO15 .... 6 C6
Vespasian Rd WEND SO18 ...... 132 B3
Vespasian Wy CHFD SO53 ...... 81 K2
Vesta Wy CHFD SO53 ...... 81 K1
Vetch CI CHCH/BSGR BH23 ...... 223 M8
Vian CI LSOL/BMARY PO13 ...... 185 G4
Vian Rd WVILLE PO7 .... 164 B2
Vicarage Dr HEND SO30 ...... 133 M3
Vicarage Gdns LYMN SO41 ...... 226 E6 [2]
Vicarage La BPWT SO32 ...... 112 B2
  FHAM PO14 .... 184 A5
  LYMN SO41 .... 226 E6
  TOTT SO40 .... 103 C2
  WVILLE PO7 .... 114 C5
Vicarage Pk RSAL SP5 ...... 73 J2
Vicarage Rd
  MOOR/WNTN BH9 ...... 220 C7
  PLE BH15 .... 233 H3
  RSAL SP5 .... 73 M3
  TOTT SO40 .... 130 D7
  VWD BH31 .... 144 D2
Vicarage Wy
  CHCH/BSGR BH23 ...... 223 M6
Vice La ROMY SO51 ...... 101 M4
Viceroy Rd ITCH SO19 ...... 132 E5
Vickers CI CHAR BH8 ...... 221 M6
Vickery Wy CHCH/BSGR BH23 ... 223 J8
Victena Rd ELGH SO50 ...... 83 K6
Victoria Av HISD PO11 ...... 213 K5
  MOOR/WNTN BH9 ...... 220 C7
  WVILLE PO7 .... 163 M5
Victoria CI HLER SO31 ...... 158 E7
  WIMB BH21 .... 217 H4
Victoria Crs BKME/WDN BH12 ... 234 D4
Victoria Gdns FBDG SP6 ...... 97 J7
  FERN BH22 .... 194 B3
  RCWD BH24 .... 170 E2 [2]
Victoria Gld HLER SO31 ...... 157 C3
Victoria Gv SSEA PO5 ...... 13 K6
Victoria Park Rd
  MOOR/WNTN BH9 ...... 220 C7
Victoria PI BMTH BH1 ...... 15 M1
  GPORT PO12 .... 10 F4 [3]
  LYMN SO41 .... 228 C6
Victoria Rd BKME/WDN BH12 ... 234 B2
  BMTH BH1 .... 15 M2
  BPWT SO32 .... 85 G8
  CHCH/BSGR BH23 ...... 238 D3
  ELGH SO50 .... 82 A3
  EMRTH PO10 .... 166 C7
  FBDG SP6 .... 97 J7
  FERN BH22 .... 194 B2
  HISD PO11 .... 189 K6
  HLER SO31 .... 156 E2
  ITCH SO19 .... 132 B7 [4]
  LYMN SO41 .... 242 A4
  PSEA PO1 .... 210 D2
  WINC SO23 .... 2 F5
  WVILLE PO7 .... 164 C1 [1]
Victoria Rd North SSEA PO5 ... 13 L3
Victoria Rd South SSEA PO5 ... 13 J7
Victoria Sq GPORT PO12 ...... 11 G2
  PSEA PO1 .... 211 G1
  SHAM SO14 .... 5 L2
Victor Rd EMRTH PO10 ...... 191 H7
  HSEA PO3 .... 211 K1 [3]
Victor St WSHM SO15 ...... 106 B8 [2]
Victory Av HORN PO8 ...... 140 E2
Victory CI CHFD SO53 ...... 81 G3
Victory Crs WSHM SO15 ...... 130 F2 [1]
Victory Gn NEND PO2 ...... 187 G6 [1]
Victory Rd FHAM/STUB PO14 ... 184 B4
  PSEA PO1 .... 12 C2 [3]
  WSHM SO15 .... 130 F2
Victory Sq WSHM SO15 ...... 130 F2 [2]
Viewside CI WIMB BH21 ...... 217 G3
Viking CI FAWY SO45 ...... 180 C8
  FHAM/STUB PO14 ...... 183 M5
  ROWN SO16 .... 105 K3
  SBNE BH6 .... 237 M4
The Vikings ROMY SO51 ...... 79 G1 [3]
Viking Wy CHCH/BSGR BH23 ... 238 F3
  HORN PO8 .... 116 B5
  SBNE BH6 .... 237 M4
Villa Gdns WVILLE PO7 ...... 140 C8
Village CI FHAM/STUB PO14 ... 184 A6
Village Rd GPORT PO12 ...... 10 D7
Village St PSF GU32 ...... 64 A2
Ville De Paris Rd
  FHAM/STUB PO14 ...... 184 E3
Villette CI CHCH/BSGR BH23 ... 222 E7
Villiers Rd FAWY SO45 ...... 155 K8
  SSEA PO5 .... 13 H8
  WSHM SO15 .... 131 G1
Vimoutiers Ct FBDG SP6 ...... 97 K7 [2]
Vince CI BWD BH11 ...... 219 M4
Vincent Av ROWN SO16 ...... 106 B6
Vincent CI NMIL/BTOS BH25 ... 225 L6
Vincent Gv FHAM/PORC PO16 ... 186 A1
Vincent Rd NMIL/BTOS BH25 ... 225 K5
  WSHM SO15 .... 106 B8
Vincent's Gv WSHM SO15 ...... 106 B8 [1]
Vincent St WSHM SO15 ...... 106 A8
Vincent's Wk SHAM SO14 ...... 5 G4
Vine Bank WEND SO18 ...... 108 A8
Vine CI HLER SO31 ...... 158 B5
  LTDN BH7 .... 236 F1
Vine Coppice WVILLE PO7 ...... 164 C4
Vine Farm CI
  BKME/WDN BH12 ...... 220 A8 [3]
Vine Farm Rd
  BKME/WDN BH12 ...... 219 M8
Vinegar HI LYMN SO41 ...... 242 C3
Vineries CI WIMB BH21 ...... 192 D2
The Vineries WIMB BH21 ...... 192 D2
Vine Rd ROWN SO16 ...... 105 M5
Vinery Gdns ROWN SO16 ...... 106 A6
Vinery Rd ROWN SO16 ...... 106 B6 [1]
Vineside LSOL/BMARY PO13 ... 185 J7
The Vineyards NBAD SO52 ...... 79 M4
Viney Av ROMY SO51 ...... 51 G8
Viney Rd LYMN SO41 ...... 228 C7

Vinnells La PSF GU32 ...... 60 C1
Vinneys CI CHCH/BSGR BH23 ... 223 G6
Vinson Rd LISS GU33 ...... 36 F4
Violet CI NBAD SO52 ...... 80 F2
Violet La FHAM/STUB PO14 ... 183 M8
Violet Rd ROWN SO16 ...... 106 F4
Virginia CI BKME/WDN BH12 ... 234 B1 [1]
Virginia Park Rd GPORT PO12 ... 209 K2
Viscount Dr CHCH/BSGR BH23 ... 239 J2
Viscount Wk BWD BH11 ...... 219 H2
  WIMB BH21 .... 219 G3
Vita Rd NEND PO2 ...... 187 J5
Vitre Gdns LYMN SO41 ...... 228 C6
Vivash Rd PSEA PO1 ...... 13 L2 [4]
Vixen CI FHAM/STUB PO14 ... 183 M6
Vixen Wk NMIL/BTOS BH25 ... 225 M3
Vokes CI ITCH SO19 ...... 132 F3
Vulcan CI WSHM SO15 ...... 130 D2
Vulcan Rd EMRTH PO10 ...... 191 H7
  WSHM SO15 .... 130 D2
Vyse La SHAM SO14 ...... 4 F6 [2]

W

Wade Court Rd HAV PO9 ...... 9 G6
Wade La HAV PO9 ...... 9 G8
Wadham Rd NEND PO2 ...... 187 H6
Wadhurst Gdns ITCH SO19 ...... 132 E8
Wadhurst Rd HEND SO30 ...... 134 A2
The Wad SELS SO20 ...... 215 K7
Wagtail Dr NMIL/BTOS BH25 ... 225 K6 [3]
Wagtail Rd HORN PO8 ...... 140 B7
Wagtail Wy FHAM/PORC PO16 ... 161 K8
Wainscott Rd ENEY PO4 ...... 211 L6
Wainsford CI LYMN SO41 ...... 227 M5
Wainsford Plantation
  LYMN SO41 .... 227 J8 [2]
Wainsford Rd LYMN SO41 ...... 227 J6
Wainwright CI CHAM PO6 ...... 188 A2
Wait End Rd WVILLE PO7 ...... 164 C1
Wakefield Av FHAM/PORC PO16... 6 F1
  NBNE BH10 .... 220 A6
Wakefield Ct WEND SO18 ...... 107 M7 [2]
Wakefield Rd WEND SO18 ...... 107 M7
Wakefords Wy HAV PO9 ...... 165 M2
Wakely Gdns BWD BH11 ...... 219 L3 [3]
Wakely Rd BWD BH11 ...... 219 M3
Walberton Av CHAM PO6 ...... 163 L8
Walcheren PI PLE BH15 ...... 232 B5
Walcott Av CHCH/BSGR BH23 ... 222 D7
Waldegrave CI ITCH SO19 ...... 132 B7 [4]
Walden Gdns HORN PO8 ...... 140 F1
Walden Rd NEND PO2 ...... 187 G6
Walditch Gdns CFDH BH17 ... 218 C6
Waldon Gdns WEND SO18 ...... 108 A6 [3]
Waldren CI PLE BH15 ...... 233 J6
Wales St WINC SO23 ...... 3 J7
Walford CI WIMB BH21 ...... 192 A2
Walford Rd CHAM PO6 ...... 163 G8
Walhampton HI LYMN SO41 ... 228 D3
Walker PI LSOL/BMARY PO13 ... 185 H7 [4]
Walker Rd NEND PO2 ...... 187 G6
Walkers CI ELGH SO50 ...... 83 J6 [3]
Walkers La North FAWY SO45 ... 180 D7
Walker's La South FAWY SO45 ... 206 D1
Walkford La NMIL/BTOS BH25 ... 225 G6
Walkford Rd CHCH/BSGR BH23... 225 G6
Walkford Wy
  CHCH/BSGR BH23 ...... 224 F7 [2]
Walkwood Av LTDN BH7 ...... 221 M8
Wallace La BROC SO42 ...... 204 A2
Wallace Rd BDST BH18 ...... 217 L5
  ITCH SO19 .... 132 D7 [3]
  NEND PO2 .... 187 K8
Wallington Ct
  FHAM/STUB PO14 ...... 184 D2 [1]
Wallington Dr CHFD SO53 ...... 52 B8
Wallington HI FHAM/PORC PO16 ... 7 L4
Wallington Rd NEND PO2 ...... 187 K7
Wallington Shore Rd
  FHAM/PORC PO16 ...... 7 M4
Wallington Wy
  FHAM/PORC PO16 ...... 7 L4
Walliscott Rd BWD BH11 ...... 219 L7
Wallisdean Av
  FHAM/STUB PO14 ...... 6 E8
  HSEA PO3 .... 211 M1
Wallisdown Rd
  BKME/WDN BH12 ...... 219 H6
Wallis Gdns WVILLE PO7 ...... 140 C7
Wallis Rd NBNE BH10 ...... 219 M7
  WVILLE PO7 .... 140 C7
Walmer CI ELGH SO50 ...... 81 M1
Walmer Rd PSEA PO1 ...... 13 M2
Walnut Av WEND SO18 ...... 107 K3
Walnut CI CHFD SO53 ...... 53 H6
  NMIL/BTOS BH25 ...... 225 K5
  ROWN SO16 .... 105 L7
Walnut Dr FHAM/STUB PO14... 183 M6
Walnut Gv FUFL SO22 ...... 2 B5
  ROWN SO16 .... 105 L8
Walnut Tree CI HISD PO11 ... 213 K5 [1]
Walnut Tree Dr EMRTH PO10 ... 167 J5
Walnwright Gdns HEND SO30 ... 109 H5
Walpole La HLER SO31 ...... 158 C1
Walpole Rd BMTH BH1 ...... 236 C3
  FUFL SO22 .... 26 B3
  GPORT PO12 .... 11 H3
Walsall St GPORT PO12 ...... 10 D4
  WVILLE PO7 .... 164 C1
Walsford Rd WBNE BH4 ...... 235 F3
Walsingham CI CHAM PO6 ...... 163 H7 [5]
Walsingham Dene LTDN BH7 ... 221 K8
Walsingham Gdns WEND SO18... 107 K5
Waltham CI BPWT SO32 ...... 86 F6
  FHAM/PORC PO16 ...... 162 A6
Waltham Crs ROWN SO16 ...... 106 A4
Waltham Rd LTDN BH7 ...... 237 G1
Waltham St SSEA PO5 ...... 12 F3 [1]
Walton CI GPORT PO12 ...... 10 D4
  WVILLE PO7 .... 164 C1
Walton Ct FHAM PO15 ...... 160 B4
Walton PI FUFL SO22 ...... 26 C1
Walton Rd CHAM PO6 ...... 188 A2

  GPORT PO12 .... 10 D4
  ITCH SO19 .... 133 H4 [2]
  NBNE BH10 .... 220 A6
  PLE BH15 .... 233 M2
Waltons Av FAWY SO45 ...... 180 B4
Wandesford PI GPORT PO12 ... 185 L7
Wangfield La BPWT SO32 ...... 110 B7
Wansbeck CI CHFD SO53 ...... 81 G3
Wanstead CI RGWD BH24 ...... 146 F8
Warbler CI HORN PO8 ...... 140 E1
  ROWN SO16 .... 106 A2
  UPTN BH16 .... 216 F8
Warblington Av HAV PO9 ...... 9 K5
Warblington CI CHFD SO53 ...... 81 G5 [5]
Warblington Rd EMRTH PO10... 190 C1
Warblington St PSEA PO1 ...... 12 D4
Warborne La LYMN SO41 ...... 228 E1
Warbrook Ct HAV PO9 ...... 165 M3 [13]
Warburton CI ITCH SO19 ...... 133 J4 [3]
Warburton Rd CFDH BH17 ... 218 C8 [3]
  ITCH SO19 .... 133 H3
Ward Crs EMRTH PO10 ...... 166 E5
Warden CI HEND SO30 ...... 108 C7 [3]
Wardens CI HISD PO11 ...... 213 K3
Wardle Rd ELGH SO50 ...... 82 C1
Ward Rd ENEY PO4 ...... 211 L6
Wardroom Rd NEND PO2 ...... 186 F7
Wareham Rd WIMB BH21 ...... 216 F5
Warfield Av WVILLE PO7 ...... 164 C1
Warfield Crs WVILLE PO7 ...... 164 C1
Warland Wy WIMB BH21 ...... 217 J1
Warlock CI ITCH SO19 ...... 133 H5 [2]
Warmwell CI CFDH BH17 ...... 218 D6
Warnes La RGWD BH24 ...... 172 D6
Warnford CI GPORT PO12 ...... 10 B4
Warnford Rd HAV PO9 ...... 165 H3
Warnford Rd LTDN BH7 ...... 237 G1
Warren Av CHCH/BSGR BH23 ... 238 E3
  CHFD SO53 .... 81 K3
  ENEY PO4 .... 211 M3
  HSEA PO3 .... 187 L4
  ROWN SO16 .... 105 M6
Warren CI CHFD SO53 ...... 81 K3
  HISD PO11 .... 213 K4
  RGWD BH24 .... 170 B3
  ROWN SO16 .... 105 M6
Warren Crs ROWN SO16 ...... 105 M6
Warren Dr RGWD BH24 ...... 170 B2
Warren Edge CI SBNE BH6 ... 237 L5 [3]
Warren Edge Rd SBNE BH6 ... 237 L5
Warren La BROC SO42 ...... 205 H8
  PSF GU32 .... 35 H3
  RGWD BH24 .... 170 B3
  RWIN SO21 .... 28 D8
Warren Pk LYMN SO41 ...... 241 M2
Warren PI TOTT SO40 ...... 104 B6
Warren Rd LISS GU33 ...... 36 F1
  PSTN BH14 .... 234 C4 [6]
  WBNE BH4 .... 235 G6
  WINC SO23 .... 3 M6
Warren Side EPSF GU31 ...... 93 G5
The Warrens RSAL SP5 ...... 44 D4
Warrior CI CHFD SO53 ...... 81 G4
Warrys CI FAWY SO45 ...... 155 L8
Warsash CI HAV PO9 ...... 165 J2 [3]
Warsash Gv
  LSOL/BMARY PO13 ...... 185 G6 [7]
Warsash Rd FHAM/STUB PO14 ... 159 J7
  HLER SO31 .... 158 B7
Warspite CI NEND PO2 ...... 187 H4
Warton CI BROC SO42 ...... 204 A2
Warwick Av NMIL/BTOS BH25 ... 225 M5
Warwick CI CHFD SO53 ...... 80 F4 [2]
  LSOL/BMARY PO13 ...... 208 E4
  WINC SO23 .... 3 G3
Warwick Crs SSEA PO5 ...... 13 H4
Warwick Rd LTDN BH7 ...... 236 F3
  PSTN BH14 .... 234 B5 [2]
  TOTT SO40 .... 104 E8 [1]
  WSHM SO15 .... 106 C6
Wasdale CI HORN PO8 ...... 116 B6
Washbrook Rd CHAM PO6 ...... 163 H8
Washington Av BMTH BH1 ... 236 C2
Washington Rd EMRTH PO10... 166 D7
  NEND PO2 .... 187 H8
Watcombe Rd SBNE BH6 ...... 237 J3
Waterbeech Dr HEND SO30 ... 109 H8 [3]
Waterberry Dr WVILLE PO7 ... 140 A7
Waterditch Rd
  CHCH/BSGR BH23 ...... 223 K5
Waterford CI LYMN SO41 ...... 228 D5
Waterford La PSTN BH14 ...... 233 M6 [3]
Waterford Gdns
  CHCH/BSGR BH23 ...... 239 M1
Waterford La LYMN SO41 ...... 228 D5
Waterford PI
  CHCH/BSGR BH23 ...... 239 M1
Waterford Rd
  CHCH/BSGR BH23 ...... 224 F8
  NMIL/BTOS BH25 ...... 225 L5
Waterhouse La WSHM SO15 ... 130 F2 [6]
Waterhouse Wy WSHM SO15 ... 130 F1
Water La FAWY SO45 ...... 155 J6
  SBNE BH6 .... 237 J1
  TOTT SO40 .... 104 C6
  WINC SO23 .... 3 J7
Waterlock Gdns ENEY PO4 ...... 212 B4
Waterloo CI HORN PO8 ...... 140 B5
Waterloo Rd CFDH BH17 ...... 218 A8
  GPORT PO12 .... 11 H9
  HAV PO9 .... 8 F3
  LYMN SO41 .... 228 D4
  MOOR/WNTN BH9 ...... 235 L1
  WIMB BH21 .... 216 F2
  WSHM SO15 .... 131 G2
Waterloo St SSEA PO5 ...... 13 H3
Waterloo Ter WSHM SO15 ...... 131 K2 [7]
Waterloo Wy RGWD BH24 ...... 170 E2 [3]
Watermain Rd RGWD BH24 ... 195 L3
Watermans La FAWY SO45 ...... 155 J7
Watermead Rd CHAM PO6 ...... 188 C1 [3]
Watermill Rd
  CHCH/BSGR BH23 ...... 222 E8
Water's Edge HEND SO30 ...... 133 M2
Waters Edge Gdns
  EMRTH PO10 .... 166 D8
Watersedge Rd CHAM PO6 ...... 162 E8 [2]

Waters Gn BROC SO42 ...... 175 L6 [2]
Waters Green Ct BROC SO42 ... 175 L6 [3]
Watership Dr RGWD BH24 ...... 171 H2
Waterside CHCH/BSGR BH23 ... 238 C4
  FAWY SO45 .... 155 K3
Waterside Gdns
  FHAM/PORC PO16 ...... 161 H7 [2]
Waterside La
  FHAM/PORC PO16 ...... 186 C2
Waterside Rd ROMY SO51 ...... 50 F7 [4]
Watersmeet
  FHAM/PORC PO16 ...... 184 F2
The Waters WHAM PO17 ...... 160 C3
Waterston CI CFDH BH17 ...... 218 B7 [8]
Water Tower Rd BDST BH18 ... 218 A4
Waterworks Rd CHAM PO6 ...... 164 B8
  PSF GU32 .... 63 H2
  RWIN SO21 .... 54 B4
Watery La CHCH/BSGR BH23 ... 223 L7
Watkin Rd BOSC BH5 ...... 236 F4
  HEND SO30 .... 109 K6 [1]
Watley CI ROWN SO16 ...... 105 J3
Watley La RWIN SO21 ...... 55 G3
Watson Av CHAR BH8 ...... 221 L6
Watson CI HEND SO30 ...... 134 A1
Watton CI CHAR BH8 ...... 221 L6
Watton La BPWT SO32 ...... 87 J6
Watton Rd FAWY SO45 ...... 180 A5
Watts CI ROWN SO16 ...... 105 K6
Watts Rd HEND SO30 ...... 134 A1
  PSEA PO1 .... 211 H1
Wavell Av CFDH BH17 ...... 217 L7
Wavell Rd BWD BH11 ...... 219 M4
  LSOL/BMARY PO13 ...... 185 H5
  WEND SO18 .... 132 E1
Wavell Wy FUFL SO22 ...... 26 B3
Wavendon Av
  NMIL/BTOS BH25 ...... 225 J8
Waveney CI
  LSOL/BMARY PO13 ...... 208 D2 [2]
Waveney Gn ROWN SO16 ...... 105 K7
Waverley Av HLER SO31 ...... 157 G2
Waverley CI FBDG SP6 ...... 97 L5
  ROMY SO51 .... 51 G7 [8]
Waverley Crs PLE BH15 ...... 233 J3
Waverley Gv ENEY PO4 ...... 13 L8
Waverley Rd CHAM PO6 ...... 164 A8
  FBDG SP6 .... 97 L5
  NMIL/BTOS BH25 ...... 225 M6
  SSEA PO5 .... 13 L7
  WSHM SO15 .... 4 A1
Wayfarer CI ENEY PO4 ...... 212 A3 [6]
  HLER SO31 .... 158 D7
Wayfarers LSOL/BMARY PO13... 209 H1
Wayfarer's Wk BPWT SO32 ... 58 B7
  HAV PO9 .... 165 G6
  HORN PO8 .... 89 K6
  NARL SO24 .... 58 A3
  WVILLE PO7 .... 163 M6
Waylands PI HEND SO30 ...... 133 L4
Wayman Rd BKME/WDN BH12... 217 J2 [2]
Wayne Rd BKME/WDN BH12 ... 234 A2
Waynflete CI BPWT SO32 ...... 85 H8
Waynflete PI FUFL SO22 ...... 26 C2 [3]
Wayside HLER SO31 ...... 134 B8
Wayside CI LYMN SO41 ...... 242 C3
Wayside Rd RGWD BH24 ...... 169 J7
  SBNE BH6 .... 237 K4
Waytown CI CFDH BH17 ...... 218 B7
Weald CI HLER SO31 ...... 158 E4
Weardale Rd CHFD SO53 ...... 81 J4
Weavers CI FERN BH22 ...... 168 C7 [2]
Weavers Gn HAV PO9 ...... 9 L1
Weavers PI CHFD SO53 ...... 53 G8
Weavills Rd ELGH SO50 ...... 82 F6
Webb CI HISD PO11 ...... 213 L6
Webb La HISD PO11 ...... 213 L6
Webb Rd FHAM/PORC PO16 ... 186 B2
Webbs CI RGWD BH24 ...... 169 H2
Webbs Gn BPWT SO32 ...... 113 G5
Webburn Gdns WEND SO18 ... 107 M5 [3]
Weber CI FUFL SO22 ...... 16 A7
Webster Rd
  MOOR/WNTN BH9 ...... 220 C5 [3]
  FHAM/STUB PO14 ...... 184 A6 [1]
Wedgewood CI FAWY SO45 ... 180 A4
Wedgewood Gdns
  CHCH/BSGR BH23 ...... 198 A7 [2]
Wedgewood Wy WVILLE PO7 ... 140 C6
Wedgwood Dr PSTN BH14 ...... 233 M6
Wedmore CI FUFL SO22 ...... 25 M5
Weeke CI RSAL SP5 ...... 72 C1 [1]
Weeke Manor CI FUFL SO22 ...... 2 A3
Welbeck Av PTSW SO17 ...... 107 G6
Welch CI ENEY PO4 ...... 13 M8
  GPORT PO12 .... 209 L1
Welch Wy ROWN SO16 ...... 105 K3
Welchwood CI HORN PO8 ...... 140 C6
Weldon Av BWD BH11 ...... 219 J3
Welland Gdns WEND SO18 ...... 108 A6
Welland Gn ROWN SO16 ...... 105 K8
Welland Rd WIMB BH21 ...... 192 B4
Wellands Rd LYND SO43 ...... 151 K3 [3]
Wellbrooke Gdns CHFD SO53 ... 81 G1
Well Copse CI HORN PO8 ...... 116 B7
Wellers CI TOTT SO40 ...... 128 F1
Wellesley Av
  CHCH/BSGR BH23 ...... 239 G1
  WEND SO18 .... 132 F1
Wellesley CI WVILLE PO7 ...... 164 C1
Wellesley Rd CHFD SO53 ...... 81 J2
Well House Av FBDG SP6 ...... 71 G5
Well House La FUFL SO22 ...... 16 D3
Wellington Av
  CHCH/BSGR BH23 ...... 239 H1
  WEND SO18 .... 132 F1
Wellington CI FAWY SO45 ...... 155 H7
  HORN PO8 .... 141 H2
Wellington Gv
  FHAM/PORC PO16 ...... 186 A1
Wellington Pk HEND SO30 ...... 108 F7
Wellington Rd CHAR BH8 ...... 15 G1
  PSTN BH14 .... 234 B5
  WEND SO18 .... 132 F1
Wellington St SSEA PO5 ...... 13 G3
Wellington Wy WVILLE PO7 ...... 164 C1 [5]

Well La BPWT SO32 ...... 112 A1
  FBDG SP6 .... 98 D6
  HLER SO31 .... 157 L6
  PLE BH15 .... 233 H4
Well Meadow HAV PO9 ...... 165 J2
Wellowbrook CI CHFD SO53 ... 80 F2 [2]
Wellow CI HAV PO9 ...... 8 B1
  WEND SO18 .... 133 G1
Wellow Dro ROMY SO51 ...... 76 D1
Wellow Gdns
  FHAM/STUB PO14 ...... 159 G6
Wellow Wood Rd ROMY SO51... 48 C8
Wellsfield SELS SO20 ...... 215 L7
Wellsmoor FHAM/STUB PO14 ... 159 G5
Wells PI ELGH SO50 ...... 81 M6
Wellswood Gdns HAV PO9 ...... 142 A5
Wellsworth La HAV PO9 ...... 142 A5
Wembley Gv CHAM PO6 ...... 187 L2 [1]
Wendover CI
  NMIL/BTOS BH25 ...... 225 K7 [2]
Wendover Rd HAV PO9 ...... 8 C3
Wensley Gdns EMRTH PO10 ... 166 D5
Wentwood Gdns
  NMIL/BTOS BH25 ...... 226 B6
Wentworth Av BOSC BH5 ...... 236 F4
Wentworth CI BOSC BH5 ...... 236 F5
Wentworth Dr BDST BH18 ...... 217 L3
  CHCH/BSGR BH23 ...... 237 L2 [2]
  HORN PO8 .... 140 F1
Wentworth Gdns
  FAWY SO45 .... 180 B6 [3]
  ITCH SO19 .... 132 F7 [1]
Wentworth Gra FUFL SO22 ... 26 D2
Wentworth Gv FAWY SO45 ...... 180 D5
Wescott Wy BWD BH11 ...... 219 J4 [3]
Wesermarsch Rd HORN PO8 ... 140 E4
Wesley CI CHAR BH8 ...... 15 M1
  ITCH SO19 .... 133 H4
Wesley Gv HSEA PO3 ...... 187 K5
Wesley Rd PSTN BH14 ...... 234 B3
  WIMB BH21 .... 192 B3
  WINC SO23 .... 17 H1
Wessex Av NMIL/BTOS BH25 ... 225 L6
Wessex CI CHCH/BSGR BH23 ... 239 H1
  FAWY SO45 .... 180 C7
Wessex Dr FUFL SO22 ...... 2 C2
Wessex Est RGWD BH24 ...... 146 F8
Wessex Gdns
  FHAM/PORC PO16 ...... 185 M1
  ROMY SO51 .... 79 G1
Wessex La WEND SO18 ...... 107 J4
Wessex Rd HORN PO8 ...... 116 B5
  PSTN BH14 .... 233 M5
  RGWD BH24 .... 146 F8
Wessex Wy CHAR BH8 ...... 221 L7
  RWIN SO21 .... 54 F8
  WBNE BH4 .... 235 G4
  WCLF BH2 .... 14 C4
West Ashling Rd RCCH PO18 ... 167 M5
West Av WIMB BH21 ...... 144 B8
West Bargate SHAM SO14 ...... 4 F4 [1]
West Battery Rd NEND PO2 ... 186 F7
Westbeams Rd LYMN SO41 ... 200 F6
Westborn Rd
  FHAM/PORC PO16 ...... 7 K5
Westbourne Av EMRTH PO10 ... 166 E6
  FAWY SO45 .... 180 A4
Westbourne CI EMRTH PO10 ... 166 E6 [1]
  WBNE BH4 .... 235 H5
Westbourne Crs PTSW SO17 ... 106 E7
Westbourne Park Rd
  WBNE BH4 .... 235 G6
Westbourne Rd EMRTH PO10 ... 166 E5
  NEND PO2 .... 187 K8
Westbroke Gdns ROMY SO51 ... 50 E7 [3]
Westbrook CI HLER SO31 ...... 158 C3
Westbrooke CI HORN PO8 ...... 140 E2
Westbrook Gv WVILLE PO7 ...... 164 B3
Westbrook Rd
  FHAM/PORC PO16 ...... 186 B2
Westbrook Wy WEND SO18 ... 107 K4 [3]
Westbury CI CHAM PO6 ...... 162 F7 [3]
  CHCH/BSGR BH23 ...... 223 L1
  CHCH/BSGR BH23 ...... 224 B7
  NMIL/BTOS BH25 ...... 225 L8
Westbury Ct HEND SO30 ...... 134 A3
Westbury Rd RGWD BH24 ...... 170 F1
  WSHM SO15 .... 130 C1
West Butts St PLE BH15 ...... 233 G6 [3]
Westby Rd BOSC BH5 ...... 236 D4
Westcliff CI LSOL/BMARY PO13... 208 C1
West Cliff Gdns WCLF BH2 ...... 14 C8
West Cliff Rd WBNE BH4 ...... 235 H6
  WCLF BH2 .... 14 C7
West CI LYMN SO41 ...... 227 M6
  VWD BH31 .... 144 B2
West Common FAWY SO45 ...... 206 B1
Westcot Rd FAWY SO45 ...... 179 M5 [3]
Westcroft Pk BDST BH18 ...... 218 A4
Westcroft Rd GPORT PO12 ...... 10 A4
Westdown Rd BWD BH11 ...... 219 L3
West Downs CI
  FHAM/PORC PO16 ...... 160 E4
West Dr ELGH SO50 ...... 82 C4
West End CI FUFL SO22 ...... 2 D7
Westend Rd ITCH SO19 ...... 132 E1
  WEND SO18 .... 108 B8
West End Rd HEND SO30 ...... 133 K4
  WEND SO18 .... 107 M8
West End Ter FUFL SO22 ...... 2 D7
Westerham CI CHAM PO6 ...... 163 J8
Westerham Rd CCLF BH13 ...... 235 G5
Westering ROMY SO51 ...... 51 H7 [2]
  ROMY SO51 .... 51 H8 [2]
Westerley CI HLER SO31 ...... 158 C3
Western Av CCLF BH13 ...... 234 D6
  EMRTH PO10 .... 166 B8
  NBNE BH10 .... 220 B4
  NMIL/BTOS BH25 ...... 225 H8
Western CI NBNE BH10 ...... 220 B3
Western District Cut
  WSHM SO15 .... 131 H1 [1]
Western Esp SHAM SO14 ...... 4 D2
Western Pde EMRTH PO10 ...... 190 C1
  SSEA PO5 .... 12 F6
Western Pde CCLF BH13 ...... 234 E8
  CHAM PO6 .... 187 J2
  CHFD SO53 .... 53 K7

FHAM/PORC PO16 .... 7 J6
FUFL SO22 .... 2 C7
HAV PO9 .... 8 C3
HEND SO30 .... 108 C7
LISS GU33 .... 36 L4
LYMN SO41 .... 228 B4
Western Wy FHAM/PORC PO16 .. 7 H6
GPORT PO12 .... 209 J3
Westfield Av FHAM/STUB PO14 .. 6 B8
HISD PO11 .... 213 J5
Westfield Cl ELGH SO50 ...... 109 H1
HLER SO31 .... 157 J6
Westfield Common
HLER SO31 .... 157 H6 🖫
Westfield Crs CHFD SO53 .... 81 H5
Westfield Dr BPWT SO32 .... 112 C6
Westfield Dro NARL SO24 .... 29 M8
Westfield Gdns
CHCH/BSGR BH23 .... 223 M7
Westfield Rd CHFD SO53 .... 81 H5
ENEY PO4 .... 211 L5
FUFL SO22 .... 16 A3
GPORT PO12 .... 10 B2
LYMN SO41 .... 228 D6
SBNE BH6 .... 237 K4
TOTT SO40 .... 104 E8
WSHM SO15 .... 130 E1
Westgate FHAM/STUB PO14 .. 184 A7
Westgate Pk WBNE BH4 .... 235 G5
Westgate St SHAM SO14 ...... 4 F6
Westgrove FBDG SP6 .... 97 K7 🖫
Westham Cl CFDH BH17 ...... 218 C5
West Haye Rd HISD PO11 .... 214 B7
West Hayes LYMN SO41 .... 228 D5
Westheath Rd BDST BH18 .. 217 M4
West Hill Dr FAWY SO45 .... 155 K3
FUFL SO22 .... 2 C7
West Hill Pk FUFL SO22 .... 2 B7
West Hill Pl WCLF BH2 .... 14 C7
West Hill Rd WCLF BH2 .... 14 C7
West Hoe La BPWT SO32 .... 85 L8
West Horton La ELGH SO50 .. 82 E7
West Howe Cl BWD BH11 .. 219 L4 🖫
Westland Dr WVILLE PO7 .... 164 C4
Westland Gdns GPORT PO12 .. 10 C6
Westlands Ct
CHCH/BSGR BH23 .... 197 L8
Westlands Gv
FHAM/PORC PO16 .... 186 A1
West La HISD PO11 .... 213 J4
LYMN SO41 .... 227 J7 🖫
NBAD SO52 .... 79 K3
Westley Cl FUFL SO22 .... 2 A4
Westley Gv FHAM/STUB PO14 .. 6 A3
Westman Rd FUFL SO22 .... 2 A2
West Marlands Rd SHAM SO14 .. 4 F2
Westmead Cl HISD PO11 .... 213 H5
West Meade LIPH GU30 .... 38 E6
Westminster Rd LYMN SO41 .. 242 A4
Westminster Gdns
FHAM/STUB PO14 ...... 159 G5 🖫
Westminster Ga FUFL SO22 .. 26 A3
Westminster Rd CCLF BH13 .. 235 G7
Westminster Rd East
CCLF BH13 .... 235 G7
West Moors Rd FERN BH22 .. 194 B1
WIMB BH21 .... 168 C1
Westmorland Wy CHFD SO53 .. 81 K3
Weston Av ENEY PO4 .... 211 M4
Weston Cl ITCH SO19 .... 132 D7
Weston Crs WEND SO18 .... 133 C1
Weston Dr BMTH BH1 .... 15 K5
Weston Grove Rd ITCH SO19 .. 132 C7
Weston La ITCH SO19 .... 132 C7
PSF GU32 .... 63 G8
ROWN SO16 .... 104 F4
Weston Rd ELGH SO50 .... 81 M5
EPSF GU31 .... 63 M5
WIMB BH21 .... 192 D1 🖫
West Overcliff Dr WBNE BH4 .. 235 H6
Westover La RGWD BH24 .... 170 B2
Westover Rd BMTH BH1 ...... 14 F6
HSEA PO3 .... 187 M8
LYMN SO41 .... 242 C4
ROWN SO16 .... 105 G8
West Park Dr FBDG SP6 ...... 96 C3
West Park La FBDG SP6 .... 96 B3
West Park Rd WSHM SO15 .... 4 A2
West Quay Rd PLE BH15 .... 233 G6
WSHM SO15 .... 4 D3
Westridge Rd PTSW SO17 .. 107 J7
West Rd BOSC BH5 .... 236 F3 🖫
CHCH/BSGR BH23 .... 197 L8
EMRTH PO10 .... 166 C8
FAWY SO45 .... 155 H7
HEND SO30 .... 133 K2
ITCH SO19 .... 132 C6
LYMN SO41 .... 241 M3
SHAM SO14 .... 5 G7
WHAM PO17 .... 162 C2
Westrow Gdns WSHM SO15 .. 131 J1
Westrow Rd WSHM SO15 .... 131 J1
West Strd SELS SO20 .... 215 J8
West St BPWT SO32 .... 113 G3
EMRTH PO10 .... 166 D8
FAWY SO45 .... 155 K3
FBDG SP6 .... 97 K7
FHAM/PORC PO16 .... 7 L8
FHAM/PORC PO16 .... 162 B8
Westrow Gdns WSHM SO15 .. 131 J1
Westrow Rd WSHM SO15 .... 131 J1
West Strd SELS SO20 .... 215 J8
West St BPWT SO32 .... 113 G3
EMRTH PO10 .... 166 D8
FAWY SO45 .... 155 K3
West View Rd
CHCH/BSGR BH23 .... 238 D2
PLE BH15 .... 233 H4
Westward Rd HEND SO30 .. 109 H8
Westway BDST BH18 .... 217 K5
LYMN SO41 .... 228 A6
MOOR/WNTN BH9 .... 220 F6
ROWN SO16 .... 105 G8
West Wy FHAM PO15 .... 159 J5
West Way Cl
MOOR/WNTN BH9 .... 220 F7 🖫
Westway Cl ROWN SO16 .... 105 J2
Westways CHAM PO6 .... 164 D8
FHAM/STUB PO14 .... 184 B6

Westways Cl ROWN SO16 .. 105 J3 🖫
Westwood Av FERN BH22 .. 194 A2
Westwood Cl EMRTH PO10 .. 166 E5
Westwood Gdns CHFD SO53 .. 53 K8
Westwood Rd HLER SO31 .. 156 F1
LYND SO43 .... 151 K2
NEND PO2 .... 187 J4
PTSW SO17 .... 106 E8
Westwood Vw NARL SO24 .... 30 D7
Wetherby Cl CFDH BH17 .... 217 L6
Wetherby Gdns TOTT SO40 .. 104 B3
Wetherdown EPSF GU31 .... 63 M5
Weyhill Cl FHAM/PORC PO16 .. 162 A1
HAV PO9 .... 165 H3 🖫
Weyman's Av NBNE BH10 .. 220 A1
Weymans Dr NBNE BH10 .. 220 A2
Weymouth Av GPORT PO12 .. 185 K8
Weymouth Rd PSTN BH14 .. 234 B3
Whaddon Cha
FHAM/STUB PO14 .... 183 M6
Whaddon Cl HAV PO9 .... 165 G2
Whaddon La RWIN SO21 ...... 55 M7
Whale Island Wy NEND PO2 .. 187 G7
Whalesmead Cl ELGH SO50 .. 82 E7
Whalesmead Rd ELGH SO50 .. 82 E7
Whaley Rd NEND PO2 .... 186 F7
Wharf Cl BKME/WDN BH12 .. 234 D2
Wharfdale Rd
BKME/WDN BH12 .... 234 C2
WBNE BH4 .... 235 H4
Wharf Hl WINC SO23 .... 27 G2
Wharf Rd NEND PO2 .... 187 G8
Wharncliffe Gdns
CHCH/BSGR BH23 .... 239 M1
Wharncliffe Rd BMTH BH1 .. 236 C4
CHCH/BSGR BH23 .... 239 M1
ITCH SO19 .... 132 B5
Whartons La TOTT SO40 .... 129 C4
Whatleigh Cl PLE BH15 ...... 233 H7
Wheat Cl NBAD SO52 .... 80 E3
Wheatcroft Dr WEND SO18 .. 108 A7 🖫
Wheatcroft Rd
LSOL/BMARY PO13 .... 208 D2
Wheatear Dr EPSF GU31 .... 64 B5 🖫
Wheatears Dr ROMY SO51 .... 76 D5
Wheatland Cl FUFL SO22 .... 26 C3
Wheatlands FHAM/STUB PO14 .. 159 M8
Wheatlands Av HISD PO11 .. 214 C7
Wheatlands Crs HISD PO11 .. 214 C7 🖫
Wheaton Rd LTDN BH7 ...... 236 F3
Wheatsheaf Ct HEND SO30 .. 133 M2 🖫
Wheatsheaf Dr HORN PO8 .. 140 B5
Wheatstone Rd ENEY PO4 .... 13 M6
Wheeler Cl GPORT PO12 .... 209 M2
Wheelers La BWD BH11 .... 219 G3
Wheelers Wk FAWY SO45 .. 180 C3
Whernside Cl ROWN SO16 .. 105 L8 🖫
Wherwell Ct HAV PO9 ...... 165 M3 🖫
Whichers Cl HAV PO9 .... 141 M8
Whichers Gate Rd HAV PO9 .. 141 M8
Whimbrel Cl ENEY PO4 ...... 212 A3
Whinchat Cl FHAM PO15 .... 160 A4
ROWN SO16 .... 106 A2
Whincroft Cl FERN BH22 .... 194 C1
Whincroft Dr FERN BH22 .... 194 C2
Whinfield Rd FAWY SO45 .... 155 J7
Whinwhistle Rd ROMY SO51 .. 77 C6
Whippingham Cl CHAM PO6 .. 163 H8
Whistler Cl ITCH SO19 .... 133 G5
Whistlers Cl CHCH/BSGR BH23 .. 231 M7
Whitaker Crs LYMN SO41 .. 228 A5
Whitby Av BDST BH18 .... 217 L6
Whitby Cl CHCH/BSGR BH23 .. 222 B4 🖫
Whitby Crs BDST BH18 ...... 217 L6
Whitby Rd LYMN SO41 ...... 242 A4
Whitchurch Av BDST BH18 .. 218 A5
Whitcombe Cl TOTT SO40 .. 129 J1 🖫
Whitcombe Gdns HSEA PO3 .. 211 K2
White Barn Crs LYMN SO41 .. 226 E5
Whitebeam Cl
FHAM/STUB PO14 .... 6 C7
HORN PO8 .... 141 G3 🖫
RWIN SO21 .... 54 F8
White Beam Ri HORN PO8 .. 116 B3
Whitebeam Rd HEND SO30 .. 134 B2
Whitebeam Wy NBAD SO52 .. 79 M3
VWD BH31 .... 144 F3
Whitechimney Rw
EMRTH PO10 .... 166 F5
Whitecliff Crs PSTN BH14 .. 233 M6
Whitecliffe Av HSEA PO3 ... 211 L1
Whitecliff Rd PSTN BH14 ... 233 L6
White Cliff Rd PSTN BH14 .. 233 M6
White Cl PLE BH15 .... 233 M1 🖫
White Cloud Pk ENEY PO4 .. 211 K5 🖫
Whitecross Cl CFDH BH17 .. 218 C5
Whitecross Gdns NEND PO2 .. 187 K5
Whitedell La WHAM PO17 .. 161 H4
White Dirt La HORN PO8 .... 116 A6
White Farm Cl NBNE BH10 .. 220 B8
Whitefield Rd FAWY SO45 .. 180 A5
NMIL/BTOS BH25 .... 225 L5
PSTN BH14 .... 233 M6
White Gates BPWT SO32 .. 110 A3
Whitehall CHCH/BSGR BH23 .. 238 A3
Whitehart Flds RGWD BH24 .. 147 G8 🖫
White Hart La
FHAM/PORC PO16 .... 185 M1
TOTT SO40 .... 102 E8
White Hart Rd ELGH SO50 .. 83 H7
GPORT PO12 .... 10 F4 🖫
PSEA PO1 .... 12 C5
Whitehaven
FHAM/PORC PO16 .... 185 M1
HORN PO8 .... 141 H2
Whitehayes Cl
CHCH/BSGR BH23 .... 223 H6
Whitehayes Rd
CHCH/BSGR BH23 .... 223 G7
White Heather Ct
FAWY SO45 .... 155 L3
Whitehorn Dr RSAL SP5 ...... 75 J8
White Horse Dr PLE BH15 .. 233 H5
White Horse La WVILLE PO7 .. 139 L2
Whitehouse Gdns PSF GU32 .. 63 K3
White House Gdns
WSHM SO15 .... 130 E2
Whitehouse Rd WIMB BH21 .. 192 B6

White Knights
NMIL/BTOS BH25 .... 240 E1
White Ladies Cl HAV PO9 .... 9 G5
White La RWIN SO21 .... 26 F8
Whitelaw Rd WSHM SO15 .. 130 F1
Whiteleaf Wy PLE PO7 ...... 114 B1
Whitelegg Wy NBNE BH10 .. 220 C3
Whiteley La FHAM PO15 .... 159 K4
HLER SO31 .... 135 G7
Whiteley Wy FHAM PO15 .. 159 H2
Whitemoor La TOTT SO40 .. 103 K4
Whitemoor Rd BROC SO42 .. 175 H6
Whitenap Cl ROMY SO51 .... 79 G2
Whitenap La ROMY SO51 .... 79 H2
White Rd ELGH SO50 .... 82 C4
Whites Hl RWIN SO21 .... 55 L4
Whiteshoot RSAL SP5 .... 73 L4
Whiteshoot Hl RSAL SP5 .... 73 K4
Whiteshute La WINC SO23 .. 26 D4
Whites La FAWY SO45 .... 180 F5 🖫
Whitestone Cl ROWN SO16 .. 105 L8 🖫
White Swan Rd PSEA PO1 .. 12 F2
Whitethorn Rd HISD PO11 .. 213 H5 🖫
Whitewater Ri FAWY SO45 .. 155 K6
Whitfield Pk RGWD BH24 .. 169 M3
Whitehedowad Av WSHM SO15 .. 106 C8
Withers La BROC SO42 ...... 204 A2
Whitley Cl EMRTH PO10 .... 166 F3
Whitley Rd HORN PO8 .... 140 D2
Whitley Wy NMIL/BTOS BH25 .. 225 M3
Whitsbury Cl HAV PO9 ...... 163 J8
Whitsbury Rd FBDG SP6 ...... 97 L3
HAV PO9 .... 165 J3
Whitstable Rd CHAM PO6 .. 163 J8
Whittington Cl FAWY SO45 .. 155 K6
Whittington Ct EMRTH PO10 .. 166 D8
Whittle Av FHAM PO15 ...... 159 G3
Whittle Rd WIMB BH21 ...... 193 K1
Whittles Wy PLE BH15 ...... 233 G6
Whitwell HLER SO31 .... 157 G1 🖫
Whitwell Rd ENEY PO4 .... 13 L9
Whitworth Cl GPORT PO12 .. 10 D3
Whitworth Rd GPORT PO12 .. 10 D3
NEND PO2 .... 187 K8
WEND SO18 .... 107 J8
Whyte Cl FAWY SO45 .... 179 M5
Whyteways ELGH SO50 ...... 81 L4
Wick Cl NMIL/BTOS BH25 .. 225 J6
Wick Dr NMIL/BTOS BH25 .. 225 J6
Wicket Rd NBNE BH10 ...... 220 A3
The Wicket FAWY SO45 .... 155 K6
Wickfield Av
CHCH/BSGR BH23 .... 238 A2
Wickfield Cl
CHCH/BSGR BH23 ...... 238 A2 🖫
Wickham Dr WIMB BH21 ... 217 H4
Wickham Rd BPWT SO32 .. 112 F4
FHAM/PORC PO16 .... 7 J1
WHAM PO17 .... 160 F4
Wickham St PSEA PO1 .... 12 C1
Wick La CHCH/BSGR BH23 .. 238 A3
RSAL SP5 .... 43 M8
SBNE BH6 .... 237 M3
Wicklea Rd SBNE BH6 ...... 238 A4
Wicklow Dr CFDH BH17 ...... 80 F3
Wickmeads Rd SBNE BH6 .. 237 M3 🖫
Wickor Cl EMRTH PO10 ..... 166 E6
Wickor Wy EMRTH PO10 ... 166 D5
Wicor Mill La
FHAM/PORC PO16 .... 185 M2
Wicor Pth FHAM/PORC PO16 .. 186 C2
Widbury Rd ALDT LYMN SO41 .. 228 A6
Widden Cl LYMN SO41 ...... 200 F6
Widdicombe Av PSTN BH14 .. 234 D6
Widdicombe Dr FAWY SO45 .. 155 J4
Wide La ELGH SO50 .... 107 L1
WEND SO18 .... 107 K3
Wide Lane Cl BROC SO42 .. 175 K7 🖫
Widgeon Cl GPORT PO12 .. 209 M1
ROWN SO16 .... 106 A2
Widget Cl BWD BH11 .... 219 M6
Widlers La BPWT SO32 ...... 84 D2
Widley Ct FHAM/STUB PO14 .. 184 D2
Widley Court Dr CHAM PO6 .. 187 L1
Widley Gdns WVILLE PO7 .. 164 B5
Widley Rd CHAM PO6 .... 163 H6
NEND PO2 .... 187 G6
Widley Wk CHAM PO6 ...... 163 K6
Widworthy Dr BDST BH18 .. 217 K3
Wield Cl HAV PO9 .... 165 G4
Wigan Crs HAV PO9 .... 164 F6
Wight Wk FERN BH22 .... 194 C6
Wilberforce Cl FUFL SO22 .. 26 B2 🖫
Wilberforce Rd GPORT PO12 .. 11 G9
SSEA PO5 .... 13 G5 🖫
Wild Arum Wy NBAD SO52 .. 80 E3
Wildburn Cl TOTT SO40 .... 104 B6
Wild Cherry Wy NBAD SO52 .. 80 F2 🖫
Wild Cl TOTT SO40 .... 129 H1 🖫
Wildern Cl HLER SO31 ...... 158 D5 🖫
Wilderness Hts WEND SO18 .. 108 B7
Wilderton Rd CCLF BH13 ... 234 E5
Wilderton Rd West
CCLF BH13 .... 234 E4
Wildfell Cl CHCH/BSGR BH23 .. 222 E7
Widown Gdns SBNE BH6 ... 237 L5
Widown Rd SBNE BH6 ...... 237 M5
Wild Ridings FHAM/STUB PO14 .. 159 M8
Wild Rose Crs HLER SO31 .. 158 C6
Wilfred Rd BOSC BH5 .... 236 E4
Wilkins Cl HORN PO8 .... 116 A2
Wilkinson Dr CHAR BH8 .... 221 L6
Wilks Cl ROWN SO16 .... 105 H3
Willersley Cl CHAM PO6 .... 163 J4
William Cl CHCH/BSGR BH23 .. 224 E6
FHAM/STUB PO14 .... 184 B7
William Macleod Wy
ROWN SO16 .... 105 M8
William Price Gdns
FHAM/PORC PO16 .... 7 J3
William Rd LTDN BH7 .... 236 E1
LYMN SO41 .... 228 C3 🖫

Williams Cl FAWY SO45 .... 180 B5
LSOL/BMARY PO13 .... 209 H1
Williams Rd HSEA PO3 ...... 187 M5
William St SHAM SO14 .... 5 M1
Willis Av NBAD SO52 .... 80 A4
Willis Rd GPORT PO12 .... 11 H3
PSEA PO1 .... 13 G1
ROWN SO16 .... 107 J3
Willis Wy CFDH BH17 .... 233 G2
Willis Waye WINC SO23 ...... 17 H3
Willow Av FBDG SP6 .... 97 K6
Willow Cl HAV PO9 .... 9 K7
HEND SO30 .... 108 D6 🖫
RGWD BH24 .... 169 H4
UPTN BH16 .... 232 C3
Willow Dr CHCH/BSGR BH23 .. 237 M5
Willow Gdns EMRTH PO10 .. 166 F4
Willow Gn WRIN SO21 .... 54 F8
Willow Gv ELGH SO50 .... 83 J6
Willow Herb Cl HLER SO31 .. 158 C6
Willow La CHCH/BSGR BH23 .. 198 B5
Willow Md CHAR BH8 .... 221 H4
Willow Pk PSTN BH14 ...... 233 L5
Willow Pl GPORT PO12 ...... 10 F1
Willow Rd BPWT SO32 ...... 111 K1
LISS GU33 .... 36 E4
The Willows NMIL/BTOS BH25 .. 225 M8
WVILLE PO7 .... 139 J4
Willow Tree Av HORN PO8 .. 140 F6
Willow Tree Gdns
FHAM/PORC PO16 .... 6 C7
Willow Tree Ri BWD BH11 .. 219 M6
Willow Tree Wk ITCH SO19 .. 132 F5
Willow Wy
CHCH/BSGR BH23 .... 237 M3 🖫
FERN BH22 .... 194 B1
Willow Wood Rd HISD PO11 .. 213 L5 🖫
Wills Av HLER SO31 .... 157 H4
Wills Rd BKME/WDN BH12 .. 234 E3
Wills Wy ROMY SO51 .... 78 F2
Willwood Cl CFDH BH17 .... 218 C5 🖫
Wilmer Rd ELGH SO50 .... 81 M6
Wilmington Cl WEND SO18 .. 107 L5
Wilmot Cl ELGH SO50 .... 82 D3
Wilmott La GPORT PO12 .... 10 A2
Wilmur Crs PLE BH15 .... 233 K2
Wilson Gv SSEA PO5 .... 13 K5
Wilson Rd BMTH BH1 .... 236 C3
NEND PO2 .... 187 G6
PSTN BH14 .... 234 B4
Wilson St SHAM SO14 .... 5 L1
Wilton Av WSHM SO15 ...... 131 J2
Wilton Cl CHCH/BSGR BH23 .. 222 B7
Wilton Crs WSHM SO15 .... 106 C7
Wilton Dr HORN PO8 .... 140 E3
Wilton Gdns
NMIL/BTOS BH25 ...... 225 K5 🖫
WSHM SO15 .... 106 C7
Wilton Pl SSEA PO5 .... 13 H7
Wilton Rd LTDN BH7 .... 236 D3
WSHM SO15 .... 106 C7
Wilton Ter SSEA PO5 .... 13 J7 🖫
Wiltshire Gdns
CHCH/BSGR BH23 .... 197 K8
Wiltshire Rd
CHCH/BSGR BH23 .... 197 K8
CHFD SO53 .... 81 J5
Wiltshire St SSEA PO5 .... 12 F3
Wilverley Av CHAR BH8 .... 221 K6
HAV PO9 .... 165 L4
Wilverley Pl FAWY SO45 ... 180 C7
Wilverley Rd BROC SO42 .. 175 K7
NMIL/BTOS BH25 .... 199 K5
Wimbledon Pk Rd SSEA PO5 .. 13 K4
Wimborne Rd BWD BH11 .. 219 M2
ENEY PO4 .... 211 L4
MOOR/WNTN BH9 .... 220 D4
NBNE BH10 .... 220 E4
PLE BH15 .... 233 H2
TWDS BH3 .... 235 L1
UPTN BH16 .... 216 B4
WCLF BH2 .... 14 F3
WIMB BH21 .... 192 C2
Wimborne Rd East FERN BH22 .. 194 B2
WIMB BH21 .... 193 L2
Wimborne Rd West
WIMB BH21 .... 192 B4
Wimpole St PSEA PO1 ...... 211 H2
Wimpson Gdns ROWN SO16 .. 105 L7
Wimpson La ROWN SO16 .. 105 K8
Winchcombe Rd CHAM PO6 .. 162 F7
Winchester By-pass
WINC SO23 .... 17 J2
Winchester Hl ROMY SO51 .. 51 G8
Winchester Rd BPWT SO32 .. 84 C5
BPWT SO32 .... 109 K5
CHFD SO53 .... 81 J2
ELGH SO50 .... 83 H4
NEND PO2 .... 187 J8
NMIL/BTOS BH25 .... 226 A3
PSF GU32 .... 62 A3
ROMY SO51 .... 51 J7
ROWN SO16 .... 105 M7
RWIN SO21 .... 54 C1
WHAM PO17 .... 136 D3
Winchester St HEND SO30 .. 109 M8
WSHM SO15 .... 131 K2
Winchester Wy TOTT SO40 .. 129 G1 🖫
Winchfield Cl ITCH SO19 .. 132 E8 🖫
Winchfield Crs HAV PO9 .... 165 G4
Wincombe Cl FERN BH22 .. 194 B5 🖫
Wincombe Dr FERN BH22 .. 194 B5
Windbury Rd ROWN SO16 .. 105 K6
Windermere Av
FHAM/STUB PO14 .... 184 B4
ROWN SO16 .... 105 J6
Windermere Gdns TOTT SO40 .. 104 D8

Windermere Rd NEND PO2 .. 187 K5
TWDS BH3 .... 235 M2
WEND SO18 .... 108 A7
Windfield Dr ROMY SO51 .. 51 C8 🖫
Windham Rd BMTH BH1 .... 15 L2
Windmill Cl HORN PO8 ...... 116 B3
LYMN SO41 .... 242 C3
RGWD BH24 .... 170 B4
Windmill Copse FAWY SO45 .. 155 K7 🖫
Windmill Fld WVILLE PO7 .. 139 L4
Windmill Gv FHAM/PORC PO16 .. 185 M2
Windmill La HLER SO31 .... 133 L6
RGWD BH24 .... 170 B4
Windover Cl ITCH SO19 .... 133 G2
Windrush Gdns WVILLE PO7 .. 164 B1
Windrush Rd ROWN SO16 .. 105 K7
Windrush Wy FAWY SO45 .. 155 L5
Windsor Cl LYMN SO41 .... 226 C4
RGWD BH24 .... 169 K3
Windsor Ct ELGH SO50 .... 82 C4 🖫
Windsor Ga ELGH SO50 ..... 81 M2
Windsor Rd BOSC BH5 ...... 236 D4
CHAM PO6 .... 187 K1
CHCH/BSGR BH23 .... 198 B7
FHAM/PORC PO16 .... 186 B1
GPORT PO12 .... 10 D3
PSF GU32 .... 63 L5
PSTN BH14 .... 234 A5
WVILLE PO7 .... 140 B6
Windsor Wy FBDG SP6 ..... 121 L2
Windwhistle La RSAL SP5 .. 45 L1
Winfield Wy EMRTH PO10 .. 166 D4 🖫
Winfrith Crs
BKME/WDN BH12 .... 219 J8
Winfrith Wy ROWN SO16 .. 105 J3
Wingate Dr ITCH SO19 ...... 132 F3
Wingate Rd TOTT SO40 .... 104 C3
Wingfield Av
CHCH/BSGR BH23 .... 224 B7
PLE BH15 .... 233 J2
Wingfield St PSEA PO1 ...... 211 H1
Wingrove Rd TOTT SO40 .. 129 G5 🖫
Winifred Cl ELGH SO50 ...... 83 H5 🖫
Winifred Rd PLE BH15 ...... 233 K3
WVILLE PO7 .... 140 C8
Winkfield Rw HORN PO8 ... 140 F3
Winkle St SHAM SO14 .... 4 F7
Winkton Cl CHCH/BSGR BH23 .. 223 G5
HAV PO9 .... 8 B1
Winnall Cl WINC SO23 .... 3 M1
Winnall Manor Rd WINC SO23 .. 3 M7
Winnall Valley Rd WINC SO23 .. 3 L6
Winnards Cl FERN BH22 .... 194 C6
Winnards Pk HLER SO31 ... 158 B5
Winnham Dr
FHAM/PORC PO16 .... 161 L7
Winnington FHAM PO15 ... 160 B4
Winn Rd PTSW SO17 .... 106 F8
Winscombe Av HORN PO8 .. 140 E6
Winsford Av ELGH SO50 ..... 82 F7
Winsford Cl
CHCH/BSGR BH23 .... 224 B7 🖫
ELGH SO50 .... 82 F7 🖫
Winsford Gdns ELGH SO50 .. 82 F7 🖫
Winslade Rd FUFL SO22 .... 16 B4
HAV PO9 .... 165 H3 🖫
Winsley Av SBNE BH6 ...... 237 H4
Winsor Cl HISD PO11 .... 214 B7
Winsor La TOTT SO40 .... 103 J8
Winsor Rd TOTT SO40 ...... 127 M1
TOTT SO40 .... 129 L2
Winspit Cl PLE BH15 .... 232 D5
Winstanley Rd NEND PO2 .. 187 G2
ROWN SO16 .... 105 H3
Winston Av BKME/WDN BH12 .. 234 F2
Winston Churchill Av SSEA PO5 .. 13 H3
Winston Cl ELGH SO50 ...... 81 M4
HISD PO11 .... 213 J5
ROWN SO16 .... 105 L6
Winstone Crs NBAD SO52 .. 79 M5
Winston Gdns
BKME/WDN BH12 .... 234 F2
Winston Rd MOOR/WNTN BH9 .. 220 E5
Winston Wy FERN BH22 .... 146 F8
Winterbourne Rd
CHAM PO6 .... 162 D7
PLE BH15 .... 233 J4
ROMY SO51 .... 51 H7
Winterhayes Cl CFDH BH17 .. 218 B5
Winterhill Rd CHAM PO6 ... 163 H8
Winter Rd ENEY PO4 .... 211 L5
Winters Cl FAWY SO45 ..... 180 B5
Winterslow Dr HAV PO9 ... 165 J2
Winters Rd BPWT SO32 .... 111 M8
Winton Cl LYMN SO41 ..... 228 D5
Winton Rd NEND PO2 .... 187 K6
PSF GU32 .... 63 L5
Winton St SHAM SO14 .... 5 H2
Winton Wy NBNE BH10 ..... 220 B7
NMIL/BTOS BH25 .... 225 M3
Wisbech Av LYMN SO41 ... 226 D5
Wisborough Rd SSEA PO5 .. 13 K7
Wishart Gdns
MOOR/WNTN BH9 .... 220 F3
Wish Pl SSEA PO5 .... 13 L7
Wisteria Dr VWD BH31 ..... 145 G4
Wisteria Gdns HAV PO9 ... 165 M4
Witchampton Cl HAV PO9 .. 165 L3 🖫
Witchampton Rd BDST BH18 .. 217 H4
Witham Cl CHFD SO53 .... 80 F2
Witherbed La FHAM PO15 .. 159 H4
Withermoor Rd
MOOR/WNTN BH9 .... 220 C8
Withies Rd LSOL/BMARY PO13 .. 185 H8
Withingham Rd CCLF BH13 .. 234 E5
Withy Cl ROMY SO51 .... 50 E8 🖫
Wittensford La LYND SO43 .. 102 B3
Wittering Rd HISD PO11 .... 214 D6
ROWN SO16 .... 105 J3
Witt Rd ELGH SO50 .... 83 H6
Witts Hl WEND SO18 .... 107 M8
Wiverley Cl CHAR BH8 ...... 227 M6
Wlnton Cl FUFL SO22 .... 2 E3
Woburn Cl ELGH SO50 .... 81 M2
Woburn Rd ROWN SO16 ... 106 A3
Wode Cl HORN PO8 .... 116 B5
Wodehouse Rd ITCH SO19 .. 132 C4

Woking Rd *PSTN* BH14 .... 234 B4
Wolfe Cl *CHCH/BSGR* BH23 .... 238 D1
  FUFL SO22 .... 26 B3
Wollaston Rd *SBNE* BH6 .... 237 L5
Wollaton Rd *FERN* BH22 .... 194 A5
Wollstonecraft Rd
  BOSC BH5 .... 236 E5
Wolseley Rd *BKME/WDN* BH12 .. 234 C2
  WSHM SO15 .... 131 G1
Wolsey Wy *LYMN* SO41 .... 242 C3
Wolterton Rd
  BKME/WDN BH12 .... 234 F3
Wolverley Ct *ROWN* SO16 .. 106 C5
Wolverton Rd *HAV* PO9 .... 165 J5
  LTDN BH7 .... 236 E3
  SHAM SO14 .... 5 K1
Wolverton Wy *SHAM* SO14 ...... 5 J1
Wolvesey Pl *CHFD* SO53 ...... 80 F4
Wonston Ct *HAV* PO9 ...... 165 M2
Wonston Rd *ROWN* SO16 ...... 106 A4
Woodacre Gdns *FERN* BH22 ...... 194 C4
Wood Barn La *FHAM* PO15 ...... 6 A5
Woodberry La *EMRTH* PO10 ...... 166 D1
  HAV PO9 .... 142 B7
Woodbourne Cl *FHAM* PO15 ...... 6 A6
  LISS GU33 .... 36 F4
Woodbury Av *CHAR* BH8 ...... 221 K6
  HAV PO9 .... 8 E7
  PSF GU32 .... 63 K3
Woodbury Cl
  CHCH/BSGR BH23 ...... 222 C5
Woodbury Gv *HORN* PO8 ...... 140 D2
Wood Cl *ITCH* SO19 ...... 133 C5
Woodcock La *LYMN* SO41 ...... 226 E5
Woodcocks Crs *LTDN* BH7 ...... 236 F1
Woodcote Dr *UPTN* BH16 ...... 232 A2
Woodcote La *HAV* PO9 ...... 165 L2
  FHAM/STUB PO14 ...... 184 E6
Woodcote Rd *PTSW* SO17 ...... 107 H5
Woodcroft La *HORN* PO8 ...... 140 D3
Woodend Rd
  MOOR/WNTN BH9 ...... 235 K1
Wood End Rd *RGWD* BH24 ...... 171 J3
Wood End Wy *NBAD* SO52 ...... 80 F1
Wooden House La *LYMN* SO41 .. 202 F6
Wooderson Cl *ELGH* SO50 ...... 83 C5
Woodfern *FBDG* SP6 .... 98 C6
Woodfield Av *CHAM* PO6 ...... 164 C7
Woodfield Dr *FUFL* SO22 ...... 26 A2
Woodfield Gdns
  CHCH/BSGR BH23 ...... 224 B7
Woodfield Park Rd
  EMRTH PO10 .... 166 F7
Woodfield Rd *BWD* BH11 ...... 219 L3
Woodford Cl *RGWD* BH24 ...... 170 F1
Woodford La *BMTH* BH1 ...... 15 L4
Woodgason La *HISD* PO11 ...... 190 A7
Wood Glade Cl *TOTT* SO40 ...... 130 D7
Woodgreen Av *HAV* PO9 ...... 8 B2
Woodgreen Dr *BWD* BH11 ...... 219 H4
Woodgreen Rd *FUFL* SO22 ...... 16 C4
Woodhall Wy *FHAM* PO15 ...... 6 D1
Woodhayes Av
  CHCH/BSGR BH23 ...... 224 C6
Woodhouse La *HAV* PO9 ...... 142 A4
  HEND SO30 .... 109 K8
  HORN PO8 .... 141 L2
Woodhouse Rd *HORN* PO8 ...... 141 K1
Woodington Cl *HAV* PO9 ...... 165 L2
Woodington Rd *ROMY* SO51 ...... 77 H4
Woodlake Cl *CFDH* BH17 ...... 218 B7
Woodland Av *BOSC* BH5 ...... 236 F4
Woodland Cl *ROMY* SO51 ...... 77 G6
  WEND SO18 .... 133 H1
Woodland Dro *RWIN* SO21 ...... 54 F5
Woodland Ms *HEND* SO30 ...... 108 C7
Woodlands
  FHAM/PORC PO16 ...... 161 H6
Woodlands Av *EMRTH* PO10 ...... 166 C5
  PLE BH15 .... 232 D5

Woodlands Cl
  CHCH/BSGR BH23 ...... 197 L8
  CHFD SO53 .... 53 J6
  FAWY SO45 .... 155 J7
  HLER SO31 .... 158 D2
  LSOL/BMARY PO13 ...... 209 G2
Woodlands Ct *FAWY* SO45 ...... 155 J7
Woodlands Crs *PLE* BH15 ...... 232 E5
Woodlands Dr *HLER* SO31 ...... 157 H2
Woodlands Dro *TOTT* SO40 ...... 128 D5
Woodlands Gv *WVILLE* PO7 ...... 164 B3
Woodlands La *HISD* PO11 ...... 213 J3
  LISS GU33 .... 37 G6
  RCCH PO18 .... 143 J6
Woodlands Rd *BROC* SO42 ...... 201 K1
  NMIL/BTOS BH25 ...... 240 D1
  TOTT SO40 .... 128 C4
Woodlands Wy *HAV* PO9 ...... 165 K4
  HLER SO31 .... 133 K8
  NBAD SO52 .... 79 K4
  RGWD BH24 .... 169 K4
  WSHM SO15 .... 106 E8
Woodland Vw *HLER* SO31 ...... 133 K8
  HORN PO8 .... 140 D2
Woodland Wk *BOSC* BH5 ...... 236 F4
  FERN BH22 .... 194 D1
Woodland Wy
  CHCH/BSGR BH23 ...... 224 B8
  LYMN SO41 .... 242 B4
Wood La *BWD* BH11 ...... 219 J2
  LYMN SO41 .... 242 B4
  NARL SO24 .... 31 J3
  WHAM PO17 .... 162 E1
Woodlane Cl *NARL* SO24 ...... 31 J3
Woodlark Gdns *EPSF* GU31 ...... 64 B5
Wood Lawn Cl
  NMIL/BTOS BH25 ...... 225 K8
Woodlea Cl *FUFL* SO22 ...... 2 C2
Woodlea Gdns *HEND* SO30 ...... 108 D7
Woodlea Wy *ROMY* SO51 ...... 52 E6
Woodleaze Cl *BDST* BH18 ...... 217 M2
Woodleigh Cl *HAV* PO9 ...... 166 A5
Woodley Cl *ROMY* SO51 ...... 51 H6
Woodley La *ROMY* SO51 ...... 50 F7
Woodley Rd *GPORT* PO12 ...... 11 G4
  ITCH SO19 .... 132 B3
Woodley Wy *ROMY* SO51 ...... 51 H6
Woodling Crs *FBDG* SP6 ...... 98 C6
Woodlinken Cl *VWD* BH31 ...... 144 F4
Woodlinken Dr *VWD* BH31 ...... 144 F4
Woodlinken Wy *VWD* BH31 ...... 144 F4
Woodmancote La
  EMRTH PO10 .... 167 J4
Woodmancote Rd *ENEY* PO4 ...... 211 L4
Woodmill La *WEND* SO18 ...... 107 J5
Woodmoor Cl *TOTT* SO40 ...... 130 E7
Woodpath *SSEA* PO5 ...... 13 H6
Woodpecker Cl *HAV* PO9 ...... 9 J4
  VWD BH31 .... 144 D3
Woodpecker Copse
  HLER SO31 .... 158 F5
Woodpecker Dr *CFDH* BH17 ...... 217 J8
  FUFL SO22 .... 16 B6
  TOTT SO40 .... 130 C7
Woodpecker Wy *ELGH* SO50 ...... 81 J6
Wood Rd *TOTT* SO40 ...... 128 F6
Woodrow *WVILLE* PO7 ...... 139 J4
Woodrush Crs *HLER* SO31 ...... 158 C6
Woodsedge *WVILLE* PO7 ...... 164 E3
Woodside *LSOL/BMARY* PO13 .... 184 F3
  ROWN SO16 .... 80 D6
Woodside Av *ELGH* SO50 ...... 81 L3
  LYMN SO41 .... 228 C2
Woodside Cl *FERN* BH22 ...... 194 C2
  TOTT SO40 .... 130 C7
Woodside Crs *ROWN* SO16 ...... 80 C6

Woodside Gdns *TOTT* SO40 ...... 129 G6
Woodside La *NMIL/BTOS* BH25 ...... 228 C6
Woodside Rd *BOSC* BH5 ...... 237 G4
  ELGH SO50 .... 81 K4
  FERN BH22 .... 194 C2
  NBAD SO52 .... 79 L4
  PSTN BH14 .... 234 B5
  PTSW SO17 .... 107 G8
Woodside Wy *HEND* SO30 ...... 133 L3
Woodstock Av *HORN* PO8 ...... 140 E3
Woodstock Cl *FHAM* PO15 ...... 6 C5
  HEND SO30 .... 133 L3
Woodstock Dr *PTSW* SO17 ...... 106 F7
Woodstock La *RGWD* BH24 ...... 170 E2
Woodstock Rd
  CHCH/BSGR BH23 ...... 223 H6
  GPORT PO12 .... 11 G4
  HAV PO9 .... 165 G6
  PSTN BH14 .... 233 M6
Woods View Rd
  MOOR/WNTN BH9 ...... 220 B8
Woodthorpe Gdns *HLER* SO31 .. 158 D2
Woodvale *FHAM* PO15 ...... 6 A4
Woodvale Gdns
  NMIL/BTOS BH25 ...... 226 A4
Woodview Cl *ROWN* SO16 ...... 106 F2
Woodville Dr *PSE* PO1 ...... 12 E5
Woodville Rd *FAWY* SO45 ...... 180 F5
  HAV PO9 .... 164 F6
Woodward Cl *GPORT* PO12 ...... 10 A4
Woofferton Rd *CHAM* PO6 ...... 162 E7
Woolbeding La *MIDH* GU29 ...... 67 L3
Woolbridge Rd *RGWD* BH24 ...... 169 J4
Woolslope Cl *FERN* BH22 ...... 168 C7
Woolslope Gdns *FERN* BH22 ...... 168 D7
Woolslope Rd *FERN* BH22 ...... 168 C7
Woolston Rd *HAV* PO9 ...... 165 G2
  HLER SO31 .... 132 F8
Woolven Cl *ITCH* SO19 ...... 233 M3
Wools Br *RGWD* BH24 ...... 169 G2
Woolwich Cl *HLER* SO31 ...... 133 K6
Wooton Rd *LSOL/BMARY* PO13 .. 208 E4
Wootton *HLER* SO31 ...... 157 G1
Wootton Farm Rd
  NMIL/BTOS BH25 ...... 199 J6
Wootton Gdns *BMTH* BH1 ...... 15 G5
Wootton Mt *BMTH* BH1 ...... 15 H5
Wootton Rough
  NMIL/BTOS BH25 ...... 199 M8
Wootton St *CHAM* PO6 ...... 187 K1
Worbarrow Gdns
  BKME/WDN BH12 ...... 219 G8
Worcester Pl *ITCH* SO19 ...... 132 F6
  LYMN SO41 .... 228 D6
Wordsworth Av *CHAM* PO6 ...... 162 C7
  CHAR BH8 .... 221 J7
Wordsworth Cl *BPWT* SO32 ...... 85 K8
  FUFL SO22 .... 2 B6
Wordsworth Pl *HLER* SO31 ...... 134 F7
Wordsworth Rd *ROWN* SO16 ...... 106 B7
Worgret Rd *PLE* BH15 ...... 233 J1
Workhouse La *PSF* GU32 ...... 61 J7
Workman's La *HLER* SO31 ...... 182 C3
Workshop Rd *WVILLE* PO7 ...... 162 B4
Worldham Rd *HAV* PO9 ...... 165 M2
Worrell Dr *BKME/WDN* BH12 .. 219 G8
Worsley Rd *SSEA* PO5 ...... 13 H6
Worsley St *ENEY* PO4 ...... 211 L6
Worthing Av *GPORT* PO12 ...... 185 K8
Worthing Rd *SSEA* PO5 ...... 13 K8
Worthington Crs *PSTN* BH14 .. 233 M5
Worthy Ct *HAV* PO9 ...... 165 M3

Worthy La *WINC* SO23 ...... 2 F5
Worthy Rd *NMIL/BTOS* BH25 .. 225 L5
  WINC SO23 .... 3 G3
Wortley Rd *CHCH/BSGR* BH23 .. 239 M1
Wraxhall Cl *CFDH* BH17 ...... 218 B7
Wraysbury Park Dr
  EMRTH PO10 .... 166 D4
Wren Cl *CHCH/BSGR* BH23 ...... 239 C3
  FUFL SO22 .... 26 C3
  NMIL/BTOS BH25 ...... 225 K6
  RGWD BH24 .... 171 G2
Wren Crs *BKME/WDN* BH12 .. 235 C3
  HEND SO30 .... 109 K8
Wren Gdns *FBDG* SP6 ...... 121 M2
Wren Rd *ELGH* SO50 ...... 81 K7
Wren Wy *FHAM/PORC* PO16 .. 161 K8
Wrexham Gr *HORN* PO8 ...... 116 A6
Wright's HI *ITCH* SO19 ...... 132 E6
Wroxham Rd
  BKME/WDN BH12 ...... 234 E3
Wryneck Cl *ROWN* SO16 ...... 106 A2
Wyatts Cl *WIMB* BH21 ...... 217 H2
Wyatts La *WIMB* BH21 ...... 217 G2
Wyborn Cl *HISD* PO11 ...... 213 L6
Wych La *LSOL/BMARY* PO13 .. 184 F4
Wychwood Cl *WCLF* BH2 ...... 14 D3
Wychwood Dr *FAWY* SO45 ...... 206 C1
  WCLF BH2 .... 14 E2
Wychwood Gv *CHFD* SO53 ...... 53 K8
  WEND SO18 .... 107 M7
Wycote Rd *LSOL/BMARY* PO13 .. 184 F4
Wyeford Cl *HAV* PO9 ...... 165 M2
Wyelands Av *WIMB* BH21 ...... 193 H3
Wykeham Cl *CFDH* BH17 ...... 218 C8
  NEND PO2 .... 106 D4
Wykeham Fld *WHAM* PO17 ...... 136 E5
Wykeham Pl *FUFL* SO22 ...... 26 C3
  LYMN SO41 .... 228 C5
Wykeham Rd *HLER* SO31 ...... 156 F2
  NEND PO2 .... 187 J7
Wylde Green La *LISS* GU33 ...... 36 F3
Wylds La *PSF* GU32 ...... 63 H8
Wyllie Rd *NEND* PO2 ...... 187 J4
Wylye Cl *WEND* SO18 ...... 108 A5
Wymering La *CHAM* PO6 ...... 163 J8
Wymering Manor Cl
  CHAM PO6 .... 163 J8
Wymering Rd *NEND* PO2 ...... 187 J8
Wyncombe Rd *BOSC* BH5 ...... 237 G3
Wyndcliffe Rd *ENEY* PO4 ...... 13 M6
Wyndham Cl
  CHCH/BSGR BH23 ...... 224 F6
  HORN PO8 .... 140 F4
Wyndham Ms *PSEA* PO1 ...... 12 D5
Wyndham Pl *WSHM* SO15 ...... 4 D1
Wyndham Rd
  CHCH/BSGR BH23 ...... 224 F6
  PSTN BH14 .... 234 A5
Wynford Rd
  MOOR/WNTN BH9 ...... 220 E4
  PSTN BH14 .... 234 B5
Wynne Cl *BDST* BH18 ...... 217 K4
Wynter Cl *LTDN* BH7 ...... 236 E1
Wynter Rd *WEND* SO18 ...... 108 A8
Wynton Wy *FHAM* PO15 ...... 160 A5
Wynyards Gap *NBAD* SO52 ...... 79 L4
Wyre Cl *CHFD* SO53 ...... 81 G2
Wyvern Cl *BKME/WDN* BH12 .. 234 C1
  CHFD SO53 .... 81 J2

Yarmouth Cl
  BKME/WDN BH12 ...... 234 F3
Yarmouth Gdns *WSHM* SO15 .. 106 A7
Yarmouth Rd
  BKME/WDN BH12 ...... 234 E2
Yarrell Md *LYMN* SO41 ...... 227 M4
Yarrells Cl *UPTN* BH16 ...... 232 B2
Yarrells La *UPTN* BH16 ...... 232 B2
Yarrow Cl *CHCH/BSGR* BH23 .. 223 M8
Yarrow Rd *BKME/WDN* BH12 .. 218 E8
Yarrow Wy *HLER* SO31 ...... 158 C6
Yateley Cl *HAV* PO9 ...... 165 C3
Yaverland *HLER* SO31 ...... 157 G2
Yeatminster Rd *CFDH* BH17 .. 218 D6
Yelverton Av *FAWY* SO45 ...... 155 L7
Yelverton Rd *WCLF* BH2 ...... 14 E5
Yeo Ct *ENEY* PO4 ...... 212 A5
Yeomans Fld *RCCH* PO18 ...... 167 M7
Yeomans Rd *CHAR* BH8 ...... 221 J5
Yeomans Wy *CHAR* BH8 ...... 221 J5
  TOTT SO40 .... 104 E8
Yeovil Cha *WEND* SO18 ...... 108 A8
Yeovilton Cl *LYMN* SO41 ...... 227 J7
Yerville Gdns *LYMN* SO41 ...... 226 D5
Yew La *NMIL/BTOS* BH25 ...... 226 A4
Yew Rd *WEND* SO18 ...... 107 M8
Yewside *LSOL/BMARY* PO13 .. 185 J7
The Yews *HORN* PO8 ...... 141 H1
Yewtree Cl *FAWY* SO45 ...... 155 L8
Yew Tree Cl *ELGH* SO50 ...... 83 H5
  HEND SO30 .... 133 M2
  WIMB BH21 .... 192 A3
Yew Tree Dr *FHAM* PO15 ...... 135 G8
  HLER SO31 .... 158 F1
Yew Tree Gdns *WVILLE* PO7 .. 139 J4
Yewtree La *ROWN* SO16 ...... 105 H5
Yew Tree Pl *LISS* GU33 ...... 36 F4
Yew Tree Rd *HISD* PO11 ...... 189 L8
Yoells Crs *HORN* PO8 ...... 140 D2
Yoells La *HORN* PO8 ...... 140 D2
Yokesford HI *ROMY* SO51 ...... 50 D3
Yonge Cl *ELGH* SO50 ...... 82 A5
York Av *NMIL/BTOS* BH25 ...... 225 M5
York Buildings *SHAM* SO14 ...... 5 G4
York Cl *BDST* BH18 ...... 217 L6
  CHCH/BSGR BH23 ...... 237 L1
  ELGH SO50 .... 109 J1
  NBAD SO52 .... 80 E4
  PSF GU32 .... 63 J5
  SHAM SO14 .... 132 A2
  TOTT SO40 .... 104 F8
York Crs *LSOL/BMARY* PO13 .. 208 E4
York Dro *RSAL* SP5 ...... 75 H8
  WEND SO18 .... 132 F1
Yorke St *SSEA* PO5 ...... 12 F4
Yorke Wy *HLER* SO31 ...... 157 J5
York Gdns *FHAM/PORC* PO16 .. 186 B2
York Pl *LTDN* BH7 ...... 236 F5
  PSEA PO1 .... 210 F2
York Rd *BMTH* BH1 ...... 15 K4
  CFDH BH17 .... 217 L7
  ELGH SO50 .... 81 M7
  WSHM SO15 .... 131 G1
Yorkwood *LISS* GU33 ...... 36 F4
Youngs Rd *BWD* BH11 ...... 219 L3
Yves Ms *SSEA* PO5 ...... 13 J7

Y

Yaldhurst Ct *HAV* PO9 ...... 165 M2
Yaldhurst La *LYMN* SO41 ...... 227 M4
Yapton St *PSEA* PO1 ...... 13 G1
Yarborough Rd *SSEA* PO5 ...... 13 G6
Yardlea Cl *HAV* PO9 ...... 141 M7
Yardley Cl *HSEA* PO3 ...... 188 A4
Yardley Rd *HEND* SO30 ...... 133 M3

Z

Zamek Cl *BWD* BH11 ...... 219 L3
Zetland Rd *CHAM* PO6 ...... 188 B1
  GPORT PO12 .... 10 E2
Zeus La *WVILLE* PO7 ...... 164 D5
Zinnia Cl *NBNE* BH10 ...... 220 C6

Index - featured places

Abbey Chiropractic Clinic
  ROMY SO51 .... 78 D1
Abbey Mead Surgery
  ROMY SO51 .... 78 C1
Abbotswood Junior School
  TOTT SO40 .... 129 H1
ABC Cinema
  BMTH BH1 .... 14 F6
Abraham Gallery
  SSEA PO5 .... 13 H6
Acorn Business Centre
  CHAM PO6 .... 163 H8
Ad Astra County First School
  CFDH BH17 .... 218 C7
Adeline Road Surgery
  BOSC BH5 .... 236 D4
Admiral Lord Nelson School
  HSEA PO3 .... 187 M7
Albany Business Centre
  WHAM PO17 .... 160 F1
Alderman Quilley
  Secondary School
  ELGH SO50 .... 81 L7
Aldermoor Health Centre
  ROWN SO16 .... 106 B4
Alderney Middle School
  BKME/WDN BH12 ...... 219 H7
Allington Manor
  Business Centre
  ELGH SO50 .... 108 D1
All Saints C of E Primary School
  RSAL SP5 .... 47 G5
All Saints Community
  Primary School
  WINC SO23 .... 27 G2
Alma Road Surgery
  PTSW SO17 .... 106 F8
Alma Road Surgery
  ROMY SO51 .... 78 E1
The Alpha Business Park
  SHAM SO14 .... 131 M1

Alverstoke C of E Junior School
  GPORT PO12 .... 10 C6
Alverstoke County
  Infant School
  GPORT PO12 .... 10 C8
Amey Industrial Estate
  PSF GU32 .... 63 K5
A M F Bowling
  ITCH SO19 .... 132 D2
A M F Bowling
  PSEA PO1 .... 13 H1
Ampfield Primary School
  ROMY SO51 .... 52 B4
Anchor Business Centre
  CHFD SO53 .... 81 G2
Andover Road Retail Park
  FUFL SO22 .... 2 E5
The Andrew Isaacs Practice
  BMTH BH1 .... 15 J4
Anne Dale County Junior &
  Infant School
  FHAM/STUB PO14 ...... 184 A6
Apple Industrial Estate
  FHAM PO15 .... 159 G3
Applemore College
  FAWY SO45 .... 155 G6
Applemore Recreation Centre
  FAWY SO45 .... 155 G5
Arch Farm Industrial Estate
  NBAD SO52 .... 97 K5
The Arnewood Practice
  NMIL/BTOS BH25 ...... 225 L5
Arnewood School
  NMIL/BTOS BH25 ...... 225 K7
The Art Gallery
  EMRTH PO10 .... 166 F4
Art Space School
  PSEA PO1 .... 211 G1
Arundel Court Junior &
  Infant School
  PSEA PO1 .... 211 H2

Ashdown School
  CFDH BH17 .... 218 C7
Ashley County Infant School
  NMIL/BTOS BH25 ...... 226 B5
Ashley Heath Industrial Estate
  WIMB BH21 .... 169 G1
Ashley Junior School
  NMIL/BTOS BH25 ...... 226 A5
Ashurst Hospital
  TOTT SO40 .... 128 F7
Associated Football Club
  TOTT SO40 .... 104 F8
Atherley House Surgery
  WSHM SO15 .... 131 H2
The Atherley School
  ROWN SO16 .... 105 G2
Avenue Clinic
  WSHM SO15 .... 131 K2
Avenue Shopping Centre
  WCLF BH2 .... 14 D5
Avonbourne Girls School
  LTDN BH7 .... 236 F1
Avon Castle
  RGWD BH24 .... 170 B5
Avonlea Preparatory School
  RGWD BH24 .... 146 F8
Awbridge County School
  ROMY SO51 .... 49 J3
Baddesley Park Industrial Estate
  NBAD SO52 .... 80 A4
Baden Powell & St Peters
  C of E (VC) School
  PSTN BH14 .... 234 A5
Badger Farm Surgery
  FUFL SO22 .... 26 B4
Ballard College
  NMIL/BTOS BH25 ...... 225 L5
Ballard Lake
  Preparatory School
  NMIL/BTOS BH25 ...... 225 L4

Banister School
  WSHM SO15 .... 131 K1
Bargate Museum
  SHAM SO14 .... 5 G4
Bargate Shopping Centre
  SHAM SO14 .... 5 G4
Barncroft Infant School
  HAV PO9 .... 165 H4
Barncroft Junior School
  HAV PO9 .... 165 G4
Barratt Industrial Park
  FHAM PO15 .... 159 G3
Bartley C of E Middle School
  TOTT SO40 .... 127 M1
Barton Peveril College
  ELGH SO50 .... 81 L7
Barton Surgery
  NMIL/BTOS BH25 ...... 225 L7
Bassett Green Junior School
  ROWN SO16 .... 107 G4
Baycroft School
  FHAM/STUB PO14 ...... 184 B6
Bay House School
  GPORT PO12 .... 209 J6
BBC South TV & Radio Solent
  WSHM SO15 .... 4 E1
The Bear Museum
  EPSF GU31 .... 63 L6
Bearwood County
  Primary School
  WIMB BH21 .... 219 G2
Beaucroft School
  WIMB BH21 .... 192 C2
Beaufort Road Surgery
  SBNE BH6 .... 237 H3
Beaulieu CP School
  BROC SO42 .... 178 D7
Bedales School
  PSF GU32 .... 63 K1

Bedenham County
  Junior & Infant School
  LSOL/BMARY PO13 ...... 185 H5
Beechwood Middle School
  WEND SO18 .... 132 D1
Belbins Business Park
  ROMY SO51 .... 50 F5
Belgrave Industrial Estate
  PTSW SO17 .... 107 H6
Bellemoor Secondary School
  ROWN SO16 .... 106 C6
Berrywood Primary School
  HEND SO30 .... 109 J7
Bethany C of E (VA)
  Junior School
  BMTH BH1 .... 236 C3
Bevois Town Primary School
  SHAM SO14 .... 131 L1
Bicknell Boys
  Residential School
  LTDN BH7 .... 236 F1
Bidbury Junior & Infant School
  HAV PO9 .... 8 A2
Birchwood Medical Centre
  CFDH BH17 .... 217 K8
Bishops Waltham County
  Infant School
  BPWT SO32 .... 85 J8
Bitterne C of E First School
  ITCH SO19 .... 132 D2
Bitterne C of E Infant School
  ITCH SO19 .... 132 D2
Bitterne Health Centre
  WEND SO18 .... 132 E1
Bitterne Leisure Centre
  WEND SO18 .... 132 E1
Bitterne Manor
  Primary School
  ITCH SO19 .... 132 B1
Bitterne Middle School
  ITCH SO19 .... 132 D2

Bitterne Park Clinic
WEND SO18 .... 107 K8
Bitterne Park Junior &
Infant School
WEND SO18 .... 107 J6
Bitterne Park
Secondary School
WEND SO18 .... 107 K6
Bitterne Park Surgery
WEND SO18 .... 107 K8
Blackbrook Business Park
FHAM PO15 .... 6 C5
Blackfield Health Centre
FAWY SO45 .... 180 B6
Blackfield Junior &
Infant School
FAWY SO45 .... 180 C7
Blue Fish Zoo
BMTH BH1 .... 14 E6
The Boatyard Industrial Estate
FHAM/PORC PO16 .... 7 H8
The Bold Gallery
CHCH/BSGR BH23 .... 238 A1
Boscombe Dental
Health Centre
BOSC BH5 .... 236 E3
Boscombe Manor
Medical Centre
BOSC BH5 .... 236 E4
Bosmere Junior School
HAV PO9 .... 8 E5
Botley Junior & Infant School
HEND SO30 .... 134 E1
Botley Park Hotel &
Country Club
BPWT SO32 .... 109 L6
Boundary Oak School
WHAM PO17 .... 160 F3
The Bourne Community College
EMRTH PO10 .... 167 G7
Bournemouth Borough Council
BMTH BH1 .... 15 K5
Bournemouth Business Centre
BMTH BH1 .... 15 J4
Bournemouth College
BMTH BH1 .... 15 M4
Bournemouth County Council
BMTH BH1 .... 15 J4
Bournemouth County Court
BMTH BH1 .... 15 H4
Bournemouth
International Airport
CHCH/BSGR BH23 .... 195 K8
Bournemouth
Magistrates Court
BMTH BH1 .... 15 H5
Bournemouth Mosque
MOOR/WNTN BH9 .... 220 D8
The Bournemouth
Nuffield Hospital
BMTH BH1 .... 15 G1
Bournemouth & Poole College
BMTH BH1 .... 15 H5
Bournemouth & Poole College
BMTH BH1 .... 15 J5
Bournemouth & Poole College
PSTN BH14 .... 233 L3
Bournemouth & Poole
College of Further Education
PSTN BH14 .... 233 L4
Bournemouth School for Boys
CHAR BH8 .... 221 G7
Bournemouth School for Girls
CHAR BH8 .... 221 G6
Bournemouth Sports Club
CHCH/BSGR BH23 .... 195 G7
Bournemouth University
BKME/WDN BH12 .... 220 A8
Bournemouth University
BMTH BH1 .... 15 J5
Bournemouth University
BMTH BH1 .... 15 K5
Boveridge House School
WIMB BH21 .... 95 H6
Boyatt Shopping Centre
ELGH SO50 .... 81 M3
Boyatt Wood Surgery
ELGH SO50 .... 81 L3
Braemore C of E
Primary School
FBDG SP6 .... 72 A8
Braishfield CP School
ROMY SO51 .... 51 J2
Bramshaw Golf Club
LYND SO43 .... 101 M7
Branksome Heath
Middle School
BKME/WDN BH12 .... 234 B2
Bransgore Primary School
CHCH/BSGR BH23 .... 198 A8
Breamore House
FBDG SP6 .... 71 M5
Brickfield Trading Estate
CHFD SO53 .... 81 G3
Brickyards Industrial Estate
PSF GU32 .... 35 M7
Bridge Gallery
WSHM SO15 .... 131 K2
Bridgemary Community School
LSOL/BMARY PO13 .... 185 G6
The Bridge Shopping Centre
PSEA PO1 .... 13 K1
Broad Chalke Primary School
RSAL SP5 .... 40 B1
Broadlands House
ROMY SO51 .... 78 D3
Broadstone First School
BDST BH18 .... 217 M4
Broadstone Middle School
BDST BH18 .... 218 A3
Brockenhurst College
BROC SO42 .... 175 L6
Brockenhurst Primary School
BROC SO42 .... 175 K7
Brockhurst County
Infant School
GPORT PO12 .... 209 K1
Brockhurst County
Junior School
GPORT PO12 .... 209 L2
Brockhurst Medical Centre
GPORT PO12 .... 209 K1

Brokenhurst Manor Golf Club
BROC SO42 .... 201 J2
Brompton Gallery
SHAM SO14 .... 5 H2
Brookes Hill Industrial Estate
TOTT SO40 .... 104 A4
Brookfield Secondary School
HLER SO31 .... 158 C4
Brookwood Industrial Estate
ELGH SO50 .... 81 L5
The Brownhill Surgery
CHFD SO53 .... 81 J1
Brownsea Open Air Theatre
CFDH BH17 .... 217 L8
Brune Park Community School
LSOL/BMARY PO13 .... 185 J8
Buckholme School
PSTN BH14 .... 233 M4
Buckland Medical Centre
NEND PO2 .... 187 H8
The Burgate School
FBDG SP6 .... 97 L5
Burgess Road Surgery
ROWN SO16 .... 107 H4
Buriton Business Park
EPSF GU31 .... 91 H1
Buriton CP School
EPSF GU31 .... 91 J3
Burley CP School
RGWD BH24 .... 172 E6
Burley Golf Club
RGWD BH24 .... 172 F5
Burnfields Retail Park
HSEA PO3 .... 187 M7
Burridge Social & Sports Club
HLER SO31 .... 134 F6
Bursledon C of E
Junior & Infant School
HLER SO31 .... 133 L8
Bursledon Windmill Museum
HLER SO31 .... 133 L6
Burton Primary School
CHCH/BSGR BH23 .... 223 G5
Business Centre
SHAM SO14 .... 5 J7
The Business Centre
RSAL SP5 .... 73 J1
Byngs Business Park
WVILLE PO7 .... 139 M6
By Pass Football Club
ROMY SO51 .... 78 E2
Cadnam Surgery
TOTT SO40 .... 127 L1
Calmore County Junior & Infant
School
TOTT SO40 .... 104 B6
Calmore Industrial Estate
TOTT SO40 .... 104 D6
Calmore Sports Club
TOTT SO40 .... 103 M6
Calshot Castle
FAWY SO45 .... 181 M7
Cameleon Theatre
WSHM SO15 .... 131 H2
Campbell Surgery
SSEA PO5 .... 13 K5
Cams Hill School
FHAM/PORC PO16 .... 161 J8
Canada House Business Centre
NMIL/BTOS BH25 .... 226 A6
Canford Heath First School
CFDH BH17 .... 233 K1
Canford Heath Middle School
CFDH BH17 .... 233 J1
Canford School
WIMB BH21 .... 192 E6
Cantell Secondary School
ROWN SO16 .... 106 F4
The Canute Surgery
ITCH SO19 .... 132 C5
The Carpet Gallery
WBNE BH4 .... 235 H5
Carter Community School
PLE BH15 .... 232 E6
Carvers Trading Estate
RGWD BH24 .... 170 E1
Castle County Primary School
FHAM/PORC PO16 .... 186 B1
Castle Court School
WIMB BH21 .... 216 F1
Catherine Corbett Clinic
HAV PO9 .... 8 F3
Catherington C of E
Controlled Infant School
HORN PO8 .... 116 A7
The Cedar School
ROWN SO16 .... 105 K4
Central Business Park
BMTH BH1 .... 15 M2
Central Trading Estate
SHAM SO14 .... 5 L3
Centurion Industrial Park
SHAM SO14 .... 132 A1
Chamberlayne Park School
ITCH SO19 .... 132 E7
Chandlers Ford Infant School
CHFD SO53 .... 81 J1
Charles Dickens Junior &
Infant School
PSEA PO1 .... 211 H2
Chawton House Surgery
LYMN SO41 .... 228 C5
Chesil Theatre
WINC SO23 .... 3 J9
Chevron Business Park
FAWY SO45 .... 179 M2
Christchurch Infant School
CHCH/BSGR BH23 .... 237 M1
Christchurch Junior School
CHCH/BSGR BH23 .... 237 L1
Christchurch Medical Centre
HAV PO9 .... 166 A5
Christchurch Ski &
Leisure Centre
CHCH/BSGR BH23 .... 195 M5
Christ the King RC
Primary School
BWD BH11 .... 219 L3
Churchers College
EPSF GU31 .... 63 M4
Churchers College Junior School
PSF GU32 .... 63 K5

Churchill Yard Industrial Estate
WVILLE PO7 .... 140 C7
City Business Centre
WINC SO23 .... 3 C5
City Grove Trading Estate
ELGH SO50 .... 81 K4
City Industrial Park
WSHM SO15 .... 4 C3
City Museum
PSEA PO1 .... 12 E5
City Museum & Art Gallery
PSEA PO1 .... 12 E5
City Offices
WINC SO23 .... 3 H8
The City of Portsmouth
Boys School
NEND PO2 .... 187 J4
The City of Portsmouth
Girls School
PSEA PO1 .... 211 J2
City of Portsmouth Sports Club
NEND PO2 .... 187 H5
Civil Service Sports Ground
ENEY PO4 .... 211 K3
Civil Service Sports Ground
HSEA PO3 .... 187 L5
Clanfield Junior School
HORN PO8 .... 116 A1
Clanfield Surgery
HORN PO8 .... 116 B4
Clayfields Sports Centre
FAWY SO45 .... 155 H4
Cliffdale Primary School
NEND PO2 .... 187 K6
The Club House
LISS GU33 .... 37 K4
Cluster Industrial Estate
HSEA PO3 .... 211 L3
The Coast Clinic
FAWY SO45 .... 180 F5
Colden Common
Primary School
RWIN SO21 .... 54 E7
College Art School
WINC SO23 .... 26 E2
College Park Infant School
NEND PO2 .... 187 K6
Collingwood Business Park
FHAM/STUB PO14 .... 184 F2
Commercial Business Centre
CHFD SO53 .... 81 H2
Compton All Saints
C of E Primary School
RWIN SO21 .... 26 C8
Compton & Upmarden
C of E Primary School
RCCH PO18 .... 118 E6
Continental Ferry Port
NEND PO2 .... 187 G8
Copnor Infant School
HSEA PO3 .... 187 L7
Copnor Junior School
NEND PO2 .... 187 K7
Copythorne First School
TOTT SO40 .... 103 G6
Corfe Hills School
WIMB BH21 .... 217 K2
Corhampton Golf Club
BPWT SO32 .... 86 D4
Cornerways Surgery
RGWD BH24 .... 169 J4
Corpus Christie School
BOSC BH5 .... 236 E3
Corpus Christi RC
Primary School
NEND PO2 .... 187 H7
Cosham Health Centre
CHAM PO6 .... 187 K1
Cottage Grove Primary School
SSEA PO5 .... 13 H5
County and Magistrates Court
PSEA PO1 .... 13 G3
Courthill First School
PSTN BH14 .... 234 C4
Court Lane Junior &
Infant School
CHAM PO6 .... 187 L1
Cowplain School
HORN PO8 .... 140 C6
Cranewater Junior School
ENEY PO4 .... 13 M7
Crescent Primary School
ELGH SO50 .... 81 M5
The Crestwood
Community School
ELGH SO50 .... 81 L3
Crofton School
FHAM/STUB PO14 .... 184 C6
The Crookhorn
Community School
WVILLE PO7 .... 164 D4
Crow Arch Lane
Industrial Estate
RGWD BH24 .... 170 E3
Cumberland Business Centre
SSEA PO5 .... 13 K2
Cumberland Infant School
ENEY PO4 .... 211 L5
Cupernham County
Junior & Infants School
ROMY SO51 .... 51 G7
Curdridge Primary School
BPWT SO32 .... 110 C7
Cutlers Gallery
BMTH BH1 .... 14 F5
David Hart Business Centre
RSAL SP5 .... 44 F5
Dawkins Business Centre
PLE BH15 .... 232 C5
D Day Museum
SSEA PO5 .... 211 G7
Deacon Trading Estate
ELGH SO50 .... 82 B6
Dean Court (Bournemouth FC)
LTDN BH7 .... 236 E2
Deanery Campus
SHAM SO14 .... 5 J5
Dean Farm Estate
WHAM PO17 .... 160 E3
Delta Business Park
FHAM/PORC PO16 .... 184 F1

Denmead Health Centre
WVILLE PO7 .... 139 J3
Denmead Infant School
WVILLE PO7 .... 139 L4
Denmead Junior School
WVILLE PO7 .... 139 K4
Derby Road Surgery
NEND PO2 .... 187 H7
Devonshire Infant School
ENEY PO4 .... 211 K4
Devonshire Infant School
ENEY PO4 .... 13 M4
Devonshire Practice
ENEY PO4 .... 211 M5
Discover Bible School
WSHM SO15 .... 131 G2
Dockyard Apprentice
Exhibition
PSEA PO1 .... 12 B1
Dorset County Council
BMTH BH1 .... 15 H4
Dorset County Council
FERN BH22 .... 194 B3
Dorset County Council
WIMB BH21 .... 193 K1
Dorset County Council
WIMB BH21 .... 192 A3
Dorset Health Authority
FERN BH22 .... 194 B3
Dorset Healthcare NHS Trust
WEND SO18 .... 133 C1
Dorset Magistrates Court
BMTH BH1 .... 15 G4
Dorset Medical Centre
SHAM SO14 .... 5 G2
Down House
RSAL SP5 .... 45 J8
Downton C of E Primary School
RSAL SP5 .... 44 D8
Downton County
Secondary School
RSAL SP5 .... 72 D1
Downton Industrial Estate
RSAL SP5 .... 44 D8
Dr Hughes & Partners
RGWD BH24 .... 170 D1
Dr Munroe & Partners
TOTT SO40 .... 104 E8
Droxford Junior School
BPWT SO32 .... 86 F7
Droxford Primary School
BPWT SO32 .... 86 F7
Dunhurst School
PSF GU32 .... 63 K2
Dunwood Manor Golf Club
ROMY SO51 .... 49 J6
Durley Primary School
BPWT SO32 .... 109 M2
Durlston Court School
NMIL/BTOS BH25 .... 240 F1
Eagle House School
PSTN BH14 .... 233 M3
East Dorset Area
Health Authority
FERN BH22 .... 194 B3
Eastern Industrial Centre
CHAM PO6 .... 188 A2
East Hants District Council
PSF GU32 .... 63 K5
Eastleigh Borough Council
ELGH SO50 .... 81 L5
Eastleigh College of Further
Education
ELGH SO50 .... 81 M6
Eastleigh Football Club
ELGH SO50 .... 107 K1
Eastleigh Health Centre
ELGH SO50 .... 81 M5
Eastleigh Museum
ELGH SO50 .... 81 M6
Eastleigh Rugby Club
ELGH SO50 .... 82 B5
East Meon Controlled
Primary School
PSF GU32 .... 61 J7
Eastney Health Centre
ENEY PO4 .... 211 L5
Eastney Swimming Baths
ENEY PO4 .... 212 A6
Easton Lane Business Park
WINC SO23 .... 3 L6
East Shore School
HSEA PO3 .... 211 M2
East Street Shopping Centre
SHAM SO14 .... 5 H4
Ebblake Industrial Estate
RGWD BH24 .... 145 H4
Eling County Infant School
TOTT SO40 .... 129 L2
Elmhurst Business Park
GPORT PO12 .... 10 F3
Elmrise Junior & Infant School
BWD BH11 .... 219 K4
Elson County Infant School
GPORT PO12 .... 185 L8
Elson County Junior School
GPORT PO12 .... 185 L8
Embley Park School
ROMY SO51 .... 77 K2
Emsworth Museum
EMRTH PO10 .... 166 D7
Emsworth Primary School
EMRTH PO10 .... 166 C7
Emsworth Surgery
EMRTH PO10 .... 166 D8
English Gallery
HAV PO9 .... 142 A6
Enterprise Industrial Estate
HORN PO8 .... 116 B8
The Epiphany School
MOOR/WNTN BH9 .... 220 F4
Fairfield Infant School
HAV PO9 .... 9 G4
Fairisle Junior & Infant School
ROWN SO16 .... 105 K4
Fairlands Montessori School
BPWT SO32 .... 136 C1
Fair Oak Junior &
Infant School
ELGH SO50 .... 83 J7
Fairway Business Centre
HSEA PO3 .... 188 A5

Fareham Borough Council
FHAM PO15 .... 159 H3
Fareham Borough Council
FHAM/PORC PO16 .... 185 L1
Fareham Borough Council
FHAM/PORC PO16 .... 7 K5
Fareham College
FHAM/STUB PO14 .... 6 D6
The Fareham Gallery
FHAM/PORC PO16 .... 7 J6
Fareham Leisure Centre
FHAM/PORC PO16 .... 7 H4
Fareham Megabowl
FHAM/STUB PO14 .... 184 F3
Fareham Park C of E
Controlled Junior School
FHAM PO15 .... 160 A5
Fareham Park Infant School
FHAM PO15 .... 160 A5
Far Horizons Gallery
PSF GU32 .... 63 K5
Fawley Business Centre
FAWY SO45 .... 180 E5
Fawley County First School
FAWY SO45 .... 180 E5
Fenwick Hospital
LYND SO43 .... 151 J2
Ferndown First School
FERN BH22 .... 194 A3
Ferndown Medical Centre
FERN BH22 .... 194 B3
Ferndown Middle School
FERN BH22 .... 193 M3
Ferndown Sports Centre
FERN BH22 .... 193 M2
Ferndown Town Council
FERN BH22 .... 194 A2
Ferndown Upper School
FERN BH22 .... 193 M2
Fernhurst Junior School
ENEY PO4 .... 211 K4
Fernside Business Park
WIMB BH21 .... 193 L1
Fish Farm
RSAL SP5 .... 44 F5
Flanders Industrial Park
HEND SO30 .... 109 G8
Fleming Park Leisure Centre
ELGH SO50 .... 81 K5
Flying Bull Junior &
Infant School
NEND PO2 .... 187 H8
Fordingbrdge Junior &
Infant School
FBDG SP6 .... 97 L5
Fordingbridge Hospital
FBDG SP6 .... 97 L7
Forest Edge School
TOTT SO40 .... 129 J1
Forest End Surgery
WVILLE PO7 .... 164 B1
Forest Gate Surgery
TOTT SO40 .... 129 G4
Forestside Medical Practice
FAWY SO45 .... 155 J8
Fort Brockhurst
LSOL/BMARY PO13 .... 185 K7
Fort Cumberland
ENEY PO4 .... 212 C5
Forton Road Surgery
GPORT PO12 .... 209 M2
Fort Wallington
Industrial Estate
FHAM/PORC PO16 .... 161 H6
Foundry Lane Middle & Primary
School
WSHM SO15 .... 106 A8
Foxhills County First School
TOTT SO40 .... 129 H4
Freeground Junior &
Infant School
HEND SO30 .... 134 D2
Freemantle Business Centre
WSHM SO15 .... 131 G3
Friarsgate Medical Centre
WINC SO23 .... 3 H8
Frobisher Industrial Centre
ROMY SO51 .... 50 C7
Front Lawn GM Junior School
HAV PO9 .... 165 K2
Front Lawn Infant School
HAV PO9 .... 165 K4
Froxfield Endowed
Controlled Infant School
PSF GU32 .... 34 D6
Fryern Junior & Infant School
CHFD SO53 .... 81 K2
The Fryern Surgery
CHFD SO53 .... 81 K1
The Futcher School
CHAM PO6 .... 164 A8
The Gallery
LYMN SO41 .... 200 F7
The Gallery
SSEA PO5 .... 13 H7
Gasholders
SHAM SO14 .... 5 K2
Gatcombe Park Infant School
NEND PO2 .... 187 K4
George & Dragon Surgery
EMRTH PO10 .... 166 F5
George Street School
Branch Clinic
PSEA PO1 .... 211 K1
Glenfield Infant School
WEND SO18 .... 132 D1
Glenhurst School
HAV PO9 .... 9 G4
Glenmoor School for Girls
NBNE BH10 .... 220 B7
Glenwood School
EMRTH PO10 .... 166 C7
Goldfield Gallery
BPWT SO32 .... 113 H7
Goldfield Gallery
PSEA PO1 .... 12 D5
Goldsmith Infant School
ENEY PO4 .... 13 M5
Gomer County Junior &
Infant School
GPORT PO12 .... 209 J8

Goodway Sea School
GPORT PO12.................... 185 L8
Goodwyn Gallery
PSEA PO1.................... 13 L1
Gordleton Industrial Estate
LYMN SO41.................... 227 K3
Gosport Health Centre
GPORT PO12.................... 10 C4
Gosport Ice Rink
LSOL/BMARY PO13.................... 185 J7
Gosport Museum
GPORT PO12.................... 11 K3
Gosport War Memorial Hospital
GPORT PO12.................... 10 C4
Grange Comprehensive School
CHCH/BSGR BH23.................... 223 J8
Grange County Junior &
Infant School
LSOL/BMARY PO13.................... 209 G1
Grange Farm Business Park
BPWT SO32.................... 111 H8
Gravatom Business Centre
BPWT SO32.................... 85 G8
Greatbridge Business Park
ROMY SO51.................... 50 C7
Greenacres School
FUFL SO22.................... 2 E3
The Gregg School
WEND SO18.................... 107 M5
Greggs School
PTSW SO17.................... 106 F7
Grey Welles Surgery
HAV PO9.................... 165 K4
Group Surgery
ROWN SO16.................... 107 J4
Grove Medical Practice
WSHM SO15.................... 131 G1
Gudge Heath Surgery
FHAM PO15.................... 6 B2
Gundrymoor Trading Estate
WIMB BH21.................... 168 D3
Gurdwara Sikh Temple
SHAM SO14.................... 131 L2
Hadleigh Practice
WIMB BH21.................... 217 G4
Hale Primary School
FBDG SP6.................... 73 H5
Hall of Aviation
SHAM SO14.................... 5 K6
Halterworth CP School
ROMY SO51.................... 79 H1
Hamble County
Primary School
HLER SO31.................... 157 J4
Hamble County
Secondary School
HLER SO31.................... 157 J3
Hambledon Cricket Club
WVILLE PO7.................... 114 D3
Hambledon Infant School
WVILLE PO7.................... 114 C5
Hambrook Business Centre
RCCH PO18.................... 167 M4
Hammond County
Junior & Infant School
FHAM/STUB PO14.................... 184 A6
Hammond Industrial Estate
FHAM/STUB PO14.................... 184 B7
Hampreston Primary School
WIMB BH21.................... 193 J5
Hampshire County Council
ELGH SO50.................... 82 A5
Hampshire County Council
ELGH SO50.................... 81 K5
Hampshire County Council
FHAM/PORC PO16.................... 7 K5
Hampshire County Council
GPORT PO12.................... 11 G4
Hampshire County Council
HAV PO9.................... 9 G5
Hampshire County Council
LYMN SO41.................... 228 C4
Hampshire County Council
RGWD BH24.................... 170 E2
Hampshire County Council
TOTT SO40.................... 129 K4
Hampshire County Council
WINC SO23.................... 2 E7
Hampshire County
Cricket Club
WSHM SO15.................... 106 E8
Hampshire Gallery
BMTH BH1.................... 15 H4
Hamwic College
SHAM SO14.................... 5 H4
Hamworthy Community Clinic
PLE BH15.................... 232 D5
Hamworthy First School
PLE BH15.................... 232 E7
Hamworthy Middle School
PLE BH15.................... 232 E7
Hanway Group Practice
NEND PO2.................... 187 J7
Hanway Surgery
PSEA PO1.................... 211 H1
Harbridge School
RGWD BH24.................... 122 B8
Hardley School
FAWY SO45.................... 180 A3
Harefield Clinic
WEND SO18.................... 132 E1
Harefield Junior &
Infant School
WEND SO18.................... 108 A8
Harestock Infant School
FUFL SO22.................... 16 C5
Harrison County
Primary School
FHAM/PORC PO16.................... 7 K4
Hart Plain Infant School
HORN PO8.................... 140 C6
Hart Plain Junior School
WVILLE PO7.................... 140 C6
Haselworth County
Primary School
GPORT PO12.................... 10 F5
Havant Business Centre
HAV PO9.................... 8 A4
Havant College
HAV PO9.................... 8 D1
Havant Leisure Centre
HAV PO9.................... 8 E2

Havant Museum
HAV PO9.................... 8 F5
Havant Retail Park
HAV PO9.................... 164 F7
Havant Rugby Football Club
HAV PO9.................... 8 A2
Havant Sports Club
HAV PO9.................... 8 E3
Havant Town Football Club
HAV PO9.................... 165 L3
Havant War Memorial Hospital
HAV PO9.................... 8 D3
Hayeswood County
First School
WIMB BH21.................... 192 E2
Hayling Billy Business Centre
HISD PO11.................... 213 H4
Hayling Island Health Centre
HISD PO11.................... 213 L5
Haymoor Middle School
CFDH BH17.................... 218 C7
Hayward Business Centre
HAV PO9.................... 165 M5
Hazel Wood First School
TOTT SO40.................... 129 G1
Headlands Business Park
RGWD BH24.................... 146 E6
Heatherlands First School
BKME/WDN BH12.................... 234 C3
Heathfield Infant &
Middle School
ITCH SO19.................... 133 G6
Heathfield School
FHAM/STUB PO14.................... 160 A8
Heathlands Primary School
BWD BH11.................... 219 L5
Hedge End Business Centre
HEND SO30.................... 109 G8
Hedge End Retail Park
HEND SO30.................... 133 L1
Hedge End Town Council
HEND SO30.................... 133 M2
Henbury View First School
WIMB BH21.................... 217 G2
Henry Beaufort School
FUFL SO22.................... 16 D5
Henry Cort Community School
FHAM/STUB PO14.................... 159 M5
The Heritage Centre &
Museum
TOTT SO40.................... 129 M2
Herne County Junior School
EPSF SO19.................... 63 M4
The Herne Farm
Leisure Centre
EPSF SO19.................... 63 M4
Highbury College
CHAM PO6.................... 187 L3
Highbury College
PSEA PO1.................... 13 H1
Highbury College of
Technology
PSEA PO1.................... 210 F2
Highbury Primary School
CHAM PO6.................... 187 L2
Highcliffe Castle Golf Club
CHCH/BSGR BH23.................... 239 K1
Highcliffe County
Junior School
CHCH/BSGR BH23.................... 224 E7
Highcliffe GM
Comprehensive School
CHCH/BSGR BH23.................... 224 B7
Highcliffe Medical Centre
CHCH/BSGR BH23.................... 224 D8
Highcroft Industrial Estate
HORN PO8.................... 116 B8
Highfield C of E (A)
Primary School
PTSW SO17.................... 106 F6
Highgrove Industrial Park
HSEA PO3.................... 187 M5
Highlands Medical Centre
FHAM PO15.................... 160 A5
Highlands Medical Centre
FHAM PO15.................... 6 A2
Hightown Industrial Estate
RGWD BH24.................... 170 F2
Hightown Primary School
ITCH SO19.................... 133 J4
Hillbourne First School
CFDH BH17.................... 217 L6
Hillbourne Middle School
CFDH BH17.................... 217 L6
Hill House School
LYMN SO41.................... 202 B7
Hill Lane Surgery
WSHM SO15.................... 131 J1
Hill Park Clinic
FHAM PO15.................... 6 D1
Hillside County First School
VWD BH31.................... 144 E1
Hillside Industrial Estate
HORN PO8.................... 116 B8
Hill View First School
NBNE BH10.................... 220 C5
Hill View Junior School
NBNE BH10.................... 220 C5
Hiltingbury County
Junior & Infant School
CHFD SO53.................... 53 H7
Hindu Temple
SHAM SO14.................... 131 M2
Hiscock Gallery
SSEA PO5.................... 13 H7
H M Coroners Court
BMTH BH1.................... 15 H4
HMS Victory
PSEA PO1.................... 210 D2
Holbrook County
Junior & Infant School
LSOL/BMARY PO13.................... 185 G5
Holbrook Recreation Centre
LSOL/BMARY PO13.................... 185 J7
Holbury County JMI School
FAWY SO45.................... 180 A5
Hollybrook First School
ROWN SO16.................... 106 C5
Hollybrook Middle School
ROWN SO16.................... 106 C5
Hollycombe School
LIPH GU30.................... 38 F4

Holy Family RC Primary School
ROWN SO16.................... 105 H6
Homefield School
CHCH/BSGR BH23.................... 223 G4
Homeopathic Surgery
NMIL/BTOS BH25.................... 240 E1
Homewood
Chiropractic Health Centre
FHAM/PORC PO16.................... 7 K4
Hook with Warsash
Primary School
HLER SO31.................... 158 B8
Hordle C of E GM
Primary School
LYMN SO41.................... 226 E5
Hordle House School
LYMN SO41.................... 241 M3
Horndean C of E Junior School
HORN PO8.................... 141 G1
Horndean Community School
HORN PO8.................... 140 F1
Horndean Football Club
HORN PO8.................... 140 F1
Horndean Health Centre
HORN PO8.................... 141 H1
Horndean Infant School
HORN PO8.................... 141 G1
Hounsdown School
TOTT SO40.................... 129 K4
Hulbert Junior School
WVILLE PO7.................... 164 D2
Hunter Simmonds Gallery
CCLF BH13.................... 235 C4
Hyde (C of E Controlled)
Primary School
FBDG SP6.................... 123 H3
Hythe CP School
FAWY SO45.................... 155 L4
Hythe Medical Centre
FAWY SO45.................... 155 K6
Imax Cinema
BMTH BH1.................... 14 F7
International Centre &
Leisure Pool
WCLF BH2.................... 14 E8
Isambard Brunel Junior School
NEND PO2.................... 187 J8
Isle of Wight
Car Ferry Terminal
PSEA PO1.................... 12 C4
Itchen College
ITCH SO19.................... 132 E3
Jellicoe Theatre
PSTN BH14.................... 233 L3
J M L Trading Estate
WSHM SO15.................... 4 C2
Jubilee Business Centre
WVILLE PO7.................... 140 C8
Jubilee Surgery
FHAM/STUB PO14.................... 159 K8
Kanes Hill Primary School
ITCH SO19.................... 133 J2
Keble Memorial
Primary School
RWIN SO21.................... 53 C2
Kelseys Doctors Surgery
LISS GU33.................... 36 E4
King Alfred College
FUFL SO22.................... 2 B8
King Alfreds College of Higher
Education
FUFL SO22.................... 2 C9
King Edward VI School
WSHM SO15.................... 106 D8
King Richard School
CHAM PO6.................... 162 D8
Kings Copse Primary School
HEND SO30.................... 134 A3
Kings Junior School
SBNE BH6.................... 237 L3
Kingsland Market
SHAM SO14.................... 5 H3
Kingsleigh First School
NBNE BH10.................... 220 A5
Kingsleigh Junior School
NBNE BH10.................... 220 A5
Kingsleigh Secondary School
NBNE BH10.................... 220 A5
Kings Park Primary School
BMTH BH1.................... 236 D2
The Kings Primary School
HEND SO30.................... 108 C5
Kings School
ELGH SO50.................... 83 G7
Kings School
FUFL SO22.................... 26 A2
Kings Theatre
SSEA PO5.................... 13 K6
Kingsworthy Primary School
WINC SO23.................... 17 H2
Kin Hon Clinic
SSEA PO5.................... 12 F3
Kinson Primary School
BWD BH11.................... 219 M3
Knightwood Primary School
NBAD SO52.................... 80 E1
Lacey Lodge School
WIMB BH21.................... 211 M2
Lake Road Health Centre
PSEA PO1.................... 211 J2
Landford C of E Primary School
RSAL SP5.................... 75 J4
Langdown County
Infants School
FAWY SO45.................... 155 M6
Langdown County
Junior School
FAWY SO45.................... 155 M5
Langrish CP School
PSF GU32.................... 62 F5
Langstone Infant School
HSEA PO3.................... 211 L2
Langstone Junior School
HSEA PO3.................... 211 L1
Lankhills School
WINC SO23.................... 2 F4
Lansdowne Clinic
BMTH BH1.................... 15 H2
Lee on Solent Health Centre
LSOL/BMARY PO13.................... 208 C2

Lee-on-the-solent
Infant School
LSOL/BMARY PO13.................... 208 D3
Lee-on-the-solent
Junior School
LSOL/BMARY PO13.................... 208 D3
Leesland C of E Infant School
GPORT PO12.................... 10 E3
Leesland C of E Junior School
GPORT PO12.................... 10 E3
Leigh House Hospital
CHFD SO53.................... 53 G8
Leisure Centre
HAV PO9.................... 8 F2
Leisure Centre
SHAM SO14.................... 131 L2
Lido Sports Club
WINC SO23.................... 3 G5
Lilliput First School
PSTN BH14.................... 234 B8
Liner Industrial Estate
WSHM SO15.................... 131 G2
Linwood School
MOOR/WNTN BH9.................... 235 M1
Liss Business Centre
LISS GU33.................... 36 D3
Liss County Infant &
Junior School
LISS GU33.................... 36 E5
Littledown Leisure Centre
LTDN BH7.................... 221 L8
Little Green School
RCCH PO18.................... 118 D4
Lockerley C of E (A)
Primary School
ROMY SO51.................... 20 F7
Locksheath County Infants &
Primary School
HLER SO31.................... 158 E7
Locks Road Surgery
HLER SO31.................... 158 E6
Lockswood Surgery
HLER SO31.................... 158 E5
Longbridge Industrial Park
SHAM SO14.................... 5 K6
Longdown Estates
TOTT SO40.................... 129 J8
Longfleet C of E VC
Combined School
PLE BH15.................... 233 K4
Longspee School
CFDH BH17.................... 233 J1
Lordshill Health Centre
ROWN SO16.................... 105 L4
L S U College of
Higher Education
WSHM SO15.................... 131 K1
Lucia Foster Welch College
SHAM SO14.................... 5 J6
Ludlow Infant School
ITCH SO19.................... 132 C5
Ludlow Middle School
ITCH SO19.................... 132 C4
Lulworth Business Centre
TOTT SO40.................... 104 D6
Lydlynch County First School
TOTT SO40.................... 129 J1
Lymington Community
Hospitals
LYMN SO41.................... 228 C4
Lymington County
Junior & Infant School
LYMN SO41.................... 228 B4
Lymington Hospital
LYMN SO41.................... 228 B4
Lymington Recreation Centre
LYMN SO41.................... 228 A5
Lyndhurst Infant School
LYND SO43.................... 151 K3
Lyndhurst Junior School
NEND PO2.................... 187 K7
Lyndhurst Surgery
LYND SO43.................... 151 K3
Lytchett Minster Upper School
UPTN BH16.................... 216 C8
Magpies Sports Club
WIMB BH21.................... 144 D8
Mainline Business Centre
LISS GU33.................... 36 E4
Malmesbury Park School
CHAR BH8.................... 236 A2
Malmesbury Park School
CHAR BH8.................... 15 J1
Malvern Business Centre
ROWN SO16.................... 106 C6
Manor Infant School
FAWY SO45.................... 180 A3
Manor Infant School
PSEA PO1.................... 211 J1
Manor Road Surgery
VWD BH31.................... 144 C2
Mansbridge Primary School
WEND SO18.................... 107 K4
Mansel Infant & Junior Schools
ROWN SO16.................... 105 J6
Maple Business Park
WIMB BH21.................... 193 K1
Marchwood C of E
Infant School
TOTT SO40.................... 130 C8
Marchwood Junior School
TOTT SO40.................... 130 D7
Marchwood Priory Hospital
TOTT SO40.................... 154 E1
Maritime Museum
BROC SO42.................... 205 H4
Marlands Shopping Centre
SHAM SO14.................... 4 F3
The Martin Kemp Welch School
BKME/WDN BH12.................... 219 H8
Marwell Zoological Park
RWIN SO21.................... 55 L8
Marycourt Co-educational
School
GPORT PO12.................... 10 D9
Mary Rose Exhibition
PSEA PO1.................... 12 B1
Mary Rose Ship Hall
PSEA PO1.................... 210 D2
Mason Manor Primary School
ROWN SO16.................... 105 L8

Mayfield Gallery
MOOR/WNTN BH9.................... 220 D6
Mayflower Theatre
WSHM SO15.................... 4 D1
Mayville High School
SSEA PO5.................... 13 K8
Meadowlands Infant School
HORN PO8.................... 140 C3
Meadowlands Junior School
HORN PO8.................... 140 C3
Medina Primary School
CHAM PO6.................... 187 J1
Mengham Infant School
HISD PO11.................... 213 L4
Mengham Junior School
HISD PO11.................... 213 L4
Meoncross School
FHAM/STUB PO14.................... 184 B4
Meon Infant School
ENEY PO4.................... 211 M4
Meon Junior School
ENEY PO4.................... 211 M3
Meonstoke School
BPWT SO32.................... 87 H4
Meon Valley Golf &
Country Club
BPWT SO32.................... 111 J8
Meon Valley Police Station
BPWT SO32.................... 85 J8
Merdon Junior School
CHFD SO53.................... 81 J1
Meredith Infant School
NEND PO2.................... 187 J8
Meridian TV studios
SHAM SO14.................... 132 A2
Middle Park Medical Centre
HAV PO9.................... 165 G4
Milford C of E School
LYMN SO41.................... 242 D2
Millbrook Clinic
ROWN SO16.................... 105 K8
Millbrook Community School
ROWN SO16.................... 105 K5
Millbrook Secondary School
ROWN SO16.................... 105 K5
Millbrook Trading Estate
WSHM SO15.................... 130 C1
Millers Dale Surgery
CHFD SO53.................... 53 G8
Millhouse Business Centre
ITCH SO19.................... 132 B4
Millstream Trading Estate
RGWD BH24.................... 170 D3
Milton Park Infant School
ENEY PO4.................... 211 M4
Milton Park Junior School
ENEY PO4.................... 211 M4
M L S College
BMTH BH1.................... 14 E5
Monks Brook Industrial Park
CHFD SO53.................... 81 G3
Moordown C of E
Primary School
MOOR/WNTN BH9.................... 220 D7
Moorgreen Hospital
HEND SO30.................... 108 E6
Moorings Way Infant School
ENEY PO4.................... 212 A2
Moorlands College
CHCH/BSGR BH23.................... 222 F2
Moorlands Infant School
WEND SO18.................... 107 M7
Morelands Primary School
WVILLE PO7.................... 164 C6
Moreton House School
PSF GU32.................... 63 K5
Morgans Vale & Woodfalls
Primary School
RSAL SP5.................... 73 J1
Mortimers Farm
Industrial Estate
ROMY SO51.................... 103 K2
Mottisfont Abbey
ROMY SO51.................... 21 L5
Mottisfont Club House
ROMY SO51.................... 21 K6
Mountbatten Business Centre
WSHM SO15.................... 4 B1
Mountbatten Secondary School
ROMY SO51.................... 79 H2
The Mount Hospital
ELGH SO50.................... 82 C3
Mount Pleasant
Industrial Estate
SHAM SO14.................... 131 M1
Mount Pleasant Junior School
SHAM SO14.................... 131 M1
Moyles Court School
RGWD BH24.................... 147 G2
Mudeford County
Primary School
CHCH/BSGR BH23.................... 238 D2
Mudeford Junior School
CHCH/BSGR BH23.................... 238 E2
Muscliff C Primary School
MOOR/WNTN BH9.................... 221 G5
Music Gallery
MOOR/WNTN BH9.................... 220 F8
National Motor Museum
BROC SO42.................... 178 D6
National Museum of Artillery
WHAM PO17.................... 161 M5
Natural Sciences Museum
ENEY PO4.................... 211 K7
Nelson Industrial Park
HEND SO30.................... 109 G7
Nethercliffe School
FUFL SO22.................... 2 D5
Netley Abbey Infant School
HLER SO31.................... 156 F1
Netley Court School
HLER SO31.................... 156 F3
Netley Marsh C of E
Controlled Infant School
TOTT SO40.................... 128 E1
Neville Lovett
Community School
FHAM/STUB PO14.................... 6 E8
Newbridge Junior School
NEND PO2.................... 211 K1
New Forest District Council
NMIL/BTOS BH25.................... 225 L6

New Forest District Council
  RGWD BH24 .... 170 D2
New Forest Golf Club
  LYND SO43 .... 151 M2
New Forest Museum &
  Visitors Centre
  LYND SO43 .... 151 L3
Newlands Infant &
  Middle School
  ROWN SO16 .... 105 K7
New Milton Junior School
  NMIL/BTOS BH25 .... 225 L7
New Milton Recreation Centre
  NMIL/BTOS BH25 .... 225 K6
New Milton Sports Club
  NMIL/BTOS BH25 .... 226 A5
New Milton Town Council
  NMIL/BTOS BH25 .... 225 L6
New Theatre Royal
  PSEA PO1 .... 12 F2
The Newton Health Clinic
  SHAM SO14 .... 131 L2
Newtown Soberton
  County Primary School
  WHAM PO17 .... 137 M2
Nightingale County
  Junior & Infant School
  ELGH SO50 .... 81 J7
Nightingale Surgery
  ROMY SO51 .... 50 F8
Nomansland & Hamptworth
  C of E Primary School
  RSAL SP5 .... 75 G8
Northam Business Centre
  SHAM SO14 .... 132 A2
Northam Primary School
  SHAM SO14 .... 5 L1
North Baddesley County Infants
  School
  NBAD SO52 .... 80 A4
North Baddesley Junior School
  NBAD SO52 .... 80 A4
Northbrook Industrial Estate
  ROWN SO16 .... 106 B6
Northern County
  Junior & Infant School
  FHAM/PORC PO16 .... 162 A7
Northern Parade Clinic
  NEND PO2 .... 187 J5
Northern Parade Infant School
  NEND PO2 .... 187 J5
Northern Parade Junior School
  NEND PO2 .... 187 J5
Northview Gallery
  HLER SO31 .... 134 A8
Norwood CP School
  ELGH SO50 .... 81 M5
Nova Business Park
  NMIL/BTOS BH25 .... 225 J6
Nuffield Theatre
  PTSW SO17 .... 106 F5
Nursling C of E Primary School
  ROWN SO16 .... 105 J3
Nursling Industrial Estate
  ROWN SO16 .... 105 C5
Oakdale South Road
  Middle School
  PLE BH15 .... 233 J3
Oakfield Primary School
  TOTT SO40 .... 104 D8
Oaklands Community School
  ROWN SO16 .... 105 L3
Oaklands RC School
  WVILLE PO7 .... 164 D3
Oak Lodge School
  FAWY SO45 .... 155 C5
Oakmead College of
  Technology
  BWD BH11 .... 219 K3
Oakwood First School
  ROWN SO16 .... 106 A3
Oakwood Junior School
  ROWN SO16 .... 106 A3
Oatlands House Health Clinic
  ROWN SO16 .... 106 B6
Oceanographic Centre
  SHAM SO14 .... 5 K8
Odeon Cinema
  BMTH BH1 .... 14 F6
Odeon Cinema
  NEND PO2 .... 187 H7
Odeon Cinema
  WSHM SO15 .... 4 D4
Oil Refinery
  FAWY SO45 .... 180 D4
O Jays Industrial Park
  HSEA PO3 .... 187 L6
Old Anchor Inn Surgery
  ELGH SO50 .... 82 B5
Old Dames School
  FBDG SP6 .... 73 H5
Oldfield Gallery
  SSEA PO5 .... 13 H5
The Old Fire Station Surgery
  ITCH SO19 .... 132 C5
Old Hambledonians Cricket Club
  HORN PO8 .... 89 K6
Olivers Battery Primary School
  FUFL SO22 .... 26 B5
On Line Gallery
  WSHM SO15 .... 131 K2
Orchard County Infant & Junior
  School
  FAWY SO45 .... 155 J6
Orchard Lea Junior &
  Infant Schools
  FHAM PO15 .... 160 C4
Orion Business Centre
  WEND SO18 .... 107 K3
The Osborn Clinic
  FHAM/PORC PO16 .... 7 L5
Osborne Practice Surgery
  SSEA PO5 .... 13 G7
Otterbourne Primary School
  RWIN SO21 .... 54 A6
Our Lady & St Joseph RC
  Primary School
  LYMN SO41 .... 228 D4
Owslebury CP School
  RWIN SO21 .... 55 M4
Padnell Infant School
  HORN PO8 .... 140 E6

Padnell Junior School
  HORN PO8 .... 140 F5
Palace House
  BROC SO42 .... 178 C7
Palmerston Business Park
  FHAM/STUB PO14 .... 184 E1
Park Community School
  HAV PO9 .... 165 G3
Park Gate Business Centre
  HLER SO31 .... 158 F2
Park Gate Junior School
  HLER SO31 .... 158 F3
Park House Primary School
  HAV PO9 .... 165 G3
Parklands Business Park
  WVILLE PO7 .... 139 K5
Park Lane Medical Centre
  HAV PO9 .... 165 H5
Parkstone Grammar
  School for Girls
  CFDH BH17 .... 217 M8
Parkway Retail Park
  BMTH BH1 .... 15 J2
Parley First School
  FERN BH22 .... 194 B5
The Pascoe Practice
  PSEA PO1 .... 12 E4
Paulsgrove Industrial Centre
  CHAM PO6 .... 162 F8
Paulsgrove Primary School
  CHAM PO6 .... 162 F8
Pavilion
  BMTH BH1 .... 15 G3
Pavilion Theatre
  BMTH BH1 .... 14 E6
Pavillion Theatre
  BMTH BH1 .... 14 F7
Peacock Trading Estate
  ELGH SO50 .... 81 L3
Peel Common County
  Junior & Infant School
  LSOL/BMARY PO13 .... 184 E6
Pegham Industrial Park
  FHAM PO15 .... 159 M2
Penhale Infant School
  PSEA PO1 .... 13 M1
Pennington County
  Junior & Infant School
  LYMN SO41 .... 228 A5
Peter Dyer Gallery
  SSEA PO5 .... 13 H7
Petersfield Business Park
  PSF GU32 .... 63 J5
Petersfield Community
  Hospital
  PSF GU32 .... 63 K5
Petersfield County
  Infant School
  EPSF GU31 .... 63 L5
Petersfield Golf Club
  PSF GU32 .... 36 B8
Petersfield Rugby Football Club
  EPSF GU31 .... 64 C4
Petersfield School
  PSF GU32 .... 63 K6
Petersfield Swimming Pool
  EPSF GU31 .... 63 L5
Petersfield Town Council
  EPSF GU31 .... 63 M5
Petersfield Town Football Club
  EPSF GU31 .... 63 M4
Petersgate Infant School
  HORN PO8 .... 116 B4
Peter Symonds College
  FUFL SO22 .... 2 E4
Phoenix Industrial Park
  ELGH SO50 .... 82 B6
Pier Theatre
  BMTH BH1 .... 14 F8
Pilgrims School
  WINC SO23 .... 3 H9
Pipers Wood Industrial Park
  WVILLE PO7 .... 140 A8
Pitmore School
  CHFD SO53 .... 53 L8
Plaza Theatre
  ROMY SO51 .... 78 E1
Pokesdown Primary School
  BOSC BH5 .... 237 G3
The Polygon School
  WSHM SO15 .... 131 J2
Poole Grammar School
  CFDH BH17 .... 218 B6
Poole Road Medical Centre
  WBNE BH4 .... 14 A6
Poole Technical High School
  PLE BH15 .... 233 H4
Portcastrian R F C
  SBNE BH6 .... 237 K2
Portchester Castle
  FHAM/PORC PO16 .... 186 C3
Portchester
  Community School
  FHAM/PORC PO16 .... 186 A1
Portchester Health Centre
  FHAM/PORC PO16 .... 162 A8
Portchester School
  LTDN BH7 .... 236 F1
Portsdown Group Practice
  WVILLE PO7 .... 164 C5
Portsmouth City Council
  CHAM PO6 .... 187 J1
Portsmouth City Council
  CHAM PO6 .... 163 K8
Portsmouth City Council
  CHAM PO6 .... 162 F7
Portsmouth City Council
  HAV PO9 .... 165 K4
Portsmouth City Council
  PSEA PO1 .... 211 J1
Portsmouth City Council
  PSEA PO1 .... 12 D5
Portsmouth City Council
  SSEA PO5 .... 13 G6
Portsmouth City Council
  SSEA PO5 .... 13 H7
Portsmouth City Council
  SSEA PO5 .... 13 J5
Portsmouth County Court
  PSEA PO1 .... 13 G2
Portsmouth Crown Court
  PSEA PO1 .... 13 G3

Portsmouth Grammar School
  PSEA PO1 .... 12 E4
Portsmouth High School
  SSEA PO5 .... 12 F6
Portsmouth Natural
  Health Centre
  SSEA PO5 .... 12 F4
Portsmouth Rugby
  Football Club
  HSEA PO3 .... 187 L4
Portsmouth Sixth Form
  College
  HSEA PO3 .... 212 A1
Portswood Primary School
  PTSW SO17 .... 107 H6
Portswood Road Surgery
  PTSW SO17 .... 107 G2
Poulner Junior & Infant School
  RGWD BH24 .... 147 G6
The Practice Doctors Surgery
  FHAM/PORC PO16 .... 7 H5
Premier Business Park
  FHAM/STUB PO14 .... 6 C7
Priestlands County
  Secondary School
  LYMN SO41 .... 228 A5
Priets House Museum
  WIMB BH21 .... 192 A4
Princes Mead School
  RWIN SO21 .... 17 K2
Princess Anne Hospital
  ROWN SO16 .... 106 A5
Priory C of E VA
  Primary School
  CHCH/BSGR BH23 .... 238 A2
Priory School
  SSEA PO5 .... 13 L3
Private Medical Centre
  BMTH BH1 .... 15 C5
Purbrook Cricket Club
  WVILLE PO7 .... 163 M4
Purbrook Junior &
  Infant School
  WVILLE PO7 .... 164 B3
Purbrook Park School
  WVILLE PO7 .... 164 B5
Queen Alexandra Hospital
  CHAM PO6 .... 163 J7
Queens Enclosure
  WVILLE PO7 .... 140 E7
Queens
  Primary School
  ROWN SO16 .... 106 A5
Queens Road Surgery
  NEND PO2 .... 187 J3
Rachel Madocks School
  HORN PO8 .... 140 B4
Rake C of E Controlled
  First School
  LISS GU33 .... 37 L3
Ranvilles Junior & Infant School
  FHAM/STUB PO14 .... 160 A8
Red Barn County
  Primary School
  FHAM/PORC PO16 .... 161 M4
Redbridge Community School
  ROWN SO16 .... 105 J8
Redbridge Primary School
  ROWN SO16 .... 105 J8
Red Funnel Ferry Terminal
  SHAM SO14 .... 4 F7
Red Gallery
  SSEA PO5 .... 13 J7
Red House Museum & Gardens
  CHCH/BSGR BH23 .... 238 A2
Redlands County
  Primary School
  FHAM/PORC PO16 .... 7 H9
Red Lodge School
  ROWN SO16 .... 106 D4
Redlynch C of E
  Primary School
  RSAL SP5 .... 73 M3
Redwood Park School
  CHAM PO6 .... 187 M2
Regents Park Girls School
  ROWN SO16 .... 105 M8
Regents Park Surgery
  WSHM SO15 .... 106 A8
Regional Film Theatre
  SHAM SO14 .... 5 J8
Rex Industrial Estate
  CHFD SO53 .... 81 J3
Richard Martin
  Gallery & Bookshop
  GPORT PO12 .... 11 H4
Riders Junior & Infant School
  HAV PO9 .... 165 H3
Ridgemede Junior School
  BPWT SO32 .... 85 J8
Ridgeway House
  Special School
  ITCH SO19 .... 132 C3
Ringwood C of E Infant School
  RGWD BH24 .... 170 E1
Ringwood County
  Junior School
  RGWD BH24 .... 170 E2
Ringwood Recreation Centre
  RGWD BH24 .... 170 E1
Ringwood Town Council
  RGWD BH24 .... 170 E2
Ringwood Trading Estate
  RGWD BH24 .... 170 E2
Ringwood Waldorf School
  RGWD BH24 .... 169 M2
River Park Leisure Centre
  WINC SO23 .... 3 H5
Riverside Business Park
  PSEA PO1 .... 228 D4
Riverside Close Surgery
  LISS GU33 .... 36 D4
Riverside School
  WVILLE PO7 .... 164 D5
Robert King Gallery
  SSEA PO5 .... 13 J8
Rogate C of E Controlled School
  .... 65 L4
Romsey Abbey C of E
  Primary School
  ROMY SO51 .... 78 C1

Romsey County Junior School
  ROMY SO51 .... 50 F8
Romsey Cricket Club
  ROMY SO51 .... 78 E2
Romsey Hospital
  ROMY SO51 .... 78 F1
Romsey Industrial Estate
  ROMY SO51 .... 50 D7
Romsey Infant School
  ROMY SO51 .... 78 E1
Romsey Rugby Football Club
  ROMY SO51 .... 78 E2
The Romsey School
  ROMY SO51 .... 50 D8
Romsey Sports Centre
  ROMY SO51 .... 78 E2
Rookesbury Park School
  WHAM PO17 .... 137 H4
Rowans House
  Industrial Estate
  ROWN SO16 .... 105 K2
Rowner County Infant School
  LSOL/BMARY PO13 .... 185 H7
Rowner County Junior School
  LSOL/BMARY PO13 .... 185 H7
Rowner Health Centre
  LSOL/BMARY PO13 .... 185 G8
Rowner Swimming Centre
  LSOL/BMARY PO13 .... 209 G2
Royal Hampshire
  County Hospital
  FUFL SO22 .... 2 B8
Royal Hampshire
  Regiment Museum
  WINC SO23 .... 2 F8
Royal Hospital Haslar
  GPORT PO12 .... 11 K7
Royal Marines Museum
  ENEY PO4 .... 211 M6
Royal Naval Museum
  PSEA PO1 .... 12 A1
Royal Navy Submarine Museum
  Offices
  GPORT PO12 .... 11 L6
Royal South Hants Hospital
  SHAM SO14 .... 131 L2
Royal Winchester Golf Club
  FUFL SO22 .... 26 A1
Rushcombe County
  First School
  WIMB BH21 .... 217 H2
Rushington Business Park
  TOTT SO40 .... 129 J3
Russell Cotes Art
  Gallery & Museum
  BMTH BH1 .... 15 G7
Russell Hicks & Temple
  ROMY SO51 .... 78 D1
St Albans C of E
  Primary School
  HAV PO9 .... 165 L5
St Aldhelms C of E
  Combined School
  BKME/WDN BH12 .... 234 F2
St Andrews Surgery
  ELGH SO50 .... 81 M6
St Annes School
  LSOL/BMARY PO13 .... 208 C1
St Anns Hospital
  CCLF BH13 .... 245 K2
St Anthonys RC Primary School
  FHAM/STUB PO14 .... 159 H6
St Barbe Museum
  LYMN SO41 .... 228 C4
St Bedes C of E Primary School
  WINC SO23 .... 3 H6
St Catherines RC Primary School
  WIMB BH21 .... 192 E2
St Catherines Road
  Junior School
  ELGH SO50 .... 81 M3
St Christophers Hospital
  FHAM/PORC PO16 .... 7 L2
St Christophers School
  WEND SO18 .... 107 K8
St Clements C of E School
  BMTH BH1 .... 236 C3
St Cuthmans School
  MIDH GU29 .... 67 K2
St Denys Primary School
  PTSW SO17 .... 107 H7
St Edmunds Catholic School
  PSEA PO1 .... 13 J1
St Edward
  Comprehensive School
  PLE BH15 .... 233 L1
St Edwards School
  ROMY SO51 .... 47 M7
St Faiths Primary School
  WINC SO23 .... 26 E3
St Francis Primary School
  NBAD SO52 .... 80 E3
St Francis School
  FHAM/STUB PO14 .... 160 A7
St Georges Beneficial C of E
  Primary School
  PSEA PO1 .... 12 D2
St Georges Business Centre
  PSEA PO1 .... 12 D2
St Georges Catholic Boys School
  ELGH SO50 .... 107 H2
St Georges Hospital
  LYMN SO41 .... 242 B4
St Georges Industrial Estate
  ENEY PO4 .... 211 L3
St Georges University
  School of Medicine
  WINC SO23 .... 3 G7
St Ives CP School
  RGWD BH24 .... 169 L3
St James C of E Primary School
  EMRTH PO10 .... 166 C6
St James C of E Primary School
  LTDN BH7 .... 237 G3
St James C of E (VC)
  First School
  FBDG SP6 .... 121 L2
St James Hospital
  ENEY PO4 .... 211 M3
St James Primary School
  HEND SO30 .... 108 E6

St Johns Cathedral
  PSEA PO1 .... 210 F2
St Johns Cathedral
  Primary School
  PSEA PO1 .... 13 K1
St Johns C of E Infant School
  HLER SO31 .... 159 G6
St Johns C of E Primary School
  GPORT PO12 .... 209 M1
St Johns C of E
  Primary School
  HAV PO9 .... 141 M8
St Johns College
  SSEA PO5 .... 13 J6
St Johns School
  WIMB BH21 .... 192 B4
St John the Baptist School
  BPWT SO32 .... 111 K6
St Josephs House
  BKME/WDN BH12 .... 234 D1
St Josephs RC School
  CHCH/BSGR BH23 .... 223 L8
St Judes Catholic
  Primary School
  FHAM/STUB PO14 .... 6 C6
St Judes C of E Primary School
  PSEA PO1 .... 12 E5
St Katherines C of E
  Primary School
  SBNE BH6 .... 238 A4
St Leonards C of E School
  RGWD BH24 .... 169 G7
St Lukes C of E School
  MOOR/WNTN BH9 .... 220 D8
St Lukes C of E School
  SSEA PO5 .... 13 H2
St Lukes Surgery
  HEND SO30 .... 109 G7
St Marks C of E County
  Infant School
  CHCH/BSGR BH23 .... 224 D7
St Marks C of E Junior School
  WSHM SO15 .... 131 H1
St Marks C of E Primary School
  NBNE BH10 .... 220 A7
St Marys C of E Primary School
  SHAM SO14 .... 5 K2
St Marys C of E Primary School
  SHAM SO14 .... 5 K2
St Marys College
  WEND SO18 .... 107 K8
St Marys First School
  FERN BH22 .... 168 B5
St Marys Hospital
  HSEA PO3 .... 211 L2
St Marys RC Primary School
  GPORT PO12 .... 10 C1
St Marys RC School
  PLE BH15 .... 233 K3
St Marys Surgery
  SHAM SO14 .... 5 J3
St Michaels C of E School
  WCLF BH2 .... 14 B6
St Michaels Middle School
  WIMB BH21 .... 192 C1
St Monica Infant School
  ITCH SO19 .... 132 E5
St Monica Middle School
  ITCH SO19 .... 132 E5
St Patricks RC Primary School
  ITCH SO19 .... 132 C5
St Pauls Hospital
  FUFL SO22 .... 2 E6
St Pauls RC Primary School
  CHAM PO6 .... 162 F8
St Peter's Church
  BMTH BH1 .... 14 F6
St Peters School
  FUFL SO22 .... 26 A3
St Peters School
  LTDN BH7 .... 221 H7
St Peters School
  SBNE BH6 .... 237 H3
St Swithuns RC Primary School
  SSEA PO5 .... 13 K4
St Swithuns School
  RWIN SO21 .... 17 J8
St Swithun Wells RC
  Primary School
  CHFD SO53 .... 81 J3
St Thomas Clinic
  LYMN SO41 .... 228 B5
St Thomas Mores RC
  Primary School
  HAV PO9 .... 8 A1
St Vincent College
  GPORT PO12 .... 10 F1
St Walburgas RC Primary School
  MOOR/WNTN BH9 .... 220 D6
Salterns School
  TOTT SO40 .... 104 D7
The Sanatorium
  Canford School
  WIMB BH21 .... 192 E7
Sandleheath Industrial Estate
  FBDG SP6 .... 97 G5
Sandle Manor School
  FBDG SP6 .... 97 J6
Sarisbury Green C of E
  Primary School
  HLER SO31 .... 158 C3
Sarisbury Infant School
  HLER SO31 .... 158 C4
Sarum Road Hospital
  FUFL SO22 .... 26 B1
Saxon Shore Infant School
  CHAM PO6 .... 162 C8
Scantabout Primary School
  CHFD SO53 .... 81 L1
Scaplens Court Museum
  PLE BH15 .... 233 H5
Shakespeare Business Centre
  ELGH SO50 .... 82 A4
Shakespeare County
  Infant School
  ELGH SO50 .... 81 M4
Shamblehurst CP School
  HEND SO30 .... 109 H8
Sharps Copse Junior &
  Infant School
  HAV PO9 .... 165 M3

Shawcross Industrial Park
HSEA PO3 .... 187 L3
Sheet CP School
PSF GU52 .... 64 A2
Shelley Museum
BOSC BH5 .... 236 E4
Shepherds Down School
RWIN SO21 .... 54 B2
Sherborne House School
CHFD SO53 .... 53 J7
Shirley Business Park
WSHM SO15 .... 131 G1
Shirley First & Middle School
WSHM SO15 .... 106 B7
The Shirley Health Centre
WSHM SO15 .... 131 G1
Shirley Swimming Pool
WSHM SO15 .... 131 G1
Shirley Warren Primary School
ROWN SO16 .... 105 M6
Sholing First School
ITCH SO19 .... 132 E4
Sholing Girls School
ITCH SO19 .... 132 E4
Sholing Infants School
ITCH SO19 .... 132 E3
Sholing Middle School
ITCH SO19 .... 132 E3
Sidings Industrial Estate
HLER SO31 .... 157 H3
Sikh Temple
SSEA PO5 .... 13 J4
Simcoe Clinic
WSHM SO15 .... 131 J1
Sinclair First & Junior School
ROWN SO16 .... 105 M3
Siskin County Junior &
Infant School
LSOL/BMARY PO13 .... 209 H2
Slades Farm Special School
NBNE BH10 .... 220 B7
Solent Business Centre
WSHM SO15 .... 130 F2
Solent Industrial Centre
WSHM SO15 .... 131 G1
Solent Industrial Estate
HEND SO30 .... 109 G7
Solent Infant School
CHAM PO6 .... 164 B8
Solent Junior School
CHAM PO6 .... 164 B8
Solent Peoples Theatre
ITCH SO19 .... 133 G5
Somerford County
Infant School
CHCH/BSGR BH23 .... 238 D1
Somerford County
Junior School
CHCH/BSGR BH23 .... 238 D1
Somers Park Primary School
SSEA PO5 .... 13 J2
Somers Town Health Centre
SSEA PO5 .... 13 J5
Sopley CP School
CHCH/BSGR BH23 .... 197 C7
Southampton Airport Parkway
Station
ELGH SO50 .... 107 L2
Southampton Central Mosque
SHAM SO14 .... 131 M2
Southampton City College
SHAM SO14 .... 5 J4
Southampton City Council
PTSW SO17 .... 107 H6
Southampton City Council
ROWN SO16 .... 106 A7
Southampton City Council
ROWN SO16 .... 106 C3
Southampton City Council
ROWN SO16 .... 105 H6
Southampton City Council
SHAM SO14 .... 5 J2
Southampton City Council
SHAM SO14 .... 5 K3
Southampton City Council
SHAM SO14 .... 4 F5
Southampton City Council
SHAM SO14 .... 4 F6
Southampton City Council
WSHM SO15 .... 4 C2
Southampton Football Club
WSHM SO15 .... 131 J2
Southampton
General Hospital
ROWN SO16 .... 106 A5
Southampton
Institute & Millais Gallery
WSHM SO15 .... 5 G1
Southampton
Magistrates Court
WSHM SO15 .... 131 L2
Southampton & New Forest
Magistrates Courts
WSHM SO15 .... 4 D1
Southampton Sports Centre
ROWN SO16 .... 106 C4
Southampton Sports Club
ROWN SO16 .... 105 H6
Southampton
Technical College
SHAM SO14 .... 5 M5
Southampton University
ROWN SO16 .... 80 B7
South Baddesley C of E Primary
School
LYMN SO41 .... 229 H2
Southbourne County
Junior & Infant School
EMRTH PO10 .... 167 J8
Southbourne Surgery
EMRTH PO10 .... 167 J8
Southdown School
RWIN SO21 .... 54 B2
The South Downs College
WVILLE PO7 .... 164 E5
Southern Electric Museum
CHCH/BSGR BH23 .... 238 A1
South Hants Country Club
WHAM PO17 .... 137 L7
Southlands School
LYMN SO41 .... 228 C1

South Parade Pier
PSEA PO1 .... 211 J7
Southsea Castle Museum
SSEA PO5 .... 211 G7
Southsea Infant School
SSEA PO5 .... 13 L7
South West Health Authority
HEND SO30 .... 133 M4
Southwick Park
Naval Recreation Centre
WHAM PO17 .... 162 E3
Spectrum Sports Club
SBNE BH6 .... 237 H4
Spitfire Court Surgery
SHAM SO14 .... 5 M6
Springdale First School
BDST BH18 .... 217 J4
Springfield School
CHAM PO6 .... 188 A1
Springhill RC Primary School
WSHM SO15 .... 131 J2
Stag Business Park
RGWD BH24 .... 170 E3
Stakes Hill Infant School
WVILLE PO7 .... 164 D2
Stakes Lodge Surgery
WVILLE PO7 .... 164 E2
Stamshaw Infant School
NEND PO2 .... 187 H6
Stamshaw Junior School
NEND PO2 .... 187 G5
Stamshaw & Tipner
Leisure Centre
NEND PO2 .... 187 G6
Stanbridge Earls School
ROMY SO51 .... 50 A5
Stanley Green First School
PLE BH15 .... 233 H2
Stanmore Primary School
FUFL SO22 .... 26 D3
Stanton Industrial Estate
WSHM SO15 .... 130 E1
Stapehill Abbey
WIMB BH21 .... 193 J3
Station Theatre
HISD PO11 .... 213 H4
Staunton Park
Community School
HAV PO9 .... 165 M1
Stedham CP School
MIDH GU29 .... 67 J7
Steep School
PSF GU32 .... 63 K1
Stephen's Castle
VWD BH31 .... 120 E8
Stoke Gallery
GPORT PO12 .... 10 F5
Stoke Park County
Junior School
ELGH SO50 .... 82 D5
Stoke Park Infant School
ELGH SO50 .... 82 D6
Stokewood Surgery
ELGH SO50 .... 82 F6
Stourfield First School
SBNE BH6 .... 237 J2
Stroud School
ROMY SO51 .... 51 K8
Summerbee First School
CHAR BH8 .... 221 G7
Summerbee Junior School
CHAR BH8 .... 221 G7
Summerbee Secondary School
CHAR BH8 .... 221 H7
Sunnyside Doctors Surgery
PSEA PO1 .... 13 L1
Sun Valley Business Park
WINC SO23 .... 3 M5
Super Bowl
BMTH BH1 .... 15 G5
Super Bowl
WSHM SO15 .... 130 D1
Superstore
BMTH BH1 .... 15 J3
Superstore
SHAM SO14 .... 4 E2
Superstore
SHAM SO14 .... 4 E3
Surrey House First School
ITCH SO19 .... 133 G5
Surrey House Health Centre
ITCH SO19 .... 133 G5
Swanmore Business Park
BPWT SO32 .... 111 L3
Swanmore C of E School
BPWT SO32 .... 112 A2
Swanmore County
Secondary School
BPWT SO32 .... 111 M3
Swan Street Surgery
PSF GU32 .... 63 K5
Swanwick Business Park
HLER SO31 .... 158 B1
Sway Park Industrial Estate
LYMN SO41 .... 200 F7
Sway St Lukes Primary School
LYMN SO41 .... 200 F6
Swaythling Clinic
PTSW SO17 .... 107 H5
Swaythling Primary School
PTSW SO17 .... 107 G5
Sylvan First School
BKME/WDN BH12 .... 234 A2
Synagogue
BMTH BH1 .... 15 G5
The Synagogue
PTSW SO17 .... 131 K1
Talbot Heath School
WBNE BH4 .... 235 H3
Talbot House
Preparatory School
MOOR/WNTN BH9 .... 220 C8
Talbot School
BKME/WDN BH12 .... 219 M8
Talisman Business Centre
HLER SO31 .... 158 F2
Tankerville School
ELGH SO50 .... 82 A5
Tanners Brook Infant School
WSHM SO15 .... 130 D1
Tanners Brook Junior School
ROWN SO16 .... 130 D1

Tatchbury Manor House
TOTT SO40 .... 103 L7
Tatchbury Mount Hospital
TOTT SO40 .... 103 M6
Tauntons College
WSHM SO15 .... 106 D7
Terminus Industrial Estate
PSEA PO1 .... 13 J2
Test Vale Surgery
TOTT SO40 .... 104 E8
Test Valley Business Centre
TOTT SO40 .... 105 G6
Testwood School
TOTT SO40 .... 104 E7
Thornden School
CHFD SO53 .... 53 L8
Thorney County
Primary School
EMRTH PO10 .... 190 E5
Thornhill Clinic
ITCH SO19 .... 133 H3
Thornhill First School
ITCH SO19 .... 133 G3
Thornhill Junior School
ITCH SO19 .... 133 G3
Thornhill Park Surgery
ITCH SO19 .... 133 H2
Three Legged Cross Country
First School
WIMB BH21 .... 144 C7
Tiptoe CP School
LYMN SO41 .... 200 B8
Titchfield County
Primary School
FHAM/STUB PO14 .... 159 K7
Totton College
TOTT SO40 .... 129 J3
Totton College
TOTT SO40 .... 104 C8
Totton Recreation Centre
TOTT SO40 .... 104 C8
Tower Industrial Estate
FAWY SO45 .... 82 B6
Townhill Infant School
WEND SO18 .... 107 M6
Townhill Middle School
WEND SO18 .... 107 M6
Townhill Park Health Clinic
WEND SO18 .... 107 M6
Townhill Surgery
WEND SO18 .... 108 A1
The Toynbee School
CHFD SO53 .... 81 J3
Treadgold Museum
PSEA PO1 .... 12 D1
Trinidad First School
BKME/WDN BH12 .... 219 G8
Trinity Business Centre
TOTT SO40 .... 104 D6
Trinity Industrial Estate
WSHM SO15 .... 130 D1
Trojans Sports Club
ELGH SO50 .... 107 H1
Tudor House Museum
SHAM SO14 .... 4 F5
Turlin Moor First School
UPTN BH16 .... 232 B4
Turlin Moor Middle School
UPTN BH16 .... 232 B4
Turnpike Business Park
FHAM/PORC PO16 .... 7 K3
Turnpike Gallery
PSF GU32 .... 63 L5
Two Riversmeet
Leisure Centre
CHCH/BSGR BH23 .... 238 B2
Twyford C of E
Primary School
RWIN SO21 .... 54 E2
Twyford School
RWIN SO21 .... 54 F2
Twyford Surgery
RWIN SO21 .... 54 E7
Twynham
Comprehensive School
CHCH/BSGR BH23 .... 237 M2
United Services
Cricket Ground
PSEA PO1 .... 12 D3
United Services Rugby Club
PSEA PO1 .... 12 E2
University of Portsmouth
ENEY PO4 .... 211 M4
University of Portsmouth
HISD PO11 .... 212 D4
University of Portsmouth
PSEA PO1 .... 13 K2
University of Portsmouth
PSEA PO1 .... 12 D1
University of Portsmouth
PSEA PO1 .... 12 D4
University of Portsmouth
PSEA PO1 .... 12 E2
University of Portsmouth
PSEA PO1 .... 12 E3
University of Portsmouth
SSEA PO5 .... 13 G3
University of Portsmouth
SSEA PO5 .... 13 H4
University of Portsmouth
SSEA PO5 .... 12 F6
University of Southampton
PTSW SO17 .... 107 G3
University of Southampton
ROWN SO16 .... 106 E5
University Practice
SSEA PO5 .... 12 F4
Upham School
BPWT SO32 .... 84 D3
Uplands County
Primary School
FHAM/PORC PO16 .... 7 G2
Uplands School
PSTN BH14 .... 234 B5
Upton Health Centre
UPTN BH16 .... 232 B1
Venture Industrial Park
LSOL/BMARY PO13 .... 185 H5
Vermont School
ROWN SO16 .... 106 D4
Verwood C of E First School
VWD BH31 .... 144 C3

Verwood C of E School
VWD BH31 .... 144 C3
Verwood Industrial Estate
VWD BH31 .... 144 F2
Verwood Leisure Centre
VWD BH31 .... 144 D2
Verwood Sports Centre
VWD BH31 .... 144 E2
Verwood Town Council
VWD BH31 .... 144 D1
Victoria Cottage Hospital
EMRTH PO10 .... 166 D8
Victoria Park
Swimming Centre
PSEA PO1 .... 12 F1
Victor Street Surgery
WSHM SO15 .... 106 A7
Victory Business Centre
PSEA PO1 .... 13 L2
Victory Retail Park
PSEA PO1 .... 211 G1
Victory Trading Estate
HSEA PO3 .... 187 M6
Village Medical Practice
FERN BH22 .... 168 B6
The Vine School
BPWT SO32 .... 110 C8
Vintage Motorcycle Museum
NMIL/BTOS BH25 .... 225 J3
Virgin Cinemas
SHAM SO14 .... 5 J7
Wallisdean County
Infant School
FHAM/STUB PO14 .... 6 D7
Wallisdean County
Junior School
FHAM/STUB PO14 .... 6 E7
Waltham Business Park
BPWT SO32 .... 111 M4
Warblington School
HAV PO9 .... 9 J4
War Memorial Hospital
LYMN SO41 .... 242 D4
Warren Avenue
Industrial Estate
ENEY PO4 .... 211 M3
Warren Park Primary School
HAV PO9 .... 165 H1
Warrior Business Centre
CHAM PO6 .... 188 C1
Waterfront Garden Surgery
FAWY SO45 .... 155 L3
Waterfront Museum
PLE BH15 .... 233 G7
Waterloo Industrial Estate
HEND SO30 .... 109 G7
The Waterloo School
WVILLE PO7 .... 164 C1
Waterlooville Football Club
WVILLE PO7 .... 140 C8
Waterlooville Health Centre
WVILLE PO7 .... 140 B6
The Waterside Health Centre
FAWY SO45 .... 155 L6
Waterside School
FHAM/PORC PO16 .... 186 F5
Webb Peploe House Surgery
LYMN SO41 .... 228 C5
Weeke CP School
FUFL SO22 .... 2 A2
Wellington Sports Club
ELGH SO50 .... 107 J1
Wellow County
Primary School
ROMY SO51 .... 76 E5
Wentworth College
BOSC BH5 .... 236 F4
Wessex Nuffield Hospital
CHFD SO53 .... 53 L7
Wessex Nuffield Hospital
ELGH SO50 .... 82 A5
Wessex Regional
Health Authority
HEND SO30 .... 109 G7
Wessex Superbowl
CHAM PO6 .... 164 E7
Westbourne County
Primary School
EMRTH PO10 .... 166 F4
Westbourne Galleries
CCLF BH13 .... 235 G5
Westbourne Surgery
EMRTH PO10 .... 166 F5
West Cliff Medical Centre
WCLF BH2 .... 14 C8
West End Surgery
HEND SO30 .... 108 D6
Western Community Hospital
ROWN SO16 .... 105 M7
Western Downland
Primary School
FBDG SP6 .... 96 C4
Western Downland School
FBDG SP6 .... 70 E7
Western Primary School
FUFL SO22 .... 2 B6
Westfield Junior School
CHAM PO6 .... 162 C8
The Westgate School
FUFL SO22 .... 2 C5
West Hill Park School
FHAM/STUB PO14 .... 159 J8
Westlands Medical Centre
FHAM/PORC PO16 .... 186 A1
West Meon Controlled
Primary School
PSF GU32 .... 60 A3
West Moors Group Practice
FERN BH22 .... 168 B6
West Moors Middle School
FERN BH22 .... 168 D7
Weston Park Boys School
ITCH SO19 .... 132 F7
Weston Park First School
ITCH SO19 .... 132 E7
Weston Park Junior School
ITCH SO19 .... 132 E7
Weston Shore First School
ITCH SO19 .... 132 D8
Westover Gallery
BMTH BH1 .... 14 F6

Westover Primary School
HSEA PO3 .... 187 M8
West Quay Retail Park
WSHM SO15 .... 4 D3
West Quay Shopping Centre
SHAM SO14 .... 4 E3
West Wittering
Parochial School
SELS PO20 .... 215 K7
Westwood Business Park
TOTT SO40 .... 104 E6
Whiteley County
Primary School
FHAM PO15 .... 159 G1
The Whiteley Surgery
HLER SO31 .... 134 F8
Whiteparish Surgery
RSAL SP5 .... 47 G5
Wickham C of E
Controlled Primary School
WHAM PO17 .... 136 D3
Wickham Park Golf Club
WHAM PO17 .... 136 C4
Wickham Riding School
WHAM PO17 .... 137 J6
Wickham Surgery
WHAM PO17 .... 136 E4
Wick 1 Industrial Estate
NMIL/BTOS BH25 .... 225 J5
Wick 2 Industrial Estate
NMIL/BTOS BH25 .... 225 J5
Wicor County Primary School
FHAM/PORC PO16 .... 161 L8
Wildern Clinic
HEND SO30 .... 134 A1
The Wildern School
HEND SO30 .... 134 A1
Wildground County
Infant School
FAWY SO45 .... 155 K7
Wildground County
Junior School
FAWY SO45 .... 155 K7
William Gilpin C of E
Primary School
LYMN SO41 .... 202 D7
Willments Industrial Estate
ITCH SO19 .... 132 B3
Wimbledon Park Sports Centre
SSEA PO5 .... 13 K8
Wimborne Industrial Estate
WIMB BH21 .... 192 A3
Wimborne Junior &
Infant School
ENEY PO4 .... 211 L4
Winchester
Agricultural Museum
WINC SO23 .... 3 G5
Winchester City Museum
WINC SO23 .... 3 G8
Winchester College
WINC SO23 .... 26 F2
The Winchester Gallery
ROWN SO16 .... 106 D5
Winchester Lawn Tennis Club
FUFL SO22 .... 2 B3
Winchester Recreation Centre
WINC SO23 .... 3 H6
Winchester Rugby Football Club
WINC SO23 .... 3 J4
Winchester School of Art
WINC SO23 .... 3 J6
Winnall CP School
WINC SO23 .... 3 L7
Winnall Farm Industrial Estate
WINC SO23 .... 3 K6
The Wishing Well Gallery
CHCH/BSGR BH23 .... 197 M7
The Wishing Well Gallery
RGWD BH24 .... 172 E5
Wolvesey Palace
WINC SO23 .... 3 H9
Woodhill Preparatory School
CHFD SO53 .... 81 J1
Woodhills School
HEND SO30 .... 134 D1
Woodlands Community School
WEND SO18 .... 108 C8
Wool House Maritime Museum
SHAM SO14 .... 4 F6
Woolsbridge Industrial Estate
WIMB BH21 .... 168 F2
Woolsbridge Small
Business Centre
WIMB BH21 .... 168 E2
Woolston First School
ITCH SO19 .... 132 C6
Woolston School
ITCH SO19 .... 132 D5
Wordsworth Infant School
WSHM SO15 .... 106 B7
Wykeham House School
FHAM/PORC PO16 .... 7 M5
Wykeham Industrial Estate
WINC SO23 .... 3 L4
Wynford Farm Industrial Estate
ROMY SO51 .... 50 E4
The Wyvern Community Secondary
School
ELGH SO50 .... 83 H7
Yarrells Preparatory School
UPTN BH16 .... 232 A1
Yeoman Industrial Park
TOTT SO40 .... 105 G6

Notes